Readings in
Christian Ethics

Readings in
Christian Ethics
A HISTORICAL SOURCEBOOK

Edited by
J. PHILIP WOGAMAN
and
DOUGLAS M. STRONG

Westminster John Knox Press
Louisville, Kentucky

Book design by Jennifer K. Cox
Cover design by Kim Wohlenhaus

First edition

Published by Westminster John Knox Press
Louisville, Kentucky

This book is printed on acid-free paper that meets the American National Standards Institute Z39.48 standard. ♾

PRINTED IN THE UNITED STATES OF AMERICA

00 01 02 03 04 05 — 10 9 8 7 6 5 4 3

Library of Congress Cataloging-in-Publication Data

Readings in Christian ethics : a historical sourcebook / edited by J. Philip
    Wogaman and Douglas Strong. — 1st ed.
       p.   cm.
    Companion text to Wogaman's Christian ethics, c 1993.
    Includes bibliographical references and index.
    ISBN 0-664-25574-4 (alk. paper)
    1. Christian ethics—History.   2. Christian ethics—History—
Sources.   I. Wogaman, J. Philip.   II. Strong, Douglas, 1956– .
III. Wogaman, J. Philip. Christian ethics.
BJ1201.R42   1996
241—dc20   96-399

Contents

Introduction

As Christianity enters its third millennium, numerous crises face both church and society—crises that call for thoughtful inquiry and straightforward action. Where can one find the scholarly resources necessary for this critical ethical task? Recently, much intellectual energy in the broader society has been spent searching for a common mode of discourse that would bring a measure of order to the multiplicity of diverse ideologies and value systems of our time. So far, however, this discussion has provided little substantive grounding for dealing with the "culture wars" that are raging. The church, meanwhile, is facing its own questions of identity and is consumed with the task of institutional maintenance. Such preoccupations hinder it from being engaged in the creative reflection necessary to do the hard theological work that undergirds complex ethical decision making. Too often, the result (in civil and ecclesial settings alike) is superficial and reductionistic moral reasoning.

Much of the difficulty regarding the shallow and uninformed ethical thinking of our day is related to the historical amnesia of our culture. It is a commonplace observation, for instance, that Americans and other Westerners only live for (and think about) the present. Rather than drawing upon the past as a resource for our moral deliberations, we approach present-day crises bereft of the lessons of yesteryear—a situation that contributes to the problem of an ungrounded ethic.

"Only [one] who is an heir is qualified to be a pioneer," wrote Jewish ecumenist Abraham Heschel. Heschel was describing the essential aptitude of an effective social activist: the willingness to be instructed by the wisdom of one's religious ancestors. Any attempt to effect lasting social change will falter without a firm understanding of the ways in which various men and women, institutions and movements, have struggled over the years to live out the ethical implications of their faith—in ways that are both similar to and different from our own moral struggles.

This sourcebook offers a broad collection of original documents that will assist contemporary students of ethics in their discovery of the relevance of Christian history. As an anthology of primary texts, this book serves as a useful companion volume to J. Philip Wogaman, *Christian Ethics: A Historical Introduction* (Westminster John Knox Press, 1993), which describes and analyzes the social, political, and theological milieu from which the texts were derived.

Of course, instruction from the past cannot be received uncritically. Concerned activists (the abolitionists, the social gospelers, and the liberation theologians, for example) have often emphasized the historical contingency of Christian praxis. "New occasions teach new duties," wrote antislavery advocate James Russell Lowell. "Time makes ancient good uncouth." Liberation theologian Gustavo Gutiérrez has made a similar observation about the particularity of each contextual situation: "not to acknowledge the newness of [ethical] issues raised . . . is to detach oneself dangerously from reality."

Nonetheless, Gutiérrez and most other thoughtful ethicists recognize the importance of being well-grounded in Christian history. Gutiérrez insists on the need to base one's ethical activity on a clear comprehension of the tradition.

> To acknowledge nothing but the new aspects of the contemporary statement of the problem is to forego the contribution of the life and reflection of the Christian community in its historical pilgrimage. Its successes, its omissions, and its errors are our heritage (*A Theology of Liberation*, 50).

Gutiérrez understands that we are products of a unique contextual social location and, at the same time, heirs to the multiplicity of contexts that have come before us.

For Christians, the critical appropriation of our long and varied history is important because we claim a faith that is based not only on the present activity of God the Spirit but also on the concrete historical actions of God enfleshed in Jesus Christ. Many of the Christians who have been most instrumental in transforming society have been those who have recognized their indebtedness to (and gleaned aspects of their ethical systems from) their forebears in the Christian tradition. To name just a few examples, Augustine harkened back to Paul; Martin Luther evoked the ideas of Augustine; John Wesley looked back to Luther and Paul, as well as to Clement and many others; and Martin Luther King, Jr. recaptured the spirit of Walter Rauschenbusch, Reinhold Niebuhr, and even Luther (his family's self-designated spiritual forefather).

The lack of a historical base for contemporary moral discussions has been fostered by the misperception common among theological students that the academic disciplines of Christian ethics and church history belong in different spheres—the one concerned with normative questions derived from the challenges of today and the other concerned with descriptive information derived from the issues of yesterday. The representation of these fields as academic polar opposites is a caricature, of course, and has not always been the case. Until the twentieth century, both history and ethics were understood generally as parts of the larger field of theology. The history of Christianity was studied under the rubric of historical theology, while social ethics was a subdiscipline of moral theology (an academic classification still used by many Catholic scholars). While this broader view of the complementarity of the two fields has continued to some degree, the rise of the social sciences in the later nineteenth and early twentieth centuries encouraged church history and Christian ethics to develop self-consciously as separate disciplines, each eager to protect its own academic territory.

Fortunately, some of the best scholars in church history and Christian ethics have countered this trend by achieving competence in both areas of knowledge. One obvious model of such a historically informed ethicist was Walter Rauschenbusch, who for many years was professor of church history at the same time that he was writing several influential works on the social gospel. This combination was no accident; Rauschenbusch bridged the two fields and was able to make a significant impact on the theological discourse of the twentieth century because he understood the importance of culture and its effect on moral behavior. He knew that the best historians of the church were those who were unconvinced by the notion of an unbiased history and thus were willing to offer (with appropriate humility) a moral judgment of the past. He also knew that the best ethicists were those who understood the limitations imposed on them by their cultural contingencies. In our moral deliberations, according to Rauschenbusch,

> We are like a swimmer in a stormy sea. To negotiate the next wave is the great object of his concern, but whether that wave is part of a tidal current sweeping him toward shore or out to sea, his narrow horizon does not tell him (*Christianizing the Social Order*, 157).

In order to move beyond the "narrow horizon" of one's contextual frame of reference, Rauschenbusch believed, it is essential that ethicists incorporate a clear "historical perspective" in their theorizing.

Rauschenbusch's disciplinary synthesis is helpful as we approach the reading of primary documents in the history of Christian ethics. On the one hand, it is important to realize that a person's ethical commitments are inescapably drawn from his or her historical circumstances. This realization provides a corrective to any sort of intellectual history that would attempt to understand the development of moral thought simply as a succession of the ideas of individuals who built on one another's systems of thought. Ideas do not exist apart from the cultural context of each person's tradition. In this sourcebook, we have tried to give some indication of the broader framework of the writers by providing preliminary comments before each selection as well as introductory comments that help to set the stage before each major period of church history.

On the other hand, primary documents also remind us that ethical ideas are not merely the product of cultures but are also the result of particular persons seeking to live out the gospel faithfully. The signatory aspects of an individual's work are evident in his or her writing. The unique emphases and even the writing style of the persons included in this volume are inseparable from their work as moral theologians, for imbedded in their prose is their personality and, for good or for ill, their ethic. In each primary text, we meet someone in a way that would be impossible if we only read about that individual in a secondary text—somewhat like the difference between a photograph and an actual human face. Primary sources are read because in them we can better understand what it is that drives someone's ethical system, and what it means to embody Christian morality. Such a reading may also result in a more sympathetic interpretation of a writer's ideas. Consequently, in many cases we have provided selections that are large enough to assist the reader in discerning the difference between a cursory secondary description and the essential thought structure of a person.

This collection of sources intentionally includes a variety of voices. The reading of primary documents reminds us that we are in a conversation with ideas that have been passed down through many centuries. Some voices have been loud. Others have been softer, or have been silenced. In the writings that tell how previous generations have responded to the gospel mandate to make one's faith active in love, some of the voices may seem to have spoken more faithfully than others. Nevertheless, all the voices need to be heard, for the greater the number of participants, the richer the dialogue. We are invited to be engaged in the historical discussion as well, and as we do, it will become evident that it is the responsibility of each new generation to pick up the conversation and carry it along.

Part 1

Early Christianity

The second-century "Letter to Diognetus" acknowledges that "Christians cannot be distinguished from the rest of the human race by country or language or customs." Nevertheless, according to that same writing, the life of Christians is extraordinary. "What the soul is in the body, that Christians are in the world." There are some differences of opinion among the earliest Christian writers, but all take the moral life with utmost seriousness. All likewise find the source of moral teaching in Christ, who is considered, by all, to embody the nature and purposes of God.

The earliest Christian writings are readily found in the New Testament (so easily available there that we shall not select any for reproduction in this volume). New Testament writings play a dual role in the history of Christian ethics. On the one hand, they reflect the church's earliest conception of the meaning of Christian life. (The New Testament writers were all members of the church and the decisions about which writings should be included in the sacred canon were ultimately made by the church.) So the New Testament itself provides something of a portrait of the ethical teachings of earliest Christianity. On the other hand, those writings were used as an authoritative source by noncanonical writings from the earliest centuries.

Early Christian writings teach high standards of personal morality. While Christians were not the only people in the ancient world to advocate highly disciplined moral living, they are noteworthy in grounding personal morality in a love ethic. Their writings frequently alluded to the two commandments—

1

love of God and of neighbor—and echoes of Paul's great love poem in 1 Corinthians 13 are frequently encountered along with Jesus' teachings. Christians are admonished by their moral teachers to live lives of sexual self-discipline (if not total abstinence), to care for widows and orphans and other vulnerable people, and repay evil with good. In defense of their faith, Christian writers were able to cite the exemplary lives typical of ordinary Christians.

As the writings included in Part 1 demonstrate, Christian thinkers in the first centuries struggled with momentous social questions. In some respects, the most elemental of these was the attitude to be taken toward the material world itself. Should Christians follow the example of highly "spiritual" religious movements of the time in denying a positive place for physical reality? Early Gnosticism posed the question, and some Christians—most notably the second-century Marcion—responded that the God worshiped through Jesus Christ had nothing to do with the creation of the material world. A number of the early writings, including some reproduced here, evidence the bitter struggle over that question. Had the "spiritualists" won out, the new faith would have evolved in vastly different ways if it had survived at all. Evolving Christian thought about creation was able to combine deep spiritual piety with the understanding that the God worshiped spiritually is the one also responsible for the awesome wonders of the universe. So *Clement's First Letter* includes a lovely passage depicting the profound harmonies of the natural world: "The heavens move at his direction and peacefully obey him. . . . The tiniest creatures come together in harmony and peace. All these things the great Creator and Master of the universe ordained to exist in peace and harmony."

Another issue was the attitude to be taken toward political power. On the one hand, Christians of the first two centuries seem characteristically to have renounced use of coercive force, even in self-defense. On the other hand, many Christian writings, beginning with Paul's Romans 13, gave substantial support to the state in *its* exercise of power. Conventional understandings of early Christian attitudes toward the state emphasize the Constantinian watershed. Before A.D. 313, when Constantine became Emperor of Rome under the Christian ensign, Christianity (it is alleged) was generally pacifist and unconformed to the world. After Constantine's victory, when Christianity became the established religion of the Roman Empire, the faith was thoroughly compromised by its investment with power. But careful reading of the earliest Christian writings suggests that this conventional picture of early Christian ethics is greatly oversimplified. The Constantinian watershed was indeed important in defining the possibilities available to Christians in the Roman world. But we should not overstate the extent to which their fundamental ethic changed.

One important shift of emphasis did occur in the second century A.D., with the development of deeper intellectual presentations of the faith. First-century and early second-century writings are based more on authoritative revelation and less upon a process of reasoning. With the emergence of the great Alexandrians Clement and Origen, and such subsequent thinkers as Tertullian, Ambrose, and Augustine, Christian ethics gained highly sophisticated expression, fully availing itself of the highest philosophical traditions and methods in the ancient world. The greatest of these thinkers was Augustine, whose work drew the best of earlier Christian thought into focus, while laying the foundations for a millennium of subsequent writing on moral questions. Footnotes cited in Part 1 are from the editors of the primary sources.

1. Clement's First Letter

Despite uncertainties about its authorship, the so-called Clement's First Letter *is clearly a message from the church at Rome to the Corinthian church and may
be dated around* A.D. *96. It strongly and beautifully defends the orthodox Christian view that the material universe is God's handiwork while warmly advocating
a disciplined life of Christian love.*

19. . . . Let us fix our eyes on the Father and Creator of the universe and
cling to his magnificent and excellent gifts of peace and kindness to us. Let
us see him in our minds and look with the eyes of our souls on his patient
purpose. Let us consider how free he is from anger toward his whole creation.

20. The heavens move at his direction and peacefully obey him. Day and
night observe the course he has appointed them, without getting in each
other's way. The sun and the moon and the choirs of stars roll on harmo-
niously in their appointed courses at his command, and with never a devi-
ation. By his will and without dissension or altering anything he has decreed the earth becomes fruitful at the proper seasons and brings forth
abundant food for men and beasts and every living thing upon it. The un-
searchable, abysmal depths and the indescribable regions* of the under-
world are subject to the same decrees. The basin of the boundless sea is by
his arrangement constructed to hold the heaped up waters, so that the sea
does not flow beyond the barriers surrounding it, but does just as he bids
it. For he said, "Thus far you shall come, and your waves shall break within
you" [Job 38:11]. The ocean which men cannot pass, and the worlds beyond
it, are governed by the same decrees of the Master. The seasons, spring,
summer, autumn, and winter, peacefully give way to each other. The
winds from their different points perform their service at the proper time
and without hindrance. Perennial springs, created for enjoyment and
health, never fail to offer their life-giving breasts to men. The tiniest creatures come together in harmony and peace. All these things the great Creator and Master of the universe ordained to exist in peace and harmony.
Thus, he showered his benefits on them all, but most abundantly on us who
have taken refuge in his compassion through our Lord Jesus Christ, to
whom be glory and majesty forever and ever. Amen.[†]

21. Take care, dear friends, that his many blessings do not turn out to be
our condemnation, which will be the case if we fail to live worthily of him,
to act in concert, and to do what is good and pleasing to him. For he says

---

*Emending *krimata* to *klimata*.
[†]This chapter bears some relation to the Christian thanksgiving for creation, which
opened the consecration prayer of the primitive Eucharist. There is an affinity of
ideas, and even some verbal parallels, with later liturgies. But the spirit of the chapter is Clement's.

somewhere, "The Spirit of the Lord is a lamp which searches the hidden depths of the heart" [Prov. 20:27]. Let us realize how near he is, and that none of our thoughts or of the ideas we have escapes his notice. It is right, therefore, that we should not be deserters, disobeying his will. Rather than offend God, let us offend foolish and stupid men who exalt themselves and boast with their pretensions to fine speech. Let us reverence the Lord Jesus Christ whose blood was given for us. Let us respect those who rule over us. Let us honor our elders. Let us rear the young in the fear of God. Let us direct our women to what is good. Let them show a purity of character we can admire. Let them reveal a genuine sense of modesty. By their reticence let them show that their tongues are considerate. Let them not play favorites in showing affection, but in holiness let them love all equally, who fear God. Let our children have a Christian training. Let them learn the value God sets on humility, what power pure love has with him, how good and excellent it is to fear him, and how this means salvation to everybody who lives in his fear with holiness and a pure conscience. For he is the searcher of thoughts and of desires. It is his breath which is in us; and when he wants to, he will take it away. . . .

30. Since, then, we are a holy portion, we should do everything that makes for holiness. We should flee from slandering, vile and impure embraces, drunkenness, rioting, filthy lusts, detestable adultery, and disgusting arrogance. "For God," says Scripture, "resists the arrogant, but gives grace to the humble" [Prov. 3:34; James 4:6; 1 Pet. 5:5]. We should attach ourselves to those to whom God's grace has been given. We should clothe ourselves with concord, being humble, self-controlled, far removed from all gossiping and slandering, and justified by our deeds, not by words. For it says: "He who talks a lot will hear much in reply. Or does the prattler imagine he is right? Blessed is the one his mother bore to be short-lived. Do not indulge in talking over-much" [Job 11:2, 3].* We should leave God to praise us and not praise ourselves. For God detests self-praisers. Let others applaud our good deeds, as it was with our righteous forefathers. Presumption, audacity, and recklessness are traits of those accursed by God. But considerateness, humility, and modesty are the traits of those whom God has blessed. . . .

34. The good laborer accepts the bread he has earned with his head held high; the lazy and negligent workman cannot look his employer in the face. We must, then, be eager to do good; for everything comes from Him. For he warns us: "See, the Lord is coming. He is bringing his reward with him, to pay each one according to his work."† He bids us, therefore, to believe on him with all our heart, and not to be slack or negligent in "every good deed" [Titus 3:10]. He should be the basis of our boasting and assurance. We should be subject to his will. We should note how the whole throng of his angels stand ready to serve his will. For Scripture says: "Ten thousand times ten thousand stood by him, and thousands of thousands ministered

*The text is corrupt in the LXX, which Clement cites.
†A conflation from: Isa. 40:10; 62:11; Prov. 24:12; Rev. 22:12.

to him and cried out: Holy, holy, holy is the Lord of Hosts: all creation is full of his glory" [Dan. 7:10; Isa. 6:3]. We too, then, should gather together for worship in concord and mutual trust, and earnestly beseech him as it were with one mouth, that we may share in his great and glorious promises. For he says, "Eye has not seen and ear has not heard and man's heart has not conceived what he has prepared for those who patiently wait for him" [1 Cor. 2:9; Isa. 64:4].*

35. How blessed and amazing are God's gifts, dear friends! Life with immortality, splendor with righteousness, truth with confidence, faith with assurance, self-control with holiness! And all these things are within our comprehension. What, then, is being prepared for those who wait for him? The Creator and Father of eternity, the all-holy, himself knows how great and wonderful it is. We, then, should make every effort to be found in the number of those who are patiently looking for him, so that we may share in the gifts he has promised. And how shall this be, dear friends? If our mind is faithfully fixed on God; if we seek out what pleases and delights him; if we do what is in accord with his pure will, and follow in the way of truth. If we rid ourselves of all wickedness, evil, avarice, contentiousness, malice, fraud, gossip, slander, hatred of God, arrogance, pretension, conceit, and inhospitality [cf. Rom. 1:29–32]. God hates those who act in this way; "and not only those who do these things but those who applaud them" [Ibid.]. For Scripture says: "But God told the sinner: Why do you speak of my statutes and have my covenant on your lips? You hated discipline and turned your back on my words. If you saw a thief you went along with him, and you threw in your lot with adulterers. Your mouth overflowed with iniquity, and your tongue wove deceit. You sat there slandering your brother and putting a stumbling block in the way of your mother's son. This you did, and I kept silent. You suspected, you wicked man, that I would be like you. I will reproach you and show you your very self. Ponder, then, these things, you who forget God, lest he seize you like a lion and there be no one to save you. A sacrifice of praise will glorify me, and that is the way by which I will show him God's salvation" [Ps. 50:16–23]. . . .

38. Following this out, we must preserve our Christian body too in its entirety. Each must be subject to his neighbor, according to his special gifts. The strong must take care of the weak; the weak must look up to the strong. The rich must provide for the poor; the poor must thank God for giving him someone to meet his needs. The wise man must show his wisdom not in words but in good deeds. The humble must not brag about his humility; but should give others occasion to mention it. He who is continent must not put on airs. He must recognize that his self-control is a gift from another. We must take to heart, brothers, from what stuff we were created, what kind of creatures we were when we entered the world, from what a dark grave he who fashioned and created us brought us into his world. And we

---

*This does not imply that Clement viewed 1 Corinthians as canonical. He merely cites an OT text via a rendering in Paul.

must realize the preparations he so generously made before we were born. Since, then, we owe all this to him, we ought to give him unbounded thanks. To him be glory forever and ever. Amen. . . .

48. . . . Let a man be faithful, let him be capable of uttering "knowledge,"* let him be wise in judging arguments, let him be pure in conduct. But the greater he appears to be, the more humble he ought to be, and the more ready to seek the common good in preference to his own. Whoever has Christian love must keep Christ's commandments. Who can describe the bond of God's love? Who is capable of expressing its great beauty? The heights to which love leads are beyond description. Love unites us to God. "Love hides a multitude of sins" [Prov. 10:12; 1 Pet. 4:8]. Love puts up with everything and is always patient. There is nothing vulgar about love, nothing arrogant. Love knows nothing of schism or revolt. Love does everything in harmony. By love all God's elect were made perfect. Without love nothing can please God. By love the Master accepted us. Because of the love he had for us, and in accordance with God's will, Jesus Christ our Lord gave his blood for us, his flesh for our flesh, and his life for ours.

60. . . . Deliver us, too, from all who hate us without good reason. Give us and all who live on the earth harmony and peace, just as you did to our fathers when they reverently "called upon you in faith and truth" [Ps. 145:18; 1 Tim. 2:7]. And grant that we may be obedient to your almighty and glorious name, and to our rulers and governors on earth.

61. You, Master, gave them imperial power through your majestic and indescribable might, so that we, recognizing it was you who gave them the glory and honor, might submit to them, and in no way oppose your will. Grant them, Lord, health, peace, harmony, and stability, so that they may give no offense in administering the government you have given them. For it is you, Master, the heavenly "King of eternity" [1 Tim. 1:17; Tob. 13:6, 10], who give the sons of men glory and honor and authority over the earth's people. Direct their plans, O Lord, in accord with "what is good and pleasing to you" [Deut. 12:25, 28; 13:18], so that they may administer the authority you have given them, with peace, considerateness, and reverence, and so win your mercy. We praise you, who alone are able to do this and still better things for us, through the high priest and guardian of our souls, Jesus Christ. Through him be the glory and the majesty to you now and for all generations and forevermore. Amen.

From "Letters in Crises," in *Early Christian Fathers*, The Library of Christian Classics, vol. 1, newly translated and edited by Cyril C. Richardson in collaboration with Eugene R. Fairweather, Edward Rochie Hardy, and Massey Hamilton Shepherd (Philadelphia: The Westminster Press), pp. 53–54, 57–61, 66, 72. First published MCMLIII by SCM Press, Ltd., London, and The Westminster Press, Philadelphia. Used by permission of the publishers.

Gnosis in its technical sense of mystical knowledge.

2. Ignatius,
Letter to Polycarp

The seven letters of Ignatius, Biship of Antioch, were evidently written by him around the beginning of the second century A.D. *when he was being conducted to Rome as a prisoner facing martyrdom. His letter to Polycarp exemplifies the early Christian exhortation to a disciplined life of Christian love.*

4. Widows must not be neglected. After the Lord you must be their protector. Do not let anything be done without your consent; and do not do anything without God's, as indeed you do not. Stand firm. Hold services more often. Seek out everybody by name. Do not treat slaves and slave girls contemptuously [cf. 1 Tim. 6:2]. Neither must they grow insolent. But for God's glory they must give more devoted service, so that they may obtain from God a better freedom. Moreover, they must not be overanxious to gain their freedom at the community's expense, lest they prove to be slaves of selfish passion. Flee from such wicked practices—nay, rather, preach against them.

5. Tell my sisters to love the Lord and to be altogether contented with their husbands. Similarly urge my brothers in the name of Jesus Christ "to love their wives as the Lord loves the Church" [Eph. 5:25, 29]. If anyone can live in chastity for the honor of the Lord's flesh, let him do so without ever boasting. If he boasts of it, he is lost; and if he is more highly honored than the bishop, his chastity is as good as forfeited. It is right for men and women who marry to be united with the bishop's approval. In that way their marriage will follow God's will and not the promptings of lust. Let everything be done so as to advance God's honor. . . .

10. . . . All of you submit yourselves to one another [1 Pet. 5:5], having your manner of life above reproach from the heathen, so that you may receive praise for your good works and the Lord may not be blasphemed on your account [1 Pet. 2:12]. "Woe to them, however, through whom the name of the Lord is blasphemed" [Isa. 52:5; Ignatius, *Letter to the Trallians,* 8:2]. Therefore, all of you teach the sobriety in which you are yourselves living. . . .

12. I am confident, indeed, that you are well versed in the sacred Scriptures and that nothing escapes you [1 Clem. 53:1; cf. Ignatius, *Ephesians* 14:1]—something not granted to me—only, as it is said in these Scriptures, "be angry but sin not" and "let not the sun go down on your anger" [Ps. 4:5, LXX; Eph. 4:26]. Blessed is he who remembers this. I believe it is so with you. May God and the Father of our Lord Jesus Christ, and the eternal High Priest himself, the Son of God, Jesus Christ, build you up in faith and truth and in all gentleness, without anger and in patient endurance, in long-suffering, forbearance, and purity; and give you a portion and share [Acts 8:21] among his saints, and to us also along with you, and to all under heaven who are destined to believe [Col. 1:23, cf. 1 Tim. 1:16] in our Lord Jesus Christ and in "his Father who raised him from the dead" [Gal. 1:1;

Col. 2:12; 1 Pet. 1:21]. "Pray for all the saints" [Eph. 6:18]. "Pray also for emperors and magistrates and rulers" [1 Tim. 2:1, 2; cf. 1 Clem. 61], and for "those who persecute and hate you" [Matt. 5:44; Luke 6:27], and for "the enemies of the cross" [Phil. 3:18], that your fruit may be manifest in all [1 Tim. 4:15], so that you may be perfected in him [Col. 2:10; James 1:4].

From "Letters in Crises," in *Early Christian Fathers*, The Library of Christian Classics, vol. 1, newly translated and edited by Cyril C. Richardson in collaboration with Eugene R. Fairweather, Edward Rochie Hardy, and Massey Hamilton Shepherd (Philadelphia: The Westminster Press), pp. 119, 135–36. First published MCMLIII by SCM Press, Ltd., London, and The Westminster Press, Philadelphia. Used by permission of the publishers.

3. Polycarp,
Letter to the Philippians

Polycarp was bishop of Smyrna during the first half of the second century. His letter to the Philippians exhorts his readers to lead a well-disciplined, faithful life as an example to the "heathen." Noteworthy is his call for prayer "for emperors and magistrates."

3. I write these things about righteousness, brethren, not at my own instance, but because you first invited me to do so. Certainly, neither I nor anyone like me can follow the wisdom of the blessed and glorious Paul, who, when he was present among you face to face with the generation of his time [Acts 16:12, 13], taught you accurately and firmly "the word of truth" [Eph. 1:13]. Also when absent he wrote you letters that will enable you, if you study them carefully [cf. 1 Clem. 45:2], to grow in the faith delivered to you—"which is a mother of us all" [Gal. 4:26],* accompanied by hope, and led by love to God and Christ and our neighbor.† For if anyone is occupied in these, he has fulfilled the commandment of righteousness; for he who possesses love is far from all sin.

4. But "the love of money is the beginning of all evils" [1 Tim. 6:10]. Knowing, therefore, that "we brought nothing into the world, and we cannot take anything out" [1 Tim. 6:7; cf. Job 1:21], let us arm ourselves "with the weapons of righteousness" [2 Cor. 6:7], and let us first of all teach ourselves to live by the commandment of the Lord.

Then you must teach your wives in the faith delivered to them and in love and purity—to cherish their own husbands [1 Clem. 1:3] in all fidelity, and to love all others equally in all chastity, and to educate their children in the fear of God [1 Clem. 21:6, 8]. And the widows should be discreet in their faith pledged to the Lord, praying unceasingly on behalf of all [1 Tim. 5:5; cf. 1 Thess. 5:17], refraining from all slander, gossip, false witness, love of

*(The word "all" is not read in the best MSS. of the New Testament, but is a reading of the Textus Receptus.)
†Col. 1:4, 5; cf. 1 Thess. 1:4 for the order: faith, love, hope.

money—in fact, from evil of any kind—knowing that they are God's altar, that everything is examined for blemishes [1 Clem. 41:2], and nothing escapes him whether of thoughts or sentiments [1 Clem. 21:3], or any of "the secrets of the heart" [1 Cor. 14:25]. Knowing, then, that "God is not mocked" [1 Gal. 6:7], we ought to live worthily of his commandment and glory.

5. Likewise the deacons should be blameless [cf. 1 Tim. 3:8–13] before his righteousness, as servants of God and Christ and not of men; not slanderers, or double-tongued, not lovers of money, temperate in all matters, compassionate, careful, living according to the truth of the Lord, who became "a servant of all" [Mark 9:35]*; to whom, if we are pleasing in the present age, we shall also obtain the age to come, inasmuch as he promised to raise us from the dead. And if we bear our citizenship worthy of him [1 Clem. 21:1; cf. Phil. 1:27; Col. 1:10], "we shall also reign with him" [2 Tim. 2:12; 1 Cor. 4:8]—provided, of course, that we have faith.

Similarly also the younger ones must be blameless in all things, especially taking thought of purity and bridling themselves from all evil. It is a fine thing to cut oneself off from the lusts that are in the world, for "every passion of the flesh wages war against the Spirit" [1 Pet. 2:11; Gal. 5:17], and "neither fornicators nor the effeminate nor homosexuals will inherit the Kingdom of God" [1 Cor. 6:9, 10], nor those who do perverse things. Wherefore it is necessary to refrain from all these things, and be obedient to the presbyters and deacons as unto God and Christ [cf. Ignatius, *Letter to the Magnesians*, chs. 2; 6:1; 13:2; *Letter to the Trallians*, 2:2; 3:1; *Letter to the Smyrnaeans*, 8:1; *Letter to Polycarp*, 6:1]. And the young women must live with blameless and pure conscience [1 Clem. 1:3].

6. Also the presbyters must be compassionate, merciful to all, turning back those who have gone astray, looking after the sick [1 Clem. 59:4], not neglecting widow [cf. Ignatius, *Polycarp*, 4:1; *Smyrnaeans*, 6:2] or orphan or one that is poor; but "always taking thought for what is honorable in the sight of God and of men" [2 Cor. 8:21; Rom. 12:27; Prov. 3:4], refraining from all anger, partiality, unjust judgment, keeping far from all love of money, not hastily believing evil of anyone, nor being severe in judgment [cf. 1 Tim. 5:19 ff], knowing that we all owe the debt of sin. If, then,we pray the Lord to forgive us, we ourselves ought also to forgive [Matt. 6:12, 14, 15]; for we are before the eyes of the Lord and God, and "everyone shall stand before the judgment seat of Christ and each of us shall give an account of himself" [Rom. 14:10, 12; cf. 2 Cor. 5:10]. So then let us "serve him with fear and all reverence" [cf. chap. 2:1; Ps. 2:11; Heb. 12:28], as he himself has commanded, and also the apostles who preached the gospel to us and the prophets who foretold [Acts 7:52; 1 Clem. 17:1] the coming of the Lord.

7. Let us be zealous for that which is good, refraining from occasions of scandal and from false brethren, and those who bear in hypocrisy the name of the Lord, who deceive empty-headed people. For "whosoever does not confess that Jesus Christ has come in the flesh is antichrist" [1 John 4:2, 3;

*There is a play here on the word "deacon," which means literally "a servant."

2:22; 2 John 7]; and whosoever does not confess the testimony of the cross "is of the devil" [1 John 3:8]; and whosoever perverts the sayings of the Lord [cf. 1 Clem. 53:1] to suit his own lusts and says there is neither resurrection nor judgment—such a one is the first-born of Satan [See Irenaeus, *Adversus Haereses, 3*, 3:4; Eusebius, *Historia Eccelesiastica, 4*, chap. 14; and *Martyrdom of Polycarp*, Epilogue, 3]. Let us, therefore, forsake the vanity of the crowd and their false teachings [cf. chap. 2:1; 1 Clem. 7:2; 9:1] and turn back to the word delivered to us from the beginning, "watching unto prayer" [1 Pet. 4:7] and continuing steadfast in fasting, beseeching fervently the all-seeing God [1 Clem. 55:6; 64:1] "to lead us not into temptation" [Matt. 6:13], even as the Lord said, "The spirit indeed is willing, but the flesh is weak" [Matt. 26:41; cf. Mark 14:38].

8. Let us, then, hold steadfastly and unceasingly to our Hope [Col. 1:27; 1 Tim. 1:1; Ignatius, *Letter to Magnesians*, chap. 11; *Trallians*, pref.; chap. 2:2] and to the Pledge [Eph. 1:14; 2 Cor. 1:22; 5:5] of our righteousness, that is, Christ Jesus, "who bore our sins in his own body on the tree, who committed no sin, neither was guile found on his lips" [1 Pet. 2:24, 22]; but for our sakes he endured everything that we might live in him. Therefore let us be imitators of his patient endurance, and if we suffer for the sake of his name, let us glorify him [1 Pet. 14:15, 16]. For he set us this example [1 Pet. 2:21; 1 Clem. 16:17] in his own Person, and this is what we believed.

9. Now I exhort all of you to be obedient to the word of righteousness [Heb. 5:13] and to exercise all patient endurance, such as you have seen with your very eyes, not only in the blessed Ignatius and Zosimus and Rufus, but also in others who were of your membership, and in Paul himself and the rest of the apostles; being persuaded that all these·"did not run in vain" [Phil. 2:16; cf. Gal. 2:2], but in faith and righteousness, and that they are now in their deserved place [1 Clem. 5:4, 7] with the Lord, in whose suffering they also shared. For they "loved not this present world" [2 Tim. 4:10], but Him who died on our behalf and was raised by God for our sakes [2 Cor. 5:15; cf. 1 Thess. 5:10].

10. Stand* firm, therefore, in these things and follow the example of the Lord, "steadfast and immovable" [1 Cor. 15:58; Col. 1:23] in the faith, "loving the brotherhood" [1 Pet. 2:17], "cherishing one another" [1 Pet. 3:8; Rom. 12:10], "fellow companions in the truth" [3 John 8]; in "the gentleness of the Lord preferring one another" [2 Cor. 10:1; Rom. 12:10] and despising no one. "Whenever you are able to do a kindness, do not put it off" [Prov. 3:28], because "almsgiving frees from death" [Tobit 4:10ff]. All of you submit yourselves to one another [1 Pet. 5:5], having your manner of life above reproach from the heathen, so that you may receive praise for your good works and the Lord may not be blasphemed on your account [1 Pet. 2:12]. "Woe to them, however, through whom the name of the Lord is blasphemed" [Isa. 52:5; Ignatius, *Trallians*, 8:2]. Therefore, all of you teach the sobriety in which you are yourselves living.

---

*With this chapter the original Greek text is no longer extant (except for ch. 13). The translation is from the Latin.

11. I have been exceedingly grieved on account of Valens, who was sometime a presbyter among you, because he so forgot the office that was given him. I warn you, therefore, to refrain from the love of money and be pure and truthful. "Shun evil of every kind" [1 Thess. 5:22]. For how shall he who cannot govern himself in these things teach another [1 Tim. 3:5]? If anyone does not refrain from the love of money he will be defiled by idolatry [Col. 3:5; Eph. 5:5] and so be judged as if he were one of the heathen, "who are ignorant of the judgment of the Lord" [Jer. 5:4]. Or "do we not know that the saints will judge the world," as Paul teaches [1 Cor. 6:2]? However, I have neither observed nor heard of any such thing among you, with whom blessed Paul labored and who were his epistles in the beginning.* Of you he was wont to boast in all the churches [Phil. 2:16; 2 Thess. 1:4] which at that time alone knew God; for we did not as yet know him. I am, therefore, very grieved indeed for that man and his wife. "May the Lord grant them true repentance" [2 Tim. 2:25; 1:18]. But you, too, must be moderate in this matter; and "do not consider such persons as enemies" [2 Thess. 3:15], but reclaim them as suffering and straying members [1 Clem. 59:4], in order that you may save the whole body of you [1 Clem. 37:5]. For in doing this you will edify yourselves [1 Thess. 5:11].

12. I am confident, indeed, that you are well versed in the sacred Scriptures and that nothing escapes you [1 Clem. 53:1; cf. Ignatius, *Ephesians,* 14:1]—something not granted to me—only, as it is said in these Scriptures, "be angry but sin not" and "let not the sun go down on your anger" [Ps. 4:5, LXX; 4:26]. Blessed is he who remembers this. I believe it is so with you. May God and the Father of our Lord Jesus Christ, and the eternal High Priest himself, the Son of God, Jesus Christ, build you up in faith and truth and in all gentleness, without anger and in patient endurance, in long-suffering, forbearance, and purity; and give you a portion and share [Acts 8:21] among his saints, and to us also along with you, and to all under heaven who are destined to believe [Col. 1:23; cf. 1 Tim. 1:16] in our Lord Jesus Christ and in "his Father who raised him from the dead" [Gal. 1:1; Col. 2:12; 1 Pet. 1:21]. "Pray for all the saints" [Eph. 6:18]. "Pray also for emperors and magistrates and rulers" [1 Tim. 2:1, 2; cf. 1 Clem. 61], and for "those who persecute and hate you" [Matt. 5:44; Luke 6:27], and for "the enemies of the cross" [Phil. 3:18], that your fruit may be manifest in all [1 Tim. 4:15], so that you may be perfected in him [Col. 2:10; James 1:4].

From "Letters in Crises," in *Early Christian Fathers*, The Library of Christian Classics, vol. 1, newly translated and edited by Cyril C. Richardson in collaboration with Eugene R. Fairweather, Edward Rochie Hardy, and Massey Hamilton Shepherd (Philadelphia: The Westminster Press), pp. 132–36. First published MCMLIII by SCM Press, Ltd., London, and The Westminster Press, Philadelphia. Used by permission of the publishers.

*Or, "who were mentioned in the beginning of his epistle." Phil. 4:15; cf. 2 Cor. 3:2; 1 Clem. 47:2.

4. The *Didache*

The Didache is an early second-century Christian manual of instruction, possibly embodying a still earlier catechism. Contrasting the "way of life" and the "way of death," the Didache catalogues a series of sins to be avoided and attitudes and practices to be embraced by Christians. The influence of such gospel teachings as the Sermon on the Mount is obvious.

The Lord's Teaching to the Heathen by the Twelve Apostles:

1. There are two ways, one of life and one of death; and between the two ways there is a great difference.

Now, this is the way of life: "First, you must love God who made you, and second, your neighbor as yourself" [Matt. 22:37–39; Lev. 19:18]. And whatever you want people to refrain from doing to you, you must not do to them [cf. Matt. 7:12].

What these maxims teach is this: "Bless those who curse you," and "pray for your enemies." Moreover, fast "for those who persecute you." For "what credit is it to you if you love those who love you? Is that not the way the heathen act?" But "you must love those who hate you" [Matt. 5:44, 46, 47; Luke 6:27, 28, 32, 33], and then you will make no enemies. "Abstain from carnal passions" [1 Pet. 2:11]. If someone strikes you "on the right cheek, turn to him the other too, and you will be perfect" [Matt. 5:39, 48; Luke 6:29]. If someone "forces you to go one mile with him, go along with him for two"; if someone robs you "of your overcoat, give him your suit as well" [Matt. 5:40, 41]. If someone deprives you of "your property, do not ask for it back" [Luke 6:30]. (You could not get it back anyway!) "Give to everybody who begs from you, and ask for no return" [Ibid]. For the Father wants his own gifts to be universally shared. Happy is the man who gives as the commandment bids him, for he is guiltless! But alas for the man who receives! If he receives because he is in need, he will be guiltless. But if he is not in need he will have to stand trial why he received and for what purpose. He will be thrown into prison and have his action investigated; and "he will not get out until he has paid back the last cent."* Indeed, there is a further saying that relates to this: "Let your donation sweat in your hands until you know to whom to give it."†

2. The second commandment of the Teaching: "Do not murder; do not commit adultery"; do not corrupt boys; do not fornicate; "do not steal"; do not practice magic; do not go in for sorcery; do not murder a child by abortion or kill a newborn infant. "Do not covet your neighbor's property; do not commit perjury; do not bear false witness" [Ex. 20:13–17; cf. Matt. 19:18; 5:33]; do not slander; do not bear grudges. Do not be double-minded or double-tongued, for a double tongue is "a deadly snare" [Prov. 21:6]. Your words shall not be dishonest or hollow, but substantiated by action. Do not

---

*Matt. 5:26. This whole section 5 should be compared with *Hermas, Mandates* 2:4–7, on which it is apparently dependent.
†Source unknown.

be greedy or extortionate or hypocritical or malicious or arrogant. Do not plot against your neighbor. Do not hate anybody; but reprove some, pray for others, and still others love more than your own life.

3. My child, flee from all wickedness and from everything of that sort. Do not be irritable, for anger leads to murder. Do not be jealous or contentious or impetuous, for all this breeds murder.

My child, do not be lustful, for lust leads to fornication. Do not use foul language or leer, for all this breeds adultery.

My child, do not be a diviner, for that leads to idolatry. Do not be an enchanter or an astrologer or a magician. Moreover, have no wish to observe or heed such practices, for all this breeds idolatry.

My child, do not be a liar, for lying leads to theft. Do not be avaricious or vain, for all this breeds thievery.

My child, do not be a grumbler, for grumbling leads to blasphemy. Do not be stubborn or evil-minded, for all this breeds blasphemy.

But be humble since "the humble will inherit the earth" [Ps. 37:11; Matt. 5:5]. Be patient, merciful, harmless, quiet, and good; and always "have respect for the teaching" [Isa. 66:2] you have been given. Do not put on airs or give yourself up to presumptuousness. Do not associate with the high and mighty; but be with the upright and humble. Accept whatever happens to you as good, in the realization that nothing occurs apart from God.

4. My child, day and night "you should remember him who preaches God's word to you" [Heb. 13:7], and honor him as you would the Lord. For where the Lord's nature is discussed, there the Lord is. Every day you should seek the company of saints to enjoy their refreshing conversation. You must not start a schism, but reconcile those at strife. "Your judgments must be fair" [Deut. 1:16, 17; Prov. 31:9]. You must not play favorites when reproving transgressions. You must not be of two minds about your decision.*

Do not be one who holds his hand out to take, but shuts it when it comes to giving. If your labor has brought you earnings, pay a ransom for your sins. Do not hesitate to give and do not give with a bad grace; for you will discover who He is that pays you back a reward with a good grace. Do not turn your back on the needy, but share everything with your brother and call nothing your own. For if you have what is eternal in common, how much more should you have what is transient!

Do not neglect your responsibility† to your son or your daughter, but from their youth you shall teach them to revere God. Do not be harsh in giving orders to your slaves and slave girls. They hope in the same God as you, and the result may be that they cease to revere the God over you both. For when he comes to call us, he will not respect our station, but will call those whom the Spirit has made ready. You slaves, for your part, must obey your masters with reverence and fear, as if they represented God.

You must hate all hypocrisy and everything which fails to please the

---

*Meaning uncertain.
†Literally, "Do not withhold your hand from. . ."

Lord. You must not forsake "the Lord's commandments," but "observe" the ones you have been given, "neither adding nor subtracting anything" [Deut. 4:2; 12:32]. At the church meeting you must confess your sins, and not approach prayer with a bad conscience. That is the way of life.

5. But the way of death is this: First of all, it is wicked and thoroughly blasphemous: murders, adulteries, lusts, fornications, thefts, idolatries, magic arts, sorceries, robberies, false witness, hypocrisies, duplicity, deceit, arrogance, malice, stubbornness, greediness, filthy talk, jealousy, audacity, haughtiness, boastfulness [cf. Matt. 15:19; Mark 7:21, 22; Rom. 1:29–31; Gal. 5:19–21].

Those who persecute good people, who hate truth, who love lies, who are ignorant of the reward of uprightness, who do not "abide by goodness" [Rom. 12:9] or justice, and are on the alert not for goodness but for evil: gentleness and patience are remote from them. "They love vanity" [Ps. 4:2], "look for profit" [Isa. 1:23], have no pity for the poor, do not exert themselves for the oppressed, ignore their Maker, "murder children" [Wisd. Sol. 12:6], corrupt God's image, turn their backs on the needy, oppress the afflicted, defend the rich, unjustly condemn the poor, and are thoroughly wicked. My children, may you be saved from all this!

6. See "that no one leads you astray" [Matt. 24:4] from this way of the teaching, since such a one's teaching is godless.

If you can bear the Lord's full yoke, you will be perfect. But if you cannot, then do what you can.

Now about food: undertake what you can. But keep strictly away from what is offered to idols, for that implies worshiping dead gods.

From "A Church Manual," in *Early Christian Fathers*, The Library of Christian Classics, vol. 1, newly translated and edited by Cyril C. Richardson in collaboration with Eugene R. Fairweather, Edward Rochie Hardy, and Massey Hamilton Shepherd (Philadelphia: The Westminster Press), pp. 171–74. First published MCMLIII by SCM Press, Ltd., London, and The Westminster Press, Philadelphia. Used by permission of the publishers.

5. *Clement's Second Letter*

The so-called Second Letter of Clement is actually an anonymous sermon from the first half of the second century, possibly of Egyptian origin. In the course of an admonition to Christians to prepare for the Lord's coming, this writing includes a striking affirmation of gender equality before God. God's kingdom will come when we no longer perceive one another as male or female.

12. Loving and doing what is right, we must be on the watch for God's Kingdom hour by hour, since we do not know the day when God will appear. For when someone asked the Lord when his Kingdom was going to come, he said, "When the two shall be one, and the outside like the inside, and the male with the female, neither male nor female."* Now "the two" are "one" when we tell each other the truth and two bodies harbor a single mind with no deception. "The outside like the inside" means this: "the inside" means the soul and "the outside" means the body. Just as your body is visible, so make your soul evident by your good deeds. Furthermore "the male with the female, neither male nor female," means this: that when a brother sees a sister† he should not think of her sex, any more than she should think of his. When you do these things, he says, my Father's Kingdom will come.

13. Right now, my brothers, we must repent, and be alert for the good, for we are full of much stupidity and wickedness. We must wipe off from us our former sins and by heartfelt repentance be saved. And we must not seek to please men or desire to please only ourselves, but by doing what is right to please even outsiders, so that the Name‡ may not be scoffed at on our account. For the Lord says, "My name is continually scoffed at by all peoples" [Isa. 52:5]; and again, "Alas for him through whom my name is scoffed at!"§ How is it scoffed at? By your failing to do what I want. For when the heathen hear God's oracles on our lips they marvel at their beauty and greatness. But afterwards, when they mark that our deeds are unworthy of the words we utter, they turn from this to scoffing, and say that it is a myth and a delusion. When, for instance, they hear from us that God says, "It is no credit to you if you love those who love you, but it is to your credit if you love your enemies and those who hate you" [Luke 6:32, 5], when they hear these things, they are amazed at such surpassing goodness. But when they see that we fail to love not only those who hate us, but even those who love us, then they mock at us and scoff at the Name.

From "An Early Christian Sermon," in *Early Christian Fathers*, The Library of Christian Classics, vol. 1, newly translated and edited by Cyril C. Richardson in collaboration with Eugene R. Fairweather, Edward Rochie Hardy, and Massey Hamilton Shepherd (Philadelphia: The Westminster Press), pp. 187–98. First published MCMLIII by SCM Press, Ltd., London, and The Westminster Press, Philadelphia. Used by permission of the publishers.

6. *Epistle to Diognetus*

Written during the latter part of the second century (or early in the third century), the Epistle to Diognetus *is of unknown authorship. Its portrait of the paradoxical relationship between Christians and the world remains a classic statement of the distinctiveness of early Christian ethics. While exhibiting some awareness of*

*Source unknown, probably the Gospel of the Egyptians. Both Clement of Alexandria (*Stromata* 3. 13:92, citing Julius Cassianus) and the Oxyrhynchus papyri (ed. Grenfell and Hunt, Vol. 4, pp. 22f.) have a similar saying. Clement directly attributes it to the Gospel of the Egyptians.
†The terms refer, not to family, but to Christian, relations.
‡I.e., the name "Christian."
§Source unknown. Possibly the Gospel of the Egyptians.

classical philosophical traditions, the letter affirms the decisiveness of God's revelation in Christ as revelation of the meaning of human existence.

The Church in the World*

5. For Christians cannot be distinguished from the rest of the human race by country or language or customs. They do not live in cities of their own; they do not use a peculiar form of speech; they do not follow an eccentric manner of life. This doctrine of theirs has not been discovered by the ingenuity or deep thought of inquisitive men, nor do they put forward a merely human teaching, as some people do. Yet, although they live in Greek and barbarian cities alike, as each man's lot has been cast, and follow the customs of the country in clothing and food and other matters of daily living, at the same time they give proof of the remarkable and admittedly extraordinary constitution of their own commonwealth. They live in their own countries, but only as aliens. They have a share in everything as citizens, and endure everything as foreigners. Every foreign land is their fatherland, and yet for them every fatherland is a foreign land. They marry, like everyone else, and they beget children, but they do not cast out their offspring. They share their board with each other, but not their marriage bed. It is true that they are "in the flesh," but they do not live "according to the flesh."[†] They busy themselves on earth, but their citizenship is in heaven.[‡] They obey the established laws, but in their own lives they go far beyond what the laws require. They love all men, and by all men are persecuted. They are unknown, and still they are condemned; they are put to death, and yet they are brought to life. They are poor, and yet they make many rich; they are completely destitute, and yet they enjoy complete abundance. They are dishonored, and in their very dishonor are glorified; they are defamed, and

---

*The heading is chosen quite deliberately, despite Meecham's criticism of Puech's reference to the *"onction ecclésiastique"* of the Epistle. Cf. A. Puech, *Les Apologistes grecs*, p. 252; *Histoire de la littérature grecque chrétienne*, 2, p. 219; H.G. Meecham, *The Epistle to Diognetus*, p. 31. In support of his criticism Meecham is compelled to quote an obscure upholder of the ultraspiritual doctrine of the Church (more judiciously defended by Sohm). Altogether apart, however, from the Hippolytean fragment, the whole discussion of the Christian's citizenship in the Epistle rests on those great churchly documents, Ephesians and First Peter—most notably, perhaps, on Eph. 2:19–22.

†Cf. 2 Cor. 10:3; 5:16; Rom. 8:4; John 17:13–19; 18:36, 37. Note this passage's vivid contrast between the created world, in which we live, and its corruption, which both affects our attitude toward it and conditions our life. The Pauline-Johannine doctrine of original sin, the full meaning of which some other Apologists failed to grasp, is here clearly implied.

‡Cf. Phil. 3:20; Eph. 2:19–22; 1 Pet. 2:9–17. The translation of Phil. 3:20, which refers to Christians as a "colony of heaven" (Moffatt), expresses most aptly the point of our Epistle, with its simultaneous recognition of the transcendent destiny and the earthly responsibility of the Christian.

17

are vindicated. They are reviled, and yet they bless; when they are affronted, they still pay due respect. When they do good, they are punished as evildoers; undergoing punishment, they rejoice because they are brought to life. They are treated by the Jews as foreigners and enemies, and are hunted down by the Greeks; and all the time those who hate them find it impossible to justify their enmity.*

6. To put it simply: What the soul is in the body, that Christians are in the world. The soul is dispersed through all the members of the body, and Christians are scattered through all the cities of the world. The soul dwells in the body, but does not belong to the body, and Christians dwell in the world, but do not belong to the world. The soul, which is invisible, is kept under guard in the visible body; in the same way, Christians are recognized when they are in the world, but their religion remains unseen. The flesh hates the soul and treats it as an enemy, even though it has suffered no wrong, because it is prevented from enjoying its pleasures; so too the world hates Christians, even though it suffers no wrong at their hands, because they range themselves against its pleasures. The soul loves the flesh that hates it, and its members; in the same way, Christians love those who hate them. The soul is shut up in the body, and yet itself holds the body together; while Christians are restrained in the world as in a prison, and yet themselves hold the world together. The soul, which is immortal, is housed in a mortal dwelling; while Christians are settled among corruptible things, to wait for the incorruptibility that will be theirs in heaven. The soul, when faring badly as to food and drink, grows better; so too Christians, when punished, day by day increase more and more. It is to no less a post than this that God has ordered them, and they must not try to evade it.

The Christian Revelation

7. As I have indicated, it is not an earthly discovery that was committed to them; it is not a mortal thought that they think of as worth guarding with such care, nor have they been entrusted with the stewardship of merely human mysteries. On the contrary, it was really the Ruler of all, the Creator of all, the invisible God himself, who from heaven established the truth and the holy, incomprehensible word among men, and fixed it firmly in their hearts. Nor, as one might suppose, did he do this by sending to men some subordinate—an angel, or principality, or one of those who administer earthly affairs, or perhaps one of those to whom the government of things in heaven is entrusted. Rather, he sent the Designer and Maker of the universe himself, by whom he created the heavens and confined the sea within

*2 Cor. 6:4–10 is obviously the pattern of this passage; cf. Diog. 5:13; 2 Cor. 6:10. The influence of John 15:25 should also be noted; the parallel destiny of the Vine and the branches (John 15:1, 5), implied in John 15:24 to 16:3, is the hidden background of our text. Here, as so often in the Epistle, we can sense a profound theological interest which, because of the aim of the work, must not become too obvious.

its own bounds—him whose hidden purposes all the elements of the world faithfully carry out, him from whom the sun has received the measure of the daily rounds that it must keep, him whom the moon obeys when he commands her to shine by night, and whom the stars obey as they follow the course of the moon. He sent him by whom all things have been set in order and distinguished and placed in subjection—the heavens and the things that are in the heavens, the earth and the things in the earth, the sea and the things in the sea, fire, air, the unfathomed pit, the things in the heights and in the depths and in the realm between; God sent him to men.

Now, did he send him, as a human mind might assume, to rule by tyranny, fear, and terror? Far from it! He sent him out of kindness and gentleness, like a king sending his son who is himself a king. He sent him as God; he sent him as man to men. He willed to save man by persuasion, not by compulsion, for compulsion is not God's way of working. In sending him, God called men, but did not pursue them; he sent him in love, not in judgment. Yet he will indeed send him someday as our Judge, and who shall stand when he appears?*

Do you not see how they are thrown to wild animals to make them deny the Lord, and how they are not vanquished? Do you not see that the more of them are punished, the more do others increase? These things do not seem to come from a human power; they are a mighty act of God, they are proofs of his presence.

8. As a matter of fact, before he came, what man had any knowledge of God at all? Or do you really accept the ideal nonsense talked by those plausible philosphers, some of whom asserted that God was fire—the very thing that they are on the point of going to, they call God!—while others claimed that he was water, and others said that he was yet another one of the elements created by God? And yet, if any one of these lines of argument is acceptable, then each and every one of the other creatures could in the same way be shown to be God. No, this is just quackery and deceit practiced by wizards. No man has ever seen God or made him known, but he has manifested himself. And he manifested himself through faith, by which alone it has been made possible for us to see God.

From "In Defense of the Faith," in *Early Christian Fathers*, The Library of Christian Classics, vol. 1, newly translated and edited by Cyril C. Richardson in collaboration with Eugene R. Fairweather, Edward Rochie Hardy, and Massey Hamilton Shepherd (Philadelphia: The Westminster Press), pp. 216–19. First published MCMLIII by SCM Press, Ltd., London, and The Westminster Press, Philadelphia. Used by permission of the publishers.

*For the last clause, cf. Mal. 3:2. At this point there is a lacuna, indicated by a marginal note in the MS. Dom Andriessen would insert the Eusebian fragment of the Apology of Quadratus here. A full statement of God's mighty acts through Christ, culminating, like many other Apologetic arguments (cf. Justin, *Dialogue with Trypho*, chs. 110; 121; Apol. 1, ch. 39; Irenaeus, *Adversus Haereses*, 4. 34:3; 33:9), in a description of Christian fidelity in tribulation, would certainly not be inappropriate at this point.

7. Justin,
First Apology

The "First Apology of Justin," to be dated around A.D. 155, is one of the earliest Christian writings to defend the faith to outsiders. While reserving ultimate worship to God alone, Justin also affirms loyalty and obedience to the "emperors and rulers of men." Justin specifically condemns Marcion, who denied that the physical universe was created by the Christian God. Among other things, the writing also supplies evidence of early Christian care for the orphans and widows and sick.

14. We warn you in advance to be careful, lest the demons whom we have attacked should deceive you and prevent your completely grasping and understanding what we say. For they struggle to have you as their slaves and servants, and now by manifestations in dreams, now by magic tricks, they get hold of all who do not struggle to their utmost for their own salvation— as we do who, after being persuaded by the Word, renounced them* and now follow the only unbegotten God through his Son. Those who once rejoiced in fornication now delight in continence alone; those who made use of magic arts have dedicated themselves to the good and unbegotten God; we who once took most pleasure in the means of increasing our wealth and property now bring what we have into common fund and share with everyone in need; we who hated and killed one another and would not associate with men of different tribes because of [their different] customs, now after the manifestation of Christ live together and pray for our enemies and try to persuade those who unjustly hate us, so that they, living according to the fair commands of Christ, may share with us the good hope of receiving the same things [that we will] from God, the master of all. So that this may not seem to be sophistry, I think fit before giving our demonstration to recall a few of the teachings which have come from Christ himself. It is for you then, as mighty emperors, to examine whether we have been taught and do teach these things truly. His sayings were short and concise, for he was no sophist, but his word was the power of God . . .

16. About being long-suffering and servants to all and free from anger, this is what he said: "To him that smites you on one cheek turn the other also, and to him that takes away your cloak do not deny your tunic either [Luke 6:29 (Matt. 5:39, 40)]. Whoever is angry is worthy of the fire. And whoever compels you to go one mile, follow him for two. Let your good works shine before men, that they as they see may wonder at your Father who is in heaven" [Matt. 5:22, 41, 16].

For we ought not to quarrel; he has not wished us to imitate the wicked, but rather by our patience and meekness to draw all men from shame and evil desires. This we can show in the case of many who were once on your side but have turned from the ways of violence and tyranny, overcome by observing

---

*Specifically in the baptismal renunciation of the devil and all his works.

the consistent lives of their neighbors, or noting the strange patience of their injured acquaintances, or experiencing the way they did business with them.

About not swearing at all, but always speaking the truth, this is what he commanded: "Swear not at all; but let your yea be yea and your nay nay. What is more than these is from the evil one" [Matt. 5:34, 37]. . . .

17. More even than others we try to pay the taxes and assessments to those whom you appoint, as we have been taught by him. For once in his time some came to him and asked whether it were right to pay taxes to Caesar. And he answered, "Tell me, whose image is on the coin." They said, "Caesar's." And he answered them again, "Then give what is Caesar's to Caesar and what is God's to God" [Matt. 22:20, 21 (Mark 12:14–17; Luke 20: 22–25)]. So we worship God only, but in other matters we gladly serve you recognizing you as emperors and rulers of men, and praying that along with your imperial power you may also be found to have a sound mind. If you pay no attention to our prayers and our frank statements about everything, it will not injure us, since we believe, or rather are firmly convinced, that every man will suffer in eternal fire in accordance with the quality of his actions, and similarly will be required to give account for the abilities which he has received from God, as Christ told us when he said, "To whom God has given more, from him more will be required" [Luke 12:48]. . . .

26. . . . [T]here is a certain Marcion of Pontus, who is still teaching his converts that there is another God greater than the Fashioner. By the help of the demons he has made many in every race of men to blaspheme and to deny God the Maker of the universe, professing that there is another who is greater and has done greater things than he. As we said, all who derive [their opinions] from these men are called Christians, just as men who do not share the same teachings with the philosophers still have in common with them the name of philosophy, thus brought into disrepute. Whether they commit the shameful deeds about which stories are told— the upsetting of the lamp, promiscuous intercourse, and the meals of human flesh,* we do not know; but we are sure that they are neither persecuted nor killed by you, on account of their teachings anyway. I have compiled and have on hand a treatise against all the heresies which have arisen, which I will give you if you would like to consult it.

27. That we may avoid all injustice† and impiety, we have been taught that to expose the newly born is the work of wicked men—first of all because we observe that almost all [foundlings], boys as well as girls, are brought up for prostitution. As the ancients are said to have raised herds of oxen or goats or sheep or horses in their pastures, so now [you raise children] just for shameful purposes, and so in every nation a crowd of females and hermaphrodites and doers of unspeakable deeds are exposed as public prostitutes. You even

---

*A reference to the charges of incest (facilitated by darkness) and cannibalism which other Apologists (Athenagoras, Tertullian, Minucius Felix) treat at length.
†Following the emendation *mēden adikomen* for *mēdena diōkomen* ("that we may persecute no one") proposed by Stephanus in 1551.

collect pay and levies and taxes from these, whom you ought to exterminate from your civilized world.* And anyone who makes use of them may in addition to [the guilt of] godless, impious, and intemperate intercourse, by chance be consorting with his own child or relative or brother. Some even prostitute their own children and wives, and others are admittedly mutilated for purposes of sodomy, and treat this as part of the mysteries of the mother of the gods—while beside each of those whom you think of as gods a serpent is depicted as a great symbol and mystery. You charge against us the actions that you commit openly and treat with honor, as if the divine light were overthrown and withdrawn—which of course does no harm to us, who refuse to do any of these things, but rather injures those who do them and then bring false witness [against us]. . . .

43. So that none may infer from what we have said that the events we spoke of, because they were foreknown and predicted, took place according to inevitable destiny—I can explain this too. We have learned from the prophets, and declare as the truth, that penalties and punishments and good rewards are given according to the quality of each man's actions. If this were not so, but all things happened in accordance with destiny, nothing at all would be left up to us. For if it is destined that one man should be good and another wicked, then neither is the one acceptable nor the other blameworthy. And if the human race does not have the power by free choice to avoid what is shameful and to choose what is right, then there is no responsibility for actions of any kind. But that [man] walks upright or falls by free choice we may thus demonstrate. We [often] observe the same man in pursuit of opposite things. If he were destined to be either wicked or virtuous, he would not be thus capable of opposites, and often change his mind. Nor would some be virtuous and others wicked, for then we would have to declare fate to be the cause of evils and [at the same time] to act in opposition to itself†—or to accept as true the opinion referred to above, that there is no real virtue or vice, but only by opinion are things considered good or bad; which, as the true Reason shows us, is the greatest impiety and wickedness. But we do say that deserved rewards are irrevocably destined for those who have chosen the good, and likewise their just deserts for those [who have chosen] the opposite. But God did not make man like other [beings], such as trees and animals, which have no power of choice. For he would not be worthy of rewards or praise if he did not choose the good of himself, but was so made, nor if he were evil would he justly deserve punishment, if he were not such of himself, but was unable to be anything different from that for which he was formed. . . .

46. . . . We have been taught that Christ is the First-begotten of God, and have previously testified that he is the Reason of which every race of man

---

*Oikoumenē, the inhabited or civilized world, assumed by Greeks and Romans to be identical with the Empire.

†I.e., by also being the cause of good—Otto conjectures "goods and" before evils, which is certainly the sense, though I doubt whether one can be sure that Justin was so clear.

partakes. Those who lived in accordance with Reason are Christians, even though they were called godless, such as, among the Greeks, Socrates and Heraclitus and others like them; among the barbarians, Abraham, Ananiah, Azariah, and Mishael,* and Elijah, and many others, whose deeds and names I forbear to list, knowing that this would be lengthy. So also those who lived without Reason were ungracious and enemies to Christ, and murderers of those who lived by Reason. But those who lived by Reason, and those who so live now, are Christians, fearless and unperturbed. For what cause a man was conceived of a virgin by the power of the Word according to the will of God, the Father and Master of all, and was named Jesus, and after being crucified and dying rose again and ascended into heaven, an intelligent man will be able to comprehend from the words that were spoken in various ways. But since the further demonstration of this does not seem necessary at the moment, I will pass on to more needed demonstrations. . . .

58. As I said before, the wicked demons have also put forward Marcion of Pontus, who is even now teaching men to deny that God is the Maker of all things in heaven and earth and that the Christ predicted by the prophets is his Son. He preaches another God besides the Fashioner of the universe, and likewise another Son. Many are persuaded by him, as if he alone knew the truth, and make fun of us, though they have no proof of the things they say, but are irrationally snatched away, like lambs by a wolf [cf. John 10:12], and become the prey of godless teachings and of demons. For those who are called demons strive for nothing else than to draw men away from God who made [them] and from Christ his First-begotten. Those who cannot rise above the earth they have nailed down by [the worship of] earthly things and the works of men's hands. They even push back those who aim at the contemplation of things divine, unless their thinking is prudent and pure and their life free from passion, and drive them into ungodliness. . . .

65. . . . When the president has given thanks and the whole congregation has assented, those whom we call deacons give to each of those present a portion of the consecrated† bread and wine and water, and they take it to the absent. . . .

67. After these [services] we constantly remind each other of these things. Those who have more come to the aid of those who lack, and we are constantly together. Over all that we receive we bless the Maker of all things through his Son Jesus Christ and through the Holy Spirit.‡ And on the day called Sunday there is a meeting in one place of those who live in cities or the country, and the memoirs of the apostles or the writings of the prophets are read as long as time permits. When the reader has finished, the president in a discourse urges and

---

*The original names of the "three holy children" (Dan. 1:7) are the ones commonly used in Greek.

†Literally, "eucharistized," i.e., blessed by the solemn prayer of thanksgiving, in accordance with the Jewish form of prayer, in which offering thanks to God for his gifts also blesses them for human use (cf. Mark 14:22, 23 and 1 Tim. 4:4, 5); but *eucharistea* as a transitive verb in this connection seems to be Christian and Gentile.

‡Not merely a general statement, but a reference to the custom, binding on Christians as on Jews, of giving thanks to God before receiving his gifts, which makes every meal a sacred act.

invites [us] to the imitation of these noble things. Then we all stand up together and offer prayers. And, as said before, when we have finished the prayer, bread is brought, and wine and water, and the president similarly sends up prayers and thanksgivings to the best of his ability, and the congregation assents, saying the Amen; the distribution, and reception of the consecrated [elements] by each one, takes place and they are sent to the absent by the deacons. Those who prosper, and who so wish, contribute, each one as much as he chooses to.* What is collected is deposited with the president, and he takes care of orphans and widows, and those who are in want on account of sickness or any other cause, and those who are in bonds, and the strangers who are sojourners among [us], and, briefly, he is the protector of all those in need.

From "In Defense of the Faith," in *Early Christian Fathers,* The Library of Christian Classics, vol. 1, newly translated and edited by Cyril C. Richardson in collaboration with Eugene R. Fairweather, Edward Rochie Hardy, and Massey Hamilton Shepherd (Philadelphia: The Westminster Press), pp. 249–53, 258–59, 269–70, 272, 280, 286, 287. First published MCMLIII by SCM Press, Ltd., London, and The Westminster Press, Philadelphia. Used by permission of the publishers.

8. Athenagoras,
A Plea Regarding Christians

Written around A.D. 177, Athenagoras's "Plea" is a fairly sophisticated appeal to the intellectual and political elites of the Antonine period. The actual authorship is unknown but is attributed to an "Athenagoras". This document seeks to demonstrate the irrationality of the persecution of Christians, the very people who are most constructive, least threatening of all.

"A Plea Regarding Christians" by Athenagoras, the Athenian, a Philosopher and a Christian†

To the Emperors Marcus Aurelius Antoninus and Lucius Aurelius Commodus, conquerors of Armenia and Sarmatia, and—what is more important—philosophers.

1. In your Empire, Your Most Excellent Majesties, different peoples observe

---

*The emphasis on the purely voluntary character of these contributions may have a legal purpose, to stress that the unlicensed Christian societies did not profess to collect dues (cf. Tertullian, *Apology,* 39:5).

†The word "plea" in the title is sometimes wrongly translated (as by the Latin) "legation" or "embassy." While this is the original meaning of the Greek word *presbeia,* it is used here in the derived sense of a "plea" or "apology." *Owing to the difficulties of the text it has seemed inappropriate to mark every emendation. Only where the text and meaning are in serious doubt has this been noted. Where, moreover, a significant lacuna appears it has been indicated thus: . . .*

different laws and customs; and no one is hindered by law or fear of punishment from devotion to his ancestral ways, even if they are ridiculous. . . .

. . . [W]hile everyone admires your mildness and gentleness and your peaceful and kindly attitude toward all, they enjoy equal rights under the law. The cities, according to their rank, share in equal honor, and the whole Empire through your wisdom enjoys profound peace.

But you have not cared for us who are called Christians in this way. Although we do no wrong, but, as we shall show, are of all men most religiously and rightly disposed toward God and your Empire, you allow us to be harassed, plundered, and persecuted, the mob making war on us only because of our name. We venture, therefore, to state our case before you. From what we have to say you will gather that we suffer unjustly and contrary to all law and reason. Hence we ask you to devise some measures to prevent our being the victims of false accusers.

The injury we suffer from our persecutors does not concern our property or our civil rights or anything of less importance. For we hold these things in contempt, although they appear weighty to the crowd. We have learned not only not to return blow for blow, nor to sue those who plunder and rob us, but to those who smite us on one cheek to offer the other also, and to those who take away our coat to give our overcoat as well. But when we have given up our property, they plot against our bodies and souls, pouring upon us a multitude of accusations which have not the slightest foundation, but which are the stock in trade of gossips and the like.

2. If, indeed, anyone can convict us of wrongdoing, be it trifling or more serious, we do not beg off punishment, but are prepared to pay the penalty however cruel and unpitying. But if the accusation goes no farther than a name—and it is clear that up to today the tales about us rest only on popular and uncritical rumor, and not a single Christian has been convicted of wrongdoing—it is your duty, illustrious, kind, and most learned Emperors, to relieve us of these calumnies by law. Thus, as the whole world, both individuals and cities, shares your kindness, we too may be grateful to you, rejoicing that we have ceased to be defamed.

It does not befit your sense of justice that others, accused of wrongdoing, are not punished before they have been convicted, while with us the mere name is of more weight than legal proof. Our judges, moreover, do not inquire if the accused has committed any wrong, but let loose against the name as if it were a crime. But no name in and of itself is good or bad. It is by reason of the wicked or good actions associated with names that they are bad or good. You know all that better than anyone, seeing you are versed in philosophy and thoroughly cultured.

That is why those who are tried before you, though arraigned on the most serious charges, take courage. For they know that you will examine their life and not be influenced by names if they mean nothing, or by accusations if they are false. Hence they receive a sentence of condemnation on a par with one of acquittal. We claim for ourselves, therefore, the same treatment as others. We should not be hated and punished because we are called Christians, for what has a name to do with our being criminals?

Rather should we be tried on charges brought against us, and either acquitted on our disproving them or punished on our being convicted as wicked men, not because of a name (for no Christian is wicked unless he is a hypocrite), but because of a crime. . . .

Christian Moral Teaching

11. Do not be surprised that I go into detail about our teaching. I give a full report to prevent your being carried away by popular and irrational opinion, and so that you may know the truth. Moreover, by showing that the teachings themselves, to which we are attached, are not human, but were declared and taught by God, we can persuade you not to hold us for atheists. What, then, are these teachings in which we are reared? "I say to you, love your enemies, bless those who curse you, pray for those who persecute you, that you may be sons of your Father in heaven, who makes his sun to shine on the evil and on the good, and sends his rain on the just and on the unjust [Matt. 5:44, 45; Luke 6:27, 28].

Although what I have said has raised a loud clamor,* permit me here to proceed freely, since I am making my defense to emperors who are philosophers. Who of those who analyze syllogisms, resolve ambiguities, explain etymologies, or [teach] homonyms, synonyms, predicates, axioms, and what the subject is and what the predicate—who of them do not promise to make their disciples happy through these and similar disciplines? And yet who of them have so purified their own hearts as to love their enemies instead of hating them; instead of upbraiding those who first insult them (which is certainly more usual), to bless them; and to pray for those who plot against them? On the contrary, they ever persist in delving into the evil mysteries of their sophistry, ever desirous of working some harm, making skill in oratory rather than proof by deeds their business. With us, on the contrary, you will find unlettered people, tradesmen and old women, who, though unable to express in words the advantages of our teaching, demonstrate by acts the value of their principles. For they do not rehearse speeches, but evidence good deeds. When struck, they do not strike back; when robbed, they do not sue; to those who ask, they give, and they love their neighbors as themselves.

12. If we did not think that a God ruled over the human race, would we live in such purity? The idea is impossible. But since we are persuaded that we must give an account of all our life here to God who made us and the world, we adopt a temperate, generous, and despised way of life. For we think that, even if we lose our lives, we shall suffer here no evil to be compared with the reward we shall receive from the great Judge for a gentle, generous, and modest life.

Plato, indeed, has said that Minos and Rhadamanthus† will judge and punish the wicked; but we say that, even if a man were Minos or Rhadamanthus or their father, he could not escape God's judgment.

---

*Following a rhetorical device, Athenagoras imagines that his speech has been met by hostile gibes.
†Sons of Zeus, and just men who judged the dead.

Then there are those who think that life is this: "Eat and drink, for tomorrow we shall die" [Isa. 22:13]. They view death as a deep sleep and a forgetting—"sleep and death, twin brothers" [Homer, *Iliad*, 16:672]. . . . And men think them religious! But there are others who reckon this present life of very little value. They are guided by this alone—to know the true God and his Word, to know the unity of the Father with the Son, the fellowship of the Father with the Son, what the Spirit is, what unity exists between these three, the Spirit, the Son, and the Father, and what is their distinction in unity. These it is who know that the life for which we look is far better than can be told, if we arrive at it pure from all wrongdoing. These it is whose charity extends to the point of loving not only their friends, for, the Scripture says, "If you love those who love you, and lend to those who lend to you, what credit is it to you [Luke 6:32, 34]? Since we are such and live this way to escape condemnation, can anyone doubt that we are religious?

From "In Defense of the Faith," in *Early Christian Fathers*, The Library of Christian Classics, vol. 1, newly translated and edited by Cyril C. Richardson in collaboration with Eugene R. Fairweather, Edward Rochie Hardy, and Massey Hamilton Shepherd (Philadelphia: The Westminster Press), pp. 300–302, 309–11. First published MCMLIII by SCM Press, Ltd., London, and The Westminster Press, Philadelphia. Used by permission of the publishers.

9. Tertullian, *Apology*

In the late second and early third centuries, several formidable minds emerged within the church to give powerful intellectual expression to Christian faith. Among these, Tertullian of Carthage is striking for his combination of intellectual sophistication with uncompromising rejection of worldliness. His Apology, *written in A.D. 197, includes his condemnation of all violence, including the killing of unwanted children and abortion, all military activity, and theatrical events.*

Chapter 9. . . . But in regard to child murder, as it does not matter whether it is committed for a sacred object, or merely at one's own self-impulse—although there is a great difference, as we have said, between parricide and homicide—I shall turn to the people generally. How many, think you, of those crowding around and gaping for Christian blood,—how many even of your rulers, notable for their justice to you and for their severe measures against us, may I charge in their own consciences with the sin of putting their offspring to death? As to any difference in the kind of murder, it is certainly the more cruel way to kill by drowning, or by exposure to cold and hunger and dogs. A maturer age has always preferred death by the sword. In our case, murder being once for all forbidden, we may not destroy even the fœtus in the womb, while as yet the human being derives blood from other parts of the body for its sustenance. To hinder a birth is merely a speedier man-killing; nor does it matter whether you take away a life that is born, or destroy one that is coming to the birth. . . . You first of all expose your children, that they may be taken up by any compassionate passer-by, to whom they are quite unknown; or you give them away, to be adopted by those who will do better to them the part of parents. Well, some time or other, all memory of the alienated progeny must be lost; and when once a mistake has been made, the transmission of incest thence will still go on—the race and the crime creeping on together. Then, further, wherever you are—at home, abroad, over the seas—your lust is an attendant, whose general indulgence, or even its indulgence in the most limited scale, may easily and unwittingly anywhere beget children, so that in this way a progeny scattered about in the commerce of life may have intercourse with those who are their own kin, and have no notion that there is any incest in the case. A persevering and steadfast chastity has protected us from anything like this: keeping as we do from adulteries and all postmatrimonial unfaithfulness, we are not exposed to incestuous mishaps. Some of us, making matters still more secure, beat away from them entirely the power of sensual sin, by a virgin continence, still boys in this respect when they are old. If you would but take notice that such sins as I have mentioned prevail among you, that would lead you to see that they have no existence among Christians. The same eyes would tell you of both facts. But the two blindnesses are apt to go together; so that those who do not see what is, think they see what is not. I shall show it to be so in everything. But now let me speak of matters which are more clear. . . .

Chapter 37. If we are enjoined, then, to love our enemies, as I have remarked above, whom have we to hate? If injured, we are forbidden to retaliate, lest we become as bad ourselves: who can suffer injury at our hands? In regard to this, recall your own experiences. How often you inflict gross cruelties on Christians, partly because it is your own inclination, and partly in obedience to the laws! How often, too, the hostile mob, paying no regard to you, takes the law into its own hand, and assails us with stones and flames! With the very frenzy of the Bacchanals, they do not even spare the Christian dead, but tear them, now sadly changed, no longer entire, from the rest of the tomb, from the asylum we might say of death, cutting them in pieces, rending them asunder. Yet, banded together as we are, ever so ready to sacrifice our lives, what single case of revenge for injury are you able to point to, though, if it were held right among us to repay evil by evil, a single night with a torch or two could achieve an ample vengeance? But away with the idea of a sect divine avenging itself by human fires, or shrinking from the sufferings in which it is tried. If we desired, indeed, to act the part of open enemies, not merely of secret avengers, would there be any lacking in strength, whether of numbers or resources? The Moors, the Marcomanni, the Parthians themselves, or any single people, however great, inhabiting a distinct territory, and confined within its own boundaries, surpasses, forsooth, in numbers, one spread over all the world! We are but of yesterday, and we have filled every place among you—cities, islands, fortresses, towns, market-places, the very camp, tribes, companies, palace, senate, forum,—we have left nothing to you but the temples of your gods. For what wars should we not be fit, not eager, even with unequal forces, we who so willingly yield ourselves to the sword, if in our religion it were not counted better to be slain than to slay? Without arms even, and raising no insurrectionary banner, but simply in enmity to you, we could carry on the contest with you by an ill-willed severance alone. For if such multitudes of men were to break away from you, and betake themselves to some remote corner of the world, why, the very loss of so many citizens, whatever sort they were, would cover the empire with shame; nay, in the very forsaking, vengeance would be inflicted. Why, you would be horror-struck at the solitude in which you would find yourselves, at such an all-prevailing silence, and that stupor as of a dead world. You would have to seek subjects to govern. You would have more enemies than citizens remaining. For now it is the immense number of Christians which makes your enemies so few,—almost all the inhabitants of your various cities being followers of Christ. . . .

Chapter 38. Ought not Christians, therefore, to receive not merely a somewhat milder treatment, but to have a place among the law-tolerated societies, seeing they are not chargeable with any such crimes as are commonly dreaded from societies of the illicit class? For, unless I mistake the matter, the prevention of such associations is based on a prudential regard to public order, that the state may not be divided into parties, which would naturally lead to disturbance in the electoral assemblies, the councils, the curiae, the special conventions, even in the public shows by the hostile collisions of rival parties; especially when now, in pursuit of gain, men have begun to consider their violence an article to be bought and sold. But as those in whom all ardour in the pursuit of glory and honour is dead, we have no pressing inducement to take part in your public meetings; nor is there aught more entirely foreign to us than affairs of state. We acknowledge one all-embracing commonwealth—the world. We renounce all your spectacles, as strongly as we renounce the matters originating them, which we know were conceived of superstition, when we give up the very things which are the basis of their representations. Among us nothing is ever said, or seen, or heard, which has anything in common with the madness of the circus, the immodesty of the theatre, the atrocities of the arena, the useless exercises of the wrestling-ground. Why do you take offense at us because we differ from you in regard to your pleasures? If we will not partake of your enjoyments, the loss is ours, if there be loss in the case, not yours. We reject what pleases you. You, on the other hand, have no taste for what is our delight. The Epicureans were allowed by you to decide for themselves one true source of pleasure—I mean equanimity; the Christian, on his part, has many such enjoyments—what harm in that?

Chapter 39. I shall at once go on, then, to exhibit the peculiarities of the Christian society, that, as I have refuted the evil charged against it, I may point out its positive good. We are a body knit together as such by a common religious profession, by unity of discipline, and by the bond of a common hope. We meet together as an assembly and congregation, that, offering up prayer to God as with united force, we may wrestle with Him in our supplications. This violence God delights in. We pray, too, for the emperors, for their ministers and for all in authority, for the welfare of the world, for the prevalence of peace, for the delay of the final consummation.* We assemble to read our sacred writings, if any peculiarity of the times makes either forewarning or reminiscence needful.[†] However it be in that respect, with the sacred words we nourish our faith, we animate our hope, we make our confidence more steadfast; and no less by inculcations of God's precepts we confirm good habits. In the same place also exhortations are made, rebukes and sacred censures are administered. For with a great gravity is the work of judging carried on among us, as befits those who feel assured that they are in the sight of God; and you have the most notable example of judgment to come when any one has sinned so grievously as to require his severance from us in prayer, in the congregation and in all sacred intercourse. The tried men of our elders preside over us, obtaining that honour not by purchase, but by established character. There is no buying and selling of any sort in the things of God. Though we have our treasure-chest, it is not made up of purchase-money, as of a religion that has its price. On the monthly day,[‡] if he likes, each puts in a small donation; but only if it be his pleasure, and only if he be able: for there is no compulsion; all is voluntary. These gifts are, as it were, piety's deposit fund. For they are not taken thence and spent on feasts, and drinking-bouts, and eating-houses, but to support and bury poor people, to supply the wants of boys and girls destitute of means and parents, and of old persons confined now to the house; such, too, as have suffered shipwreck; and if there happen to be any in the mines, or banished to the islands, or shut up in the prisons, for nothing but their fidelity to the cause of God's Church, they become the nurslings of their confession. But it is mainly the deeds of a love so noble that lead many to put a brand upon us. *See,* they say, *how they love one[§] another,* for themselves are animated by mutual hatred; how they are ready even to die for one another, for they themselves will sooner put to death. And they are wroth with us, too, because we call each other brethren; for no other reason, as I think, than because among themselves names of consanguinity are assumed in mere pretence of affection. But we are your brethren as well, by the law of our common mother nature, though you are hardly men, because brothers so unkind. At the same time, how much more fittingly they are called and counted brothers who have been led to the knowledge of God as their common Father, who have drunk in one spirit of holiness, who from the same womb of a common ignorance have agonized into the same light of truth! But on this very account, perhaps, we are regarded as having less claim to be held true brothers, that no tragedy makes a noise about our brotherhood, or

*Chap. 32.
[†][An argument for Days of Public Thanksgiving, Fasting and the like.]
[‡][On ordinary Sundays, "they laid by in store," apparently: once a month they offered.]
[§][A precious testimony, although the caviller asserts that afterwards the heathen used this expression derisively.]

that the family possessions, which generally destroy brotherhood among you, create fraternal bonds among us. One in mind and soul, we do not hesitate to share our earthly goods with one another. All things are common among us but our wives. . . .

Chapter 17. The object of our worship is the One God, He who by His commanding word, His arranging wisdom, His mighty power, brought forth from nothing this entire mass of our world, with all its array of elements, bodies, spirits, for the glory of His majesty; whence also the Greeks have bestowed on it the name of Κόσμος [*Kosmos*]. The eye cannot see Him, though He is (spiritually) visible. He is incomprehensible, though in grace He is manifested. He is beyond our utmost thought, though our human faculties conceive of Him. He is therefore equally real and great. But that which, in the ordinary sense, can be seen and handled and conceived, is inferior to the eyes by which it is taken in, and the hands by which it is tainted, and the faculties by which it is discovered; but that which is infinite is known only to itself. This it is which gives some notion of God, while yet beyond all our conceptions—our very incapacity of fully grasping Him affords us the idea of what He really is. He is presented to our minds in His transcendent greatness, as at once known and unknown. And this is the crowning guilt of men, that they will not recognize One, of whom they cannot possibly be ignorant. Would you have the proof from the works of His hands, so numerous and so great, which both contain you and sustain you, which minister at once to your enjoyment, and strike you with awe; or would you rather have it from the testimony of the soul itself? Though under the oppressive bondage of the body, though led astray by depraving customs, though enervated by lusts and passions, though in slavery to false gods; yet, whenever the soul comes to itself, as out of a surfeit, or a sleep, or a sickness, and attains something of its natural soundness, it speaks of God; using no other word, because this is the peculiar name of the true God. "God is great and good"—"Which may God give," are the words on every lip. It bears witness, too, that God is judge, exclaiming, "God sees," and, "I commend myself to God," and, "God will repay me." O noble testimony of the soul by nature* Christian! Then, too, in using such words as these, it looks not to the Capitol, but to the heavens. It knows that there is the throne of the living God, as from Him and from thence itself came down. . . .

Chapter 19. [D]ecision may seem to have been given likewise concerning military service, which is between dignity and power. But now inquiry is made about this point, whether a believer may turn himself unto military service, and whether the military may be admitted unto the faith, even the rank and file, or each inferior grade, to whom there is no necessity for taking part in sacrifices or capital punishments. There is no agreement between the divine and the human sacrament,† the standard of Christ and the standard of the devil, the camp of light and the camp of darkness. One soul

---

*Though we are not by nature good, in our present estate; this is elsewhere demonstrated by Tertullian, as see chap. [18].
†"Sacramentum" in Latin is, among other meanings, "a military oath."

cannot be due to two *masters*—God and Caesar. And yet Moses carried a rod,* and Aaron wore a buckle,† and John (Baptist) is girt with leather,‡ and Joshua the son of Nun leads a line of march; and the People warred: if it pleases you to sport with the subject. But how will *a Christian man* war, nay, how will he serve even in peace, without a sword, which the Lord has taken away [Matt. 26:52; 2 Cor. 10:4; John 18:30]. For albeit soldiers had come unto John, and had received the formula of their rule [See Luke 3:12, 13]; albeit, likewise, a centurion had believed [Matt. 8:5ff; Luke 7:1ff]; *still* the Lord afterward, in disarming Peter, unbelted every soldier. No dress is lawful among us, if assigned to any unlawful action.

From *The Ante-Nicene Fathers: Translations of The Writings of the Fathers down to A.D. 325*, vol. 3, edited by The Reverend Alexander Roberts and James Donaldson (Grand Rapids, Mich.: William B. Eerdmans Publishing Co., 1976, reprinted), pp. 25, 26, 31, 32, 45, 46, 73.

10.   Clement of Alexandria, *Stromata, Who Is the Rich Man that Shall Be Saved?*, and *The Instructor*

Deeply steeped in Hellenistic philosophical traditions, Clement of Alexandria (d. ca. A.D. 215) gave urbane and sophisticated form to Christian theology, including Christian ethics. His Stromata *includes an extraordinary passage— included here—on the transcendence of God; Clement concludes that all names for God are imperfect representations of God's greater reality. His* Who Is the Rich Man that Shall Be Saved? *seeks a less literal, more spiritual interpretation of Gospel warnings about wealth. His* The Instructor *illustrates Clement's penchant for equating good ethics with good manners.*

STROMATA

Book 5

Chapter 12. . . . And John the apostle says: "No man hath seen God at any time. The only-begotten God, who is in the bosom of the Father, He hath declared Him," [John 1:18]—calling invisibility and ineffableness the bosom of God. Hence some have called it the Depth, as containing and embosoming all things, inaccessible and boundless.

---

*"Virgam." The vine switch, or rod, in the Roman army was a mark of the centurion's (i.e., captain's) rank.
†To fasten the ephod; hence the buckle worn by soldiers here referred to would probably be the belt buckle. Buckles were sometimes given as military rewards.
‡As soldiers with belts.

This discourse respecting God is most difficult to handle. For since the first principle of everything is difficult to find out, the absolutely first and oldest principle, which is the cause of all other things being and having been, is difficult to exhibit. For how can that be expressed which is neither genus, nor difference, nor species, nor individual, nor number; nay more, is neither an event, nor that to which an event happens? No one can rightly express Him wholly. For on account of His greatness He is ranked as the All, and is the Father of the universe. Nor are any parts to be predicated of Him. For the One is indivisible; wherefore also it is infinite, not considered with reference to inscrutability, but with reference to its being without dimensions, and not having a limit. And therefore it is without form and name. And if we name it, we do not do so properly, terming it either the One, or the Good, or Mind, or Absolute Being, or Father, or God, or Creator, or Lord. We speak not as supplying His name; but for want, we use good names, in order that the mind may have these as points of support, so as not to err in other respects. For each one by itself does not express God; but all together are indicative of the power of the Omnipotent. For predicates are expressed either from what belongs to things themselves, or from their mutual relation. But none of these are admissible in reference to God. Nor any more is He apprehended by the science of demonstration. For it depends on primary and better known principles. But there is nothing antecedent to the Unbegotten.

It remains that we understand, then, the Unknown, by divine grace, and by the word alone that proceeds from Him; as Luke in the Acts of the Apostles relates that Paul said, "Men of Athens, I perceive that in all things ye are too superstitious. For in walking about, and beholding the objects of your worship, I found an altar on which was inscribed, To the Unknown God. Whom therefore ye ignorantly worship, Him declare I unto you" [Acts 3:22, 23].

From *The Ante-Nicene Fathers: Translations of The Writings of the Fathers down to A.D. 325*, vol. 2, edited by The Reverend Alexander Roberts and James Donaldson (New York: Charles Scribner's Sons, 1926), pp. 463–64. Copyright © 1885 by The Christian Literature Publishing Company.

WHO IS THE RICH MAN THAT SHALL BE SAVED?

1. Those who bestow laudatory addresses on the rich* appear to me to be rightly judged not only flatterers and base, in vehemently pretending

*[The solemn words of our Lord about the perils of wealth and "the deceitfulness of riches" are much insisted on by Hermas, especially in the beautiful opening of the *Similitudes* (book 3); and it seems remarkable, that, even in the age of martyrs and confessors, such warnings should have seemed needful. Clement is deeply impressed with the duty of enforcing such doctrine; and perhaps the term of this very interesting essay is to be found in that eloquent passage in his *Stromata* (book 2, chap. 5, pp. 351, 352), to which the reader may do well to recur, using it as a preface to the following pages.]

that things which are disagreeable give them pleasure, but also godless and treacherous. . . . For it appears to me to be far kinder, than basely to flatter the rich and praise them for what is bad, to aid them in working out their salvation in every possible way; asking this of God, who surely and sweetly bestows such things on His own children; and thus by the grace of the Saviour healing their souls, enlightening them and leading them to the attainment of the truth. . . .

2. Perhaps the reason of salvation appearing more difficult to the rich than to poor men, is not single but manifold. For some, merely hearing, and that in an off-hand way, the utterance of the Saviour, "that it is easier for a camel to go through the eye of a needle than for a rich man to enter into the kingdom of heaven" [Matt. 19:24], despair of themselves as not destined to live, surrender all to the world, cling to the present life as if it alone was left to them, and so diverge more from the way to the life to come, no longer inquiring either whom the Lord and Master calls rich, or how that which is impossible to man becomes possible to God. But others rightly and adequately comprehend this, but attaching slight importance to the works which tend to salvation, do not make the requisite preparation for attaining to the objects of their hope. And I affirm both of these things of the rich who have learned both the Saviour's power and His glorious salvation. With those who are ignorant of the truth I have little concern.

3. Those then who are actuated by a love of the truth and love of their brethren, and neither are rudely insolent towards such rich as are called, nor, on the other hand, cringe to them for their own avaricious ends, must first by the word relieve them of their groundless despair, and show with the requisite explanation of the oracles of the Lord that the inheritance of the kingdom of heaven is not quite cut off from them if they obey the commandments; then admonish them that they entertain a causeless fear, and that the Lord gladly receives them, provided they are willing; and then, in addition, exhibit and teach how and by what deeds and dispositions they shall win the objects of hope. . . . So also let not the man that has been invested with worldly wealth proclaim himself excluded at the outset from the Saviour's lists, provided he is a believer and one who contemplates the greatness of God's philanthropy; nor let him, on the other hand, expect to grasp the crowns of immortality without struggle and effort, continuing untrained, and without contest. But let him go and put himself under the Word as his trainer, and Christ the President of the contest; and for his prescribed food and drink let him have the New Testament of the Lord; and for exercises, the commandments; and for elegance and ornament, the fair dispositions, love, faith, hope, knowledge of the truth, gentleness, meekness, pity, gravity: so that, when by the last trumpet the signal shall be given for the race and departure hence, as from the stadium of life, he may with a good conscience present himself victorious before the judge who confers the rewards, confessedly worthy of the Fatherland on high, to which he returns with crowns and the acclamations of angels.

4. May the Saviour then grant to us that, having begun the subject from this point, we may contribute to the brethren what is true, and suitable, and saving, first touching the hope itself, and, second, touching the access to the hope. He indeed grants to those who beg, and teaches those who ask, and dissipate[s] ignorance and dispels despair, by introducing again the same words about the rich, which become their own interpreters and infallible expounders. For there is nothing like listening again to the very same statements, which till now in the Gospels were distressing you, hearing them as you did without examination, and erroneously through puerility: "And going forth into the way, one approached and kneeled, saying, Good Master, what good thing shall I do that I may inherit everlasting life? And Jesus saith, Why callest thou Me good? There is none good but one, *that is,* God. Thou knowest the commandments. Do not commit adultery, Do not kill, Do not steal, Do not bear false witness, Defraud not, Honour thy father and thy mother. And he answering saith to Him, All these have I observed. And Jesus, looking upon him, loved him, and said, One thing thou lackest. If thou wouldest be perfect, sell what thou hast and give to the poor, and thou shalt have treasure in heaven: and come, follow Me. And he was sad at that saying, and went away grieved: for he was rich, having great possessions. And Jesus looked round about, and saith to His disciples, How hardly shall they that have riches enter into the kingdom of God! And the disciples were astonished at His words. . . .

11. What then was it which persuaded him to flight and made him depart from the Master, from the entreaty, the hope, the life, previously pursued with ardour?— "Sell thy possessions." And what is this? He does not, as some conceive off-hand, bid him throw away the substance he possessed, and abandon his property; but bids him banish from his soul his notions about wealth, his excitement and morbid feeling about it, the anxieties, which are the thorns of existence, which choke the seed of life. For it is no great thing or desirable to be destitute of wealth, if without a special object,—not except on account of life. For thus those who have nothing at all, but are destitute, and beggars for their daily bread, the poor dispersed on the streets, who know not God and God's righteousness, simply on account of their extreme want and destitution of subsistence, and lack even of the smallest things, were most blessed and most dear to God, and sole possessors of everlasting life.

Nor was the renunciation of wealth and the bestowment of it on the poor or needy a new thing; for many did so before the Saviour's advent,—some because of the leisure (thereby obtained) for learning, and on account of a dead wisdom; and others for empty fame and vain-glory, as the Anaxagorases, the Democriti, and the Crateses.

12. Why then command as new, as divine, as alone life-giving, what did not save those of former days? And what peculiar thing is it that the new creature the Son of God intimates and teaches? It is not the outward act that others have done, but something else indicated by it, greater, more godlike, more perfect, the stripping off of the passions from the soul itself and from the disposition, and the cutting up by the roots and casting out of what is alien to the mind. For this is the lesson peculiar to the believer, and the instruction worthy of the Saviour. For those who formerly despised external things relinquished and squandered the property, but the passions of the soul, I believe, they intensified. For they indulged in arrogance, pretension, and vainglory, and in contempt of the rest of mankind, as if they had done something superhuman. How then would the Saviour have enjoined on those destined to live for ever what was injurious and hurtful with reference to the life which He promised? For although such is the case, one, after ridding himself of the burden of wealth, may none the less have still the lust and desire for money innate and living; and may have abandoned the use of it, but being at once destitute of and desiring what he spent, may doubly grieve both on account of the absence of attendance and the presence of regret. For it is impossible and inconceivable that those in want of the necessaries of life should not be harassed in mind, and hindered from better things in the endeavour to provide them somehow, and from some source.

13. And how much more beneficial the opposite case, for a man, through possessing competency, both not himself to be in straits about money, and also to give assistance to those to whom it is requisite to do so! For if no one had anything, what room would be left among men for giving. . . . How could one give food to the hungry, and drink to the thirsty, clothe the naked, and shelter the houseless, for not doing which He threatens with fire and the outer darkness, if each man first divested himself of all these things? Nay, He bids Zaccheus and Matthew, the rich tax-gathers, entertain Him hospitably. And he does not bid them part with their property, but, applying the just and removing the unjust judgment, He subjoins, "To-day salvation has come to this house, forasmuch as he also is a son of Abraham" [Luke 5:29; 19:9]. He so praises the use of property as to enjoin, along with this addition, the giving a share of it, to give drink to the thirsty, bread to the hungry, to take the houseless in, and clothe the naked. But if it is not possible to supply those needs without substance, and He bids people abandon their substance, what else would the Lord be doing than exhorting to give and not to give the same things, to feed and not to feed, to take in and to shut out, to share and not to share? which were the most irrational of all things.

14. Riches, then, which benefit also our neighbours, are not to be thrown away. For they are possessions, inasmuch as they are possessed, and goods, inasmuch as they are useful and provided by God for the use of men; and they lie to our hand, and are put under our power, as material and instruments which are for good use to those who know the instrument. . . .

16. . . . For he who holds possessions, and gold, and silver, and houses, as the gifts of God; and ministers from them to the God who gives them for the salvation of men; and knows that he possesses them more for the sake of the brethren than his own; and is superior to the possession of them, not the slave of the things he possesses; and does not carry them about in his soul, nor bind and circumscribe his life within them, but is ever labouring at some good and divine work, even should he be necessarily some time or other deprived of them, is able with cheerful mind to bear their removal equally with their abundance. This is he who is blessed by the Lord, and

called poor in spirit, a meet heir of the kingdom of heaven, not one who could not live rich.

17. But he who carries his riches in his soul, and instead of God's Spirit bears in his heart gold or land, and is always acquiring possessions without end, and is perpetually on the outlook for more, bending downwards and fettered in the toils of the world, being earth and destined to depart to earth,—whence can he be able to desire and to mind the kingdom of heaven,—a man who carries not a heart, but land or metal, who must perforce be found in the midst of the objects he has chosen? For where the mind of man is, there is also his treasure. The Lord acknowledges a twofold treasure,—the good: "For the good man, out of the good treasure of his heart, bringeth forth good;" and the evil: for "the evil man, out of the evil treasure, bringeth forth evil: for out of abundance of the heart the mouth speaketh. . . .

18. So that (the expression) rich men that shall with difficulty enter into the kingdom, is to be apprehended in a scholarly* way, not awkwardly, or rustically, or carnally. For if the expression is used thus, salvation does not depend on external things, whether they be many or few, small or great, or illustrious or obscure, or esteemed or disesteemed; but on the virtue of the soul, on faith, and hope, and love, and brotherliness, and knowledge, and meekness, and humility, and truth, the reward of which is salvation. For it is not on account of comeliness of body that any one shall live, or, on the other hand, perish. But he who uses the body given to him chastely and according to God, shall live; and he that destroys the temple of God shall be destroyed. An ugly man can be profligate, and a good-looking man temperate. Neither strength and great size of body makes alive, nor does any of the members destroy. But the soul which uses them provides the cause for each. Bear then, it is said, when struck on the face [Matt. 5:39]; which a man strong and in good health can obey. And again, a man who is feeble may transgress from refractoriness of temper. So also a poor and destitute man may be found intoxicated with lusts; and a man rich in worldly goods temperate, poor in indulgences, trustworthy, intelligent, pure, chastened.

From *The Ante-Nicene Fathers: Translations of The Writings of the Fathers down to A.D. 325*, vol. 2, edited by The Reverend Alexander Roberts and James Donaldson (New York: Charles Scribner's Sons, 1926), pp. 591–96. Copyright © 1885 by The Christian Literature Publishing Company.

THE INSTRUCTOR
Book 2

Chapter 1. . . . Some men, in truth, live that they may eat, as the irrational creatures, "whose life is their belly, and nothing else." But the Instructor

---

*μαθματικῶς [mathematikos]. Fell suggests instead of this reading of the text, πνευματικῶς [pneumatikos] or μεμελημένως [memelemenos].

enjoins us to eat that we may live. For neither is food our business, nor is pleasure our aim; but both are on account of our life here, which the Word is training up to immortality. Wherefore also there is discrimination to be employed in reference to food. And it is to be simple, truly plain, suiting precisely simple and artless children—as ministering to life, not to luxury. And the life to which it conduces consists of two things—health and strength; to which plainness of fare is most suitable, being conducive both to digestion and lightness of body, from which come growth, and health, and right strength, not strength that is wrong or dangerous and wretched, as is that of athletes produced by compulsory feeding.

We must therefore reject different varieties, which engender various mischiefs, such as a depraved habit of body and disorders of the stomach, the taste being vitiated by an unhappy art—that of cookery, and the useless art of making pastry. For people dare to call by the name of food their dabbling in luxuries, which glides into mischievous pleasures. Antiphanes, the Delian physician, said that this variety of viands was the one cause of disease; there being people who dislike the truth, and through various absurd notions abjure moderation of diet, and put themselves to a world of trouble to procure dainties from beyond seas.

. . . . "Whatever earth and the depths of the sea, and the unmeasured space of the air produce," they cater for their gluttony. In their greed and solicitude, the gluttons seem absolutely to sweep the world with a drag-net to gratify their luxurious tastes. These gluttons, surrounded with the sound of hissing frying-pans, and wearing their whole life away at the pestle and mortar, cling to matter like fire. More than that, they emasculate plain food, namely bread, by straining off the nourishing part of the grain, so that the necessary part of food becomes matter of reproach to luxury. There is no limit to epicurism among men. For it has driven them to sweet-meats, and honey-cakes, and sugar-plums; inventing a multitude of desserts, hunting after all manner of dishes. A man like this seems to me to be all jaw, and nothing else. . . .

For it were not seemly that we, after the fashion of the rich man's son in the Gospel [Luke 15:2], should, as prodigals, abuse the Father's gifts; but we should use them, without undue attachment to them, as having command over ourselves. For we are enjoined to reign and rule over meats, not to be slaves to them. . . .

We are not, then, to abstain wholly from various kinds of food, but only are not to be taken up about them. We are to partake of what is set before us, as becomes a Christian, out of respect to him who has invited us, by a harmless and moderate participation in the social meeting; regarding the sumptuousness of what is put on the table as a matter of indifference, despising the dainties, as after a little destined to perish. . . . And how foolish for people to raise themselves on the couches, all but pitching their faces into the dishes, stretching out from the couch as from a nest, according to the common saying, "that they may catch the wandering steam by breathing it in!" And how senseless, to besmear their hands with the condiments, and to be constantly reaching to the sauce, cramming them-

selves immoderately and shamelessly, not like people tasting, but raven-
ously seizing! . . .

From all slavish habits* and excess we must abstain, and touch what is
set before us in a decorous way; keeping the hand and couch and chin free
of stains; preserving the grace of the countenance undisturbed, and com-
mitting no indecorum in the act of swallowing; but stretching out the hand
at intervals in an orderly manner. We must guard against speaking anything while eating: for the voice becomes disagreeable and inarticulate
when it is confined by full jaws; and the tongue, pressed by the food and
impeded in its natural energy, gives forth a compressed utterance. Nor is
it suitable to eat and to drink simultaneously. For it is the very extreme of
intemperance to confound the times whose uses are discordant. . . . It is
therefore disgraceful to set one's self to do this; since the conversation of
wags of this description is not fit for our ears, inasmuch as by the very expressions used it familiarizes us with shameful actions.[†]

Pleasantry is allowable, not waggery. Besides, even laughter must be
kept in check; for when given vent to in the right manner it indicates or-
derliness, but when it issues differently it shows a want of restraint.

For, in a word, whatever things are natural to men we must not eradi-
cate from them, but rather impose on them limits and suitable times.

From *The Ante-Nicene Fathers: Translations of The Writings of the Fathers down to A.D.
325,* vol. 2, edited by The Reverend Alexander Roberts and James Donaldson (New York:
Charles Scribner's Sons, 1926), pp. 237–40, 250. Copyright © 1885 by The Christian Literature
Publishing Company.

11.   Origen, *Against Celsus*

*Clement's pupil and successor as head of the Christian catechetical school at
Alexandria, Origen (ca. 182–ca. 251), continued Clement's project of interpreting
Christian faith in Hellenistic thought forms.* Against Celsus *is a reply to a searching criticism of Christian ideas and behavior by an earlier pagan. Here, Origen defends the civic loyalty and responsible citizenship of Christians.*

Book 5

Chapter 37. As there are, then, generally two laws presented to us, the
one being the law of nature, of which God would be the legislator, and
the other being the written law of cities, it is a proper thing, when the written law is not opposed to that of God, for the citizens not to abandon it under pretext of foreign customs; but when the law of nature, that is, the law
of God, commands what is opposed to the written law, observe whether

---

*Literally, "slave-manners," the conduct to be expected from slaves.
[†]Our author is a terrible satirist; but it is instructive to see Christianity thus prescribing the minor morals, and banishing pagan brutality with holy scorn.

reason will not tell us to bid a long farewell to the written code, and to the desire of its legislators, and to give ourselves up to the legislator God, and to choose a life agreeable to His word, although in doing so it may be necessary to encounter dangers, and countless labours, and even death and dishonour. For when there are some laws in harmony with the will of God, which are opposed to others which are in force in cities, and when it is impracticable to please God (and those who administer laws of the kind referred to), it would be absurd to condemn those acts by means of which we may please the Creator of all things, and to select those by which we shall become displeasing to God, though we may satisfy unholy laws, and those who love them. But since it is reasonable in other matters to prefer the law of nature, which is the law of God, before the written law, which has been enacted by men in a spirit of opposition to the law of God, why should we not do this still more in the case of those laws which relate to God? . . .

Book 8

Chapter 68. Celsus goes on to say: "We must not disobey the ancient writer, who said long ago,

> 'Let one be king, whom the son of crafty Saturn
>   appointed;'"

Homer, Iliad, 2:205

and adds: "If you set aside this maxim, you will deservedly suffer for it at the hands of the king. For if all were to do the same as you, there would be nothing to prevent his being left in utter solitude and desertion, and the affairs of the earth would fall into the hands of the wildest and most lawless barbarians; and then there would no longer remain among men any of the glory of your religion or of the true wisdom." If, then, "there shall be one lord, one king," he must be, not the man "whom the son of crafty Saturn appointed," but the man to whom He gave the power, who "removeth kings and setteth up kings" [Dan. 2:21], and who "raiseth up the useful man in time of need upon earth" [Eccl. 10:4 (LXX)]. For kings are not appointed by that son of Saturn, who, according to Grecian fable, hurled his father from his throne, and sent him down to Tartarus (whatever interpretation may be given to this allegory), but by God, who governs all things, and who wisely arranges whatever belongs to the appointment of kings. We therefore do set aside the maxim contained in the line,

> "Whom the son of crafty Saturn appointed;"

for we know that no god or father of a god ever devises anything crooked or crafty. But we are far from setting aside the notion of a providence, and of things happening directly or indirectly through the agency of providence. And the king will not "inflict deserved punishment" upon us, if we say that not the son of crafty Saturn gave him his kingdom, but He who "removeth and setteth up kings." And would that all were to follow my example in rejecting the maxim of Homer, maintaining the divine origin of the kingdom, and observing the precept to honour the king! In these circumstances the king will not "be left in utter solitude and desertion," neither will "the affairs of the world fall into the hands of the most impious and wild barbarians." For if, in the words of Celsus, "they do as I do," then it is evident that even the barbarians, when they yield obedience to the word of God, will become most obedient to the law, and most humane; and every form of worship will be destroyed except the religion of Christ, which will alone prevail. And indeed it will one day triumph, as its principles take possession of the minds of men more and more every day. . . .

Chapter 70. But if all the Romans, according to the supposition of Celsus, embrace the Christian faith, they will, when they pray, overcome their enemies; or rather, they will not war at all, being guarded by that divine power which promised to save five entire cities for the sake of fifty just persons. For men of God are assuredly the salt of the earth: they preserve the order of the world [cf. Cowper, *Task,* book 6, *sub finem*]; and society is held together as long as the salt is uncorrupted: for "if the salt have lost its savour, it is neither fit for the land nor for the dunghill; but it shall be cast out, and trodden under foot of men. He that hath ears, let him hear" [Luke 14:34, 35; Matt. 5:13] the meaning of these words. When God gives to the tempter permission to persecute us, then we suffer persecution; and when God wishes us to be free from suffering, even in the midst of a world that hates us, we enjoy a wonderful peace, trusting in the protection of Him who said, "Be of good cheer, I have overcome the world" [John 16:33]. And truly He has overcome the world. Wherefore the world prevails only so long as it is the pleasure of Him who received from the Father power to overcome the world; and from His victory we take courage. Should He even wish us again to contend and struggle for our religion, let the enemy come against us, and we will say to them, "I can do all things, through Christ Jesus our Lord, which strengtheneth me" [Phil. 4:13]. For of "two sparrows which are sold for a farthing," as the Scripture says, "not one of them falls on the ground without our Father in heaven" [Matt. 10:29–30]. And so completely does the Divine Providence embrace all things, that not even the hairs of our head fail to be numbered by Him. . . .

Chapter 72. Afterwards he says: "If it were possible," implying at the same time that he thought it most desirable, "that all the inhabitants of Asia, Europe, and Libya, Greeks and Barbarians, all to the uttermost ends of the earth, were to come under one law;" but judging this quite impossible, he adds, "Any one who thinks this possible, knows nothing." It would require careful consideration and lengthened argument to prove that it is not only possible, but that it will surely come to pass, that all who are endowed with reason shall come under one law. However, if we must refer to this subject, it will be with great brevity. The Stoics, indeed, hold that, when the strongest of the elements prevails, all things shall be turned into fire. But our belief is, that the Word shall prevail over the entire rational creation, and change every soul into His own perfection; in which state every one, by the mere exercise of his power, will choose what he desires, and obtain what he chooses. For although, in the diseases and wounds of the body, there are some which no medical skill can cure, yet we hold that in the mind there is no evil so strong that it may not be overcome by the Supreme Word and God. . . . Let them also carefully consider the promise, that all shall call upon the name of the Lord, and serve Him with one consent; also that all contemptuous reproach shall be taken away, and there shall be no longer any injustice, or vain speech, or a deceitful tongue. And thus much it seemed needful for me to say briefly, and without entering into elaborate details, in answer to the remark of Celsus, that he considered any agreement between the inhabitants of Asia, Europe, and Libya, as well Greeks as Barbarians, was impossible. And perhaps such a result would indeed be impossible to those who are still in the body, but not to those who are released from it.

Chapter 73. In the next place, Celsus urges us "to help the king with all our might, and to labour with him in the maintenance of justice, to fight for him; and if he requires it, to fight under him, or lead an army along with him." To this our answer is, that we do, when occasion requires, give help to kings, and that, so to say, a divine help, "putting on the whole armour of God" [Eph. 6:2]. And this we do in obedience to the injunction of the apostle, "I exhort, therefore, that first of all, supplications, prayers, intercessions, and giving of thanks, be made for all men; for kings, and for all that are in authority" [1 Tim. 2–8]; and the more any one excels in piety, the more effective help does he render to kings, even more than is given by soldiers, who go forth to fight and slay as many of the enemy as they can. And to those enemies of our faith who require us to bear arms for the commonwealth, and to slay men, we can reply: "Do not those who are priests at certain shrines, and those who attend on certain gods, as you account them, keep their hands free from blood, that they may with hands unstained and free from human blood offer the appointed sacrifices to your gods; and even when war is upon you, you never enlist the priests in the army. If that, then, is a laudable custom, how much more so, that while others are engaged in battle, these too should engage as the priests and ministers of God, keeping their hands pure, and wrestling in prayers to God on behalf of those who are fighting in a righteous cause, and for the king who reigns righteously, that whatever is opposed to those who act righteously may be destroyed!" And as we by our prayers vanquish all demons who stir up war, and lead to the violation of oaths, and disturb the peace, we in this way are much more helpful to the kings than those who go into the field to fight for them. And we do take our part in public affairs, when along with righteous prayers we join self-denying exercises and meditations, which teach us to despise pleasures, and not to be led away by them. And none fight better for king than we do. We do not indeed fight under him, although he require it; but we fight on his behalf, forming a special army—an army of piety—by offering our prayers to God.

Chapter 74. And if Celsus would have us to lead armies in defence of our country, let him know that we do this too, and that not for the purpose of being seen by men, or of vainglory. For "in secret," and in our own hearts, there are prayers which ascend as from priests in behalf of our fellow-citizens. And Christians are benefactors of their country more than others. For they train up citizens, and inculcate piety to the Supreme Being; and they promote those whose lives in the smallest cities have been good and worthy, to a divine and heavenly city, to whom it may be said, "Thou hast been faithful in the smallest city, come into a great one [Luke 19:17], where "God standeth in the assembly of the gods, and judgeth the gods in the midst;" and He reckons thee among them, if thou no more "die as a man, or fall as one of the princes" [Ps. 82:1, 7].

Chapter 75. Celsus also urges us to "take office in the government of the country, if that is required for the maintenance of the laws and the support of religion." But we recognize in each state the existence of another national organization* founded by the Word of God, and we exhort those who are mighty in word and of blameless life to rule over Churches. Those who are ambitious of ruling we reject; but we constrain those who, through excess of modesty, are not easily induced to take a public charge in the Church of God. And those who rule over us well are under the constraining influence of the great King, whom we believe to be the Son of God, God the Word. And if those who govern in the Church, and are called rulers of the divine nation—that is, the Church—rule well, they rule in accordance with the divine commands, and never suffer themselves to be led astray by worldly policy. And it is not for the purpose of escaping public duties that Christians decline public offices, but that they may reserve themselves for a diviner and more necessary service in the Church of God—for the salvation of men. And this service is at once necessary and right. They take charge of all—of those that are within, that they may day by day lead better lives, and of those that are without, that they may come to abound in holy words and in deeds of piety; and that, while thus worshipping God truly, and training up as many as they can in the same way, they may be filled with the word of God and the law of God, and thus be united with the Supreme God through His Son the Word, Wisdom, Truth, and Righteousness, who unites to God all who are resolved to conform their lives in all things to the law of God.

From *The Ante-Nicene Fathers: Translations of The Writings of the Fathers down to A.D. 325*, vol. 4, edited by The Reverend Alexander Roberts and James Donaldson (New York: Charles Scribner's Sons, 1926), pp. 559–60, 665–66, 667–68. Copyright © 1885 by the Christian Literature Publishing Company.

*σύστημα πατρίδος [systema patridos]. [A very notable passage as to the autonomy of the primitive Churches in their divers nations.]

12. Lactantius,
The Divine Institutes

The triumph of the Emperor Constantine in A.D. 313 was a watershed event in the history of Christian ethics. Formerly a suspected and often persecuted minority, Christians now enjoyed imperial patronage and, increasingly, "establishment" status. The writings of Lactantius illustrate the change. Tutor to the emperor's own son, Lactantius in his principal work, The Divine Institutes, *flattered Constantine while also exploring the meaning of justice and condemning injustices and false conceptions of the good.*

Book 1

Chapter 1. . . . And we now commence this work under the auspices of your name, O mighty Emperor Constantine, who were the first of the Roman princes to repudiate errors, and to acknowledge and honour the majesty of the one and only true God.* For when that most happy day had shone upon the world, in which the Most High God raised you to the prosperous height of power, you entered upon a dominion which was salutary and desirable for all, with an excellent beginning; when, restoring justice which had been overthrown and taken away, you expiated the most shameful deed of others. In return for which action God will grant to you happiness, virtue, and length of days, that even when old you may govern the state with the same justice with which you began in youth, and may hand down to your children the guardianship of the Roman name, as you yourself received it from your father. For to the wicked, who still rage against the righteous in other parts of the world, the Omnipotent will also repay the reward of their wickedness with a severity proportioned to its tardiness; for as He is a most indulgent Father towards the godly, so is He a most upright Judge against the ungodly. And in my desire to defend His religion and divine worship, to which can I rather appeal, whom can I address, but him by whom justice and wisdom have been restored to the affairs of men? . . .

Book 3

Chapter 9. . . . I now come to the chief good of true wisdom, the nature of which is to be determined in this manner; first, it must be the property of man alone, and not belong to any other animal; secondly, it must belong to the soul only, and not be shared with the body; lastly, it cannot fall to the lot of any one without knowledge and virtue. Now this limitation excludes and does away with all the opinions of those *whom I have mentioned;* for their sayings contain nothing of this kind. I will now say what this is, that I may

*[It thrills me to compare this modest tribute of Christian confidence, with Justin's unheeded appeal to the Stoical Antonine.]

show, as I designed, that all philosophers were blind and foolish, who could neither see, nor understand, nor surmise at any time what was fixed as the chief good for man. Anaxagoras, when asked for what purpose he was born, replied that he might look upon the heaven and the sun. . . . You believe that it is a great thing to behold the heaven and the sun: why, therefore, do you not give thanks to Him who is the author of this benefit? why do you not measure with your mind the excellence, the providence, and the power of Him whose works you admire? For it must be, that He who created objects worthy of admiration, is Himself much more to be admired. . . . Therefore it is not the world which is to be contemplated by the eye, for each is a body,* but it is God who is to be contemplated by the soul: for God, being Himself immortal, willed that the soul also should be everlasting. But the contemplation of God is the reverence and worship of the common Parent of mankind. And if the philosophers were destitute of this, and in their ignorance of divine things prostrated themselves to the earth, we must suppose that Anaxagoras neither beheld the heaven nor the sun, though he said that he was born that he might behold them. The object proposed to man is therefore plain† and easy, if he is wise; and to it especially belongs humanity.‡ For what is humanity itself, but justice? what is justice, but piety? And piety§ is nothing else than the recognition of God as a parent. . . .

Chapter 10. . . . Therefore the chief good of man is in religion only; for the other things, even those which are supposed to be peculiar to man, are found in the other animals also. . . .

Chapter 11. . . . It is agreed upon, therefore, by the general consent of all mankind, that religion ought to be undertaken; but we have to explain what errors are committed on this subject. God willed this to be the nature of man, that he should be desirous and eager for two things, religion and wisdom. But men are mistaken in this, that they either undertake religion and pay no attention to wisdom, or they devote themselves to wisdom alone, and pay no attention to religion, though the one cannot be true without the other. The consequence is, that they fall into a multiplicity of religions, but false ones, because they have left wisdom, which could have taught them that there cannot be many gods; or they devote themselves to wisdom, but a false wisdom, because they have paid no attention to the religion of the Supreme God, who might have instructed them to the knowledge of the truth. Thus men who undertake either of these courses follow a devious path, and one full of the greatest errors, inasmuch as the duty of man, and all truth, are included in these two things which are inseparably connected. I wonder, therefore, that there was none at all of the philosophers who discovered the abode and dwelling-place of the chief good. For they might have sought it in this manner. Whatever the

*Each, viz., the world and the eye.
†Expedita, "free from obstacles," "unembarrassed."
‡Humanity, properly that which is characteristic of man, then kindness and humaneness.
§Pietas. The word denotes not only piety towards God, but also the affection due to a parent.

greatest good is, it must be an object proposed to all men. There is pleasure, which is desired by all; but this is common also to man with the beasts, and has not the force of the honourable, and brings a feeling of satiety, and when it is in excess is injurious, and it is lessened by advance of age, and does not fall to the lot of many: for they who are without resources, who constitute the greater part of men, must also be without pleasure. Therefore pleasure is not the chief good; but it is not even a good. What shall we say of riches? This is much more* true of them. For they fall to the lot of fewer men, and that generally by chance; and they often fall to the indolent, and sometimes by guilt, and they are desired by those who already possess them. What shall we say of sovereignty itself? That does not constitute the chief good: for all cannot reign, but it is necessary that all should be capable of attaining the chief good. . . .

. . . Can it be that that which is admitted to be good and honourable should be requited with no reward, and be so unproductive as to procure no advantage from itself? That great labour and difficulty and struggling against evils with which this life is filled, must of necessity produce some great good. But what shall we say that it is? Pleasure? But nothing that is base can arise from that which is honourable. Shall we say that it is riches? or commands? But these things are frail and uncertain.† Is it glory? or honour? or a lasting name? But all these things are not contained in virtue itself, but depend upon the opinion and judgment of others. For virtue is often hated and visited with evil. But the good which arises from it ought to be so closely united with it as to be incapable of being separated or disunited from it; and it cannot appear to be the chief good in any other way than if it belongs peculiarly to virtue, and is such that nothing can be added to it or taken from it. Why should I say that the duties of virtue consist in the despising of all these things? For not to long for, or desire, or love pleasures, riches, dominions, and honours, and all those things which are esteemed as goods, as others do overpowered by desire, that assuredly is virtue. Therefore it effects something else more sublime and excellent; nor does anything struggle against these present goods but that which longs for greater and truer things. Let us not despair of being able to find it, if we turn our thoughts in all directions; for no slight or trifling rewards are sought. . . .

Chapter 12. . . . [I]f no reward, such as it deserves, is found on earth, inasmuch as it despises all things which are frail and transitory, what else remains but that it may effect some heavenly reward, since it treats with contempt all earthly things, and may aim at higher things, since it despises things that are humble? And this *reward* can be nothing else but immortality. . . .

Book 5

Chapter 5. . . . [T]he worship of God being taken away, men lost the knowledge of good and evil. Thus the common intercourse of life perished from among men, and the bond of human society was destroyed. Then they

---

*Multo magis is the reading of the MSS.; but multo minus—"much less"—seems preferable.
†Liable to fall, perishable.

began to contend with one another, and to plot, and to acquire for themselves glory from the shedding of human blood.

Chapter 6. . . . And the source of all these evils was lust; which, indeed, burst forth from the contempt of true majesty. For not only did they who had a superfluity fail to bestow a share upon others, but they even seized the property of others, drawing everything to their private gain; and the things which formerly even individuals laboured to obtain for the common use of men,* were now conveyed to the houses of a few. For, that they might subdue others by slavery, they began especially to withdraw and collect together the necessaries of life, and to keep them firmly shut up, that they might make the bounties of heaven their own; not on account of kindness,† a feeling which had no existence in them, but that they might sweep together all the instruments of lust and avarice. They also, under the name of justice, passed most unequal and unjust laws, by which they might defend their plunder and avarice against the force of the multitude. They prevailed, therefore, as much by authority as by strength, or resources, or malice. And since there was in them no trace of justice, the offices of which are humanity, equity, pity, they now began to rejoice in a proud and swollen inequality, and made‡ themselves higher than other men, by a retinue of attendants, and by the sword, and by the brilliancy of their garments. For this reason they invented for themselves honours, and purple robes, and fasces, that, being supported by the terror produced by axes and swords, they might, as it were by the right of masters, rule them, stricken with fear, and alarmed. Such was the condition in which the life of man was placed by that king who, having defeated and put to flight a parent, did not seize his kingdom, but set up an impious tyranny by violence and armed men, and took away that golden age of justice, and compelled men to become wicked and impious. . . .

. . . But the change of the age and the expulsion of justice is to be deemed nothing else, as I have said, than the laying aside of divine religion, which alone effects that man should esteem man dear, and should know that he is bound to him by the tie of brotherhood, since God is alike a Father to all, so as to share the bounties of the common God and Father with those who do not possess them; to injure no one, to oppress no one, not to close his door against a stranger, nor his ear against a suppliant, but to be bountiful, beneficent, and liberal, which Tullius§ thought to be praises suitable to a king. This truly is justice.

From *The Ante-Nicene Fathers: Translations of The Writings of the Fathers down to A.D. 325*, vol. 7, edited by The Reverend Alexander Roberts and James Donaldson (Grand Rapids, Mich.: William B. Eerdmans Publishing Co., 1975, reprinted), pp. 10, 76–79, 141–42.

*Hominum. Another reading is "omnium," of all, as opposed to the few.
†Propter humanitatem.
‡Altiores se . . . faciebant. Another reading is, "altiores cæteris . . . fulgebant."
§[Compare Cicero, *De Officiis*, i, 14, with Luke 22:25.]

13. Ambrose,
Letters to Priests

In his Letters to Priests, *Bishop Ambrose of Milan (ca. 339–397) offers pastoral advice on moral issues, including the discussion here on the moral problems of wealth and greed. Ambrose combined unusual gifts as a preacher, theologian, and administrator, but he is also remembered for his great influence upon a greater theologian, Augustine.*

What better pattern of righteousness is there than the divine, for the Son of God says: 'Love your enemies' and again: 'Pray for those who persecute and calumniate you' [Matt. 5:44]. He so far removes from the perfect the desire for vengeance that He commands charity for those who do them harm. And since He had said in the old Scriptures: 'Revenge is mine and I will repay' [Deut. 32:55], He says in the Gospel that we must pray for those who have done us harm, so that He who said He will have to punish will not punish them; it is His wish to pardon by your consent with which He agrees according to His promise. For, if you seek revenge, you know that the unrighteous is punished more severely by his own convictions than by the severity of his judges.

Since no one can be without some trouble, let us strive not to have our troubles caused by our sin. And no one is so severely condemned by another's judgment as the fool by his own, for he is the author of his own evils. Therefore, let us keep away from tasks which are troublesome and fraught with discord, having no advantage, producing only added weight. Yet, we should live so as not to regret our decisions or our actions. A wise man usually looks ahead, so he will not often have to repent, for only God never repents. What is the advantage of righteousness but peace of mind? What is the meaning of living righteously but living with peace? As the pattern of the master is, so is the condition of the whole house. If these are needed for a home, how much more for the Church, 'Where there is rich and poor, slave and freeman, Greek and Syrian, patrician and plebeian, we are all one in Christ' [Col. 3:11].

Let no one think that he is to be paid more deference because he is rich [cf. Prov. 17:5]. In the Church a man is rich if he is rich in faith, for the faithful man has a whole world of riches. Is it strange that the faithful man owns the world, since he owns Christ's inheritance, which is more priceless than the world? 'You were redeemed with the precious blood' surely was said to all, not only to the rich. But, if you wish to be rich, follow Him who says: 'Be you also holy in all your behavior.' This He says not only to the rich but to all, because He judges without respect of persons as His faithful witness, the Apostle, says: 'Spend the time of your sojourning not in luxury, nor in fastidiousness, nor haughtiness of heart, but in fear [1 Pet. 1:18, 19, 15, 17]. You have been given time on this earth, not eternity; use the time as those who know they are going to set out from here.

Trust not in riches, because they must all be left here; only faith will go with you. Righteousness will be your companion if faith leads the way. Why do riches flatter you? 'You were not redeemed with gold or silver,' with possessions or silk garments, 'from your vain manner of life, but by the precious blood of Christ Jesus' [1 Pet. 1:18, 19]. He is rich who is an heir of God, a joint-heir of Christ. Despise not a poor man, for He made you rich. Despise not a man in want, for 'The poor man cried, and the Lord heard' [Ps. 33:7]. Reject not the needy, for Christ even became poor although He was rich, but He became poor for you so that He might with His poverty enrich you. Exalt not yourself as rich; He sent forth His Apostles without money.

And the first of them said: 'Silver and gold I have none [Acts 3:6]. He glories in poverty as if escaping contamination. 'Silver and gold,' says he, 'I have none,' nor gold and silver. He does not know their order, for he does not know their use. 'Silver and gold I have none, but faith I do have. I am rich enough in the name of Jesus, which is above every name' [cf. Phil. 2:9]. I have not silver, neither do I desire it; I have not gold, neither do I want it. But I have what you rich men do not have, I have what even you consider of more value, and I give it to the poor, so that I say in the name of Jesus: 'Strengthen ye feeble hands, and weak knees' [Isa. 35:3].

But, if you wish to be rich, you must be poor. Then you will be rich in all things, if you are poor in spirit. Not property, but the spirit, makes one rich.

There are some who abase themselves amid many riches, and they do so rightly and wisely, for the law of nature is sufficiently rich to all, whereby one quickly finds what is more than enough, but for lust all the abundance of riches is poverty. Finally, no one is born poor, he becomes so. Poverty is not in nature, but in our feelings; therefore it is easy for nature to be found rich, difficult for greed to be so. For, the more each one acquires, the more he thirsts and is parched by a certain intoxication of his desire.

Why do you seek for a heap of riches as if it were necessary? Nothing is so necessary as to know what is not necessary. Why do you turn the blame upon the flesh? It is not the belly of the body, but greed of mind that makes a man unsatisfied. Does the flesh take away the hope of the future? Does the flesh destroy the sweetness of spiritual grace? Does the flesh hinder faith? Does the flesh concede anything to vain opinions, as to harsh masters? Rather does the flesh love moderate frugality, by which it is stripped of a burden, and is clothed in good health, because it lays down its concern and takes on tranquility.

Riches themselves are not to be censured. 'The ransom of a man's life are his riches' [Prov. 13:8], for one who gives to the poor ransoms his soul. Therefore, even in riches there is scope for virtue. You are like helmsmen on a great sea. If one steers his course well, he passes quickly over the sea to reach harbor. But one who does not know how to manage his property is drowned by his load. Therefore it is written: 'The substance of the rich is a very strong city' [Prov. 10:15].

What is that city but Jerusalem which is in heaven where there is the kingdom of God? This is the good possession which produces everlasting fruit; the good possession which is not left here, but is possessed there. One who will have this possession says: 'The Lord is my portion' [Ps. 72:26]. He says not: My portion extends from this boundary to that. He says not: My portion is among certain neighbors, except, perhaps, among the Apostles, among the Prophets, among the Lord's saints. This is the righteous man's portion. He says not: My portion is in meadows, in forests, in plains, except perhaps in the plains of the forest where is found the Church of which it is written: 'We have found it in the fields of the forest' [Ps. 131:6]. He says not: My portion consists of herds of horses, for 'Untrustworthy is the steed for safety' [Ps. 32:17]. He says not: My portion consists of herds of oxen, asses, or sheep, except, perhaps, he counts himself among those herds which know their owner, and wishes to consort with that ass which does not shun the crib of Christ' [cf. Isa. 1:3], and that sheep is his portion which was led to the slaughter and the 'Lamb which was dumb before his shearer and did not open his mouth' [Isa. 53:7], in whose humiliation judgment has been exalted. Well does he say: 'Before his shearer,' because He laid on the cross what was superfluous, not His own essence; when He was stripped of His body, He did not lose His Godhead.

Not everyone, therefore, says: 'The Lord is my portion.' The greedy man does not say this, because greed comes and says: You are my portion; I have you under my sway, you are become my slave, you sold yourself to me in that gold of yours, you turned yourself over to me in that possession of yours. The luxury-loving man does not say: Christ is my portion, because luxury comes and says: You are my portion; I made you my slave in that banquet, I caught you in the net of those feasts, I have you bound to payment by the surety of your gluttony. Do you not know that you valued your table more than your life? I convict you by your own judgment. Deny it if you can, but you cannot. Finally, you kept nothing for life, you spent all for your table. The adulterer cannot say: 'The Lord is my portion,' because passion comes and says: I am your portion; you bound yourself to me by your love for that maiden, by a night with a harlot you came under my laws and into my power. The traitor does not say: Christ is my portion, because at once the vileness of sin rushes upon him and says: He is deceiving you, Lord Jesus, he is mine. . . .

Love hospitality, by which blessed Abraham found favor, and received Christ as his guest, and Sara already worn with age deserved to have a son. Lot also escaped the destructive fire of Sodom [cf. Gen. 18:1, 2; 19:2, 3, 13–22], and you can entertain angels if you offer your hospitality to strangers. What shall I say of Rahob who by this means found salvation [cf. Josh. 2:1–19]?

Show compassion for those who are bound by chains, as if you yourself were bound with them. Console those who grieve: 'It is better to go to the house of mourning, than to the house of joy' [Eccl. 7:3]. From one is borne the merit of a good work; from the other, a lapse into sin. Lastly, from the one you hope for a reward; in the other you receive it. Suffer with those who are in trouble, as if being in trouble with them.

Let a woman show deference, not be a slave to her husband; let her show she is ready to be guided, not coerced. She is not worthy of wedlock who is worthy of chiding. Let the husband, too, manage his wife like a steersman, pay honor to her as his life partner, share with her as the co-heir of grace.

Mothers, wean your children, love them, but pray for them that they may be long-lived above the earth, not on it, but above it. Nothing is long-lived on this earth, and that which lasts long is brief and more hazardous. Warn them rather to take up the cross of the Lord than to love this life.

From Ambrose, "Letters to Priests," in *Fathers of the Church,* translated by Sister Mary Melchior Beyenka (Washington, D.C.: Catholic University of America Press, 1954), pp. 352–61.

14. Augustine, *Morals of the Catholic Church, The City of God,* and *Against the Manichaeans*

The thought of Augustine of Hippo (354–430) was to dominate Christian theology for a thousand years, and it continues to exert great direct and indirect influence on Christian thinking. In his Morals of the Catholic Church, *Augustine reflects upon love, the ultimate object of which is always God, and upon the classical virtues, each of which is also interpreted by him in relation to the love of God. In his magisterial* City of God, *Augustine explores the nature of sin and the freedom of the will and offers an overarching theological interpretation of human society. Implicitly, his contrast between the city of God and the human city, intertwined as they are in earthly existence, suggests a high doctrine of the church in relation to the world—though Augustine is aware of the presence of sin in the church. This selection from the* City of God *also contains his reflections on peace, and the following selection from his writings against the Manichaeans contains the heart of his formulation of "just war" doctrine.*

MORALS OF THE CATHOLIC CHURCH

For other than this, that which really is I knew not; and was, as it were, through sharpness of wit, persuaded to assent to foolish deceivers, when they asked me, "whence is evil?" "is God bounded by a bodily shape, and has hairs and nails?" "are they to be esteemed righteous who had many wives at once, and did kill men, and sacrificed living creatures" [1 Kings 18:40]? At which I, in my ignorance, was much troubled, and departing from the truth, seemed to myself to be making towards it; because as yet I knew not that evil was nothing but a privation of good, until at last a thing ceases altogether to be; which how should I see, the sight of whose eyes reached only to bodies, and of my mind to a phantasm? . . .

For hence I believed Evil also to be some such kind of substance, and to have its own foul and hideous bulk; whether gross, which they called earth, or thin and subtile (like the body of the air), which they imagine to be some malignant mind, creeping through that earth. And because a piety, such as it was, constrained me to believe that the good God never created any evil nature, I conceived two masses, contrary to one another, both unbounded, but the evil narrower, the good more expansive. And from this pestilent beginning, the other sacrilegious conceits followed on me. For when my mind endeavoured to recur to the Catholic faith, I was driven back, since that was not the Catholic faith which I thought to be so. And I seemed to myself more reverential, if I believed of Thee, my God (to whom Thy mercies confess out of my mouth), as unbounded, at least on other sides, although on that where the mass of evil was opposed to Thee, I was constrained to confess Thee bounded; than if on all sides I should imagine Thee to be bounded by the form of a human body. And it seemed to me better to believe Thee to have created no evil (which to me ignorant seemed not some only, but a bodily substance, because I could not conceive of mind unless as a subtile body, and that diffused in definite spaces), than to believe the nature of evil, such as I conceived it, could come from Thee. Yea, and our Saviour Himself, Thy Only Begotten, I believed to have been reached forth (as it were) for our salvation, out of the mass of Thy most lucid substance, so as to believe nothing of Him, but what I could imagine in my vanity. His Nature then, being such, I thought could not be born of the Virgin Mary, without being mingled with the flesh: and how that which I had so figured to myself could be mingled, and not defiled, I saw not. I feared therefore to believe Him born in the flesh, lest I should be forced to believe Him defiled by the flesh. Now will Thy spiritual ones mildly and lovingly smile upon me, if they shall read these my confessions. Yet such was I. . . .

What innumerable toys, made by divers arts and manufactures in our apparel, shoes, utensils and all sort of works, in pictures also in divers images, and these far exceeding all necessary and moderate use and all pious meaning, have men added to tempt their own eyes withal; outwardly following what themselves make, inwardly forsaking Him by whom themselves were made, and destroying that which themselves have been made! But I, my God and my Glory, do hence also sing a hymn to Thee, and do consecrate praise to Him who consecrateth me, because beautiful patterns which through men's souls are conveyed into their cunning hands, come from that Beauty, which is above our souls, which my soul day and night sigheth after. But the framers and followers of the outward beauties derive thence the rule of judging of them, but not of using them. And He is there, though they perceive Him not, that so they might not wander, but *keep their strength for Thee* [Ps. 58—Vulg.], and not scatter it abroad upon pleasurable wearinesses. And I, though I speak and see this, entangle my steps with these outward beauties; but Thou pluckest me out, O Lord, thou pluckest me out; *because Thy loving-kindness is before my eyes* [Ps. 25:3]. For I am taken miserably, and Thou pluckest me out mercifully; sometimes not perceiving it, when I had but lightly lighted upon them; otherwhiles with pain, because I had stuck fast in them. . . .

But, O Lord, Thou alone Lord without pride, because Thou art the only true Lord, who hast no Lord; hath this third kind of temptation also ceased from me, or can it cease through this whole life? To wish, namely, to be feared and loved of men, for no other end, but that we may have a joy therein which is no joy? A miserable life this and a foul boastfulness? Hence especially it comes that men do neither purely love nor fear Thee. And therefore *dost Thou resist the proud, and givest grace to the humble* [Jam. 4:6]: yea, Thou thunderest down upon the ambitions of the world, and *the foundations of the mountains tremble* [Ps. 18:7]. Because now certain offices of human society make it necessary to be loved and feared of men, the adversary of our true blessedness layeth hard at us, every where spreading his snares of "well-done, well-done;" that greedily catching at them, we may be taken unawares, and sever our joy from Thy truth, and set it in the deceivingness of men; and be pleased at being loved and feared, not for Thy sake, but in Thy stead.

From *The Confessions of St. Augustine*, The Harvard Classics, vol. 7, translated by Edward B. Pusey and edited by Charles W. Eliot (New York: P. F. Collier & Son Corp.), pp. 37, 75, 188, 191. Copyright © 1909 by P. F. Collier & Son; 1937 by P. F. Collier & Son Corporation.

THE CITY OF GOD

Book 5

Chapter 10. . . . Wherefore, neither is that necessity to be feared, for dread of which the Stoics labored to make such distinctions among the causes of things as should enable them to rescue certain things from the dominion of necessity, and to subject others to it. Among those things which they wished not to be subject to necessity they placed our wills, knowing that they would not be free if subjected to necessity. For if that is to be called *our necessity* which is not in our power, but even though we be unwilling effects what it can effect,—as, for instance, the necessity of death,—it is manifest that our wills by which we live uprightly or wickedly are not under such a necessity; for we do many things which, if we were not willing, we should certainly not do. This is primarily true of the act of willing itself,—for if we will, it *is*; if we will not, it *is* not,—for we should not will if we were unwilling. But if we define necessity to be that according to which we say that it is necessary that anything be of such or such a nature, or be done in such and such a manner, I know not why we should have any dread of that necessity taking away the freedom of our will. For we do not put the life of God or the foreknowledge of God under necessity if we should say that it is necessary that God should live forever, and foreknow all things; as neither is His power diminished when we say that He cannot die or fall into error,—for this is in such a way impossible to Him, that if it were possible for Him, He would be of less power. But assuredly He is rightly called omnipotent, though He can neither die nor fall into error. For He is called omnipotent on account of His doing what he wills, not on account of His suffering what He wills not; for if that should befall Him, He would by no means be omnipotent. Wherefore, He cannot do some things for the very reason that He is omnipotent. So also, when we say that it is necessary that, when we will, we will by free choice, in so saying we both affirm what is true beyond doubt, and do not still subject our wills thereby to a necessity which destroys liberty. Our wills, therefore, *exist* as *wills*, and do themselves whatever we do by willing, and which would not be done if we were unwilling. But when any one suffers anything, being unwilling, by the will of another, even in that case will retains its essential validity,—we do not mean the will of the party who inflicts the suffering, for we resolve it into the power of God. For if a will should simply exist, but not be able to do what it wills, it would be overborne by a more powerful will. Nor would this be the case unless there had existed will, and that not the will of the other party, but the will of him who willed, but was not able to accomplish what he willed. Therefore, whatsoever a man suffers contrary to his own will, he ought not to attribute to the will of men, or of angels, or of any created spirit, but rather to His will who gives power to wills. It is not the case, therefore, that because God foreknew what would be in the power of our wills, there is for that reason nothing in the power of our wills. For he who foreknew this did not foreknow nothing. Moreover, if He who foreknew what would be in the power of our wills did not foreknow nothing, but something, assuredly, even though He did foreknow, there is something in the power of our wills. Therefore we are by no means compelled, either, retaining the prescience of God, to take away the freedom of the will, or, retaining the freedom of the will, to deny that He is prescient of future things, which is impious. But we embrace both. We faithfully and sincerely confess both. The former, that we may believe well; the latter, that we may live well. For he lives ill who does not believe well concerning God. Wherefore, be it far from us, in order to maintain our freedom, to deny the prescience of Him by whose help we are or shall be free. Consequently, it is not in vain that laws are enacted, and that reproaches, exhortations, praises, and vituperations are had recourse to; for these also He foreknew, and they are of great avail, even as great as He foreknew that they would be of. Prayers, also, are of avail to procure those things which He foreknew that He would grant to those who offered them; and with justice have rewards been appointed for good deeds, and punishments for sins. For a man does not therefore sin because God foreknew that he would sin. Nay, it cannot be doubted but that it is the man himself who sins when he does sin, because He, whose foreknowledge is infallible, foreknew not that fate, or fortune, or something else would sin, but that the man himself would sin, who, if he wills not, sins not. But if he shall not will to sin, even this did God foreknow. . . .

Book 14

Chapter 4. . . . When, therefore, man lives according to man, not according to God, he is like the devil. Because not even an angel might live according to an angel, but only according to God, if he was to abide in the truth, and speak God's truth and not his own lie. And of man, too, the same apostle says in another place, "If the truth of God hath more abounded through my lie;" [Rom. 3:7]—"my lie," he said, and "God's truth." When, then, a man lives according to the truth, he lives not according to himself, but according to God; for He was God who said, "I am the truth" [John 14:6]. When, therefore, man lives according to himself,—that is, according to man, not according to God,—assuredly he lives according to a lie; not that man himself is a lie, for God is his author and creator; who is certainly not the author and creator of a lie, but because man was made upright, that he might not live according to himself, but according to Him that made him,—in other words, that he might do His will and not his own; and not to live as he was made to live, that is a lie. For he certainly desires to be blessed even by not living so that he may be blessed. And what is a lie if this desire be not? Wherefore it is not without meaning said that all sin is a lie. For no sin is committed save by that desire or will by which we desire that it be well with us, and shrink from it being ill with us. That, therefore, is a lie which we do in order that it may be well with us, but which makes us more miserable than we were. And why is this, but because the source of man's happiness lies only in God, whom he abandons when he sins, and not in himself, by living according to whom he sins?

In enunciating this proposition of ours, then, that because some live according to the flesh and others according to the spirit, there have arisen two diverse and conflicting cities, we might equally well have said, "because some live according to man, others according to God.". . .

Chapter 13. . . .Our first parents fell into open disobedience because already they were secretly corrupted; for the evil act had never been done had not an evil will preceded it. And what is the origin of our evil will but pride? For "pride is the beginning of sin" [Eccl. 10:13]. And what is pride but the craving for undue exaltation? And this is undue exaltation, when the soul abandons Him to whom it ought to cleave as its end, and becomes a kind of end to itself. This happens when it becomes its own satisfaction. And it does so when it falls away from that unchangeable good which ought to satisfy it more than itself. This falling away is spontaneous; for if the will had remained steadfast in the love of that higher and changeless good by which it was illumined to intelligence and kindled into love, it would not have turned away to find satisfaction in itself, and so become frigid and benighted; the woman would not have believed the serpent spoke the truth, nor would the man have preferred the request of his wife to the command of God, nor have supposed that it was a venial transgression to cleave to the partner of his life even in a partnership of sin. The wicked deed, then,—that is to say, the transgression of eating the forbidden fruit,—was committed by persons who were already wicked. That "evil fruit" [Matt 7:18] could be brought forth only by "a corrupt tree." But that the tree was evil was not the result of nature; for certainly it could become so only by the vice of the will, and vice is contrary to nature. Now, nature could not have been depraved by vice had it not been made out of nothing. Consequently, that it is a nature, this is because it is made by God;

55

but that it falls away from Him, this is because it is made out of nothing. But man did not so fall away* as to become absolutely nothing; but being turned towards himself, his being became more contracted than it was when he clave to Him who supremely is. Accordingly, to exist in himself, that is, to be his own satisfaction after abandoning God, is not quite to become a nonentity, but to approximate to that. And therefore the holy Scriptures designate the proud by another name, "self-pleasers." For it is good to have the heart lifted up, yet not to one's self, for this is proud, but to the Lord, for this is obedient, and can be the act only of the humble. There is, therefore, something in humility which, strangely enough, exalts the heart, and something in pride which debases it. This seems, indeed, to be contradictory, that loftiness should debase and lowliness exalt. But pious humility enables us to submit to what is above us; and nothing is more exalted above us than God; and therefore humility, by making us subject to God, exalts us. But pride, being a defect of nature, by the very act of refusing subjection and revolting from Him who is supreme, falls to a low condition; and then comes to pass what is written: "Thou castedst them down when they lifted up themselves" [Ps. 73:18]. For he does not say, "when they had been lifted up," as if first they were exalted, and then afterwards cast down; but "when they lifted up themselves" even then they were cast down,—that is to say, the very lifting up was already a fall. And therefore it is that humility is specially recommended to the city of God as it sojourns in this world, and is specially exhibited in the city of God, and in the person of Christ its King; while the contrary vice of pride, according to the testimony of the sacred writings, specially rules his adversary the devil. And certainly this is the great difference which distinguishes the two cities of which we speak, the one being the society of the godly men, the other of the ungodly, each associated with the angels that adhere to their party, and the one guided and fashioned by love of self, the other by love of God.

The devil, then, would not have ensnared man in the open and manifest sin of doing what God had forbidden, had man not already begun to live for himself. It was this that made him listen with pleasure to the words, "Ye shall be as gods" [Gen 3:5], which they would much more readily have accomplished by obediently adhering to their supreme and true end than by proudly living to themselves. For created gods are gods not by virtue of what is in themselves, but by a participation of the true God. By craving to be more, man becomes less; and by aspiring to be self-sufficing, he fell away from Him who truly suffices him. Accordingly, this wicked desire which prompts man to please himself as if he were himself light, and which thus turns him away from that light by which, had he followed it, he would himself have become light,—this wicked desire, I say, already secretly existed in him, and the open sin was but its consequence. For that is true which is written, "Pride goeth before destruction, and before honor is humility" [Prov. 18:12]; that is to say, secret ruin precedes open ruin, while the former is not counted ruin. For who counts exaltation ruin, though no sooner

Defecit.

is the Highest forsaken than a fall is begun? But who does not recognize it as ruin, when there occurs an evident and indubitable transgression of the commandment? And consequently, God's prohibition had reference to such an act as, when committed, could not be defended on any pretence of doing what was righteous.* And I make bold to say that it is useful for the proud to fall into an open and indisputable transgression, and so displease themselves, as already, by pleasing themselves, they had fallen. For Peter was in a healthier condition when he wept and was dissatisfied with himself, than when he boldly presumed and satisfied himself. And this is averred by the sacred Psalmist when he says, "Fill their faces with shame, that they may seek Thy name, O Lord" [Ps. 83:16]; that is, that they who have pleased themselves in seeking their own glory may be pleased and satisfied with Thee in seeking Thy glory. . . .

Chapter 28. . . . Accordingly, two cities have been formed by two loves: the earthly by the love of self, even to the contempt of God; the heavenly by the love of God, even to the contempt of self. The former, in a word, glories in itself, the latter in the Lord. For the one seeks glory from men; but the greatest glory of the other is God, the witness of conscience. The one lifts up its head in its own glory; the other says to its God, "Thou art my glory, and the lifter up of mine head" [Ps. 3:3]. In the one, the princes and the nations it subdues are ruled by the love of ruling; in the other, the princes and the subjects serve one another in love, the latter obeying, while the former take thought for all. The one delights in its own strength, represented in the persons of its rulers; the other says to its God, "I will love Thee, O Lord, my strength" [Ps. 28:1]. And therefore the wise men of the one city, living according to man, have sought for profit to their own bodies or souls, or both, and those who have known God "glorified Him not as God, neither were thankful, but became vain in their imaginations, and their foolish heart was darkened; professing themselves to be wise,"—that is, glorying in their own wisdom, and being possessed by pride,—"they became fools, and changed the glory of the incorruptible God into an image made like to corruptible man, and to birds, and four-footed beasts, and creeping things." For they were either leaders or followers of the people in adoring images, "and worshipped and served the creature more than the Creator, who is blessed for ever" [Rom. 1:21–25]. But in the other city there is no human wisdom, but only godliness, which offers due worship to the true God, and looks for its reward in the society of the saints, of holy angels as well as holy men, "that God may be all in all" [1 Cor. 15:28]. . . .

Book 15

Chapter 4. . . . But the earthly city, which shall not be everlasting (for it will no longer be a city when it has been committed to the extreme penalty), has its good in this world, and rejoices in it with such joy as such things can afford. But as this is not a good which can discharge its devotees of all distresses,

---

*That is to say, it was an obvious and indisputable transgression.

this city is often divided against itself by litigations, wars, quarrels, and such victories as are either life-destroying or short-lived. For each part of it that arms against another part of it seeks to triumph over the nations though itself in bondage to vice. If, when it has conquered, it is inflated with pride, its victory is life-destroying; but if it turns its thoughts upon the common casualties of our mortal condition, and is rather anxious concerning the disasters that may befall it than elated with the successes already achieved, this victory, though of a higher kind, is still only short-lived; for it cannot abidingly rule over those whom it has victoriously subjugated. But the things which this city desires cannot justly be said to be evil, for it is itself, in its own kind, better than all other human good. For it desires earthly peace for the sake of enjoying earthly goods, and it makes war in order to attain to this peace; since, if it has conquered, and there remains no one to resist it, it enjoys a peace which it had not while there were opposing parties who contested for the enjoyment of those things which were too small to satisfy both. This peace is purchased by toilsome wars; it is obtained by what they style a glorious victory. Now, when victory remains with the party which had the juster cause, who hesitates to congratulate the victor, and style it a desirable peace? These things, then, are good things, and without doubt the gifts of God. But if they neglect the better things of the heavenly city, which are secured by eternal victory and peace never-ending, and so inordinately covet these present good things that they believe them to be the only desirable things, or love them better than those things which are believed to be better,—if this be so, then it is necessary that misery follow and ever increase. . . .

Book 19

Chapter 7. . . . After the state or city comes the world, the third circle of human society,—the first being the house, and the second the city. And the world, as it is larger, so it is fuller of dangers, as the greater sea is the more dangerous. And here, in the first place, man is separated from man by the difference of languages. For if two men, each ignorant of the other's language, meet, and are not compelled to pass, but, on the contrary, to remain in company, dumb animals, though of different species, would more easily hold intercourse than they, human beings though they be. For their common nature is no help to friendliness when they are prevented by diversity of language from conveying their sentiments to one another; so that a man would more readily hold intercourse with his dog than with a foreigner. But the imperial city has endeavored to impose on subject nations not only her yoke, but her language, as a bond of peace, so that interpreters, far from being scarce, are numberless. This is true; but how many great wars, how much slaughter and bloodshed, have provided this unity! And though these are past, the end of these miseries has not yet come. For though there have never been wanting, nor are yet wanting, hostile nations beyond the empire, against whom wars have been and are waged, yet, supposing there were no such nations, the very extent of the empire itself has produced wars of a more obnoxious description—social and civil wars—and with these the whole race has been agitated, either by the actual conflict or the fear of a renewed outbreak. If I attempted to give an adequate description of these manifold disasters, these stern and lasting necessities, though I am quite unequal to the task, what limit could I set? But, say they, the wise man will wage just wars. As if he would not all the rather lament the necessity of just wars, if he remembers that he is a man; for if they were not just he would not wage them, and would therefore be delivered from all wars. For it is the wrong-doing of the opposing party which compels the wise man to wage just wars; and this wrong-doing, even though it gave rise to no war, would still be matter of grief to man because it is man's wrong-doing. Let every one, then, who thinks with pain on all these great evils, so horrible, so ruthless, acknowledge that this is misery. And if any one either endures or thinks of them without mental pain, this is a more miserable plight still, for he thinks himself happy because he has lost human feeling. . . .

Chapter 12. . . . Whoever gives even moderate attention to human affairs and to our common nature, will recognize that if there is no man who does not wish to be joyful, neither is there any one who does not wish to have peace. For even they who make war desire nothing but victory,—desire, that is to say, to attain to peace with glory. For what else is victory than the conquest of those who resist us? and when this is done there is peace. It is therefore with the desire for peace that wars are waged, even by those who take pleasure in exercising their warlike nature in command and battle. And hence it is obvious that peace is the end sought for by war. For every man seeks peace by waging war, but no man seeks war by making peace. For even they who intentionally interrupt the peace in which they are living have no hatred of peace, but only wish it changed into a peace that suits them better. They do not, therefore, wish to have no peace, but only one more to their mind. And in the case of sedition, when men have separated themselves from the community, they yet do not effect what they wish, unless they maintain some kind of peace with their fellow-conspirators. And therefore even robbers take care to maintain peace with their comrades, that they may with greater effect and greater safety invade the peace of other men. And if an individual happen to be of such unrivalled strength, and to be so jealous of partnership, that he trusts himself with no comrades, but makes his own plots, and commits depredations and murders on his own account, yet he maintains some shadow of peace with such persons as he is unable to kill, and from whom he wishes to conceal his deeds. In his own home, too, he makes it his aim to be at peace with his wife and children, and any other members of his household; for unquestionably their prompt obedience to his every look is a source of pleasure to him. And if this be not rendered, he is angry, he chides and punishes; and even by this storm he secures the calm peace of his own home, as occasion demands. For he sees that peace cannot be maintained unless all the members of the same domestic circle be subject to one head, such as he himself is in his own house. And therefore if a city or nation offered to submit itself to him, to serve him in the same style as he had made his household serve him, he would no longer lurk in a brigand's hiding-places, but lift his head in open day as a king, though the same coveteousness and wickedness should remain in him. . . .

. . . For the most savage animals . . . encompass their own species with a ring of protecting peace. They cohabit, beget, produce, suckle, and bring up their young, though very many of them are not gregarious, but solitary,— not like sheep, deer, pigeons, starlings, bees, but such as lions, foxes, eagles, bats. . . . How much more powerfully do the laws of man's nature move him to hold fellowship and maintain peace with all men so far as in him lies, since even wicked men wage war to maintain the peace of their own circle, and wish that, if possible, all men belonged to them, that all men and things might serve but one head, and might, either through love or fear, yield themselves to peace with him! It is thus that pride in its perversity apes God. It abhors equality with other men under Him; but, instead of His rule, it seeks to impose a rule of its own upon its equals. It abhors, that is to say, the just peace of God, and loves its own unjust peace; but it cannot help loving peace of one kind or other. For there is no vice so clean contrary to nature that it obliterates even the faintest traces of nature.

He, then, who prefers what is right to what is wrong, and what is well-ordered to what is perverted, sees that the peace of unjust men is not worthy to be called peace in comparison with the peace of the just. And yet even what is perverted must of necessity be in harmony with, and in dependence on, and in some part of the order of things, for otherwise it would have no existence at all. . . .

Chapter 15. . . . The origin of the Latin word for slave is supposed to be found in the circumstance that those who by the law of war were liable to be killed were sometimes preserved by their victors, and were hence called servants.* And these circumstances could never have arisen save through sin. For even when we wage a just war, our adversaries must be sinning; and every victory, even though gained by wicked men, is a result of the first judgment of God, who humbles the vanquished either for the sake of removing or of punishing their sins. Witness that man of God, Daniel, who, when he was in captivity, confessed to God his own sins and the sins of his people, and declares with pious grief that these were the cause of the captivity [Dan. 9]. The prime cause, then, of slavery is sin, which brings man under the dominion of his fellow,—that which does not happen save by the judgment of God, with whom is no unrighteousness, and who knows how to award fit punishments to every variety of offence. But our Master in heaven says, "Every one who doeth sin is the servant of sin" [John 8:34]. And thus there are many wicked masters who have religious men as their slaves, and who are yet themselves in bondage; "for of whom a man is overcome, of the same is he brought in bondage" [2 Pet. 2:19]. And beyond question it is a happier thing to be the slave of a man than of a lust; for even this very lust of ruling, to mention no others, lays waste men's hearts with the most ruthless dominion. Moreover, when men are subjected to one another in a peaceful order, the lowly position does as much good to the servant as the proud position does harm to the master. But by nature, as God first created us, no one is the slave either of man or of sin. This servitude is,

Servus, "a slave," from *servare*, "to preserve."

however, penal, and is appointed by that law which enjoins the preservation of the natural order and forbids its disturbance; for if nothing had been done in violation of that law, there would have been nothing to restrain by penal servitude. And therefore the apostle admonishes slaves to be subject to their masters, and to serve them heartily and with good-will, so that, if they cannot be freed by their masters, they may themselves make their slavery in some sort free, by serving not in crafty fear, but in faithful love, until all unrighteousness pass away, and all principality and every human power be brought to nothing, and God be all in all.

From *A Select Library of the Nicene and Post-Nicene Fathers of the Christian Church*, vol. 2, edited by Philip Schaff (Buffalo, N.Y.: The Christian Literature Company, 1887), pp. 92, 93, 264, 273–74, 282, 405, 407, 411, 498.

AGAINST THE MANICHAEANS

Chapter 11. ¶18. Following after God is the desire of happiness; to reach God is happiness itself. We follow after God by loving Him; we reach Him, not by becoming entirely what He is, but in nearness to Him, and in wonderful and immaterial contact with Him, and in being inwardly illuminated and occupied by His truth and holiness. He is light itself; we get enlightenment from Him. The greatest commandment, therefore, which leads to happy life, and the first, is this: "Thou shalt love the Lord thy God with all thy heart, and soul, and mind." For to those who love the Lord all things issue in good. . . . If, then, to those who love God all things issue in good, and if, as no one doubts, the chief or perfect good is not only to be loved, but to be loved so that nothing shall be loved better, as is expressed in the words, "With all thy soul, with all thy heart, and with all thy mind," who, I ask, will not at once conclude, when these things are all settled and most surely believed, that our chief good which we must hasten to arrive at in preference to all other things is nothing else than God? And then, if nothing can separate us from His love, must not this be surer as well as better than any other good? . . .
Chapter 12. ¶21. The farther, then, the mind departs from God, not in space, but in affection and lust after things below Him, the more it is filled with folly and wretchedness. So by love it returns to God,—a love which places it not along with God, but under Him. And the more ardor and eagerness there is in this, the happier and more elevated will the mind be, and with God as sole governor it will be in perfect liberty. Hence it must know that it is a creature. It must believe what is the truth,—that its Creator remains ever possessed of the inviolable and immutable nature of truth and wisdom, and must confess, even in view of the errors from which it desires deliverance, that it is liable to folly and falsehood. But then again, it must take care that it be not separated by the love of the other creature, that is, of this visible world, from the love of God Himself, which sanctifies it in order to lasting happiness. No other creature, then,—for we are ourselves a creature,—separates us from the love of God which is in Christ Jesus our Lord.

Chapter 13. ¶22. Let this same Paul tell us who is this Christ Jesus our Lord. "To them that are called," he says, "we preach Christ the virtue of God, and the wisdom of God" [1 Cor. 1:23, 24]. And does not Christ Himself say, "I am the truth?" If, then, we ask what it is to live well,—that is, to strive after happiness by living well,—it must assuredly be to love virtue, to love wisdom, to love truth, and to love with all the heart, with all the soul, and with all the mind; virtue which is inviolable and immutable, wisdom which never gives place to folly, truth which knows no change or variation from its uniform character. Through this the Father Himself is seen; for it is said, "No man cometh unto the Father but by me" [John 14:6]. To this we cleave by sanctification. For when sanctified we burn with full and perfect love, which is the only security for our not turning away from God, and for our being conformed to Him rather than to this world; for "He has predestinated us," says the same apostle, "that we should be conformed to the image of His Son" [Rom. 8:29].

23. It is through love, then, that we become conformed to God; and by this conformation, and configuration, and circumcision from this world we are not confounded with the things which are properly subject to us. And this is done by the Holy Spirit. "For hope," he says, "does not confound us; for the love of God is shed abroad in our hearts by the Holy Spirit, which is given unto us" [Rom. 5:5]. But we could not possibly be restored to perfection by the Holy Spirit, unless He Himself continued always perfect and immutable. And this plainly could not be unless He were of the nature and of the very substance of God, who alone is always possessed of immutability and invariableness. "The creature," it is affirmed, not by me but by Paul, "has been made subject to vanity" [Rom. 8:20]. And what is subject to vanity is unable to separate us from vanity, and to unite us to the truth. But the Holy Spirit does this for us. He is therefore no creature. For whatever is, must be either God or the creature. . . .

Chapter 15. ¶25. As to virtue leading us to a happy life, I hold virtue to be nothing else than perfect love of God. For the fourfold division of virtue I regard as taken from four forms of love. For these four virtues (would that all felt their influence in their minds as they have their names in their mouths!), I should have no hesitation in defining them: that temperance is love giving itself entirely to that which is loved; fortitude is love readily bearing all things for the sake of the loved object; justice is love serving only the loved object, and therefore ruling rightly; prudence is love distinguishing with sagacity between what hinders it and what helps it. The object of this love is not anything, but only God, the chief good, the highest wisdom, the perfect harmony. So we may express the definition thus: that temperance is love keeping itself entire and incorrupt for God; fortitude is love bearing everything readily for the sake of God; justice is love serving God only, and therefore ruling well all else, as subject to man; prudence is love making a right distinction between what helps it towards God and what might hinder it.* . . .

---

*[It would be difficult to find in Christian literature a more beautiful and satisfactory exposition of love to God. The Neo-Platonic influence is manifest, but it is Neo-Platonism thoroughly Christianized.—A. H. N.]

Chapter 26. ¶48. To proceed to what remains. It may be thought that there is nothing here about man himself, the lover. But to think this, shows a want of clear perception. For it is impossible for one who loves God not to love himself. For he alone has a proper love for himself who aims diligently at the attainment of the chief and true good; and if this is nothing else but God, as has been shown, what is to prevent one who loves God from loving himself? And then, among men should there be no bond of mutual love? Yea, verily; so that we can think of no surer step towards the love of God than the love of man to man.

49. Let the Lord then supply us with the other precept in answer to the question about the precepts of life; for He was not satisfied with one as knowing that God is one thing and man another, and that the difference is nothing less than that between the Creator and the thing created in the likeness of its Creator. He says then that the second precept is, "Thou shalt love thy neighbor as thyself" [Matt. 22:39]. Now you love yourself suitably when you love God better than yourself. What, then, you aim at in yourself you must aim at in your neighbor, namely, that he may love God with a perfect affection. For you do not love him as yourself, unless you try to draw him to that good which you are yourself pursuing. For this is the one good which has room for all to pursue it along with thee. From this precept proceed the duties of human society, in which it is hard to keep from error. But the first thing to aim at is, that we should be benevolent, that is, that we cherish no malice and no evil design against another. For man is the nearest neighbor of man.

50. Hear also what Paul says: "The love of our neighbor," he says, "worketh no ill" [Rom. 13:10]. The testimonies here made use of are very short, but, if I mistake not, they are to the point, and sufficient for the purpose. And every one knows how many and how weighty are the words to be found everywhere in these books on the love of our neighbor. But as a man may sin against another in two ways, either by injuring him or by not helping him when it is in his power, and as it is for these things which no loving man would do that men are called wicked, all that is required is, I think, proved by these words, "The love of our neighbor worketh no ill." And if we cannot attain to good unless we first desist from working evil, our love of our neighbor is a sort of cradle of our love to God, so that, as it is said, "the love of our neighbor worketh no ill," we may rise from this to these other words, "We know that all things issue in good to them that love God" [Rom. 8:28].

51. But there is a sense in which these either rise together to fullness and perfection, or, while the love of God is first in beginning, the love of our neighbor is first in coming to perfection. For perhaps divine love takes hold on us more rapidly at the outset, but we reach perfection more easily in lower things. However that may be, the main point is this, that no one should think that while he despises his neighbor he will come to happiness and to the God whom he loves. And would that it were as easy to seek the good of our neighbor, or to avoid hurting him, as it is for one well trained and kindhearted to love his neighbor! These things require more than mere good-will, and can be done only by a high degree of thoughtfulness and prudence, which belongs only to those to whom it is given by God, the source of all good. On this topic—which is one, I think, of great difficulty—I will try to say a few words such as my plan admits of, resting all my hope in Him whose gifts these are.

From *A Select Library of the Nicene and Post-Nicene Fathers of the Christian Church*, vol. 2, edited by Philip Schaff (Grand Rapids, Mich.: William B. Eerdmans Publishing Co., 1956, reprinted), pp. 46–48, 55.

Part 2

Medieval Christianity

Great themes in Augustinian thought dominated the ethic of medieval Christianity: single-minded devotion to God as source of all good, an ascetic attitude toward the weaknesses of the flesh (honored even when not followed), a high conception of the church as mediator of divine salvation and arbiter of God's moral commandments.

Great mystics, like Catherine of Siena and Bernard of Clairvaux, sought direct union with God. But the mystical quest was not escapism. It was permeated by love for fellow humanity as for God, and its consequence was much engagement with the world. Both Catherine and Bernard were deeply involved in the political debates of their times; both had extraordinary influence with secular and ecclesiastical leaders. Catherine confronted political and economic power centers head-on while also spending her life in direct ministrations to the victims of plague.

The monastic ideal, illustrated here by selections from the Rule of St. Benedict, was to achieve perfect devotion to God—loving God, as Augustine's *City of God* had said, even to the point of contempt of self. The monastic ethic was thoroughly, even ruthlessly, ascetic. The point of ascetic self-denial and mortification of the flesh was to put aside every lesser love for the sake of the love of God alone. The constant danger of that ethic was, however, that it should become an end in itself.

Monastic and mystical tendencies in medieval Christianity might well have fractured the church, with this or that religious elite separating itself from those considered less worthy. On the whole, however, this did not occur. The greater devotion and discipline of the monastic communities was taken into the life of the greater church as a spiritual and moral resource for all. The church, as keeper of the sacramental means of salvation, had authority understood by all to have been given directly by God. But the prayers and rigorous moral example of saints and monastics were understood to help the church in its ministry to ordinary people.

A very important part of the church's moral teaching developed through the penitential system. In order to be worthy of the Mass, one had to be cleansed of sin. Through the confessional, the faithful confessed their sins to priests, who then prescribed appropriate penances. When these had been discharged, the faithful could be granted absolution and admitted to the Mass. Since the receiving of communion was understood to be definitively important as a means to salvation, the church thus had great leverage on the moral behavior of believers. It could define and determine the relative degrees of seriousness of sins, and it could specify penalties. At stake, for believers, was salvation itself.

A literature developed for the guidance of priest-confessors in the medieval church. The penitential manuals, at first resisted by church hierarchy, were perhaps inevitable in assuring that sins and penances would not be interpreted differently by different confessors. These manuals played a very important role in shaping the ethic of medieval Christianity. While the manuals give every appearance of outright legalism, one must remember that the whole system of confession and penance was understood as a means to the end of salvation and not as an end in itself. Underneath it all, Augustine's vision of love of God supplied the ultimate theological rationale for requirements and penances often appearing very remote from love.

The rediscovery of the writings of Aristotle during the later centuries of the medieval period helped stimulate a revival of critical thought. Thomas Aquinas was particularly important as a creative theological and philosophical mind, and his contributions to Christian ethics, like those of Augustine, were destined to have a commanding influence. The rebirth of critical thought also had the consequence of stimulating theological minds like the English John Wyclif and the Bohemian Jan Hus, who were important precursors of the Protestant Reformation.

15. The Rule of St. Benedict

The most important and enduring of the medieval monastic communities was the Benedictine order, established by Benedict of Nursia (born ca. A.D. 480). The Rule of St. Benedict is a particularly good illustration of medieval monastic ethics. The rule sets forth ways by which a monk can become truly humble and single-mindedly devoted to God.

Chapter 4. The Tools for Good Works

¹ First of all, *love the Lord God with your whole heart, your whole soul and all your strength, ²and love your neighbor as yourself* [Matt. 22:37–39; Mark 12:30–31; Luke 10:27]. ³Then the following: *You are not to kill, ⁴not to commit adultery; ⁵you are not to steal ⁶nor to covet* [Rom. 13:9]; *⁷you are not to bear false witness* [Matt. 19:18; Mark 10:19; Luke 18:20]. *⁸You must honor everyone* [1 Pet. 2:17], *⁹and never do to another what you do not want done to yourself* [Tob. 4:16; Matt. 7:12; Luke 6:31].

¹⁰*Renounce yourself in order to follow Christ* [Matt. 16:24; Luke 9:23]; ¹¹*discipline your body* [1 Cor. 9:27]; ¹²do not pamper yourself, ¹³but love fasting. ¹⁴You must relieve the lot of the poor, ¹⁵*clothe the naked,* ¹⁶*visit the sick* [Matt. 25:36], ¹⁷and bury the dead. ¹⁸Go to help the troubled ¹⁹and console the sorrowing.

²⁰Your way of acting should be different from the world's way; ²¹the love of Christ must come before all else. ²²You are not to act in anger ²³or nurse a grudge. ²⁴Rid your heart of all deceit. ²⁵Never give a hollow greeting of peace ²⁶or turn away when someone needs your love. ²⁷Bind yourself to no oath lest it prove false, ²⁸but speak the truth with heart and tongue.

²⁹*Do not repay one bad turn with another* [1 Thess. 5:15; 1 Pet. 3:9]. ³⁰Do not injure anyone, but bear injuries patiently. ³¹*Love your enemies* [Matt. 5:44; Luke 6:27]. ³²If people curse you, do not curse them back but bless them instead. ³³*Endure persecution for the sake of justice* [Matt. 5:10].

³⁴You must *not be proud,* ³⁵*nor be given to wine* [Titus 1:7; 1 Tim. 3:3]. ³⁶Refrain from too much eating ³⁷or sleeping, ³⁸and *from laziness* [Rom. 12:11]. ³⁹Do not grumble ⁴⁰or speak ill of others.

⁴¹Place your hope in God alone. ⁴²If you notice something good in yourself, give credit to God, not to yourself, ⁴³but be certain that the evil you commit is always your own and yours to acknowledge.

⁴⁴Live in fear of judgment day ⁴⁵and have a great horror of hell. ⁴⁶Yearn for everlasting life with holy desire. ⁴⁷Day by day remind yourself that you are going to die. ⁴⁸Hour by hour keep careful watch over all you do, ⁴⁹aware that God's gaze is upon you, wherever you may be. ⁵⁰As soon as wrongful thoughts come into your heart, dash them against Christ and disclose them to your spiritual father. ⁵¹Guard your lips from harmful or deceptive

speech. [52]Prefer moderation in speech [53]and speak no foolish chatter, nothing just to provoke laughter; [54]do not love immoderate or boisterous laughter. . . .

Chapter 5. Obedience

[1]The first step of humility is unhesitating obedience, [2]which comes naturally to those who cherish Christ above all. [3]Because of the holy service they have professed, or because of dread of hell and for the glory of everlasting life, [4]they carry out the superior's order as promptly as if the command came from God himself. [5]The Lord says of men like this: *No sooner did he hear than he obeyed me* [Ps. 17(18):45]; [6]again, he tells teachers: *Whoever listens to you, listens to me* [Luke 10:16]. [7]Such people as these immediately put aside their own concerns, abandon their own will, [8]and lay down whatever they have in hand, leaving it unfinished. With the ready step of obedience, they follow the voice of authority in their actions. [9]Almost at the same moment, then, as the master gives the instruction the disciple quickly puts it into practice in the fear of God; and both actions together are swiftly completed as one.

[10]It is love that impels them to pursue everlasting life; [11]therefore, they are eager to take the narrow road of which the Lord says: *Narrow is the road that leads to life* [Matt. 7:14]. [12]They no longer live by their own judgment, giving in to their whims and appetites; rather they walk according to another's decisions and directions, choosing to live in monasteries and to have an abbot over them. [13]Men of this resolve unquestionably conform to the saying of the Lord: *I have come not to do my own will, but the will of him who sent me* [John 6:38].

[14]This very obedience, however, will be acceptable to God and agreeable to men only if compliance with what is commanded is not cringing or sluggish or half-hearted, but free from any grumbling or any reaction of unwillingness. [15]For the obedience shown to superiors is given to God, as he himself said: *Whoever listens to you, listens to me* [Luke 10:16]. [16]Furthermore, the disciples' obedience must be given gladly, for *God loves a cheerful giver* [2 Cor. 9:7]. [17]If a disciple obeys grudgingly and grumbles, not only aloud but also in his heart, [18]then, even though he carries out the order, his action will not be accepted with favor by God, who sees that he is grumbling in his heart. [19]He will have no reward for service of this kind; on the contrary, he will incur punishment for grumbling, unless he changes for the better and makes amends. . . .

Chapter 7. Humility

[1]Brothers, divine Scripture calls to us saying: *Whoever exalts himself shall be humbled, and whoever humbles himself shall be exalted* [Luke 14:11; 18:14]. [2]In saying this, therefore, it shows us that every exaltation is a kind of pride, [3]which the Prophet indicates he has shunned, saying: *O Lord, my heart is not*

exalted; my eyes are not lifted up and I have not walked in the ways of the great nor gone after marvels beyond me [Ps. 130(131):1]. ⁴*And why? If I had not a humble spirit, but were exalted instead, then you would treat me like a weaned child on its mother's lap* [Ps. 130(131):2].

⁵Accordingly, brothers, if we want to reach the highest summit of humility, if we desire to attain speedily that exaltation in heaven to which we climb by the humility of this present life, ⁶then by our ascending actions we must set up that ladder on which Jacob in a dream saw *angels descending and ascending* [Gen. 28:12]. ⁷Without doubt, this descent and ascent can signify only that we descend by exaltation and ascend by humility. ⁸Now the ladder erected is our life on earth, and if we humble our hearts the Lord will raise it to heaven. ⁹We may call our body and soul the sides of this ladder, into which our divine vocation has fitted the various steps of humility and discipline as we ascend.

¹⁰The first step of humility, then, is that a man keeps the *fear of God* always *before his eyes* [Ps. 35(36):2] and never forgets it. ¹¹He must constantly remember everything God has commanded, keeping in mind that all who despise God will burn in hell for their sins, and all who fear God have everlasting life awaiting them. ¹²While he guards himself at every moment from sins and vices of thought or tongue, of hand or foot, of self-will or bodily desire, ¹³let him recall that he is always seen by God in heaven, that his actions everywhere are in God's sight and are reported by angels at every hour. . . .

²³As for the desires of the body, we must believe that God is always with us, for *All my desires are known to you* [Ps. 37(38):10], as the Prophet tells the Lord. ²⁴We must then be on guard against any base desire, because death is stationed near the gateway of pleasure. ²⁵For this reason Scripture warns us, *Pursue not your lusts* [Sir. 18:30]. . . .

³¹The second step of humility is that a man loves not his own will nor takes pleasure in the satisfaction of his desires; ³²rather he shall imitate by his actions that saying of the Lord: *I have come not to do my own will, but the will of him who sent me* [John 6:38]. ³³Similarly we read, "Consent merits punishment; constraint wins a crown."

³⁴The third step of humility is that a man submits to his superior in all obedience for the love of God, imitating the Lord of whom the Apostle says: *He became obedient even to death* [Phil. 2:8].

³⁵The fourth step of humility is that in this obedience under difficult, unfavorable, or even unjust conditions, his heart quietly embraces suffering ³⁶and endures it without weakening or seeking escape. For Scripture has it: *Anyone who perseveres to the end will be saved* [Matt. 10:22], ³⁷and again, *Be brave of heart and rely on the Lord* [Ps. 26(27):14]. ³⁸Another passage shows how the faithful must endure everything, even contradiction, for the Lord's sake, saying in the person of those who suffer, *For your sake we are put to death continually; we are regarded as sheep marked for slaughter* [Rom. 8:36; Ps. 43(44):22]. ³⁹They are so confident in their expectation of reward from God that they continue joyfully and say, *But in all this we overcome because of him who so greatly loved us* [Rom. 8:37]. ⁴⁰Elsewhere Scripture says: *O God, you*

have tested us, you have tried us as silver is tried by fire; you have led us into a snare, you have placed afflictions on our backs [Ps. 65(66):10–11]. [41]Then, to show that we ought to be under a superior, it adds: *You have placed men over our heads* [Ps. 65(66):12].

[42]In truth, those who are patient amid hardships and unjust treatment are fulfilling the Lord's command: *When struck on one cheek, they turn the other; when deprived of their coat, they offer their cloak also; when pressed into service for one mile, they go two* [Matt. 5:39–41]. [43]With the Apostle Paul, they bear with *false brothers, endure persecution,* and *bless those who curse them* [2 Cor. 11:26; 1 Cor. 4:12].

[44]The fifth step of humility is that a man does not conceal from his abbot any sinful thoughts entering his heart, or any wrongs committed in secret, but rather confesses them humbly. [45]Concerning this, Scripture exhorts us: *Make known your way to the Lord and hope in him* [Ps. 36(37):5]. [46]And again, *Confess to the Lord, for he is good; his mercy is forever* [Ps. 105(106):1; Ps. 117 (118):1]. [47]So too the Prophet: *To you I have acknowledged my offense; my faults I have not concealed.* [48]*I have said: Against myself I will report my faults to the Lord, and you have forgiven the wickedness of my heart* [Ps. 31(32):5].

[49]The sixth step of humility is that a monk is content with the lowest and most menial treatment, and regards himself as a poor and worthless workman in whatever task he is given, [50]saying to himself with the Prophet: *I am insignificant and ignorant, no better than a beast before you, yet I am with you always* [Ps. 72(73):22–23].

[51]The seventh step of humility is that a man not only admits with his tongue but is also convinced in his heart that he is inferior to all and of less value, [52]humbling himself and saying with the Prophet: *I am truly a worm, not a man, scorned by men and despised by the people* [Ps. 21(22):7]. [53]*I was exalted, then I was humbled and overwhelmed with confusion* [Ps. 87(88):16]. [54]And again, *It is a blessing that you have humbled me so that I can learn your commandments* [Ps. 118(119):71, 73].

[55]The eighth step of humility is that a monk does only what is endorsed by the common rule of the monastery and the example set by his superiors.

[56]The ninth step of humility is that a monk controls his tongue and remains silent, not speaking unless asked a question, [57]for Scripture warns, *In a flood of words you will not avoid sinning* [Prov. 10:19], [58]and, *A talkative man goes about aimlessly on earth* [Ps. 139(140):12].

[59]The tenth step of humility is that he is not given to ready laughter, for it is written: *Only a fool raises his voice in laughter* [Sir. 21:23].

[60]The eleventh step of humility is that a monk speaks gently and without laughter, seriously and with becoming modesty, briefly and reasonably, but without raising his voice, [61]as it is written: "A wise man is known by his few words."

[62]The twelfth step of humility is that a monk always manifests humility in his bearing no less than in his heart, so that it is evident [63]at the Work of God, in the oratory, the monastery or the garden, on a journey or in the field, or anywhere else. Whether he sits, walks or stands, his head must be bowed and his eyes cast down. [64]Judging himself always guilty on account

of his sins, he should consider that he is already at the fearful judgment, [65]and constantly say in his heart what the publican in the Gospel said with downcast eyes: *Lord, I am a sinner, not worthy to look up to heaven* [Luke 18:13]. [66]And with the Prophet: *I am bowed down and humbled in every way* [Ps. 37(38):7–9; Ps. 118(119):107].

[67]Now, therefore, after ascending all these steps of humility, the monk will quickly arrive at that *perfect love* of God which *casts out fear* [1 John 4:18]. [68]Through this love, all that he once performed with dread, he will now begin to observe without effort, as though naturally, from habit, [69]no longer out of fear of hell but out of love for Christ, good habit and delight in virtue. [70]All this the Lord will by the Holy Spirit graciously manifest in his workman now cleansed of vices and sins. . . .

Chapter 33. Monks and Private Ownership

[1]Above all, this evil practice must be uprooted and removed from the monastery. [2]We mean that without an order from the abbot, no one may presume to give, receive [3]or retain anything as his own, nothing at all—not a book, writing tablets or stylus—in short, not a single item, [4]especially since monks may not have the free disposal even of their own bodies and wills. [5]For their needs, they are to look to the father of the monastery, and are not allowed anything which the abbot has not given or permitted. [6]*All things should be the common possession* of all, as it is written, so *that no one* presumes to *call anything his own* [Acts 4:32].

[7]But if anyone is caught indulging in this most evil practice, he should be warned a first and a second time. [8]If he does not amend, let him be subjected to punishment.

Chapter 34. Distribution of Goods According to Need

[1]It is written: *Distribution was made to each one as he had need* [Acts 4:35]. [2]By this we do not imply that there should be favoritism—God forbid—but rather consideration for weaknesses. [3]Whoever needs less should thank God and not be distressed, [4]but whoever needs more should feel humble because of his weakness, not self-important because of the kindness shown him. [5]In this way all the members will be at peace. [6]First and foremost, there must be no word or sign of the evil of grumbling.

From *The Rule of St. Benedict: In Latin and English with Notes,* edited by Timothy Fry (Collegeville, Minn.: The Liturgical Press, 1981), pp. 181–89, 191–99, 201, 203, 231. Copyright © 1981 by The Order of St. Benedict, Inc., Collegeville, Minnesota.

16. Hildegard of Bingen, *The Visions*

Hildegard of Bingen (1098–1179) was one of several women religious leaders whose influence on the ethic of the medieval world went well beyond the confines of their own monastic communities. In this selection, Hildegard reflects broadly on the marriage bond and the relationships of men and women.

Book One

11. . . . . [T]here should be perfect love in these two as there was in those first two. For Adam could have blamed his wife because by her advice she brought him death, but nonetheless he did not dismiss her as long as he lived in this world, because he knew she had been given to him by divine power. Therefore, because of perfect love, let a man not leave his wife except for the reason the faithful Church allows. And let them never separate, unless both with one mind want to contemplate My Son, and say with burning love for Him: "We want to renounce the world and follow Him Who suffered for our sake!" But if these two disagree as to whether they should renounce the world for one devotion, then let them by no means separate from each other, since, just as the blood cannot be separated from the flesh as long as the spirit remains in the flesh, so the husband and wife cannot be divided from each other but must walk together in one will.

But if either husband or wife breaks the law by fornication, and it is made public either by themselves or by their priests, they shall undergo the just censure of the spiritual magisterium. For the husband shall complain of the wife, or the wife of the husband, about the sin against their union before the Church and its prelates, according to the justice of God; but not so that the husband or wife can seek another marriage; either they shall stay together in righteous union, or they shall both abstain from such unions, as the discipline of church practice shows. And they shall not tear each other to pieces by viperous rending, but they shall love with pure love, since both man and woman could not exist without having been conceived in such a bond, as My friend Paul witnesses when he says:

12. . . . . "As the woman is of the man, so is the man for the woman; but all are from God" [1 Cor. 11:12]. Which is to say: Woman was created for the sake of man, and man for the sake of woman. As she is from the man, the man is also from her, lest they dissent from each other in the unity of making their children; for they should work as one in one work, as the air and the wind intermingle in their labor. In what way? The air is moved by the wind, and the wind is mingled with the air, so that in their movement all verdant things are subject to their influence. What does this mean? The wife must cooperate with the husband and the husband with the wife in making children. Therefore the greatest crime and wickedest act is to make by fornication a division in the days of creating children, since the husband and wife cut off their own blood from its rightful place, sending it to an alien place. They will certainly incur the deceit of the Devil and the wrath of God, because they have transgressed that bond God ordained for them. Woe to them, therefore, if their sins are not forgiven!

From *Hildegard of Bingen: Scivias*, translated by Mother Columba Hart and Jane Bishop (Mahwah, N.J.: Paulist Press, 1990), p. 78. © by the Abbey of Regina Laudis. Used by permission of Paulist Press.

17. Bernard of Clairvaux, *On Loving God*

Bernard of Clairvaux (1090–1153) well illustrates the deep involvement of medieval mystics in the problems of the world. His major contribution to Christian ethics is in this reflection on Christian love.

The First Degree of Love:
When Man Loves Himself for His Own Sake

But because nature has become rather frail and weak, man is driven by necessity to serve nature first. This results in bodily love, by which man loves himself for his own sake. He does not yet know anything but himself, as it is written, "First came what is animal, then what is spiritual" [1 Cor. 15:46]. This love is not imposed by rule but is innate in nature. For who hates his own flesh [Eph. 5:29]? But if that same love begins to get out of proportion and headstrong, as often happens, and it ceases to be satisfied to run in the narrow channel of its needs, but floods out on all sides into the fields of pleasure, then the overflow can be stopped at once by the commandment "You shall love your neighbor as yourself" [Matt. 22:39].

It is wholly right that he who is your fellow in nature [2 Pet. 1:4] should not be cut off from you in grace, especially in that grace which is innate in nature. If a man feels it a heavy burden to help his brothers in their need and to share in their pleasures, let him keep his desires in check all by himself if he does not want to fall into sin. He can indulge himself as much as he likes as long as he remembers to show an equal tolerance to his neighbor. O man, the law of life and discipline impose restraint [Sir. 45:6] to prevent you chasing after your desires until you perish [Sir. 18:30], and to save you from making of nature's good things a way to serve the soul's enemy through lust.

Is it not much more right and honest to share nature's goods with your fellow man, that is, your neighbor, than with an enemy? If you take the advice of Wisdom and turn away from your pleasures [Sir. 18:30] and make yourself content with food and clothing as the Apostle teaches [1 Tim. 6:8], soon you will find that your love is not impeded by carnal desires which fight against the soul [1 Pet. 2:11]. I think you will not find it a burden to share with your fellow man what you withhold from the enemy of your soul. Then will your love be sober and just, when you do not deny your brother what he needs from the pleasures you have denied yourself. It is in this way that bodily love is shared, when it is extended to the community.

8.24. But what are you to do if when you share with your neighbor you yourself are left without something you need? What but ask in full faith [Acts 4:29; 28:31] from him who gives generously to everyone and does not grudge [James 1:5], who opens his hand and pours blessing on every creature [Ps. 144:16]. There is no doubt that he will come to your aid generously when you are in need, since he is so generous in time of plenty. Scripture says, "First seek the Kingdom of God and his justice and all these things will be added to you" [Matt. 6:33; Luke 12:31]. He promises without being asked to give what is needed to whoever is not greedy for himself and loves his neighbor. This is to seek the kingdom of God and to implore his help against the tyranny of sin, to take on the yoke of chastity and sobriety rather than to let sin rule in your mortal body [Rom. 6:12]. More: This is righteousness, to share what is common to your nature with him who has the same gift of nature.

8.25. But to love one's neighbor with perfect justice it is necessary to be prompted by God. How can you love your neighbor with purity if you do not love him in God? But he who does not love God cannot love in God. You must first love God, so that in him you can love your neighbor too [Mark 12:30–31].

God therefore brings about your love for him, just as he causes other goods. This is how he does it: He who made nature also protects it. For it was so created that it needs its Creator as its Protector, so that what could not have come into existence without him cannot continue in existence without him. So that no rational creature might be in ignorance of this fact and (dreadful thought) claim for himself the gifts of the Creator, that same Creator willed by a high and saving counsel that man should endure tribulation; then when man fails and God comes to his aid and sets him free, man will honor God as he deserves. For this is what he says, "Call upon me in the day of tribulation. I will deliver you, and you shall honor me" [Ps. 49:15]. And so in that way it comes about that man who is a bodily animal [1 Cor. 2:14], and does not know how to love anything but himself, begins to love God for his own benefit, because he learns from frequent experience that in God he can do everything which is good for him [Phil. 4:13], and that without him he can do nothing [John 15:5].

The Second Degree of Love:
When Man Loves God for His Own Good

9.26. Man therefore loves God, but as yet he loves him for his own sake, not God's. Nevertheless the wise man ought to know what he can do by himself and what he can do only with God's help; then you will avoid hurting him who keeps you from harm.

If a man has a great many tribulations and as a result he frequently turns to God and frequently experiences God's liberation, surely even if he had a breast of iron or a heart of stone [Ezek. 11:19; 36:26], he must soften toward the generosity of the Redeemer and love God not only for his own benefit, but for himself?

The Third Degree of Love:
When Man Loves God for God's Sake

Man's frequent needs make it necessary for him to call upon God often, and to taste by frequent contact, and to discover by tasting how sweet the Lord is [Ps. 33:9]. It is in this way that the taste of his own sweetness leads us to love God in purity more than our need alone would prompt us to do. The Samaritans set us an example when they said to the woman who told them the Lord was there, "Now we believe, not because of your words, but because we have heard him for ourselves and we know that truly he is the Savior of the world" [John 4:42]. In the same way, I urge, let us follow their example and rightly say to our flesh, "Now we love God not because he meets your needs; but we have tasted and we know how sweet the Lord is" [Ps. 33:9].

There is a need of the flesh which speaks out, and the body tells by its actions of the kindnesses it has experienced. And so it will not be difficult for the man who has had that experience to keep the commandment to love his neighbor [Mark 12:31]. He truly loves God, and therefore he loves what is God's. He loves chastely, and to the chaste it is no burden to keep the commandments; the heart grows purer in the obedience of love, as it is written [1 Pet. 1:22]. Such a man loves justly and willingly keeps the just law.

This love is acceptable because it is given freely. It is chaste because it is not made up of words or talk, but of truth and action [1 John 3:18]. It is just because it gives back what it has received. For he who loves in this way loves as he is loved. He loves, seeking in return not what is his own [1 Cor. 13:5], but what is Jesus Christ's, just as he has sought not his own but our good, or rather, our very selves [2 Cor. 12:14]. He who says, "We trust in the Lord for he is good" [Ps. 117:1] loves in this way. He who trusts in the Lord not because he is good to him but simply because he is good truly loves God for God's sake and not for his own. He of whom it is said, "He will praise you when you do him favors" [Ps. 48:19] does not love in this way.

That is the third degree of love, in which God is already loved for his own sake.

The Fourth Degree of Love:
When Man Loves Himself for the Sake of God

9.27. Happy is he who has been found worthy to attain to the fourth degree, where man loves himself only for God's sake. "O God, your justice is like the mountains of God" [Ps. 35:7]. That love is a mountain, and a high mountain of God. Truly, "a rich and fertile mountain" [Ps. 67:16]. "Who will climb the mountain of the Lord" [Ps. 23:3]? "Who will give me wings like a dove, and I shall fly there and rest" [Ps. 54:7]? That place was made a place of peace and it has its dwelling-place in Sion [Ps. 75:3]. "Alas for me, my exile has been prolonged!" [Ps. 119:5]. When will flesh and blood [Matt. 16:17], this vessel of clay [2 Cor. 4:7], this earthly dwelling [Wisd. Sol. 9:15], grasp this? When will it experience this kind of love, so that the mind, drunk with divine love and forgetting itself, making itself like a broken vessel [Ps. 30:13], throw itself wholly on God and, clinging to God [1 Cor. 6:17], become one with him in spirit and say, "My body and my heart have fainted, O God of my heart; God, my part in eternity" [Ps. 72:26]? I should call him blessed and holy to whom it is given to experience even for a single instant something which is rare indeed in this life. To lose yourself as though you did not exist and to have no sense of yourself, to be emptied out of yourself [Phil. 2:7] and almost annihilated, belongs to heavenly not to human love.

And if indeed any mortal is rapt for a moment or is, so to speak, admitted for a moment to this union, at once the world presses itself on him [Gal. 1:4], the day's wickedness troubles him, the mortal body weighs him down, bodily needs distract him, he fails because of the weakness of his corruption and—more powerfully than these—brotherly love calls him back. Alas, he is forced to come back to himself, to fall again into his affairs, and to cry out wretchedly, "Lord, I endure violence; fight back for me" [Isa. 38:14], and, "Unhappy man that I am, who will free me from the body of this death?" [Rom. 7:24].

9.28. But since Scripture says that God made everything for himself [Prov. 16:4; Rev. 4:11] there will be a time when he will cause everything to conform to its Maker and be in harmony with him. In the meantime, we must make this our desire: that as God himself willed that everything should be for himself, so we, too, will that nothing, not even ourselves, may be or have been except for him, that is according to his will, not ours. The satisfaction of our needs will not bring us happiness, not chance delights, as does the sight of his will being fulfilled in us and in everything which concerns us. This is what we ask every day in prayer when we say, "Your will be done, on earth as it is in heaven" [Matt. 6:10]. O holy and chaste love! O sweet and tender affection! O pure and sinless intention of the will—the more pure and sinless in that there is no mixture of self-will in it, the more sweet and tender in that everything it feels is divine.

To love in this way is to become like God. As a drop of water seems to disappear completely in a quantity of wine, taking the wine's flavor and color; as red-hot iron becomes indistinguishable from the glow of fire and its own original form disappears; as air suffused with the light of the sun seems transformed into the brightness of the light, as if it were itself light rather than merely lit up; so, in those who are holy, it is necessary for human affection to dissolve in some ineffable way, and be poured into the will of God. How will God be all in all [1 Cor. 15:26] if anything of man remains in man? The substance remains, but in another form, with another glory, another power.

When will this be? Who will see this? Who will possess it? "When shall I come and when shall I appear in God's presence" [Ps. 41:3]? O Lord my God, "My heart said to you, 'My face has sought you. Lord, I will seek your face' " [Ps. 26:8]. Shall I see your holy temple [Ps. 26:4]?

9.29. I think that cannot be until I do as I am bid. "Love the Lord your God with all your heart and with all your soul and with all your strength" [Mark 12:30]. Then the mind will not have to think of the body. The soul will no longer have to give the body life and feeling, and its power will be set free of these ties and strengthened by the power of God. For it is impossible to draw together all that is in you and turn toward the face of God as long as the care of the weak and miserable body demands one's attention. So it is in a spiritual and immortal body, a perfect body, beautiful and at peace and subject to the spirit in all things, that the soul hopes to attain the fourth degree of love, or rather, to be caught up to it; for it lies in God's power to give to whom he will. It is not to be obtained by human effort. That, I say, is when a man will easily reach the fourth degree: when no entanglements of the flesh hold him back and no troubles will disturb him, as he hurries with great speed and eagerness to the joy of the Lord [Matt. 25:21; 25].

But do we not think that the holy martyrs received this grace while they were still in their victorious bodies—at least in part? They were so moved within by the great force of their love that they were able to expose their bodies to outward torments and think nothing of them. The sensation of outward pain could do no more than whisper across the surface of their tranquility; it could not disturb it.

11.30. But what of those who are already free of the body? We believe that they are wholly immersed in that sea of eternal light and bright eternity.

Reprinted from *Bernard of Clairvaux: Selected Works*, translated by G. R. Evans (Mahwah, N.J.: Paulist Press, 1987), pp. 192–97. © by Gillian R. Evans. Used by permission of Paulist Press.

18. Catherine of Siena, *The Dialogue*

Numbered among the foremost medieval mystics, Catherine of Siena (1347–1380) exerted enormous influence upon the political and ecclesiastical leaders of her time. Her mystical writings contain substantial ethical content. The "I" in this selection represents God; "you," Catherine. God ("I") is speaking to her ("you").

6. I would have you know that every virtue of yours and every vice is put into action by means of your neighbors. If you hate me, you harm your neighbors and yourself as well (for you are your chief neighbor), and the harm is both general and particular.

I say general because it is your duty to love your neighbors as your own self [Lev. 19:18; Mark 12:33]. In love you ought to help them spiritually with prayer and counsel, and assist them spiritually and materially in their need—at least with your good will if you have nothing else. If you do not love me you do not love your neighbors, nor will you help those you do not love. But it is yourself you harm most, because you deprive yourself of grace. And you harm your neighbors by depriving them of the prayer and loving desires you should be offering to me on their behalf. Every help you give them ought to come from the affection you bear them for love of me.

In the same way, every evil is done by means of your neighbors, for you cannot love them if you do not love me. This lack of charity for me and for your neighbors is the source of all evils, for if you are not doing good you are necessarily doing evil. And to whom is this evil shown and done? First of all to yourself and then to your neighbors—not to me, for you cannot harm me except insofar as I count whatever you do to them as done to me [Matt. 25:40]. You do yourself the harm of sin itself, depriving yourself of grace, and there is nothing worse you can do. You harm your neighbors by not giving them the pleasure of the love and charity you owe them, the love with which you ought to be helping them by offering me your prayer and holy desire on their behalf. Such is the general help that you ought to give to every reasoning creature.

More particular are the services done to those nearest you, under your very eyes. Here you owe each other help in word and teaching and good example, indeed in every need of which you are aware, giving counsel as sincerely as you would to yourself, without selfishness. If you do not do this because you have no love for your neighbors, you do them special harm, and this as persistently as you refuse them the good you could do. How? In this Way:

Sin is both in the mind and in the act. You have already sinned in your mind when you have conceived a liking for sin and hatred for virtue. (This is the fruit of that sensual selfishness which has driven out the loving charity you ought to have for me and your neighbors.) And once you have conceived you give birth to one sin after another against your neighbors, however it pleases your perverse sensual will. Sometimes we see cruelty, general or particular, born. It is a general sort of cruelty to see yourself and others damned and in danger of death for having lost grace. What cruelty, to refuse to help either oneself or others by loving virtue and hating vice! But some actually extend their cruelty even further, not only refusing the good example of virtue but in their wickedness assuming the role of the devil by dragging others as much as they can from virtue and leading them to vice. This is spiritual cruelty: to make oneself the instrument for depriving others of life and dealing out death.

Bodily cruelty springs from greed, which not only refuses to share what is one's own but takes what belongs to others, robbing the poor, playing the overlord, cheating, defrauding, putting up one's neighbors' goods— and often their very persons—for ransom.

O wretched cruelty! You will find yourself deprived of my mercy unless you turn to compassion and kindness! At times you give birth to hurtful words, followed often enough by murder. At other times you give birth to indecency toward others, and the sinner becomes a stinking beast, poisoning not only one or two but anyone who might approach in love or fellowship.

And who is hurt by the offspring of pride? Only your neighbors. For you harm them when your exalted opinion of yourself leads you to consider yourself superior and therefore to despise them. And if pride is in a position of authority, it gives birth to injustice and cruelty, and becomes a dealer in human flesh.

O dearest daughter, grieve that I am so offended, and weep over these dead so that your prayer may destroy their death! For you see that everywhere, on every level of society, all are giving birth to sin on their neighbors' heads. For there is no sin that does not touch others, whether secretly by refusing them what is due them, or openly by giving birth to the vices of which I have told you.

It is indeed true, then, that every sin committed against me is done by means of your neighbors.

7. . . . For all virtues are built on charity for your neighbors. So I have told you, and such is the truth: Charity gives life to all the virtues, nor can any virtue exist without charity. In other words, virtue is attained only through love of me.

After the soul has come to know herself she finds humility and hatred for her selfish sensual passion, recognizing the perverse law that is bound up in her members and is always fighting against the spirit [cf. Gal. 5:17]. So she rises up with hatred and contempt for that sensuality and crushes it firmly under the foot of reason. And through all the blessings she has received from me she discovers within her very self the breadth of my goodness. She humbly attributes to me her discovery of this self-knowledge, because she knows that my grace has drawn her from darkness and carried her into the light of true knowledge. Having come to know my goodness, the soul loves it both with and without intermediary. I mean she loves it without the intermediary of herself or her own advantage. But she does have as intermediary that virtue which is conceived through love of me, for she sees that she cannot be pleasing or acceptable to me except by conceiving hatred of sin and love of virtue.

Virtue, once conceived, must come to birth. Therefore, as soon as the soul has conceived through loving affection, she gives birth for her neighbors' sake. And just as she loves me in truth, so also she serves her neighbors in truth. Nor could she do otherwise, for love of me and love of neighbor are one and the same thing: Since love of neighbor has its source in me, the more the soul loves me, the more she loves her neighbors.

Such is the means I have given you to practice and prove your virtue. The service you cannot render me you must do for your neighbors. Thus it will be evident that you have me within your soul by grace, when with tender loving desire you are looking out for my honor and the salvation of your neighbors by bearing fruit for them in many holy prayers.

I showed you earlier how suffering alone, without desire, cannot atone for sin. Just so, the soul in love with my truth never ceases doing service for all the world, universally and in particular, in proportion to her own burning desire and to the disposition of those who receive. Her loving charity benefits herself first of all, as I have told you, when she conceives that virtue from which she draws the life of grace. Blessed with this unitive love she reaches out in loving charity to the whole world's need for salvation. But beyond a general love for all people she sets her eye on the specific needs of her neighbors and comes to the aid of those nearest her according to the graces I have given her for ministry: Some she teaches by word, giving sincere and impartial counsel; others she teaches by her example—as everyone ought to—edifying her neighbors by her good, holy, honorable life.

These are the virtues, with innumerable others, that are brought to birth in love of neighbor. But why have I established such differences? Why do I give this person one virtue and and that person another, rather than giving them all to one person? It is true that all the virtues are bound together, and it is impossible to have one without having them all. But I give them in different ways so that one virtue might be, as it were, the source of all the others. So to one person I give charity as the primary virtue, to another justice, to another humility, to another a lively faith or prudence or temperance or patience, and to still another courage.

These and many other virtues I give differently to different souls, and the soul is most at ease with that virtue which has been made primary for her. But through her love of that virtue she attracts all the other virtues to herself, since they are all bound together in loving charity.

The same is true of many of my gifts and graces, virtue and other spiritual gifts, and those things necessary for the body and human life. I have distributed them all in such a way that no one has all of them. Thus have I given you reason—necessity, in fact—to practice mutual charity. For I could well have supplied each of you with all your needs, both spiritual and material. But I wanted to make you dependent on one another so that each of you would be my minister, dispensing the graces and gifts you have received from me. So whether you will it or not, you cannot escape the exercise of charity! Yet, unless you do it for love of me, it is worth nothing to you in the realm of grace.

So you see, I have made you my ministers, setting you in different positions and in different ranks to exercise the virtue of charity. For there are many rooms in my house [John 14:2]. All I want is love. In loving me you will realize love for your neighbors, and if you love your neighbors you have kept the law [cf. Matt. 22:37–40]. If you are bound by this love you will do everything you can to be of service wherever you are.

8. I have told you how to serve your neighbors, and how that service proves your love for me. Now I will go further:

You test the virtue of patience in yourself when your neighbors insult you. Your humility is tested by the proud, your faith by the unfaithful, your hope by the person who has no hope. Your justice is tried by the unjust, your compassion by the cruel, and your gentleness and kindness by the wrathful. Your neighbors are the channel through which all your virtues are tested and come to birth, just as the evil give birth to all their vices through their neighbors.

Attend well. When I say that humility is tested by pride, I mean that a proud person cannot harm one who is humble, for the humble person smothers pride. If you are faithful to me your faith cannot be lessened by the infidelity of the wicked who neither love nor trust me. Nor can these lessen your hope once you have conceived it through love of me; rather it will be strengthened and proved in your affectionate love for your neighbors.

Those who do not love me cannot believe or trust me; rather they believe and trust in their selfish sensuality, which they do love. They have no faith or trust in my servants either. But though they do not love me faithfully or with constant hope seek their salvation in me, my faithful servant will not abandon them. You see, in the face of their unfaithfulness and lack of hope you prove your own faith. And whenever it may be necessary to prove your virtue, you prove it both in yourself and through your neighbors.

So your justice is not lessened but proved by the injustices of others. That is, you show you are just through the virtue of patience. Likewise, your kindness and mildness are revealed through gentle patience in the presence of wrath. And in the face of envy, spite, and hatred your loving charity is revealed in hungry desire for the salvation of souls.

I tell you, moreover, when you return good for evil you not only prove your own virtue, but often you send out coals ablaze with charity that will melt hatred and bitterness from the heart and mind of the wrathful, even turning their hatred to benevolence. Such is the power of charity and perfect patience in one who takes up the burden of the sins of the wicked and bears with their anger.

Then consider the virtue of steadfast courage. It is tested when you have to suffer much from people's insults and slanders, which would like to drag you away from the way and teaching of the truth either by abuse or flattery. But if you have conceived the virtue of courage within you, you will always be strong and constant, and you will prove your courage externally through your neighbors. If, on the other hand, your virtue could not give solid proof of itself when tried by all these contrary things, then it could not be grounded in truth. . . .

51. *Then divine Goodness looked with the eye of his mercy upon that soul's hungry longing and said:*

My dearest daughter, I am not scornful of desire. No, I am the one who answers holy longings. Therefore I want to explain to you what you ask.

You ask me to explain to you the image of the three stairs, and to tell you how people must act to be able to escape from the river and mount the bridge. I did describe for you earlier people's delusion and blindness, and how they taste even in this life the pledge of hell and, like martyrs of the devil, reap eternal damnation. I told you what fruit they harvest from their evil actions. And when I told you these things, I showed you how they ought to behave. Still, to satisfy your longing, I will now explain it to you more fully.

You know that every evil is grounded in selfish love of oneself. This love is a cloud that blots out the light of reason. It is in reason that the light of faith is held, and one cannot lose the one without losing the other.

I made the soul after my own image and likeness, giving her memory, understanding, and will. The understanding is the most noble aspect of the soul. It is moved by affection, and it in turn nourishes affection. Affection is love's hand, and this hand fills the memory with thoughts of me and of the blessings I have given. Such remembrance makes the soul caring instead of indifferent, grateful instead of thankless. So each power lends a hand to the other, thus nourishing the soul in the life of grace.

The soul cannot live without love. She always wants to love something because love is the stuff she is made of, and through love I created her. This is why I said that it is affection that moves the understanding, saying, as it were, "I want to love, because the food I feed on is love." And the understanding, feeling itself awakened by affection, gets up, as it were, and says, "If you want to love, I will give you something good that you can love." And at once it is aroused by the consideration of the soul's dignity and the indignity into which she has fallen through her own fault. In the dignity of her existence she tastes the immeasurable goodness and uncreated love with which I created her. And in the sight of her own wretchedness she discovers and tastes my mercy, for in mercy I have lent her time and drawn her out of darkness.

Affection in turn is nourished by love, opening its mouth, holy desire, and eating hatred and contempt for its selfish sensuality seasoned with the oil of true humility and perfect patience, which it has drawn from this holy hatred. After the virtues have been conceived, they are born either perfect or imperfect, according to how the soul exercises the perfection within her, as I will tell you further on.

So also, on the other hand, if sensual affection wants to love sensual things, the eye of understanding is moved in that direction. It takes for its object only passing things with selfish love, contempt for virtue, and love of vice, drawing from these pride and impatience. And the memory is filled only with what affection holds out to it.

This love so dazzles the eye that it neither discerns nor sees anything but the glitter of these things. Such is their glitter that understanding sees and affection loves them all as if their brightness came from goodness and loveliness. Were it not for this glitter, people would never sin, for the soul by her very nature cannot desire anything but good. But vice is disguised as something good for her, and so the soul sins. Her eyes, though, cannot tell the difference because of her blindness, and she does not know the truth. So she wanders about searching for what is good and lovely where it is not to be found.

I have already told you that the world's pleasures are all venomous thorns. Understanding is deluded at the sight of them, and the will in loving them (for it loves what it should not love), and the memory in holding on to them. Understanding is acting like a thief who robs someone else, and so the memory holds on to the constant thought of things that are apart from me, and in this way the soul is deprived of grace.

Such is the unity of these three powers of the soul that I cannot be offended by one without all three offending me. The one lends a hand to the other, for good or for evil, by free choice. This free choice is bound up with affection. So it moves as it pleases, whether by the light of reason or unreasonably. Your reason is bound to me, unless free choice cuts you off through disordered love. And you have that perverse law that is always fighting against the spirit [Rom. 7:23].

There are, then, two aspects to yourself: sensuality and reason. Sensuality is a servant, and it has been appointed to serve the soul, so that your body may be your instrument for proving and exercising virtue. The soul is free, liberated from sin in my Son's blood, and she cannot be dominated unless she consents to it with her will, which is bound up with free choice. Free choice is one with the will, and agrees with it. It is set between sensuality and reason and can turn to whichever one it will.

It is true that when the soul decides to gather her powers with the hand of free choice in my name, all the actions that person does, whether spiritual or temporal, are gathered in. Free choice cuts itself off from sensuality and binds itself to reason. And then I dwell in their midst through grace. This is what my Truth, the Word incarnate, meant when he said: "Whenever two or three are gathered in my name, I will be in their midst" [Matt. 18:20], and this is the truth. I have already told you that no one can come to me except through him. That is why I have made of him a bridge with three stairs, the latter being an image of the three spiritual stages.

From *Catherine of Siena: The Dialogue,* translated by Suzanne Noffke (Mahwah, N.J.: Paulist Press, 1980), pp. 33–39, 103–5. © 1980 by The Missionary Society of St. Paul the Apostle in the State of New York. Used by permission of Paulist Press.

19. *The Penitential of Cummean*

Illustrative of the penitential manuals, The Penitential of Cummean *(ca. A.D. 950) is attributed to an Irish monk by that name. The manual offers guidance to the confessor in diagnosing sins and prescribing penances.*

1. Of Gluttony

1. Those who are drunk with wine or beer, contrary to the Savior's prohibition (as it is said, "Take heed that your hearts be not overcharged with surfeiting and drunkenness or with the cares of this life lest perchance that day come upon you suddenly, for as a snare shall it come upon all that dwell upon the face of the whole earth" [Luke 21:34–35]) and [that] of the Apostle; ("Be not drunk with wine wherein is luxury") [Eph. 5:18]—if they have taken the vow of sanctity, they

shall expiate the fault for forty days with bread and water; laymen, however, for seven days.

2. He who compels anyone, for the sake of good fellowship, to become drunk shall do penance in the same manner as one who is drunk.

3. If he does this on account of hatred, he shall be judged as a homicide.

4. He who is not able to sing psalms, being benumbed in his organs of speech, shall perform a special fast.

5. He who anticipates the canonical hour, or only on account of appetite takes something more delicate than the others have, shall go without supper or live for two days on bread and water.

6. He who suffers excessive distention of the stomach and the pain of satiety [shall do penance] for one day.

7. If he suffers to the point of vomiting, though he is not in a state of infirmity, for seven days.

8. If, however, he vomits the host, for forty days.

9. But if [he does this] by reason of infirmity, for seven days.

10. If he ejects it into the fire, he shall sing one hundred psalms.

11. If dogs lap up this vomit, he who has vomited shall do penance for one hundred days.

12. [One who] steals food [shall do penance] for forty days; if [he does it] again, for three forty-day periods; if a third time, for a year; if, indeed, [he does it] a fourth time, he shall do penance in the yoke of exile under another abbot. . . .

2. Of Fornication

1. A bishop who commits fornication shall be degraded and shall do penance for twelve years. . . .

9. So shall those who commit sodomy do penance for seven years.

10. For femoral masturbation, two years.

11. He who merely desires in his mind to commit fornication, but is not able, shall do penance for one year, especially in the three forty-day periods.

12. He who is polluted by an evil word or glance, yet did not wish to commit bodily fornication, shall do penance for twenty or forty days according to the degree of his sin.

13. But if he is polluted by a violent assault of the imagination he shall do penance for seven days.

14. He who for a long time is lured by imagination to commit fornication, and repels the thought too gently, shall do penance for one or two or more days, according to the duration of the imagination. . . .

18. He who loves any woman, [but is] unaware of any evil beyond a few conversations, shall do penance for forty days.

19. But he who kisses and embraces, one year, especially in the three forty-day periods.

20. He who loves in mind only, seven days.

21. If, however, he has spoken but has not been accepted by her, forty [days].

22. A layman who turns to fornication and the shedding of blood shall do penance for three years; in the first, and in three forty-day periods of the others, with bread and water, and in all [three years] without wine, without flesh, without arms, without his wife.

23. A layman who defiles his neighbor's wife or virgin [daughter] shall do penance for one year with bread and water, without his own wife.

24. But if he defiles a vowed virgin and begets a son, [he shall do penance] for three years without arms; in the first, with bread and water, in the others without wine and flesh.

25. If he does not beget, but defiles, he shall do penance for one year and one-half without delicacies and without his wife.

26. But if he enters in unto his woman-slave, he shall sell her and shall do penance for one year.

27. If he begets a son by her, he shall liberate her.

28. In the case of one whose wife is barren, both he and she shall live in continence. . . .

3. Of Avarice

1. He who commits theft once shall do penance for one year; if [he does it] a second time, for two years.

2. If he is a boy, forty or thirty days, according to his age or state of knowledge.

3. He who hoards what is left over until the morrow through ignorance shall give these things to the poor. But if [he does this] through contempt of those who censure him, he shall be cured by alms and fasting according to the judgment of a priest. If, indeed, he persists in his avarice he shall be sent away.

4. He who recovers from one who is carrying them off things that are his own, against the contrary command of the Lord and of the Apostle, shall give to the poor those things which he has recovered.

5. He who plunders another's goods by any means, shall restore fourfold to him whom he has injured.

6. If he has not the means of making restitution, he shall do penance as we have stated above. . . .

14. A cleric who has an excess of goods shall give these to the poor; but if he does not, he shall be excommunicated.

15. If he afterwards does penance, he shall live secluded in penance for the same [length of] time as that in which he was recalcitrant.

16. One who lies because of cupidity shall make satisfaction in liberality to him whom he has cheated.

17. One who lies through ignorance, however, and does not know it, shall confess to him to whom he has lied and to a priest and shall be condemned to an hour of silence or fifteen psalms.

18. If [he] verily [did it] by intention, he shall do penance by three days of silence, or three psalms if he can [sing].

4. Of Anger

1. He who, justly or unjustly, makes his brother sad shall mollify by a satisfaction the rancor he has conceived, and so he shall be able to pray.

2. But if it is impossible to be reconciled with him, then at least he shall do penance, his priest being judge.

3. He who refuses to be reconciled shall live on bread and water for as long a time as he has been implacable.

4. He who hates his brother shall go on bread and water as long as he has not overcome his hatred; and he shall be joined to him whom he hates in sincere charity.

5. He who commits murder through nursing hatred in his mind, shall give up his arms until his death, and dead unto the world, shall live unto God.

6. But if it is after vows of perfection, he shall die unto the world with perpetual pilgrimage.

7. But he who does this through anger, not from premeditation, shall do penance for three years with bread and water and with alms and prayers.

8. But if he kills his neighbor unintentionally, by accident, he shall do penance for one year.

9. He who by a blow in a quarrel renders a man incapacitated or maimed shall take care of [the injured man's] medical expenses and shall make good the damages for the injury and shall do his work until he is healed and do penance for half a year. . . .

12. One who curses his brother in anger shall both make satisfaction to him whom he has cursed and live secluded for seven days on bread and water.

13. He who utters in anger harsh but not injurious words shall make satisfaction to his brother and keep a special fast.

14. But if [he expresses his anger] with pallor or flush or tremor, yet remains silent, he shall go for a day on bread and water.

15. He who [does not betray it but] nevertheless feels incensed in his mind shall make satisfaction to him who has incensed him.

16. He who will not confess to him who has incensed him, that pestilential person shall be sent away from the company of the saints; if he repents, he shall do penance for as long as he was recalcitrant.

5. Of Dejection

1. He who long harbors bitterness in his heart shall be healed by a joyful countenance and a glad heart.
2. But if he does not quickly lay this aside, he shall correct himself by fasting according to the decision of a priest.
3. But if he returns to it, he shall be sent away until, on bread and water, he willingly and gladly acknowledges his fault. . . .

7. Of Vainglory

1. The contentious also shall subject himself to the decision of another; otherwise he shall be anathematized, since he is among the strangers to the Kingdom of God.
2. One who boasts of his own good deeds shall humble himself; otherwise any good he has done he shall lose on account of human glory.

8. Of Pride

1. He who takes up any novelty outside the Scriptures, such as might lead to heresy, shall be sent away.
2. But if he repents, he shall publicly condemn his own opinion and convert to the faith those whom he has deceived, and he shall fast at the decision of his priest.
3. He who proudly censures others for any kind of contempt shall first make satisfaction to them and then fast according to the judgment of his priest. . . .
8. He who for envy's sake defames [another] or willingly listens to a defamer shall be put apart and shall fast for four days on bread and water.
9. If the offense is against a superior, he shall do penance thus for seven days and shall serve him willingly thereafter. . . .
18. He who intentionally disdains to bow to any senior shall go without supper. . . .
21. He who rebukes others boldly shall first conciliate them and then sing thirty psalms.
22. He who imputes a shameful sin to his brother, especially before he rebukes him, shall make satisfaction to him and do penance for three days.
23. He who speaks with a woman alone, or remains under the same roof [with her] at night, shall go without supper. . . .

9. Of Petty Cases

1. If by some accident anyone negligently lose the host, leaving it for beasts and birds to devour, if it is excusable he shall do penance for three forty-day periods; if not, for a year.

2. He who not without knowing it gives the communion to one who is excommunicate, shall do penance for forty [days].

3. So [shall] he [do penance] who eats of a dead thing unaware; but if not [unaware], he shall do penance for a year.

4. Now let it be noted that for whatever time anyone remains in his sins, for so long shall he do penance.

5. If any work is imposed on anyone and he does it not, on account of contempt, he shall go without supper. . . .

13. Those who furnish guidance to the barbarians shall do penance for fourteen years, even if it does not result in the slaughter of the Christians; but if [it turns out] otherwise they shall give up their arms and until death, being dead to the world, shall live unto God.

14. He who despoils monasteries, falsely saying that he is redeeming captives, [shall] go for one year on bread and water, and everything that he has taken he shall give to the poor, and he shall do penance for two years without wine and flesh.

15. He who loses a consecrated object shall do penance for seven days.

16. He who eats of the flesh of a dead animal, of whose [manner of] death he is unaware, shall live the third part of a year on bread and water and the rest [of it] without wine and flesh.

10. Let Us Now Set Forth the Determinations of Our Fathers before Us on the Misdemeanors of Boys

1. Boys talking alone and transgressing the regulations of the elders, shall be corrected by three special fasts.

2. Those who kiss simply shall be corrected with six special fasts; those who kiss licentiously without pollution, with eight special fasts; if with pollution or embrace, with ten special fasts. . . .

6. But boys of twenty years who practice masturbation together and confess [shall do penance] twenty or forty days before they take communion. . . .

10. A small boy, if he eats anything that has been stolen, shall do penance for seven days.

11. If after his twentieth year he adds to this any considerable theft, he shall do penance for twenty days. . . .

13. A man who practices masturbation by himself, for the first offense, one hundred days; if he repeats it, a year.

14. Men guilty of homosexual practices, for the first offense, a year; if they repeat it, two years. . . .

21. Small boys who strike one another shall do penance for seven days; but if [they are] older, for twenty days; if [they are] adolescents, they shall do penance for forty days.

11. Of Questions concerning the Host

1. He who fails to guard the host carefully, so that a mouse eats it, shall do penance for forty days.

2. But he who loses it in the church, that is, so that a part falls and is not found, twenty days. . . .

23. If the host fall from the hands of the celebrant to the ground and is not found, everything that is found in the place in which it fell shall be burned and the ashes concealed as above, and then the priest shall be sentenced to half a year [of penance].

24. If the host is found, the place shall be cleaned up with a broom, and the straw, as we have said above, burned with fire, and the priest shall do penance for twenty days. . . .

29. If the priest stammers over the Sunday prayer which is called "the perilous," if once, he shall be cleansed with fifty strokes; if a second time, one hundred; if a third time, he shall keep a special fast.

But this is to be carefully observed in all penance: the length of time anyone remains in his faults; with what learning he is instructed; with what passion he is assailed; with what courage he stands; with what tearfulness he seems to be afflicted; and with what oppression he is driven to sin. For Almighty God who knows the hearts of all and has bestowed diverse natures will not estimate [various] weights of sins as [worthy] of equal penance. . . . Whence a certain wise man saith: "To whom more is intrusted, from him shall more be exacted." Thus the priests of the Lord learn, who preside over the churches; for a part is given to them together with those for whose faults they make satisfaction. What is it then to make satisfaction for a fault unless when thou receive the sinner to penance, [and] by warning, exhortation, teaching, lead him to penance, correct him of his error, amend him of his faults, and make him such that God is rendered favorable to him after conversion, thou art said to make satisfaction for his fault? When, therefore, thou art such a priest, and such is thy teaching and thy word, there is given to thee a part of those whom thou correctest, that their merit may be thy reward and their salvation thy glory.

20. Thomas Aquinas,
Summa Theologica and Summa Contra Gentiles

Indisputably the dominant mind of the later Middle Ages, Thomas Aquinas (1225–1274) created a vast synthesis of the rediscovered Aristotle, the theology of Augustine, the monastic and mystical movements, and evolving conceptions of church and sacrament. His formulations of Christian ethics, while ultimately cast in a theological frame of reference, are dominated by an Aristotelian form of natural law.

SUMMA THEOLOGICA

Question 5. Article 1. *Whether Goodness Differs Really from Being?*. . . Goodness and being are really the same, and differ only in idea; which is clear from the following argument. The essence of goodness consists in this, that it is in some way desirable. Hence the Philosopher says: *Goodness is what all desire* [Aristotle, *Nichomachean Ethics*, book 1, 1 (1094a 3)]. Now it is clear that a thing is desirable only in so far as it is perfect, for all desire their own perfection. But everything is perfect so far as it is actual. Therefore it is clear that a thing is perfect so far as it is being; for being is the actuality of everything, as is clear from the foregoing [question 3, article 4; question 4, articles 1 and 3]. Hence it is clear that goodness and being are the same really. But goodness expresses the aspect of desirableness, which being does not express.

Reply Obj. 1. Although goodness and being are the same really, nevertheless, since they differ in thought, they are not predicated of a thing absolutely in the same way. For since being properly signifies that something actually is, and actuality properly correlates to potentiality, a thing is, in consequence, said absolutely to have being accordingly as it is primarily distinguished from that which is only in potentiality; and this is precisely each thing's substantial being. Hence it is by its substantial being that everything is said to have being absolutely; but by any further actuality it is said to have being relatively. Thus to be white signifies being relatively, for to be white does not take a thing out of absolutely potential being, since it is added to a thing that actually has being. But goodness expresses perfection, which is something desirable, and hence it expresses something final. Hence, that which has ultimate perfection is said to be absolutely good, but that which has not the ultimate perfection it ought to have (although, in so far as it is at all actual, it has some perfection) is not said to be perfect absolutely nor good absolutely, but only relatively. . . .

Question 5. Article 3. *Whether Every Being Is Good?*. . . Every being, as being, is good. For all being, as being, has actuality and is in some way perfect, since every act is some sort of perfection, and perfection implies desirability and goodness, as is clear from what has been said. Hence it follows that every being as such is good. . . .

. . . No being is said to be evil, considered as being, but only so far as it lacks being. Thus a man is said to be evil, because he lacks the being of virtue; and an eye is said to be evil, because it lacks the power to see well. . . .

Question 48. Article 2. *Whether Evil Is Found in Things?*. . . . As was said above, the perfection of the universe requires that there should be inequality in things, so that every grade of goodness may be realized [question 47, article 2]. Now, one grade of goodness is that of the good which cannot fail. Another grade of goodness is that of the good which can fail in goodness. These grades of goodness are to be found in being itself; for there are some things which cannot lose their being, as incorruptible things, while there are some which can lose it, as corruptible things. As, therefore, the perfection of the universe requires that there should be not only incorruptible beings, but also corruptible beings, so the perfection of the universe requires that there should be some which can fail in goodness and which sometimes do fail. Now it is in this that evil consists, namely, in the fact that a thing fails in goodness. Hence it is clear that evil is found in things in the way that corruption also is found; for corruption itself is an evil. . . .

Question 55. Article 1. *Whether Human Virtue Is Habit?* . . . Virtue denotes a certain perfection of a power. Now a thing's perfection is considered chiefly in relation to its end. But the end of power is act. Therefore power is said to be perfect according as it is determined to its act. Now there are some powers which of themselves are determined to their acts, for instance, the active natural powers. And therefore these natural powers are in themselves called virtues. But the rational powers, which are proper to man, are not determined to one particular action, but are inclined indifferently to many; but they are determined to acts by means of habits, as is clear from what we have said above [question 49, article 4]. Therefore human virtues are habits. . . .

Question 58. Article 2. . . . It is stated in *Ethics* [1]. that *there are two kinds of virtue: some we call intellectual, some, moral* [Aristotle, *Ethics*, book 1, 13 (1103a 3)].

. . . Reason is the first principle of all human acts, and whatever other principles of human acts may be found, they obey reason in some way, but diversely. For some obey reason instantaneously and without any contradiction whatever. Such are the members of the body, provided they be in a healthy condition, for as soon as reason commands, the hand or the foot proceeds to action. Hence the Philosopher says that *the soul rules the body with a despotic rule* [cf. Aristotle, *Politics*, book 1, 2 (1254b 4)], *i.e.*, as a master rules his slave, who has no right to rebel. Accordingly, some held that all the active principles in man are subordinate to reason in this way. If this were true, for a man to act well it would suffice that his reason be perfect. Consequently, since virtue is a habit perfecting man in view of his doing good actions, it would follow that virtue existed only in the reason, so that there would be none but intellectual virtues. This was the opinion of Socrates, who said *every virtue is a kind of prudence,* as is stated in *Ethics* [Aristotle, *Ethics*, 6, 13 (1144b 19)]. Hence he maintained that as long as a man was in possession of knowledge, he could not sin, and that every one who sinned did so through ignorance [Ibid., book 7, 2 (1145b 23); cf. also Plato, *Protagoras* (pp. 352B; 355A; 357B)].

Now this is based on a false supposition. For the appetitive part obeys the reason, not instantaneously, but with a certain power of opposition; and so the Philosopher says that *reason commands the appetitive part by a political rule* [Aristotle, *Politics*, book 1, 5 (1254b 4)], whereby a man rules over subjects that are free, having a certain right of opposition. Hence Augustine says on *Ps.* [98] that *sometimes the intellect marks the way, while desire lags, or follows not at all* [St. Augustine, *Enarrationes in Psalmos*, sermon 8, super Ps. 98, 20 (PL 37, 1522)]; so much so, that sometimes the habits or passions of the appetitive part cause the use of reason to be impeded in some particular action. And in this way, there is some truth in the saying of Socrates that so long as a man is in possession of knowledge he does not sin: provided, however, that this knowledge is made to include the use of reason in this individual act of choice.

Accordingly, for a man to do a good deed, it is requisite not only that his reason be well disposed by means of a habit of intellectual virtue, but also that his appetite be well disposed by means of a habit of moral virtue. And so moral differs from intellectual virtue, even as the appetite differs from the reason. Hence, just as the appetite is the principle of human acts, in so far as it partakes of reason, so moral habits are to be considered human virtues in so far as they are in conformity with reason. . . .

Question 61. Article 2. . . . Things may be numbered either in respect of their formal principles, or according to the subjects in which they are; and in either way we find that there are four cardinal virtues.

For the formal principle of the virtue of which we speak now is the good as defined by reason. This good can be considered in two ways. First, as existing in the consideration itself of reason, and thus we have one principal virtue called *prudence*.—Secondly, according as the reason puts its order into something else, and this either into operations, and then we have *justice*, or into passions, and then we need two virtues. For the need of putting the order of reason into the passions is due to their thwarting reason; and this occurs in two ways. First, when the passions incite to something against reason, and then they need a curb, which we thus call *temperance*; secondly, when the passions withdraw us from following the dictate of reason, *e.g.*, through fear of danger or toil, and then man needs to be strengthened for that which reason dictates, lest he turn back, and to this end there is *fortitude*. . . .

In like manner, we find the same number if we consider the subjects of virtue. For there are four subjects of the virtue of which we now speak, viz., the power which is rational in its essence, and this is perfected by *prudence*; and that which is rational by participation, and is threefold, the will, subject of *justice*, the concupiscible power, subject of *temperance*, and the irascible power, subject of *fortitude*. . . .

Question 62. Article 1. *Whether There Are Theological Virtues?* . . . The precepts of law are about acts of virtue. But the divine law contains precepts about the acts of faith, hope and charity: for it is written ([*Eccl.* 2:]8, seqq.): *Ye that fear the Lord believe Him,* and again, *hope in Him,* and again, *love Him.* Therefore faith, hope and charity are virtues directing us to God. Therefore they are theological virtues.

. . . Man is perfected by virtue for those actions by which he is directed to happiness, as was explained above [question 5, article 7]. Now man's happiness or felicity is twofold, as was also stated above [question 5, article 5]. One is proportioned to human nature, a happiness, namely, which man can obtain by means of the principles of his nature. The other is a happiness surpassing man's nature, and which man can obtain by the power of God alone, by a kind of participation of the Godhead; and thus it is written (2 *Pet.* [1:]4) that by Christ we are made *partakers of the divine nature.* And because such happiness surpasses the power of human nature, man's natural principles, which enable him to act well according to his power, do not suffice to direct man to this same happiness. Hence it is necessary for man to receive from God some additional principles, by which he may be directed to supernatural happiness, even as he is directed to his connatural end by means of his natural principles, albeit not without the divine assistance. Such principles are called *theological virtues* [cf. William of Auxerre, *Summa Aurea*, book 3, tr. 2, ch. 2 (fol. 130ra)]. They are so called, first, because their object is God, inasmuch as they direct us rightly to God; secondly, because they are infused in us by God alone; thirdly, because these virtues are not made known to us, save by divine revelation, contained in Holy Scripture. . . .

Question 62. Article 3. *Whether Faith, Hope and Charity are Fittingly Reckoned as Theological Virtues?* . . . As was stated above, the theological virtues direct man to supernatural happiness in the same way as by the natural inclination man is directed to his connatural end. Now the latter direction happens in two respects. First, according to the reason or intellect, in so far as it contains the first universal principles which are known to us through the natural light of the intellect, and which are reason's starting-point, both in speculative and in practical matters. Secondly, through the rectitude of the will tending naturally to the good as defined by reason.

But these two fall short of the order of supernatural happiness, according to [1 Cor. 2:9]: *The eye hath not seen, nor ear heard, neither hath it entered into the heart of man, what things God hath prepared for them that love Him.* Consequently, in relation to both intellect and will, man needed to receive in addition something supernatural to direct him to a supernatural end. First, as regards the intellect, man receives certain supernatural principles, which are held by means of a divine light; and these are the things which are to be believed, about which is *faith.*—Secondly, the will is directed to this end, both as to the movement of intention, which tends to that end as something attainable,—this pertains to *hope*—and as to a certain spiritual union, whereby the will is, in a way, transformed into that end—and this belongs to *charity.* For the appetite of a thing is naturally moved and tends towards its connatural end and this movement is due to a certain conformity of the thing with its end. . . .

But in the order of perfection, charity precedes faith and hope, because both faith and hope are quickened by charity, and receive from charity their full complement as virtues. For thus charity is the mother and the root of all the virtues, inasmuch as it is the form of them all, as we shall state further on [Aquinas, *Summa Theologica*, II–II, question 23, article 8]. . . .

Question 64. Article 1. *Whether the Moral Virtues Consist in a Mean?* . . . *Objection* 1. It would seem that moral virtue does not consist in a mean. For the nature of a mean is incompatible with that which is extreme. Now the nature of virtue is to be something extreme; for it is stated in *De Caelo* [1]. that *virtue is the peak of power* [Aristotle, *De Caelo*, book 1, 11 (281a 11; a 18); cf., St. Thomas, *In De Caelo*, book 1, lecture 25]. Therefore moral virtue does not consist in a mean.

Obj. 2. Further, the maximum is not a mean. Now some moral virtues tend to a maximum: for instance, magnanimity to very great honors, and magnificence to very large expenditures, as is stated in *Ethics* [Aristotle, *Ethics,* book 4, 2 (1122a 18); 3 (1123a 34)]. Therefore not every moral virtue consists in a mean.

Obj. 3. Further, if it is essential to a moral virtue to consist in a mean, it follows that a moral virtue is not perfected, but on the contrary corrupted, through tending to something extreme. Now some moral virtues are perfected by tending to something extreme. Thus virginity, which abstains from all sexual pleasure, observes the extreme, and is the most perfect chastity. In the same way, to give all to the poor is the most perfect mercy or liberality. Therefore it seems that it is not essential to moral virtue that is should consist in a mean.

On the contrary, The Philosopher says that *moral virtue is an elective habit consisting in the mean* [Ibid., book 2, 6 (1106b 36)].

I answer that, As has already been explained, the nature of virtue is that it should direct man to good [question 55, article 3]. Now moral virtue is properly a perfection of the appetitive part of the soul in regard to some determinate matter; and the measure and rule of the appetitive movement in relation to appetible objects is the reason. But the good of that which is measured or ruled consists in its conformity with its rule; and, thus, the good of things made by art is that they follow the rule of art. Consequently, in things of this sort, evil consists in discordance from their rule or measure. Now this may happen either by their exceeding the measure or by their falling short of it; as we may clearly observe in all things ruled or measured. Hence it is evident that the good of moral virtue consists in conformity with the rule of reason. Now it is clear that between excess and deficiency the mean is equality or conformity. Therefore it is evident that moral virtue consists in a mean.

Reply Obj. 1. Moral virtue derives its goodness from the rule of reason, while its matter consists in passions or operations. If, therefore, we compare moral virtue to reason, then, if we look at that which it has of reason, it holds the position of one extreme, viz., conformity; while excess and defect take the position of the other extreme, viz., deformity. But if we consider moral virtue in respect of its matter, then it has the nature of a mean, in so far as it makes the passion conform to the rule of reason. Hence the Philosopher says that *virtue, as to its essence, is a mean,* in so far as the rule of virtue is imposed on its proper matter; *but it is an extreme in reference to the "best" and "the excellent,"* viz., as to its conformity with reason [Ibid., book 4, 3 (1123b 13)].

Reply Obj. 2. In actions and passions, the mean and the extremes depend on various circumstances. Hence nothing hinders something from being extreme in a particular virtue according to one circumstance, while the same thing is a mean according to other circumstances, through its conformity with reason. This is the case with magnanimity and magnificence. For if we look at the absolute quantity of the respective objects of these virtues, we shall call it an extreme and a maximum; but if we consider the quantity in relation to other circumstances, then it has the character of a mean, since these virtues tend to this maximum in accordance with the rule of reason, *i.e., where* it is right, *when* it is right, and for an *end* that is right. There will be excess, if one tends to this maximum *when* it is not right, or *where* it is not right, or for an undue *end;* and there will be deficiency if one fails to tend thereto *where* one ought, and *when* one ought. This agrees with the saying of the Philosopher that the *magnanimous man observes the extreme in quantity, but the mean in the right mode of his action* [Aristotle, *Ethics*, book 2, 6 (1107a 7)].

Reply Obj. 3. The same is to be said of virginity and poverty as of magnanimity. For virginity abstains from all sexual matters, and poverty from all wealth, for a right end, and in a right manner, *i.e.,* according to God's commandment, and for the sake of eternal life. But if this be done in an undue manner, *i.e.,* out of unlawful superstition, or again for vainglory, it will be in excess. And if it be not done when it ought to be done, or as it ought to be done, it is a vice by deficiency; as for instance, in those who break their vows of virginity or poverty. . . .

Question 90. Article 2. *Whether Law is Always Directed to the Common Good?* . . . As we have stated above, law belongs to that which is a principle of human acts, because it is their rule and measure. Now as reason is a principle of human acts, so in reason itself there is something which is the principle in respect of all the rest. Hence to this principle chiefly and mainly law must needs be referred. Now the first principle in practical matters, which are the object of the practical reason, is the last end: and the last end of human life is happiness or beatitude, as we have stated above [question 2, article 7; question 3, article 1; question 69, article 1]. Consequently, law must needs concern itself mainly with the order that is in beatitude. Moreover, since every part is ordained to the whole as the imperfect to the perfect, and since one man is a part of the perfect community, law must needs concern itself properly with the order directed to universal happiness. Therefore the Philosopher, in the above definition of legal matters, mentions both happiness and the body politic, since he says that we call those legal matters *just which are adapted to produce and preserve happiness and its parts for the body politic* [Aristotle, *Ethics*, book 5, 1 (1129b 17)]. For the state is a perfect community, as he says in *Politics* 1 [Aristotle, *Politics*, book 1, 1 (1252a 5)].

. . . [S]ince law is chiefly ordained to the common good, any other precept in regard to some individual work must needs be devoid of the nature of a law, save in so far as it regards the common good. Therefore every law is ordained to the common good. . . .

Question 90. Article 3. *Whether The Reason of Any Man Is Competent to Make Laws?* . . . A law, properly speaking, regards first and foremost the order to the common good. Now to order anything to the common good belongs either to the whole people, or to someone who is the vicegerent of the whole people. Hence the making of a law belongs either to the whole people or to a public personage who has care of the whole people; for in all other matters the directing of anything to the end concerns him to whom the end belongs. . . .

Question 91. Article 1. *Whether There Is an Eternal Law?* . . . As we have stated above, law is nothing else but a dictate of practical reason emanating from the ruler who governs a perfect community [question 90, articles 1–4]. Now it is evident, granted that the world is ruled by divine providence, as was stated in the First Part [Aquinas, *Summa Theologica*, book 1, question 22, articles 1 and 2], that the whole community of the universe is governed by the divine reason. Therefore the very notion of the government of things in God, the ruler of the universe, has the nature of a law. And since the divine reason's conception of things is not subject to time, but is eternal, according to *Prov.* [8:]23, therefore it is that this kind of law must be called eternal. . . .

Question 91. Article 2. *Whether There Is in Us a Natural Law?* . . . [L]aw, being a rule and measure, can be in a person in two ways: in one way, as in him that rules and measures; in another way, as in that which is ruled and measured, since a thing is ruled and measured in so far as it partakes of the rule or measure. Therefore, since all things subject to divine providence are ruled and measured by the eternal law, as was stated above, it is evident that all things partake in some way in the eternal law, in so far as, namely, from its being imprinted on them, they derive their respective inclinations to their proper acts and ends. Now among all others, the rational creature is subject to divine providence in a more excellent way, in so far as it itself partakes a share of providence, by being provident both for itself and for others. Therefore it has a share of the eternal reason, whereby it has a natural inclination to its proper act and end; and this participation of the eternal law in the rational creature is called the natural law. Hence the Psalmist, after saying (*Ps.* [4:]6): *Offer up the sacrifice of justice,* as though someone asked what the works of justice are, adds: *Many say, Who showeth us good things?* in answer to which question he says: *The light of Thy countenance, O Lord, is signed upon us.* He thus implies that the light of natural reason, whereby we discern what is good and what is evil, which is the function of the natural law, is nothing else than an imprint on us of the divine light. It is therefore evident that the natural law is nothing else than the rational creature's participation of the eternal law. . . .

Question 91. Article 3. *Whether There Is a Human Law?* . . . Now it is to be observed that the same procedure takes place in the practical and in the speculative reason, for each proceeds from principles to conclusions, as was stated above [Ibid.]. Accordingly, we conclude that, just as in the speculative reason, from naturally known indemonstrable principles we draw the conclusions of the various sciences, the knowledge of which is not imparted to us by nature, but acquired by the efforts of reason, so too it is that from the precepts of the natural law, as from common and indemonstrable principles, the human reason needs to proceed to the more particular determination of certain matters. These particular determinations, devised by human reason, are called human laws, provided that the other essential conditions of law be observed, as was stated above [question 90]. Therefore Tully says in his *Rhetoric* that *justice has its source in nature; thence certain things came into custom by reason of their utility; afterwards these things which emanated from nature, and were approved by custom, were sanctioned by fear and reverence for the law* [Cicero, *De Inventione,* book 2, 53 (p. 148b)]. . . .

Question 91. Article 4. *Whether There Was any Need for a Divine Law?*
. . . Besides the natural and the human law it was necessary for the directing of human conduct to have a divine law. And this for four reasons. First, because it is by law that man is directed how to perform his proper acts in view of his last end. Now if man were ordained to no other end than that which is proportionate to his natural ability, there would be no need for man to have any further direction, on the part of his reason, in addition to the natural law and humanly devised law which is derived from it. But since man is ordained to an end of eternal happiness which exceeds man's natural ability, as we have stated above [question 5, article 5], therefore it was necessary that, in addition to the natural and the human law, man should be directed to his end by a law given by God.

Secondly, because, by reason of the uncertainty of human judgment, especially on contingent and particular matters, different people form different judgments on human acts; whence also different and contrary laws result. In order, therefore, that man may know without any doubt what he ought to do and what he ought to avoid, it was necessary for man to be directed in his proper acts by a law given by God, for it is certain that such a law cannot err.

Thirdly, because man can make laws in those matters of which he is competent to judge. But man is not competent to judge of interior movements, that are hidden, but only of exterior acts which are observable; and yet for the perfection of virtue it is necessary for man to conduct himself rightly in both kinds of acts. Consequently, human law could not sufficiently curb and direct interior acts, and it was necessary for this purpose that a divine law should supervene.

Fourthly, because, as Augustine says [St. Augustine, *De Libero Arbitrio*, book 1, 5 (PL 32, 1228)], human law cannot punish or forbid all evil deeds, since, while aiming at doing away with all evils, it would do away with many good things, and would hinder the advance of the common good, which is necessary for human living. In order, therefore, that no evil might remain unforbidden and unpunished, it was necessary for the divine law to supervene, whereby all sins are forbidden. . . .

Question 96. Article 2. . . . As was stated above, law is framed as a rule or measure of human acts. [question 90, article 1 and 2]. Now a measure should be homogeneous with that which it measures, as is stated in *Metaphysics* [Aristotle, *Metaphysics*, book 9, 1 (1053a 24)], since different things are measured by different measures. Therefore laws imposed on men should also be in keeping with their condition, for, as Isidore says, law should be *possible both according to nature, and according to the customs of the country* [Isidore, *Etymologiae*, book 2, 10; book 5, 21 (PL 82, 131, 203)]. Now the ability or facility of action is due to an interior habit or disposition, since the same thing is not possible to one who has not a virtuous habit, as is possible to one who has. Thus the same thing is not possible to a child as to a full-grown man, and for which reason the law for children is not the same as for adults, since many things are permitted to children, which in an adult are punished by law or at any rate are open to blame. In like manner, many things are permissible to men not perfect in virtue, which would be intolerable in a virtuous man.

Now human law is framed for the multitude of human beings, the majority of whom are not perfect in virtue. Therefore human laws do not forbid all vices, from which the virtuous abstain, but only the more grievous vices, from which it is possible for the majority to abstain; and chiefly those that are injurious to others, without the prohibition of which human society could not be maintained. Thus human law prohibits murder, theft and the like. . . .

. . . The purpose of human law is to lead men to virtue, not suddenly, but gradually. Therefore it does not lay upon the multitude of imperfect men the burdens of those who are already virtuous, viz., that they should abstain from all evil. Otherwise these imperfect ones, being unable to bear such precepts, would break out into yet greater evils. As it is written [*Prov.* 30:33]: *He that violently bloweth his nose, bringeth out blood;* again [*Matt.* 9:17]: if *new wine, i.e.,* precepts of a perfect life, is *put into old bottles, i.e.,* into imperfect men, *the bottles break, and the wine runneth out, i.e.,* the precepts are despised, and those men, from contempt, break out into evils worse still. . . .

Question 96. Article 4. *Whether Human Law Binds a Man in Conscience?*
. . . Laws framed by man are either just or unjust. If they be just, they have the power of binding in conscience from the eternal law whence they are derived, according to [*Prov.* 8:15]: *By Me kings reign, and lawgivers decree just things.* Now laws are said to be just, both from the end (when, namely, they are ordained to the common good), from their author (that is to say, when the law that is made does not exceed the power of the lawgiver), and from their form (when, namely, burdens are laid on the subjects according to an equality of proportion and with a view to the common good). For, since one man is a part of the community, each man, in all that he is and has, belongs to the community; just as a part, in all that it is, belongs to the whole. So, too, nature inflicts a loss on the part in order to save the whole; so that for this reason such laws as these, which impose proportionate burdens, are just and binding in conscience, and are legal laws.

On the other hand, laws may be unjust in two ways: first, by being contrary to human good, through being opposed to the things mentioned above:—either in respect of the end, as when an authority imposes on his subjects burdensome laws, conducive, not to the common good, but rather to his own cupidity or vainglory; or in respect of the author, as when a man makes a law that goes beyond the power committed to him; or in respect of the form, as when burdens are imposed unequally on the community, although with a view to the common good. Such are acts of violence rather than laws, because, as Augustine says, *a law that is not just seems to be no law at all* [St. Augustine, *De Libero Arbitrio,* book 1, 5 (PL 32, 1227)]. Therefore, such laws do not bind in conscience, except perhaps in order to avoid scandal or disturbance, for which cause a man should even yield his right, according to *Matt.* [5:]40, 41: *If a man . . . take away thy coat, let go thy cloak also unto him; and whosoever will force thee one mile, go with him other two.*

Secondly, laws may be unjust through being opposed to the divine good. Such are the laws of tyrants inducing to idolatry, or to anything else contrary to the divine law. Laws of this kind must in no way be observed, because, as is stated in Acts [5:]29, *we ought to obey God rather than men.* . . .

Question 92. Article 1. *Whether Woman Should Have Been Made.* . . . It was necessary for woman to be made, as the Scripture says, as *a helper* to man; not, indeed, as a helpmate in other works, as some say,* since man can be more efficiently helped by another man in other works; but as a helper in the work of generation. This can be made clear if we observe the mode of generation carried out in various living things. Some living things do not possess in themselves the power of generation, but are generated by an agent of another species; and such are those plants and animals which are generated, without seed, from suitable matter through the active power of the heavenly bodies. Others possess the active and passive generative power together, as we see in plants which are generated from seed. For the noblest vital function in plants is generation, and so we observe that in these the active power of generation invariably accompanies the passive power. Among perfect animals, the active power of generation belongs to the male sex, and the passive power to the female. And as among animals there is a vital operation nobler than generation, to which their life is principally directed, so it happens that the male sex is not found in continual union with the female in perfect animals, but only at the time of coition; so that we may consider that by coition the male and female are one, as in plants they are always united, even though in some cases one of them preponderates, and in some the other. But man is further ordered to a still nobler work of life, and that is intellectual operation. Therefore there was greater reason for the distinction of these two powers in man; so that the female should be produced separately from the male, and yet that they should be carnally united for generation. Therefore directly after the formation of woman, it was said: *And they shall be two in one flesh* (Gen. [2:]24).

. . . As regards the individual nature, woman is defective and misbegotten, for the active power in the male seed tends to the production of a perfect likeness according to the masculine sex; while the production of woman comes from defect in the active power, or from some material indisposition, or even from some external influence, such as that of a south wind, which is moist, as the Philosopher observes [Aristotle, *De Generatione Animalium*, book 4, 2 (766b 33)]. On the other hand, as regards universal human nature, woman is not misbegotten, but is included in nature's intention as directed to the work of generation. Now the universal intention of nature depends on God, Who is the universal Author of nature. Therefore, in producing nature, God formed not only the male but also the female.

. . . Subjection is twofold. One is servile, by virtue of which a superior makes use of a subject for his own benefit; and this kind of subjection began after sin. There is another kind of subjection, which is called economic or civil, whereby the superior makes use of his subjects for their own ben-

---

*Anonymously reported by St. Augustine, *De Genesi ad Litteram*, book 9, 3 (PL 34, 395).

efit and good; and this kind of subjection existed even before sin. For the good of order would have been wanting in the human family if some were not governed by others wiser than themselves. So by such a kind of subjection woman is naturally subject to man, because in man the discernment of reason predominates. Nor is inequality among men excluded by the state of innocence. . . .

Question 93. Article 4. . . . Since man is said to be to the image of God by reason of his intellectual nature, he is the most perfectly like God according as his intellectual nature can most imitate God. Now the intellectual nature imitates God chiefly in this, that God understands and loves Himself. Therefore the image of God may be considered in man in three ways. First, inasmuch as man possesses a natural aptitude for understanding and loving God; and this aptitude consists in the very nature of the mind, which is common to all men. Secondly, inasmuch as man actually or habitually knows and loves God, though imperfectly; and this image consists in the conformity of grace. Thirdly, inasmuch as man knows God actually and loves Him perfectly; and this image consists in the likeness of glory. Therefore on the words, *The light of Thy countenance, O Lord, is signed upon us* [*Ps.* 4:7], the *Gloss* distinguishes a threefold image, of *creation*, of *recreation*, and of *likeness* [*Glossa Ordinaria*, book 3, 92a]. The first is found in all men, the second only in the just, the third only in the blessed.

Reply Obj. 1. The image of God, in its principal signification, namely the intellectual nature, is found both in man and in woman. Hence after the words, *To the image of God He created him,* it is added, *Male and female He created them* [*Gen.* 1:27]. Moreover it is said *them* in the plural, as Augustine remarks, lest it should be thought that both sexes were united in one individual [St. Augustine, *De Genesi ad Litteram*, book 3, 22 (PL 34, 294)]. But in a secondary sense the image of God is found in man, and not in woman, for man is the beginning and end of woman, just as God is the beginning and end of every creature. So when the Apostle had said that *man is the image and glory of God, but woman is the glory of man,* he adds his reason for saying this: *For man is not of woman, but woman of man; and man was not created for woman, but woman for man.*

Reply Objs. 2 and 3. These reasons refer to the image consisting in the conformity of grace and glory.

From "The Summa Theologica," in *The Basic Writings of St. Thomas Aquinas*, vol. 1, edited by Anton C. Pegis (New York: Random House, 1945), pp. 42–46, 413, 442–43, 467, 468, 475–80, 488–90, 744–53, 792–95, 879–81, 890.

SUMMA CONTRA GENTILES

Chapter 2. . . . every agent, by its action, intends an end.

For in those things which clearly act for an end, we declare the end to be that towards which the movement of the agent tends; for when this is reached, the end is said to be reached, and to fail in this is to fail in the end intended. This may be seen in the physician who aims at health, and in a man who runs towards an appointed goal. Nor does it matter, as to this, whether that which tends to an end be endowed with knowledge or not; for just as the target is the end of the archer, so is it the end of the arrow's flight. Now the movement of every agent tends to something determinate, since it is not from any force that any action proceeds, but heating proceeds from heat, and cooling from cold; and therefore actions are differentiated by their active principles. Action sometimes terminates in something made, as for instance building terminates in a house, and healing in health; while sometimes it does not so terminate, as for instance, in the case of understanding and sensation. And if action terminates in something made, the movement of the agent tends by that action towards the thing made; while if it does not terminate in something made, the movement of the agent tends to the action itself. It follows therefore that every agent intends an end while acting, which end is sometimes the action itself, sometimes a thing made by the action.

Again. In all things that act for an end, that is said to be the last end beyond which the agent seeks nothing further; and thus the physician's action goes as far as health, and when this is attained, his efforts cease. But in the action of every agent, a point can be reached beyond which the agent does not desire to go; or else actions would tend to infinity, which is impossible, for since *it is not possible to pass through an infinite medium* [Aristotle, *Posterior Analytics,* book 1, 22 (82b 38)], the agent would never begin to act, because nothing moves towards what it cannot reach. Therefore every agent acts for an end. . . .

Chapter 16. . . . . Accordingly if every agent acts for some good, as we have shown above, it follows that good is the end of each thing. For everything is directed by its action to some end; for either the action itself is an end, or the end of the action is also the end of the agent: and this is its good.

Again. The end of a thing is the term of its appetite. Now the appetite of a thing terminates in a good, for the philosophers define good as *the object of all appetite* [e.g., Aristotle, *Ethics,* book 1, 1 (1094a 2)]. Therefore the end of everything is a good.

Moreover. That toward which a thing tends while it is without it, and wherein it rests when it has it, is its end. Now anything that is without its proper perfection is moved towards it, as far as in it lies; and if it have that perfection, it rests therein. Therefore the end of a thing is its perfection. But the perfection of a thing is its good. Therefore every thing is directed to good as its end. . . .

Chapter 17. . . . . From the foregoing it is clear that all things are directed to one good as their last end.

For if nothing tends to something as its end, except in so far as this is good, it follows that good, as such, is an end. Consequently that which is the supreme good is supremely the end of all. Now there is but one supreme good, namely God, as we have shown in the First Book [Aquinas, *Summa Contra Gentiles,* book 1, 42]. Therefore all things are directed to the highest good, namely God, as their end. . . .

Chapter 25. . . . Besides. Man naturally desires to know the cause of any known effect. But the human intellect knows universal being. Therefore it naturally desires to know its cause, which is God alone, as we proved in the Second Book [Aquinas, *Contra Gentiles*, book 2, 15]. Now one has not attained to one's last end until the natural desire is at rest. Therefore the knowledge of any intelligible object is not enough for man's happiness, which is his last end, unless he know God also, which knowledge terminates his natural desire as his last end. Therefore this very knowledge of God is man's last end.

Further. A body that tends by its natural appetite to its place is moved all the more vehemently and rapidly the nearer it approaches its end. Hence Aristotle proves that a natural straight movement cannot be towards an indefinite point, because it would not be more moved afterwards than before [Aristotle, *De Caelo*, book 1, 8 (277a 18)]. Hence that which tends more vehemently to a thing afterwards than before is not moved towards an indefinite point but towards something fixed. Now this we find in the desire of knowledge, for the more one knows, the greater one's desire to know. Consequently, man's natural desire in knowledge tends to a definite end. This can be none other than the highest thing knowable, which is God. Therefore the knowledge of God is man's last end.

Now the last end of man and of any intelligent substance is called *happiness* or *beatitude,* for it is this that every intellectual substance desires as its last end, and for its own sake alone. Therefore the last beatitude or happiness of any intellectual substance is to know God. . . .

Chapter 27. . . . From what has been said it is clearly impossible that human happiness consist in pleasures of the body, the chief of which are pleasures of the table and of sex.

It has been shown that according to nature's order pleasure is for the sake of operation, and not conversely. Therefore, if an operation be not the ultimate end, the consequent pleasure can neither be the ultimate end, nor accompany the ultimate end. Now it is manifest that the operations which are followed by the pleasures mentioned above are not the last end; for they are directed to certain manifest ends: eating, for instance, to the preservation of the body, and carnal intercourse to the begetting of children. Therefore the aforesaid pleasures are not the last end, nor do they accompany the last end. Therefore happiness does not consist in them.

Again. The will is higher than the sensitive appetite, for it moves the sensitive appetite, as was stated above. But happiness does not consist in an act of the will, as we have already proved. Much less therefore does it consist in the aforesaid pleasures which are seated in the sensitive appetite.

Moreover. Happiness is a good proper to man, for it is an abuse of terms to speak of brute animals as being happy. Now these pleasures are common to man and brute. Therefore we must not assign happiness to them.

The last end is the most noble of things belonging to a reality, for it has the nature of that which is best. But the aforementioned pleasures do not befit man according to what is most noble in him, namely, the intellect, but according to the sense. Therefore happiness is not to be located in such pleasures.

Besides. The highest perfection of man cannot consist in his being united to things lower than himself, but consists in his being united to something above him; for the end is better than that which tends to the end. Now the above pleasures consist in man's being united through his senses to things beneath him, namely, certain sensible things. Therefore we must not assign happiness to such pleasures. . . .

Chapter 28. . . . From the foregoing it is also clear that neither does man's highest good, or happiness, consist in honors.

For man's ultimate end and happiness is his most perfect operation, as we have shown above. But man's honor does not consist in something done by him, but in something done to him by another who shows him respect [cf. Aristotle, Ethics, book 1, 5 (1095b 25)]. Therefore man's happiness must not be placed in honors.

Again. That which is for the sake of another good and desirable thing is not the last end. Now such is honor, for a man is not rightly honored, except because of some other good in him. For this reason men seek to be honored, as though wishing to have a voucher for some good that is in them; so that they rejoice more in being honored by the great and the wise. Therefore we must not assign man's happiness to honors.

Besides. Happiness is obtained through virtue. Now virtuous deeds are voluntary, or else they would not be praiseworthy. Therefore happiness must be a good obtainable by man through his will. But it is not in a man's power to secure honor, rather is it in the power of the man who pays honor. Therefore happiness is not to be assigned to honors.

Moreover. Only the good can be worthy of honor, and yet it is possible even for the wicked to be honored. Therefore it is better to become worthy of honor, than to be honored. Therefore honor is not man's supreme good.

Furthermore. The highest good is the perfect good. Now the perfect good is incompatible with any evil. But that which has no evil in it cannot possibly be evil. Therefore that which is in possession of the highest good cannot be evil. Yet it is possible for an evil person to receive honor. Therefore honor is not man's supreme good.

Chapter 29. . . . Therefore it is evident also that man's supreme good does not consist in glory, which is the recognition of one's good name.

For glory, according to Cicero, is the general recognition and praise of a person's good name, [Cicero, De Inventione, book 2, 55 (p. 150b)] and, in the words of Ambrose, consists in being well known and praised [cf. St. Augustine, Contra Maximinum Arium, book 2, 13 (PL 42, 770)]. Now men seek praise and distinction through being famous, so that they may be honored by those whom their fame reaches. Therefore glory is sought for the sake of honor, and consequently if honor be not the highest good, much less is glory.

Again. Those goods are worthy of praise, whereby a man shows himself to be ordered to his end. Now he who is directed to his end has not yet reached his last end. Therefore praise is not bestowed on one who has reached his last end; rather does he receive honor, as the Philosopher says

[Aristotle, *Ethics,* book 1, 12 (1101b 24)]. Therefore glory cannot be the highest good, since it consists chiefly in praise.

Besides. It is better to know than to be known, because only the higher realities know, whereas the lowest are known. Therefore man's highest good cannot be glory, which consists in a man's being known. . . .

Chapter 30. . . . Hence it is evident that neither is wealth man's highest good. For wealth is not sought except for the sake of something else, because of itself it brings us no good, but only when we use it, whether for the support of the body or for some similar purpose. Now the highest good is sought for its own, and not for another's sake. Therefore wealth is not man's highest good.

Again. Man's highest good cannot consist in the possession or preservation of things whose chief advantage for man consists in their being spent. Now the chief advantage of wealth is in its being spent, for this is its use. Therefore the possession of wealth cannot be man's highest good. . . .

Chapter 31. . . . In like manner, neither can worldly power be man's highest happiness, since in the achievement thereof chance can effect much. Again, it is unstable, and not subject to man's will; and it is often obtained by evil men. These are incompatible with the highest good, as was already stated.

Again. Man is said to be good especially according as he approaches the highest good. But in respect to his having power, he is not said to be either good or evil, since not everyone who can do good deeds is good, nor is a person evil because he can do evil deeds. Therefore the highest good does not consist in being powerful.

Besides. Every power implies reference to something else. But the highest good is not referred to anything further. Therefore power is not man's highest good. . . .

Chapter 32. . . . Like arguments avail to prove that man's highest good does not consist in goods of the body, such as health, beauty and strength. For they are common to good and evil, they are unstable, and they are not subject to the will.

Besides. The soul is better than the body, which neither lives nor possesses these goods without the soul. Therefore, the soul's good, such as understanding and the like, is better than the body's good. Therefore the body's good is not man's highest good. . . .

Chapter 37. . . . Accordingly, if man's ultimate happiness does not consist in external things, which are called goods of fortune; nor in goods of the body; nor in goods of the soul, as regards the sensitive part; nor as regards the intellectual part, in terms of the life of moral virtue; nor in terms of the intellectual virtues which are concerned with action, namely, art and prudence:—it remains for us to conclude that man's ultimate happiness consists in the contemplation of truth.

For this operation alone is proper to man, and it is in it that none of the other animals communicates.

Again. This is not directed to anything further as to its end, since the contemplation of the truth is sought for its own sake.

Again. By this operation man is united to beings above him, by becoming like them; because of all human actions this alone is both in God and in the separate substances. Also, by this operation man comes into contact with those higher beings, through knowing them in any way whatever.

Besides, man is more self-sufficing for this operation, seeing that he stands in little need of the help of external things in order to perform it.

Further. All other human operations seem to be ordered to this as to their end. For perfect contemplation requires that the body should be disencumbered, and to this effect are directed all the products of art that are necessary for life. Moreover, it requires freedom from the disturbance caused by the passions, which is achieved by means of the moral virtues and of prudence; and freedom from external disturbance, to which the whole governance of the civil life is directed. So that, if we consider the matter rightly, we shall see that all human occupations appear to serve those who contemplate the truth.

Now, it is not possible that man's ultimate happiness consist in contemplation based on the understanding of first principles; for this is most imperfect, as being most universal, containing potentially the knowledge of things. Moreover, it is the beginning and not the end of human inquiry, and comes to us from nature, and not through the pursuit of the truth. Nor does it consist in contemplation based on the sciences that have the lowest things for their object, since happiness must consist in an operation of the intellect in relation to the most noble intelligible objects. It follows then that man's ultimate happiness consists in wisdom, based on the consideration of divine things.

It is therefore evident also by way of induction that man's ultimate happiness consists solely in the contemplation of God, which conclusion was proved above by arguments.

Chapter 40. . . . There is yet another knowledge of God, in one respect superior to the knowledge we have been discussing, namely, that whereby God is known by men through faith. Now this knowledge surpasses the knowledge of God through demonstration in this respect, namely, that by faith we know certain things about God which are so sublime that reason cannot reach them by means of demonstration, as we have stated at the beginning of this work [Aquinas, *Contra Gentiles*, Book 1, 5]. But not even in this knowledge of God can man's ultimate happiness consist.

For happiness is the intellect's perfect operation, as was already declared. But in knowledge by faith, the operation of the intellect is found to be most imperfect as regards the contribution of the intellect, although it is most perfect on the part of the object; for the intellect in believing does not grasp the object of its assent. Therefore neither does man's happiness consist in this knowledge of God.

Again. It has been shown that ultimate happiness does not consist chiefly in an act of the will. Now in knowledge by faith, the will has the leading place; for the intellect assents by faith to things proposed to it, because it so wills, and not through being constrained by the evidence of their truth. Therefore man's final happiness does not consist in this knowledge.

Besides. A believer assents to things proposed to him by another, but not seen by himself; so that the knowledge of faith resembles hearing rather than seeing. Now a man would not believe in what is unseen by him, and proposed to him by another, unless he thought this other to have a more perfect knowledge of the things proposed than he himself has who sees not. Either therefore the judgment of the believer is wrong, or the proposer must have more perfect knowledge of the things proposed. And if the latter also knows these things only through hearing them from another, we cannot proceed thus indefinitely, for then the assent of faith would be without foundation or certitude, since we should not come to some first principle certain in itself, to give certitude to the faith of believers. Now, in reality, it is not possible that the assent of faith be false and without foundation, as is clear from what we have said at the beginning of this work [Aquinas, *Contra Gentiles,* book 1, 7], and yet if it were false and baseless, happiness could not consist in such knowledge. There is therefore some knowledge of God that is higher than the knowledge of faith, whether he who proposes faith sees the truth immediately, as when we believe Christ, or whether he receives the truth from him who sees it immediately, as when we believe the Apostles and Prophets. Since, then, man's happiness consists in the highest knowledge of God, it cannot consist in the knowledge of faith.

Moreover. Since happiness is the last end, the natural desire is set at rest thereby. But the knowledge of faith does not set the desire at rest, but inflames it; for everyone desires to see what he believes. Therefore man's ultimate happiness does not consist in the knowledge of faith.

Further. The knowledge of God has been declared to be the end inasmuch as it unites us to the last end of all, namely, God. Now the knowledge of faith does not make the thing believed to be perfectly present to the intellect, since faith is of absent, and not present, things. Hence the Apostle says [2 *Cor.* 6:7] that *so long as we walk by faith, we are pilgrims from the Lord.* Yet faith makes God to be present to love, since the believer assents to God voluntarily, according to the saying of [*Eph.* 3:17]: *That Christ may dwell by faith in our hearts.* Therefore the knowledge of faith cannot be man's ultimate happiness.

From "The Summa Contra Gentiles," in *The Basic Writings of St. Thomas Aquinas,* vol. 2, edited by Anton C. Pegis (New York: Random House, 1945), pp. 5, 26–27, 46, 51–60, 64–65.

21. Marsilius of Padua, *Defensor Pacis*

Marsilius of Padua (ca. 1280–1343) was one of the truly revolutionary minds of the late medieval world. Chiefly noted for his contributions to political thought, Marsilius developed a covenantal understanding of both secular and ecclesiastical governance.

Discourse 1

Chapter 1. ¶4. The fruits of peace or tranquility, then, are the greatest goods, as we have said, while those of its opposite, strife, are unbearable evils. Hence we ought to wish for peace, to seek it if we do not already have it, to conserve it once it is attained, and to repel with all our strength the strife which is opposed to it. To this end individual brethren, and in even greater degree groups and communities, are obliged to help one another, both from the feeling of heavenly love and from the bond or law of human society. This admonition Plato also gives us, as Tully attests in the first book of his treatise *On Duties*, when he said: "We were not born for ourselves alone; to part of us our native land lays claim, and to part, our friends." To this sentence Tully adds: "And so, as the Stoics were wont to say, the things that grow in the earth are all created for the use of men; but men are born for the sake of men. In this we ought to follow the lead of nature, and to bring forth common utilities for all." But it would be no small common utility, indeed it is rather a necessity, to unmask the sophism of this singular cause of wars which threatens no small harm to all states and communities. Hence, whoever is willing and able to discern the common utility is obliged to give this matter his vigilant care and diligent efforts. For while this sophism remains concealed, this pestilence can in no way be avoided, nor its pernicious effect be completely uprooted from states or cities. . . .

Chapter 9. ¶5. To make clearer these concepts of Aristotle, and to summarize all the methods of establishing the other kinds of government, we shall say that every government is over either voluntary or involuntary subjects. The first is the genus of well-tempered governments, the second of diseased governments. Each of these genera is divided into three species or kinds, as was said in Chapter [8]. And since one of the species of well-tempered government, and perhaps the more perfect, is kingly monarchy, let us resume our previous statements about its various kinds or methods, by saying that the king or monarch either is named by the election of the inhabitants or citizens, or duly obtains the rulership without their election. If without the election of the citizens, this is either because he or his ancestors first inhabited the region, or because he bought the land and jurisdiction, or acquired it by a just war or by some other lawful method, such as by gift made to him for some great service. Each of these kinds of monarchy participates so much the more in true kingship, the more it is over voluntary subjects and according to law made for the common benefit of the subjects; and it savors so much the more of tyranny the more it departs from these features, that is, the consent of the subjects and law established for their common benefit. Hence it is written in the *Politics* [Book 4, chap. 8]: "These," that is, monarchies, "were kingly because they were according to law, and ruled voluntary subjects; but they were tyrannical because they ruled despotically and in accordance with their," that is, the monarchs', "own judgment." These two features, then, distinguish temperate from diseased government, as is apparent from the clear statement of Aristotle, but absolutely or in greater degree it is the consent of the subjects which is the distinguishing criterion. Now if the ruling monarch is elected by the inhabitants, it is either with all his posterity succeeding him or not. If the latter, this may be in several ways, as he is named either for his own lifetime alone, or for his own lifetime and that of one or more of his successors, or not for the whole lifetime either of himself or of any of his successors but only for some determinate period, such as one or two years, more or less. Again, he is named to exercise either every judicial office, or only one office such as leading the army.

6. The elected and the non-elected kingly monarchs agree in that each rules voluntary subjects. They differ, however, in that the non-elected kings rule less voluntary subjects, and by laws which are less politic for the common benefit, as we said before in the case of the barbarians. The elected kings, on the other hand, rule more voluntary subjects, and by laws which are more politic, in that they are made for the common benefit, as we have said.

7. From these considerations it is clear, and will be even more apparent in the sequel, that the elected kind of government is superior to the non-elected. This is also the view of Aristotle in that passage of the *Politics* [Book 3, chap. 8], which we cited above with reference to those who were made rulers in the heroic days. Again, this method of establishing governments is more permanent in perfect communities. For at some time or other it becomes necessary to have recourse to this from among all the other methods of establishing governments, but not conversely. For example, if hereditary succession fails, or if for some reason the multitude cannot bear the excessive malice of that family's rule, they must then turn to the method of election, which can never fail so long as the generation of men does not fail. Moreover, by the method of election alone is the best ruler obtained. For it is expedient that the ruler be the best man in the polity, since he must regulate the civil acts of all the rest.

8. The method of establishing the other species of temperate government is usually election; in some cases the ruler is chosen by lot, without subsequent hereditary succession. Diseased governments, on the other hand, are usually established by fraud or force or both.

9. Which of the temperate governments is better, monarchy or one of the other two species, aristocracy or polity; and again, which of the monarchies is better, the elected or the non-elected; and moreover, which of the elected monarchies, that established with hereditary succession ensuing or that in which one man alone is named without such succession; which in turn is divided into the further alternatives of whether it is better to name the ruler for a whole lifetime, either of himself alone or of some of his successors also, or only for some determinate period, such as one or two years, more or less—in all these questions there is room for inquiry and reasonable doubt. It must be held without doubt, however, in accordance with the truth and the manifest view of Aristotle, that election is the more certain standard of government, as will be more fully shown in Chapters [12, 16, 17] of this discourse.

10. We must not overlook, however, that different multitudes in different times and places are inclined toward different kinds of polity and government, as Aristotle says in the *Politics* [Book 3, chap. 9]. Legislators and institutors of governments must hearken to this fact. For just as not every man is inclined toward the best discipline or study, whereupon it is appropriate that he be directed toward the acquisition not of that discipline but of some other good one for which he is more fitted, so too a multitude in some time or place may perhaps not be inclined to accept the best kind of government, and therefore recourse must first be had to that kind of temperate government which is more appropriate to it. For example, before the monarchy of Julius Caesar, the Roman people were for a long time unwilling to accept any definite monarch, either with hereditary succession or even one who was named only for his own lifetime. The reason for this was perhaps that there was a larger number of heroic men worthy of rulership among them, both families and individuals. . . .

Chapter 12. ¶4. . . . [C]hildren, slaves, aliens, and women are distinguished from citizens, although in different ways. For the sons of citizens are citizens in proximate potentiality, lacking only in years. The weightier part of the citizens should be viewed in accordance with the honorable custom of polities, or else it should be determined in accordance with the doctrine of Aristotle in the *Politics* [Book 6, chap. 2].

5. Having thus defined the citizen and the weightier part of the citizens, let us return to our proposed objective, namely, to demonstrate that the human authority to make laws belongs only to the whole body of the citizens or to the weightier part thereof. Our first proof is as follows. The absolutely primary human authority to make or establish human laws belongs only to those men from whom alone the best laws can emerge. But these are the whole body of the citizens, or the weightier part thereof, which represents that whole body; since it is difficult or impossible for all persons to agree upon one decision, because some men have a deformed nature, disagreeing with the common decision through singular malice or ignorance. The common benefit should not, however, be impeded or neglected because of the unreasonable protest or opposition of these men. The authority to make or establish laws, therefore, belongs only to the whole body of the citizens or to the weightier part thereof.

. . . .The second proposition [is] that the best law is made only through the hearing and command of the entire multitude. . . . That at which the entire body of the citizens aims intellectually and emotionally is more certainly judged as to its truth and more diligently noted as to its common utility. For a defect in some proposed law can be better noted by the greater number than by any part thereof, since every whole, or at least every corporeal whole, is greater in mass and in virtue than any part of it taken separately. Moreover, the common utility of a law is better noted by the entire multitude, because no one knowingly harms himself. Anyone can look to see whether a proposed law leans toward the benefit of one or a few persons more than of the others or of the community, and can protest against it. Such, however, would not be the case were the law made by one or a few persons, considering their own private benefit rather than that of the community. . . .

6. Another argument to the principal conclusion is as follows. The authority to make the law belongs only to those men whose making of it will

cause the law to be better observed or observed at all. Only the whole body of the citizens are such men. To them, therefore, belongs the authority to make the law. The first proposition of this demonstration is very close to self-evident, for a law would be useless unless it were observed. . . . That law is better observed by every citizen which each one seems to have imposed upon himself. But such is the law which is made through the hearing and command of the entire multitude of the citizens. . . . every citizen must be free, and not undergo another's despotism, that is, slavish dominion. But this would not be the case if one or a few of the citizens by their own authority made the law over the whole body of citizens. For those who thus made the law would be despots over the others, and hence such a law, however good it was, would be endured only with reluctance, or not at all, by the rest of the citizens, the more ample part. Having suffered contempt, they would protest against it, and not having been called upon to make it, they would not observe it. On the other hand, a law made by the hearing or consent of the whole multitude, even though it were less useful, would be readily observed and endured by every one of the citizens, because then each would seem to have set the law upon himself, and hence would have no protest against it, but would rather tolerate it with equanimity. . . .

Discourse 2

Chapter 2. ¶2. . . . In another sense this word "church" means all the priests or bishops, deacons, and others who minister in the temple or the church taken in the preceding sense. And according to this meaning, only clergymen or ministers are commonly called persons of the church or churchmen.

Again in another sense, and especially among the moderns, this word "church" means those ministers, priests or bishops and deacons, who minister in and preside over the metropolitan or principal church. This usage was long since brought about by the church of the city of Rome, whose ministers and overseers are the Roman pope and his cardinals. Through custom they have brought it about that they are called the "church" and that one says the "church" has done or received something when it is these men who have done or received or otherwise ordained something.

3. But the word "church" has also another meaning which is the truest and the most fitting one of all, according to the first imposition of the word and the intention of these first imposers, even though this meaning is not so familiar nor in accord with modern usage. According to this signification, the "church" means the whole body of the faithful who believe in and invoke the name of Christ, and all the parts of this whole body in any community, even the household. And this was the first imposition of this term and the sense in which it was customarily used among the apostles and in the primitive church. Hence the Apostle, in the first epistle to the Corinthians, Chapter 1, wrote: "To the church of God that is at Corinth, to them that are sanctified in Christ Jesus, called to be saints, with all that invoke the name of our Lord Jesus Christ." Whereon the gloss according to Ambrose: "Sanctified in baptism, and this in Christ Jesus." And it was in accordance with this meaning that the Apostle spoke in the twentieth chapter of the Acts, to the Ephesian priests, when he said: "Take heed to yourselves and to the whole flock, wherein the Holy Ghost hath placed you bishops, to rule the church of God which he hath purchased with his own blood" [Acts 20:28]. And therefore all the Christian faithful, both priests and non-priests, are and should be called churchmen according to this truest and most proper signification, because Christ purchased and redeemed all men with his blood. . . .

5. Again, and more pertinently, this word "spiritual" refers to the divine law, and the teaching and learning of the commands and counsels in accordance with it and through it. Under this signification also come all ecclesiastic sacraments and their effects, all divine grace, all theological virtues, and the gifts of the Holy Spirit ordering us toward eternal life. For it was in this way, and appropriately, that the Apostle used this word in the epistle to the Romans, Chapter 15 [Rom. 15:27], and in the first epistle to the Corinthians, Chapter 9, when he said: "If we have sown unto you spiritual things, is it a great matter if we reap your carnal things" [1 Cor. 9:11]? Whereon the gloss according to Ambrose: "Spiritual things, that is, those things which vivify your spirit, or which were given by the Holy Spirit, namely, the word of God, and the mystery of the kingdom of the heavens."

Moreover, in another sense this word is used for any voluntary human action or passion, whether in oneself or directed toward another, which is done for the purpose of meriting a blessed life in the future world. Such are the contemplation of God, love of God and of one's neighbors, abstinence, mercy, meekness, prayer, offerings for piety or divine worship, hospitality, pilgrimage, castigation of one's own body, contempt for and flight from worldly and carnal pleasures, and generally all similar actions and passions done for the aforesaid purpose.

Again, this word refers, although not so properly as in the second and third sense, to the temple or the church taken in its second sense; and to all the utensils and ornaments which serve therein for divine worship. . . .

Chapter 4. ¶3. Therefore for the present purpose it suffices to show, and I shall first show, that Christ himself came into the world not to dominate men, nor to judge them by judgment in the third sense, nor to wield temporal rule, but rather to be subject as regards the status of the present life; and moreover, that he wanted to and did exclude himself, his apostles and disciples, and their successors, the bishops or priests, from all such coercive authority or worldly rule, both by his example and by his words of counsel or command. I shall also show that the leading apostles, as Christ's true imitators, did this same thing and taught their successors to do likewise; and moreover, that both Christ and the apostles wanted to be and were continuously subject in property and in person to the coercive jurisdiction of secular rulers, and that they taught and commanded all others, to whom they preached or wrote the law of truth, to do likewise, under pain of eternal damnation. Then I shall write a chapter on the power or authority of the keys which Christ gave to the apostles and their successors in office, bishops and priests, so that it may be clear what is the nature, quality, and extent of such power, both of the Roman bishop and of the others. For ignorance on this point has hitherto been and still is the source of many questions and damnable controversies among the Christian faithful, as was mentioned in the first chapter of this discourse.

4. And so in pursuit of these aims we wish to show that Christ, in his purposes or intentions, words, and deeds, wished to exclude and did exclude himself and the apostles from every office of rulership, contentious jurisdiction, government, or coercive judgment in this world. This is first shown clearly beyond any doubt by the passage in the eighteenth chapter of the gospel of John. For when Christ was brought before Pontius Pilate, vicar of the Roman ruler in Judaea, and accused of having called himself king of the Jews, Pontius asked him whether he had said this, or whether he did call himself a king, and Christ's reply included these words, among others: "My kingdom is not of this world," that is, I have not come to reign by temporal rule or dominion, in the way in which worldly kings reign. And proof of this was given by Christ himself through an evident sign when he said: "If my kingdom were of this world, my servants would certainly fight, that I should not be delivered to the Jews," as if to argue as follows: If I had come into this world to reign by worldly or coercive rule, I would have ministers for this rule, namely, men to fight and to coerce transgressors, as the other kings have; but I do not have such ministers, as you can clearly see. Hence the interlinear gloss: "It is clear that no one defends him." And this is what Christ reiterates: "But now my kingdom is not from hence," that is, the kingdom about which I have come to teach. . . .

Chapter 18. ¶8. . . . Having thus given a brief recital of the development of the matters under consideration from their origin, we now enter more fully upon a definitive discussion of them, first making, with the Apostle, this indubitable assumption: that the Catholic faith is one, not many; whence in Ephesians, Chapter 4, it is written: "One lord, one faith" [Eph. 4:5]. And all the faithful must believe and profess this faith in unity, that is, according to the same meaning. . . .

Chapter 20. ¶2. . . . [T]he principal authority, direct or indirect, for such determination of doubtful questions belongs only to a general council composed of all Christians or of the weightier part of them, or to those persons who have been granted such authority by the whole body of Christian believers. The procedure is as follows: Let all the notable provinces or communities of the world, in accordance with the determination of their human legislators whether one or many, and according to their proportion in quantity and quality of persons, elect faithful men, first priests and then non-priests, suitable persons of the most blameless lives and the greatest experience in divine law. These men are to act as judges in the first sense of the word, representing the whole body of the faithful by virtue of the authority which these whole bodies have granted to them, and they are to assemble at a place which is most convenient according to the decision of the majority of them, where they are to settle those matters pertaining to divine law which have appeared doubtful, and which it seems useful, expedient, and necessary to define. There too they are to make such other decrees with regard to church ritual or divine worship as will be conducive to the quiet and tranquility of the believers. For it would be needless and harmful for the multitude of inexperienced believers thus to assemble: harmful, because they would be distracted from their tasks which are necessary for the sustenance of corporeal life, which would be burdensome or perhaps unbearable.

3. However, divine law lays upon all believers obligations toward such a council assembled for the afore-mentioned purpose, although the obligation takes different forms. The priests are obligated because their function is to teach the law in its true sense, to see to it that its integrity and truth are maintained, to condemn errors made regarding it, and to recall men from these errors by exhortations, arguments, and threats. Hence in the last chapter of Matthew, the Truth says to all the priests, in the person of the apostles: "Go ye therefore and teach all nations." Hence too the Apostle Paul, speaking in the person of all the apostles, wrote in 1 Corinthians, Chapter 9: "Necessity is laid upon me; yea, woe is me if I preach not the gospel!" Besides the priests, those persons who are learned in divine law are also obligated, more so than are the other believers, for they have to call upon the others and to come together with the priests, especially if they have been sufficiently requested or enjoined to do so; for "to him that knoweth to do good, and doth it not, to him it is sin," as it is written in James, Chapter 4. Also, in order to settle other matters, outside divine law, which are important for the common utility and peace of the believers, persons who have been appointed for this purpose by the faithful human legislator can and must be present at the council. And the legislators also have obligations toward the council: namely, to elect suitable persons to make up the council, to provide them with the necessary temporal goods, and, if necessary, to compel, for the public welfare, the attendance of those who, although they are suitable and have been elected to this council, yet refuse to come, whether priests or non-priests.

Translation and introduction by Alan Gewirth. From *Marsilius of Padua, Defensor Pacis*, general editor W.T.H. Jackson (Toronto, Canada: University of Toronto Press, 1980), pp. 5, 31–34, 46–47, 102–5, 114–15, 272, 280–81. Copyright © 1980 by the Mediaeval Academy of America. Copyright © 1990 by Columbia University Press. Reprinted with permission from the publisher.

22. Jan Hus, *The Church*

The Bohemian Jan Hus (ca. 1372–1415) was leader of a church reform movement strongly influenced by the reemphasis upon biblical authority of John Wyclif and the Lollards. In this selection, Hus calls upon the laity to hold the ecclesiastical hierarchy accountable. Hus was summoned to the Council of Constance in 1414 and condemned by that body to be burned at the stake in 1415.

Chapter 7. *The Faith which Is the Foundation of the Church.* . . . [T]here is one faith which is the explicit belief of a faithful man and . . . there is another faith which is implicit faith as the catholic, who has the disposition—

habitus—of faith infused or explicitly acquired, believes in the catholic church in common with others and by reason of that common faith believes implicitly whatever single thing is included under holy mother church. Likewise in believing whatsoever Christ wished to be believed about himself and refusing to believe what he did not wish to be believed about himself, he believes every article, affirmative or negative, which is to be believed about Christ. This faith Peter had implicitly when he expressly confessed Christ to be true God and true man, saying: "Thou art Christ, the Son of the living God." And yet the same Peter explicitly set himself against Christ and his Gospel when, after Christ had said, "All ye shall be offended in me this night" [Matt. 26:31], he denied and said: "Though all be offended in thee, yet will I never be offended." Thus also many of the faithful in common [that is, as a body] believe implicitly all the truth of Scripture, and when a truth unknown to them is proposed, they search to see if it is laid down in holy Scripture, and if this is shown to be the case they at once acknowledge the sense which the Holy Spirit insists on. Therefore, whoever has in common with others faith formed in love, this suffices for salvation when accompanied with the grace of perseverance. For God, who gave the first faith, will give to his soldier clearer faith, unless he puts some hindrance in the way. For God does not demand of all his children that they should continuously during their sojourn here be in the particular act of thought about any particular point of faith, but it is enough that, putting aside inertia and callousness, they have faith formed as a habit.

Faith, therefore, we must understand, is twofold: the one unformed, which is exercised by the demons who believe and tremble; the other faith formed in love. The latter, accompanied with perseverance, saves, but not the former. . . . This faith is the foundation of the other virtues which the church of Christ practices. Likewise it is to be noted that, inasmuch as faith is not of things which appear to the senses but of hidden things and inasmuch as it is difficult to believe hidden things, therefore two elements are necessary to faith in order that we may believe anything truly: (1) the truth which illumines the mind, (2) the authority [evidence] which conforms the mind. Here belongs one property of faith, that it is concerned alone with the truth—all falsehood being excluded—the truth which the faithful ought to defend even unto death. The second property of faith is, that without proof and special knowledge it is obscure to the faithful, for what we see with the eye we cannot be said to believe. . . . For now we hope for our blessedness and believe, but do not see with the eyes of the flesh. And, because it is not possible without faith to please God, therefore every one who is to be saved ought first of all to be faithful—*fidelis*—[have faith]. A faithful person, however, is he who has faith infused by God and has no fear of ill to himself mixed with his faith. But all open offenders according to the law of present unrighteousness are unfaithful—*infideles*—[without faith], for it is impossible for any one to sin mortal sin except to obey contrary to God; the second, when the work is voluntary; the third, when it is pure from the standpoint of a holy purpose, in accordance with the Saviour's teaching, when he said: "If thine eye is single, thy whole body shall be full of light," [Matt. 6:22]. The fourth condition is when the work is judicious, because neither defect nor excess infects it, and the fifth, when it is permanently persevered in, as an obligation, even to the end. From this it is clear that an inferior, recognizing a superior's injudicious command, that it is known or should be known as fitted to hurt the church, by drawing away from the worship of God and the profit of souls unto salvation,—he ought to resist that superior. For such resistance is true obedience done not only to God in view of the law of fraternal correction but also to the superior himself, for no superior has the right to command anything except what is good. Since, therefore, an inferior is obligated, for obedience's sake, to do that which is generically good and commanded by the superior, it follows that he is obeying in so resisting him, as he ought; for he thereby does what is good, and turns away from what is evil. Hence, it is clear that a subject, in obeying his prelate in that which is evil, is not excused from sin, for the Saviour says: "If the blind guide the blind, both fall into the pit," [Matt. 15:14].

This means that if a "blind man," that is, an ignorant or bad prelate, guides "a blind man," that is, an ignorant or bad subject, by commanding him to do something, they both fall into the pit of error. Hence, Christ aptly says to his disciples in regard to the scribes and Pharisees—who taught that it is a sin to eat bread with unwashen hands, when it is nevertheless not a sin:—"Let them alone, they are blind leaders of the blind." What does "let them alone" mean? The Gloss says, "Leave them to their own will; they are blind," that is, they are obscured by traditions.

And this rule of Christ the very brute animals observe, for the horse or the ass, discerning the hole in front of them and urged on by spurs, avoid the ditch so far as they can, as is clear from the case of the ass, which discerned the angel forbidding, lest it go the way Balaam wanted to go [Num. 22:22], and, with a man's voice, admonished the prophet's unwisdom. Hence, Bernard says ironically in his letter to the monk Adam: "Thou, that most obedient son, thou, that most devoted disciple—as for that thy father and teacher, whom neither by an instant of time nor a turn of the foot, as they say, thou didst suffer to be removed from thee as long as he lived—after him not with blind eyes, but after the manner of Balaam, with open eyes, thou didst not hesitate to fall down into the pit!" So much Bernard.

From these truths, however, it follows further that clerical inferiors, and much more laics, may sit in judgment on the works of their superiors. From this it follows that the judgment by discreet and hidden arbitrament in the court of conscience is one thing, and the judgment in virtue of the empowered jurisdiction in the court of the church is another. . . . The laic also ought to examine and judge the works of his superior, as the apostle judged the works of Peter, when he corrected him and said: "When I saw that they walked not uprightly according to the truth of the Gospel, I said unto Cephas before them all, If thou, who art a Jew, livest as do the Gentiles and not as do the Jews, how compellest thou the Gentiles to walk as do the Jews?" [Gal. 2:14]. Secondly, the laic ought to examine and judge his superior for the purpose of fleeing, for Christ said: "Beware of false prophets which come unto you in sheep's clothing, but inwardly they are ravening wolves," [Matt. 7:15]. Thirdly, he ought to examine and judge that the superior may attend to spiritual offices and bodily nourishment or other good works to be done. For not otherwise should clergymen ever be chosen by laics as their curates and confessors and the dispensers of their alms.

Therefore, it is lawful for the rich of this world with diligent scrutiny to examine by what and what kind of superiors they shall administer their alms and in what way they shall administer them, guarding against rapacious wolves, because according to the apostle, in Acts 20:29, and according to Chrysostom, *in Imperfecto,* Homily 20, it is clear that in this way they seek more the money of those subject to them than their salvation and this is at variance with the apostle, who says: "I seek not yours, but you," [2 Cor. 12:14]. And looking ahead with prophetic vision and seeing such false apostles, he affirmed, "I know that after my departing rapacious wolves shall enter in among you, not sparing the flock," [Acts 20:29]. And because this wolfishness is clearly discerned in the robbing of temporal things and in the infliction of punishments for the very purpose of plundering temporal goods more abundantly, he declares that he had himself pursued the opposite course. No man's gold and silver, he says, or vestments have I coveted, as ye yourselves know, because for those things that were needful for me and for those that were with me these hands have ministered.

Therefore, subjects living piously in Christ ought to pay heed to the life of the apostles and see to it whether their superiors live conformably to the apostles. For, if in their spiritual ministry they are out of accord with the apostles, if they are busy in exacting money, spurn evangelical poverty and incline to the world, nay, if they evidently sow offences, then they know by their works that they have departed from the religion of Jesus Christ the Lord. Therefore, O ye who love Christ's law from the heart, first note their works and see if they [the superiors] incline to the world, second give heed to their commands, whether they savor of avarice or the gain of this world, and third consult holy Scripture whether they command in accordance with Christ's counsel. And in the light of this counsel believe them; or disbelieve them, if they command contrary to this counsel. But let not curates say to laics, 'What concern is it of yours to take note of our life or works,' for did not our Saviour say: "Do not according to their works"? [Matt. 23]. And afterwards he exposed the works of the prelates to the multitude that they might know them and to their advantage avoid them. Yea, much more to the prelates, who say, 'What concern is it of yours to take note of our life and works?' it is pertinent for laics to reply: 'What concern is it of yours that ye should receive our alms?' for the apostle says: "We command you in the name of Jesus Christ that ye withdraw yourselves from every brother that walketh disorderly and not after the tradition which they received of us, for ye yourselves know how ye ought to imitate us, for we behaved not ourselves disorderly among you, neither did we eat bread for naught at any man's hands, but in labor and travail, for even when we were with you, this we commanded you, If any man will not work, neither let him eat" [2 Thess. 3:6, 10].

23.   Julian of Norwich, *Showings*

For Julian (1342–ca. 1420), the moral life centers on her experience of the over-whelming love of God for the world revealed to her in mystical experience. Julian sees the love of Mother Jesus working to destroy human faults and to offer virtues in their place. The love of God is so great a force that it must triumph over all ob-stacles in the end.

Chapter 58. God the blessed Trinity, who is everlasting being, just as he is eternal from without beginning, just so was it in his eternal purpose to create human nature, which fair nature was first prepared for his own Son, the second person; and when he wished, by full agreement of the whole Trinity he created us all once. And in our creating he joined and united us to himself, and through this union we are kept as pure and as noble as we were created. . . .

And so in our making, God almighty is our loving Father, and God all wisdom is our loving Mother, with the love and the goodness of the Holy Spirit, which is all one God, one Lord. And in the joining and the union he is our very true spouse and we his beloved wife and his fair maiden, with which wife he was never displeased; for he says: I love you and you love me, and our love will never divide in two.

I contemplated the work of all the blessed Trinity, in which contempla-tion I saw and understood these three properties: the property of the fa-therhood, and the property of the motherhood, and the property of the lordship in one God. In our mighty Father we have our protection and our bliss, as regards our natural substance, which is ours by our creation from without beginning; and in the second person, in knowledge and wisdom we have our perfection, as regards our sensuality, our restoration and our salvation, for he is our Mother, brother and saviour; and in our good Lord the Holy Spirit we have our reward and our gift for our living and our labour, endlessly surpassing all that we desire in his marvellous courtesy, out of his great plentiful grace. For all our life consists of three: In the first we have our being, and in the second we have our increasing, and in the third we have our fulfillment. The first is nature, the second is mercy, the third is grace. . . .

Chapter 59. . . . As truly as God is our Father, so truly is God our Mother, and he revealed that in everything, and especially in these sweet words where he says: I am he; that is to say: I am he, the power and goodness of fatherhood; I am he, the wisdom and the lovingness of motherhood; I am he, the light and the grace which is all blessed love; I am he, the Trinity; I am he, the unity; I am he, the great supreme goodness of every kind of

117

thing; I am he who makes you to love; I am he who makes you to long; I am he, the endless fulfilling of all true desires. For where the soul is highest, noblest, most honourable, still it is lowest, meekest and mildest.

And from this foundation in substance we have all the powers of our sensuality by the gift of nature, and by the help and the furthering of mercy and grace, without which we cannot profit. Our great Father, almighty God, who is being, knows us and loved us before time began. Out of this knowledge, in his most wonderful deep love, by the prescient eternal counsel of all the blessed Trinity, he wanted the second person to become our Mother, our brother and our saviour. From this it follows that as truly as God is our Father, so truly is God our Mother. Our Father wills, our Mother works, our good Lord the Holy Spirit confirms. And therefore it is our part to love our God in whom we have our being, reverently thanking and praising him for our creation, mightily praying to our Mother for mercy and pity, and to our Lord the Holy Spirit for help and grace. For in these three is all our life: nature, mercy and grace, of which we have mildness, patience and pity, and hatred of sin and wickedness; for the virtues must of themselves hate sin and wickedness.

And so Jesus is our true Mother in nature by our first creation, and he is our true Mother in grace by his taking our created nature. All the lovely works and all the sweet loving offices of beloved motherhood are appropriated to the second person, for in him we have this godly will, whole and safe forever, both in nature and in grace, from his own goodness proper to him.

I understand three ways of contemplating motherhood in God. The first is the foundation of our nature's creation; the second is his taking of our nature, where the motherhood of grace begins; the third is the motherhood at work. And in that, by the same grace, everything is penetrated, in length and in breadth, in height and in depth without end; and it is all one love. . . .

Chapter 60. But now I should say a little more about this penetration, as I understood our Lord to mean: How we are brought back by the motherhood of mercy and grace into our natural place, in which we were created by the motherhood of love, a mother's love which never leaves us. . . .

. . . The mother's service is nearest, readiest and surest: nearest because it is most natural, readiest because it is most loving, and surest because it is truest. No one ever might or could perform this office fully, except only him. We know that all our mothers bear us for pain and for death. O, what is that? But our true Mother Jesus, he alone bears us for joy and for endless life, blessed may he be. So he carries us within him in love and travail, until the full time when he wanted to suffer the sharpest thorns and cruel pains that ever were or will be, and at the last he died. And when he had finished, and had borne us so for bliss, still all this could not satisfy his wonderful love. And he revealed this in these great surpassing words of love: If I could suffer more, I would suffer more. He could not die any more, but he did not want to cease working; therefore he must needs nourish us, for the precious love of motherhood has made him our debtor.

The mother can give her child to suck of her milk, but our precious Mother Jesus can feed us with himself, and does, most courteously and most tenderly, with the blessed sacrament, which is the precious food of true life; and with all the sweet sacraments he sustains us most mercifully and graciously, and so he meant in these blessed words, where he said: I am he whom Holy Church preaches and teaches to you. That is to say: All the health and the life of the sacraments, all the power and the grace of my word, all the goodness which is ordained in Holy Church for you, I am he.

The mother can lay her child tenderly to her breast, but our tender Mother Jesus can lead us easily into his blessed breast through his sweet open side, and show us there a part of the godhead and of the joys of heaven, with inner certainty of endless bliss. And that he revealed in the tenth revelation, giving us the same understanding in these sweet words which he says: See, how I love you, looking into his blessed side, rejoicing.

This fair lovely word 'mother' is so sweet and so kind in itself that it cannot truly be said of anyone or to anyone except of him and to him who is the true Mother of life and of all things. To the property of motherhood belong nature, love, wisdom and knowledge, and this is God. For though it may be so that our bodily bringing to birth is only little, humble and simple in comparison with our spiritual bringing to birth, still it is he who does it in the creatures by whom it is done. The kind, loving mother who knows and sees the need of her child guards it very tenderly, as the nature and condition of motherhood will have. And always as the child grows in age and in stature, she acts differently, but she does not change her love. And when it is even older, she allows it to be chastised to destroy its faults, so as to make the child receive virtues and grace. This work, with everything which is lovely and good, our Lord performs in those by whom it is done. So he is our Mother in nature by the operation of grace in the lower part, for love of the higher part. And he wants us to know it, for he wants to have all our love attached to him; and in this I saw that every debt which we owe by God's command to fatherhood and motherhood is fulfilled in truly loving God, which blessed love Christ works in us. And this was revealed in everything, and especially in the great bounteous words when he says: I am he whom you love.

Part 3

The Reformation Era

By the 1500s—and, to some degree, long before that—the carefully nuanced penitential system so central to the medieval church began to disintegrate; abuses such the fraudulent sale of indulgences and the ostentatious display of institutional wealth and power led to great disaffection with the church. Earlier critics like Wyclif and Hus had already challenged various aspects of accepted Catholic belief. But it was the dramatic sixteenth-century reforms instituted by Martin Luther and the other Protestant Reformers that were most disruptive to the structure, theology, and practice of the Roman church.

Luther was persuaded that salvation was based solely on the grace of God received by faith in Christ, rather than on meritorious good works. In his seminal treatise *Concerning Christian Liberty* he stressed the distinction between the freedom of grace and the bondage of the will. Since the requirements of the moral law are endless, efforts to fulfill them are fruitless. The law serves a necessary but ultimately negative function, by pointing out to us what we are completely unable to do by ourselves. Because a person cannot buy or achieve pardon, trust must be placed in God's promise of grace. The person who is in such a relationship of trust is freed from the anxiety of attempting to obtain moral perfection by his or her own efforts.

In contrast to Luther's sharp dichotomy between grace and law, but also in contrast to the Roman hierarchy's defense of the traditional penitential means to justification, the great humanist scholar Desiderius Erasmus sought a middle position. Erasmus viewed the efforts of the human will—

when in cooperation with God's grace—as a source of freedom, not of bondage. According to Erasmus, Luther's "freedom" seemed to be an excuse for Christian complacency and inaction.

Luther responded that Christians lived in the midst of a paradox, in which they were sinners and justified believers at the same time. When Luther applied this theological paradox to the realm of social relations, he was led to espouse a concept known as the "two kingdoms," the simultaneity of the kingdom of God and the kingdom of this world. These parallel kingdoms, Luther wrote, will coexist until the coming of Christ. As believers, we must function within both kingdoms, practicing one ethic in our life before God and a different ethic in our life before the world. The idea of the two kingdoms could (and did) lead toward a conservative approach in regard to the state; specifically for Luther, these views caused him to back away from and, eventually, to denounce the more extreme religious and political aspirations of the German peasants.

Some of the radical reformers believed that Luther had not gone far enough. Thomas Müntzer was convinced that God's answer to the peasants' misfortune lay in the violent overthrow of their oppressors. Taking a very different approach, Michael Sattler and the Swiss Anabaptists believed in the separation of Christians from the world; in the Schleitheim Confession they declared their commitment to pacifism, their withdrawal from carnality (including the government), and their insistence on a visible identification of believers with the gathered community of faith through adult baptism.

Second-generation Protestants were faced with the task of consolidating the theological and ethical advances of the Reformation. While Luther had written primarily in opposition to the monolithic presence of institutional Catholicism, John Calvin had to address the multiform religious situation of the mid-sixteenth century—which included Catholics, Lutherans, the Reformed, and various kinds of radical Protestants. Calvin's soteriological views were close to Luther's, but, in response to those who accused the Reformers of antinomianism, Calvin enunciated a more positive role for the moral law in the life of the justified believer. Also similar to Luther, Calvin stressed that believers had a "calling" to serve God according to their respective positions in life. But Calvin's particular emphasis on how persons should work out their election in terms of their vocation was modified by his historical situation. Calvin's opinions regarding the attitudes that persons should take in respect to the magistrates, for example, were written in direct opposition to the Anabaptists.

There were, of course, voices other than those of the Protestant leaders speaking on ethical issues during the Reformation era. Some of the most significant expressions included Teresa of Ávila, the mystical founder of the Discalced Carmelites, and Francisco de Suárez, the great Jesuit moral theologian. In the next century, the Quakers, the Levellers, and the Diggers represented some of the various forms of Reformed radicalism that developed in the English-speaking world. Footnotes cited in Part 3 are from editors of the primary sources.

24. Martin Luther, *Concerning Christian Liberty, On Temporal Authority,* and *Against the Robbing and Murdering Hordes of Peasants*

Concerning Christian Liberty *is Luther's classic statement on the freedom enjoyed by a believer from the burden of the law and the anxiety of self-reliance. In* On Temporal Authority, *Luther offers his description of the two kingdoms. Finally, Luther's conservative stance regarding rebellion against lawfully instituted governmental authorities is stated in* Against the Robbing and Murdering Hordes of Peasants.

CONCERNING CHRISTIAN LIBERTY

. . . I shall set down the following two propositions concerning the freedom and the bondage of the spirit:

A Christian is a perfectly free lord of all, subject to none.

A Christian is a perfectly dutiful servant of all, subject to all.

These two theses seem to contradict each other. If however, they should be found to fit together they would serve our purpose beautifully. . . .

First, let us consider the inner man to see how a righteous, free and pious Christian, that is, a spiritual, new and inner man, becomes what he is. It is evident that no external thing has any influence in producing Christian righteousness or freedom, or in producing unrighteousness or servitude. A simple argument will furnish the proof of this statement. What can it profit the soul if the body is well, free, and active, and eats, drinks, and does as it pleases? For in these respects even the most godless slaves of vice may prosper. On the other hand, how will poor health or imprisonment or hunger or thirst or any other external misfortune harm the soul? Even the most godly men, and those who are free because of clear consciences, are afflicted with these things. None of these things touch either the freedom or the servitude of the soul. It does not help the soul if the body is adorned with the sacred robes of priests or dwells in sacred places or is occupied with sacred duties or prays, fasts, abstains from certain kinds of food, or does any work that can be done by the body and in the body. The righteousness and the freedom of the soul require something far different since the things which have been mentioned could be done by any wicked person. Such works produce nothing but hypocrites. On the other hand, it will not harm the soul if the body is clothed in secular dress, dwells in unconsecrated places, eats and drinks as others do, does not pray aloud, and neglects to do all the above-mentioned things which hypocrites can do.

Furthermore, to put aside all kinds of works, even contemplation, meditation, and all that the soul can do, does not help. One thing, and only one thing, is necessary for Christian life, righteousness, and freedom. That one thing is the most holy Word of God, the gospel of Christ, as Christ says, John 11 [:25], "I am the resurrection and the life; he who believes in me, though he die, yet shall he live"; and John 8 [:36], "So if the Son makes you free, you will be free indeed"; and Matt. 4 [:4], "Man shall not live by bread alone, but by every word that proceeds from the mouth of God." Let us then consider it certain and firmly established that the soul can do without anything except the Word of God and that where the Word of God is missing there is no help at all for the soul. If it has the Word of God it is rich and lacks nothing since it is the Word of life, truth, light, peace, righteousness, salvation, joy, liberty, wisdom, power, grace, glory, and of every incalculable blessing. . . .

You may ask, "What then is the Word of God, and how shall it be used, since there are so many words of God?" I answer: The Apostle explains this in Romans 1. The Word is the gospel of God concerning his Son, who was made flesh, suffered, rose from the dead, and was glorified through the Spirit who sanctifies. To preach Christ means to feed the soul, make it righteous, set it free, and save it, provided it believes the preaching. Faith alone is the saving and efficacious use of the Word of God, according to Rom. 10 [:9]: "If you confess with your lips that Jesus is Lord and believe in your heart that God raised him from the dead, you will be saved." Furthermore, "Christ is the end of the law, that every one who has faith may be justified" [Rom. 10:4]. Again, in Rom. 1 [:17], "He who through faith is righteous shall live." The Word of God cannot be received and cherished by any works whatever but only by faith. Therefore it is clear that, as the soul needs only the Word of God for its life and righteousness, so it is justified by faith alone and not any works; for if it could be justified by anything else, it would not need the Word, and consequently it would not need faith.

This faith cannot exist in connection with works—that is to say, if you at the same time claim to be justified by works, whatever their character. . . .

. . . It is clear, then, that a Christian has all that he needs in faith and needs no works to justify him; and if he has no need of works, he has no need of the law; and if he has no need of the law, surely he is free from the law. It is true that "the law is not laid down for the just" [1 Tim. 1:9]. This is that Christian liberty, our faith, which does not induce us to live in idleness or wickedness but makes the law and works unnecessary for any man's righteousness and salvation. . . .

Let this suffice concerning the inner man, his liberty, and the source of his liberty, the righteousness of faith. He needs neither laws nor good works but, on the contrary, is injured by them if he believes that he is justified by them.

Now let us turn to the second part, the outer man. Here we shall answer all those who, offended by the word "faith" and by all that has been said, now ask, "If faith does all things and is alone sufficient unto righteousness, why then are good works commanded? We will take our ease and do no works and be content with faith." I answer: not so, you wicked men, not so. That would indeed be proper if we were wholly inner and perfectly spiritual men. But such we shall be only at the last day, the day of the resurrection of the dead. As long as we live in the flesh we only begin to make some progress in that which shall be perfected in the future life. For this reason the Apostle in Rom. 8 [:23] calls all that we attain in this life "the first fruits of the Spirit" because we shall indeed receive the greater portion, even the fulness of the Spirit, in the future. This is the place to assert that which was said above, namely, that a Christian is the servant of all and made subject to all. Insofar as he is free he does no works, but insofar as he is a servant he does all kinds of works. How this is possible we shall see.

Although, as I have said, a man is abundantly and sufficiently justified by faith inwardly, in his spirit, and so has all that he needs, except insofar as this faith and these riches must grow from day to day even to the future life; yet he remains in this mortal life on earth. In this life he must control his own body and have dealings with men. Here the works begin; here a man cannot enjoy leisure; here he must indeed take care to discipline his body by fastings, watchings, labors, and other reasonable discipline and to subject it to the Spirit so that it will obey and conform to the inner man and faith and not revolt against faith and hinder the inner man, as it is the nature of the body to do if it is not held in check. . . .

The following statements are therefore true: "Good works do not make a good man, but a good man does good works; evil works do not make a wicked man, but a wicked man does evil works." Consequently it is always necessary that the substance or person himself be good before there can be any good works, and that good works follow and proceed from the good person, as Christ also says, "A good tree cannot bear evil fruit, nor can a bad tree bear good fruit" [Matt. 7:18]. It is clear that the fruits do not bear the tree and that the tree does not grow on the fruits, also that, on the contrary, the trees bear the fruits and the fruits grow on the trees. As it is necessary, therefore, that the trees exist before their fruits and the fruits do not make trees either good or bad, but rather as the trees are, so are the fruits they bear; so a man must first be good or wicked before he does a good or wicked work, and his works do not make him good or wicked, but he himself makes his works either good or wicked. . . .

From this it is easy to know how far good works are to be rejected or not, and by what standard all the teachings of men concerning works are to be interpreted. If works are sought after as a means to righteousness, are burdened with this perverse leviathan,* and are done under the false impression that through them one is justified, they are made necessary and freedom and faith are destroyed; and this addition to them makes them no longer good but truly damnable works. They are not free, and they blaspheme the grace of God since to justify and to save by faith belongs to the grace of God alone. What the works have no power to do they nevertheless—by a godless presumption through this folly of ours—pretend to do and thus violently force themselves into the office and glory of grace. We do not, therefore, reject good works; on the contrary, we cherish and teach them as much as possible. We do not condemn them for their own sake but

*Probably a reminiscence of Leviathan, the twisting serpent, in Isa. 27:1.

on account of this godless addition to them and the perverse idea that righteousness is to be sought through them; for that makes them appear good outwardly, when in truth they are not good. They deceive men and lead them to deceive one another like ravening wolves in sheep's clothing [Matt. 7:15].

But this leviathan, or perverse notion concerning works, is unconquerable where sincere faith is wanting. Those work-saints cannot get rid of it unless faith, its destroyer, comes and rules in their hearts. Nature of itself cannot drive it out or even recognize it, but rather regards it as a mark of the most holy will. If the influence of custom is added and conforms this perverseness of nature, as wicked teachers have caused it to do, it becomes an incurable evil and leads astray and destroys countless men beyond all hope of restoration. Therefore, although it is good to preach and write about penitence, confession, and satisfaction, our teaching is unquestionably deceitful and diabolical if we stop with that and do not go on to teach about faith. . . .

Let this suffice concerning works in general and at the same time concerning the works which a Christian does for himself. Lastly, we shall also speak of the things which he does toward his neighbor. A man does not live for himself alone in this mortal body to work for it alone, but he lives also for all men on earth; rather, he lives only for others and not for himself. To this end he brings his body into subjection that he may the more sincerely and freely serve others. . . .

. . . [H]e should be guided in all his works by this thought and contemplate this one thing alone, that he may serve and benefit others in all that he does, considering nothing except the need and the advantage of his neighbor. Accordingly the Apostle commands us to work with our hands so that we may give to the needy, although he might have said that we should work to support ourselves. He says, however, "that he may be able to give to those in need" [Eph. 4:28]. This is what makes caring for the body a Christian work, that through its health and comfort we may be able to work, to acquire, and lay by funds with which to aid those who are in need, that in this way the strong member may serve the weaker, and we may be sons of God, each caring for and working for the other, bearing one another's burdens and so fulfilling the law of Christ [Gal. 6:2]. This is a truly Christian life. Here faith is truly active through love [Gal. 5:6], that is, it finds expression in works of the freest service, cheerfully and lovingly done, with which a man willingly serves another without hope of reward; and for himself he is satisfied with the fullness and wealth of his faith. . . .

. . . Although the Christian is thus free from all works, he ought in this liberty to empty himself, take upon himself the form of a servant, be made in the likeness of men, be found in human form, and to serve, help, and in every way deal with his neighbor as he sees that God through Christ has dealt and still deals with him. This he should do freely, having regard for nothing but divine approval.

He ought to think: "Although I am an unworthy and condemned man, my God has given me in Christ all the riches of righteousness and salvation without any merit on my part, out of pure, free mercy, so that from now on I need nothing except faith which believes that this is true. Why should I not therefore freely, joyfully, with all my heart, and with an eager will do all things which I know are pleasing and acceptable to such a Father who has overwhelmed me with his inestimable riches? I will therefore give myself as a Christ to my neighbor, just as Christ offered himself to me; I will do nothing in this life except what I see is necessary, profitable, and salutary to my neighbor, since through faith I have an abundance of all good things in Christ."

Behold, from faith thus flow forth love and joy in the Lord, and from love a joyful, willing, and free mind that serves one's neighbor willingly and takes no account of gratitude or ingratitude, of praise or blame, of gain or loss. For a man does not serve that he may put men under obligations. He does not distinguish between friends and enemies or anticipate their thankfulness or unthankfulness, but he most freely and most willingly spends himself and all that he has, whether he wastes all on the thankless or whether he gains a reward. . . .

We conclude, therefore, that a Christian lives not in himself, but in Christ and in his neighbor. Otherwise he is not a Christian. He lives in Christ through faith, in his neighbor through love. By faith he is caught up beyond himself into God. By love he descends beneath himself into his neighbor. Yet he always remains in God and in his love, as Christ says in John 1 [:51], "Truly, truly, I say to you, you will see heaven opened, and the angels of God ascending and descending upon the Son of man."

Enough now of freedom. As you see, it is a spiritual and true freedom and makes our hearts free from all sins, laws and commands, as Paul says, 1 Tim 1 [:9], "The law is not laid down for the just." It is more excellent than all other liberty, which is external, as heaven is more excellent than earth. May Christ give us this liberty both to understand and to preserve. Amen.

Finally, something must be added for the sake of those for whom nothing can be said so well that they will not spoil it by misunderstanding it. It is questionable whether they will understand even what will be said here. There are very many who, when they hear of this freedom of faith, immediately turn it into an occasion for the flesh and think that now all things are allowed them. They want to show that they are free men and Christians only by despising and finding fault with ceremonies, traditions, and human laws; as if they were Christians because on stated days they do not use the accustomed prayers, and with upturned nose scoff at the precepts of men, although they utterly disregard all else that pertains to the Christian religion. The extreme opposite of these are those who rely for their salvation solely on their reverent observance of ceremonies, as if they would be saved because on certain days they fast or abstain from meats, or pray certain prayers; these make a boast of the precepts of the church and of the fathers, and do not care a fig for the things which are of the essence of our faith. Plainly, both are in error because they neglect the weightier things which are necessary to salvation, and quarrel so noisily about trifling and unnecessary matters.

How much better is the teaching of the Apostle Paul who bids us take a middle course and condemns both sides when he says, "Let not him who eats despise him who abstains, and let not him who abstains pass judgment on him who eats" [Rom. 14:3]. Here you see that they who neglect and disparage ceremonies, not out of piety, but out of mere contempt, are reproved, since the Apostle teaches us not to despise them. Such men are puffed up by knowledge. On the other hand, he teaches those who insist on the ceremonies not to judge the others, for neither party acts toward the other according to the love that edifies. Wherefore we ought to listen to Scripture which teaches that we should not go aside to the right or to the left [Deut. 28:14] but follow the statutes of the Lord which are right, "rejoicing the heart" [Ps. 19:8]. As a man is not righteous because he keeps and clings to the works and forms of the ceremonies, so also will a man not be counted righteous merely because he neglects and despises them.

Our faith in Christ does not free us from works but from false opinions concerning works, that is, from the foolish presumption that justification is acquired by works. Faith redeems, corrects, and preserves our consciences so that we know that righteousness does not consist in works, although works neither can nor ought to be wanting; just as we cannot be without food and drink and all the works of this mortal body, yet our righteousness is not in them, but in faith; and yet those works of the body are not to be despised or neglected on that account.

Reprinted from *Luther's Works*, vol. 31, pp. 344–50, 358–67, 371–73. Edited and translated by Harold J. Grimm. General editor, Helmut T. Lehmann. Copyright © 1959 by Fortress Press. Used by permission of Augsburg Fortress.

ON TEMPORAL AUTHORITY

. . . . [W]e must divide the children of Adam and all mankind into two classes, the first belonging to the kingdom of God, the second to the kingdom of the world. Those who belong to the kingdom of God are all the true believers who are in Christ and under Christ, for Christ is King and Lord in the kingdom of God. . . .

Now observe, these people need no temporal law or sword. If all the world were composed of real Christians, that is, true believers, there would be no need for or benefits from prince, king, lord, sword, or law. They would serve no purpose, since Christians have in their heart the Holy Spirit, who both teaches and makes them to do injustice to no one, to love everyone, and to suffer injustice and even death willingly and cheerfully at the hands of anyone. Where there is nothing but the unadulterated doing of right and bearing of wrong, there is no need for any suit, litigation, court, judge, penalty, law, or sword. For this reason it is impossible that the temporal sword and law should find any work to do among Christians, since they do of their own accord much more than all laws and teachings can demand, just as Paul says in 1 Timothy 1 [:9], "The law is not laid down for the just but for the lawless."

Why is this? It is because the righteous man of his own accord does all and more than the law demands. But the unrighteous do nothing that the law demands; therefore, they need the law to instruct, constrain, and compel them to do good. . . .

. . . All who are not Christians belong to the kingdom of the world and are under the law. There are few true believers and still fewer who live a Christian life, who do not resist evil and indeed themselves do no evil. For this reason God has provided for them a different government beyond the Christian estate and kingdom of God. He has subjected them to the sword so that, even though they would like to, they are unable to practice their wickedness, and if they do practice it they cannot do so without fear or with success and impunity. In the same way a savage wild beast is bound with chains and ropes so that it cannot bite and tear as it would normally do, even though it would like to; whereas a tame and gentle animal needs no restraint, but is harmless despite the lack of chains and ropes.

If this were not so, men would devour one another, seeing that the whole world is evil and that among thousands there is scarcely a single true Christian. No one could support wife and child, feed himself, and serve God. The world would be reduced to chaos. For this reason God has ordained two governments; the spiritual, by which the Holy Spirit produces Christians and righteous people under Christ; and the temporal, which restrains the un-Christian and wicked so that—no thanks to them—they are obliged to keep still and to maintain an outward peace. Thus does St. Paul interpret the temporal sword in Romans 13 [:3], when he says it is not a terror to good conduct but to bad. And Peter says it is for the punishment of the wicked [2 Pet. 2:14].

If anyone attempted to rule the world by the gospel and to abolish all temporal law and sworn on the plea that all are baptized and Christian, and that, according to the gospel, there shall be among them no law or sword—or need for either—pray tell me, friend, what would he be doing? He would be loosing the ropes and chains of the savage wild beasts and letting them bite and mangle everyone, meanwhile insisting that they were harmless, tame, and gentle creatures; but I would have the proof in my wounds. Just so would the wicked under the name of Christian abuse evangelical freedom, carry on their rascality, and insist that they were Christians subject neither to law nor sword, as some are already raving and ranting.*

To such a one we must say: Certainly it is true that Christians, so far as they themselves are concerned, are subject neither to law nor sword, and have need of neither. But take heed and first fill the world with real Christians before you attempt to rule it in a Christian and evangelical manner. This you will never accomplish; for the world and the masses are and always will be un-Christian, even if they are all baptized and Christian in

*The allusion is to the Anabaptists.

name. Christians are few and far between (as the saying is). Therefore, it is out of the question that there should be a common Christian government over the whole world, or indeed over a single country or any considerable body of people, for the wicked always outnumber the good. Hence, a man who would venture to govern an entire country or the world with the gospel would be like a shepherd who should put together in one fold wolves, lions, eagles, and sheep, and let them mingle freely with one another saying, "Help yourselves, and be good and peaceful toward one another. The fold is open, there is plenty of food. You need have no fear of dogs and clubs." The sheep would doubtless keep the peace and allow themselves to be fed and governed peacefully, but they would not live long, nor would one beast survive another.

For this reason one must carefully distinguish between these two governments. Both must be permitted to remain; the one to produce righteousness, the other to bring about external peace and prevent evil deeds. Neither one is sufficient in the world without the other. No one can become righteous in the sight of God by means of the temporal government, without Christ's spiritual government. Christ's government does not extend over all men; rather, Christians are always a minority in the midst of non-Christians. Now where temporal government or law alone prevails, there sheer hypocrisy is inevitable, even though the commandments be God's very own. For without the Holy Spirit in the heart no one becomes truly righteous, no matter how fine the works he does. On the other hand, where the spiritual government alone prevails over land and people, there wickedness is given free rein and the door is open for all manner of rascality, for the world as a whole cannot receive or comprehend it. . . .

. . . But you say: if Christians then do not need the temporal sword or law, why does Paul say to all Christians in Romans 13 [:1], "Let all souls be subject to the governing authority," and St. Peter, "Be subject to every human ordinance" [1 Pet. 2:13], etc., as quoted above? Answer: I have just said that Christians, among themselves and by and for themselves need no law or sword since it is neither necessary nor useful for them. Since a true Christian lives and labors on earth not for himself alone but for his neighbor, he does by the very nature of his spirit even what he himself has no need of, but is needful and useful to his neighbor. Because the sword is most beneficial and necessary for the whole world in order to preserve peace, punish sin, and restrain the wicked, the Christian submits most willingly to the rule of the sword, pays his taxes, honors those in authority, [cf. Rom. 13:6–7], serves, helps, and does all he can to assist the governing authority, that it may continue to function and be held in honor and fear. Although he has no need of these things for himself—to him they are not essential—nevertheless, he concerns himself about what is serviceable and of benefit to others, as Paul teaches in Ephesians 5 [:21–6:9].

Just as he performs all other works of love which he himself does not need—he does not visit the sick in order that he himself may be made well, or feed others because he himself needs food—so he serves the governing authority not because he needs it but for the sake of others, that they may be protected and that the wicked may not become worse. He loses nothing by this; such service in no way harms him, yet it is of great benefit to the world. If he did not so serve he would be acting not as a Christian but even contrary to love; he would also be setting a bad example to others who in like manner would not submit to authority, even though they were not Christians. . . .

. . . You ask whether a Christian too may bear the temporal sword and punish the wicked, since Christ's words, "Do not resist evil," are so clear and definite that the sophists have had to make of them a "counsel." Answer: You have now heard two propositions. One is that the sword can have no place among Christians; therefore, you cannot bear it among Christians or hold it over them, for they do not need it. The question, therefore, must be referred to the other group, the non-Christians, whether you may bear it there in a Christian manner. Here the other proposition applies, that you are under obligation to serve and assist the sword by whatever means you can, with body, goods, honor, and soul. For it is something which you do not need, but which is very beneficial and essential for the whole world and for your neighbor. Therefore, if you see that there is a lack of hangmen, constables, judges, lords, or princes, and you find that you are qualified, you should offer your services and seek the position, that the essential governmental authority may not be despised and become enfeebled or perish. The world cannot and dare not dispense with it.

Here is the reason why you should do this: In such a case you would be entering entirely into the service and work of others, which would be of advantage neither to yourself nor your property or honor, but only to your neighbor and to others. You would be doing it not with the purpose of avenging yourself or returning evil for evil, but for the good of your neighbor and for the maintenance of the safety and peace of others. For yourself, you would abide by the gospel and govern yourself according to Christ's word [Matt. 5:39–40], gladly turning the other cheek and letting the cloak go with the coat when the matter concerned you and your cause.

In this way the two propositions are brought into harmony with one another: at one and the same time you satisfy God's kingdom inwardly and the kingdom of the world outwardly. You suffer evil and injustice, and yet at the same time you punish evil and injustice; you do not resist evil, and yet at the same time, you do resist it. In the one case, you consider yourself and what is yours; in the other, you consider your neighbor and what is his. In what concerns you and yours, you govern yourself by the gospel and suffer injustice toward yourself as a true Christian; in what concerns the person or property of others, you govern yourself according to love and tolerate no injustice toward your neighbor. The gospel does not forbid this; in fact, in other places it actually commands it.

AGAINST THE ROBBING AND MURDERING HORDES OF PEASANTS

. . . .The peasants have taken upon themselves the burden of three terrible sins against God and man; by this they have abundantly merited death in body and soul. In the first place, they have sworn* to be true and faithful, submissive and obedient, to their rulers, as Christ commands when he says, "Render to Caesar the things that are Caesar's" [Luke 20:25]. And Romans 13 [:1] says, "Let every person be subject to the governing authorities." Since they are now deliberately and violently breaking this oath of obedience and setting themselves in opposition to their masters, they have forfeited body and soul, as faithless, perjured, lying, disobedient rascals and scoundrels usually do. . . .

In the second place, they are starting a rebellion, and are violently robbing and plundering monasteries and castles which are not theirs; by this they have doubly deserved death in body and soul as highwaymen and murderers. Furthermore, anyone who can be proved to be a seditious person is an outlaw before God and the emperor; and whoever is the first to put him to death does right and well. For if a man is in open rebellion, everyone is both his judge and his executioner; just as when a fire starts, the first man who can put it out is the best man to do the job. For rebellion is not just simple murder; it is like a great fire, which attacks and devastates a whole land. Thus rebellion brings with it a land filled with murder and bloodshed; it makes widows and orphans, and turns everything upside down, like the worst disaster. . . .

In the third place, they cloak this terrible and horrible sin with the gospel, call themselves "Christian brethren," take oaths and submit to them, and compel people to go along with them in these abominations. Thus they become the worst blasphemers of God and slanderers of his holy name. . . .

It does not help the peasants when they pretend that according to Genesis 1 and 2 all things were created free and common and that all of us alike have been baptized. . . .

For baptism does not make men free in body and property, but in soul; and the gospel does not make goods common, except in the case of those who, of their own free will, do what the apostles and disciples did in Acts 4 [:32–37]. They did not demand, as do our insane peasants in their raging, that the goods of others—of Pilate and Herod—should be common, but only their own goods. Our peasants, however, want to make the goods of other men common, and keep their own for themselves. Fine Christians they are! I think there is not a devil left in hell; they have all gone into the peasants. Their raving has gone beyond all measure.

Now since the peasants have brought [the wrath of] both God and man down upon themselves and are already many times guilty of death in body and soul, and since they submit to no court and wait for no verdict, but only rage on, I must instruct the temporal authorities on how they may act with a clear conscience in this matter.

*All men took this oath under the feudal system.

First, I will not oppose a ruler who, even though he does not tolerate the gospel, will smite and punish these peasants without first offering to submit the case to judgment.* He is within his rights, since the peasants are not contending any longer for the gospel, but have become faithless, perjured, disobedient, rebellious murderers, robbers, and blasphemers, whom even a heathen ruler has the right and authority to punish. . . .

But if the ruler is a Christian and tolerates the gospel,† so that the peasants have no appearance of a case against him, he should proceed with fear. First he must take the matter to God, confessing that we have deserved these things, and remembering that God may, perhaps, have thus aroused the devil as a punishment upon all Germany. Then he should humbly pray for help against the devil, for we are contending not only "against flesh and blood" but "against the spiritual hosts of wickedness in the air" [Eph. 6:12, 2:2], which must be attacked with prayer. Then, when our hearts are so turned to God that we are ready to let his divine will be done, whether he will or will not have us to be princes and lords, we must go beyond our duty, and offer the mad peasants an opportunity to come to terms, even though they are not worthy of it. Finally, if that does not help, then swiftly take to the sword.

For in this case a prince and lord must remember that according to Romans 13 [:4] he is God's minister and the servant of his wrath and that the sword has been given him to use against such people. If he does not fulfil the duties of his office by punishing some and protecting others, he commits as great a sin before God as when someone who has not been given the sword commits murder. If he is able to punish and does not do it—even though he would have had to kill someone or shed blood—he becomes guilty of all the murder and evil that these people commit. For by deliberately disregarding God's command he permits such rascals to go about their wicked business, even though he was able to prevent it and it was his duty to do so. This is not a time to sleep. And there is no place for patience or mercy. This is the time of the sword, not the day of grace.

Reprinted from *Luther's Works*, vol. 46, pp. 49–53. Edited and translated by Robert C. Schultz. General editor, Helmut T. Lehmann. Copyright © 1967 by Fortress Press. Used by permission of Augsburg Fortress.

25. Desiderius Erasmus, *On the Freedom of the Will*

Erasmus (ca. 1466–1536), the great scholar of the Renaissance, wrote this important response to Luther in 1524. Erasmus tried to encourage moderation in the raging debates of the period, but he was rebuffed in his attempt by Protestant and Catholic leaders alike.

---

*In other words, a ruler need not wait for a judicial verdict against the peasants.
†I.e., has evangelical sympathies.

Let us, . . . suppose that there is some truth in the doctrine which Wyclif taught and Luther asserted, that whatever is done by us is done not by free choice but by sheer necessity. What could be more useless than to publish this paradox to the world? Again, suppose for a moment that it were true in a certain sense, as Augustine says somewhere, that "God works in us good and evil, and rewards his own good works in us, and punishes his evil works in us"; what a window to impiety would the public avowal of such an opinion open to countless mortals! Especially in view of the slowness of mind of mortal men, their sloth, their malice, and their incurable propensity toward all manner of evil. What weakling will be able to bear the endless and wearisome warfare against his flesh? What evildoer will take pains to correct his life? Who will be able to bring himself to love God with all his heart when He created hell seething with eternal torments in order to punish his own misdeeds in his victims as though he took delight in human torments? For that is how most people will interpret them. For the most part, men are by nature dull-witted and sensual, prone to unbelief, inclined to evil, with a bent to blasphemy, so that there is no need to add fuel to the furnace. . . .

. . . [I]t is not wrong to say that man does something, and yet attributes the sum of all that he does to God as its author, from whom it has come about that he was able to ally his own effort with the grace of God. So Paul says: "But by the grace of God I am what I am" [1 Cor. 15:10]. He recognizes the author of his being, but when you hear him say: "And his grace toward me was not in vain," you recognize the human will relying on the divine assistance. . . . Thus to those who maintain that man can do nothing without the help of the grace of God, and conclude that therefore no works of men are good—to these we shall oppose a thesis to me much more probable, that there is nothing that man cannot do with the help of the grace of God and that therefore all the works of man can be good. . . .

. . . [W]hen I hear that the merit of man is so utterly worthless that all things, even the works of godly men, are sins, when I hear that our will does nothing more than clay in the hand of a potter, when I hear all that we do or will referred to absolute necessity, my mind encounters many a stumbling block. First, why does one so often read that godly men, full of good works, have wrought righteousness and walked in the presence of God, turning neither to the right nor to the left, if the deeds of even the most godly men are sin, and sin of such character that, did the mercy of God not intervene, it would have plunged into hell even him for whom Christ died? How is it that we hear so much about reward if there is no such thing as merit? With what impudence is the obedience of those who obey the divine commands praised, and the disobedience of those who do not obey condemned? Why is there so frequent a mention of judgment in Holy Scriptures if there is no weighing of merits? Or are we compelled to be present at the Judgment Seat if nothing has happened through our own will, but all things have been done in us by sheer necessity? There is the further objection: What is the point of so many admonitions, so many precepts, so many threats, so many exhortations, so many expostulations, if of ourselves we do nothing, but God in accordance with his immutable will does everything in us, both to will and to perform the same? He wishes us to pray without ceasing, to watch, to fight, to contend for the prize of eternal life. Why does he wish anything to be unceasingly prayed for which he has already decreed either to give or not to give, and cannot change his decrees, since he is immutable? Why does he command us to seek with so many labors what he has decided freely to bestow? We are afflicted, we are cast out, we are reviled, we are tortured, we are killed, and thus the grace of God in us strives, conquers, and triumphs. The martyr suffers these torments and yet there is no merit given him, nay, rather, he may be said to sin in exposing his body to torments in hope of eternal life. But why has the most merciful God so willed to work in the martyrs? For a man would seem cruel, if he had decided to give something as a free gift to a friend, not to give it unless that friend were tortured to the point of despair.

But when we come to so dark a depth of the divine counsel, perhaps we shall be ordered to adore that which it is not right to pursue. The human mind will say: "He is God, he can do what he wills, and since his nature is altogether the best, everything that he wills must also be for the best." This, too, can be said plausibly enough, that God crowns his gifts in us, and orders his benefit to be our reward and what he has worked in us that he wills by his free goodness to be imputed to those who trust in him as though it were a debt to them, wherewith they may attain eternal life. But I know not how they are to appear consistent who so exaggerate the mercy of God to the godly that as regards others they almost make him cruel. Pious ears can admit the benevolence of one who imputes his own good to us; but it is difficult to explain how it can be a mark of his justice (for I will not speak of mercy) to hand over others to eternal torments in whom he has not deigned to work good works, when they themselves are incapable of doing good, since they have no free choice or, if they have, it can do nothing but sin. . . .

. . . [I]n my opinion free choice could have been so established as to avoid that confidence in our merits and the other dangers which Luther avoids . . . and without losing those benefits that Luther admires. That is to my mind the advantage of the view of those who attribute entirely to grace the first impulse which stirs the soul, yet in the performance allow something to human choice which has not withdrawn itself from the grace of God. For since there are three stages in all things— beginning, progress, and end—they attribute the first and last to grace, and only in progress say that free choice achieves anything, yet in such wise that in each individual action two causes come together, the grace of God and the will of man: in such a way, however, that grace is the principal cause and the will secondary, which can do nothing apart from the principal cause, since the principal is sufficient in itself. Just as fire burns by its native force, and yet the principal cause is God who acts through the fire, and this cause would of itself be sufficient, without which the fire could do nothing if he withdrew from it.

On this more accommodating view, it is implied that a man owes all his salvation to divine grace, since the power of free choice is exceedingly trivial in this regard and this very thing which it can do is a work of the grace of God who first created free choice and then freed it and healed it. And so we can appease, if they are capable of being appeased, those who cannot bear that man should own anything good which he does not owe to God. . . .

Let us try to express our meaning in a parable. . . . A father lifts up a child who has fallen and has not yet strength to walk, however much it tries, and shows it an apple which lies over against it; the child longs to run, but on account of the weakness of its limbs it would have fallen had not its father held its hand and steadied its footsteps, so that led by its father it obtains the apple which the father willingly puts in its hand as a reward for running. The child could not have stood up if the father had not lifted it, could not have seen the apple had the father not shown it, could not advance unless the father had all the time assisted its feeble steps, could not grasp the apple had the father not put it into his hand. What, then, can the infant claim for itself? And yet it does something. But it has nothing to glory about in its own powers, for it owes its very self to its father. Let us apply this analogy to our relation with God. What, then, does the child do here? It relies with all its powers on the one who lifts it, and it accommodates as best it can its feeble steps to him who leads. No doubt the father could have drawn the child against its will, and the child could have resisted by refusing the outstretched apple; the father could have given the apple without the child's having to run to get it, but he preferred to give it in this way, as this was better for the child. I will readily allow that less is due to our industry in following after eternal life than to the boy who runs to his father's hand. . . .

But although we see so little attributed to free choice, yet to some even this seems to be too much. For they would have grace alone to be working in us and our mind in all things to be only passive as an instrument of the divine Spirit, so that good can in no way be said to be ours save insofar as the divine benevolence freely imputes it to us; for grace does not work in us *through*, so much as *in*, free choice, in the same way as a potter works in the clay and not through the clay. But where, then, is there any room for mention of the crown and of the reward? God, they say, crowns his own gifts in us and orders his benefit to be our reward, and what he has wrought in us, he deigns to impute to us making us a partner in his Heavenly Kingdom. This I do not see, how they maintain a free choice which is quite inactive. For if they were to say that it is acted upon by grace in such a way as to cooperate with it, that would be an easier explanation. . . . those who deny free choice entirely, but say that all things happen by absolute necessity, aver that God works in all men not only good but even evil works. Whence it would seem to follow that just as man can by no reason be said to be the author of good works, so he can in no way be said to be the author of evil works. Although this view seems plainly to ascribe cruelty and injustice to God, a sentiment offensive to pious ears (for he would not be God if there were found in him any blemish or imperfection), yet its champions can make this plea in support of their unconvincing case: "He is God. His work must necessarily be of supreme excellence and beauty; so if you look at the order of the universe, even things evil in themselves are good seen as a whole, and show forth the glory of God, nor is it for any creature to pass judgment on the counsel of God but to submit himself entirely to it; and so, if God chooses to condemn this or that man, he ought not to complain, but embrace whatever is His good pleasure, being fully persuaded that all things are done by Him for the best, nor could they be done in any other way than the best. . . ."

. . . They immeasurably exaggerate original sin, by which they would have even the most excellent powers of human nature to be so corrupt that they can do nothing of themselves except to be ignorant of God and to hate him. And they aver that, even though justified by faith, a man cannot of himself do anything but sin. And that very proneness toward sin which is left in us by the sin of our first parents, they will have it to be sin and indeed invincible sin, so that there is no precept of God which even a man justified by faith can fulfill; but so many commandments of God have no other end than to magnify the grace of God, which bestows salvation upon men without consideration of merit.

Meanwhile, these people seem to me in one place to restrict the divine mercy that in another they may widen it, as though one should provide for one's guests a very slender lunch so that the dinner may seem more sumptuous, in a way imitating those artists who, when they want to give the illusion of light in one part of their picture, darken with shadows the parts next to it. They begin, therefore, by making God almost cruel, since on account of another's sin he thus rages against the whole human race, especially when they have repented of their sins and have grievously expiated them all their days. But when they say that even those who are justified by faith do nothing but sin, nay, that in loving and trusting God we earn God's hatred, do they not here make extremely niggardly the grace of God, who so justifies man by faith that he still does nothing but sin? . . .

I will not now examine the reasons why they say that all the commandments of God are impossible to us, for that was not my intention; I simply wished to show by the way that these men, by their excess of zeal of enlarging in one place the role of grace in the plan of salvation, obscure it in other places. And I fail to see how these points of view can be consistent. Having cut the throat of free choice, they teach that a man is now led by the Spirit of Christ, whose nature will not suffer any association with sin. And yet these same people assert that even when he has received grace, a man does nothing but sin. Luther seems to delight in this kind of extravagant statement, for he seeks to put down the extravagances of others, in the words of the proverb, by cutting a poor knot with a blunt chopper.* This boldness on the part of some goes as far as hyperbole, for they sell not only their own merits, but those of all the saints. And what works are these? Singing, the murmuring of psalms, the eating of fish, fasting, clothes, titles. This nail Luther has driven out with another when he says that all the merits of the saints are nothing but that all the deeds of men, however holy, have been sins, bringing eternal damnation, unless the mercy of God came to the rescue. . . .

*A proverb expounded by Erasmus in the *Adagia*.

One party has made a considerable profit out of confessions and satis-
factions, with which they marvelously encumbered the consciences of men,
and likewise out of purgatory, concerning which they have asserted certain
paradoxes. This fault the other side corrected by saying that confession is
an invention of Satan; the most moderate of them say that confession is not
compulsory and there is no need of satisfaction for sins, since Christ has
paid the penalty for all sins; and finally that there is no purgatory. The one
side go so far as to profess that the commands of petty priors are obligatory
on pain of hellfire, nor do they hesitate to promise eternal life to him who
shall obey. The opposite party meet this extravagance by saying that all
the decrees of popes, councils, bishops, are heretical and anti-Christian.
Thus one party has enlarged the power of the pontiff beyond all bounds,
the other speaks openly of him in terms that I would not dare repeat. Again,
one party says that the vows of monks and priests are perpetually binding
on pain of hellfire, the other says that such vows are thoroughly wicked,
that they are not to be undertaken, and if undertaken are not to be kept.

It is from the conflict of such exaggerated views that have been born the
thunders and lightnings which now shake the world. And if each side continues to defend bitterly its own exaggerations, I can see such a fight coming as was that between Achilles and Hector whom, since they were both
equally ruthless, only death could divide. It is commonly said that the only
way to make a crooked stick straight is to bend it in the opposite direction:
that may be right for the correction of morals, but whether it is tolerable in
the matter of doctrine I do not know. . . . in these matters it is moderation
which pleases me at any rate. Pelagius has no doubt attributed too much to
free choice, and Scotus quite enough, but Luther first mutilated it by cutting off its right arm: then not content with this he thoroughly cut the throat
of free choice and despatched it. I prefer the view of those who do attribute
much to free choice, but most to grace.

Nor was it necessary, in avoiding the Scylla of arrogance, that you
should be wrecked on the Charybdis of despair or indolence. Nor in mending a dislocated limb need you twist another, but rather put it back into
place; nor is it necessary so to fight with an enemy in front that incautiously
you receive a wound in the back. The result of this moderation will be the
achievement of some good work, albeit imperfect, from which no man can
arrogate anything to himself: there will be some merit, but such that the
sum *is* owed to God. There is an abundance in human life of weakness,
vices, crimes, so that if any man wishes to look at himself he can easily put
down his conceit, although we do not assert that man however justified can
do nothing but sin, especially since Christ calls him reborn, and Paul, a new
creature. Why, you will say, grant anything to free choice? In order to have
something to impute justly to the wicked who have voluntarily come short
of the grace of God, in order that the calumny of cruelty and injustice may
be excluded from God, that despair may be kept away from us, that complacency may be excluded also, and that we may be incited to endeavor.
For these reasons, almost everyone admits free choice, but as inefficacious
apart from the perpetual grace of God, lest we arrogate aught to ourselves.

One may object, to what does free choice avail if it accomplishes nothing? I reply, to what does the whole man avail if God so works in him as a potter with clay and just as he could act on a pebble?

From *Luther and Erasmus: Free Will and Salvation*, The Library of Christian Classics, vol. 17, translated and edited by E. Gordon Rupp and Philip S. Watson in collaboration with A. N. Marlow and B. Drewery (Philadelphia: The Westminster Press), pp. 41, 84–88, 90–96. Copyright © MCMLXIX The Westminster Press. Published simultaneously by The Westminster Press, Philadelphia, and the SCM Press, Ltd., London.

26. Thomas Müntzer, *Sermon before the Princes*

In this 1524 sermon, Müntzer (ca. 1490–1525) advocated one of the most radical forms of the Reformation ethic. Convinced that Luther had not gone far enough in his changes, Müntzer supported the establishment of a theocracy on the basis of direct inspiration and millennial expectation. This theocracy was to be created, if necessary, by the violent elimination of the ungodly, and would be led (he hoped) by the princes.

It is known that poor, ailing, disintegrating Christendom can be neither counseled nor aided unless the diligent, untroubled servants of God daily work through the Scriptures, singing, reading, and preaching. But therewith the head of many a pampered priest will continuously have to suffer great blows or [he will] miss out in his handiwork. But how ought one otherwise to deal with him at a time when Christendom is being so wretchedly devastated by ravenous wolves . . .?

Yea, so nicely that the real friends of God are thereby misled; and even with the diligence of the most intense application, they are scarcely able to detect their error, as Matthew [24:24] clearly shows. This is what the simulated sanctity and the flattering absolution of the godless enemies of God accomplish. For they say the Christian church cannot err.* . . . Christ the Son of God and his apostles and indeed, before him, his holy prophets began a real pure Christianity, having sown pure wheat in the field, that is, [they] planted the precious Word of God in the hearts of the elect as Matthew [12:24–30], Mark [4:26–29], and Luke [8:5–15] have written, and Ezekiel [36:29]. But the lazy, neglectful ministers of this same church have not wished to accomplish this and maintain it by dint of diligent watchfulness; but rather they have sought their own [ends], not what was Jesus Christ's [Phil. 2:4, 21]. For this reason they have allowed the harmfulness of the godless vigorously to take over, that is, the weeds [Ps. 80:9–14].† . . . Thus, ye

---

*A reference to Gregory VII's *Dictatus Papae*: it held that the Roman Church cannot err.
†Ps. 79 in the Vulgate. The reference is to the weeds choking the [true] vine of Israel (=the church).

amiable princes, it is necessary that we apply utmost diligence in these par-
lous days [1 Tim. 4], as all the dear fathers have delineated in the Bible from
the beginning of the world, in order to cope with this insidious evil. For the
age is dangerous and the days are wicked [2 Tim. 3:1; Eph. 5:15 f.]. Why?
Simply because the noble power of God is so wretchedly disgraced and dishonored that the poor common people are misled by the ungodly divines
all with such rigmarole, as the prophet Micah [3:5–37] says of it: This is now
the character of almost all divines with mighty few exceptions. They teach
and say that God no longer reveals his divine mysteries to his beloved
friends by means of valid visions or his audible Word, etc. Thus they stick
with their inexperienced way [cf. Eccl. 34:9] and make into the butt of sar-
casm those persons who go around in possession of revelation, as the godless did to Jeremiah [20:7f.]. . . . O beloved, yea, the great Stone there is
about to fall and strike these schemes of [mere] reason and dash them to
the ground, for he says [Matt. 10:34]: I am not come to send peace but
a sword. What should be done, however, with the same?* Nothing different from [what is done with] the wicked who hinder the gospel: Get them
out of the way and eliminate them, unless you want to be ministers of the
devil rather than of God, as Paul calls you [Rom. 13:4]. You need not doubt
it. God will strike to pieces all your adversaries who undertake to persecute
you, for his hand is by no means shortened, as Isaiah [59:1] says. Therefore he can still help you and wishes to, as he supported the elect King
Josiah and others who defended the name of God. Thus you are angels,
when you wish to do justly, as Peter says [2 Pet. 1:4]. Christ commanded in
deep gravity, saying [Luke 19:27]: Take mine enemies and strangle them
before mine eyes. Why? Ah! because they ruin Christ's government for him
and in addition want to defend their rascality under the guise of Christian
faith and ruin the whole world with their insidious subterfuge.†. . . Now if
you want to be true governors, you must begin government at the roots,
and, as Christ commanded, drive his enemies from the elect. For you are
the means to this end.‡ Beloved, don't give us any old jokes about how
the power of God should do it without your application of the sword. Otherwise may it rust away for you in its scabbard! May God grant it, whatever any divine may say to you! Christ says it sufficiently [Matt. 7:19]; John
15:2, 6]. Every tree that bringeth not forth good fruit is rooted out and cast
into the fire. If you do away with the mask of the world, you will soon rec-

---

*The text reads *mit demselbigen* and may refer specifically to Luther.
†Here Müntzer is reinterpreting the politically conservative text of Rom. [chap.] 13,
into a revolutionary document. By reversing the sequence of [chap.] 13:1–4 and con-
struing vs. 1 f. as the sequel of vs. 3 f., he would make the Ernestine princes, by hor-
tatory anticipation, the executors of God's wrath against the godless and the pro-
tectors of the revolutionary saints. But he warns them that if they fail to identify
themselves with the covenantal people, the sword will revert to the people.
‡The princes possess the sword whereby the decision against the ungodly can be
made.

ognize it with a righteous judgment [John 7:24]. Perform a righteous judgment at God's command! You have help enough for the purpose [Wisd. Sol. 6], for Christ is your Master [Matt. 23:8]. Therefore let not the evildoers live longer who make us turn away from God [Deut. 13:5]. For the godless person has no right to live when he is in the way of the pious. In Ex. 22:18 God says: Thou shalt not suffer evildoers* to live. Saint Paul also means this where he says of the sword of rulers that is bestowed upon them for the retribution of the wicked as protection for the pious [Rom. 13:4]. . . . the sword is necessary to wipe out the godless [Rom. 13:4]. That this might now take place, however, in an orderly and proper fashion, our cherished fathers, the princes, should do it, who with us confess Christ. If, however, they do not do it, the sword will be taken from them [Dan. 7:26 f.] For they confess him all right with words and deny him with the deed [Titus 1:16].

From the "Sermon before the Princes by Thomas Müntzer," in *Spiritual and Anabaptist Writers*, The Library of Christian Classics, vol. 25, edited by George H. Williams and Angel M. Mergal (Philadelphia: Westminster/John Knox Press), pp. 49, 50, 54, 65–68. First published MCMLVII.

27. The Schleitheim Confession of Faith

The Schleitheim Confession (written in 1527) formulated the theological and ethical concerns of that segment of the radical, Anabaptist reformation that produced and influenced the later Mennonite and Baptist traditions. In the confession, emphasis is placed on the clear distinction between behavior appropriate to the world and behavior appropriate to the church—which is entered only through adult baptism. The principal author of the confession was probably Michael Sattler.

Dear brethren and sisters, we who have been assembled in the Lord at Schleitheim on the Border, make known in points and articles to all who love God that as concerns us we are of one mind to abide in the Lord as God's obedient children, [His] sons and daughters, we who have been and shall be separated from the world in everything [and] completely at peace. . . .

A very great offense has been introduced by certain false brethren among us, so that some have turned aside from the faith, in the way they intend to practice and observe the freedom of the Spirit and of Christ. But such have missed the truth and to their condemnation are given over to the lasciviousness and self-indulgence of the flesh. They think faith and love may do and permit everything and nothing will harm them nor condemn them, since they are believers. . . .

The articles which we discussed and on which we were of one mind are these[:] 1. Baptism; 2. The Ban [Excommunication]; 3. Breaking of Bread; 4. Separation from the Abomination; 5. Pastors in the Church; 6. The Sword; and 7. The Oath.

*The Vulgate has *maleficos* for the modern rendering "witch" or "sorceress."

First. Observe concerning baptism: Baptism shall be given to all those who have learned repentance and amendment of life, and who believe truly that their sins are taken away by Christ, and to all those who walk in the resurrection of Jesus Christ, and wish to be buried with Him in death, so that they may be resurrected with Him, and to all those who with this significance request it [baptism] of us and demand it for themselves. This excludes all infant baptism, the highest and chief abomination of the pope. . . .

Second. We are agreed as follows on the ban: The ban shall be employed with all those who have given themselves to the Lord, to walk in His commandments, and with all those who are baptized into the one body of Christ and who are called brethren or sisters, and yet who slip sometimes and fall into error and sin, being inadvertently overtaken. The same shall be admonished twice in secret and the third time openly disciplined or banned according to the command of Christ [Matt. 18]. But this shall be done according to the regulation of the Spirit [Matt. 5] before the breaking of bread, so that we may break and eat one bread, with one mind and in one love, and may drink of one cup.

Third. In the breaking of bread we are of one mind and are agreed [as follows]: All those who wish to break one bread in remembrance of the broken body of Christ, and all who wish to drink of one drink as a remembrance of the shed blood of Christ, shall be united beforehand by baptism in one body of Christ which is the church of God and whose Head is Christ. For as Paul points out we cannot at the same time be partakers of the Lord's table and the table of devils; we cannot at the same time drink the cup of the Lord and the cup of the devil. That is, all those who have fellowship with the dead works of darkness have no part in the light. Therefore all who follow the devil and the world have no part with those who are called unto God out of the world. . . .

Fourth. We are agreed [as follows] on separation: A separation shall be made from the evil and from the wickedness which the devil planted in the world; in this manner, simply that we shall not have fellowship with them [the wicked] and not run with them in the multitude of their abominations. . . .

From all this we should learn that everything which is not united with our God and Christ cannot be other than an abomination which we should shun and flee from. By this is meant all popish and antipopish works and church services, meetings and church attendance, drinking houses, civic affairs, the commitments [made in] unbelief and other things of that kind, which are highly regarded by the world and yet are carried on in flat contradiction to the command of God, in accordance with all the unrighteousness which is in the world. From all these things we shall be separated and have no part with them for they are nothing but an abomination, and they are the cause of our being hated before our Christ Jesus. Who has set us free from the slavery of the flesh and fitted us for the service of God through the Spirit Whom He has given us.

Therefore there will also unquestionably fall from us the unchristian, devilish weapons of force—such as sword, armor and the like, and all their use [either] for friends or against one's enemies—by virtue of the word of Christ, Resist not [him that is] evil.

Fifth. We are agreed as follows on pastors in the church of God: The pastor in the church of God shall, as Paul has prescribed, be one who out-and-out has a good report of those who are outside the faith. . . .

This one moreover shall be supported of the church which has chosen him, wherein he may be in need, so that he who serves the Gospel may live of the Gospel as the Lord has ordained. . . .

Sixth. We are agreed as follows concerning the sword: The sword is ordained of God outside the perfection of Christ. It punishes and puts to death the wicked, and guards and protects the good. In the Law the sword was ordained for the punishment of the wicked and for their death, and the same [sword] is [now] ordained to be used by the wordly magistrates.

In the perfection of Christ, however, only the ban is used for a warning and for the excommunication of the one who has sinned, without putting the flesh to death,—simply the warning and the command to sin no more.

Now it will be asked by many who do not recognize [this as] the will of Christ for us, whether a Christian may or should employ the sword against the wicked for the defense and protection of the good, or for the sake of love.

Our reply is unanimously as follows: Christ teaches and commands us to learn of Him, for He is meek and lowly in heart and so shall we find rest to our souls. Also Christ says to the heathenish woman who was taken in adultery, not that one should stone her according to the law of His Father (and yet He says, As the Father has commanded me, thus I do), but in mercy and forgiveness and warning, to sin no more. Such [an attitude] we also ought to take completely according to the rule of the ban.

Secondly, it will be asked concerning the sword, whether a Christian shall pass sentence in worldly dispute and strife such as unbelievers have with one another. This is our united answer: Christ did not wish to decide or pass judgment between brother and brother in the case of the inheritance, but refused to do so. Therefore we should do likewise.

Thirdly, it will be asked concerning the sword, Shall one be a magistrate if one should be chosen as such? The answer is as follows: They wished to make Christ king, but He fled and did not view it as the arrangement of His Father. Thus shall we do as He did, and follow Him, and so shall we not walk in darkness. For He Himself says, He who wishes to come after me, let him deny himself and take up his cross and follow me. Also, He Himself forbids the [employment of] the force of the sword saying, The worldly princes lord it over them, etc., but not so shall it be with you. Further, Paul says, Whom God did foreknow He also did predestinate to be conformed to the image of His Son, etc. Also Peter says, Christ has suffered (not ruled) and left us an example, that ye should follow His steps.

Finally it will be observed that it is not appropriate for a Christian to serve as a magistrate because of these points: The government magistracy is according to the flesh, but the Christians' is according to the Spirit; their houses and dwelling remain in this world, but the Christians' are in heaven; their citizenship is in this world, but the Christians' citizenship is in heaven; the weapons of their conflict and war are carnal and against the flesh only, but the Christians' weapons are spiritual, against the fortification of the devil. The worldlings are armed with steel and iron, but the Christians are armed with the armor of God, with truth, righteousness, peace, faith, salvation and the Word of God. In brief, as is the mind of Christ toward us, so shall the mind of the members of the body of Christ be through Him in all things, that there may be no schism in the body through which it would be destroyed. For every kingdom divided against itself will be destroyed. Now since Christ is as it is written of Him, His members must also be the same, that His body may remain complete and united to its own advancement and upbuilding.

Seventh. We are agreed as follows concerning the oath: The oath is a confirmation among those who are quarreling or making promises. In the Law it is commanded to be performed in God's Name, but only in truth, not falsely. Christ, who teaches the perfection of the Law, prohibits all swearing to His [followers], whether true or false,—neither by heaven, nor by the earth, nor by Jerusalem, nor by our head,—and that for the reason which He shortly thereafter gives. For you are not able to make one hair white or black. So you see it is for this reason that all swearing is forbidden: we cannot fulfill that which we promise when we swear, for we cannot change [even] the very least thing on us.

From J. C. Wenger, ed. "Brotherly Union of a Number of Children of God concerning Seven Articles," *The Mennonite Quarterly Review,* 19, no. 4 (October 1947):247–51.

28: John Calvin,
The Institutes of the Christian Religion

Calvin (1509–1564) wrote many editions of the Institutes, *his final one in 1559. In these passages from Books 2, 3, and 4, Calvin speaks about the positive obligations of the moral law in the life of the believer (the so-called third use of the law), the vocation of the Christian, and the attitude that the Christian should take toward the state.*

Book 2

Chapter 7. ¶6. . . . [L]et us survey briefly the function and use of what is called the "moral law." Now, so far as I understand it, it consists of three parts.

The first part is this: while it shows God's righteousness, that is, the righteousness alone acceptable to God, it warns, informs, convicts, and lastly condemns, every man of his own unrighteousness. For man, blinded and drunk with self-love, must be compelled to know and to confess his own feebleness and impurity. . . .

7. . . . The law is like a mirror. In it we contemplate our weakness, then the iniquity arising from this, and finally the curse coming from both—just as a mirror shows us the spots on our face. . . .

10. . . . The second function of the law is this: at least by fear of punishment to restrain certain men who are untouched by any care for what is just and right unless compelled by hearing the dire threats in the law. But they are restrained, not because their inner mind is stirred or affected, but because, being bridled, so to speak, they keep their hands from outward activity, and hold inside the depravity that otherwise they would wantonly have indulged. Consequently, they are neither better nor more righteous before God. Hindered by fright or shame, they dare neither execute what they have conceived in their minds, nor openly breathe forth the rage of their lust. Still, they do not have hearts disposed to fear and obedience toward God. Indeed, the more they restrain themselves, the more strongly are they inflamed; they burn and boil within, and are ready to do anything or burst forth anywhere—but for the fact that this dread of the law hinders them. . . .

But this constrained and forced righteousness is necessary for the public community of men, for whose tranquillity the Lord herein provided when he took care that everything be not tumultuously confounded. This would happen if everything were permitted to all men. Nay, even for the children of God, before they are called and while they are destitute of the Spirit of sanctification, so long as they play the wanton in the folly of the flesh, it is profitable for them to undergo this tutelage. . . .

12. . . . The third and principal use, which pertains more closely to the proper purpose of the law, finds its place among believers in whose hearts the Spirit of God already lives and reigns. For even though they have the law written and engraved upon their hearts by the finger of God, that is, have been so moved and quickened through the directing of the Spirit that they long to obey God, they still profit by the law in two ways.

Here is the best instrument for them to learn more thoroughly each day the nature of the Lord's will to which they aspire, and to conform them in the understanding of it. It is as if some servant, already prepared with all earnestness of heart to commend himself to his master, must search out and observe his master's ways more carefully in order to conform and accommodate himself to them. And not one of us may escape from this necessity. For no man has heretofore attained to such wisdom as to be unable, from the daily instruction of the law, to make fresh progress toward a purer knowledge of the divine will.

Again, because we need not only teaching but also exhortation, the servant of God will also avail himself of this benefit of the law: by frequent meditation upon it to be aroused to obedience, be strengthened in it, and be drawn back from the slippery path of transgression. In this way the saints must press on; for, however eagerly they may in accordance with the Spirit strive toward God's righteousness, the listless flesh always so burdens them that they do not proceed with due readiness. A law is to the flesh like a whip to an idle and balky ass, to arouse it to work. Even for a spiritual man not yet free of the weight of the flesh the law remains a constant sting that will not let him stand still. . . .

Chapter 8. ¶5. . . . Now it will not be difficult to decide the purpose of the whole law: the fulfillment of righteousness to form human life to the archetype of divine purity. For God has so depicted his character in the law that if any man carries out in deeds whatever is enjoined there, he will express the image of God, as it were, in his own life. For this reason, Moses, wishing to remind the Israelites of the gist of the law, said: "And now, Israel, what does the Lord your God require of you, but to fear the Lord . . . , to walk in his ways, to love him, to serve him with all your heart and with all your soul, and to keep his commandments?" [Deut. 10:12–13]. And Moses did not cease to harp on this same thought to them whenever he had to point out the arm of the law. Here is the object of the teaching of the law: to join man by holiness of life to his God, and, as Moses elsewhere says, to make him cleave to God [cf. Deut. 11:22 or 30:20].

Now the perfection of that holiness comes under the two headings already mentioned: "That we should love the Lord God with all our heart, with all our soul, and with all our strength" [Deut 6:5], "and our neighbor as ourselves" [Lev. 19:18]. First, indeed, our soul should be entirely filled with the love of God. From this will flow directly the love of neighbor. This is what the apostle shows when he writes that "the aim of the law is love from a pure conscience and a faith unfeigned" [1 Tim. 1:5 f.]. You see how conscience and sincere faith are put at the head. In other words, here is true piety, from which love is derived.

It would, therefore, be a mistake for anyone to believe that the law teaches nothing but some rudiments and preliminaries of righteousness by which men begin their apprenticeship, and does not also guide them to the true goal, good works, since you cannot desire a greater perfection than that expressed in the statements of Moses and Paul. For whither, I submit, will any man wish to go who will not be content to be taught to fear God, to worship spiritually, to obey the commandments, to follow the Lord's upright way, and lastly, to have a pure conscience, sincere faith, and love? From this is confirmed that interpretation of the law which seeks and finds in the commandments of the law all the duties of piety and love. For those who follow only dry and bare rudiments—as if the law taught them only half of God's will—do not at all understand its purpose, as the apostle testifies. . . .

53. . . . But you will ask: "Does the essence of righteousness lie more in living innocently with men than in honoring God with piety?" Not at all! But because a man does not easily maintain love in all respects unless he earnestly fears God, here is proof also of his piety. Besides, since the Lord well knows, and also attests through his prophets, that no benefit can come from us to him, he does not confine our duties to himself, but he exercises us "in good works toward our neighbor." The apostle consequently has good reason to place the whole perfection of the saints in love [Eph. 3:19; 1:5; Col. 3:14]. Elsewhere he quite rightly calls it the "fulfillment of the law," adding that "he who loves his neighbor has fulfilled the law" [Rom. 13:8]. Again, "The whole law is comprehended in one word, 'Love your neighbor as yourself.'" [Gal. 5:14 f.] Paul teaches only what Christ himself teaches when he says: "Whatever you wish that men would do to you, do so to them; for this is the law and the prophets" [Matt. 7:12]. It is certain that the Law and the Prophets give first place to faith and whatever pertains to the lawful worship of God, relegating love to a subordinate position. But the Lord means that the law only enjoins us to observe right and equity toward men, that thereby we may become practiced in witnessing to a pious fear of men, if we have any of it in us.

54. . . . Here, therefore, let us stand fast: our life shall best conform to God's will and the prescription of the law when it is in every respect most fruitful for our brethren. . . .

55. . . . Now, since Christ has shown in the parable of the Samaritan that the term "neighbor" includes even the most remote person [Luke 10:36], we are not expected to limit the precept of love to those in close relationships. I do not deny that the more closely a man is linked to us, the more intimate obligation we have to assist him. It is the common habit of mankind that the more closely men are bound together by the ties of kinship, of acquaintanceship, or of neighborhood, the more responsibilities for one another they share. This does not offend God; for his providence, as it were, leads us to it. But I say: we ought to embrace the whole human race without exception in a single feeling of love; here there is no distinction between barbarian and Greek, worthy and unworthy, friend and enemy, since all should be contemplated in God, not in themselves. When we turn aside from such contemplation, it is no wonder we become entangled in many errors. Therefore, if we rightly direct our love, we must first turn our eyes not to man, the sight of whom would more often engender hate than love, but to God, who bids us extend to all men the love we bear to him, that this may be an unchanging principle: whatever the character of the man, we must yet love him because we love God. . . .

Book 3

Chapter 10. ¶4. . . . [T]here is no surer or more direct course than that which we receive from contempt of the present life and meditation upon heavenly immortality. . . . [T]hose who use this world should be so affected as if they did not use it; those who marry, as if they did not marry; those who buy, as if they did not buy, just as Paul enjoins [1 Cor. 7:29–31]. . . . [T]hey should know to bear poverty peaceably and patiently, as well as to bear abundance moderately. He who bids you use this world as if you used it not destroys not only the intemperance of gluttony in food and drink, and excessive indulgence at table, in buildings and clothing, ambition, pride, arrogance, and overfastidiousness, but also all care and inclination that either diverts or hinders you from thought of the heavenly life and zeal to cultivate the soul. Long ago Cato truly said: "There is great care about dress, but great carelessness about virtue." To use the old proverb: those who are much occupied with the care of the body are for the most part careless about their own souls.

Therefore, even though the freedom of believers in external matters is not to be restricted to a fixed formula, yet it is surely subject to this law: to indulge oneself as little as possible; but, on the contrary, with unflagging effort to mind to insist upon cutting off all show of superfluous wealth, not to mention licentiousness, and diligently to guard against turning helps into hindrances.

5. . . . . [T]hey who have narrow and slender resources should know how to go without things patiently, lest they be troubled by an immoderate desire for them. If they keep this rule of moderation, they will make considerable progress in the Lord's school. So, too, they who have not progressed, in some degree at least, in this respect have scarcely anything to prove them disciples of Christ. For besides the fact that most other vices accompany the desire for earthly things, he who bears poverty impatiently also when in prosperity commonly betrays the contrary disease. This is my point: he who is ashamed of mean clothing will boast of costly clothing; he who, not content with a slender meal, is troubled by the desire for a more elegant one, will also intemperately abuse those elegances if they fall to his lot. He who will bear reluctantly, and with a troubled mind, his deprivation and humble condition if he be advanced to honors will by no means abstain from arrogance. To this end, then, let all those for whom the pursuit of piety is not a pretense strive to learn, by the Apostle's example, how to be filled and to hunger, to abound and to suffer want [Phil. 4:12].

. . . Scripture. . . .decrees that all those things were so given to us by the kindness of God, and so destined for our benefit, that they are, as it were, entrusted to us, and we must one day render account of them. Thus, therefore, we must so arrange it that this saying may continually resound in our ears: "Render account of your stewardship" [Luke 16:2]. At the same time let us remember by whom such reckoning is required: namely, him who has greatly commended abstinence, sobriety, frugality, and moderation, and has also abominated excess, pride, ostentation, and vanity; who approves no other distribution of good things than one joined with love; who has already condemned with his own lips all delights that draw man's spirit away from chastity and purity, or befog his mind.

6. . . . . Finally, this point is to be noted: the Lord bids each one of us in all life's actions to look to his calling. For he knows with what great restlessness human nature flames, with what fickleness it is borne hither and thither, how its ambition longs to embrace various things at once. Therefore, lest through our stupidity and rashness everything be turned topsy-turvy, he has appointed duties for every man in his particular way of life. And that no one may thoughtlessly transgress his limits, he has named these various kinds of living "callings." Therefore, each individual has his own kind of living assigned to him by the Lord as a sort of sentry post so that he may not heedlessly wander about throughout life. Now, so necessary is this distinction that all our actions are judged in his sight by it, often indeed far otherwise than in the judgment of human and philosophical reason. No deed is considered more noble, even among philosophers, than to free one's country from tyranny. Yet a private citizen who lays his hand upon a tyrant is openly condemned by the heavenly judge [1 Sam. 24:7, 11; 26:9].

But I will not delay to list examples. It is enough if we know that the

Lord's calling is in everything the beginning and foundation of well-doing. And if there is anyone who will not direct himself to it, he will never hold to the straight path in his duties. Perhaps, sometimes, he could contrive something laudable in appearance; but whatever it may be in the eyes of men, it will be rejected before God's throne. Besides, there will be no harmony among the several parts of his life. Accordingly, your life will then be best ordered when it is directed to this goal. For no one, impelled by his own rashness, will attempt more than his calling will permit, because he will know that it is not lawful to exceed its bounds. A man of obscure station will lead a private life ungrudgingly so as not to leave the rank in which he has been placed by God. Again, it will be no slight relief from cares, labors, troubles, and other burdens for a man to know that God is his guide in all these things. The magistrate will discharge his functions more willingly; the head of the household will confine himself to his duty; each man will bear and swallow the discomforts, vexations, weariness, and anxieties in his way of life, when he has been persuaded that the burden was laid upon him by God. From this will arise also a singular consolation: that no task will be so sordid and base, provided you obey your calling in it, that it will not shine and be reckoned very precious in God's sight. . . .

. . . Paul . . . states both that power is an ordinance of God [Rom. 13:2], and that there are no powers except those ordained by God [Rom. 13:1]. Further, that princes are ministers of God, for those doing good unto praise; for those doing evil, avengers unto wrath [Rom. 13:3–4]. To this may be added the examples of holy men, of whom some possessed kingdoms, as David, Josiah, and Hezekiah; others, lordships, as Joseph and Daniel; others, civil rule among a free people, as Moses, Joshua, and the judges. The Lord has declared his approval of their offices. Accordingly, no one ought to doubt that civil authority is a calling, not only holy and lawful before God, but also the most sacred and by far the most honorable of all callings in the whole life of mortal men. . . .

Book 4

Chapter 20. ¶ 5. . . . Those who desire to usher in anarchy object that, although in antiquity kings and judges ruled over ignorant folk, yet that servile kind of governing is wholly incompatible today with the perfection which Christ brought with his gospel. In this they betray not only their ignorance but devilish arrogance, when they claim a perfection of which not even a hundredth part is seen in them. But whatever kind of men they may be, the refutation is easy. For where David urges all kings and rulers to kiss the Son of God [Ps. 2:12], he does not bid them lay aside their authority and retire to private life, but submit to Christ the power with which they have been invested, that he alone may tower over all. Similarly, Isaiah, when he promises that kings shall be foster fathers of the church, and queens its nurses [Isa. 49:23], does not deprive them of their honor. Rather, by a noble title he makes them defenders of God's pious worshipers; for that prophecy looks to the coming of Christ. I knowingly pass over very many passages which occur frequently, and especially in the psalms, in which the right of rulers is asserted for them all [Pss. 21; 22; 45; 72; 89; 110; 132]. But most notable of all is the passage of Paul where, admonishing Timothy that prayers be offered for kings in public assembly, he immediately adds the reason: "That we may lead a peaceful life under them with all godliness and honesty" [1 Tim. 2:2]. By these words he entrusts the condition of the church to their protection and care.

6. . . .This consideration ought continually to occupy the magistrates themselves, since it can greatly spur them to exercise their office and bring them remarkable comfort to mitigate the difficulties of their task, which are indeed many and burdensome. For what great zeal for uprightness, for prudence, gentleness, self-control, and for innocence ought to be required of themselves by those who know that they have been ordained ministers of divine justice? How will they have the brazenness to admit injustice to their judgment seat, which they are told is the throne of the living God? How will they have the boldness to pronounce an unjust sentence, by that mouth which they know has been appointed an instrument of divine truth? With what conscience will they sign wicked decrees by that hand which they know has been appointed to record the acts of God? To sum up, if they remember that they are vicars of God, they should watch with all care, earnestness, and diligence, to represent in themselves to men some image of divine providence, protection, goodness, benevolence, and justice. And they should perpetually set before themselves the thought that "if all are cursed who carry out in deceit the work of God's vengeance" [Jer. 48:10], much more gravely cursed are they who deceitfully conduct themselves in a righteous calling. . . . This is to hearten them for their task when they learn that they are deputies of God, to whom they must hereafter render account of the administration of their charge. And this admonition deserves to have great weight with them. For if they commit some fault, they are not only wrongdoers to men whom they wickedly trouble, but are also insulting toward God himself, whose most holy judgments they defile. Again, they have the means to comfort themselves greatly when they ponder in themselves that they are occupied not with profane affairs or those alien to a servant of God, but with a most holy office, since they are serving as God's deputies. . . .

7. . . . Those who, unmoved by so many testimonies of Scripture, dare rail against his holy ministry as a thing abhorrent to Christian religion and piety—what else do they do but revile God himself, whose ministry cannot be reproached without dishonor to himself? And these folk do not just reject the magistrates, but cast off God that he may not reign over them. For if the Lord truly said this of the people of Israel because they refused Samuel's rule [1 Sam. 8:7], why will it less truly be said today of these who let themselves rage against all governments ordained by God? The Lord said to his disciples that the kings of the Gentiles exercise lordship over Gentiles, but it is not so among the disciples, where he who is first ought to become the least [Luke 22:25–26]; by this saying, they tell us, all Christians are forbidden to take kingdoms or governments. O skillful interpreters!

There arose a contention among the disciples over which one would excel the others. To silence this vain ambition, the Lord taught them that their ministry is not like kingdoms, in which one is pre-eminent above the rest. What dishonor, I ask you, does this comparison do to kingly dignity? Indeed, what does it prove at all, except that the kingly office is not the ministry of an apostle? Moreover, among magistrates themselves, although there is a variety of forms, there is no difference in this respect, that we must regard all of them as ordained of God. . . .

10. . . . But here a seemingly hard and difficult question arises: if the law of God forbids all Christians to kill [Ex. 20:13; Deut. 5:17; Matt. 5:21], and the prophet prophesies concerning God's holy mountain (the church) that in it men shall not afflict or hurt [Isa. 11:9; 65:25]—how can magistrates be pious men and shedders of blood at the same time?

Yet if we understand that the magistrate in administering punishments does nothing by himself, but carries out the very judgments of God, we shall not be hampered by this scruple. The law of the Lord forbids killing; but, that murders may not go unpunished, the Lawgiver himself puts into the hand of his ministers a sword to be drawn against all murderers. It is not for the pious to afflict and hurt; yet to avenge, at the Lord's command, the afflictions of the pious is not to hurt or to afflict. Would that this were ever before our minds—that nothing is done here from men's rashness, but all things are done on the authority of God who commands it; and while his authority goes before us, we never wander from the straight path! Unless perhaps restraint is laid upon God's justice, that it may not punish misdeeds. But if it is not right to impose any law upon him, why should we try to reproach his ministers? They do not bear the sword in vain, says Paul, for they are ministers of God to execute his wrath, avengers of wrongdoers [Rom. 13:4]. Therefore, if princes and other rulers recognize that nothing is more acceptable to the Lord than their obedience, let them apply themselves to this ministry, if, indeed, they are intent on having their piety, righteousness, and uprightness approved of God [cf. 2. Tim. 2:15]. . . .

. . . Now if their true righteousness is to pursue the guilty and the impious with drawn sword, should they sheathe their sword and keep their hands clean of blood, while abandoned men wickedly range about with slaughter and massacre, they will become guilty of the greatest impiety, far indeed from winning praise for their goodness and righteousness thereby!

Begone, now, with that abrupt and savage harshness, and that tribunal which is rightly called the reef of accused men! For I am not one either to favor undue cruelty or think that a fair judgment can be pronounced unless clemency, that best counselor of kings and surest keeper of the kingly throne (as Solomon declares) [Prov. 20:28] is always present. . . .

Yet it is necessary for the magistrate to pay attention to both, lest by excessive severity he either harm more than heal; or, by superstitious affectation of clemency, fall into the cruelest gentleness, if he should (with a soft and dissolute kindness) abandon many to their destruction. . . .

11. . . . But kings and people must sometimes take up arms to execute such public vengeance. On this basis we may judge wars lawful which are

so undertaken. For if power has been given them to preserve the tranquillity of their dominion, to restrain the seditious stirrings of restless men, to help those forcibly oppressed, to punish evil deeds—can they use it more opportunely than to check the fury of one who disturbs both the repose of private individuals and the common tranquillity of all, who raises seditious tumults, and by whom violent oppressions and vile misdeeds are perpetrated? If they ought to be the guardians and defenders of the laws, they should also overthrow the efforts of all whose offenses corrupt the discipline of the laws. Indeed, if they rightly punish those robbers whose harmful acts have affected only a few, will they allow a whole country to be afflicted and devastated by robberies with impunity? For it makes no difference whether it be a king or the lowest of the common folk who invades a foreign country in which he has no right, and harries it as an enemy. All such must, equally, be considered as robbers and punished accordingly. Therefore, both natural equity and the nature of the office dictate that princes must be armed not only to restrain the misdeeds of private individuals by judicial punishment, but also to defend by war the dominions entrusted to their safekeeping, if at any time they are under enemy attack. . . .

20. . . . We are not in any more disagreement with Christ's words in which he forbids us to resist evil, and commands us to turn the right cheek to him who has struck the left, and to give our cloak to him who has taken away our coat [Matt. 5:39–40]. He indeed wills that the hearts of his people so utterly recoil from any desire to retaliate that they should rather allow double injury to be done them than desire to pay it back. And we are not leading them away from this forbearance. For truly, Christians ought to be a kind of men born to bear slanders and injuries, open to the malice, deceits, and mockeries of wicked men. And not that only, but they ought to bear patiently all these evils. That is, they should have such complete spiritual composure that, having received one offense, they make ready for another, promising themselves throughout life nothing but the bearing of a perpetual cross. Meanwhile, let them also do good to those who do them harm, and bless those who curse them [Luke 6:28; cf. Matt. 5:44], and (this is their only victory) strive to conquer evil with good [Rom. 12:21]. So minded, they will not seek an eye for an eye, a tooth for a tooth, as the Pharisees taught their disciples to desire revenge, but, as we are instructed by Christ, they will so suffer their body to be maimed, and their possessions to be maliciously seized, that they will forgive and voluntarily pardon those wrongs as soon as they have been inflicted upon them [Matt 5:38 ff.].

Yet this equity and moderateness of their minds will not prevent them from using the help of the magistrate in preserving their own possessions, while maintaining friendliness toward their enemies; or zealous for public welfare, from demanding the punishment of a guilty and pestilent man, who, they know, can be changed only by death. . . .

22. . . . The first duty of subjects toward their magistrates is to think most honorably of their office, which they recognize as a jurisdiction bestowed by God, and on that account to esteem and reverence them as ministers and representatives of God. For you may find some who very respectfully yield

themselves to their magistrates and desire somebody whom they can obey, because they know that such is expedient for public welfare; nevertheless, they regard magistrates only as a kind of necessary evil. But Peter requires something more of us when he commands that the king be honored [1 Peter 2:17]; as does Solomon when he teaches that God and king are to be feared [Prov. 24:21]. For Peter, the word "to honor" includes a sincere and candid opinion of the king. Solomon, yoking the king with God, shows that the king is fully of a holy reverence and dignity. There is also that famous saying in Paul: that we should obey "not only because of wrath, but because of conscience" [Rom. 13:5, cf. Vulg.]. By this he means that subjects should be led not by fear alone of princes and rulers to remain in subjection under them (as they commonly yield to an armed enemy who sees that vengeance is promptly taken if they resist), but because they are showing obedience to God himself when they give it to them; since the rulers' power is from God.

I am not discussing the men themselves, as if a mask of dignity covered foolishness, or sloth, or cruelty, as well as wicked morals full of infamous deeds, and thus acquired for vices the praise of virtues; but I say that the order itself is worthy of such honor and reverence that those who are rulers are esteemed among us and receive reverence out of respect for their lordship.

23. . . . From this also something else follows: that, with hearts inclined to reverence their rulers, the subjects should prove their obedience toward them, whether by obeying their proclamations, or by paying taxes, or by undertaking public offices and burdens which pertain to the common defense, or by executing any other commands of theirs. . . .

Let no man deceive himself here. For since the magistrate cannot be resisted without God being resisted at the same time, even though it seems that an unarmed magistrate can be despised with impunity, still God is armed to avenge mightily this contempt toward himself.

Moreover, under this obedience I include the restraint which private citizens ought to bid themselves keep in public, that they may not deliberately intrude in public affairs, or pointlessly invade the magistrate's office, or undertake anything at all politically. If anything in a public ordinance requires amendment, let them not raise a tumult, or put their hands to the task—all of them ought to keep their hands bound in this respect—but let them commit the matter to the judgment of the magistrate, whose hand alone here is free. I mean, let them not venture on anything without a command. For when the ruler gives his command, private citizens receive public authority. . . .

25. . . . But if we look to God's Word, it will lead us farther. We are not only subject to the authority of princes who perform their office toward us uprightly and faithfully as they ought, but also to the authority of all who, by whatever means, have got control of affairs, even though they perform not a whit of the princes' office. For despite the Lord's testimony that the magistrate's office is the highest gift of his beneficence to preserve the safety of men, and despite his appointment of bounds to the magistrates—he still declares at the same time that whoever they may be, they have their authority solely from him. Indeed, he says that those who rule for the public

benefit are true patterns and evidences of this beneficence of his; that they who rule unjustly and incompetently have been raised up by him to punish the wickedness of the people; that all equally have been endowed with that holy majesty with which he has invested lawful power. . . .

. . . . In a very wicked man utterly unworthy of all honor, provided he has the public power in his hands, that noble and divine power resides which the Lord has by his Word given to the ministers of his justice and judgment. Accordingly, he should be held in the same reverence and esteem by his subjects, in so far as public obedience is concerned, in which they would hold the best of kings if he were given to them. . . .

29. . . . We owe this attitude of reverence and therefore of piety toward all our rulers in the highest degree, whatever they may be like. I therefore the more often repeat this: that we should learn not to examine the men themselves, but take it as enough that they bear, by the Lord's will, a character upon which he has imprinted and engraved an inviolable majesty.

But (you will say) rulers owe responsibilities in turn to their subjects. This I have already admitted. But if you conclude from this that service ought to be rendered only to just governors, you are reasoning foolishly. For husbands are also bound to their wives, and parents to their children, by mutual responsibilities. Suppose parents and husbands depart from their duty. Suppose parents show themselves so hard and intractable to their children, whom they are forbidden to provoke to anger [Eph. 6:4], that by their rigor they tire them beyond measure. Suppose husbands most despitefully use their wives, whom they are commanded to love [Eph. 5:25] and to spare as weaker vessels [1 Peter 3:7]. Shall either children be less obedient to their parents or wives to their husbands? They are still subject even to those who are wicked and undutiful.

Indeed, all ought to try not to "look at the bag hanging from their back," that is, not to inquire about another's duties, but every man should keep in mind that one duty which is his own. This ought particularly to apply to those who have been put under the power of others. Therefore, if we are cruelly tormented by a savage prince, if we are greedily despoiled by one who is avaricious or wanton, if we are neglected by a slothful one, if finally we are vexed for piety's sake by one who is impious and sacrilegious, let us first be mindful of our own misdeeds, which without doubt are chastised by such whips of the Lord. . . .

30. . . . Here are revealed his goodness, his power, and his providence. For sometimes he raises up open avengers from among his servants, and arms them with his command to punish the wicked government and deliver his people, oppressed in unjust ways, from miserable calamity. Sometimes he directs to this end the rage of men with other intentions and other endeavors. . .

For the first kind of men, when they had been sent by God's lawful calling to carry out such acts, in taking up arms against kings, did not at all violate that majesty which is implanted in kings by God's ordination; but, armed from heaven, they subdued the lesser power with the greater, just as it is lawful for kings to punish their subordinates. But the latter kind of men, although they were directed by God's hand whither he pleased, and executed his work unwittingly, yet planned in their minds to do nothing but an evil act.

32. . . . But in that obedience which we have shown to be due the authority of rulers, we are always to make this exception, indeed, to observe it as primary, that such obedience is never to lead us away from obedience to him, to whose will the desires of all kings ought to be subject, to whose decrees all their commands ought to yield, to whose majesty their scepters ought to be submitted. And how absurd would it be that in satisfying men you should incur the displeasure of him for whose sake you obey men themselves! The Lord, therefore, is the King of Kings, who, when he has opened his sacred mouth, must alone be heard, before all and above all men; next to him we are subject to those men who are in authority over us, but only in him. If they command anything against him, let it go unesteemed. And here let us not be concerned about all that dignity which the magistrates possess; for no harm is done to it when it is humbled before that singular and truly supreme power of God. . . . But since this edict has been proclaimed by the heavenly herald, Peter—"We must obey God rather than men" [Acts 5:29]—let us comfort ourselves with the thought that we are rendering that obedience which the Lord requires when we suffer anything rather than turn aside from piety. And that our courage may not grow faint, Paul pricks us with another goad: That we have been redeemed by Christ at so great a price as our redemption cost him, so that we should not enslave ourselves to the wicked desires of men—much less be subject to their impiety.

From *Calvin: Institutes of the Christian Religion,* The Library of Christian Classics, vol. 20, edited by John T. McNeill and translated by Ford Lewis Battles (Philadelphia: The Westminster Press), pp. 354–61, 415–19, 722–25, 1490–99, 1508–20. Copyright © MCMLX W. L. Jenkins. Published simultaneously by The Westminster Press, Philadelphia, and SCM Press, Ltd., London. Used by permission of the publishers.

29.   Teresa of Ávila,
The Interior Castle

The Interior Castle, *written in 1577, was designed as a guide to spiritual development through prayer and service. For Teresa (1515–1582), the advanced forms of contemplative union with God were not antithetical to charity and service, but were their counterpart. Her original readers were women whose lives were circumscribed by cloister or by family responsibilities, but her teaching—that the works of charity are to be evaluated not by their size but by their love—is applicable to persons in many settings.*

Chapter 5. ¶9. The diligence on our part that comes to my mind as being the most effective is the following. First, we must always ask God in prayer to sustain us, and very often think that if He abandons us we will soon end in the abyss, as is true; and we must never trust in ourselves since it would be foolish to do so. Then, we should walk with special care and attention, observing how we are proceeding in the practice of virtue: whether we are getting better or worse in some areas, especially in love for one another, in the desire to be considered the least among the Sisters, and in the performance of ordinary tasks. For if we look out for these things and ask the Lord to enlighten us, we will soon see the gain or the loss. Don't think that a soul that comes so close to God is allowed to lose Him so quickly, that the devil has an easy task. His Majesty would regret the loss of this soul so much that He gives it in many ways a thousand interior warnings, so that the harm will not be hidden from it.

10. Let this, in sum, be the conclusion: that we strive always to advance. And if we don't advance, let us walk with great fear. Without doubt the devil wants to cause some lapse, for it is not possible that after having come so far, one will fail to grow. Love is never idle, and a failure to grow would be a very bad sign. A soul that has tried to be the betrothed of God Himself, that is now intimate with His Majesty . . . must not go to sleep. . . .

12. This is what I want us to strive for, my Sisters; and let us desire and be occupied in prayer not for the sake of our enjoyment but so as to have this strength to serve. Let's refuse to take an unfamiliar path, for we shall get lost at the most opportune time. It would indeed be novel to think of having these favors from God through a path other than the one He took and the one followed by all His saints. May the thought never enter our minds. Believe me, Martha and Mary must join together in order to show hospitality to the Lord and have Him always present and not host Him badly by failing to give Him something to eat. How would Mary, always seated at His feet, provide Him with food if her sister did not help her? His food is that in every way possible we draw souls that they may be saved and praise Him always.

13. You will make two objections: one, that He said that Mary had chosen the better part. The answer is that she had already performed the task of Martha. . . . You see she wasn't always in the delight of contemplation at the feet of the Lord.

Chapter 7. ¶14. . . . The other objection you will make is that you are unable to bring souls to God, that you do not have the means; that you would do it willingly but that not being teachers or preachers as were the apostles, you do not know how. . . . sometimes the devil gives us great desires so that we will avoid setting ourselves to the task at hand, serving our Lord in possible things, and instead be content with having desired the impossible. Apart from the fact that by prayer you will be helping greatly, you need not be desiring to benefit the whole world but must concentrate on those who are in your company, and thus your deed will be greater since you are more obliged toward them. Do you think such deep humility, your mortification, service of all and great charity toward them, and love of the Lord is of little benefit? This fire of love in you enkindles their souls, and with every other virtue you will be always awakening them. Such service will not be small but very great and very pleasing to the Lord. By what you do in deed—that which you can—His Majesty will understand that you would do much more. Thus He will give you the reward He would if you had gained many souls for Him. . . .

15. . . . In sum, my Sisters, what I conclude with is that we shouldn't build castles in the air. The Lord doesn't look so much at the greatness of our works as at the love with which they are done. And if we do what we can, His Majesty will enable us each day to do more and more, provided that we do not quickly tire. But during the little while this life lasts—and perhaps it will last a shorter time than each one thinks—let us offer the Lord interiorly and exteriorly the sacrifice we can. His Majesty will join it with that which He offered on the cross to the Father for us. Thus even though our works are small they will have the value our love for Him would have merited had they been great.

Translated by Kiernan Kavanaugh Otilio Rodriguez. From the "Interior Castle," in *The Collected Works of St. Teresa of Ávila*, vols. 1 and 2 (Washington, D.C.: The Institute of Carmelite Studies Publications, 1980), pp. 357–58, 448–50. Copyright 1976, 1980 by Washington Province of Discalced Carmelites, ICS Publications, 2131 Lincoln Road, N.E., Washington, D.C. 20002 USA.

30. Francisco de Suárez, *A Work on the Three Theological Virtues: Faith, Hope, and Charity*

In this treatise, the eminent Spanish Jesuit theologian and social philosopher Francisco de Suárez (1548–1617) defended and advanced the Augustinian concept of "just war."

Disputation 13

Section 1. *Is War Intrinsically Evil?* The first heresy consists in the assertion that it is intrinsically evil and contrary to charity to wage war. . . . The second error is the assertion that war is specifically forbidden to Christians, and especially, war against Christians. . . . The conclusions that follow will elucidate the matter. . . .

Our first conclusion is that war, absolutely speaking, is not intrinsically evil, nor is it forbidden to Christians. This conclusion is a matter of faith and is laid down in the Scriptures, for in the Old Testament, wars waged by most holy men are praised [Gen. 14:19, 20]: 'Blessed be Abram. . . . And blessed be God by whose protection the enemies are in thy hands.' We find similar passages concerning Moses, Josue, Samson, Gedeon, David, the Machabees, and others, whom God often ordered to wage war upon the enemies of the Hebrews. Moreover, the apostle Paul [Heb. 11:33] said that by faith the saints conquered kingdoms. . . .

157

However, one may object, in the first place, that the Lord said to David: 'Thou shalt not build my temple because thou art a man who has shed blood.'

Secondly, it will be objected that Christ said to Peter [John 18:11]: 'Put up thy sword into the scabbard,' &c.; and that Isaias also said [Isa. 2:4]: 'They shall turn their swords into ploughshares . . . neither shall they be exercised any more to war'; and, in another Chapter [11:9]: 'They shall not hurt nor shall they kill in all [my] holy mountain.' The Prophet is speaking, indeed, of the time of the coming of the Messiah, at which time, especially, it will be made clear, what is permissible and what is not permissible.

Thirdly, at the council of Nicaea [chap. 11], a penalty was imposed upon Christians who, after having received the faith, enrolled themselves for military service. Furthermore, Pope Leo (*Letters* [92]) wrote that war was forbidden to Christians, after a solemn penance.

Fourthly, war morally brings with it innumerable sins; and a given course of action is considered in itself evil and forbidden, if it is practically always accompanied by unseemly circumstances and harm to one's neighbours. One may add that war is opposed to peace, to the love of one's enemies, and to the forgiveness of injuries. . . .

The Council of Nicaea, indeed, dealt especially with those Christians who, for a second time, were assuming the uniforms of pagan soldiers which they had once cast off. And Pope Leo . . . was speaking of those Christians who, after a public penance had been imposed upon them, were returning to war, before the penance had been completed. Furthermore, it may have been expedient for the early Church to forbid those who had recently been converted to the faith to engage in military service immediately, in company with unbelievers, and under pagan officers.

To the argument drawn from reason, Augustine replies (*On the City of God*, Bk. [19:7]) that he deems it advisable to avoid war in so far as is possible, and to undertake it only in cases of extreme necessity, when no alternative remains; but he also holds that war is not entirely evil, since the fact that evils follow upon war is incidental, and since greater evils would result if war were never allowed.

Wherefore, in reply to the confirmation of the argument in question one may deny that war is opposed to an honourable peace; rather, it is opposed to an unjust peace, for it is more truly a means of attaining peace that is real and secure. Similarly, war is not opposed to the love of one's enemies; for whoever wages war honourably hates, not individuals, but the actions which he justly punishes. And the same reasoning is true of the forgiveness of injuries, especially since this forgiveness is not enjoined under every circumstance, for punishment may sometimes be exacted, by legitimate means, without injustice.

Secondly, I hold that defensive war not only is permitted, but sometimes is even commanded. The first part of this proposition follows from the first conclusion, which even the Doctors cited above accept; and it holds true not only for public officials, but also for private individuals, since all laws allow the repelling of force with force. . . .The reason supporting it is that the right of self-defence is natural and necessary. Whence the second part of our second proposition is easily proved. For self-defence may sometimes be prescribed, at least in accordance with the order of charity; a fact which I have elsewhere pointed out. . . . The same is true of the defence of the state, especially if such defence is an official duty. . . .

My third conclusion is, that even when war is aggressive, it is not an evil in itself, but may be right and necessary. . . .

The reason supporting our third conclusion is that such a war is often necessary to a state, in order to ward off acts of injustice and to hold enemies in check. Nor would it be possible, without these wars, for states to be maintained in peace. Hence, this kind of warfare is allowed by natural law; and even by the law of the Gospel, which derogates in no way from natural law, and contains no new divine commands save those regarding faith and the Sacraments. The statement of Luther that it is not lawful to resist the punishment of God is indeed ridiculous; for God does not will the evils but merely permits them; and therefore He does not forbid that they should be justly repelled.

It remains for us to explain what constitutes an aggressive war, and what, on the other hand, constitutes a defensive war; for sometimes that which is merely an act of defence may present the appearance of an aggressive act. Thus, for example, if enemies seize the houses or the property of others, but have themselves suffered invasion from the latter, that is no aggression but defence. To this extent, civil laws are . . . justified in conscience also, when they provide that if any one tries to dispossess me of my property, it is lawful for me to repel force with force. For such an act is not aggression, but defence, and may be lawfully undertaken even on one's own authority. The laws in question are extended to apply to him who, while absent, has been ejected from a tenure which they call a natural one, and who, upon his return, is prevented from recovering that tenure. For . . . any one who has been despoiled may, even on his own authority, have recourse to arms, because such an act is not really aggression, but a defence of one's legal possession. . . .

Consequently, we have to consider whether the injustice is, practically speaking, simply about to take place; or whether it has already done so, and redress is sought through war. In this second case, the war is aggressive. In the former case, war has the character of self-defence, provided that it is waged with a moderation of defence which is blameless. Now, the injury is considered as beginning, when the unjust act itself, even physically regarded, is beginning; as when a man has not been entirely deprived of his rightful possession; or even when he has been so deprived, but immediately—that is, without noteworthy delay—attempts to defend himself and to reinstate himself in possession. The reason for this is as follows: When any one is, to all intents and purposes, in the very act of resisting, and attempts—in so far as is possible—to protect his right, he is not considered as having, in an absolute sense, suffered wrong, nor as having been deprived of his possession. . . .

Our fourth proposition is this: in order that a war may be justly waged, a number of conditions must be observed, which may be grouped under three heads. First, the war must be waged by a legitimate power; secondly, the cause itself and the reason must be just; thirdly, the method of its conduct must be proper, and due proportion must be observed at its beginning, during its prosecution and after victory. . . . The underlying principle of this general conclusion, indeed, is that, while a war is not in itself evil, nevertheless, on account of the many misfortunes which it brings in its train, it is one of those undertakings that are often carried on in evil fashion; and that therefore, it requires many [justifying] circumstances to make it righteous.

From *Selections from Three Works of Francisco Suárez, S.J.*, vol. 2, translated by Gwladys L. Williams, Ammi Brown, and John Waldron (Oxford, London: Clarendon Press, 1944), pp. 800–805.

31. William Penn, *Fruits of Solitude*

The "historical testimonies" of Friends (also known as the Quakers) have traditionally included commitments to peace, simplicity of lifestyle, truth-telling, equality, and community. These precepts might be described both as spiritual disciplines and as ethical principles. As in these examples from Fruits of Solitude, *written in 1693 by William Penn (1644–1718), authority for the precepts is usually drawn more from lived experience than from scriptural analysis.*

Pride

18. And yet we are very apt to be full of our selves, instead of Him that made what we so much value; and, but for whom we can have no Reason to value our selves. For we have nothing that we can call our own; no, not our selves: For we are all but Tenants, and at Will too, of the great Lord of our selves, and the rest of this great Farm, the World that we live upon.

19. But methinks we cannot answer it to our Selves as well as our Maker, that we should live and die ignorant of our Selves, and thereby of Him and the Obligations we are under to Him for our Selves. . . .

Luxury

28. Such is now become our Delicacy, that we will not eat ordinary Meat, nor drink small, pall'd Liquor; we must have the best, and the best cook'd for our Bodies, while our Souls feed on empty or corrupted Things. . . .

Frugality or Bounty

50. Frugality is good if Liberality be join'd with it. The first is leaving off superfluous Expences; the last bestowing them to the Benefit of others that need. The first without the last begins Covetousness; the last without the first begins Prodigality: Both together make an excellent Temper. Happy the Place where ever that is found.

51. Were it universal, we should be Cur'd of two Extreams, Want and Excess: and the one would supply the other, and so bring both nearer to a Mean; the just Degree of earthly Happiness.

52. It is a Reproach to Religion and Government to suffer so much Poverty and Excess. . . .

Discipline

55. If though wouldst be happy and easie in thy Family, above all things observe Discipline.

56. Every one in it should know their Duty; and there should be a Time and Place for every thing; and whatever else is done or omitted, be sure to begin and end with God.

Industry

57. Love Labor: For if thou dost not want it for Food, thou mayest for Physick. It is wholesom for thy Body, and good for thy Mind. It prevents the Fruits of Idleness, which many times comes of nothing to do, and leads too many to do what is worse than nothing. . . .

Temperance

59. To this a spare Diet contributes much. Eat therefore to live and do not live to eat. That's like a Man, but this below a Beast.

60. Have wholesome, but not costly Food, and be rather cleanly than dainty in ordering it. . . .

72. All Excess is ill: But Drunkenness is of the worst Sort. It spoils Health, dismounts the Mind, and unmans Men: It reveals Secrets, is Quarrelsome, Lascivious, Impudent, Dangerous and Mad. In fine, he that is drunk is not a Man: Because he is so long void of Reason, that distinguishes a Man from a Beast.

Apparel

73. Excess in Apparel is another costly Folly. The very Trimming of the vain World would cloath all the naked one.

74. Chuse thy Cloaths by thine own Eyes, not another's. The more plain and simple they are, the better. Neither unshapely, nor fantastical; and for Use and Decency, and not for Pride.

75. If thou art clean and warm, it is sufficient; for more doth but rob the Poor, and please the Wanton. . . .

Qualities of a Friend

111. A true Friend unbosoms freely, advises justly, assists readily, adventures boldly, takes all patiently, defends courageously, and continues a Friend unchangeably.

112. These being the Qualities of a Friend, we are to find them before we chuse one.

113. The Covetous, the Angry, the Proud, the Jealous, the Talkative, cannot but make ill Friends, as well as the False. . . .

Temporal Happiness

246. Be not tempted to presume by Success: For many that have got largely, have lost all, by coveting to get more.

247. To hazard much to get much has more of Avarice than Wisdom.

248. It is great Prudence both to Bound and Use Prosperity.

249. Too few know when they have Enough; and fewer know how to employ it. . . .

Government

363. Three Things contribute much to ruin Governments; Looseness, Oppression and Envy.

364. Where the Reins of Government are too slack, there the Manners of the People are corrupted: And that destroys Industry, begets Effeminacy, and provokes Heaven against it.

365. Oppression makes a Poor Country, and a Desperate People, who always wait an Opportunity to change. . . .

Religion

454. Religion is the Fear of God, and its Demonstration on good Works; and Faith is the Root of both: For without Faith we cannot please God, nor can we fear what we do not believe.

455. The Devils also believe and know abundance: But in this is the Difference, their Faith works not by Love, nor their Knowledge by Obedience; and therefore they are never the better for them. . . .

468. To be like Christ then, is to be a Christian. And Regeneration is the only way to the Kingdom of God, which we pray for.

469. Let us to Day, therefore, hear his Voice, and not harden our Hearts; who speaks to us many ways. In the Scriptures, in our Hearts, by his Servants and his Providences. And the Sum of all is HOLINESS and CHARITY.

470. St. James gives a short Draught of this Matter, but very full and reaching, Pure Religion and undefiled before God the Father, is this, to visit the Fatherless and the Widows in their Affliction, and to keep our selves unspotted from the World. Which is compriz'd in these Two Words, CHARITY and PIETY.

471. They that truly make these their Aim, will find them their Attainment; and with them, the Peace that follows so excellent a Condition.

472. Amuse not thy self therefore with the numerous Opinions of the World, nor value thy self upon verbal Orthodoxy, Philosophy, or thy Skill in Tongues, or Knowledge of the Fathers: (too much the Business and Vanity of the World). But in this rejoyce, That thou knowest God, that is the Lord, who exerciseth loving Kindness, and Judgment, and Righteousness in the Earth.

473. Publick Worship is very commendable, if well performed. We owe it to God and good Example. But we must know, that God is not tyed to Time or Place, who is every where at the same Time: And this we shall know, as far as we are capable, if where ever we are, our Desires are to be with him.

474. Serving God, People generally confine to the Acts of Publick and Private Worship: And those, the more zealous do oftener repeat, in hopes of Acceptance.

475. But if we consider that God is an Infinite Spirit, and, as such, every where; and that our Saviour has taught us, That he will be worshipped in Spirit and in Truth; we shall see the shortness of such a Notion.

476. For serving God concerns the Frame of our Spirits, in the whole Course of our Lives; in every Occasion we have, in which we may shew our Love to his Law. . . .

517. Let us chuse, therefore, to commune where there is the warmest Sense of Religion; where Devotion exceeds Formality, and Practice most corresponds with Profession; and where there is at least as much Charity as Zeal: For where this Society is to be found, there shall we find the Church of God. . . .

543. We are too ready to retaliate, rather than forgive, or gain by Love and Information.

544. And yet we could hurt no Man that we believe loves us.

545. Let us then try what Love will do: For if Men did once see we Love them, we should soon find they would not harm us.

546. Force may subdue, but Love gains: And he that forgives first, wins the Lawrel.

547. If I am even with my Enemy, the Debt is paid; but if I forgive it, I oblige him for ever.

548. Love is the hardest Lesson in Christianity, but, for that reason, it should be most our care to learn it. . . .

555. What we Love, we'll Hear; what we Love, we'll Trust; and what we Love, we'll serve, ay, and suffer for too. If you love me (says our Blessed Redeemer) keep my Commandments. Why? Why then he'll Love us; then we shall be his Friends; then he'll send us the Comforter; then whatsoever we ask, we shall receive; and then where he is we shall be also, and that for ever. Behold the Fruits of Love; the Power, Vertue, Benefit and Beauty of Love!

556. Love is above all; and when it prevails in us all, we shall all be Lovely, and in Love with God and one with another.

From William Penn, *Fruits of Solitude*, The Harvard Classics, vol. 1, edited by Charles W. Eliot (New York: P. F. Collier & Son Corp., 1937, reprinted), pp. 323–34, 344, 352, 359–67.

32.   The Levellers,
The Putney Debates

The English "radical reformation" is here represented in a great debate conducted within the army of Oliver Cromwell on October 29, 1647. Colonel Thomas Rainsborough and John Wildman argued the "Leveller" case for political equality against General Ireton.

MR. PETTUS [MAXIMILIAN PETTY]: We judge, that all inhabitants that have not lost their birthright should have an equal voice in elections.

RAINSBOROUGH: I desired that those that had engaged in it, for really I think that the poorest he that is in England hath a life to live as the greatest he; and therefore truly, sir, I think it's clear, that every man that is to live under a government ought first by his own consent to put himself under that government; and I do think that the poorest man in England is not at all bound in a strict sense to that government that he hath not had a voice to put himself under; and I am confident that, when I have heard the reasons against it, that something will be said to answer those reasons, insomuch that I should doubt whether I was an Englishman or no, that should doubt of these things.

IRETON: That's this.

Give me leave to tell you, that if you make this the rule, I think you must fly for refuge to an absolute natural right, and you must deny all civil right; and I am sure it will come to that in the consequence. . . . For my part, I think it is no right at all. I think that no person hath a right to an interest or share in the disposing of the affairs of the kingdom, and in determining or choosing those that shall determine what laws we shall be ruled by here, no person hath a right to this that hath not a permanent fixed interest in this kingdom, and those persons together are properly the represented of this kingdom, who taken together, and consequently are to make up the representers of this kingdom, are the representers, who taken together do comprehend whatsoever is of real or permanent interest in the kingdom, and I am sure there is otherwise (I cannot tell what), otherwise any man can say why a foreigner coming in amongst us, or as many as will coming in amongst us, or by force or otherwise settling themselves here, or at least by our permission having a being here, why they should not as well lay claim to it as any other. We talk of birthright. Truly birthright there is thus much claim: men may justly have by birthright, by their very being born in England, that we should not seclude them out of England. That we should not refuse to give them air and place and ground, and the freedom of the highways and other things, to live amongst us, not any man that is born here, though he in birth, or by his birth there come nothing at all that is part of the permanent interest of this kingdom to him. That I think is due to a man by birth. But that by a man's being born here he shall have a share in that power that shall dispose of the lands here, and of all things here, I do not think it a sufficient ground. . . . There is all the reason and justice that can be: if I will come to live in a kingdom, being a foreigner to it, or live in a kingdom, having no permanent interest in it, if I will desire as a stranger, or claim as one freeborn here, the air, the free passage of highways, the protection of laws, and all such things, and if I will either desire them, or claim them, I (if I have no permanent interest in that kingdom) must submit to those laws and those rules, who taken together do comprehend the whole interest of the kingdom. . . .

WILDMAN: . . . The case is different from the native inhabitant and foreigner. If a foreigner shall be admitted to be an inhabitant in the nation, he may so he will submit to that form of government as the natives do; he hath the same right as the natives but in this particular. Our case is to be considered thus: that we have been under slavery, that's acknowledged by all. Our very laws were made by our conquerors; and whereas it's spoken much of chronicles, I conceive there is no credit to be given to any of them; and the reason is because those that were our lords, and made us their vassals, would suffer nothing else to be chronicled. We are now engaged for our freedom; that's the end of parliaments, not to constitute what is already according to the just rules of government. Every person in England hath as clear a right to elect his representative as the greatest person in England. I conceive that's the undeniable maxim of government: that all government is in the free consent of the people. If then upon that account, there is no person that is under a just government, or hath justly his own, unless he by his own free consent be put under that government. This he cannot be unless he be consenting to it, and therefore, according to this maxim, there is never a person in England; if, as that gentleman says be true, there are no laws that in this strictness and rigour of justice, that are not made by those who he doth consent to. And therefore I should humbly move, that if the question be stated, which would soonest bring things to an issue, it might rather be this: Whether any person can justly be bound by law not by his own consent, who doth not give his consent that such persons shall make laws for him.

From *The Levellers in the English Revolution,* edited by G. E. Aylmer (Ithaca, N.Y.: Cornell University Press, 1965), pp. 99–101, 109. Copyright © 1965 by G. E. Aylmer.

33. Gerrard Winstanley, *The Communism of the "Diggers"*

Gerrard Winstanley (1609–1676) was the dominant figure in the "Digger" movement of mid–seventeenth-century England. This selection from Winstanley argues for a commonwealth in which all goods will be held in common.

There Shall Be No Buying and Selling of the Earth, Nor of the Fruits Thereof

For by the Government under Kings the cheaters hereby have cozened the plain-hearted of their Creation Birth-rights, and have possessed themselves in the Earth, and call it theirs, and not the others, and so have brought in that poverty and misery which lies upon many men. And whereas the wise should help the foolish, and the strong help the weak, the wise and strong destroy the weak and simple . . . and so the Proverb is made true—*Plain dealing is a jewel, but he who uses it shall die a beggar.* And why? Because this buying and selling is the nursery of cheats; it is the Law of the Conqueror, the Righteousness of the Scribes and Pharisees. . . . And these cunning cheaters commonly become the Rulers of the Earth. . . . For not the wise poor man, but the cunning rich man was always made an Officer and a Ruler; such a one as by his stolen interests in the Earth would be sure to hold others in bondage of poverty and servitude to him and his party. Therefore there shall be no buying and selling in a free Common-wealth, neither shall anyone hire his Brother to work for him. . . .

If the Common-wealth might be governed without buying and selling, here is a Platform of Government for it, which is the ancientest Law of Righteousness to Mankind in the use of the Earth, and which is the very height of Earthly Freedom. But if the minds of the people, through covetousness and proud ignorance, will have the Earth governed by buying and selling still, this same Platform, with some few things subtracted, declares an easy way of Government of the Earth for the quiet of people's minds, and the preserving of peace in the Land.

How Must the Earth Be Planted?

The Earth is to be planted and the fruits reaped and carried into Barns and Storehouses by the assistance of every family. If any man or family want corn or other provisions, they may go to the Storehouses and fetch without money. If they want a horse to ride, go into the fields in Summer, or to the Common Stables in Winter, and receive one from the Keepers, and when your journey is performed, bring him where you had him, without money. If any want food or victuals, they may either go to the butchers' shops and receive what they want without money, or else go to the flocks of sheep or herds of cattle, and take and kill what meat is needful for their families, without buying and selling. The reason why all the riches of the Earth are a Common Stock is this: Because the Earth and the labors thereupon are managed by common assistance of every family, without buying and selling, as is shown more largely in the Office of Overseers for Trades and the Law for Storehouses. The Laws for the right ordering thereof, and the Officers to see the Laws executed, to preserve the peace of every family, and to improve and promote every trade, is shown in the work of Officers and the Laws following.

Who Alone Will Object

None will be an enemy to this Freedom, which, indeed, is to do to another as a man would have another do to him, but Covetousness and Pride, the spirit of the old grudging, snapping Pharisees, who give God abundant of good words in their sermons, in their prayers, in their fasts, and in their thanksgivings, as though none should be more faithful servants to Him than they. Nay, they will shun the company, imprison, and kill every one that will not worship God, they are so zealous. Well now, God and Christ hath enacted an everlasting Law, which is Love, not only one another of your own mind, but love your enemies too, such as are not of your mind: and having food and raiment therewith be content.

From Lewis H. Berens, *The Digger Movement in the Days of the Commonwealth As Revealed in the Writings of Gerrard Winstanley, the Digger: Mystic and Rationalist, Communist and Social Reformer* (London: Holland Press and Merlin Press, 1961), pp. 216–17. First published in 1906. Copyright © 1961 by Holland Press and The Merlin Press.

Part 4

Christian Ethics in the Eighteenth and Nineteenth Centuries

Part of the unintended legacy of the Reformation, particularly during the seventeenth century, was the development of a new strain of doctrinal scholasticism (among both Catholics and Protestants) and a series of bloody sectarian wars throughout Europe. A listing of the most notorious of these conflicts would include the decades of struggle between the monarchy and the Puritan-dominated Parliament in Britain and the Hundred Years' War between various Catholic and Protestant princes in Germany. By the last half of the seventeenth century, many Europeans sought an intellectual framework that could assist them in moving beyond this sectarian impasse. The result of their search was the Enlightenment, a period of great intellectual fervor that helped usher in the modern era.

Some of the principles of the Enlightenment that issued forth from this social context had a great impact on Christian ethics: the desire for religious toleration, the development of moral rather than dogmatic bases for determining religious truth claims, and the questioning of the legitimacy of arbitrary human institutions and authorities (such as despotic governments, hierarchical churches, humanly constructed creeds and, for some, even scripture). Natural laws, discernible by any educated person, could be discovered for every field of human inquiry—such as science, politics, economics, and religion. Self-evident empirical verification was the test for the validity of truth claims. Knowledge was highly valued if it was gained by "common sense," that is, if there was mutual consensus resulting from an analysis of sensory data available to everyone. Continuing the Reformation stress on the priesthood of all believers, an emphasis was placed on the inherent ability of the individual self. All people were "endowed by their Creator with certain inalienable rights." Human potential, cooperation with God, and a progressive view of truth were preferred over concepts based on divine election and static understandings of reality. Revelation and mystery were replaced with reason and scientific certainty.

The eighteenth and nineteenth centuries can be characterized as that period in the history of ethics when Christians came to terms with the precepts of the Enlightenment—sometimes by accommodation to its central tenets, at other times by reaction to it. John Locke was one of those who articulated a religious accommodation to empiricism; just before the beginning of the eighteenth century, he attempted to demonstrate that Christianity was the most reasonable of faiths. In a similar vein, Joseph Butler sought to show that religion was analogous to the natural order.

Not all Christians in this period found empirical verification for their faith through reason alone; some combined the contemporary interest in a reasonable religion with a stress on the subjective experience of God—an "experimental" faith, often expressed in evangelical terms as the "new birth" of conversion. John Wesley's ethical concerns, for example, while partially a product of Anglican and nonconformist piety inherited from his parents, were also affected by the Pietist spirituality of the Moravians. Nineteenth-century American evangelicals used a similar experiential base for their ethical understandings.

For many Christians during this period, certain cultural mores of Western society seemed contrary to the modern concept of natural law. Although institutionalized practices such as slavery, patriarchy, and industrial capitalism (resulting in a permanent underclass) were encoded in human law, it was asserted that these practices were against the "higher law" of God. Another Enlightenment principle—the concept that the social utility of all cultural conventions needed to be demonstrated—was appropriated to prove that these patterns of behavior were not useful for society. John Wesley, Luther Lee, Frederick Douglass, and others used both "higher law" and utilitarian arguments for their attacks on luxury, intemperance, and enslavement.

Many of the Enlightenment ideals that were just beginning to be expressed in the eighteenth century were made more definitive in the nineteenth. Optimism regarding human nature, for example, sometimes resulted in a particularly high view of human ability. Friedrich Schleiermacher, an heir of Pietism, emphasized inward feeling and a personal sense of dependence on the Infinite. Christian ethics was a result of each person's identification with the God-consciousness of Jesus. Leo Tolstoy, influenced by Romanticism, tried to live a sinless life of social justice advocacy, pacifism, and self-imposed simplicity. Jesus, for Tolstoy, was a great man who should be imitated. God was supreme Good and Reason, but the concept of a personal deity was left behind.

The leading nineteenth-century social issues addressed by F. D. Maurice and the British Christian socialists were poverty, unemployment, and malnutrition, while in the United States, the rhetoric of the American Revolution meant that issues of equality were uppermost in the minds of many Christian people. African Americans such as David Walker and Frederick Douglass, white abolitionists such as Charles Grandison Finney and Luther Lee, and women's rights activists such as Lucretia Mott, Sojourner Truth, and Frances Willard struggled to expand the horizon of equal rights in a variety of ways.

For some Christians, the social implications of the Enlightenment were so threatening they felt the need to react defensively. The Roman Catholic Church, for instance, faced with direct challenges to its temporal and spiritual authority, issued the *Syllabus of Errors*. The claims of modernity caused others to question the utility of Christianity altogether. Elizabeth Cady Stanton found the traditional Christian message to be intrinsically oppressive; hence, she believed, it should be rejected by modern women.

34. John Locke,
The Reasonableness of Christianity

The empiricist John Locke (1632–1704) wrote this treatise in 1695 to demonstrate that Christianity is the most reasonable of all religions. Given this fact, Locke asserted, the most important task for the Christian is to lead a righteous, moral life.

172. These two, faith and repentance, i.e., believing Jesus to be the Messiah, and a good life, are the indispensable conditions of the new covenant, to be performed by all those who would obtain eternal life. The reasonableness, or rather necessity of which, that we may the better comprehend, we must a little look back to what was said in the beginning.

173. Adam being the son of God, and so St. Luke calls him, [3:]38, had this part also of the likeness and image of his father, viz. that he was immortal. But Adam transgressing the command given him by his heavenly Father, incurred the penalty, forfeited that state of immortality, and became mortal. . . .

(174). God nevertheless, out of his infinite mercy, willing to bestow eternal life on mortal men, sends Jesus Christ into the world; who being conceived in the womb of a virgin (that had not known man) by the immediate power of God, was properly the Son of God.

(178). God therefore, out of his mercy to mankind, and for the erecting of the kingdom of his Son, and furnishing it with subjects out of every kindred, and tongue, and people, and nation, proposed to the children of men, that as many of them as would believe Jesus his Son (whom he sent into the world) to be the Messiah, the promised Deliverer; and would receive him for their King and Ruler; should have all their past sins, disobedience, and rebellion forgiven them: and if for the future they lived in a sincere obedience to his law, to the utmost of their power; the sins of human frailty for the time to come, as well as all those of their past lives, should, for his Son's sake, because they gave themselves up to him, to be his subjects, be forgiven them, and so their faith, which made them be baptized into his name (i.e. enrol themselves in the kingdom of Jesus the Messiah, and profess themselves his subjects, and consequently live by the laws of his kingdom) should be accounted to them for righteousness; i.e. should supply the defects of a scanty obedience in the sight of God; who, counting this faith to them for righteousness, or complete obedience, did thus justify, or make them just, and thereby capable of eternal life.

(179). [So] believing him to be the Messiah their King, it was further required, that those who would have the privilege, advantage and deliverance of his kingdom, should enter themselves into it; and by baptism being made denizens, and solemnly incorporated into that kingdom, live as became subjects obedient to the laws of it. For if they believed him to be the Messiah, their King, but would not obey his laws, and would not have him to reign over them, they were but the greater rebels; and God would not justify them for a faith that did but increase their guilt, and oppose diametrically the kingdom and design of the Messiah; "Who gave himself for us, that he might redeem us from all iniquity, and purify unto himself a peculiar people, zealous of good works" [Titus 2:14]. And therefore St. Paul tells the Galatians, that that which availeth is faith; but faith working by love. And that faith without works, i.e. the works of sincere obedience to the law and will of Christ, is not sufficient for our justification, St. James shews at large, Ch.[2].

180. Neither, indeed, could it be otherwise, for life, eternal life being the reward of justice or righteousness only, appointed by the righteous God (who is of purer eyes than to behold iniquity) to those only who had no taint or infection of sin upon them, it is impossible that he should justify those who had no regard to justice at all, whatever they believed. This would have been to encourage iniquity, contrary to the purity of his nature, and to have condemned that eternal law of right, which is holy, just, and good: of which no one precept or rule is abrogated or repealed; nor indeed can be, whilst God is an holy, just, and righteous God, and man a rational creature. The duties of that law arising from the constitution of his very nature, are of eternal obligation; nor can it be taken away, or dispensed with, without changing the nature of things, or overturning the measures of right and wrong, and thereby introducing and authorizing irregularity, confusion, and disorder in the world. Christ's coming into the world was not for such an end as that; but on the contrary, to reform the corrupt state of degenerate man; and out of those who would mend their lives, and bring forth fruit meet for repentance, erect a new kingdom.

From John Locke, *The Reasonableness of Christianity*, edited and abridged by I. T. Ramsey (Stanford, Calif.: Stanford University Press, 1958), pp. 45–46.

35.   Joseph Butler,
Upon the Love of Our Neighbour

Butler (1692–1752), a bishop of the Church of England, is well known in the history of Christian ethics for his doctrine of benevolence. This is best set forth in a series of sermons, most notable in Upon the Love of our Neighbor *of ca. 1729. Butler exemplifies the nationalistic spirit of Enlightenment religious and ethical thought.*

Sermon 12. The precept may be understood as requiring only that we have the same kind of affection to our fellow-creatures, as to ourselves.

That, as every man has the principle of self-love, which disposes him to avoid misery, and consult his own happiness: so we should cultivate the affection of good-will to our neighbour, and that it should influence us to have the same kind of regard to him. This, at least, must be commanded: and this will not only prevent our being injurious to him, but will also put us upon promoting his good. There are blessings in life, which we share in common with others; peace, plenty, freedom, healthful season. But real benevolence to our fellow-creatures would give us the notion of a common interest in a stricter sense: for in the degree we love another, his interest, his joys, and sorrows, are our own. It is from self-love that we form the notion of private good, and consider it as our own: love of our neighbour will teach us thus to appropriate to ourselves his good and welfare; to consider ourselves as having a real share in his happiness. Thus the principle of benevolence would be an advocate within our own breasts, to take care of the interests of our fellow-creatures, in all the interfering and competitions which cannot but be, from the imperfection of our nature, and the state we are in. It would, likewise, in some measure, lessen that interfering; and hinder men from forming so strong a notion of private good, exclusive of the good of others, as we commonly do. Thus, as the private affection makes us in a peculiar manner sensible of humanity, justice, or injustice, when exercised towards ourselves; love of our neighbour would give us the same kind of sensibility in his behalf. This would be the greater security of our uniform obedience to that most equitable rule: 'Whatsoever ye would that men should do unto you, do ye even so unto them.'

. . . . That which we more strictly call piety, or the love of God, and which is an essential part of a right temper, some may perhaps imagine no way connected with benevolence: yet, surely, they must be connected, if there be indeed in being an object infinitely good. Human nature is so constituted, that every good affection implies the love of itself; i.e., becomes the object of a new affection in the same person. Thus, to be righteous, implies in it the love of righteousness; to be benevolent, the love of benevolences; to be good, the love of goodness; whether this righteousness, benevolence, or goodness, be viewed as in our own mind, or in another's: and the love of God, as a Being perfectly good, is the love of perfect goodness, contemplated in a being or person. Thus morality and religion, virtue and piety, will at last necessarily coincide, run up into one and the same point, and love will be in all senses *the end of the commandment*.

From Joseph Butler, *Fifteen Sermons Preached at the Rolls Chapel* (London: Thomas Tegg & Son, 1836), pp. 119, 120, 130.

36.   John Wesley,
A Plain Account of Christian Perfection,
The Use of Money, Thoughts on the Present
Scarcity of Provisions, and *Thoughts upon Slavery*

The founder of Methodism and the leading figure of the evangelical revival in eighteenth-century Britain, John Wesley (1703–1791) did not write a systematic compendium of his theology or of his social ethic. But through his various sermons and treatises, Wesley's approach to moral issues becomes clear: one's faith must be active in love. Wesley's rather unique stress on the sanctified life is described in A Plain Account of Christian Perfection, *the last revision of which was made in 1777. More specific issues are addressed in* The Use of Money *(1760),* Thoughts on the Present Scarcity of Provisions *(1773), and* Thoughts upon Slavery *(1774).*

A PLAIN ACCOUNT OF CHRISTIAN PERFECTION

I think it was in the latter end of the year 1740, that I had a conversation with Dr. Gibson, then Bishop of London, at Whitehall. He asked me what I meant by perfection. I told him without any disguise or reserve. When I ceased speaking, he said, "Mr. Wesley, if this be all you mean, publish it to all the world. If any one then can confute what you say, he may have free leave." I answered, "My Lord, I will;" and accordingly wrote and published the sermon on Christian perfection.

In this I endeavored to show, (1.) In what sense Christians are not, (2.) In what sense they are, perfect.

(1.) In what sense they are not. They are not perfect in knowledge. They are not free from ignorance, no, nor from mistake. We are no more to expect any living man to be infallible, than to be omniscient. They are not free from infirmities, such as weakness or slowness of understanding, irregular quickness or heaviness of imagination. Such in another kind are impropriety of language, ungracefulness of pronunciation; to which one might add a thousand nameless defects, either in conversation or behaviour. From such infirmities as these none are perfectly freed till their spirits return to God; neither can we expect till then to be wholly freed from temptation; for 'the servant is not above his master.' But neither in this sense is there any absolute perfection on earth. There is no perfection of degrees, none which does not admit of a continual increase.

(2.) In what sense then are they perfect? Observe, we are not now speaking of babes in Christ, but adult Christians. . . .

. . . [I]t is only of grown Christians it can be affirmed, they are in such a sense perfect, as, . . . to be freed from evil thoughts and evil tempers. First, from evil or sinful thoughts. Indeed, whence should they spring? 'Out of the heart of man,' if at all, 'proceed evil thoughts.' If, therefore, the heart be no longer evil, then evil thoughts no longer proceed out of it: For 'a good tree cannot bring forth evil fruit.'

And as they are freed from evil thoughts, so likewise from evil tempers. Every one of these can say, with St. Paul, 'I am crucified with Christ; nevertheless I live; yet not I, but Christ liveth in me'—words that manifestly describe a deliverance from inward as well as from outward sin. This is expressed both negatively, 'I live not,' my evil nature, the body of sin, is destroyed; and positively, 'Christ liveth in me,' and therefore all that is holy, and just, and good. Indeed, both these, 'Christ liveth in me,' and, 'I live not,' are inseparably connected. For what communion hath light with darkness, or Christ with Belial?

He, therefore, who liveth in these Christians hath 'purified their hearts by faith;' insomuch that every one that has Christ in him, 'the hope of glory, purifieth himself even as he is pure.' He is purified from pride; for Christ was lowly in heart: He is pure from desire and self-will; for Christ desired only to do the will of his Father: And he is pure from anger, in the common sense of the word; for Christ was meek and gentle. I say, *in the common sense of the word*; for he is angry at sin, while he is grieved for the sinner. He feels a displacency at every offence against God, but only tender compassion to the offender.

Thus doth Jesus save his people from their sins, not only from outward sins, but from the sins of their hearts. 'True,' say some, 'but not till death, not in this world.' Nay, St. John says, 'Herein is our love made perfect, that we may have boldness in the day of judgment; because, as he is, so are we in this world.' The Apostle here, beyond all contradiction, speaks of himself and other living Christians, of whom he flatly affirms, that, not only at or after death, but 'in this world,' they are 'as their Master.' . . .

Not long after, I think in the spring, 1741, we published a second volume of Hymns. As the doctrine was still much misunderstood, and consequently misrepresented, I judged it needful to explain yet farther upon the head; which was done in the preface to it as follows:—

This great gift of God, the salvation of our souls, is no other than the image of God fresh stamped on our hearts. It is a 'renewal of believers in the spirit of their minds, after the likeness of Him that created them.' God hath now laid 'the axe unto the root of the tree, purifying their hearts by faith,' and 'cleansing all the thoughts of their hearts by the inspiration of his Holy Spirit.' Having this hope, that they shall see God as he is, they 'purify themselves even as he is pure,' and are 'holy, as he that hath called them is holy, in all manner of conversation.' Not that they have already attained all that they shall attain, either are already in this sense perfect. But they daily 'go on from strength to strength; beholding' now, 'as in a glass, the glory of the Lord, they are changed into the same image, from glory to glory, by the Spirit of the Lord.'

And 'where the Spirit of the Lord is, there is liberty;' such liberty 'from the law of sin and death,' as the children of this world will not believe, though a man declare it unto them. 'The Son hath made them free' who are thus 'born of God,' from that great root of sin and bitterness, pride. They feel that all their 'sufficiency is of God,' that it is He alone who 'is in all their thoughts,' and 'worketh in them both to will and to do of his good pleasure,' They feel that 'it is not they' that 'speak, but the Spirit of' their 'Father who speaketh' in them, and that whatsoever is done by their hands, 'the Father who is in them, he doeth the works.' So that God is to them all in all, and they are nothing in his sight. They are freed from self-will, as desiring nothing but the holy and perfect will of God; not supplies in want, not ease in pain, nor life, or death, or any creature; but continually crying in their inmost soul, 'Father, thy will be done.' They are freed from evil thoughts, so that they cannot enter into them, no, not for a moment. Aforetime, when an evil thought came in, they looked up, and it vanished away. But now it does not come in, there being no room for this, in a soul which is full of God. . . .

. . . [L]ove is the highest gift of God; humble, gentle, patient love . . . all visions, revelations, manifestations whatever, are little things compared to love. . . .

It were well you should be thoroughly sensible of this,—'the heaven of heavens is love.' There is nothing higher in religion; there is, in effect, nothing else; if you look for anything but more love, you are looking wide of the mark, you are getting out of the royal way. And when you are asking others, 'Have you received this or that blessing?' if you mean anything but more love, you mean wrong; you are leading them out of the way, and putting them upon a false scent. Settle it then in your heart, that from the moment God has saved you from all sin, you are to aim at nothing more, but more of that love described in the thirteenth of the Corinthians. You can go no higher than this, till you are carried into Abraham's bosom. . . .

1. By perfection I mean the humble, gentle, patient love of God, and our neighbour, ruling our tempers, words, and actions.

I do not include an impossibility of falling from it, either in part or in whole. . . .

And I do not contend for the term *sinless*, though I do not object against it.

2. As to the manner. I believe this perfection is always wrought in the soul by a simple act of faith; consequently, in an instant.

But I believe a gradual work, both preceeding and following that instant.

3. As to the time. I believe this instant generally is the instant of death, the moment before the soul leaves the body. But I believe it may be ten, twenty, or forty years before.

I believe it is usually many years after justification; but that it may be within five years or five months after it, I know no conclusive argument to the contrary.

From *The Works of the Reverend John Wesley, A.M.*, vol. 11, edited by Thomas Jackson (London: Wesleyan Methodist Book Room, 1872), 374–79, 430, 446.

The Use of Money

2. . . . [L]et the world be as corrupt as it will, is gold or silver to blame? "The love of money," we know, "is the root of all evil;" but not the thing itself. The fault does not lie in the money, but in them that use it. It may be used ill: And what may not? But it may likewise be used well: It is full as applicable to the best, as to the worst uses. It is of unspeakable service to all civilized nations, in all the common affairs of life: It is a most compendious instrument of transacting all manner of business, and (if we use it according to Christian wisdom) of doing all manner of good. It is true, were man in a state of innocence, or were all men "filled with the Holy Ghost," so that, like the infant Church at Jerusalem, "no man counted any thing he had his own," but "distribution was made to every one as he had need," the use of it would be superseded; as we cannot conceive there is any thing of the kind among the inhabitants of heaven. But, in the present state of mankind, it is an excellent gift of God, answering the noblest ends. In the hands of his children, it is food for the hungry, drink for the thirsty, raiment for the naked: It gives to the traveller and the stranger where to lay his head. By it we may supply the place of an husband to the widow, and of a father to the fatherless. We may be a defence for the oppressed, a means of health to the sick, of ease to them that are in pain; it may be as eyes to the blind, as feet to the lame; yea, a lifter up from the gates of death!

3. It is therefore, of the highest concern, that all who fear God know how to employ this valuable talent; that they be instructed how it may answer these glorious ends, and in the highest degree. And, perhaps, all the instructions which are necessary for this may be reduced to three plain rules, by the exact observance whereof we may approve ourselves faithful stewards of "the mammon of unrighteousness."

I. 1. The First of these is, (he that heareth, let him understand!) "Gain all you can." Here we may speak like the children of the world: We meet them on their own ground. And it is our bounden duty to do this: We ought to gain all we can gain, without buying gold too dear, without paying more for it than it is worth. But this it is certain we ought not to do; we ought not to gain money at the expense of life, nor (which is in effect the same thing) at the expense of our health. Therefore, no gain whatsoever should induce us to enter into, or to continue in, any employ, which is of such a kind, or is attended with so hard or so long labour, as to impair our constitution. Neither should we begin or continue in any business which necessarily deprives us of proper seasons for food and sleep, in such a proportion as our nature requires. . . .

2. We are, Secondly, to gain all we can without hurting our mind, any more than our body. For neither may we hurt this: We must preserve, at all events, the spirit of an healthful mind. Therefore, we may not engage or continue in any sinful trade; any that is contrary to the law of God, or of our country. . . .

3. We are, Thirdly, to gain all we can, without hurting our neighbour.

But this we may not, cannot do, if we love our neighbour as ourselves. We cannot, if we love every one as ourselves, hurt any one *in his substance*. . . . We cannot, consistent with brotherly love, sell our goods below the market-price; we cannot study to ruin our neighbour's trade, in order to advance our own; much less can we entice away, or receive, any of his servants or workmen whom he has need of. None can gain by swallowing up his neighbour's substance, without gaining the damnation of hell!

4. Neither may we gain by hurting our neighbour *in his body.* Therefore we may not sell anything which tends to impair health. Such is, eminently, all that liquid fire, commonly called drams, or spirituous liquors. . . .

6. This is dear-bought gain. And so is whatever is procured by hurting our neighbour *in his soul*; by ministering, suppose, either directly or indirectly, to his unchastity, or intemperance; which certainly none can do, who has any fear of God, or any real desire of pleasing Him. It nearly concerns all those to consider this, who have anything to do with taverns, victualling-houses, opera-houses, play-houses, or any other places of public, fashionable diversion. If these profit the souls of men, you are clear; your employment is good, and your gain innocent; but if they are either sinful in themselves, or natural inlets to sin of various kinds, then, it is to be feared, you have a sad account to make. O beware, lest God say in that day, "These have perished in their iniquity, but their blood do I require at thy hands!"

7. These cautions and restrictions being observed, it is the bounden duty of all who are engaged in worldly business to observe that first and great rule of Christian wisdom, with respect to money, "Gain all you can." Gain all you can by honest industry. Use all possible diligence in your calling. Lose no time. If you understand yourself, and your relation to God and man, you know you have none to spare. If you understand your particular calling, as you ought, you will have no time that hangs upon your hands. Every business will afford some employment sufficient for every day and every hour. That wherein you are placed, if you follow it in earnest, will leave you no leisure for silly, unprofitable diversions. You have always something better to do, something that will profit you, more or less. And "whatsoever thy hand findeth to do, do it with thy might." Do it as soon as possible: No delay! No putting off from day to day, or from hour to hour! Never leave anything till to-morrow, which you can do to-day. And do it as well as possible. Do not sleep or yawn over it: Put your whole strength to the work. Spare no pains. Let nothing be done by halves, or in a slight and careless manner. Let nothing in your business be left undone, if it can be done by labour or patience.

8. Gain all you can, by common sense, by using in your business all the understanding which God has given you. It is amazing to observe, how few do this; how men run on in the same dull track with their forefathers. But whatever they do who know not God, this is no rule for you. It is a shame for a Christian not to improve upon *them,* in whatever he takes in hand. You should be continually learning, from the experience of others, or from your own experience, reading, and reflection, to do everything you have to do better to-day than you did yesterday. And see that you practice whatever you learn, that you may make the best of all that is in your hands.

II. 1. Having gained all you can, by honest wisdom, and unwearied diligence, the Second rule of Christian prudence is, "Save all you can." Do not throw precious talent into the sea: Leave that folly to heathen philosophers. Do not throw it away in idle expenses, which is just the same as throwing it into the sea. Expend no part of it merely to gratify the desire of the flesh, the desire of the eye, or the pride of life.

2. Do not waste any part of so precious a talent, merely in gratifying the desires of the flesh; in procuring the pleasures of sense, of whatever kind; particularly, in enlarging the pleasure of tasting. I do not mean, avoid gluttony and drunkenness only: An honest Heathen would condemn these. But there is a regular, reputable kind of sensuality, an elegant epicurism, which does not immediately disorder the stomach, nor (sensibly at least) impair the understanding; and yet (to mention no other effects of it now) it cannot be maintained without considerable expense. Cut off all this expense! Despise delicacy and variety, and be content with what plain nature requires.

3. Do not waste any part of so precious a talent, merely in gratifying the desire of the eye, by superfluous or expensive apparel, or by needless ornaments. Waste no part of it in curiously adorning your houses; in superfluous or expensive furniture; in costly pictures, painting, gilding, books; in elegant rather than useful gardens. . . .

4. Lay out nothing to gratify the pride of life, to gain the admiration or praise of men. This motive of expense is frequently interwoven with one or both of the former. Men are expensive in diet, or apparel, or furniture, not barely to please their appetite, or to gratify their eye, or their imagination, but their vanity too. . . .

III. 1. But let not any man imagine that he has done anything, barely by going thus far, by "gaining and saving all he can," if he were to stop here. All this is nothing, if a man go not forward, if he does not point all this at a farther end. Nor, indeed, can a man properly be said to save anything, if he only lays it up. You may as well throw your money into the sea, as bury it in the earth. And you may as well bury it in the earth, as in your chest, or in the bank of England. Not to use, is effectually to throw it away. If, therefore, you would indeed "make yourselves friends of the mammon of unrighteousness," add the Third rule to the two preceding. Having, First, gained all you can, and Secondly, saved all you can, Then "give all you can."

2. In order to see the ground and reason of this, consider, when the Possessor of heaven and earth brought you into being, and placed you in this world, he placed you here, not as a proprietor, but a steward: As such he entrusted you, for a season, with goods of various kinds; but the sole property of these still rests in him, nor can ever be alienated from him. As you yourself are not your own, but his, such is, likewise, all that you enjoy. Such is your soul and your body, not your own, but God's. And so is your substance in particular. And he has told you, in the most clear and express terms, how you are to employ it for him, in such a manner, that it may be all an holy sacrifice, acceptable through Christ Jesus. And this light, easy service, he hath promised to reward with an eternal weight of glory.

3. The directions which God has given us, touching the use of our worldly substance, may be comprised in the following particulars. If you desire to be faithful and a wise steward, out of that portion of your Lord's goods which he has for the present lodged in your hands, but with the right of resuming whenever it pleases him, First, provide things needful for yourself; food to eat, raiment to put on, whatever nature moderately requires for preserving the body in health and strength. Secondly, provide these for your wife, your children, your servants, or any others who pertain to your household. If, when this is done, there be an overplus left, then "do good to them that are of the household of faith." If there be an overplus still, "as you have opportunity, do good unto all men." In so doing, you give all you can; nay, in a sound sense, all you have: For all that is laid out in this manner is really given to God. You "render unto God the things that are God's," not only by what you give to the poor, but also by that which you expend in providing things needful for yourself and your household. . . .

6. . . . You see the nature and extent of truly Christian prudence, so far as it relates to the use of that great talent, money. Gain all you can, without hurting either yourself or your neighbour, in soul or body, by applying hereto with unintermitted diligence, and with all the understanding which God has given you;—save all you can, by cutting off every expense which serves only to indulge foolish desire; to gratify either the desire of the flesh, the desire of the eye, or the pride of life; waste nothing, living or dying, on sin or folly, whether for yourself or your children;—and then, give all you can, or, in other words, give all you have to God.

From *The Works of the Reverend John Wesley, A. M.*, vol. 6, edited by Thomas Jackson (London: Wesleyan Methodist Book Room, 1872), pp. 126–35.

THOUGHTS ON THE PRESENT SCARCITY OF PROVISIONS

I. 1. Why are thousands of people starving, perishing for want, in every part of the nation? The fact I know; I have seen it with my eyes, in every corner of the land. I have known those who could only afford to eat a little coarse food once every other day. I have known one in London (and one that a few years before had all the conveniences of life) picking up from a dunghill stinking sprats, and carrying them home for herself and her children. I have known another gathering the bones which the dogs had left in the streets, and making broth of them, to prolong a wretched life! I have heard a third artlessly declare, "Indeed I was very faint, and so weak I could hardly walk, until my dog, finding nothing at home, went out, and brought in a good sort of bone, which I took out of his mouth, and made a pure dinner!" Such is the case at this day of multitudes of people, in a land flowing, as it were, with milk and honey! abounding with all the necessaries, the conveniences, the superfluities of life!

Now, why is this? Why have all these nothing to eat? Because they have nothing to do. The plain reason why they have no meat is, because they have no work.

2. But why have they no work? Why are so many thousand people, in London, in Bristol, in Norwich, in every county, from one end of England to the other, utterly destitute of employment?

Because the persons that used to employ them cannot afford to do it any longer. Many that employed fifty men, now scarce employ ten; those that employed twenty, now employ one, or none at all. They cannot, as they have no vent for their goods; food being so dear, that the generality of people are hardly able to buy anything else.

3. But why is food so dear? To come to particulars: Why does bread-corn bear so high a price? To set aside partial causes, . . . the grand cause is because such immense quantities of corn are continually consumed by distilling. . . . [L]ittle less than half the wheat produced in the kingdom is every year consumed, not by so harmless a way as throwing it into the sea, but by converting it into deadly poison; poison that naturally destroys not only the strength and life, but also the morals, of our countrymen . . .

4. But why are oats so dear? Because there are four times as many horses kept . . . for coaches and chaises in particular, as were a few years ago. . . .

5. Why are beef and mutton so dear? Because many considerable farmers, particularly in the northern counties, who used to breed large numbers of sheep, or horned cattle, and very frequently both, now breed none at all: They no longer trouble themselves with either sheep, or cows, or oxen; as they can turn their land to far better account by breeding horses alone. Such is the demand, not only for coach and chaise horses, which are bought and destroyed in incredible numbers, but much more for bred horses, which are yearly exported by hundreds, yea, thousands, to France.

6. But why are pork, poultry, and eggs so dear? Because of the monopolizing of farms; perhaps as mischievous a monopoly as was ever introduced into these kingdoms. The land which was some years ago divided between ten or twenty little farmers, and enabled them comfortably to provide for their families, is now generally engrossed by one great farmer. One farms an estate of a thousand a year, which formerly maintained ten or twenty. Every one of these little farmers kept a few swine, with some quantity of poultry; and, having little money, was glad to send his bacon, or pork, or fowls and eggs to market continually. Hence the markets were plentifully served; and plenty created cheapness. But at present, the great, the gentlemen-farmers are above attending to these little things. They breed no poultry or swine, unless for their own use; consequently they send none to market. Hence it is not strange if two or three of these, living near a market-town, occasion such a scarcity of these things, by preventing the former supply, that the price of them is double or treble to what it was before. . . .

Another cause (the most terrible one of all, and the most destructive both of personal and social happiness) why not only beef, mutton, and pork, but all kinds of victuals, are so dear, is luxury. What can stand against this? Will it not waste and destroy all that nature and art can produce? If a person of quality will boil down three dozen of neats' tongues, to make two or three quarts of soup, (and so proportionably in other things,) what wonder that provisions fail? Only look into the kitchens of the great, the nobility and gentry, almost without exception; (considering withal, that "the toe of the peasant treads upon the heel of the courtier;") and when you have observed the amazing waste which is made there, you will no longer wonder at the scarcity, and consequently dearness, of the things which they use so much art to destroy.

7. But why is land so dear? Because, on all these accounts, gentlemen cannot live as they have been accustomed to do without increasing their income; which most of them cannot do, but by raising their rents. And then the farmer, paying an higher rent for the land, must have an higher price for the produce of it. This again tends to raise the price of land; and so the wheel runs round.

8. But why is it, that not only provisions and land, but well nigh everything else, is so dear? Because of the enormous taxes, which are laid on almost everything that can be named. . . .

9. But why are the taxes so high? Because of the national debt. They must be so while this continues. I have heard that the national expense, seventy years ago, was, in time of peace, three millions a year. And now the bare interest of the public debt amounts yearly to above four millions! to raise which, with the other stated expenses of government, those taxes are absolutely necessary.

To sum up the whole: Thousands of people throughout the land are perishing for want of food. This is owing to various causes; but above all, to distilling, taxes, and luxury.

Here is the evil, and the undeniable causes of it. But where is the remedy?

Perhaps it exceeds all the wisdom of man to tell: But it may not be amiss to offer a few hints on the subject.

II. 1. What remedy is there for this sore evil—many thousand poor people are starving? Find them work, and you will find them meat. They will then earn and eat their own bread.

2. But how can the masters give them work without ruining themselves? Procure vent for what is wrought, and the masters will give them as much work as they can do. And this would be done by sinking the price of provisions; for then people would have money to buy other things too.

3. But how can the price of wheat and barley be reduced? By prohibiting for ever, by making a full end of that bane of health, that destroyer of strength, of life, and of virtue,—distilling. Perhaps this alone might go a great way toward answering the whole design. . . .

6. How can the price of pork and poultry be reduced? Whether it ever will, is another question. But it can be done, (1.) By letting no farms of above an hundred pounds a year: (2.) By repressing luxury; whether by laws, by

example, or by both. I had almost said, by the grace of God; but to mention this has been long out of fashion.

7. How may the price of land be reduced? By all the methods above-named, as each tends to lessen the expense of housekeeping: But especially the last; by restraining luxury, which is the grand and general source of want.

8. How may the taxes be reduced? (1.) By discharging half the national debt, and so saving, by this single means, above two million a year. . . .

But will this ever be done? I fear not: At least, we have no reason to hope for it shortly; for what good can we expect (suppose the Scriptures are true) for such a nation as this, where there is no fear of God, where there is such a deep, avowed, thorough contempt of all religion, as I never saw, never heard or read of, in any other nation, whether Christian, Mahometan, or Pagan? It seems as if God must shortly arise and maintain his own cause. But, if so, let us fall into the hands of God, and not into the hands of men.

From *The Works of the Reverend John Wesley, A.M.*, vol. 11, edited by Thomas Jackson (London: Wesleyan Methodist Book Room, 1872), pp. 53–59.

THOUGHTS UPON SLAVERY

11. . . . Upon the whole, . . . the Negroes who inhabit the coast of Africa, from the river Senegal to the southern bounds of Angola, are so far from being the stupid, senseless, brutish, lazy barbarians, the fierce, cruel, perfidious savages they have been described, that, on the contrary, they are represented, by them who have no motive to flatter them, as remarkably sensible, considering the few advantages they have for improving their understanding; as industrious to the highest degree, perhaps more so than any other natives of so warm a climate; as fair, just, and honest in all their dealings, unless where white men have taught them to be otherwise; and as far more mild, friendly, and kind to strangers, than any of our forefathers were. *Our forefathers!* Where shall we find at this day, among the fair-faced natives of Europe, a nation generally practising the justice, mercy, and truth, which are found among these poor Africans? . . . [W]e may leave England and France, to seek genuine honesty in Benin, Congo, or Angola. . . .

III. 7. . . . [W]hat can be more wretched than the condition they then enter upon? Banished from their country, from their friends and relations for ever, from every comfort of life, they are reduced to a state scarce anyway preferable to that of beasts of burden. In general, a few roots, not of the nicest kind, usually yams or potatoes, are their food; and two rags, that neither screen them from the heat of the day, nor the cold of the night, their covering. Their sleep is very short, their labour continual, and frequently above their strength; so that death sets many of them at liberty before they have lived out half their days. The time they work in the West Indies, is from day-break to noon, and from two o'clock till dark; during which time, they are attended by overseers, who, if they think them dilatory, or think anything not so well done as it should be, whip them most unmercifully, so that you may see their bodies long after wealed and scarred usually from the shoulders to the waist. And before they are suffered to go to their quarters, they have commonly something to do, as collecting herbage for the horses, or gathering fuel for the boilers; so that it is often past twelve before they can get home. Hence, if their food is not prepared, they are sometimes called to labour again, before they can satisfy their hunger. And no excuse will avail. If they are not in the field immediately, they must expect to feel the lash. Did the Creator intend that the noblest creatures in the visible world should live such a life as this? . . .

IV. 1. This is the plain, unaggravated matter of fact. Such is the manner wherein our African slaves are . . . treated in our plantations. I would now inquire, whether these things can be defended, on the principles of even heathen honesty; whether they can be reconciled (setting the Bible out of the question) with any degree of either justice or mercy.

2. The grand plea is, "They are authorized by law." But can law, human law, change the nature of things? Can it turn darkness into light, or evil into good? By no means. Notwithstanding ten thousand laws, right is right, and wrong is wrong still. There must still remain an essential difference between justice and injustice, cruelty and mercy. So that I still ask, Who can reconcile this treatment of the Negroes, first and last, with either mercy or justice?

Where is the justice of inflicting the severest evils on those that have done us no wrong? of depriving those that never injured us in word or deed, of every comfort of life? of tearing them from their native country, and depriving them of liberty itself, to which an Angolan has the same natural right as an Englishman, and on which he sets as high a value? Yea, where is the justice of taking away the lives of innocent, inoffensive men; murdering thousands of them in their own land, by the hands of their own countrymen; many thousands, year after year, on shipboard, and then casting them like dung into the sea; and tens of thousands in that cruel slavery to which they are so unjustly reduced?

3. But waving, for the present, all other considerations, I strike at the root of this complicated villany; I absolutely deny all slave-holding to be consistent with any degree of natural justice. . . .

IV. 6. . . . I deny that villany is ever necessary. It is impossible that it should ever be necessary for any reasonable creature to violate all the laws of justice, mercy, and truth. No circumstances can make it necessary for a man to burst in sunder all the ties of humanity. It can never be necessary for a rational being to sink himself below a brute. A man can be under no necessity of degrading himself into a wolf. The absurdity of the supposition is so glaring, that one would wonder any one can help seeing it.

This in general. But, to be more particular, I ask, . . . What is necessary? . . . It may be answered, "The whole method now used by the original purchasers of Negroes is necessary to the furnishing our colonies yearly with a hundred thousand slaves." I grant, this is necessary to that end. But how is that end necessary? How will you prove it necessary that one hundred, that one, of those slaves should be procured? "Why, it is necessary to my gaining an hundred thousand pounds." Perhaps so: But how is this necessary?

It is very possible you might be both a better and a happier man, if you had not a quarter of it. I deny that your gaining one thousand is necessary either to your present or eternal happiness. "But, however, you must allow, these slaves are necessary for the cultivation of our islands; inasmuch as white men are not able to labour in hot climates." I answer, it were better that all those islands should remain uncultivated for ever; yea, it were more desirable that they were altogether sunk in the depth of the sea, than that they should be cultivated at so high a price as the violation of justice, mercy, and truth. . . . Better no trade, than trade procured by villany. It is far better to have no wealth, than to gain wealth at the expense of virtue. Better is honest poverty, than all the riches bought by the tears, and sweat, and blood, of our fellow-creatures.

8. "However this be, it is necessary, when we have slaves, to use them with severity." What, to whip them for every petty offence, till they are all in gore blood? to take that opportunity of rubbing pepper and salt into their raw flesh? to drop burning sealing-wax upon their skin? to castrate them? to cut off half their foot with an axe? to hang them on gibbets, that they may die by inches, with heat, and hunger, and thirst? to pin them down to the ground, and then burn them by degrees, from the feet to the head? to roast them alive? When did a Turk or a Heathen find it necessary to use a fellow-creature thus?

I pray, to what end is this usage necessary? "Why, to prevent their running away; and to keep them constantly to their labour, that they may not idle away their time: So miserably stupid is this race of men, yea, so stubborn, and so wicked." Allowing them to be as stupid as you say, to whom is that stupidity owing? Without question, it lies altogether at the door of their inhuman masters; who give them no means, no opportunity, of improving their understanding; and, indeed, leave them no motive, either from hope or fear, to attempt any such thing. They were no way remarkable for stupidity while they remained in their own country: The inhabitants of Africa, where they have equal motives and equal means of improvement, are not inferior to the inhabitants of Europe: to some of them they are greatly superior. . . .

V. 5. . . . [T]his equally concerns every gentleman that has an estate in our American plantations; yea, all slave-holders, of whatever rank and degree; seeing men-buyers are exactly on a level with men-stealers. Indeed you say, "I pay honestly for my goods; and I am not concerned to know how they are come by." Nay, but you are; you are deeply concerned to know they are honestly come by. Otherwise you are a partaker with a thief, and are not a jot honester than him. But you know they are not honestly come by; you know they are procured by means nothing near so innocent as picking of pockets, house-breaking, or robbery upon the highway. You know they are procured by a deliberate series of more complicated villany (of fraud, robbery, and murder) than was ever practised either by Mahometans or Pagans; in particular, by murders, of all kinds, by the blood of the innocent poured upon the ground like water. Now, it is your money that pays the merchant, and through him the captain and the African butchers. You therefore are guilty, yea, principally guilty, of all these frauds, robberies, and murders. You are the spring that puts all the rest in notion; they would not stir a step without you; therefore, the blood of all these wretches who die before their time, whether in their country or elsewhere, lies upon your head. "The blood of thy brother" (for, whether thou wilt believe it or no, such he is in the sight of Him that made him) "crieth against thee from the earth," from the ship, and from the waters. O, whatever it costs, put a stop to its cry before it be too late: Instantly, at any price, were it the half of your goods, deliver thyself from blood-guiltiness! Thy hands, thy bed, thy furniture, thy house, thy lands, are at present stained with blood. Surely it is enough; accumulate no more guilt; spill no more the blood of the innocent! Do not hire another to shed blood; do not pay him for doing it! Whether you are a Christian or no, show yourself a man! Be not more savage than a lion or a bear!

6. Perhaps you will say, "I do not buy any Negroes; I only use those left me by my father." So far is well; but is it enough to satisfy your own conscience? Had your father, have you, has any man living, a right to use another as a slave? It cannot be, even setting Revelation aside. It cannot be, that either war, or contract, can give any man such a property in another as he has in his sheep and oxen. Much less is it possible, that any child of man should ever be born a slave. Liberty is the right of every human creature, as soon as he breathes the vital air; and no human law can deprive him of that right which he derives from the law of nature.

If, therefore, you have any regard to justice, (to say nothing of mercy, nor the revealed law of God,) render unto all their due. Give liberty to whom liberty is due, that is, to every child of man, to every partaker of human nature. Let none serve you but by his own act and deed, by his own voluntary choice. Away with all whips, all chains, all compulsion! Be gentle toward all men; and see that you invariably do unto every one as you would he should do unto you.

7. O thou God of love, thou who art loving to every man, and whose mercy is over all thy works; thou who art the Father of the spirits of all flesh, and who art rich in mercy unto all; thou who has mingled of one blood all the nations upon earth; have compassion upon these outcasts of men, who are trodden down as dung upon the earth! Arise, and help these that have no helper, whose blood is spilt upon the ground like water! Are not these also the work of thine own hands, the purchase of thy Son's blood? Stir them up to cry unto thee in the land of their captivity; and let their complaint come up before thee; let it enter into thy ears! Make even those that lead them away captive to pity them, and turn their captivity as the rivers in the south. O burst thou all their chains in sunder; more especially the chains of their sins! Thou Savior of all, make them free, that they may be free indeed!

From *The Works of the Reverend John Wesley, A.M.*, vol. 11, edited by Thomas Jackson (London: Wesleyan Methodist Book Room, 1872), pp. 64–65, 68, 70–74, 78–79.

37. Friedrich Schleiermacher, *Introduction to Christian Ethics*

Arguably the greatest nineteenth-century theologian, Friedrich Schleiermacher (1768–1834) understood the essence of Christian faith and life to be God-consciousness. Christian ethics, in this transcription of his lecture notes by a student, is the expression of the God-consciousness of Christ in life, an ethic to be contrasted with an imperative ethic based upon law.

The Consciousness of God as Principle of Action

Now a further word about the separation of the two disciplines [of Christian theology and Christian Ethics] insofar as it is something incidental. The distinctive nature of the propositions of Christian theology is that they contain expressions of the Christian consciousness to the extent that the highest reality is set forth in them. The propositions of Christian ethics are expressions of the Christian consciousness as it expresses itself as moral feeling. Those are not different explanations. One can easily imagine a conceptually rigorous grouping of a complex of propositions of one or the other. If we returned to the time when theology and ethics were not yet separated, that explanation would seem unsuitable, and it might be concluded that such union should never have happened. However, since we said the separation of the two disciplines is nothing essential, but only incidental, the implication clearly is that the propositions of one discipline must be analogous and homogeneous with those of the other. Still a unity must be found here. It is this: When it is said that Christian ethics contains expressions about the Christian moral feeling, that does not mean that the consciousness of God should thereby have been excluded; on the contrary, it is the character of the Christian moral feeling that the principle of behavior should be nothing else but the consciousness of God. As far as Christian theology is concerned, it has not been said that the Christian consciousness has not always included the principles of Christian behavior. For example, if we adhere to the propositions of the Christian consciousness that affirm the attributes of God, then we must certainly proceed from the fact that these are always understandable only in relation to one another. However, if we construct only one combination—for example, between divine omnipotence and divine love—then we must say that this combination leads to trust in God, and that is already a principle of behavior. It must be possible in the Christian sphere to accomplish in form what Spinoza accomplished in the philosophical sphere, namely, to treat everything as ethics. Theology could appear in ethics, albeit incompletely, just as ethics has appeared in theology.

Thus, in the most precise accord, we must imagine that Christian consciousness as that in which the highest reality is set forth and Christian consciousness as that which includes the source of actions are entirely one and the same. . . .

The Use of the Moral in Holy Scripture

Having asserted that Christian ethics should be nothing but the manifestation of the Christian life, how do we establish that what we take up in Christian ethics is actually the pure expression of the Christian principle? Here we can give only the following answer: We have to establish this from its agreement with Scripture. This answer has its ground in what we as Protestant Christians believe about the standard authority of Scripture. In practice we find here a significant distinction between the respective methods of Christian ethics and theology. The same theologians who use a number of biblical texts in their dogmatic works use very few appeals to Scripture in their discussions of morality. Why is that? Is Scripture more sparing in moral than in theological concerns? That is not the case. Certainly the social relationships of that time were entirely different from what they are presently. The vital mistakes that had to be resisted no longer occur to us, and the same is true in connection with those things that gave value to other regulations. Not due to scarcity but in the applicability to the present situation—therein lies the issue. Here the *ignara ratio theologica* [ignorance of theological principles] meets us halfway. If we cannot make direct use of the specific regulations, we do have the general principles that we can employ in our situation and which we can then verify with Scripture passages. The specific regulations are to be made applicable for us by way of analogy. Therefore we do not need to pass over into the philosophical sphere, which will always govern Christian theology and ethics in form but never in substance. From where, however, do we originally derive the substance? The intellectually rigorous method requires that substance originate conjointly with form and that both be developed from the same thing. Tracing its origin to Scripture gives the method its final confirmation. That is the way that we must distinguish our approach from rational ethics. That to which we appeal fundamentally is the pure Christian principle of life, which we find manifested in the Christian life itself. Having found this principle, we will be able to go to work entirely analytically. In this way it is only the rigor of form for which we have presupposed the rule of the philosophical method. We do not have to appeal directly to anything speculative and rational.

The Relationship of What Is "Pleasing to God" to the Fact of Redemption

. . . The common element of all Christian doctrine is that the fact of redemption is acknowledged through Christ, and without this there is no Christian doctrine. The question is: What kind of effect does this have generally on Christian ethics, and how is this doctrine derived? Here we must go back to the still more general religious character of doctrine where it must be agreed that ethics is religious when it manifests and sanctions the activity as pleasing to God and so constructs it. But how should the fundamental fact of redemption through Christ be viewed in this respect? It is easy to show that it can take place in a twofold way. First, one says: The recognition of what is pleasing to God is independent of the fact of redemption through Christ, but in this fact Christianity has given assistance, which is not found outside of Christianity, for realizing the God-pleasing action. Does this fundamental belief of the Christian have an effect on the construction of ethics? No, because nothing is incumbent upon ethics in and for itself except to construct the whole range of human activity that satisfies a certain idea of the right and good. If recognition of the divine will has always existed prior to redemption, then no change can take place in the construction of ethics. At most it would be of influence in asceticism. Here we can return again to the attempt to reduce Christian ethics to philosophical ethics. Beginning with that presupposition, one should abandon the attempt to construct Christian ethics and simply add the individual propositions of dogmatics as postscripts. The question is whether another presupposition is possible. By all means, if we put the matter as follows: The idea of "pleasing to God" has itself emerged in another way through the fact of the divine revelation in the person of Christ, and adhering to this revelation of God in Christ was also a manifestation of the idea of "pleasing to God." In that case it is clear that there must be a Christian ethics. What exactly is this that has continually emerged in the Christian church as the Christian consciousness? If we begin with Christ himself, he lays the most certain claim to the fact that he has knowledge of God that can be communicated only through him, and that he sets forth a knowledge of God's will that did not exist before him.

The Ethical Consequences of a Superhuman Representation of the Person of Christ

This is indeed clear, but those who proceed from the other presupposition offer another explanation: Christ was right because his knowledge of God was at that time not yet available. He spoke to his people, among whom there could not yet be the knowledge of what is pleasing to God; neither could it have been known by the Gentiles. Many have said: Christian ethics needs only to be assimilated to what is already available (Stoicism). Christ has revealed what is of God and the divine will, and without him that could not have become known until later. Thus the same thing is said, but now one adds an appendix: After we have considered how much Christ's teachings about God concur with human reason, it is natural to jettison the historical element and build solely upon human reason. Then it would be time to abandon Christian ethics and to explain what appears there as pure rational instruction. Now the question becomes: Is there another explanation of those words of Christ, and can one decide between the two? As long as reason has not attained this self-standing knowledge, it is clear that the moral teachings of Christ must be perceived as belonging exclusively to him. Suppose, however, that after reason has attained this self-understanding, Christian ethics expounds this unequivocally as rational instruction. This happens because the intelligence is very reticent to relinquish its customary form, and there may be a certain wisdom in leading the soul to retain the form even now in practice. But it is clear that another interpretation is possible. Once it has been conceded that the moral prescriptions of Christ were available before him among neither the Jews nor the Gentiles, and that they have been made valid only in connection with Christianity, then one can assert correctly: Human reason would not have attained that by itself, and if it were to attain that in the present, that is to be ascribed only to the influence which Christ has had on it. This all depends upon the conception that one has of the person of Christ. If one has a purely natural conception, one must say: Christ can bring forth nothing except what human reason would also have discovered at a later time. However, if one says that with the person of Christ and through Christ something real has entered human nature, that something has appeared that was not previously there and that even now can come forth only insofar as the union with Christ persists, then one must concede that human reason does not yet have that on its own. Therefore the existence of a special Christian ethics stands or falls with the superhuman conception of the person of Christ. From a purely naturalistic view of Christianity, it is always contradictory to pursue a distinctly Christian ethics, and it is always consistent to turn it into the pure instruction of reason. . . .

The Replacement of the Imperative by the Descriptive Form

Beginning from the distinction between the Protestant and Catholic churches, let us ask what form the particular propositions of our ethics should take. What first suggests itself is that they should have the form of commandment. Then again one could insist that another form would be more appropriate. Since not all commandments are stated explicitly in Scripture, this approach seems to lean toward Catholicism. In that case, who is the one giving commands? If propositions were always the pure words of Scripture, then one would know that Scripture is the one giving commands. But propositions are often developed from Scripture, and then the developer—namely, the theologian—appears as the one giving commands, and this must not happen. The more the church is ruled by the civil arm, the less each will be upheld. If something is commanded in relation to the Christian life, the Christian will then see that it proceeds more from the civil arm. Though we have no obligation to choose the giving of commands as the form for Christian ethics, it would still be good to do in order to breathe new life into the distinction between clergy and laity. In addition to the commandment, we find another form already in Scripture which alone is sufficient reason to prefer it to the other. This twofold form found in the New Testament consists of the already mentioned commandment (in the maxims of the apostolic letters and the teachings of Christ) and then the purely descriptive form, which we find in the most crucial passages—as, for example, in [1] Corinthians 13 where we find the description of *agape*, which still occupies a major place in morality. There nothing is commanded, but simply stated that it is such and such. The same is true in Galatians where the *karpoi tou pneumatos* [fruits of the Spirit] are described. From this passage [Gal. 5:16–24], in which Paul renounces the law, one could draw a further conclusion and assert that he meant not only the Mosaic Law—though surely that is the main point—but also the legal form in general. One must think of the moral law generally. How else can it cohere with Paul's statement that "You are not under the law"? One cannot think of the Mosaic law without thinking of the moral law of the Decalogue. In that case, what is the essence and the distinguishing feature of law? Law is given where it is presupposed that the content of the law would not be followed if the law were not given. The contrary is always presupposed. The same is true in politics. According to Paul, that statement can refer only to the form, not to the content, of the law, and then one sees clearly how this encompasses the whole of human life. Wherever the Spirit is and wherever human beings develop for themselves the fruit of the Spirit, there is no longer any connection with law. For such persons the law no longer exists. If we conceive the task of Christian ethics as assembling those propositions which are actually followed as a result of the operation of that Spirit, then we see how the form of law is unsuitable for this content. As Paul said: "You are not under the law." If now and again the imperative form creates the impression of a commandment-giving faction in the church, it seems most appropriate to renounce that form and adhere to the other. If now, based on Paul himself, it can be ascertained that he made use of the imperative form, we will discover that this is natural where he writes generally to *neophutous* [neophytes] in Christianity, for whom the Spirit does not yet have power over the whole of life. Surely this is continually the case in the Christian church, and there is none for whom the law is not necessary, at least at times, though it is purely ascetic for each individual. We conclude that the form of Christian ethics that most clearly expresses the spirit of Christianity is the antithesis to law. However, one is free to put oneself or another under the form of law where it is necessary.

Considering the usual practice, we find the commandment to be the dominant form, and so it is natural to ask how that could have originated, inasmuch as we consider it incorrect. On the one hand, this draws its main support from the relationship that one seeks to give to Christian and philosophical ethics. This has taken a different form in different times. During ancient times the descriptive form more often prevailed. Thus in Stoicism the archetype was the description of the wise custom, while in Aristotelian thought it was the description of virtue. However, in more recent moral philosophy the ethics of duty has generally predominated, and there the form of commandment emerges. If we want to investigate whence this has come, we will hardly know where to begin except with this: The development of universal ethics has, on the one hand, been joined to politics (where law rightly dominates). History offers still another clue: Philosophical ethics has developed, not from what exists in science, but more from what is found in the common public life. Through the medium of rational ethics it has returned, via the practice of Christianity, in the didactic form of academic theology. That practice, however, was catechetical, and thus that ethics was developed from the practice of pedagogy, where even the commandment has its natural place. Two very different things have to be considered here.

The Overcoming of the Old Testament Economy in "Adoption": The Spiritual Coming of Age

Since we base Christian ethics on Scripture, we must ask what Scripture is. Is it the New Testament alone? Or both testaments together? Or the New Testament as an appendix to the Old Testament? The more one concedes and assigns to the Old Testament, the more the command-giving form will dominate, because this is what carries weight in the Old Testament. However, Paul's cardinal passage in the Epistle to the Galatians should provide the ground to deny the Old Testament the right to determine the form. When Judaism was a theocracy, there was a confusion of politics and religion. The main form in which God was held in consciousness was political, for God was conceived as sovereign. The natural development of this general consciousness in the individual included the notion that the divine will appeared in the form of commandment. In Christianity this necessarily must be otherwise, not only because particularism is abandoned, but because the relationship is conceived differently from the very beginning. In Christianity the will of God does not come to us so much as it arises within us through the union in which Christ stands with God. Each individual is in the Christian church only to the extent that there exists between him and Christ a unity of will like that between Christ and God. The true essence of Christianity and the way in which redemption should be conceived in moral terms is this: The will of God arises within us through communion with Christ. Therefore a form that represents the will of God as something external can no longer be regarded as correct. Rather we must say that in the State itself the greater the unity between the individual and the whole, the less laws are necessary. The more we stress this characteristic Christian standpoint, the more the imperative form appears unsuitable. The form of pure statement, however, implies in each moment that something gains validity only by virtue of the Spirit ruling in the Christian church. On the other hand, it can still be said that in one passage Christ himself lays down his entire will for his disciples in the form of a commandment, *entole:* "A *kaine entole* [new commandment] I give to you" (John 13:34). But what is the content of the commandment? In a literal sense the form [of the commandment] cannot be applied at all to this content because the content is love. Love is a disposition, and a disposition can never be commanded. Therefore, that is either a figurative or an elliptical expression, or the content is to be understood indirectly. But, no, Christ wanted to set forth love as that by which he would recognize his disciples; therefore, *entole* is not to be taken literally.

From Friedrich Schleiermacher, *Introduction to Christian Ethics,* translated by John C. Shelley (Nashville, Abingdon Press, 1989, English translation), pp. 44–46, 49–51, 62–65. Copyright © 1983 by Verlag W. Kohlhammer GmbH, Stuttgart.

38. F. D. Maurice,
The Kingdom of Christ

Prominent among mid–nineteenth-century British theologians, Frederick Deni-
son Maurice (1805–1872) styled himself a Christian socialist, even while criticiz-
ing the secular socialisms and utilitarianisms of his time alike. This selection il-
lustrates both his critical views and his grounding of Christian social ethics in the
life and sacraments of the church.

The impossibility of distinguishing social utilitarianism from individual
utilitarianism, of reconciling the acknowledgment of a certain ultimate end
in one region of thought with the positive denial of it in another, became
apparent to those whose minds were most real, most impatient of mere artificial boundaries, as well as to those who were strictly and formally logical. Poets found that if their art could be defended at all, it must be merely
as a kind of amusement, upon the same grounds as cards or horse-racing;
religious men, however reluctant they might be to acknowledge any relation between such topics, were driven to ask themselves whether the doctrine of Paley and Bentham could be reconciled with that of the Sermon on
the Mount, and if not, which was to be abandoned? This school, therefore,
found itself unexpectedly assailed by all those new and strange thoughts
respecting literature, metaphysics, and the spiritual universe, which had
been gradually working themselves out in the minds of men in the different parts of Europe, while Mr. Bentham had been occupied in his study
with the rationale of evidence, and having nothing to oppose to them, it
could only sound a retreat, and endeavour, at whatever risk of theoretical
or practical inconsistency, to defend the existence of its philosophy by cir-
cumscribing the application of it within very narrow limits. But even
within these limits it has no safe dwelling-place. For while the desire of
man for a universal polity has grown every day more strong, this desire has
connected itself more and more with deep feelings and passions, has had
less and less to do with the mere calculating understanding. But to this calculating understanding the Benthamites make their sole appeal; by this
they would fashion the whole scheme of human life, and of the universe.
The right thing is that the will of the majority should be omnipotent. But
what calculus have they discovered for measuring the strength which lies
in that word—*will*—or for ascertaining what is to become of all theories and
axioms of legislation when it has obtained supremacy?

Far more profound in its conception, and I think also, more interesting in
its details, than the system of which I have been speaking, was that which
was proclaimed in France about twelve years ago, under the name of St.
Simonianism. In their project of society the Benthamites discarded, or treated
as mere accidents, all national distinctness. But, there was one circumstance
in the condition of man which could not be wholly accidental, or entirely the

fruit of bad legislation. Men do exist in families; it would seem that in the most fortunate societies the principle of family life has been most recognized, its limits most accurately defined. Without taking any cognizance of this fact, the Benthamites created a society upon the hypothesis that mankind is an aggregate of individual atoms. The St. Simonians felt at once that such a scheme was a practical delusion: so long as the notions of mankind continue what they are, so long as the morality which maintains these notions, and is maintained by them, subsists, men will be continually acting, speaking, voting, *per stirpes*, and not *per capita*. Thus the aristocratical idea intrudes itself; the existence of a perfect democratical fellowship is impossible. . . .

. . . [D]oes the churchman I am supposing find himself in one of our awful manufacturing districts? Of course, the sense of his own utter inadequacy to deal with the mass of evil which he meets there is the first which will take hold of him, and will grow stronger every day. Yet he is there, and he knows that there is One who cares for this mass of living beings infinitely more than he does. Nay, his own coldness and heartlessness will continually remind him that if he is to care for them at all, the feeling must be communicated to him by him who often seems to these unhappy creatures utterly heedless of their sorrows and complainings. And then he has the consolation which the Athenian orator found when he reflected on the reverses of his countrymen, and the resistless march of Philip. 'If we had done such and such things and they had failed, we might despair; we have not done them, therefore let us hope.' A Church which was looked upon, and almost looked upon itself, as a tool of the aristocracy, which compared its own orders with the ranks in civil society, and forgot that it existed to testify that man as man is the object of his Creator's sympathy; such a Church had no voice which could reach the hearts of these multitudes. The Liberal proclamation which says, 'Teach them; impart to them a few of the things that we know', was more genial, and humane. But there are thoughts ever at work in these Englishmen, in these human beings, thoughts quickened by hunger and suffering, which such instruction could not appease. More impressive far was the speech of the Methodist and the Evangelical: 'You have immortal souls, they are perishing; oh! ask how they may be saved.' Such words spoken with true earnestness are very mighty. But they are not enough; men feel that they are not merely lost creatures; they look up to heaven above them, and ask whether it can be true that this is the whole account of their condition; that their sense of right and wrong, their cravings for fellowship, their consciousness of being creatures having powers which no other creatures possess, are all nothing. If religion, they say, will give us no explanation of these feelings, if it can only tell us about a fall for the whole race, and an escape for a few individuals of it, then our wants must be satisfied without religion. Then begin Chartism and Socialism, and whatever schemes make rich men tremble. Surely, what the modern assertors of a church system say about the duty of administering active charity to these sufferers, of showing that we do not merely regard them as pensioners on the national bounty, but as fellow-men for whom we are to make sacrifices—surely this language is far more to the purpose. Surely if acted upon even imperfectly, it must produce most happy effects. But how would the proclamation to our Chartists and Socialists, that they had baptismal purity once, and that they have lost it now; that they must recover their ground by repentance, by prayer and fasting; that they must submit to discipline, and be deprived of privileges which they never exercised nor cared for; how can such a proclamation as this meet any of the confused, disorderly notions which are stirring in their minds, or set them right?

On the other hand, if the new and unwonted proclamation were to go forth, 'God has cared for you, you are indeed his children; his Son has redeemed you, his Spirit is striving with you; there is a fellowship larger, more irrespective of outward distinctions, more democratical, than any which you can create; but it is a fellowship of mutual love, not mutual selfishness, in which the chief of all is the servant of all'—may not one think that a result would follow as great as that which attended the preaching of any Franciscan friar in the twelfth century, or any Methodist preacher in the eighteenth? For these are true words, everlasting words, and yet words which belong especially to our time; they are words which interpret, and must be interpreted by, that regular charity, that ministerial holiness, those sacraments, prayers, discipline, of which the Catholic speaks. They connect his words about repentance with those of the Evangelical, making it manifest, that nothing but an accursed nature and a depraved will could have robbed any of the blessings which God has bestowed upon us all. They translate into meaning and life all the liberal plans for the education of adults and children; they enable us to fulfil the notion, which statesmen have entertained, that the Church is to be the supporter of the existing orders, by making her a teacher and example to those orders respecting their duties and responsibilities; by removing the hatred which their forgetfulness of those duties and responsibilities is threatening to create in the minds of the lower classes.

But a churchman, such as I have supposed, would be both compelled by his circumstances, and urged by his principles, to change these convictions into action, by enlisting all the wealthier inhabitants of his parish in different services and occupations for the benefit of their inferiors. I am unwilling to enlarge upon this subject; first, because my practical ignorance makes me unfit to offer any suggestions upon it; and, secondly, because I am certain that our English political wisdom, guided by Catholic feeling, is already doing much in many parts of this land, in the accomplishment of such a design. I must, however, refer to it for the purpose of remarking how the notion that party organization is necessary, is at once explained and refuted the moment we aim at an ecclesiastical organization. It is explained when the truth, that no man is meant to work alone, which is the truth that is implied in this strange maxim, is made the principle of our action. It is refuted, for we find how infinitely freer from friction a society is which is held together by sacramental bonds, and is moving under the direction of an appointed pastor, than all societies constructed upon a party model, or acknowledging a party motive, ever have been or ever can be. For the one seeks to preserve all existing ranks and relations, the other sets them all aside. The one is continually endeavouring to understand how the middle classes may be brought most to act upon the lower, so as to be their guides and not their tyrants; how the upper classes may be brought to act upon the middle, so as not to be their fawning slaves and at the same time the betrayers of their consciences at elections—cold and distant and the objects of their servile imitation at other times; how each portion of the community may preserve its proper position to the rest, and may be fused together by the spiritual power which exists for each, the minister of all, the creature of none. The other confounds all orders, and yet does not the least diminish their mutual repulsion, or make them feel that they have a common object. Above all, the churchman is ever longing to discover how the handmaidens of the Church may be brought to do her the services which they alone can do, without departing for a moment from their own true estate, as wives, as sisters, as mothers; how the whole sex may be an order of Sisters of Charity; and how, in each particular neighbourhood, this order may be at work in lowliness and meekness, softening and healing the sorrows of the world. The partisan acknowledges no difference of vocation in man and woman; all are to be equally feverish and restless; careful about many things, unfit alike for quiet contemplation or regular activity.

From Frederick Denison Maurice, *The Kingdom of Christ or Hints to a Quaker: Respecting the Principles, Constitution and Ordinances of the Catholic Church*, vols. 1 and 2 (London: SCM Press Ltd., 1958), pp. 196–97, 335–38.

39.   Leo Tolstoy,
The Kingdom of God Is within You

The famous Russian novelist Leo Tolstoy (1828–1910) is important to the history of Christian ethics for his pacifist and anarchist views. Tolstoy believed that the renunciation of violence and abandonment of military, police, and penal institutions would enable the universal reign of love.

Response to Critics

The critics upon my books, both the Russian and the foreign critics, can be divided into two classes: into the religious critics—people who consider themselves to be believers—and lay critics, who are freethinkers.

I shall begin with the first:

In my book I accuse the church teachers of teaching contrary to Christ's commandments, which are clearly and definitely expressed in the Sermon on the Mount, and especially contrary to the commandment about nonresistance to evil, thus depriving Christ's teaching of all significance. The church teachers recognize the Sermon on the Mount with the commandment about non-resistance to evil as a divine revelation, and so, if they have found it necessary to write about my book at all, they ought, it would seem, first of all to answer this chief point of accusation and say outright whether they consider the teaching of the Sermon on the Mount and of the commandment about non-resistance to evil obligatory for a Christian, or not,—and they must not answer it as this is generally done, that is, by saying that, although on the one hand it cannot properly be denied, on the other it cannot be affirmed, the more so that, and so forth,—but must answer it just as the question is put by me in my book: did Christ actually demand from His disciples the fulfilment of what He taught in the Sermon on the Mount? and so, can a Christian, remaining a Christian, go to court, taking part in it and condemning people, or seeking in it defence by means of violence, or can he not? Can a Christian, still remaining a Christian, take part in the government, using violence against his neighbours, or not? And the chief question, which now, with the universal military service, stands before all men,—can a Christian, remaining a Christian, contrary to Christ's injunction, make any promises as to future acts, which are directly contrary to the teaching, and, taking part in military service, prepare himself for the murder of men and commit it?

The questions are put clearly and frankly, and, it would seem, they ought to be answered clearly and frankly. But nothing of the kind has been done in all the criticisms upon my book, just as nothing of the kind has been done in the case of all those arraignments of the church teachers for departing from Christ's law, with which history is filled since the time of Constantine.

Very much has been said in reference to my book about how incorrectly I interpret this or that passage in the Gospel, how I err in not acknowledging the Trinity, the redemption, and the immortality of the soul; very much has been said, but this one thing, which for every Christian forms the chief, essential question of life: how to harmonize what was clearly expressed in the teacher's words and is clearly expressed in the heart of every one of us,—the teaching about forgiveness, humility, renunciation, and love of all men, of our neighbours and of our enemies,—with the demand of military violence exerted against the men of one's own nation or another nation.

Everything which may be called semblances of answers to this question may be reduced to the five following divisions. I have tried in this respect to collect everything I could, not only in reference to the criticisms upon my book, but also in reference to what has been written upon the subject in former times.

The first, the rudest way of answering, consists in the bold assertion that violence does not contradict Christ's teaching, and that it is permitted and even prescribed by the Old and the New Testament.

Assertions of this kind issue for the most part from people high up in the governmental or ecclesiastic hierarchy, who are, therefore, quite convinced that no one will dare to contradict their assertions, and that if one actually dared to do so, they would not hear these objections. These men have, in consequence of their intoxication with their power, for the most part to such an extent lost the concept of what that Christianity is, in the name of which they occupy their places, that everything of a Christian nature in Christianity presents itself to them as sectarian; but everything which in the writings of the Old and the New Testament may be interpreted in an anti-Christian and pagan sense, they consider to be the foundation of Christianity. In favour of their assertion that Christianity does not contradict violence, these men with the greatest boldness generally bring forward the most offensive passages from the Old and the New Testament, and interpret them in the most non-Christian manner: the execution of Ananias and Sapphira, the execution of Simon Magus, and so forth. They adduce all those words of Christ which may be interpreted as a justification of cruelty, such as the expulsion from the temple, "It shall be more tolerable on that day for Sodom, than for that city," and so forth.

According to the concepts of these men, the Christian government is not in the least obliged to be guided by the spirit of humility, forgiveness of offenses, and love of our enemies.

It is useless to refute such an assertion, because the men who assert this refute themselves, or rather, turn away from Christ, inventing their own Christ and their own Christianity in place of Him in whose name the church exists and also the position which they occupy in it. If all men knew that the church preaches Christ punishing, and not forgiving, and warring, no one would be believing in this church, and there would be no one to prove what it is proving.

The second method is a little less rude. It consists in asserting that, although Christ really taught to offer one's cheek and give up a shirt, and this is a very high moral demand, there are malefactors in the world, and if these are not curbed by the exercise of force, the whole world and all good men will perish. This proof I found for the first time in John Chrysostom and I pointed out its incorrectness in my book, *My Religion.*

This argument is ungrounded, because, in the first place, if we allow ourselves to recognize any men as special malefactors (Raca), we thus destroy the whole meaning of the Christian teaching, according to which we are all equal and brothers, as the sons of one heavenly Father; in the second place, because, even if God permitted the exertion of violence against malefactors, it is absolutely impossible to find that safe and indubitable sign by which a malefactor may be unerringly told from one who is not, and so every man, or society of men, would recognize another as a malefactor, which is the case now; in the third place, because even if it were possible unerringly to tell malefactors from those who are not malefactors, it would still not be possible in a Christian society to execute, or maim, or lock up these malefactors, because in Christian society there would be no one to do this, because every Christian, as a Christian, is enjoined not to use violence against a malefactor.

The third method of answering is still shrewder than the previous one. It consists in asserting that, although the commandment of non-resistance to evil is obligatory for a Christian when the evil is directed against him personally, it ceases to be obligatory when the evil is directed against his neighbours, and that then a Christian is not only not obliged to fulfil the commandments, but is also obliged in the defence of his neighbours, contrary to the commandment, to use violence against the violators.

This assertion is quite arbitrary, and in the whole of Christ's teaching no confirmation of such an interpretation can be found. Such an interpretation is not only a limitation of the commandment, but a direct negation and annihilation of it. If any man has a right to use violence when another is threatened by danger, then the question as to the use of violence reduces itself to the question of defining what constitutes a danger for another person. But if my private judgment decides the question of danger for another, then there does not exist such a case of violence that it could not be explained on the basis of a danger with which another is threatened. Wizards were executed and burned, aristocrats and Girondists were executed, and so were their enemies, because those who were in power considered them to be dangerous for others.

If this important limitation, which radically undermines the meaning of the commandment, entered Christ's mind, there ought somewhere to be mention made of it. But in all the preaching and the life of the teacher there is not only no such limitation, but, on the contrary, there is expressed a particular caution against such a false and offensive limitation, which destroys the commandment. The mistake and the blunder of such a limitation is with particular clearness shown in the Gospel in connection with the judgment of Caiaphas, who made this very limitation. He recognized that it was not good to execute innocent Jesus, but he saw in Him danger, not for himself, but for the whole nation, and so he said: "It is expedient for us that one man should die for the people, and that the whole nation perish not." And more clearly still was the negation of such a limitation expressed in the words said to Peter when he attempted with violence to resist the evil which was directed against Jesus [Matt. 26:52]. Peter was not defending himself, but his beloved and divine teacher. And Christ directly forbade him to do so, saying that he who takes the sword shall perish with the sword.

Besides, the justification of violence used against a neighbour for the sake of defending another man against worse violence is always incorrect, because in using violence against an evil which is not yet accomplished, it is impossible to know which evil will be greater—whether the evil of my violence or of that against which I wish to defend my neighbour. We execute a criminal, thus freeing society from him, and we are positively unable to tell whether the criminal would not have changed on the morrow and whether our execution is not a useless cruelty. We lock up a man whom we suppose to be a dangerous member of society, but beginning with to-morrow this man may cease to be dangerous, and his incarceration is futile. I see that a man whom I know to be a robber is pursuing a girl, and I have a gun in my hand,—I kill the robber and save the girl; the robber has certainly been killed or wounded, but it is unknown to me what would happen if that were not the case. What an enormous amount of evil must take place, as it actually does, as the result of arrogating to ourselves the right to prevent an evil that may occur! Ninety-nine hundredths of the evil of the world, from the Inquisition to dynamite bombs and the executions and sufferings of tens of thousands of so-called political criminals, are based on this reflection.

40.   Pope Pius IX,
The Syllabus of Errors

The Syllabus of Errors, *promulgated by Pope Pius IX in 1864, presents and condemns eighty theses attributed to modern thinkers on the themes of rationalism, liberalism, the church's rights, and the church's relationship to the state. In subsequent years the teachings of the* Syllabus *were nuanced, but at the time they highlighted the conservative trend of ethical thought within nineteenth-century Roman Catholicism. Each of the statements listed here was considered to be an "error" that all faithful Catholics were expected to reject.*

10. As the philosopher is one thing, and philosophy is another, so it is the right and duty of the philosopher to submit to the authority which he shall have recognized as true; but philosophy neither can nor ought to submit to any authority.

11. The Church not only ought never to animadvert upon philosophy, but ought to tolerate the errors of philosophy, leaving to philosophy the care of their correction.

12. The decrees of the Apostolic See and the Roman Congregations fetter the free progress of science.

13. The method and principles by which the old scholastic doctors cultivated theology are no longer suitable to the demands of the age and the progress of science. . . .

15. Every man is free to embrace and profess the religion he shall believe true, guided by the light of reason.

16. Men may, in any religion, find the way of eternal salvation, and obtain eternal salvation.

17. We may entertain at least a well-founded hope for the eternal salvation of all those who are in no manner in the true Church of Christ.

18. Protestantism is nothing more than another form of the same true Christian religion, in which it is possible to be equally pleasing to God as in the Catholic Church. . . .

21. The Church has not the power of defining dogmatically that the religion of the Catholic Church is the only true religion. . . .

23. The Roman Pontiffs and oecumenical Councils have exceeded the limits of their power, have usurped the rights of princes, and have even committed errors in defining matters of faith and morals.

24. The Church has not the power of availing herself of force, or any direct or indirect temporal power. . . .

27. The ministers of the Church, and the Roman Pontiff, ought to be absolutely excluded from all charge and dominion over temporal affairs. . . .

38. Roman Pontiffs have, by their too arbitrary conduct, contributed to the division of the Church into eastern and western. . . .

47. The best theory of civil society requires that popular schools open to the children of all classes, and, generally, all public institutes intended for instruction in letters and philosophy, and for conducting the education of the young, should be freed from all ecclesiastical authority, government, and interference, and should be fully subject to the civil and political power, in conformity with the will of rulers and the prevalent opinions of the age.

48. This system of instructing youth, which consists in separating it from the Catholic faith and from the power of the Church, and in teaching exclusively, or at least primarily, the knowledge of natural things and the earthly ends of social life alone, may be approved by Catholics. . . .

55. The Church *ought to be separated* from the State, and the State from the Church. . . .

63. It is allowable to refuse obedience to legitimate princes: nay, more, to rise in insurrection against them. . . .

76. The abolition, of the temporal power, of which the Apostolic See is possessed, would contribute in the greatest degree to the liberty and prosperity of the Church.

77. In the present day, it is no longer expedient that the Catholic religion shall be held as the only religion of the State, to the exclusion of all other modes of worship.

78. Whence it has been wisely provided by law, in some countries called Catholic, that persons coming to reside therein shall enjoy the public exercise of their own worship.

79. Moreover, it is false that the civil liberty of every mode of worship, and the full power given to all of overtly and publicly manifesting their opinions and their ideas, of all kinds whatsoever, conduce more easily to corrupt the morals and minds of the people, and to the propagation of the pest of indifferentism.

80. The Roman Pontiff can and ought to reconcile himself to, and agree with, progress, liberalism, and civilization as lately introduced.

From Robert R. Hull, *The Syllabus of Errors of Pope Pius IX: The Scourge of "Liberalism"* (Huntington, Ind.: Our Sunday Visitor, 1926), pp. 32, 34, 39, 42, 46, 47, 53–54, 60, 71–72. Copyright © 1926 by Our Sunday Visitor Press.

41. David Walker,
Appeal to the Coloured Citizens of the World

*Walker (1785–1830), a free black living in Boston, Massachusetts, was out-
raged by the oppression of his fellow African Americans, and was particularly distressed by the complicity of white Christians in that oppression. His* Appeal *(1829)
was one of the earliest black jeremiads against white America; it may have provided
the inspiration for Nat Turner's famous slave revolt of 1831.*

Article 3. . . . Religion, my brethren, is a substance of deep consideration
among all nations of the earth. The Pagans have a kind, as well as the Mahometans, the Jews and the Christians. But pure and undefiled religion, such
as was preached by Jesus Christ and his apostles, is hard to be found in all
the earth. God, through his instrument, Moses, handed a dispensation of his
Divine will, to the children of Israel after they had left Egypt for the land of
Canaan or of Promise, who through hypocrisy, oppression and unbelief, departed from the faith.—He then, by his apostles, handed a dispensation of
his, together with the will of Jesus Christ, to the Europeans in Europe, who,
in open violation of which, have made *merchandise* of us, and it does appear
as though they take this very dispensation to aid them in their *infernal* depredations upon us. Indeed, the way in which religion was and is conducted by
the Europeans and their descendants, one might believe it was a plan fabri-
cated by themselves and the *devils* to oppress us. But hark! My master has
taught me better than to believe it—he has taught me that his gospel as it was
preached by himself and his apostles remains the same, notwithstanding Europe has tried to mingle blood and oppression with it. . . .

The Pagans, Jews and Mahometans try to make proselytes to their religions, and whatever human beings adopt their religions they extend to
them their protection. But Christian Americans, not only hinder their fellow
creatures, the Africans, but thousands of them *will absolutely beat a coloured
person nearly to death, if they catch him on his knees, supplicating the throne of
grace.* This barbarous cruelty was by all the heathen nations of antiquity, and
is by the Pagans, Jews and Mahometans of the present day, left entirely to
Christian Americans to inflict on the Africans and their descendants, that
their cup which is nearly full may be completed. I have known tyrants or
usurpers of human liberty in different parts of this country to take their fellow creatures, the coloured people, and beat them until they would scarcely
leave life in them; what for? Why they say "The black devils had the audacity to be found *making prayers and supplications to the God who made
them!!!!*" Yes, I have known small collections of coloured people to have con-
vened together, for no other purpose than to worship God Almighty, in spirit
and in truth, to the best of their knowledge; when tyrants, calling themselves *patrols,* would also convene and wait almost in breathless silence for
the poor coloured people to commence singing and praying to the Lord our

God, as soon as they had commenced, the wretches would burst in upon them and drag them out and commence beating them as they would rattle-snakes—many of whom, they would beat so unmercifully, that they would hardly be able to crawl for weeks and sometimes for months. Yet the American ministers send out missionaries to convert the heathen, while they keep us and our children sunk at their feet in the most abject ignorance and wretchedness that ever a people was afflicted with since the world began. Will the Lord suffer this people to proceed much longer? Will he not stop them in their career? Does he regard the heathens abroad, more than the heathens among the Americans? Surely the Americans must believe that God is partial, notwithstanding his Apostle Peter, declared before Cornelius and others that he has no respect to persons, but in every nation he that feareth God and worketh righteousness is accepted with him.—"The word," said he, "which God sent unto the children of Israel, preaching peace, by Jesus Christ, (he is Lord of all.") Have not the Americans the Bible in their hands? Do they believe it? Surely they do not. See how they treat us in open viola-tion of the Bible! They no doubt will be greatly offended with me, but if God does not awaken them, it will be, because they are superior to other men, as they have represented themselves to be. Our divine Lord and Master said, "all things whatsoever ye would that men should do unto you, do ye even so unto them." But an American minister, with the Bible in his hand, holds us and our children in the most abject slavery and wretchedness. Now I ask them, would they like for us to hold them and their children in abject slav-ery and wretchedness? No, says one, that never can be done—you are too abject and ignorant to do it—you are not men—you were made to be slaves to us, to dig up gold and silver for us and our children. Know this, my dear sirs, that although you treat us and our children now, as you do your do-mestic beast—yet the final result of all future events are known but to God Almighty alone, who rules in the armies of heaven and among the inhabi-tants of the earth, and who dethrones one earthly king and sits up another, as it seemeth good in his holy sight. We may attribute these vicissitudes to what we please, but the God of armies and of justice rules in heaven and in earth, and the whole American people shall see and know it yet, to their sat-isfaction. I have known pretended preachers of the gospel of my Master, who not only held us as their natural inheritance, but treated us with as much rigor as any Infidel or Deist in the world—just as though they were intent only on taking our blood and groans to glorify the Lord Jesus Christ. The wicked and ungodly, seeing their preachers treat us with so much cru-elty, they say: our preachers, who must be right, if any body are, treat them like brutes, and why cannot we?—They think it is no harm to keep them in slavery and put the whip to them, and why cannot we do the same!—They being preachers of the gospel of Jesus Christ, if it were any harm, they would surely preach against their oppression and do their utmost to erase it from the country; not only in one or two cities, but one continual cry would be raised in all parts of this confederacy, and would cease only with the com-plete overthrow of the system of slavery, in every part of the country. But how far the American preachers are from preaching against slavery and oppression, which have carried their country to the brink of a precipice; to save them from plunging down the side of which, will hardly be affected, will appear in the sequel of this paragraph, which I shall narrate just as it transpired. I remember a Camp Meeting in South Carolina, for which I embarked in a Steam Boat at Charleston, and having been five or six hours on the water, we at last arrived at the place of hearing, where was a very great concourse of people, who were no doubt, collected together to hear the word of God, (that some had collected barely as spectators to the scene, I will not here pretend to doubt, however, that is left to themselves and their God.) Myself and boat companions, having been there a little while, we were all called up to hear; I among the rest went up and took my seat—being seated, I fixed myself in a complete position to hear the word of my Saviour and to receive such as I thought was authenticated by the Holy Scriptures; but to my no ordinary astonishment, our Reverend gentleman got up and told us (coloured people) that slaves must be obedient to their masters—must do their duty to their masters or be whipped—the whip was made for the backs of fools, &c. Here I pause for a moment, to give the world time to consider what was my surprise, to hear such preaching from a minister of my Master, whose very gospel is that of peace and not of blood and whips, as this pretended preacher tried to make us believe. What the American preachers can think of us, I aver this day before my God, I have never been able to define. They have newspapers and monthly periodicals, which they receive in continual succession, but on the pages of which, you will scarcely ever find a paragraph respecting slavery, which is ten thousand times more injurious to this country than all the other evils put together; and which will be the final overthrow of its government, unless something is very speedily done; for their cup is nearly full—Perhaps they will laugh at or make light of this; but I tell you Americans! that unless you speedily alter your course, *you* and your *Country are gone!!!!!!* For God Almighty will tear up the very face of the earth!!! Will not that very remarkable passage of Scripture be fulfilled on Christian Americans? Hear it Americans!! "He that is unjust, let him be unjust still:—and he which is filthy, let him be filthy still: and he that is righteous, let him be righteous still: and he that is holy, let him be holy still." I hope that the Americans may hear, but I am afraid that they have done us so much injury, and are so firm in the belief that our Creator made us to be an inheritance to them for ever, that their hearts will be hardened, so that their destruction may be sure. This language, perhaps is too harsh for the American's delicate ears. But Oh Americans! Americans!! I warn you in the name of the Lord, (whether you will hear, or forbear,) to repent and reform, or you are ruined!!! Do you think that our blood is hidden from the Lord, because you can hide it from the rest of the world, by sending out missionaries, and by your charitable deeds to the Greeks, Irish, &c.? Will he not publish your secret crimes on the house top? Even here in Boston, pride and prejudice have got to such a pitch, that in the very houses erected to the Lord, they have built little places for the reception of coloured people, where they must sit during meeting, or keep away from the house of God, and the preachers say nothing about it—much less go into the hedges and highways seeking the lost sheep of the house of Israel, and try to bring them in to their Lord and Master. There are not a more wretched, ignorant, miserable, and abject set of beings in all the world, than the blacks in the Southern and Western sections of this country, under tyrants and devils. The preachers of America cannot see them, but they can send out missionaries to convert the heathens, notwithstanding. Americans! unless you speedily alter your course of proceeding, if God Almighty does not stop you, I say it in his name, that you may go on and do as you please for ever, both in time and eternity—never fear any evil at all!!!!!!!! . . .

How can the preachers and people of America believe the Bible? Does it teach them any distinction on account of a man's colour? Hearken, Americans! to the injunctions of our Lord and Master, to his humble followers.

"And Jesus came and spake unto them, saying, all power is given unto me in Heaven and in earth.

"Go ye, therefore, and teach all nations, baptizing them in the name of the Father, and of the Son, and of the Holy Ghost.

"Teaching them to observe all things whatsoever I have commanded you; and lo, I am with you alway, even unto the end of the world. Amen."

I declare, that the very face of these injunctions appear to be of God and not of man. They do not show the slightest degree of distinction. "Go ye therefore" (says my divine Master) "and teach all nations," (or in other words, all people) "baptizing them in the name of the Father, and of the Son, and of the Holy Ghost." Do you understand the above, Americans? We are a people, notwithstanding many of you doubt it. You have the Bible in your hands, with this very injunction.—Have you been to Africa, teaching the inhabitants thereof the words of the Lord Jesus? "Baptizing them in the name of the Father, and of the Son and of the Holy Ghost." Have you not, on the contrary, entered among us, and learnt us the art of throat-cutting, by setting us to fight, one against another, to take each other as prisoners of war, and sell to you for small bits of calicoes, old swords, knives, &c. to make slaves for you and your children? This being done, have you not brought us among you, in chains and hand-cuffs, like brutes, and treated us with all the cruelties and rigour your ingenuity could invent, consistent with the laws of your country, which (for the blacks) are tyrannical enough? Can the American preachers appeal unto God, the Maker and Searcher of hearts, and tell him, with the Bible in their hands, that they make no distinction on account of men's colour? Can they say, O God! thou knowest all things—thou knowest that we make no distinction between thy creatures, to whom we have to preach thy Word? Let them answer the Lord; and if they cannot do it in the affirmative, have they not departed from the Lord Jesus Christ, their master? But some may say, that they never had, or were in possession of religion, which made no distinction, and of course they could not have departed from it. I asked you then, in the name of the Lord, of what kind can your religion be? Can it be that which was preached by our Lord Jesus Christ from Heaven? I believe you cannot be so wicked as to tell him that his Gospel was that of *distinction*. What can the American preachers and people take God to be? Do they believe his words?

If they do, do they believe that he will be mocked? Or do they believe, because they are whites and we blacks, that God will have respect to them? Did not God make us all as it seemed best to himself? What right, then, has one of us, to despise another, and treat them cruel, on account of his colour, which none, but the God who made it can alter? Can there be a greater absurdity in nature, and particularly in a free republican country? But the Americans, having introduced slavery among them, their hearts have become almost seared, as with hot iron, and God has nearly given them up to believe a lie in preference to the truth!!! And I am awfully afraid that pride, prejudice, avarice and blood, will, before long prove the final ruin of this happy republic, or land of *liberty!!!!* Can any thing be a greater mockery of religion than the way in which it is conducted by the Americans? It appears as though they are bent only on daring God Almighty to do his best—they chain and handcuff us and our children and drive us around the country like brutes, and go into the house of the God of justice to return him thanks for having aided them in their infernal cruelties inflicted upon us. Will the Lord suffer this people to go on much longer, taking his holy name in vain? Will he not stop them, PREACHERS and all? O Americans! Americans!! I call God—I call angels—I call men, to witness, that your DESTRUCTION *is at hand,* and will be speedily consummated unless you REPENT.

42. Frederick Douglass, *Life and Writings*

Douglass (1817–1895) was a former slave who became a vocal abolitionist, speaking on behalf of the American Anti-Slavery Society. In these excerpts from three speeches delivered in the 1840s, Douglass issues a stinging rebuke of the hypocrisy evident in the American church.

. . . [P]eople in general will say they liked colored men as well as any other, *but in their proper place!* They assign us that place; they don't let us do it for ourselves, nor will they allow us a voice in the decision. They will not allow that we have a head to think, and a heart to feel, and a soul to aspire. They treat us not as men, but as dogs—they cry "Stu-boy!" and expect us to run and do their bidding. That's the way we are liked. You degrade us, and then ask why we are degraded—you shut our mouths, and then ask why we don't speak—you close your colleges and seminaries against us, and then ask why we don't know more.

But all this prejudice sinks into insignificance in *my* mind, when compared with the enormous iniquity of the system which is its cause—the system that sold my four sisters and my brothers into bondage—and which calls in its priests to defend it even from the Bible! The slave-holding ministers preach up the divine right of the slaveholders to property in their fellow-men. The southern preachers say to the poor slave, "Oh! if you wish to be happy in time, happy in eternity, you must be obedient to your masters; their interest is yours. God made one portion of men to do the working, and another to do the thinking; how good God is! Now, you have no trouble or anxiety; but ah! you can't imagine how perplexing it is to your masters and mistresses to have so much thinking to do in your behalf! You cannot appreciate your blessings; you know not how happy a thing it is for you, that you were born of that portion of the human family which has the working, instead of the thinking to do! Oh! how grateful and obedient you ought to be to your masters! How beautiful are the arrangements of Providence! Look at your hard, horny hands—see how nicely they are adapted to the labor you have to perform! Look at our delicate fingers, so exactly fitted for our station, and see how manifest it is that God designed us to be His thinkers, and you the workers—Oh! the wisdom of God!"—I used to attend a Methodist church, in which my master was a class-leader; he would talk most sanctimoniously about the dear Redeemer, who was sent "to preach deliverance to the captives, and set at liberty them that are bruised"—he could pray at morning, pray at noon, and pray at night; yet he could lash up my poor cousin by his two thumbs, and inflict stripes and blows upon his bare back, till the blood streamed to the ground! all the time quoting scripture, for his authority, and appealing to that passage of the Holy Bible which says, "He that knoweth his master's will, and doeth it not, shall be beaten with many stripes!" Such was the amount of this good Methodist's piety. . . .

. . . I have to inform you that the religion of the southern states, at this time, is the great supporter, the great sanctioner of the bloody atrocities to which I have referred. While America is printing tracts and Bibles; sending missionaries abroad to convert the heathen; expending her money in various ways for the promotion of the Gospel is foreign lands—the slave not only lies forgotten, uncared for, but is trampled under foot by the very churches of the land. What have we in America? Why, we have slavery made part of the religion of the land. Yes, the pulpit there stands up as the great defender of this cursed institution, as it is called. Ministers of religion come forward and torture the hallowed pages of inspired wisdom to sanction the bloody deed. They stand forth as the foremost, the strongest defenders of this "institution."

As a proof of this, I need not do more than state the general fact, that slavery has existed under the droppings of the sanctuary of the south for the last two hundred years, and there has not been any war between the religion and the slavery of the south. Whips, chains, gags, and thumbscrews have all lain under the droppings of the sanctuary, and instead of rusting from off the limbs of the bondman, those droppings have served to preserve them in all their strength. Instead of preaching the Gospel against this tyranny, rebuke, and wrong, ministers of religion have sought, by all and every means, to throw in the background whatever in the Bible could be construed into opposition to slavery, and to bring forward that which they could torture into its support.

This I conceive to be the darkest feature of slavery, and the most difficult to attack, because it is identified with religion, and exposes those who denounce it to the charge of infidelity. Yes, those with whom I have been laboring, namely, the old organization anti-slavery society of America, have been again and again stigmatized as infidels, and for what reason? Why, solely in consequence of the faithfulness of their attacks upon the slaveholding religion of the southern states, and the northern religion that sympathizes with it. I have found it difficult to speak on this matter without persons coming forward and saying, "Douglass, are you not afraid of injuring the cause of Christ? You do not desire to do so, we know; but are you not undermining religion?" This has been said to me again and again, even since I came to this country, but I cannot be induced to leave off these exposures. I love the religion of our blessed Savior. I love that religion that comes from above, in the "wisdom of God, which is first pure, then peaceable, gentle, and easy to be entreated, full of mercy and good fruits, without partiality and without hypocrisy." I love that religion that sends its votaries to bind up the wounds of him that has fallen among thieves. I love that religion that makes it the duty of its disciples to visit the fatherless and the widow in their affliction. I love that religion that is based upon the glorious principle, of love to God and love to man; which makes its followers do unto others as they themselves would be done by. If you demand liberty to yourself, it says, grant it to your neighbors. If you claim a right to think for yourself, it says, allow your neighbors the same right. If you claim to act for yourself, it says, allow your neighbors the same right. It is because I love this religion that I hate the slaveholding, the woman-whipping, the mind-darkening, the soul-destroying religion that exists in the southern states of America. It is because I regard the one as good, and pure, and holy, that I cannot but regard the other as bad, corrupt, and wicked. Loving the one I must hate the other; holding to the one I must reject the other. . . .

. . . Wm. Lloyd Garrison and a noble army of the friends of emancipation have been labouring in season and out of season, amid smiles and frowns, sunshine and clouds, striving to establish the conviction through this land, that to hold and traffic in human flesh is a sin against God. They have been somewhat successful; but they have been in no wise so successful as they might have been, had the men and women at the North rallied around them as they had a right to hope from their profession. They have had to contend not only with skilful politicians, with a deeply prejudiced and pro-slavery community, but with eminent Divines, Doctors of Divinity, and Bishops. Instead of encouraging them as friends, they have acted as enemies. For many days did Garrison go the rounds of the city of Boston to ask of the minister the poor privilege of entering their chapels and lifting up his voice for the dumb. But their doors were bolted, their gates barred, and their pulpits hermetically sealed. It was not till an infidel hall was thrown open, that the voice of dumb millions could be heard in Boston.

I take it that all who have heard at all on this subject, are well convinced that the stronghold of Slavery is in the pulpit. Say what we may of politicians and political parties, the power that holds the keys of the dungeon in which the bondman is confined, is the pulpit. It is that power which is dropping, dropping, constantly dropping on the ear of this people, creating and moulding the moral sentiment of the land. This they have sufficiently under their control that they can change it from the spirit of hatred to that of love to mankind. That they do it not, is evident from the results of their teaching. The men who wield the blood-clotted cow-skin come from our Sabbath Schools in the Southern States. Who act as slave-drivers? The men who go forth from our own congregations here. Why, if the Gospel were truly preached among us, a man would as soon think of going into downright piracy as to offer himself as a slave-driver.

. . . People at the North talk coolly of uncles, cousins, and brothers who are slaveholders, and of their coming to visit them. If the Gospel were truly preached here, you would as soon talk of having an uncle or brother a brothel keeper as a slaveholder. . . .

For a long time when I was a slave, I was led to think from hearing such passages as "servants obey, &c." that if I dared to escape, the wrath of God would follow me. All are willing to acknowledge my right to be free; but after this acknowledgement, the good man goes to the Bible and says "after all I see some difficulty about this thing. You know, after the deluge, there was Shem, Ham, and Japhet; and you know that Ham was black and had a curse put upon him; and I know not but it would be an attempt to thwart the purposes of Jehovah, if these men were set at liberty." . . .

I dwell mostly upon the religious aspect, because I believe it is the religious people who are to be relied on in this Anti-Slavery movement. Do not misunderstand my railing—do not class me with those who despise religion—do not identify me with the infidel. I love the religion of Christianity—which is pure, peaceable, gentle, easy to be entreated, full of good fruits, and without hypocrisy. . . . By all the love I bear to such a Christianity as this, I hate that of the Priest and Levite, that with long-faced Phariseeism goes up to Jerusalem and worships, and leaves the bruised and wounded to die. I despise that religion that can carry Bibles to the heathen on the other side of the globe and withhold them from [the] heathen on this side—which can talk about human rights yonder and traffic in human flesh here. . . .

There is another religion. It is that which takes off fetters instead of binding them on—that breaks every yoke—that lifts up the bowed down. The Anti-Slavery platform is based on this kind of religion. It spreads its table to the lame, the halt, and the blind. It goes down after a long neglected race. It passes, link by link till it finds the lowest link in humanity's chain—humanity's most degraded form in the most abject condition. It reaches down its arm and tells them to stand up. This is Anti-Slavery—this is Christianity. It is reviving gloriously among the various denominations. It is threatening to supercede those old forms of religion having all of the love of God and none of man in it.

From Frederick Douglass, *Life and Writings of Frederick Douglass*, edited by Philip S. Foner (New York: International Universities Press, 1975), pp. 104–5, 161–62, 270–74.

43. Charles Grandison Finney, *Lectures on Revivals of Religion*

The best-known evangelist of nineteenth-century America, Finney (1792–1875) was an attorney who became a Presbyterian preacher and, later, a professor of theology and president of Oberlin College, a biracial, coeducational school in Ohio. In this 1835 manual on how to conduct a revival, Finney warns fellow ministers that resistance to temperance and antislavery reform will be a "hindrance" to the work of evangelism.

Lecture 15

It has always been the case, whenever any of the servants of God do anything in His cause, and there appears to be *a probability* that they will succeed, that Satan by his agents regularly attempts to divert their minds and nullify their labours. So it has been during the last ten years, in which there have been such remarkable revivals through the length and breadth of the land. These revivals have been very great and powerful, and extensive. It has been estimated that not less than TWO HUNDRED THOUSAND persons have been converted to God in that time. And the devil has been busy in his devices to divert and distract the people of God, and turn off their energies from pushing forward the great work of salvation. . . .

Things Which May Stop a Revival. Some have talked very foolishly on this subject, as if nothing could hinder a genuine revival. They say: "If your revival is a work of God, it cannot be stopped: can any created being stop God?" Now I ask if this is common sense? Formerly, it used to be the established belief that a revival could not be stopped, because it was the work of God. And so they supposed it would go on, whatever might be done to hinder it, in the Church or out of it. But the farmer might just as well reason so, and think he could go and cut down his wheat and not hurt the crop, because it is God that makes grain grow. A revival is the work of God, and so is a crop of wheat; and God is as much dependent on the use of means in one case as the other. And therefore a revival is as liable to be injured as a wheat field. . . .

Resistance to the Temperance reformation will put a stop to revivals in a Church. The time has come that it can no longer be innocent in a Church to stand aloof from this glorious reformation. The time was when this could be done ignorantly. The time has been when ministers and Christians could enjoy revivals, notwithstanding that ardent spirit was used among them. But since light has been thrown upon the subject, and it has been found that the use is injurious, no member or minister can be innocent and stand neutral in the cause. They must speak out and take sides. And if they do not take ground on one side, their influence is on the other. Show me a minister that has taken ground against the Temperance reformation who has had a revival. Show me one who now stands aloof from it who has a revival. Show me one who now temporises upon this point, who does not come out and take a stand in favour of Temperance, who has a revival. It used not to be so. But now the subject has come up, and has been discussed, and is understood, no man can shut his eyes upon the truth. The man's hands are RED WITH BLOOD who stands aloof from the Temperance cause. And can *he* have a revival?

Revivals are hindered when ministers and *Churches take wrong ground in regard to any question involving human rights.* Take the subject of SLAVERY, for instance. The time was when this subject was not before the public mind. John Newton continued in the slave trade after his conversion. And so had his mind been perverted, and so completely was his conscience seared, in regard to this most nefarious traffic, that the sinfulness of it never occurred to his thoughts until some time after he became a child of God. Had light been poured upon his mind previously to his conversion, he *never could* have been converted without previously abandoning this sin. And after his conversion, when convinced of its iniquity, he could no longer enjoy the presence of God without abandoning the sin for ever.

So, doubtless, many slave dealers and slave holders in our country have been converted, notwithstanding their participation in this abomination, because the sinfulness of it was not apparent to their minds. So ministers and Churches, to a great extent throughout the land, have held their peace, and borne no testimony against this abomination, existing in the Church and in the nation. But recently, the subject has come up for discussion, and the providence of God has brought it distinctly before the eyes of all men. Light is now shed upon this subject, as it has been upon the cause of Temperance. Facts are exhibited, and principles established, and light thrown in upon the minds of men, and this monster is dragged from his horrid den, and exhibited before the Church, and it is demanded of Christians: "IS THIS SIN?" Their testimony *must* be given on this subject. They are God's witnesses. They are sworn to tell "the truth, the whole truth, and nothing but the truth." It is impossible that their testimony should not be given, on one side or the other. Their silence can no longer be accounted for upon the principle of ignorance, that they have never had their attention turned to the subject. Consequently, the silence of Christians upon the subject is virtually saying *that they do not* consider slavery as a sin.

The truth is, this is a subject on which they cannot be silent without guilt. The time has come, in the providence of God, when every southern breeze is loaded down with the cries of lamentation, mourning, and woe. Two millions of degraded heathen in our own land stretch their hands, all shackled and bleeding, and send forth to the Church of God the agonising cry for help. And shall the Church, in her efforts to reclaim and save the world, deafen her ears to this voice of agony and despair? God forbid! The Church cannot turn away from this question. It is a question for the Church and for the nation to decide, and God will push it to a decision. It is in vain for us to resist it for fear of distraction, contention, and strife. It is in vain to account it an act of *piety* to turn away the ear from hearing this cry of distress.

The Church must testify, and testify "the truth, the whole truth, and nothing but the truth," on this subject, or she is perjured, and the Spirit of

God departs from her. She is under oath to testify, and ministers and Churches who do not pronounce it sin, bear false testimony for God. It is doubtless true, that one of the reasons for the low state of religion at the present time is that many Churches have taken the wrong side on the subject of slavery, have suffered prejudice to prevail over principle, and have feared to call this abomination by its true name.

From Charles Grandison Finney, *Lectures on Revivals of Religion* (New York: Fleming H. Revell Co., 1868) pp. 263–64, 272–73.

44. Luther Lee,
The Supremacy of the Divine Law and *Slavery: A Sin against God*

Lee (1800–1889) was an American evangelical abolitionist who helped to organize both the Wesleyan Methodist Church (an antislavery denomination) and the Liberty Party (a Christian antislavery political party). In the sermon The Supremacy of the Divine Law *(1846) Lee provided an early systemic understanding of the corrupting effects of social sin. In the religious tract* Slavery: A Sin against God *(1853) Lee expressed typical abolitionist arguments in a logical, persuasive manner.*

THE SUPREMACY OF THE DIVINE LAW

[Matt. 16:24, 25]—"Then said Jesus unto his disciples, If any man will come after me, let him deny himself, and take up his cross, and follow me.

For whosoever will save his life, shall lose it: and whosoever will lose his life for my sake, shall find it."

The object of quoting this text is to prove the paramount claim of the gospel, that the law of Christ is to be obeyed whatever human laws may exist to the contrary, and whatever consequences may attend obedience. The meaning is, that whosoever will save his natural life by disobeying or denying me, shall lose his moral or spiritual life, and whosoever will lose his natural life for my sake, that is, die rather than disobey me, shall find, that is, secure all the objects of life, in the possession of moral or spiritual life. If it could be right to disobey Christ under any circumstances, or to escape any consequences, even death itself, then there could be no such thing as losing life for his sake, from regard to him; hence as he in the text does teach that men may be called to sacrifice life for his sake, it follows that nothing can justify us in disregarding his law; it is paramount, and must be obeyed, should all human laws contravene. . . .

The design of divine law is to reveal or make known to man what is right; the design of human law is to secure what is already known to be right. The

213

only good reason why any human law should be enacted, is the fact, that the end to be secured by it is right. Now, as the right of the thing to be secured is the only reason why the law should be enacted which is to secure it, the right must exist before the law, and the law is based upon the right, and not the right upon the law. This view shows that human law makes nothing right which was not right previous to the enactment of the law.

The manner of constituting human legislatures may throw some light on the subject of the comparative claim of divine and human law. How are our legislatures constituted? By the suffrages of the people. The leaders of one party meet here and nominate a man, and the leaders of another party meet there, and nominate another candidate, and a third person gets upon a stump and nominates himself, and then they all go to work, and make their respective presses groan under the misrepresentations, slanders and falsehoods, with which they assail each other until the day of voting, when one of them is elected, and is thereby constituted a law maker. There are some honorable exceptions to the rule of general corruption, but still corruption is the general rule. Go to our national legislature, and of whom do you find it composed? Of tiplers, rumdrinkers, wine bibbers, beer-guzzlers, gamblers, fist-fighters, duelists, and libertines. So notoriously corrupt is Congress, that when it assembles, there is a priming up and moving on to the seat of government, among some of the higher classes of the frail sisterhood, from Maine to Georgia. Are these the men to make laws, more binding than the law of God? Is this the authority to ascend above the throne of God, their Maker, and reverse his decrees, and hush the voice that speaks his law? Will they roll up as a scroll his lightning's blaze, in which he wrapt the mount of Sinai when he delivered his law, and silence the thunders with which he then spake in the startled ear of a listening world? All this, and more too, is involved in the idea that human law can be binding when it conflicts with divine. The very thought is blasphemous!

We are to indulge in some reflections which the subject appears calculated to inspire.

How corrupt must slavery be, which needs to resort to such measures to sustain itself. The persecution and death of Mr. Torrey [an abolitionist] is but one item in a system of warfare upon human rights, designed to support and perpetuate slavery. . . . So corrupt is slavery that it could not live, even in this corrupt world, were it not for the special efforts, and the force of special legislation surrounding it with legal supports and defenses on every side. That slavery may live, the liberty of speech and the freedom of the press must die, and the voice of conscience must be silenced. Slaveholders dare not trust each other; yea, they dare not trust themselves, unrestrained by law, lest in some honest moment, under some impulse of humanity, they should emancipate the victims of their oppression. Hence all the laws against emancipation. How corrupting must such a system be, and how dangerous to all the best interests of humanity, and to social and civil relations?

From *Five Sermons and a Tract by Luther Lee*, edited by Donald W. Dayton (Chicago: Holrad House, 1975), pp. 48, 52–53.

SLAVERY: A SIN AGAINST GOD

By slavery is meant the system which reduces man to a chattel, and buys and sells him, and subjects him to the liabilities of other property, claiming the same right of property in the offspring by virtue of the right previously asserted to the parent. This is the system of American slavery, and against it and all other slavery involving the same principles, the arguments are directed.

Slavery consisting in the right of property in man, with the usual incidents of that right must be morally wrong, sin in itself, for the following reasons.

Argument First: It Is Inconsistent with Man's Relation to God, and the Obligations Growing out of That Relation

Dr. Payne, in his "Elements of Moral Science," says,—

"Virtue as it regards man, is the conformity or harmony of his affections and actions with the various relations in which he has been placed—of which conformity the perfect intellect of God, guided in its exercise by his infinitely holy nature, is the only infallible judge."

If this be a correct definition of virtue, and we believe it is; it follows, that man cannot rightfully sustain two relations at the same time, with both of which his affections and actions cannot harmonize; which is the case with the relation that all men sustain to God, and the relation of *property*, to man with its usual incidents. The relation[s] we sustain to God, are various. He is our Creator, our Preserver, our Benefactor—He is the framer of our bodies and the Father of our spirits, and he is our Governor.

. . . Dr. Payne asserts that God is the judge of the conformity of man's affections and actions to his relations, and this judgment God has expressed in the first great commandment, which reads as follows:—

"Thou shalt love the Lord thy God with all thy heart, and with all thy soul, and with all thy mind, and with all thy strength." This commandment clearly lays such a claim to the affections of the heart, and demands such an entire devotion of the soul as gives tone to, and controls the actions; it therefore contains the foundation of absolute obedience to God. This is seen in the expression, "with all thy strength." This requires a consecration of the physical powers in obedience to God, under the control of the affections of the heart.

There is but one question more to settle, which is, can these affections and *actions* exist in the same heart and life, at the same time with those affections and *actions* which are consonant with the relation of a piece of property to its owner, a personal chattel to a chattel holder? Slavery may say what it pleases; common sense says no.

To be under obligation to obey God, there must exist the right and power of devoting our lives to God, for there can be no obligation where there is not both *right* and *power* to respond to that obligation. But the slave, who is the property of man, has not and *cannot have* the power of devoting his life to God, because his life is not at his own disposal, according to the dictates of his own understanding of right; he cannot do what God *requires*, but must do what *men require*, and wicked men too, who fear not God and regard not his law. Should it be said that slave owners do not interfere with the slave's right to obey God, and liberty of conscience, every one must know that such an assumption would be false, for the extension of the right to slaves, to obey God, as free men professing the religion of the Bible deem it their duty to obey God, would overthrow the system of slavery.

Further, if it were admitted that slave owners grant their slaves the privilege of obeying God, it would not relieve the difficulty, for it would still follow that the system of property in man, takes away from the human chattel the *right* to obey God, and puts it into the hand of the owner, who has the power to close up before the chattelized traveller to eternity, the path of obedience and with authority direct his footsteps in the way of sin and death. Man cannot sustain the relation of property to man, without an infraction of the relation that he sustains to God, and of the rights and powers essential to the conformity of his affections and *actions* to this relation, hence, the *right* of property in man cannot exist.

The assumption of the relation of a chattel holder to a subject of God's moral government, is to step in between such subject and God, and disannul man's relation to his Maker, and absolve him from his allegiance to Jehovah's throne. Can this be right? Does the Bible sanction such a principle, beaming as it does with the mind of Him who declares himself to be a jealous God; flashing with the lightnings of his displeasure, and speaking in the thunder tones of his wrath against all who turn away from the claims of his law to acknowledge any other authority, to serve any other God or bow down to the likeness of any thing in heaven, earth or hell? It cannot be.

Argument Second: Slavery Conflicts with Various Specific Duties which the Bible Requires of All Men

It is the duty of all intelligent beings to use all the means within their reach to acquire a knowledge of God and his will. To remain ignorant of God and of his will concerning us through neglect of the means within our reach, is of itself a sin of the darkest shade. But from what source is the knowledge of God to be derived? The answer is plain, the *Scriptures*. "To the law and the testimony; if they speak not according to this word it is because there is no light in them."

It is clear that if the Scriptures are an expression of the mind of God, and have been inspired by his spirit, all must possess a common right of direct access to this fountain of moral light. This none will deny but the Pope and his menials. With this accords the practice of all Protestants; whenever they establish missions in any part of the world among the heathen, they put the Bible into their hands so soon as they can speak its language, or so soon as it can be translated into their own language. The only exception is found in the act of withholding the scriptures from the slaves of our own country, who might be taught to read them with far greater facility.

But God has made it our duty to know him, and to know him through this medium. . . .

The right and duty of all men to possess themselves of the scriptures and to read and study the same being established, it only remains to show that slavery is of necessity and forever inimical to this right and duty; taking away the one, and nullifying the other. The right of property in man cannot exist co-ordinate with the right and obligation to 'search the scriptures.' . . .

The right and obligation to search the scriptures includes the right to devote sufficient time to the pursuit of religious knowledge. But the right of property in a man includes the right to monopolize and dispose of his whole time, so that he cannot possess the right of devoting his time or any part of it to the study of the scriptures, from which it follows again that the right of slavery is at war with the duties which God has commanded. If the advocate of slavery will attempt to evade the force of this, by denying that the right of property in man includes the right to control the time of such property, he will ruin his own cause; for if the slaveholder has not a right to say how the slave shall improve his time, his right of property in him will not be worth contending about. If the right of property in man includes the right of controlling his time, it conflicts with duties which God requires and must be wrong; and if it does not give the master the right to control the time of the slave, the whole practical system of slavery is a violation of right.

In showing that slavery conflicts with certain specified duties, it is proper to notice the duty of publicly worshipping God. On this point we will quote but one text.

[Heb. 10:25]. "Not forsaking the assembling of yourselves together, as the manner of some is." This text clearly teaches the duty of meeting together in Christian assemblies for religious purposes, while slavery declares that the right of slaves so to assemble cannot be admitted with safety to the system.

To conclude this argument, we say that to grant the slaves the simple *right of obeying the Gospel,* by attending to all its devotional and social *duties as they are commanded and understood by Christians generally,* would *overthrow the entire system.* To give them the Scriptures to be read according to the dictates of their own consciences, and to allow them the privilege of *selecting their own ministers* from whose lips they choose to hear the words of life, which is the inalienable right of all Christians, would come so near to the abolition of slavery as to leave but little to be done to complete it. The *right of property* in man cannot exist without taking away the right *of doing the duties and enjoying the privileges of the Gospel,* and therefore the right of property in man cannot exist as a *right,* but must be *wrong,* whenever assumed.

From *Five Sermons and a Tract by Luther Lee,* edited by Donald W. Dayton (Chicago: Holrad House, 1975), pp. 123–28.

45. The Seneca Falls Convention, *Declaration of Sentiments*

Often considered the founding document of the women's rights movement, this declaration was the result of a convention held at the Wesleyan Methodist Church of Seneca Falls, New York, in 1848. Participants at the convention included Lucretia Mott, Elizabeth Cady Stanton, and Frederick Douglass. Like the Declaration of Independence after which it was modeled, this declaration adheres to the Enlightenment principle of natural rights.

When, in the course of human events, it becomes necessary for one portion of the family of man to assume among the people of the earth a position different from that which they have hitherto occupied, but one to which the laws of nature and of nature's God entitle them, a decent respect to the opinions of mankind requires that they should declare the causes that impel them to such a course.

We hold these truths to be self-evident: that all men and women are created equal; that they are endowed by their Creator with certain inalienable rights; that among these are life, liberty, and the pursuit of happiness; that to secure these rights governments are instituted, deriving their just powers from the consent of the governed. Whenever any form of government becomes destructive of these ends, it is the right of those who suffer from it to refuse allegiance to it, and to insist upon the institution of a new government, laying its foundation on such principles, and organizing its powers in such form, as to them shall seem most likely to effect their safety and happiness. Prudence, indeed, will dictate that governments long established should not be changed for light and transient causes; and accordingly all experiences hath shown that mankind are more disposed to suffer, while evils are sufferable, than to right themselves by abolishing the forms to which they were accustomed. But when a long train of abuses and usurpations, pursuing invariably the same object evinces a design to reduce them under absolute despotism, it is their duty to throw off such government, and to provide new guards for their future security. Such has been the patient sufferance of the women under this government, and such is now the necessity which constrains them to demand the equal station to which they are entitled.

The history of mankind is a history of repeated injuries and usurpations on the part of man toward woman, having in direct object the establishment of an absolute tyranny over her. To prove this, let facts be submitted to a candid world.

He has never permitted her to exercise her inalienable right to the elective franchise.

He has compelled her to submit to laws, in the formation of which she had no voice.

He has withheld from her rights which are given to the most ignorant and degraded men—both natives and foreigners.

Having deprived her of this first right of a citizen, the elective franchise, thereby leaving her without representation in the halls of legislation, he has oppressed her on all sides.

He has made her, if married, in the eye of the law, civilly dead.

He has taken from her all right in property, even to the wages she earns.

He has made her, morally, an irresponsible being, as she can commit many crimes with impunity, provided they be done in the presence of her husband. In the covenant of marriage, she is compelled to promise obedience to her husband, he becoming, to all intents and purposes, her master— the law giving him power to deprive her of her liberty, and to administer chastisement.

He has so framed the laws of divorce, as to what shall be the proper causes, and in case of separation, to whom the guardianship of the children shall be given, as to be wholly regardless of the happiness of women—the law, in all cases, going upon a false supposition of the supremacy of man, and giving all power into his hands.

After depriving her of all rights as a married woman, if single, and the owner of property, he has taxed her to support a government which recognizes her only when her property can be made profitable to it.

He has monopolized nearly all the profitable employments, and from those she is permitted to follow, she receives but a scanty remuneration. He closes against her all the avenues to wealth and distinction which he considers most honorable to himself. As a teacher of theology, medicine, or law, she is not known.

He has denied her the facilities for obtaining a thorough education, all colleges being closed against her.

He allows her in Church, as well as State, but a subordinate position, claiming Apostolic authority for her exclusion from the ministry, and, with some exceptions, from any public participation in the affairs of the Church.

He has created a false public sentiment by giving to the world a different code of morals for men and women, by which moral delinquencies which exclude women from society, are not only tolerated, but deemed of little account in man.

He has usurped the prerogative of Jehovah himself, claiming it as his right to assign for her a sphere of action, when that belongs to her conscience and to her God.

He has endeavored, in every way that he could, to destroy her confidence in her own powers, to lessen her self-respect, and to make her willing to lead a dependent and abject life.

Now, in view of this entire disfranchisement of one-half the people of this country, their social and religious degradation—in view of the unjust laws above mentioned, and because women do feel themselves aggrieved, oppressed, and fraudulently deprived of their most sacred rights, we insist that they have immediate admission to all the rights and privileges which belong to them as citizens of the United States.

In entering upon the great work before us, we anticipate no small amount of misconception, misrepresentation, and ridicule; but we shall use every instrumentality within our power to effect our object. We shall employ agents, circulate tracts, petition the State and National legislatures, and endeavor to enlist the pulpit and the press in our behalf. We hope this Convention will be followed by a series of Conventions embracing every part of the country. . . .

Whereas, The great precept of nature is conceded to be, that "man shall pursue his own true and substantial happiness." Blackstone in his Commentaries remarks, that this law of Nature being coeval with mankind, and dictated by God himself, is of course superior in obligation to any other. It is binding over all the globe, in all countries and at all times; no human laws are of any validity if contrary to this, and such of them as are valid, derive all their force, and all their validity, and all their authority, mediately and immediately, from this original; therefore,

Resolved. That such laws as conflict, in any way, with the true and substantial happiness of woman, are contrary to the great precept of nature and of no validity, for this is "superior in obligation to any other."

Resolved. That all laws which prevent woman from occupying such a station in society as her conscience shall dictate, or which place her in a position inferior to that of man, are contrary to the great precept of nature, and therefore of no force or authority.

Resolved. That woman is man's equal—was intended to be so by the Creator, and the highest good of the race demands that she should be recognized as such. . . .

Resolved. That inasmuch as man, while claiming for himself intellectual superiority, does accord to woman moral superiority, it is pre-eminently his duty to encourage her to speak and teach, as she has an opportunity, in all religious assemblies. . . .

Resolved. That woman has too long rested satisfied in the circumscribed limits which corrupt customs and a perverted application of the Scriptures have marked out for her, and that it is time she should move in the enlarged sphere which her great Creator has assigned her. . . .

Resolved. That the equality of human rights results necessarily from the fact of the identity of the race in capabilities and responsibilities.

Resolved, therefore, That, being invested by the Creator with the same capabilities, and the same consciousness of responsibility for their exercise, it is demonstrably the right and duty of woman, equally with man, to promote every righteous cause by every righteous means; and especially in regard to the great subjects of morals and religion, it is self-evidently her right to participate with her brother in teaching them, both in private and in public, by writing and by speaking, by any instrumentalities proper to be used, and in any assemblies proper to be held; and this being a self-evident truth growing out of the divinely implanted principles of human nature, any custom or authority adverse to it, whether modern or wearing the hoary sanction of antiquity, is to be regarded as a self-evident falsehood, and at war with mankind. . . .

Resolved, That the speedy success of our cause depends upon the zealous and untiring efforts of both men and women, for the overthrow of the monopoly of the pulpit, and for the securing to woman an equal participation with men in the various trades, professions, and commerce.

From Elizabeth Cady Stanton, Susan B. Anthony, and Matilda Joslyn Gage: *History of Woman Suffrage*, vol. 1 (New York: Fowler and Wells, 1881), pp. 70–73.

46.   Lucretia Mott,
Not Christianity, but Priestcraft

Mott (1793–1880), a liberal Quaker, spoke widely on behalf of abolitionism and women's rights. The following selection is taken from a speech that she delivered at a women's rights convention in Philadelphia in 1854. Mott contrasted the male dominance of institutional religion with the gender equality that she believed to be characteristic of true Christianity.

It is not Christianity, but priestcraft that has subjected woman as we find her. The Church and State have been united, and it is well for us to see it so. We have had to bear the denunciations of these reverend (irreverend) clergymen . . . of late. But if we look to their authority to see how they expound the text, quite likely we shall find a new reading. . . .

Blame is often attached to the position in which woman is found. I blame her not so much as I pity her. So circumscribed have been her limits that she does not realise the misery of her condition. Such dupes are men to custom that even servitude, the worst of ills, comes to be thought a good, till down from sire to son it is kept and guarded as a sacred thing. Woman's existence is maintained by sufferance. The veneration of man has been misdirected, the pulpit has been prostituted, the Bible has been ill-used. It has been turned over and over as in every reform. The temperance people have had to feel its supposed denunciations. Then the anti-slavery, and now this reform has met, and still continues to meet, passage after passage of the Bible, never intended to be so used. Instead of taking the truths of the Bible in corroboration of the right, the practice has been to turn over its pages to find example and authority for the wrong, for the existing abuses of society. For the usage of drinking wine, the example of the sensualist Solomon, is always appealed to. In reference to our reform, even admitting that Paul did mean preach, when he used that term, he did not say that the recommendation of that time was to be applicable to the churches of all after-time. We have been so long pinning our faith on other people's sleeves that we ought to begin examining these things daily ourselves, to see whether they are so; and we should find on comparing text with text, that a very different construction might be put upon them. Some of our early Quakers not seeing how far they were to be carried, became Greek and Hebrew scholars, and they found that the text would bear other translations as well as other constructions. . . .

It is not so Apostolic to make the wife subject to the husband as many have supposed. It has been done by law and public opinion since that time. There has been a great deal said about sending missionaries over to the East to convert women who are immolating themselves on the funeral pile of the husbands. I know this may be a very good work, but I would ask you to look at it. How many women are there now immolated upon the shrine of superstition and priestcraft, in our very midst, in the assumption that man only has a right to the pulpit, and that if a woman enters it she disobeys God; making woman believe in the misdirection of her vocation, and that it is of divine authority that she should be thus bound. . . .

I do not want to dwell too much upon Scripture authority. We too often bind ourselves by authorities rather than by the truth. We are infidel to truth in seeking examples to overthrow it. The very first act of note that is mentioned when the disciples and apostles went forth after Jesus was removed from them, was the bringing up of an ancient prophecy to prove that they were right in the position they assumed on that occasion, when men and women were gathered together on the holy day of Pentecost, when every man heard and saw those wonderful works which are recorded. Then Peter stood forth—some one has said that Peter made a great mistake in quoting the prophet Joel—but he stated that "the time is come, this day is fulfilled the prophecy, when it is said, I will pour out my spirit upon all flesh, and your sons and your daughters shall prophesy," etc.—the language of the Bible is beautiful in its repetition—"upon my servants and my handmaidens I will pour out my spirit and they shall prophesy." Now can anything be clearer than that?

From Elizabeth Cady Stanton, Susan B. Anthony, and Matilda Joslyn Gage: *History of Woman Suffrage,* vol. 1 (New York: Fowler and Wells, 1881), pp. 380–81.

47. Sojourner Truth,
Ain't I a Woman?

Sojourner Truth (ca. 1797–1883) was an illiterate former slave who became a powerful spokesperson for the elimination of race and gender discrimination. Thus, she anticipated the "womanist" concerns of many late twentieth-century African-American women. Her address before the Akron, Ohio Women's Rights Convention in 1851, was written down by her colleague Frances Gage. Gage provided some introductory comments to Truth's speech; other comments by Gage are interspersed within the text of the address.

The leaders of the movement trembled on seeing a tall, gaunt black woman in a gray dress and white turban, surmounted with an uncouth sun-bonnet, march deliberately into the church, walk with the air of a queen up the aisle, and take her seat upon the pulpit steps. A buzz of disapprobation was heard all over the house, and there fell on the listening ear, "An abolition affair!" "Woman's rights and niggers!" "I told you so!" "Go it, darkey!" . . .

. . . Again and again, timorous and trembling ones came to me and said, with earnestness, "Don't let her speak, Mrs. Gage, it will ruin us. Every newspaper in the land will have our cause mixed up with abolition and niggers, and we shall be utterly denounced." My only answer was, "We shall see when the time comes."

The second day the work waxed warm. Methodist, Baptist, Episcopal, Presbyterian, and Universalist ministers came in to hear and discuss the resolutions presented. One claimed superior rights and privileges for man, on the ground of "superior intellect"; another, because of the "manhood of Christ; if God had desired the equality of woman, He would have given some token of His will through the birth, life, and death of the Saviour." Another gave us a theological view of the "sin of our first mother."

There were very few women in those days who dared to "speak in meeting"; and the august teachers of the people were seemingly getting the better of us, while the boys in the galleries, and the sneerers among the pews, were hugely enjoying the discomfiture, as they supposed, of the "strong-minded." Some of the tender-skinned friends were on the point of losing dignity, and the atmosphere betokened a storm. When, slowly from her seat in the corner rose Sojourner Truth, who, till now, had scarcely lifted her head. "Don't let her speak!" gasped half a dozen in my ear. She moved slowly and solemnly to the front, laid her old bonnet at her feet, and turned her great speaking eyes to me. There was a hissing sound of disapprobation above and below. I rose and announced "Sojourner Truth," and begged the audience to keep silence for a few moments.

The tumult subsided at once, and every eye was fixed on this almost Amazon form, which stood nearly six feet high, head erect, and eyes piercing the upper air like one in a dream. At her first word there was a profound hush. She spoke in deep tones, which, though not loud, reached every ear in the house, and away through the throng at the doors and windows.

"Well, chilern, whar dar is so much racket dar must be somethin' out o' kilter. I think dat 'twixt de niggers of de Souf and de womin at de Norf, all talkin' 'bout rights, de white men will be in a fix pretty soon. But what's all dis here talkin' 'bout?

"Dat man ober dar say dat womin needs to be helped into carriages, and lifted ober ditches, and to hab de best place everywhar. Nobody eber helps me into carriages, or ober mud-puddles, or gibs me any best place!" And raising herself to her full height, and her voice to a pitch like rolling thunder, she asked, "And a'n't I a woman? Look at me! Look at my arm! (and she bared her right arm to the shoulder, showing her tremendous muscular power). I have ploughed, and planted, and gathered into barns, and no man could head me! And a'n't I a woman? I could work as much and eat as much as a man—when I could get it—and bear de lash as well! And a'n't I a woman? I have borne thirteen chilern, and seen 'em mos' all sold off to slavery, and when I cried out with my mother's grief, none but Jesus heard me! And a'n't I a woman?

"Den dey talks 'bout dis ting in de head; what dis dey call it?" ("Intellect," whispered some one near.) "Dat's it, honey. What's dat got to do wid womin's rights or nigger's rights? If my cup won't hold but a pint, and yours holds a quart, wouldn't ye be mean not to let me have my little half-measure full?" And she pointed her significant finger, and sent a keen glance at the minister who had made the argument. The cheering was long and loud.

"Den dat little man in black dar, he say women can't have as much rights as men, 'cause Christ wan't a woman! Whar did your Christ come from?" Rolling thunder couldn't have stilled that crowd, as did those deep, wonderful tones, as she stood there with outstretched arms and eyes of fire. Raising her voice still louder, she repeated, "Whar did your Christ come from? From God and a woman! Man had nothin' to do wid Him." Oh, what a rebuke that was to that little man.

Turning again to another objector, she took up the defense of Mother Eve. I can not follow her through it all. It was pointed, and witty, and solemn; eliciting at almost every sentence deafening applause; and she ended by asserting: "If de fust woman God ever made was strong enough to turn de world upside down all alone, dese women togedder (and she glanced her eye over the platform) ought to be able to turn it back, and get it right side up again! And now dey is asking to do it, de men better let 'em." Long-continued cheering greeted this. " 'Bleeged to ye for hearin' on me, and now ole Sojourner han't got nothin' more to say."

Amid roars of applause, she returned to her corner, leaving more than one of us with streaming eyes, and hearts beating with gratitude. She had taken us up in her strong arms and carried us safely over the slough of difficulty turning the whole tide in our favor. I have never in my life seen anything like the magical influence that subdued the mobbish spirit of the day, and turned the sneers and jeers of an excited crowd into notes of respect and admiration. Hundreds rushed up to shake hands with her, and congratulate the glorious old mother, and bid her God-speed on her mission of "testifyin' agin concerning the wickedness of this 'ere people."

From Elizabeth Cady Stanton, Susan B. Anthony, and Matilda Joslyn Gage: *History of Woman Suffrage*, vol. 1 (New York: Fowler and Wells, 1881), pp. 115–17.

48. Frances E. Willard,
Woman in the Pulpit

Willard (1839–1898), for many years president of the Women's Christian Temperance Union and a prominent spokeswoman for the movement advocating the enfranchisement of women, sought support for her feminist positions in a nuanced reading of scripture. In Woman in the Pulpit, *written in 1889, Willard states that if women were being subjugated on the basis of the Bible, then the Bible was being misinterpreted. The ethics that Willard found in the Bible were not those of subjugation but of equality.*

The First Congregational Church organized in New Jersey ordered its chorister "not to allow any females to sing in the choir, because Paul had commanded women to keep silence in the churches." This is the most illustrious instance, so far as I know, of absolute fidelity to a literal exegesis concerning woman's relation to public worship. . . . A similar degree of reverence for the letter furnished the argument upon which excellent ecclesiastical authority claimed the divine origin of African slavery, for does not Paul say, in Ephesians [6:] 5, "Servants, be obedient to them that are your masters according to the flesh, with fear and trembling, in singleness of your heart as unto Christ;" (and "bond-servants" is clearly the meaning as stated in the eighth verse).

Side by side with the method of exegesis which would enforce this literal view, and promulgated by the same class of exegetes, is another, which may be called the method of playing fast and loose, and which is thus illustrated:—

In the Sermon on the Mount (Matt. [5]) there is a specific command not to strike back when one is struck; not to go to law; to give to him that asketh; not to turn away from him that would borrow; and to suffer people to be divorced for one cause only; yet every one of these precepts coming from Christ himself is specifically and constantly violated by pastors and people, and without penalty. . . .

In 1 Tim. [2:] 9, Paul says, "I desire . . . that women adorn themselves in modest apparel, with shamefastness and sobriety; not with braided hair, and gold or pearls or costly raiment;" and adds, "Let a woman learn in quietness with all subjection. But I permit not a woman to teach, nor to have dominion over a man, but to be in quietness. For Adam was first formed, then Eve." But our exegetes and pulpit expounders, while laying the most solemn emphasis upon the last part of this command as an unchangeable rule of faith and practice for womankind in all ages and in all places, pass over the specific commands relative to braided hair, gold, pearls, and expensive attire, and have a thousand times preached to women who were violating every one of them, without uttering the slightest warning or reproof.

In Genesis, the Lord says to Cain, the elder brother, speaking to him of Abel, "Unto thee shall be his desire, and thou shalt rule over him," but our exegetes do not find here divine authorization of an elder brother's supremacy, and yet they construe the same expression when the Lord speaks to Eve, as the assertion, for all time, of a woman's subjection to her husband; moreover, they do this in face of the explicit declaration that God said, "Let *us* make man in *our* image, after our likeness: and let *them* have dominion . . . so God created man in his own image, in the image of God created he him; *male* and *female* created he *them*."

Take the sixth chapter of 1 [Corinthians] and note its explicit and reiterated commands to Christians never to go to law, beginning with Pauline vigor: "*Dare* any of you?" Where is the "sweet reasonableness" of gliding softly over these inspired mandates, and urging those of the eleventh chapter in the same epistle as though they formed part of a creed for the subjection of women? My brethren, these things ought not so to be.

In presence of these multiplied instances, and many others that might be named, what must a plain Bible-reading member of the laity conclude? For my own part, I long ago found in these two conflicting methods of exegesis, one of which strenuously insisted on a literal view, and the other played fast and loose with God's word according to personal predilection, a pointed illustration of the divine declaration that "it is not good for man to be alone." We need women commentators to bring out the women's side of the book; we need the stereoscopic view of truth in general, which can only be had when woman's eye and man's together shall discern the perspective of the Bible's full-orbed revelation.

I do not at all impugn the good intention of the good men who have been our exegetes, and I bow humbly in presence of their scholarship; but, while they turn their linguistic telescopes on truth, I may be allowed to make a correction for the "personal equation" in the results which they espy.

Study the foregoing illustrations, and find in them one more proof of that "humanness of the saints," which is a factor in all human results. Given, in heredity and environment, an established theory of the subjection of woman, and how easily one finds the same in Paul's epistles; given an appreciation of the pleasantness of wine, and how naturally one dwells upon the duty of its use at the communion, to the exclusion of special thought about the duty of retaining anything so tasteless as unleavened bread; given the charm that men find in "stylish" dress, carefully arranged hair, and beautiful jewelry, as shown in the attire of women, and it becomes perfectly natural that they should not censure these manifestations, but expatiate, instead, upon the more pleasing theory of woman's silence and subjection. Given the custom of being waited on, and slavery is readily seen to be of divine authority; given the unpleasantness of washing people's feet, and that hallowed ordinance speedily passes into innocuous desuetude; given the fathomless quantity of unconscious selfishness still regnant in good men, and the heavenly precepts of the Sermon on the Mount become "largely tinctured with oriental imagery, and not be taken in their severely literal sense." . . .

From all of which considerations the plain wayfaring woman cannot help concluding that exegesis, thus conducted, is one of the most time-serving and man-made of all sciences, and one of the most misleading of all arts. It has broken Christendom into sects that confuse and astound the heathen world, and to-day imposes the heaviest yoke now worn by woman upon that most faithful follower of Him who is her emancipator no less than humanity's Saviour. But as the world becomes more deeply permeated by the principles of Christ's Gospel, methods of exegesis are revised. The old texts stand there, just as before, but we interpret them less narrowly. Universal liberty of person and of opinion are now conceded to be Bible-precept principles; Onesimus and Canaan are no longer quoted as the slave-holder's main-stay; the theory of unfermented wine as well as bread is accepted by our temperance people generally; the great Russian writer, Count Tolstoï, stands as the representative of a school that accepts the precepts of Christ's Sermon on the Mount with perfect literalness, and theologians, not a few, find in the Bible no warrant whatever for the subjection of woman in any-thing. . . .

. . . It is men who have taken the simple, loving, tender Gospel of the New Testament, so suited to be the proclamation of a woman's lips, and translated it in terms of sacerdotalism, dogma, and martyrdom. It is men who have given us the dead letter rather than the living Gospel. The mother-heart of God will never be known to the world until translated into terms of speech by mother-hearted women. Law and love will never bal-ance in the realm of grace until a woman's hand shall hold the scales.

Men preach a creed; women will declare a life. Men deal in formulas, women in facts. Men have always tithed mint and rue and cummin in their exegesis and their ecclesiasticism, while the world's heart has cried out for compassion, forgiveness, and sympathy. Men's preaching has left heads committed to a catechism, and left hearts hard as nether millstones. The Greek bishop who said, "My creed is faultless, with my life you have noth-ing to do," condensed into a sentence two thousand years of priestly dogma. Men reason in the abstract, women in the concrete. A syllogism symbolizes one, a rule of life the other.

From Frances E. Willard, *Woman in the Pulpit* (Chicago: Woman's Temperance Publication Association, 1889), pp. 17–24, 46–47.

49.   Elizabeth Cady Stanton, *The Woman's Bible*

Stanton (1815–1902) was a popular public speaker and daring advocate for women's suffrage and political rights. In her view, as expressed in The Woman's Bible, *written in 1895, scripture stood in the way of women's well-being. Stanton saw scripture and the entire Christian tradition as flawed, due to its male trans-mission. She placed greater emphasis and hope in the extension of Enlightenment ideals of the God-given "rights of man" to include women.*

From the inauguration of the movement for woman's emancipation the Bible has been used to hold her in the "divinely ordained sphere," pre-scribed in the Old and New Testaments.

The canon and civil law; church and state; priests and legislators; all po-litical parties and religious denominations have alike taught that woman was made after man, of man, and for man, an inferior being, subject to man. Creeds, codes, Scriptures and statutes, are all based on this idea. The fash-ions, forms, ceremonies and customs of society, church ordinances and dis-cipline all grow out of this idea. . . .

The Bible teaches that woman brought sin and death into the world, that she precipitated the fall of the race, that she was arraigned before the judgment seat of Heaven, tried, condemned and sentenced. Marriage for her was to be a condition of bondage, maternity a period of suffering and anguish, and in silence and subjection, she was to play the role of a dependent on man's bounty for all her material wants, and for all the information she might desire on the vital questions of the hour, she was commanded to ask her husband at home. Here is the Bible position of woman briefly summed up.

Those who have the divine insight to translate, transpose and transfigure this mournful object of pity into an exalted, dignified personage, worthy our worship as the mother of the race, are to be congratulated as having a share of the occult mystic power of the eastern Mahatmas.

The plain English to the ordinary mind admits of no such liberal interpretation. The unvarnished texts speak for themselves. The canon law, church ordinances and Scriptures, are homogeneous, and all reflect the same spirit and sentiments.

These familiar texts are quoted by clergymen in their pulpits, by statesmen in the halls of legislation, by lawyers in the courts, and are echoed by the press of all civilized nations, and accepted by woman herself as "The Word of God." So perverted is the religious element in her nature, that with faith and works she is the chief support of the church and clergy; the very powers that make her emancipation impossible. When, in the early part of the Nineteenth Century, women began to protest against their civil and political degradation, they were referred to the Bible for an answer. When they protested against their unequal position in the church, they were referred to the Bible for an answer.

This led to a general and critical study of the Scriptures. Some, having made a fetish of these books and believing them to be the veritable "Word of God," with liberal translations, interpretations, allegories and symbols, glossed over the most objectionable features of the various books and clung to them as divinely inspired. Others, seeing the family resemblance between the Mosaic code, the canon law, and the old English common law, came to the conclusion that all alike emanated from the same source; wholly human in their origin and inspired by the natural love of domination in the historians. Others, bewildered with their doubts and fears, came to no conclusion. While their clergymen told them on the one hand, that they owed all the blessings and freedom they enjoyed to the Bible, on the other, they said it clearly marked out their circumscribed sphere of action: that the demands for political and civil rights were irreligious, dangerous to the stability of the home, the state and the church. Clerical appeals were circulated from time to time conjuring members of their churches to take no part in the anti-slavery or woman suffrage movements, as they were infidel in their tendencies, undermining the very foundations of society. No wonder the majority of women stood still, and with bowed heads, accepted the situation. . . .

Others fear that they might compromise their evangelical faith by affiliating with those of more liberal views, who do not regard the Bible as the "Word of God" but like any other book, to be judged by its merits. If the Bible teaches the equality of Woman, why does the church refuse to ordain women to preach the gospel, to fill the offices of deacons and elders, and to administer the Sacraments, or to admit them as delegates to the Synods, General Assemblies and Conferences of the different denominations? They have never yet invited a woman to join one of their Revising Committees, nor tried to mitigate the sentence pronounced on her by changing one count in the indictment served on her in Paradise. . . .

. . . Why is it more ridiculous for women to protest against her present status in the Old and New Testament, in the ordinances and discipline of the church, than in the statutes and constitution of the state? Why is it more ridiculous to arraign ecclesiastics for their false teaching and acts of injustice to women, than members of Congress and the House of Commons? Why is it more audacious to review Moses than Blackstone, the Jewish code of laws, than the English system of jurisprudence? Women have compelled their legislators in every state in this Union to so modify their statutes for women that the old common law is now almost a dead letter. Why not compel Bishops and Revising Committees to modify their creeds and dogmas? Forty years ago it seemed as ridiculous to timid, time-serving and retrograde folk for women to demand an expurgated edition of the laws, as it now does to demand an expurgated edition of the Liturgies and the Scriptures. Come, come, my conservative friend, wipe the dew off your spectacles, and see that the world is moving. Whatever your views may be as to the importance of the proposed work, your political and social degradation are but an outgrowth of your status in the Bible. When you express your aversion, based on a blind feeling of reverence in which reason has no control, to the revision of the Scriptures, you do but echo Cowper, who, when asked to read Paine's "Rights of Man," exclaimed, "No man shall convince me that I am improperly governed while I *feel* the contrary."

Others say it is not *politic* to rouse religious opposition. This much-lauded policy is but another word for *cowardice*. How can woman's position be changed from that of a subordinate to an equal, without opposition, without the broadest discussion of all the questions involved in her present degradation? For so far-reaching and momentous a reform as her complete independence, an entire revolution in all existing institutions is inevitable.

Let us remember that all reforms are interdependent, and that whatever is done to establish one principle on a solid basis, strengthens all. Reformers who are always compromising, have not yet grasped the idea that truth is the only safe ground to stand upon. The object of an individual life is not to carry one fragmentary measure in human progress, but to utter the highest truth clearly seen in all directions, and thus to round out and perfect a well balanced character. Was not the sum of influence exerted by John Stuart Mill on political, religious and social questions far greater than that of any statesman or reformer who has sedulously limited his sympathies and activities to carrying one specific measure? We have many women abundantly endowed with capabilities to understand and revise what men have thus far written. But they are all suffering from inherited ideas of their inferiority; they do not perceive it, yet such is the true explanation of their solicitude, lest they should seem to be too self-asserting. . . .

To women still believing in the plenary inspiration of the Scriptures, we say give us by all means your exegesis in the light of the higher criticism learned men are now making, and illumine the Woman's Bible, with your inspiration.

Bible historians claim special inspiration for the Old and New Testaments containing most contradictory records of the same events, of miracles opposed to all known laws, of customs that degrade the female sex of all human and animal life, stated in most questionable language that could not be read in a promiscuous assembly, and call all this "The Word of God."

The only points in which I differ from all ecclesiastical teaching is that I do not believe that any man ever saw or talked with God, I do not believe that God inspired the Mosaic-code, or told the historians what they say he did about woman, for all the religions on the face of the earth degrade her, and so long as woman accepts the position that they assign her, her emancipation is impossible. Whatever the Bible may be made to do in Hebrew or Greek, in plain English it does not exalt and dignify woman. . . .

There are some general principles in the holy books of all religions that teach love, charity, liberty, justice and equality for all the human family, there are many grand and beautiful passages, the golden rule has been echoed and re-echoed around the world. There are lofty examples of good and true men and women, all worthy our acceptance and example whose lustre cannot be dimmed by the false sentiments and vicious characters bound up in the same volume. The Bible cannot be accepted or rejected as a whole, its teachings are varied and its lessons differ widely from each other. In criticising the peccadilloes of Sarah, Rebecca and Rachel, we would not shadow the virtues of Deborah, Huldah and Vashti. In criticising the Mosaic code we would not question the wisdom of the golden rule and the fifth Commandment. Again the church claims special consecration for its cathedrals and priesthood, parts of these aristocratic churches are too holy for women to enter, boys were early introduced into the choirs for this reason, woman singing in an obscure corner closely veiled. A few of the more democratic denominations accord women some privileges, but invidious discriminations of sex are found in all religious organizations, and the most bitter outspoken enemies of woman are found among clergymen and bishops of the Protestant religion.

The canon law, the Scriptures, the creeds and codes and church discipline of the leading religions bear the impress of fallible man, and not of our ideal great first cause, "the Spirit of all Good," that set the universe of matter and mind in motion, and by immutable law holds the land, the sea, the planets, revolving round the great centre of light and heat, each in its own elliptic, with millions of stars in harmony all singing together, the glory of creation forever and ever.

From Elizabeth Cady Stanton, *The Woman's Bible: Comments on Genesis, Exodus, Leviticus, Numbers and Deuteronomy* (New York: European Publishing Company, 1895), pp. 7–13.

Part 5

Christian Ethics in the Twentieth Century

The extraordinary challenges faced by humanity and by the Christian church in the twentieth century have helped evoke extraordinary accomplishments in human thought, including Christian ethics. This has been the century of total war and explosive population growth, of startling inventions and discoveries, of space travel and information and communications revolutions. Every age flatters itself on its uniqueness; twentieth-century humanity, so far, undoubtedly has more to talk about than any other.

If the events of this century have been both sobering and exhilarating, Christian thought has also been chastened and stretched. Christian ethics in America and Europe began the twentieth century with the vigorous social gospel movement, a creative endeavor to make the gospel more relevant to the Industrial Revolution. American Protestant thinkers like Walter Rauschenbusch and Washington Gladden challenged the rugged individualism of the industrial age with a new vision of social solidarity. Continental Protestants like Christoph Blumhardt and Leonhard Ragaz espoused new forms of religious socialism. Pope Leo XIII's 1891 encyclical *Rerum Novarum* had prepared the way for a series of encyclicals by his twentieth-century successors affirming Christian social responsibility over against doctrinaire laissez-faire capitalism. The historican/theologian Ernst Troeltsch's great work, *The Social Teaching of the Christian Churches* (1911), helped set the stage for Christian social ethics to emerge as an academic discipline, especially in America.

The twentieth century was to be a period of great theological creativity, much of it in Christian ethics. Major figures like Karl Barth, Dietrich Bonhoeffer, Reinhold and Richard Niebuhr, and Paul Tillich were chastened by the persistent evils of war and totalitarianism as well as the hypocrisies of economic greed cloaked in religious garb. Their thought was greatly influenced by the social gospel movement and religious socialism, but they struggled to understand the realities of sin and grace more deeply.

Influenced by such minds, and a host of other productive thinkers and movements, the churches developed an impressive body of social teaching. By the end of the century most Protestant denominations had well-established procedures for adopting declarations on social issues and a large corpus of such teaching. The Roman Catholic Church, through the encyclicals of twentieth-century popes and the immensely productive Second Vatican Council (1962–1965), developed a large body of social teaching on a variety of subjects. Among the most significant twentieth-century developments, the ecumenical movement was largely an outgrowth of moral impulse. As the slogan of one of the early ecumenical conferences put it, "the world is too strong for a divided church." The Life and Work Movement, with pivotal world conferences in Stockholm (1925) and Oxford (1937) focused the attention of ecumenically minded churches on problems of war and peace, the emerging totalitarianism, and the ideological struggles between capitalism, socialism, and communism. The World Council of Churches, begun at the Amsterdam Assembly (1948), struggled with the meaning of "responsible society" and, in later years, with problems of sustainable economic development and social justice.

In the latter half of the twentieth century, civil rights movements and various forms of liberation theology contributed fresh insight to the meaning of social justice, and such thinkers as Martin Luther King, Jr., James Cone, and Gustavo Guitérrez emerged as major new voices. Following in the footsteps of nineteenth-century feminist thinkers, Georgia Harkness, Rosemary Radford Ruether, and others struggled for full equality for women as a part of the meaning of the gospel. Feminist thought brought new insight into the importance of language, helping Christians understand how theological metaphor and church practice can enshrine inherited conceptions of male superiority that are contradicted by the deeper meaning of Christian faith.

Christian pacifism continued as a vital force in twentieth-century Christianity, stimulated by the deeper theological contributions of thinkers like John Howard Yoder and challenged by new levels of violence and the threat of thermonuclear war. A vigorous resurgence of evangelical Christian thought, typified by Carl F. H. Henry, rekindled the traditional evangelical call for individual repentance and redemption while calling for social justice.

It is always difficult to assess one's own time with clarity. This section of the book is the largest, both because it deals with the most recent developments in Christian ethics and because, in our view, this has been an unusually productive period. Even so, it has not been possible to include more than a fraction of the immense literature contributed to Christian ethics in this century. We have sought to include a fair sampling of important and enduring material. This section includes the work of a few living Christian ethicists, but it has not been possible to include here the work of most contemporary thinkers—even some whose contributions will doubtless make a lasting mark.

50. Walter Rauschenbusch,
Christianity and the Social Crisis,
Christianizing the Social Order,
and *A Theology for the Social Gospel*

Walter Rauschenbusch (1861–1918) became the leading voice of the social gospel movement. As a young Baptist pastor, Rauschenbusch discovered that the poor New York City neighborhood surrounding his church was "not a safe place for saved souls"; a "social regeneration" was needed. Later, he became a professor at Rochester Theological Seminary. Through his teaching and through his many writings, he shared his vision for a gradual systemic transformation of society resulting in the kingdom of God on earth. In Christianity and the Social Crisis, *written in 1907, he hoped to mobilize "moral forces" for "the progressive regeneration of social life."Rauschenbusch's specific ideas on how to accomplish this social task found expression in* Christianizing the Social Order *(1912). His final work,* A Theology for the Social Gospel *(1917), was an effort to provide a systematic theological exposition that was "large enough to match" and "vital enough to back" the ambitious undertakings of the social gospelers.*

CHRISTIANITY AND THE SOCIAL CRISIS

To undertake the gradual reconstruction of social life consciously and intelligently would have required a scientific comprehension of social life which was totally lacking in the past. Sociology is still an infant science. Modern political economy may be said to have begun with Adam Smith's "Wealth of Nations," which was published in 1776. Modern historical science, which is interpreting the origins and the development of social institutions, is only about a century old.

For the ordinary man the social order as he finds it has all the sanctity and immutability of natural and divine law. Under feudalism both noble and peasant assumed that God himself had divided humanity into barons and serfs, and any contradiction of that seemed a sacrilege to the barons and a joyful surprise to the serfs. In monarchical countries the institution of kingship is regarded as the natural and divine order. In European thought it is treated as an axiom that there must be well-defined social classes. In our own country intelligent men assume that land has always been freely bought and sold by individuals as to-day; that a man has always had the power to dispose about his property even after he was dead; that business men have always bought in the cheapest market and sold in the dearest at whatever prices they could make; that workingmen have always competed with one another for wages; and that any attempt to change these social adjustments is an attempt to meddle with a natural law as universal as the law of gravitation. Yet our capitalistic organization is of comparatively recent origin, and would have been thought intolerable and immoral in times past. We are only now coming to realize that within certain limits human society is plastic, constantly changing its forms, and that the present system of social organization, as it superseded others, may itself be displaced by something better. Without such a conception of the evolution of social institutions any larger idea of social regeneration could hardly enter the minds of men. The modern socialist movement is really the first intelligent, concerted, and continuous effort to reshape society in accordance with the laws of social development. . . .

. . . We have seen that in the prophetic religion of the Old Testament and in the aims of Jesus Christ the reconstruction of the whole of human life in accordance with the will of God and under the motive power of religion was the ruling purpose. Primitive Christianity, while under the fresh impulse of Jesus, was filled with social forces. In its later history the reconstructive capacities of Christianity were paralyzed by alien influences, but through the evolution of the Christian spirit in the Church it has now arrived at a stage in its development where it is fit and free for its largest social mission. At the same time Christian civilization has arrived at the great crisis of its history and is in the most urgent need of all moral power to overcome the wrongs which have throttled other nations and civilizations. The Church, too, has its own power and future at stake in the issues of social development. Thus the will of God revealed in Christ and in the highest manifestations of the religious spirit, the call of human duty, and the motives of self-protection, alike summon Christian men singly and collectively to put their hands to the plough and not to look back till public morality shall be at least as much Christianized as private morality now is.

The question then immediately confronts us: What social changes would be involved in such a religious reorganization of life? What institutions and practices of our present life would have to cease? What new elements would have to be embodied? What social ideal should be the ultimate aim of Christian men, and what practical means and policies should they use for its attainment?

. . . [Here we] will merely undertake to suggest in what ways the moral forces latent in Christian society can be aroused and mobilized for the progressive regeneration of social life, and in what chief directions these forces should be exerted.

There are certain lines of endeavor which lead nowhere. Christian men have again and again attempted to find the way out of the maze in these directions, but experience has set up the sign, "No Thoroughfare."

One of these futile efforts is the attempt to make economic development revert to earlier stages. Christian men of conservative spirit recoil from the swift pace and impersonal hugeness of modern industry and look back to the simpler processes and more personal contact between master and men as a better and more Christian social life. The personal interest of the intelligent Christian middle class is likely to run in the same direction. Thus in our country we have the outcry of that class against the trusts and the department stores, and the insistence on returning to the simple competition of small concerns. But it is safe to say that no such return would be permanent. These great industrial undertakings extend the area within which coöperation and the correlation of forces rule, and competition is no match for coöperation. Our effort must rather be to preserve all the benefits which the elaboration of the productive machinery has worked out, but to make these benefits enrich the many instead of the few. Reform movements arising among the business class are often reactionary; they seek to revert to outgrown conditions and turn the shadow on the dial backward. Socialism is almost unique in accepting as inevitable and desirable the essential achievements of industrial organization, but only as halfway stages toward a vaster and a far juster social system.

For the same reasons it is futile to attempt to reform modern society on biblical models. The principle underlying the Mosaic land system is wholly right. The spirit pervading the Hebrew laws protecting the laborer and the poor is so tender and noble that it puts us to shame. But these legal prescriptions were adjusted to an agricultural and stationary population, organized under patriarchal and tribal coherence, and they would be wholly unworkable under modern conditions. It is rather our business to catch the bold and humane spirit of the prophetic tribunes of the people and do as well in our day as they did in theirs. Nothing could be more valuable than to understand the social contents of the Bible in their historical setting, and press home on the Christian Church the essential purpose and direction of its own inspired book. But here, too, it is true that "the letter killeth; it is the spirit that quickeneth."

One of the most persistent mistakes of Christian men has been to postpone social regeneration to a future era to be inaugurated by the return of Christ. In former chapters the origin of this hope and its original beauty and power have been discussed. It was at the outset a triumphant assertion of faith against apparent impossibilities. It still enshrines the social hope of Christianity and concedes that some time the social life of men is to pass through a radical change and be ruled by Christ. But the element of postponement in it to-day means a lack of faith in the present power of Christ and paralyzes the religious initiative. It ignores the revelation of God contained in nineteen centuries of continuous history. It is careful not to see the long succession of men and churches and movements that staked all their hopes and all their chances of social improvement on this expectation and were disappointed. It is true that any regeneration of society can come only through the act of God and the presence of Christ; but God is now acting, and Christ is now here. To assert that means not less faith, but more. It is true that any effort at social regeneration is dogged by perpetual relapses and doomed forever to fall short of its aim. But the same is true of our personal efforts to live a Christlike life; it is true, also, of every local church, and of the history of the Church at large. Whatever argument would demand the postponement of social regeneration to a future era will equally demand the postponement of personal holiness to a future life. We must have the faith of the apostolic Church in the triumph of Christ over the kingdoms of the world, *plus* the knowledge which nineteen centuries of history have given to us. Unless we add that knowledge, the faith of the apostles becomes our unbelief.

Another *cul-de-sac* of Christian endeavor is the organization of communistic colonies. There is no reason why a number of Christian people should not live in commons or organize for cooperative production if they can hope to make their life more comfortable, more free from care, and more moral in its relations. But past experience does not show that such colonies served to Christianize social life at large. The example is not widely contagious, even if the colony is successful. If the experiment fails through any of a hundred practical causes, its failure is heralded as a convincing demonstration that competition is the only orthodox and successful basis of society. Settlements with some communistic features are likely to increase in the future as the eyes of cultured people are opened to the wastefulness and unhappiness of ordinary life, and they may be exceedingly useful if they gather like-minded men and women in groups, and thus intensify and clarify their convictions by intercourse. But they will be influential on a large scale only if the ideas and experiences wrought out in these settlements find channels to run out freely into the general unregenerate life through books, newspapers, or lectures issuing from the settlement. In the main, the salt of the earth will do its work best if it is not stored in casks by itself, but rubbed in evenly and generously where it is most needed. The mass of society will ponderously move an inch where a select colony might spurt a mile toward the future; but the total gain in foot-pounds will be greater in the mass-movement. The coöperative stores in England and on the continent are a far more hopeful and influential education in the coöperative principle than the communistic colonies have been, because they are built into the mass of the general life.

If the Church should in the future really seek to Christianize social life, it will almost certainly be tempted to make itself the chief agent and beneficiary of the process. Attempts will be made to organize ecclesiastical duplicates of fraternal insurance societies, coöperative undertakings, labor bureaus, etc. There will be Christian socialist parties in politics. The Church will claim to be the only agency through which social salvation can come. It will seek to keep the social movement under clerical control. This effort will be prompted partly by the desire to put its organized power at the service of the poor; partly by the fear of non-Christian or anti-Christian influences which may dominate social radicalism; and partly by the instinct of self-assertion, self-protection, and self-aggrandizement which resides in every social organization. Just as the desire to save individuals is now frequently vitiated by the anxiety to increase church membership, so the desire to save social life may be vitiated by the anxiety to keep the Church to the front. Those ecclesiastical bodies which have the strongest church-consciousness are most likely to insist that this work shall be done through them or not at all. The history of the social movement in Europe has furnished most interesting and significant demonstrations of this tendency. But it is full of peril not only to the Church, but to the social movement itself. It beclouds the social issues by ecclesiastical interests and jealousies. It subtly and unconsciously changes the aim from the salvation of the people to the salvation of the Church. The social movement could have no more powerful ally than religious enthusiasm; it could have no more dangerous ally than ecclesiasticism. If the Church truly desires to save the social life of the people, it must be content with inspiring the social movement with religious faith and daring, and it must not attempt to control and monopolize it for its own organization. If a man wants to give honest help, he must fill himself with the spirit of Jesus and divest himself of the ecclesiastical point of view.

In personal religion the first requirement is to repent and believe in the gospel. As long as a man is self-righteous and complacently satisfied with his moral attainments, there is no hope that he will enter into the higher development, and unless he has faith that a higher level of spiritual life is attainable, he will be lethargic and stationary.

Social religion, too, demands repentance and faith: repentance for our social sins; faith in the possibility of a new social order. As long as a man sees in our present society only a few inevitable abuses and recognizes no sin and evil deep-seated in the very constitution of the present order, he is still in a state of moral blindness and without conviction of sin. Those who believe in a better social order are often told that they do not know the sinfulness of the human heart. They could justly retort the charge on the men of the evangelical school. When the latter deal with public wrongs, they often exhibit a curious unfamiliarity with the forms which sin assumes there, and sometimes reverently bow before one of the devil's spider-webs, praising it as one of the mighty works of God. Regeneration includes that a man must pass under the domination of the spirit of Christ, so that he will judge of life as Christ would judge of it. That means a revaluation of social values. Things that are now "exalted among men" must become "an abomination" to him because they are built on wrong and misery. Unless a man finds his judgment at least on some fundamental questions in opposition to the current ideas of the age, he is still a child of this world and has not "tasted the powers of the coming age." He will have to repent and believe if he wants to be a Christian in the full sense of the word. . . .

Here enters socialism. It proposes to abolish the division of industrial society into two classes and to close the fatal chasm which has separated the employing class from the working class since the introduction of power machinery. It proposes to restore the independence of the workingman by making him once more the owner of his tools and to give him the full proceeds of his production instead of a wage determined by his poverty. It has no idea of reverting to the simple methods of the old handicrafts, but heartily accepts the power machinery, the great factory, the division of labor, the organization of the men in great regiments of workers, as established facts in modern life, and as the most efficient method of producing wealth. But it proposes to give to the whole body of workers the ownership of these vast instruments of production and to distribute among them all the entire proceeds of their common labor. There would then be no capitalistic class opposed to the working class; there would be a single class which would unite the qualities of both. Every workman would be both owner and worker, just as a farmer is who tills his own farm, or a housewife who works in her own kitchen. This would be a permanent solution of the labor question. It would end the present insecurity, the constant antagonism, the social inferiority, the physical exploitation, the intellectual poverty to which the working class is now exposed even when its condition is most favorable.

If such a solution is even approximately feasible, it should be hailed with joy by every patriot and Christian, for it would put a stop to our industrial war, drain off the miasmatic swamp of undeserved poverty, save our political democracy, and lift the great working class to an altogether different footing of comfort, intelligence, security and moral strength. And it would embody the principle of solidarity and fraternity in the fundamental institutions of our industrial life. All the elements of coöperation and interaction which are now at work in our great establishments would be conserved, and in addition the hearty interest of all workers in their common factory or store would be immensely intensified by the diffused sense of ownership. Such a social order would develop the altruistic and social instincts just as the competitive order brings out the selfish instincts.

From Walter Rauschenbusch, *Christianity and the Social Crisis,* Library of Theological Ethics (Louisville, Ky.: Westminster/John Knox Press, 1992), pp. 194–195, 343–49, 407–8.

CHRISTIANIZING THE SOCIAL ORDER

Christianizing the social order means bringing it into harmony with the ethical convictions which we identify with Christ. A fairly definite body of moral convictions has taken shape in modern humanity. They express our collective conscience, our working religion. The present social order denies and flouts many of these principles of our ethical life and compels us in practice to outrage our better self. We demand therefore that the moral sense of humanity shall be put in control and shall be allowed to reshape the institutions of social life.

We call this "christianizing" the social order because these moral principles find their highest expression in the teachings, the life, and the spirit of Jesus Christ. Their present power in Western civilization is in large part directly traceable to his influence over its history. To the great majority of our nation, both inside and outside of the churches, he has become the incarnate moral law and his name is synonymous with the ideal of human goodness. To us who regard him as the unique revelation of God, the unfolding of the divine life under human forms, he is the ultimate standard of moral and spiritual life, the perfect expression of the will of God for humanity, the categorical imperative with a human heart. But very many who do not hold this belief in a formulated way or who feel compelled to deny it, including an increasing portion of our Jewish fellow-citizens, will still consent that in Jesus our race has reached one of its highest points, if not its crowning summit thus far, so that Jesus Christ is a prophecy of the future glory of humanity, the type of Man as he is to be. Christianizing means humanizing in the highest sense. I ask the consent of both classes to use his name for the undertaking which he initiated for us. To say that we want to moralize the social order would be both vague and powerless to most men. To say that we want to christianize it is both concrete and compelling. Christ's spirit is the force that drives us. His mind is the square and plumb line that must guide us in our building.

The danger in using so high a word is that we shall be led to expect too much. Even a Christian social order cannot mean perfection. As long as men are flesh and blood the world can be neither sinless nor painless. For instance, how can any form of social organization keep the tremendous electric current of sex desire from going astray and dealing misery and shame? The law of growth, which is essential to human life, itself makes any static perfection impossible. Every child is born a kicking little egotist and has to learn by its own mistakes and sins to coördinate itself with the social life of every successive group which it enters. If perfection were reached to-day, new adjustments would be demanded to-morrow by the growth of new powers. The justest and most sympathetic human society conceivable would unknowingly inflict injury and wrong, and only slowly realize it when it heard the insistent cry of pain. The structure of society can never be up to date. It is necessarily a slow historical growth, and men will always have to labor hard to rid it of antiquated and harmful customs and institutions brought down from a worse past.

I must ask my readers to keep these limitations of human life in mind as axioms in all the discussion that follows, even when they are not stated, and to assume that we are keeping within hailing distance of common sense. We shall demand perfection and never expect to get it. But by demanding it we shall get more than we now have. Straight-cut insistence on moral duty is quite compatible with the largest patience, as human frailty limps up to God's judgment seat and pleads guilty for a thousand sins. Jesus is the classical example of the combination between high-voltage moral demand and the tenderest understanding.

But within the limitations of human nature I believe that the constitutional structure of the social order can be squared with the demands of Christian morality. At every new step of moral progress the clamor has gone up that fairness and decency were utopian fanaticism and would ruin society, but instead of making the social machinery unworkable, every step toward collective Christian ethics proved an immense relief to society.

An unchristian social order can be known by the fact that it makes good men do bad things. It tempts, defeats, drains, and degrades, and leaves men stunted, cowed, and shamed in their manhood. A Christian social order makes bad men do good things. It sets high aims, steadies the vagrant impulses of the weak, trains the powers of the young, and is felt by all as an uplifting force which leaves them with the consciousness of a broader and nobler humanity as their years go on. . . .

Our business life is the seat and source of our present troubles. So much ought to be plain to all who care to see. It is in commerce and industry that we encounter the great collective inhumanities that shame our Christian feeling, such as child labor and the bloody total of industrial accidents. Here we find the friction between great classes of men which makes whole communities hot with smoldering hate or sets them ablaze with lawlessness. . . .

Business life is the unregenerate section of our social order. If by some magic it could be plucked out of our total social life in all its raw selfishness, and isolated on an island, unmitigated by any other factors of our life, that island would immediately become the object of a great foreign mission crusade for all Christendom. . . .

Our first need is to analyze our economic system so that we may understand wherein and why it is fundamentally unchristian. Most of us have accepted our economic system as we accept our stomach, without understanding its workings. Nor is it easy to understand the moral essentials of this huge and complicated social machinery. We have no such historical perspective of it as our great-grandchildren will have when they study the Great Industrial Transition of the Twentieth Century in college. . . .

. . . Nothing calls out such serious thought and discussion at present as the unsatisfactory relation of the economic life to the higher laws and values of humanity. . . . I propose throughout to think from the point of view of a Christian man. The tests that I shall apply are not technical but moral. Does our business system create sound and noble manhood? Does it make it fairly easy to do right and hard to do wrong? Does it call men upward or tempt them downward? Does it reward or penalize fraternal action? Does it furnish the material basis for the Reign of God on earth? . . .

We should get the most enlightening comments on our economic life if we could bring to life some able mind that went to sleep in A.D. 1700, or if some one could live in the year 2000 like the hero of "Looking Backward" and come back to us. By comparing our present system backward with the order out of which it has developed, or forward with the order into which it is silently passing, we should get a realization of the distinctive qualities of the life in the midst of which we are moving. . . .

In the old order the aim was to make a living, to give the children an education and a start in life, to lay something by for a rainy day, and to rise a step in life if possible. The range of possibilities and the range of ambition were both narrow. There was always a big difference between the thrifty man and the shiftless man; between the mechanic who sent his boy to college, and his cousin who went fishing and let his job wait for him. But the richest and the poorest in our old-time village communities were only a few thousand dollars apart. In the cities men of business sagacity equal to any that we now have were content if a lifetime of success won them a few hundred thousand dollars.

To-day the range of possibilities is enormous, and the unsatisfied thirst for wealth has grown correspondingly. The poorest and the richest are as far apart as the molehill and the peaks of the Sierras. In the higher reaches of business getting a living drops out of sight. The dominant concern is to get profit, and to invest it to get more profit. . . .

The moral objection lies, not against the size and complexity of the modern system, but against the fact that this wonderful product of human ability and toil with its immense powers of production has gravitated into the ownership and control of a relatively small class of men. This group is always changing; some drop out, others enter. But these personal changes are of little importance for the make-up of society. The group is permanent, and the men in it have acquired a proportion of power over their fellows which—human nature being what it is—must lead to injustice, to inequality, and to the frustration of the Christian conception of human fellowship. . . .

. . . [T]he economic interests of the capitalist revolve around his profits, and since the capitalist class is the controlling and dominant class, the desire for profit dominates our whole industrial organization. All its efforts converge on one end, to make dividends. All the parts of the great organism of production move toward profit with an overwhelming singleness of purpose. Whenever profit has collided with the higher interests of humanity, the latter have hitherto gone down with sickening regularity. This triumphant sway of profit as the end of work and existence puts the stamp of mammonism on our modern life.

From Walter Rauschenbusch, *Christianizing the Social Order* (New York: The Macmillan Company, 1926), pp. 125–27, 156–65.

A THEOLOGY FOR THE SOCIAL GOSPEL

The social gospel realizes the importance and power of the super-personal forces in the community. It has succeeded in awakening the social conscience of the nation to the danger of allowing such forces to become parasitic and oppressive. A realization of the spiritual power and value of these composite personalities must get into theology, otherwise theology will not deal adequately with the problem of sin and of redemption, and will be unrelated to some of the most important work of salvation which the coming generations will have to do. . . .

The doctrine of original sin has directed attention to the biological channels for the transmission of general sinfulness from generation to generation, but has neglected and diverted attention from the transmission and perpetuation of specific evils through the channels of social tradition. . . .

New spiritual factors of the highest significance are disclosed by the realization of the super-personal forces, or composite personalities, in society. When these backslide and become combinations for evil, they add enormously to the power of sin. Theology has utilized the terminology and results of psychology to interpret the sin and regeneration of individuals. Would it stray from its field if it utilized sociological terms and results in order to interpret the sin and redemption of these super-personal entities in human life?

The solidaristic spiritual conceptions . . . must all be kept in mind and seen together, in order to realize the power and scope of the doctrine to which they converge: the Kingdom of Evil. . . .

The new thing in the social gospel is the clearness and insistence with which it sets forth the necessity and the possibility of redeeming the historical life of humanity from the social wrongs which now pervade it and which act as temptations and incitements to evil and as forces of resistance to the powers of redemption. Its chief interest is concentrated on those manifestations of sin and redemption which lie beyond the individual soul. If our exposition of the superpersonal agents of sin and of the Kingdom of Evil is true, then evidently a salvation confined to the soul and its personal interests is an imperfect and only partly effective salvation.

Yet the salvation of the individual is, of course, an essential part of salvation. Every new being is a new problem of salvation. It is always a great and wonderful thing when a young spirit enters into voluntary obedience to God and feels the higher freedom with which Christ makes us free. It is one of the miracles of life. The burden of the individual is as heavy now as ever. The consciousness of wrong-doing, of imperfection, of a wasted life lies on many and they need forgiveness and strength for a new beginning. Modern pessimism drains the finer minds of their confidence in the world and the value of life itself. At present we gasp for air in a crushing and monstrous world. Any return of faith is an experience of salvation.

Therefore our discussion can not pass personal salvation by. We might possibly begin where the old gospel leaves off, and ask our readers to take all the familiar experiences and truths of personal evangelism and religious nurture for granted. . . .But our understanding of personal salvation itself is deeply affected by the new solidaristic comprehension furnished by the social gospel. . . .

. . . . It is time to overhaul our understanding of the kind of change we hope to produce by personal conversion and regeneration. The social gospel furnishes some tests and standards.

When we undertook to define the nature of sin, we accepted the old definition, that sin is selfishness and rebellion against God, but we insisted on putting humanity into the picture. The definition of sin as selfishness gets its reality and nipping force only when we see humanity as a great solidarity and God indwelling in it. In the same way the terms and definitions of salvation get more realistic significance and ethical reach when we see the internal crisis of the individual in connection with the social forces that play upon him or go out from him. The form which the process of redemption takes in a given personality will be determined by the historical and social spiritual environment of the man. . . .

If sin is selfishness, salvation must be a change which turns a man from self to God and humanity. His sinfulness consisted in a selfish attitude, in which he was at the centre of the universe, and God and all his fellowmen were means to serve his pleasures, increase his wealth, and set off his egotisms. Complete salvation, therefore, would consist in an attitude of love in which he would freely co-ordinate his life with the life of his fellows in obedience to the loving impulses of the spirit of God, thus taking his part in a divine organism of mutual service. When a man is in a state of sin, he may be willing to harm the life and lower the self-respect of a woman for the sake of his desires; he may be willing to take some of the mental and spiritual values out of the life of a thousand families, and lower the human level of a whole mill-town in order to increase his own dividends or maintain his autocratic sense of power. If this man came under the influence of the mind of Christ, he would see men and women as children of God with divine worth and beauty, and this realization would cool his lust or covetousness. . . .

Conversion has usually been conceived as a break with our own sinful past. But in many cases it is also a break with the sinful past of a social group. . . . In primitive Christianity baptism stood for a conscious break with pagan society. This gave it a powerful spiritual reaction. Conversion is most valuable if it throws a revealing light not only across our own past, but across the social life of which we are part, and makes our repentance a vicarious sorrow for all. . . .

The salvation of the super-personal beings is by coming under the law of Christ. The fundamental step of repentance and conversion for professions and organizations is to give up monopoly power and the incomes derived from legalized extortion, and to come under the law of service, content with a fair income for honest work. The corresponding step in the case of governments and political oligarchies, both in monarchies and in capitalistic semi-democracies, is to submit to real democracy. Therewith they step out of the Kingdom of Evil into the Kingdom of God. . . .

The fundamental first step in the salvation of mankind was the achievement of the personality of Jesus. Within him the Kingdom of God got its first foothold in humanity. It was by virtue of his personality that he became the initiator of the Kingdom. . . .

The personality which he achieved was a new type in humanity. Having the power to master and assimilate others, it became the primal cell or a new social organism. Even if there had been no sin from which mankind had to be redeemed, the life of Jesus would have dated an epoch in the evolution of the race by the introduction of a new type and consequently new social standards. He is the real revelation of God. Other conceptions have to be outlived; his has to be attained. . . .

The cross is the monumental fact telling of grace and inviting repentance and humility.

Thus the death of Christ was the conclusive and effective expression of the love of Jesus Christ for God and man, and his complete devotion to the Kingdom of God. The more his personality was understood to be the full and complete expression of the character of God, the more did his death become the assurance and guarantee that God loves us, forgives us, and is willing to do all things to save us.

It is the business of theologians and preachers to make the atonement effective in producing the characteristic of love in Christian men and women. If it does not assimilate them to the mind of Christ it has missed its purpose. We can either be saved by non-ethical sacramental methods, or by absorbing the moral character of Jesus into our own character. Let every man judge which is the salvation he wants.

The social gospel is based on the belief that love is the only true working principle of human society. It teaches that the Kingdom of Evil has thrust love aside and employed force, because love will support only a fraternal distribution of property and power, while force will support exploitation and oppression. If love is the fundamental quality in God, it must be part of the constitution of humanity. Then it can not be impossible to found society on love. The atonement is the symbol and basis of a new social order.

From Walter Rauschenbusch, *A Theology for the Social Gospel* (Nashville: Abingdon Press, 1978), pp. 75–78, 95–99, 117, 151, 152, 273–74. Copyright © 1917 by Macmillan Publishing Company; renewed 1945 by Pauline E. Rauschenbusch. Reprinted with permission of Simon & Schuster, Inc.

51. Georgia Harkness, *Women Ministers*

Harkness (1891–1974), professor at Garrett Biblical Institute (now Garrett–Evangelical Theological Seminary), was the first woman to hold a major chair in theology in the United States. Influenced by the social gospel and, later, by neo-orthodoxy, she worked tirelessly for the ordination of women in the Methodist church, achieving her goal in 1956. Women Ministers was written in 1939.

To the leadership of woman in the church many barriers have been interposed. John Calvin, spiritual forebear of much of American Protestantism, wrote: "It is not permitted to any woman to speak in church, nor to teach, nor to baptize, nor to offer sacrifice: neither to lay claim to the lot of a man or the priestly office. . . . It is plainly evident that this abuse could not become implanted without the barbarous confusion of the whole of Christianity."

Many others within the church have echoed in spirit, if not in diction, the words of Samuel Johnson, "I am very fond of the company of ladies. I like their beauty, I like their delicacy, I like their vivacity—and I like their silence."

Nevertheless women have not been silent. Women today occupy a significant and growing place in religious leadership. Yet in spite of the emancipating power of the Christian gospel which has opened to women large opportunities in education, medicine, law, politics, and the arts, the church has been reluctant to accept women into leadership on terms of parity with men.

Certainly we women ought not either militantly or plaintively to bewail our fate. Prohibition was not won by [radical American temperance advocate] Carry Nation, or woman suffrage by [radical British suffragette] Silvia Pankhurst. While I do not claim large knowledge of male nature, I am sure that no man likes to be told by a woman that women are abused.

245

On the other hand, we women must not, either through timidity or indifference, acquiesce in things as they are. Any marked change can come only through the agency of men whose sense of justice and Christian concern for personality are focused on the issue.

To tackle one of the knottiest issues, I wish to speak to the moot problem of ordination. I do not believe ordination to be all-important. I regard it as less important than that women be admitted to the governing bodies and policy-making organs of the church. Neither do I believe that large numbers of women are likely to seek ordination. Nevertheless, while ordination is not all-important, it is a crucial matter for a principle is at stake.

I believe that ordination on terms of full parity with men should be opened to women for three reasons:

The first is biblical. At the dawn of Hebrew history, Deborah seems to have had full political and religious authority—a situation which has not been duplicated since.

I base my judgment, however, not on the spirit of the Old Testament but of the New. Paul stated it when he wrote: "There is neither Jew nor Greek, there is neither bond nor free, there is neither male nor female; ye are all one in Christ Jesus."

The second reason is practical. The church ought to command the wholehearted allegiance and elicit the best services of all Christians. Every year there are trained, intelligent, and deeply Christian college women who are forced to go into various types of regular social service because they do not find within the church the opportunities open to their brothers.

The third reason is spiritual. The richest and most intimate experiences in the life of the Christian are those which have to do with reception into the membership of the church, with partaking of the sacraments, with marriage, with the baptism of children, with the consolation the minister is called upon to offer when sorrow enters a home.

As long as a person is debarred by reason of sex from acting as the agent of the church in these high moments, no matter what other opportunities are open to her she is debarred from the largest Christian service. A case might easily be made for the contention that women have a special aptitude for entering into the inner lives of persons at these sacred moments.

However, I do not say that women have more or less of tact and understanding for such situations than have men. I say only that where there is equal insight and equal consecration and therefore equal capacity to minister in Christ's name, there ought to be equality of opportunity to do so. . . .

The large contributions of women in the lay activities of the local church and in the building of Christian homes have long been recognized. They are, and ought to be, held in high esteem. There is no greater service that women can render than to rear up an oncoming Christian generation. Yet it is no disparagement of these great contributions to point out that these are not all that women have to offer.

There are men within the church—even within the Methodist church—who ask why women are so largely putting their energies into other organizations for women and are neglecting the church.

In a few sentences of the Madras Report lies the primary answer to that question:

> These agencies afford to women large scope for their varied abilities. In the official life of the church, women are offered relatively few opportunities which call forth their full allegiance and command their abilities and energies.

Men will help solve the problem when they realize that a Christian sense of the spiritual equality of all persons, brought to bear upon the facts, is an adequate spur to the removal of limitations. Barriers even now are being broken down through the agency of men, and larger opportunities await us all through their united effort.

From Georgia Harkness, "Women Ministers," *The Christian Advocate* vol. 114, no. 44 (November 1939): 1061.

52. Dorothy Day, *The Catholic Worker*

Day (1897–1960) was one of the most influential Catholic laypersons of the twentieth century. Under her leadership, the Catholic Worker movement became an influential enterprise for nonviolent social change. The core of the movement's theological ethic of gentle personalism, combining social activism and Catholic faith, was clearly displayed in Day's own life and writing. The following passages were excerpted from The Catholic Worker *from 1942.*

We are at war, a declared war, with Japan, Germany, and Italy. . . .

We are still pacifists. Our manifesto is the Sermon on the Mount, which means that we will try to be peacemakers. Speaking for many of our conscientious objectors, we will not participate in armed warfare or in making munitions, or by buying government bonds to prosecute the war, or in urging others to these efforts.

But neither will we be carping in our criticism. We love our country and we love our President. We have been the only country in the world where men and women of all nations have taken refuge from oppression. We recognize that while in the order of intention we have tried to stand for peace, for love of our brothers and sisters, in the order of execution we have failed as Americans in living up to our principles.

We will try daily, hourly, to pray for an end to the war. . . .

Let us add that unless we continue this prayer with almsgiving, in giving to the least of God's children; and fasting in order that we may help feed the hungry; and penance in recognition of our share in the guilt, our prayer may become empty words.

Our Works of Mercy may take us into the midst of war. As editor of *The Catholic Worker*, I would urge our friends and associates to care for the sick and the wounded, to the growing of food for the hungry, to the continuance of all our Works of Mercy in our houses and on our farms. . . .

247

"But we are at war," people say, "This is no time to talk of peace. It is demoralizing to the armed forces to protest, not to cheer them on in their fight for Christianity, for democracy, for civilization. Now that it is under way, it is too late to do anything about it." One reader writes to protest against our "frail" voices "blatantly" crying out against war. (The word "blatant" comes from "bleat," and we are indeed poor sheep crying out to the Good Shepherd to save us from these horrors.) Another Catholic newspaper says it sympathizes with our sentimentality. This is a charge always leveled against pacifists. We are supposed to be afraid of the suffering, of the hardships of war.

But let those who talk of softness, of sentimentality, come to live with us in cold, unheated houses in the slums. Let them come to live with the criminal, the unbalanced, the drunken, the degraded, the perverted. (It is not decent poor, it is not the decent sinner who was the recipient of Christ's love.) Let them live with rats, with vermin, bedbugs, roaches, lice (I could describe the several kinds of body lice).

Let their flesh be mortified by cold, by dirt, by vermin; let their eyes be mortified by the sight of bodily excretions, diseased limbs, eyes, noses, mouths.

Let their noses be mortified by the smells of sewage, decay, and rotten flesh. Yes, and the smell of the sweat, blood, and tears spoken of so blithely by Mr. Churchill, and so widely and bravely quoted by comfortable people. . . .

Our Catholic Worker groups are perhaps too hardened to the sufferings in the class war, living as they do in refugee camps, the refugees being, as they are, victims of the class war we live in always. We have lived in the midst of this war now these many years. It is a war not recognized by the majority of our comfortable people. They are pacifists themselves when it comes to the class war. They even pretend it is not there.

Many friends have counseled us to treat this world war in the same way. "Don't write about it. Don't mention it. Don't jeopardize the great work you are doing among the poor, among the workers. Just write about constructive things like Houses of Hospitality and Farming Communes." "Keep silence with a bleeding heart," one reader, a man, pro-war, and therefore not a sentimentalist, writes us.

But we cannot keep silent. We have not kept silence in the face of the monstrous injustice of the class war, or the race war that goes on side by side with this world war (which the Communists used to call the imperialist war).

Read the letters in this issue of the paper, the letter from the machine-shop worker as to the deadening, degrading hours of labor. Remember the unarmed steel strikers, the coal miners, shot down on picket lines. Read the letter from our correspondent in Seattle who tells of the treatment accorded agricultural workers in the Northwest. Are these workers supposed to revolt? These are Pearl Harbor incidents! Are they supposed to turn to arms in the class conflict to defend their lives, their homes, their wives and children?

53. Karl Barth,
The Doctrine of Creation

The vast Church Dogmatics *of the Swiss theologian Karl Barth (1886–1968) contributes to Christian ethics at many points, but nowhere more creatively than in vol. 3,* The Doctrine of Creation *(a major section of the* Church Dogmatics, *physically encompassing four large parts). Barth's distinction between "covenant" and "creation" is a particularly interesting solution to the relationship between spiritual and physical realities.*

Creation as the External Basis of the Covenant

Section 41. . . . The creature to whom He has bound Himself belongs to Him. It is only God's free love that makes Him bind Himself to it. In so doing, He does not in any sense discharge a debt. How can He be impelled by anything but Himself, in perfect freedom, really to love the creature which owes its existence and nature to Him alone, to enter with it into this relation and therefore to provide this sequel to His creation? But as He does this, as His love is so incomprehensibly high and deep that He is not ashamed to will and do it, His activity has its solid external basis in the fact that what He loves belongs to Him. In the partner of His covenant He does not have to do with the subject of another nor a lord in his own right, but with His own property, with the work of His will and achievement. The external dynamic of this covenant is that it rests on creation. In virtue of its being and nature, the creature is destined, prepared and equipped to be a partner of this covenant. This covenant cannot be seriously threatened or attacked by the nature of the creature or its surroundings, nor by any attribute of man and the world. By its whole nature the creature is destined and disposed for this covenant. There is no peculiarity in man and the world which does not as such aim at this covenant. As a partner of this covenant, the creature will always have to do exclusively with its Creator on God's side, and exclusively with its own God-given nature on its own.

We have to make a self-evident restriction. Creation is not itself the covenant. The existence and being of the one loved are not identical with the fact that it is loved. This can be said only in respect of the love with which God loves Himself—the Father the Son and the Son the Father in the Holy Spirit. It cannot be said of God's relationship to the creature posited in distinction from Himself. The existence and being of the creature willed and constituted by God are the object and to that extent the presupposition of His love. Thus the covenant is the goal of creation and creation the way to the covenant. Nor is creation the inner basis of the covenant. (At a later point we shall have to state conversely that the covenant is the inner basis of creation; but this relationship is not reversible.) The inner basis of the covenant is simply the free love of God, or more precisely the eternal covenant which

God has decreed in Himself as the covenant of the Father with His Son as the Lord and Bearer of human nature, and to that extent the Representative of all creation. Creation is the external—and only the external—basis of the covenant. It can be said that it makes it technically possible; that it prepares and establishes the sphere in which the institution and history of the covenant take place; that it makes possible the subject which is to be God's partner in this history, in short the nature which the grace of God is to adopt and to which it is to turn in this history. As the love of God could not be satisfied with the eternal covenant as such; as it willed to execute it and give it form outside the divine sphere, it made itself this external ground of the covenant, i.e., it made necessary the existence and being of the creature and therefore of creation. It is, however, only its external basis. . . .

The Problem of Special Ethics

Section 52. The question of the Word of God in Christian proclamation, and therefore dogmatics, embraces necessarily the ethical question as well, i.e., the question what is good human action. For Christian proclamation is the message of Jesus Christ and of the grace of God manifested and active in Him. He is the Word of God about which dogmatics enquires. Thus dogmatics asks concerning the covenant between the true God and true man established in Him from all eternity and fulfilled in Him in time. But true man is characterised by action, by good action, as the true God is also characterised by action, by good action. As dogmatics enquires concerning the action of God and its goodness, it must necessarily make thorough enquiry concerning active man and the goodness of his action. It has the problem of ethics in view from the very first, and it cannot legitimately lose sight of it. . . .

The task of theological ethics is to understand the Word of God as the command of God. Its fundamental, simplest and comprehensive answer to the ethical problem is that man's action is good in so far as it is sanctified by the Word of God which as such is also the command of God. "There is none good but one, that is, God" (Mk 10 [:18]). But the God who is active in His Word and command is good. By "God" we mean the One who is revealed, sovereign and operative in Jesus Christ. He is good. He is the fulness, measure and source of all goodness, and therefore of what is to be called good in human action. Man's action is good in so far as he is the obedient hearer of the Word and command of God. The hearing and obeying which proceeds from and by the Word of God is man's sanctification. Ethics has to understand the Word of God as the fulness, measure and source of this sanctification.

Ethics has first to attempt this with an upward look, as it were, in relation to the divine action. To that extent there is what may be called a "general" ethics, which forms part of the doctrine of God as a counterpart to the doctrine of election. In this it is a question of understanding generally the fact and extent that human sanctification and therefore good human action are effected by the action of God in His command. . . .

In "special" ethics, the first part of which we have now to treat in the context and as the conclusion of the doctrine of creation, it is a matter of varying emphases and standpoints within the same question and answer. We now look downwards, as it were, to the man who acts, i.e., who acts under the command of God, His claim and decision and judgment. We now enquire concerning sanctification as it comes to man from the God who acts towards him in His command, concerning the good which is real and recognisable in his action under the command of God. . . .

If, then, the outworking and shaping of man's sanctification by the command of God in man's real action is a problem of ethics, this necessarily means that ethics becomes concrete, particular, or special ethics. It still has to do with the Word and command of God. It still sets out from the knowledge that God alone is good, and man only through the grace of His Word and in hearing and obeying His command. But it now follows the work of grace and the Word and command of God into the distinctive lowlands of real human action and therefore into the sphere of concrete human volition, decision, action and abstention, into the events in which this particular man realises this particular condition and possibility and therefore himself, into the related sequence of events. Here in the sphere of the concrete, particular, special elements in human possibility and reality there must be seen and demonstrated the fact and extent of the existence of good human action under the lordship and efficacy of the divine command. But if ethics takes this turn, we must consider exactly what is possible or impossible, and what is thus to be undertaken or not.

"Special ethics" is sometimes taken to mean the understanding of the command of God as a prescribed text, which, partly written and partly unwritten, is made up of biblical texts in which there are believed to be seen universally binding divine ordinances and directions, of certain propositions again presumed to be universally valid, of the natural moral law generally perceptible to human reason, and finally of particular norms which have been handed down historically in the tradition of Western Christianity and which lay claim to universal validity. The grouping and blending of the various elements in this text may vary, the Bible, natural law or tradition predominating. The essential point is that God's command is regarded as in some sense a legal text known to the ethical teacher and those whom he has to instruct. . . .

One might well be tempted to call this the ideal solution to the problem of special ethics. It sheds light at once by reason of its formal clarity. It seems to effect what one might expect from ethics, and with particular eagerness from "special ethics." It rushes to the help of doubtful and groping consciences in their individual decisions, proffering its superior knowledge either before or after the event. It gives precise and detailed information about good and evil in relation to what man has done or intends doing. . . .

The way of casuistry is basically unacceptable, however enticing it might seem, and however convenient it would be both for spiritual advisers and above all for troubled souls if this way could be followed. . . .

. . . [T]here is no such thing as a casuistical ethics: no fixation of the divine command in a great or small text of ethical law; no method or technique of applying this text to the plenitude of conditions and possibilities of the activity of all men; no means of deducing good or evil in the particular instance of human conduct from the truth of this text presupposed as a universal rule and equated with the command of God. This is something which special ethics must not attempt. . . .

Why not? There are three decisive reasons.

1. If special ethics becomes casuistry, this means that the moralist wishes to set himself on God's throne, to distinguish good and evil, and always to judge things as the one or the other, not only in relation to others but also to himself. He makes himself lord, king and judge at the place where only God can be this. . . .

2. Again, whether it finds its direction in tradition, a conception of natural law or the Bible, casuistical ethics makes the objectively untenable assumption that the command of God is a universal rule, an empty form, or rather a tissue of such rules and forms. As in the case of human law, it thus requires to be filled out by concrete and specific application to come into force as a command. Now this may well be necessary for the "form of the good" and similar philosophical epitomes of the moral law. But the case is very different with the command of the living God. This is given to man not only universally and formally but in concrete fulness and with definiteness of content. . . . It is always an individual command for the conduct of this man, at this moment and in this situation; a prescription for this case of his; a prescription for the choice of a definite possibility of human intention, decision and action.

3. But casuistical ethics also involves an encroachment in relation to man's action under the command of God, a destruction of the Christian freedom, in which alone this can be a good action. In the whole concrete fulness and concentration with which it always applies to man, the command of God is an appeal to his freedom; not, of course, to a freedom of his choice, preference, or selection; but to his real freedom, which consists in his freedom for God, in his freedom to obey Him. If he receives and understands it as the command of God's free grace, he then opens and attaches himself to it in freedom, as a child does to the word of its father, because he is the father and it is the child. God's demand in relation to man is a demand of man himself: not merely, then, that he should actually will or do or not will and do this or that which God proposes; but that he should voluntarily confess what is proposed, making it a matter of his own choice and decision. God wills indeed that man should be there—there in His cause. In the fulfilment of his obedience, man is to be free for Him and therefore for eternal life. He is to act rightly as His confidant, not only in external conformity as ordered, but in genuine agreement and therefore with a good conscience. Action means not only to choose and realise this or that, but to choose and realise oneself in this or that. So, then, an action done in obedience to God cannot consist only in carrying out something that God wishes, but in man's offering himself to God in so doing. Casuistry de-

stroys the freedom of this obedience. . . . [I]t conceals from him the character of his conduct as his own, direct responsibility. It spares him what he
should not be spared—the knowledge that it is not merely his external conduct, nor his will, purpose and intention, but himself that is demanded. The
Neo-Protestant critics of this ethics used to complain that it encroached
too much upon man, his personality, etc. The very opposite is true; it en-
croaches too little upon man. It does not make clear to him, but rather conceals, what a good action is. It makes it all too easy for him to adhere to a
decision which is not that of the divine command, and even to judge himself by it—*ut aliquid fieri videatur*—but in so doing to preserve for himself the
false freedom of being somewhere else and thus refusing the obedience due
to God's command in spite of his acceptance of the casuistical decision. . . .

The Protection of Life

Section 55. . . . Whenever we dare even think that the killing of men by
men is not only not forbidden but even necessary in certain circumstances,
there is always the possibility of the same *privare*, of the same independent
construction of the exceptional case on the ground of very dubious and
quite arbitrary desires, of the same attempted self-justification by moral
sophistry. In such cases we are always in danger of approving that which
the civil law with more or less assurance and consistency condemns as a
crime and the command of God as a sin. The line which keeps us from
falling under this condemnation will always be razor sharp, and how near
we shall sometimes be to crossing it! But if this is a warning to be most circumspect, it must not deter us from being prepared point by point even in
this dangerous neighbourhood to stand by the truth that at some time or
other, perhaps on the far frontier of all other possibilities, it may have to
happen in obedience to the commandment that men must be killed by men.

We mention first the problem of the deliberate interruption of preg-
nancy usually called abortion (*abortus*, the suppression of the fruit of the
body). This question arises where conception has taken place but for varying reasons the birth and existence of the child are not desired and are perhaps even feared. . . .

Before proceeding, we must underline the fact that he who destroys germinating life kills a man and thus ventures the monstrous thing of decree-
ing concerning the life and death of a fellow-man whose life is given by
God and therefore, like his own, belongs to Him. He desires to discharge a
divine office, or, even if not, he accepts responsibility for such discharge,
by daring to have the last word on at least the temporal form of the life of
his fellow-man. Those directly or indirectly involved cannot escape this responsibility.

. . . [T]his child is a man for whose life the Son of God has died, for whose
unavoidable part in the guilt of all humanity and future individual guilt He
has already paid the price. The true light of the world shines already in the
darkness of the mother's womb. And yet they want to kill him deliberately

because certain reasons which have nothing to do with the child himself favour the view that he had better not be born! Is there any emergency which can justify this? It must surely be clear to us that until the question is put in all its gravity a serious discussion of the problem cannot even begin, let alone lead to serious results. . . .

. . . In the case of the unborn, the mother, father, doctor (whose very vocation is to serve the preservation and development of life) and all concerned, can desire only its life and healthy birth. How can they possibly will the opposite? They can do so only on the presupposition of their own blindness towards life, in bondage to the opinion that they must live rather than that they may live, and therefore out of anxiety, i.e., out of gracelessness and therefore godlessness.

On the other hand, they cannot set their will absolutely upon the preservation of this life, or rather upon the service of its preservation. They all stand in the service of God. He orders them to serve its preservation and therefore the future birth of the child. There is an almost infinite number of objections to the possibility of willing anything else in obedience to Him. But it is not quite infinite. If a man knows that he is in God's service and wills to be obedient to Him, can he really swear that he will never on any occasion will anything else as God may require? What grounds have we for the absolute thesis that in no circumstances can God will anything but the preservation of a germinating life, or make any other demand from the mother, father, doctor or others involved? If He can will that this germinating life should die in some other way, might He not occasionally do so in such a way as to involve the active participation of these other men? How can we deny absolutely that He might have commissioned them to serve Him in this way, and that their action has thus been performed, and had to be performed, in this service? How, then can we indict them in these circumstances?

This is the exceptional case which calls for discussion. In squarely facing it, we are not opening a side-door to the crime which is so rampant in this sphere. We refer to God's possibility and His specific command. We cannot try to exclude this. Otherwise the No which has to be pronounced in every other case is robbed of its force. For, as we have seen, it is truly effective only as the divine No. Hence no human No can or should be given the last word. The human No must let itself be limited. God can limit this human No, and, if He does so, it is simply human obstinacy and obduracy and transgression to be absolutely logical and to try to execute the No unconditionally. Let us be quite frank and say that there are situations in which the killing of germinating life does not constitute murder but is in fact commanded. . . .

And we can and must add that, even if only in general terms and in the sense of a guiding line, these situations may always be known by the concrete fact that in them a choice must be made for the protection of life, one life being balanced against another, i.e., the life of the unborn child against the life or health of the mother, the sacrifice of either the one or the other being unavoidable. It is hard to see why in such cases the life of the child should always be given absolute preference, as maintained in Roman Catholic ethics. To be sure, we cannot and must not maintain, on the basis of the commandment, that the life and health of the mother must always be saved at the expense of the life of the child. There may well be mothers who for their part are ready to take any risk for their unborn children, and how can we forbid them to do so? On the basis of the command, however, we can learn that when a choice has to be made between the life or health of the mother and that of the child, the destruction of the child in the mother's womb might be permitted and commanded, and with the qualifications already mentioned a human decision might thus be taken to this effect. . . .

The required calculation and venture in the decision between life and death obviously cannot be subject to any human law, because no such law can grasp the fulness of healthy or sick, happy or unhappy, preserved or neglected human life, let alone the freedom of the divine command and the obedience which we owe to it. Hence we shall have to be content with the following observations. 1. For all concerned what must be at stake must be life against life, nothing other nor less, if the decision is not to be a wrong decision and the resultant action murder either of the child or the mother. 2. There is always required the most scrupulous calculation and yet also a resolute venture with a conscience which is bound and therefore free. Where such thought as is given is only careless or clouded, and the decision weak and hesitant, sin crouches at the door. 3. The calculation and venture must take place before God and in responsibility to Him. Otherwise, how can there possibly be obedience, and how can the content be good and right, even though apparently good human reasons and justification might be found in one direction or another? 4. Since the calculation and venture, the conviction that we are dealing with the exception, are always so dangerous, they surely cannot be executed with the necessary assurance and joy except in faith that God will forgive the elements of human sin involved. . . .

. . . If there can be any question of a just war, if we can describe this undertaking and participation in it as commanded, then it can only be with the same, and indeed with even stricter reserve and caution than have been found to be necessary in relation to such things as suicide, abortion, capital punishment etc. War is to be set in this category, nor is there any point in concealing the fact that the soldier, i.e., the fighting civilian, stands in direct proximity to the executioner. At any rate, it is only in the extreme zone, and in conjunction with other human acts which come dangerously near to murder, that military action can in certain instances be regarded as approved and commanded rather than prohibited.

We must also add that in this particular case the question is indeed to be put far more strictly than in relation to the other possibilities. For (1) war is an action in which the nation and all its members are actually engaged in killing, or in the direct or indirect preparation and promotion of killing. All are involved in this action either as those who desire or as those who permit it, and in any case as those who contribute to it in some sector. All are directly responsible in respect of the question whether it is commanded killing or forbidden murder. Again, however, killing in war is (2) a killing

255

of those who for the individuals fighting in the service of the nation can be enemies only in the sense that they for their part have to wage war in the service of their country. The fact that the latter fight with approval on the other side can only make them appear guilty and criminal from this side. But whether the participants are guilty and criminal, and as such about to kill and therefore to murder, is a question which they also from their side might put to those who fight with approval on this side. Finally, killing in war (3), unlike the other possibilities already discussed, calls in question, not merely for individuals but for millions of men, the whole of morality, or better, obedience to the command of God in all its dimensions. Does not war demand that almost everything that God has forbidden be done on a broad front? To kill effectively, and in connexion therewith, must not those who wage war steal, rob, commit arson, lie, deceive, slander, and unfortunately to a large extent fornicate, not to speak of the almost inevitable repression of all the finer and weightier forms of obedience? And how can they believe and pray when at the climax of this whole world of dubious action it is a brutal matter of killing? It may be true that even in war many a man may save many things, and indeed that an inner strength may become for him a more strong and genuine because a more tested possession. But it is certainly not true that people become better in war. The fact is that war is for most people a trial for which they are no match, and from the consequences of which they can never recover. Since all this is incontestable, can it and should it nevertheless be defended and ventured?

All affirmative answers to this question are wrong from the very outset, and in Christian ethics constitute a flat betrayal of the Gospel, if they ignore the whole risk and venture of this Nevertheless, and do not rest on an exact calculation of what is here at stake and whether we can and must nevertheless reply in the affirmative. We can also put it in this way. All affirmative answers to the question are wrong if they do not start with the assumption that the inflexible negative of pacifism has almost infinite arguments in its favour and is almost overpoweringly strong. Or again, we might put it thus. All affirmative answers to the question are wrong if they do not incorporate a recognition that even *in extremis* it is far more difficult to express even a qualified affirmative at this point than when we stand on the outer margin in such matters as suicide, abortion, self-defence etc. . . .

A first essential is that war should not on any account be recognised as a normal, fixed and in some sense necessary part of what on the Christian view constitutes the just state, or the political order demanded by God. Certainly the state as such possesses power and must be able to exercise it. But it does this in any case, and it is no primary concern of Christian ethics to say that it should do so, or to maintain that the exercise of power constitutes the essence of the state, i.e., its *opus proprium*, or even a part of it. What Christian ethics must insist is that it is an *opus alienum* for the state to have to exercise power. It cannot assure the state that in the exercise of power either the state or its organs may do gaily and confidently whatever they think is right. In such cases it must always confront them with the question whether there is really any necessity for this exercise. Especially the state must not be given *carte blanche* to grasp the *ultima ratio* of organising mass slaughter in its dealings with other states. Christian ethics cannot insist too loudly that such mass slaughter might well be mass murder, and therefore that this final possibility should not be seized like any other, but only at the very last hour in the darkest of days. The Church and theology have first and supremely to make this detached and delaying movement. If they do not first and for a long time make this the burden of their message, if they do not throw in their weight decisively on this side of the scales. . . . they will be in no position authentically and authoritatively to issue a call to arms, to the political *opus alienum*. For they can do this only if they have previously held aloof, calling for peace right up to the very last moment. . . .

What Christian ethics has to emphasise is that neither inwardly nor outwardly does the normal task of the state, which is at issue even in time of war, consist in a process of annihilating rather than maintaining and fostering life. Nor should it be rashly maintained that annihilating life is also part of the process of maintaining and fostering it. Biological wisdom of this kind cannot serve as the norm or rule in ethics. The state which Christian ethics can and must affirm, which it has to proclaim as the political order willed and established by God, is not in itself and as such the mythological beast of the jungle, the monster with the Janus head, which by its very nature is prepared at any moment to turn thousands into killers and thousands more into killed. The Church does the state no honour, nor does it help it, if in relation to it it acts on this assumption concerning its nature. According to the Christian understanding, it is no part of the normal task of the state to wage war; its normal task is to fashion peace in such a way that life is served and war kept at bay. If there is a mistake in pacifism, apart from the inadvisable ethical absolutism of its thesis, it consists in its abstract negation of war, as if war could be understood and negated in isolation and not in relation to the so-called peace which precedes it. Our attention should be directed to this relation. It is when a state does not rightly pursue its normal task that sooner or later it is compelled to take up the abnormal one of war, and therefore to inflict this abnormal task on other states. It is when the power of the state is insufficient to meet the inner needs of the country that it will seek an outer safety-valve for the consequent unrest and think it is found in war. It is when interest-bearing capital rather than man is the object whose maintenance and increase are the meaning and goal of the political order that the mechanism is already set going which one day will send men to kill and be killed. Against such a perversion of peace neither the supposed, though already undermined and no longer steadfast, love of the masses for peace, nor the well-meant and vocal declaiming of idealists against war, is of any avail. For the point is that when war does break out it is usually the masses who march, and even the clearest words spoken against war, and the most painful recollections of previous wars, are rendered stale and impotent. A peace which is no real peace can make war inevitable. Hence the first, basic and decisive point which Christian ethics must make in this matter is that the state, the totality of responsible citizens, and each individual in his own conduct should so fashion peace while there is still time that it will not lead to this explosion but make war superfluous and unnecessary instead of inevitable. Relatively speaking, it requires no great faith, insight nor courage to condemn war radically and absolutely, for no one apart from leaders of the armaments industry and a few high-ranking officers really believes that war is preferable to peace. Again, it requires no faith, insight nor courage at all to howl with the wolves that unfortunately war belongs no less to the present world order, historical life and the nature of the state than does peace, so that from the very outset we must regard it as an emergency for which preparation must be made. What does require Christian faith, insight and courage—and the Christian Church and Christian ethics are there to show them—is to tell nations and governments that peace is the real emergency to which all our time, powers and ability must be devoted from the very outset in order that men may live and live properly, so that no refuge need be sought in war, nor need there be expected from it what peace has denied. Pacifists and militarists are usually agreed in the fact that for them the fashioning of peace as the fashioning of the state for democracy, and of democracy for social democracy, is a secondary concern as compared with rearmament or disarmament. It is for this reason that Christian ethics must be opposed to both. Neither rearmament nor disarmament can be a first concern, but the restoration of an order of life which is meaningful and just. When this is so, the two slogans will not disappear. They will have their proper place. They will come up for discussion at the proper time. But they will necessarily lose their fanatical tone, since far more urgent concerns will be up for discussion. And there can always be the hope that some day both will prove to be irrelevant.

It is only against the background of this first concern, and only as the Church has a good conscience that it is doing its best for a just peace among states and nations, that it can and should plead for the preservation of peace among states and nations, for fidelity and faith in their mutual dealings as the reasonable presupposition of a true foreign policy, for solid agreements and alliances and their honest observance, for international courts and conventions, and above all, and in all nations, for openness, understanding and patience towards others and for such education of young people as will lead them to prefer peace to war. The Church can and should raise its voice against the institution of standing armies in which the officers constitute *per se* a permanent danger to peace. It can and should resist all kinds of hysterical or premature war scares. It exists in this aeon. Hence it is not commissioned to proclaim that war is absolutely avoidable. But it is certainly commissioned to oppose the satanic doctrine that war is inevitable and therefore justified, that it is unavoidable and therefore right when it occurs, so that Christians have to participate in it. Even in a world in which states and nations are still in the early stages and never at the end of the long road in respect of that first concern, there is never in practice an absolute necessity of war, and the Church certainly has neither right nor obligation to affirm this necessity either in general or in detail as the occasion may arise. We do not need optimism but simply a modicum of sane intelligence to recognise that relatively if not absolutely, in practice if not in principle, war can be avoided to a very large extent. The Church must not preach pacifism, but it must see to it that this sane intelligence is voiced and heard so long as this is possible, and that the many ways of avoiding war which now exist in practice should be honestly applied until they are all exhausted. It is better in this respect that the Church should stick to its post too long and become a forlorn hope than that it should leave it too soon and then have to realise that it has become unfaithful by yielding to the general excitement, and that it is thus the accessory to an avoidable war which can only be described as mass murder.

From Karl Barth, "The Doctrine of Creation," in *Church Dogmatics*, vol. 3, part 4, edited by Rev. Prof. G. W. Bromiley and Rev. Prof. T. F. Torrance (Edinburgh: T. & T. Clark, 1961, English translation), 3–15, 96–97, 415–23, 454–60.

54.   Dietrich Bonhoeffer,
The Cost of Discipleship and *Ethics*

The German theologian Dietrich Bonhoeffer (1906–1945) was executed by the Nazis shortly before the end of World War II, and the body of his work is necessarily incomplete. His contributions to Christian ethics are nevertheless important, including sections of his The Cost of Discipleship *and his partially completed and posthumously published* Ethics. *In the former, he speaks of "cheap grace," a morally complacent contrast to the "costly grace" that demands total commitment. In the latter, Bonhoeffer offers his own solution to the problem of relating ultimate realities to what he calls the penultimate.*

THE COST OF DISCIPLESHIP

Cheap grace is the deadly enemy of our Church. We are fighting to-day for costly grace.

Cheap grace means grace sold on the market like cheapjacks' wares. The sacraments, the forgiveness of sin, and the consolations of religion are thrown away at cut prices. Grace is represented as the Church's inexhaustible treasury, from which she showers blessings with generous hands, without asking questions or fixing limits. Grace without price; grace without cost! The essence of grace, we suppose, is that the account has been paid in advance; and, because it has been paid, everything can be had for nothing. Since the cost was infinite, the possibilities of using and spending it are infinite. What would grace be if it were not cheap?

Cheap grace means grace as a doctrine, a principle, a system. It means forgiveness of sins proclaimed as a general truth, the love of God taught as the Christian "conception" of God. An intellectual assent to that idea is held to be of itself sufficient to secure remission of sins. The Church which holds the correct doctrine of grace has, it is supposed, *ipso facto* a part in that grace. In such a Church the world finds a cheap covering for its sins; no contrition is required, still less any real desire to be delivered from sin. Cheap grace therefore amounts to a denial of the living Word of God, in fact, a denial of the Incarnation of the Word of God.

Cheap grace means the justification of sin without the justification of the sinner. Grace alone does everything, they say, and so everything can remain as it was before. "All for sin could not atone." The world goes on in the same old way, and we are still sinners "even in the best life" as Luther said. Well, then, let the Christian live like the rest of the world, let him model himself on the world's standards in every sphere of life, and not presumptuously aspire to live a different life under grace from his old life under sin. That was the heresy of the enthusiasts, the Anabaptists and their kind. Let the Christian beware of rebelling against the free and boundless grace of God and desecrating it. Let him not attempt to erect a new religion of the letter by endeavouring to live a life of obedience to the commandments of Jesus Christ! The world has been justified by grace. The Christian knows that, and takes it seriously. He knows he must not strive against this indispensable grace. Therefore—let him live like the rest of the world! Of course he would like to go and do something extraordinary, and it does demand a good deal of self-restraint to refrain from the attempt and content himself with living as the world lives. Yet it is imperative for the Christian to achieve renunciation, to practice self-effacement, to distinguish his life from the life of the world. He must let grace be grace indeed, otherwise he will destroy the world's faith in the free gift of grace. Let the Christian rest content with his worldliness and with this renunciation of any higher standard than the world. He is doing it for the sake of the world rather than for the sake of grace. Let him be comforted and rest assured in his possession of this grace—for grace alone does everything. Instead of following Christ, let the Christian enjoy the consolations of his grace! That is what we mean by cheap grace, the grace which amounts to the justification of sin without the justification of the repentant sinner who departs from sin and from whom sin departs. Cheap grace is not the kind of forgiveness of sin which frees us from the toils of sin. Cheap grace is the grace we bestow on ourselves.

Cheap grace is the preaching of forgiveness without requiring repentance, baptism without church discipline, Communion without confession, absolution without personal confession. Cheap grace is grace without discipleship, grace without the cross, grace without Jesus Christ, living and incarnate.

Costly grace is the treasure hidden in the field; for the sake of it a man will gladly go and sell all that he has. It is the pearl of great price to buy which the merchant will sell all his goods. It is the kingly rule of Christ, for whose sake a man will pluck out the eye which causes him to stumble, it is the call of Jesus Christ at which the disciple leaves his nets and follows him.

Costly grace is the gospel which must be *sought* again and again, the gift which must be *asked* for, the door at which a man must *knock*.

Such grace is *costly* because it calls us to follow, and it is *grace* because it calls us to follow *Jesus Christ*. It is costly because it costs a man his life, and it is grace because it gives a man the only true life. It is costly because it condemns sin, and grace because it justifies the sinner. Above all, it is *costly* because it cost God the life of his Son; "ye were bought at a price," and what has cost God much cannot be cheap for us. Above all, it is *grace* because God did not reckon his Son too dear a price to pay for our life, but delivered him up for us. Costly grace is the Incarnation of God.

Costly grace is the sanctuary of God; it has to be protected from the world, and not thrown to the dogs. It is therefore the living word, the Word of God, which he speaks as it pleases him. Costly grace confronts us as a gracious call to follow Jesus, it comes as a word of forgiveness to the broken spirit and the contrite heart. Grace is costly because it compels a man to submit to the yoke of Christ and follow him; it is grace because Jesus says: "My yoke is easy and my burden is light."

ETHICS

The word of the justifying grace of God never departs from its position as the final word; it never yields itself simply as a result that has been achieved, a result that might just as well be set at the beginning as at the end. The way from the penultimate to the ultimate can never be dispensed with. The word remains irreversibly the last; for otherwise it would be reduced to the quality of what is calculable, a merchandise, and would thereby be robbed of its divine character. Grace would be venal and cheap. It would not be a gift.

The Penultimate

Justification by grace and faith alone remains in every respect the final word and for this reason, when we speak of the things before the last, we must not speak of them as having any value of their own, but we must bring to light their relation to the ultimate. It is for the sake of the ultimate that we must now speak of the penultimate. This must now be made clearly intelligible.

One must ask the question at this point, without answering it, whether man can live by the ultimate alone, whether faith can, so to speak, be extended in time, or whether faith does not rather always become real in life as the ultimate phase of a span of time or of many spans of time. We are not speaking here of the recollection of past faith, or of the repetition of articles of faith, but of the living faith which justifies a life. We are asking whether this faith is and ought to be realizable every day, at every hour, or whether here, too, the length of the penultimate must every time be traversed anew for the sake of the ultimate. We are asking, therefore, about the penultimate in the lives of Christians. We are asking whether to deny it is pious self-deception, or whether to take it seriously in its own way is to incur guilt. This means that we are asking also whether the word, the gospel, can be extended in time, whether it can be spoken at any time in the same way, or whether here, too, there is a difference between the ultimate and the penultimate. . . .

Two extreme solutions can be given to the problem of relation of the penultimate with the ultimate in Christian life. It may be solved 'radically' or by means of a compromise; and it is to be noted at once that the compromise solution, too, is an extreme solution.

The radical solution sees only the ultimate, and in it only the complete breaking off of the penultimate. Ultimate and penultimate are here mutually exclusive contraries. Christ is the destroyer and enemy of everything penultimate and everything penultimate is enmity towards Christ. . . .

The other solution is the compromise. Here the last word is on principle set apart from all preceding words. The penultimate retains its right on its own account, and is not threatened or imperilled by the ultimate. The world still stands; the end is not yet here; there are still penultimate things which must be done, in fulfilment of the responsibility for this world which God has created. Account must still be taken of men as they are. The ultimate remains totally on the far side of the everyday; it is thus, in fact, an eternal justification for things as they are. . . .

The two solutions are equally extreme, and both alike contain elements both of truth and of untruth. They are extreme because they place the penultimate and the ultimate in a relation of mutual exclusiveness. In the one case the penultimate is destroyed by the ultimate; and in the other case the ultimate is excluded from the domain of the penultimate. In the one case the ultimate does not admit the penultimate; and in the other case the penultimate does not admit the ultimate. In both cases thoughts which are in themselves equally right and necessary are in an inadmissible manner made absolute. The radical solution has as its point of departure the end of all things, God the Judge and Redeemer; the compromise solution bases itself upon the Creator and Preserver. On the one side it is the end that is regarded as absolute, and on the other side it is things as they are. Thus creation and redemption, time and eternity confront one another in a conflict which cannot be resolved; the unity of God Himself is sundered, and faith in God is broken apart. The answer to the exponents of the radical solution is that Christ is not radical in their sense and similarly the answer to the adherents of the compromise solution must also be that Christ does not make compromises. Christian life, therefore, is a matter neither of radicalism nor of compromise. . . .

Radicalism always springs from a conscious or unconscious hatred of what is established. Christian radicalism, no matter whether it consists in withdrawing from the world or in improving the world, arises from hatred of creation. The radical cannot forgive God His creation. He has fallen out with the created world, the Ivan Karamazov, who at the same time makes the figure of the radical Jesus in the legend of the Grand Inquisitor. When evil becomes powerful in the world, it infects the Christian, too, with the poison of radicalism. It is Christ's gift to the Christian that he should be reconciled with the world as it is, but now this reconciliation is accounted a betrayal and denial of Christ. It is replaced by bitterness, suspicion and contempt for men and the world. In the place of the love that believes all, bears all and hopes all, in the place of the love which loves the world in its very wickedness with the love of God (John [3:16]), there is now the pharisaical denial of love to evil, and the restriction of love to the closed circle of the devout. Instead of the open Church of Jesus Christ, which serves the world till the end, there is now some allegedly primitive Christian ideal of a Church, which in its turn confuses the reality of the living Jesus Christ with the realization of a Christian idea. Thus a world which has become evil succeeds in making the Christians become evil too. It is the same germ that disintegrates the world and that makes the Christians become radical. In both cases it is hatred towards the world, no matter whether the haters are the ungodly or the godly. On both sides it is a refusal of faith in the creation. But devils are not cast out through Beelzebub.

Compromise always springs from hatred of the ultimate. . . .

. . . Thus man remains man, even though he is a new, a risen man, who in no way resembles the old man. Until he crosses the frontier of his death, even though he has already risen again with Christ, he remains in the world of the penultimate, the world into which Jesus entered and the world in which the cross stands. Thus, so long as the earth continues, even the resurrection does not annul the penultimate, but the eternal life, the new life, breaks in with ever greater power into the earthly life and wins its space for itself within it. . . .

As for the question of the things before the last, it follows from what has been said so far that the Christian life means neither a destruction nor a sanctioning of the penultimate. In Christ the reality of God meets the reality of the world and allows us to share in this real encounter. It is an encounter beyond all radicalism and beyond all compromise. Christian life is participation in the encounter of Christ with the world.

It has now become clear that the ultimate—the last things—leaves open a certain amount of room for the penultimate, the things before the last. We must, therefore, consider this penultimate more closely.

The Preparing of the Way

What is this penultimate? It is everything that precedes the ultimate, everything that precedes the justification of the sinner by grace alone, everything which is to be regarded as leading up to the last thing when the last thing has been found. It is at the same time everything which follows the ultimate and yet again precedes it. There is, therefore, no penultimate in itself; as though a thing could justify itself in itself as being a thing

before the last thing a thing becomes penultimate only through the ulti-
mate, that is to say, at the moment when it has already lost its own validity. The penultimate, then, does not determine the ultimate; it is the ulti-
mate which determines the penultimate. The penultimate is not a state or
condition in itself, but it is a judgement which the ultimate passes upon that
which has preceded it. Concretely, two things are called penultimate in relation to the justification of the sinner by grace, namely being man (*Mensch-
sein*) and being good. Now it would be quite wrong, it would be robbing
the ultimate, if we were to say, for example, that to be man is a precondi-
tion of justification by grace. On the contrary, it is only on the basis of the
ultimate that we can know what it is to be man, so that manhood can be determined and established through justification. And yet the relationship is
such that manhood precedes justification, and that from the standpoint of
the ultimate it is necessary that it should precede it. The penultimate does
not therefore rob the ultimate of its freedom; but it is the freedom of the ultimate that validates the penultimate. And so, with all necessary reservations, it is now possible to speak of manhood, for example, as a penultimate
to justification by faith. Only man can be justified, precisely because only
he who is justified becomes 'man'.

Now from this there follows something which is of crucial importance.
For the sake of the ultimate the penultimate must be preserved. Any arbitrary destruction of the penultimate will do serious injury to the ultimate.
If, for example, a human life is deprived of the conditions which are proper
to it, then the justification of such a life by grace and faith, if it is not rendered impossible, is at least seriously impeded. In concrete terms, if a slave
is so far prevented from making free use of his time that he can no longer
hear the preaching of the word, then this word of God cannot in any case
lead him to the justifying faith. From this fact it follows that it is necessary
to see to it that the penultimate, too, is provided with the preaching of the
ultimate word of God, the proclamation of the justification of the sinner by
grace alone, lest the destruction of the penultimate should prove a hindrance to the ultimate. If the proclaimer of the word does not at the same
time take every measure to ensure that the word may be heard, then he is
not satisfying the claim of the word to pass freely and unhindered. The way
must be made ready for the word. It is the word itself that demands it.

Preparing the way for the word: this is the purpose of everything that
has been said about the things before the last. 'Prepare ye the way of the
Lord, make his paths straight. Every valley shall be filled; and every mountain and hill shall be brought low; and the crooked shall be made straight,
and the rough ways shall be made smooth; and all flesh shall see the salvation of God' (Luke [3:4ff.]). Christ indeed makes His own way when He
comes; He is the 'breaker' of all bonds [Micah 2:13]. 'He breaketh the gates
of brass, and cutteth the bars of iron in sunder' (Ps. [107:16]); 'He putteth
down the mighty from their seat, and exalteth the humble and meek' (Luke
[1:52]). His entry is a triumph over His enemies. But lest the might of His
coming should overwhelm mankind in anger, and in order that it may find
them humble and expectant, the entry is preceded by the summons to the

preparation of the way. Yet this making ready of the way is not merely an inward process; it is a formative activity on the very greatest visible scale. 'The valleys shall be exalted' (Isa. [40:4]). That which has been cast down into the depths of human wretchedness, that which has been abased and humbled, is now to be raised up. There is a depth of human bondage, of human poverty, of human ignorance, which impedes the merciful coming of Christ. 'The mountains and hills shall be made low' (Isa. [40:4]). If Christ is to come, then all that is proud and haughty must bow down. There is a measure of power, of wealth, of knowledge, which is an impediment to Christ and to His mercy. 'The crooked shall be made straight' (Luke [3:5]). The way of Christ is a straight way. There is a measure of entanglement in the lie, in guilt, in one's own labour, in one's own work (Ps. [9:16]) and in self-love, which makes the coming of grace particularly difficult. That is why the way had to be made straight on which Christ is to come to man. 'The rough ways shall be made smooth' (Luke [3:5]). Defiance, stubbornness and unreceptiveness may have hardened a man so much that Christ can now only destroy him in anger as one who resists Him, and so that Christ can no longer enter into him in mercy, because the door is bolted against Christ's merciful coming and is not opened to Him when He knocks.

Christ comes indeed, and opens up His own way, no matter whether man is ready beforehand or not. No one can hinder His coming, but we can resist His coming in mercy. There are conditions of the heart, of life and of the world which impede the reception of grace in a special way, namely, by rendering faith infinitely difficult. We say that they impede it and render it difficult, but not that they make it impossible. And we are well aware also that even the levelling of the way and the removal of the obstacles cannot compel the imparting of grace. The merciful coming of Christ must still 'break the gates of brass and cut the bars of iron' (Ps. [107:16]); grace must in the end itself prepare and make level its own way and grace alone must ever anew render possible the impossible. But all this does not release us from our obligation to prepare the way for the coming of grace, and to remove whatever obstructs it and makes it difficult. The state in which grace finds us is not a matter of indifference, even though it is always by grace alone that grace comes to us. We may, among other things, make it difficult for ourselves to attain to faith. For him who is cast into utter shame, desolation, poverty and helplessness, it is difficult to have faith in the justice and goodness of God. For him whose life has become a prey to disorder and indiscipline, it will be difficult to hear the commandments of God in faith. It is hard for the sated and the mighty to grasp the meaning of God's judgement and God's mercy. And for one who has been disappointed in mistaken belief, and who has become inwardly undisciplined, it is hard to attain to the simplicity of the surrender of the heart to Jesus Christ. That is not said in order either to excuse or to discourage those whom these things have befallen. They must know, on the contrary, that it is precisely to the depths of downfall, of guilt and of misery, that God stoops down in Jesus Christ; that precisely the dispossessed, the humiliated and the exploited, are especially near to the justice and mercy of God; that it is to the undisciplined that Jesus Christ offers His help and His strength; and that the truth is ready to set upon firm ground those who stray and despair.

But all this does not exclude the task of preparing the way. This task is, on the contrary, a charge of immense responsibility for all those who know of the coming of Christ. The hungry man needs bread and the homeless man needs a roof; the dispossessed need justice and the lonely need fellowship; the undisciplined need order and the slave needs freedom. To allow the hungry man to remain hungry would be blasphemy against God and one's neighbour, for what is nearest to God is precisely the need of one's neighbour. It is for the love of Christ, which belongs as much to the hungry man as to myself, that I share my bread with him and that I share my dwelling with the homeless. If the hungry man does not attain to faith, then the guilt falls on those who refused him bread. To provide the hungry man with bread is to prepare the way for the coming of grace.

But what is happening here is a thing before the last. To give bread to the hungry man is not the same as to proclaim the grace of God and justification to him, and to have received bread is not the same as to have faith. Yet for him who does these things for the sake of the ultimate, and in the knowledge of the ultimate, this penultimate does bear a relation to the ultimate. It is a pen*ultimate*. The coming of grace is the ultimate.

55. Paul Tillich,
Love, Power, and Justice

The German-American theologian Paul Tillich (1886–1965) here provides a striking solution to a recurring issue in Christian ethics, how love and justice are to be related to each other. Tillich suggests that they are not opposed; they are different aspects of the same reality.

Justice [has been] defined as the form in which power of being actualizes itself in the encounter of power with power. Justice is immanent in power, since there is no power of being without its adequate form. But whenever power of being encounters power of being, compulsion cannot be avoided. The question then is: What is the relation of justice to the compulsory element of power? The answer must be: [I]t is not compulsion which is unjust, but a compulsion which destroys the object of compulsion instead of working towards its fulfilment. If the totalitarian State dehumanizes those for the sake of whom it enforces its laws, their power of being as persons is dissolved and their intrinsic claim is denied. It is not compulsion which violates justice, but a compulsion which disregards the intrinsic claim of a being to be acknowledged as what it is within the context of all beings. It may well be that a compulsion which prevents the punishment of a law-breaker destroys his power of being and violates his claim to be reduced in his power of being according to proportional justice. This is the truth in Hegel's formula that the criminal has a right to punishment. A power structure in which compulsion works against the intrinsic justice of its elements is not strengthened but weakened. The unacknowledged, justified claims, although suppressed, do not disappear. They are effective against the whole in which they are suppressed and they may ultimately destroy a power structure which is neither able to accept them as participants, nor able to throw them out as strange bodies. The intrinsic claim in everything that is cannot be violated without violating the violator. This is equally true of biological, psychological, and of sociological structures of power. The mental power of a human being, e.g., can express itself in three forms. It can suppress elements which belong to it, as special desires or hopes or ideas. In this case the suppressed elements remain and turn the mind against itself, driving it towards disintegration. Or the mental power of a human being can receive resisting elements which belong to it, elevating them into unity with the whole. Or the mental power can throw them out radically as foreign bodies whose claim to belong to the whole is successfully rejected. In the second and the third case the human mind exercises justice in opposite directions towards the resisting elements. In the first case it violates the intrinsic claim of a being and endangers itself. This psychological example is also valid for biological and sociological structures of power and will be discussed in one of the following chapters.

As in power, justice is immanent in love. A love of any type, and love as a whole if it does not include justice, is chaotic self-surrender, destroying him who loves as well as him who accepts such love. Love is the drive for reunion of the separated. It presupposes that there is something to be reunited, something relatively independent that stands upon itself. Sometimes the love of complete self-surrender has been praised and called the fulfilment of love. But the question is: What kind of self-surrender is it and what is it that it surrenders? If a self whose power of being is weakened or vanishing surrenders, his surrender is worth nothing. He is a self which has not received from himself the justice to which he is entitled, according to his intrinsic claim for justice. The surrender of such an emaciated self is not genuine love because it extinguishes and does not unite what is estranged. The love of this kind is the desire to annihilate one's responsible and creative self for the sake of the participation in another self which by the assumed act of love is made responsible for himself and oneself. The chaotic self-surrender does not give justice to the other one, because he who surrenders did not give justice to himself. It is justice to oneself to affirm one's own power of being and to accept the claim for justice which is implied in this power. Without this justice there is no reuniting love, because there is nothing to unite.

This leads to the question of justice towards oneself, a question which is analogous to the questions of self-love and self-control. In both cases we spoke of a metaphorical use of the term. We must do so also in the case of justice towards oneself. There is no independent self which could decide about the claim for justice by another self with which it happens to be identical. But there is a definite sense in which one can speak of justice towards oneself, namely in the sense that the deciding centre is just towards the elements of which it is the centre. Justice towards oneself in this sense decides, e.g. that the puritan form of self-control is unjust because it excludes elements of the self which have a just claim to be admitted to the general balance of strivings. Repression is injustice against oneself, and it has the consequence of all injustice: it is self-destructive because of the resistance of the elements which are excluded. This, however, does not mean that the chaotic admittance of all strivings to the central decision is a demand of the justice towards oneself. It may be highly unjust, in so far as it makes a balanced centre impossible and dissolves the self into a process of disconnected impulses. This is the danger of the romantic or open type of self-control. It can become as unjust towards oneself as the puritan or closed type of self-control. To be just towards oneself means to actualize as many potentialities as possible without losing oneself in disruption and chaos.

This is a warning not to be unjust towards oneself in the relation of love. For this is always also an injustice towards him who accepts the injustice which we exercise towards ourselves. He is prevented from being just because he is forced to abuse by being abused.

Love does not do more than justice demands, but love is the ultimate principle of justice. Love reunites; justice preserves what is to be united. It is the form in which and through which love performs its work. Justice in its ultimate meaning is creative justice, and creative justice is the form of reuniting love.

From Paul Tillich, *Love, Power, and Justice: Ontological Analyses and Ethical Applications* (London: Oxford University Press, 1954), pp. 67–71. © Oxford University Press. Reprinted by permission of Oxford University Press.

56. Reinhold Niebuhr,
The Nature and Destiny of Man

Much of the "Christian realism" of Reinhold Niebuhr (1892–1971) is grounded in his reinterpretation of the doctrine of original sin. His belief in the universality of sin infuses a political ethic emphasizing the importance of political and legal structures to help assure "proximate" justice. While clearly influenced by the idealism of the social gospel movement, Niebuhr seeks to avoid any illusions of human perfectibility.

Chapter 7. Man As Sinner. "In every religion," declared Albrecht Ritschl, the most authoritative exponent of modern liberal Christianity, "what is sought with the help of the superhuman power reverenced by man is a solution of the contradiction in which man finds himself as both a part of nature and a spiritual personality claiming to dominate nature." It is perfectly true that this problem of finiteness and freedom underlies all religion. But Ritschl does not appreciate that the uniqueness of the Biblical approach to the human problem lies in its subordination of the problem of finiteness to the problem of sin. It is not the contradiction of finiteness and freedom from which Biblical religion seeks emancipation. It seeks redemption from sin; and the sin from which it seeks redemption is occasioned, though not caused, by this contradiction in which man stands. Sin is not caused by the contradiction because, according to Biblical faith, there is no absolute necessity that man should be betrayed into sin by the ambiguity of his position, as standing in and yet above nature. But it cannot be denied that this is the occasion for his sin.

Man is insecure and involved in natural contingency; he seeks to overcome his insecurity by a will-to-power which overreaches the limits of human creatureliness. Man is ignorant and involved in the limitations of a finite mind; but he pretends that he is not limited. He assumes that he can gradually transcend finite limitations until his mind becomes identical with universal mind. All of his intellectual and cultural pursuits, therefore, become infected with the sin of pride. Man's pride and will-to-power disturb the harmony of creation. The Bible defines sin in both religious and moral terms. The religious dimension of sin is man's rebellion against God, his effort to usurp the place of God. The moral and social dimension of sin is injustice. The ego which falsely makes itself the centre of existence in its pride and will-to-power inevitably subordinates other life to its will and thus does injustice to other life.

Sometimes man seeks to solve the problem of the contradiction of finiteness and freedom, not by seeking to hide his finiteness and comprehending the world into himself, but by seeking to hide his freedom and by losing himself in some aspect of the world's vitalities. In that case his sin may be defined as sensuality rather than pride. Sensuality is never the mere expression of natural impulse in man. It always betrays some aspect of his abortive effort to solve the problem of finiteness and freedom. Human passions are always characterized by unlimited and demonic potencies of which animal life is innocent. . . .

Chapter 8. *Man As Sinner (continued).* The egotism of man has been defined and illustrated thus far without a careful discrimination between group pride and the pride and egotism of individuals. This lack of discrimination is provisionally justified by the fact that, strictly speaking, only individuals are moral agents, and group pride is therefore merely an aspect of the pride and arrogance of individuals. It is the fruit of the undue claims which they make for their various social groups. Nevertheless some distinctions must be made between the collective behaviour of men and their individual attitudes. This is necessary in part because group pride, though having its source in individual attitudes, actually achieves a certain authority over the individual and results in unconditioned demands by the group upon the individual. Whenever the group develops organs of will, as in the apparatus of the state, it seems to the individual to have become an independent centre of moral life. He will be inclined to bow to its pretensions and to acquiesce in its claims of authority, even when these do not coincide with his moral scruples or inclinations.

A distinction between group pride and the egotism of individuals is necessary, furthermore, because the pretensions and claims of a collective or social self exceed those of the individual ego. The group is more arrogant, hypocritical, self-centred and more ruthless in the pursuit of its ends than the individual. An inevitable moral tension between individual and group morality is therefore created. "If," said the great Italian statesman, Cavour, "we did for ourselves what we do for our country, what rascals we would be." This tension is naturally most apparent in the conscience of responsible statesmen, who are bound to feel the disparity between the canons of ordinary morality and the accepted habits of collective and political behaviour. Frederick the Great was not, as statesmen go, a man of unique moral sensitivity. His confession of a sense of this tension is therefore the more significant. "I hope," said he, "that posterity will distinguish the philosopher from the monarch in me and the decent man from the politician. I must admit that when drawn into the vortex of European politics it is difficult to preserve decency and integrity. One feels oneself in constant danger of being betrayed by one's allies and abandoned by one's friends, of being suffocated by envy and jealousy, and is thus finally driven to the terrible alternative of being false either to one's country or to one's word.

The egotism of racial, national and socio-economic groups is most consistently expressed by the national state because the state gives the collective impulses of the nation such instruments of power and presents the imagination of individuals with such obvious symbols of its discrete collective identity that the national state is most able to make absolute claims for itself, to enforce those claims by power and to give them plausibility and credibility by the majesty and panoply of its apparatus. In the life of every political group, whether nation or empire, which articulates itself through the instrument of a state, obedience is prompted by the fear of power on the one hand and by reverence for majesty on the other. The temptation to idolatry is implicit in the state's majesty. Rationalists, with their simple ideas of government resting purely upon the consent of the governed, have never appreciated to what degree religious reverence for majesty is implicit in this consent. The political history of man begins with tribal polytheism, can be traced through the religious pretensions of empires with their inevitable concomitants of imperial religions and their priest-kings and god-kings, and ends with the immoderate and idolatrous claims of the modern fascist state. No politically crystallized social group has, therefore, ever existed without entertaining, or succumbing to, the temptation of making idolatrous claims for itself. Frequently the organs of this group pride, the state and the ruling oligarchy which bears the authority of the state, seek to detach themselves from the group pride of which their majesty is a symbol and to become independent sources of majesty. But this inversion is possible only because the original source of their majesty lies in something which transcends their individual power and prestige, namely the pride and greatness of the group itself.

Sinful pride and idolatrous pretension are thus an inevitable concomitant of the cohesion of large political groups. This is why it is impossible to regard the lower morality of groups, in comparison with individuals, as the consequence of the inertia of "nature" against the higher demands of individual reason. It is true of course that the group possesses only an inchoate "mind" and that its organs of self-transcendence and self-criticism are very unstable and ephemeral compared to its organs of will. A shifting and unstable "prophetic minority" is the instrument of this self-transcendence, while the state is the organ of the group's will. For this reason the immorality of nations is frequently regarded as in effect their unmorality, as the consequence of their existence in the realm of "nature" rather than the realm of reason."I treat government not as a conscious contrivance," wrote Professor Seeley in a sentiment which expresses the conviction of many modern political scientists, "but as an half-instinctive product of the effort of human beings to ward off from themselves certain evils to which they are exposed.

Such an interpretation has a measure of validity but it certainly does not do justice to the "spiritual" character of national pride, nor to the contribution which individuals, with all their rational and spiritual faculties, make to pride of groups and the self-deification of nations. The most conducive proof that the egotism of nations is a characteristic of the spiritual life, and not merely an expression of the natural impulse of survival, is the fact that its most typical expressions are the lust-for-power, pride (comprising considerations of prestige and "honour"), contempt toward the other (the reverse side of pride and its necessary concomitant in a world in which self-esteem is constantly challenged by the achievements of others); hypocrisy (the inevitable pretension of conforming to a higher norm than self-interest); and finally the claim of moral autonomy by which the self-deification of the social group is made explicit by its presentation of itself as the source and end of existence. . . .

Chapter 9.¶4. *Temptation and Inevitability of Sin.* The full complexity of the psychological facts which validate the doctrine of original sin must be analyzed, first in terms of the relation of temptation to the inevitability of sin. Such an analysis may make it plain why man sins inevitably, yet without escaping responsibility for his sin. The temptation to sin lies, as previously observed, in the human situation itself. This situation is that man as spirit transcends the temporal and natural process in which he is involved and also transcends himself. Thus his freedom is the basis of his creativity but it is also his temptation. Since he is involved in the contingencies and necessities of the natural process on the one hand and since, on the other, he stands outside of them and foresees their caprices and perils, he is anxious. In his anxiety he seeks to transmute his finiteness into infinity, his weakness into strength, his dependence into independence. He seeks in other words to escape finiteness and weakness by a quantitative rather than qualitative development of his life. The quantitative antithesis of finiteness is infinity. The qualitative possibility of human life is its obedient subjection to the will of God. This possibility is expressed in the words of Jesus: "He that loseth his life for my sake shall find it" [Matt. 10:39].

It will be noted that the Christian statement of the ideal possibility does not involve self-negation but self-realization. The self is, in other words, not evil by reason of being a particular self and its salvation does not consist in absorption into the eternal. Neither is the self divided, as in Hegelianism, into a particular or empirical and a universal self; and salvation does not consist in sloughing off its particularity and achieving universality. The Christian view of the self is only possible from the standpoint of Christian theism in which God is not merely the x of the unconditioned or the undifferentiated eternal. God is revealed as loving will; and His will is active in creation, judgment and redemption. The highest self-realization for the self is therefore not the destruction of its particularity but the subjection of its particular will to the universal will.

But the self lacks the faith and trust to subject itself to God. It seeks to establish itself independently. It seeks to find its life and thereby loses it. For the self which it asserts is less than the true self. It is the self in all the contingent and arbitrary factors of its immediate situation. By asserting these contingent and arbitrary factors of an immediate situation, the self loses its true self. It increases its insecurity because it gives its immediate necessities a consideration which they do not deserve and which they cannot have without disturbing the harmony of creation. By giving life a false centre, the self then destroys the real possibilities for itself and others. Hence the relation of injustice to pride, and the vicious circle of injustice, increasing as it does the insecurity which pride was intended to overcome.

The sin of the inordinate self-love thus points to the prior sin of lack of trust in God. The anxiety of unbelief is not merely the fear which comes from ignorance of God. "Anxiety," declares Kierkegaard, "is the dizziness of freedom," but it is significant that the same freedom which tempts to anxiety also contains the ideal possibility of knowing God. Here the Pauline psychology is penetrating and significant. St. Paul declares that man is without excuse because "the invisible things of him from the creation of the world are clearly seen, being understood by the things that are made, even his eternal power and Godhead" [Rom. 1:20]. The anxiety of freedom leads to sin only if the prior sin of unbelief is assumed. This is the meaning of Kierkegaard's assertion that sin posits itself.

The sin of man's excessive and inordinate love of self is thus neither merely the drag of man's animal nature upon his more universal loyalties, nor yet the necessary consequence of human freedom and self-transcendence. It is more plausibly the consequence of the latter than of the former because the survival impulse of animal nature lacks precisely those boundless and limitless tendencies of human desires. Inordinate self-love is occasioned by the introduction of the perspective of the eternal into natural and human finiteness. But it is a false eternal. It consists in the transmutation of "mutable good" into infinity. This boundless character of human desires is an unnatural rather than natural fruit of man's relation to the temporal process on the one hand and to eternity on the other. If man knew, loved and obeyed God as the author and end of his existence, a proper limit would be set for his desires including the natural impulse of survival.

The fact that the lie is so deeply involved in the sin of self-glorification and that man cannot love himself inordinately without pretending that it is not his, but a universal, interest which he is supporting, is a further proof that sin presupposes itself and that it is neither ignorance nor yet the ignorance of ignorance which forces the self to sin. Rather it "holds the truth in unrighteousness."

The idea that the inevitability of sin is not due merely to the strength of the temptation in which man stands by reason of his relation to both the temporal process and eternity, is most perfectly expressed in the scriptural words: "Let no man say when he is tempted, I am tempted of God: for God cannot be tempted with evil, neither tempteth he any man: But every man is tempted, when he is drawn away of his own lust, and enticed. Then when lust hath conceived, it bringeth forth sin: and sin, when it is finished, bringeth forth death." But on the other hand the idea that the situation of finiteness and freedom is a temptation once evil has entered it and that evil does enter it prior to any human action is expressed in Biblical thought by the conception of the devil. The devil is a fallen angel, who fell because he sought to lift himself above his measure and who in turn insinuates temptation into human life. The sin of each individual is preceded by Adam's sin: but even this first sin of history is not the first sin. One may, in other words, go farther back than human history and still not escape the paradoxical conclusion that the situation of finiteness and freedom would not lead to sin if sin were not already introduced into the situation. This is, in the words of Kierkegaard, the "qualitative leap" of sin and reveals the paradoxical relation of inevitability and responsibility. Sin can never be traced merely to the temptation arising from a particular situation or condition in which man as man finds himself or in which particular men find themselves. Nor can the temptation which is compounded of a situation of finiteness and freedom, plus the fact of sin, be regarded as leading necessarily to sin in the life of each individual, if again sin is not first presupposed in that life. For this reason even the knowledge of inevitability does not extinguish the sense of responsibility. . . .

Chapter 9.¶2. *The Relation of Justice to Love.* . . . [T]he Christian conception of the relation of historical justice to the love of the Kingdom of God is a dialectical one. Love is both the fulfillment and the negation of all achievements of justice in history. Or expressed from the opposite standpoint, the achievements of justice in history may rise in indeterminate degrees to find their fulfillment in a more perfect love and brotherhood; but each new level of fulfillment also contains elements which stand in contradiction to perfect love. There are therefore obligations to realize justice in indeterminate degrees; but none of the realizations can assure the serenity of perfect fulfillment. If we analyse the realities of history in terms of this formula it will throw light on aspects of history which would otherwise remain obscure and perplexing; and will obviate mistakes which are inevitably made under alternative interpretations. Higher realizations of historic justice would be possible if it were more fully understood that all such realizations contain contradictions to, as well as approximations of, the ideal of love. Sanctification in the realm of social relations demands recognition of the impossibility of perfect sanctification.

The paradoxical relation between justice and love is expressed on various levels. We have previously explored the relation between sacrificial and mutual love. In that analysis it became apparent that mutual love (in which disinterested concern for the other elicits a reciprocal response) is the highest possibility of history in the sense that only such love is justified by historical consequences; but also that such love can only be initiated by a type of disinterestedness (sacrificial love) which dispenses with historical justification. Thus the pinnacle of the moral ideal stands both inside and beyond history: inside in so far as love may elicit a reciprocal response and change the character of human relations; and beyond history in so far as love cannot require a mutual response without losing its character of disinterestedness. The love commandment is therefore no simple historical possibility. The full implications of the commandment illustrate the dialectical relation between history and the eternal.

3. *Laws and Principles of Justice.* The relation of justice to love contains complexities analogous to the dialectical relation of mutual to sacrificial love. These complexities may be clarified by considering them in two dimensions. The first is the dimension of rules and laws of justice. The second is the dimension of structures of justice, of social and political organizations in their relation to brotherhood. The difference between the first and second dimension obviously lies in the fact that laws and principles of justice are abstractly conceived, while structures and organizations embody the vitalities of history. The contradiction between actual social institutions and arrangements and the ideal of brotherhood is obviously greater than between love and the rules and laws of justice.

All systems, rules and laws governing social relations are on the one hand instruments of mutuality and community; and they contain on the other hand mere approximations of, and positive contradictions to, the ideal of brotherhood. These aspects of the character of rules of justice must be examined in turn.

Systems and principles of justice are the servants and instruments of the spirit of brotherhood in so far as they extend the sense of obligation towards the other, (*a*) from an immediately felt obligation, prompted by obvious need, to a continued obligation expressed in fixed principles of mutual support; (*b*) from a simple relation between a self and one "other" to the complex relations of the self and the "others"; and (*c*) finally from the obligations, discerned by the individual self, to the wider obligations which the community defines from its more impartial perspective. These communal definitions evolve slowly in custom and in law. They all contain some higher elements of disinterestedness, which would not be possible to the individual self.

In these three ways rules and laws of justice stand in a positive relation to the law of love. It is significant that the rational element is constitutive in each of them. An immediately felt obligation towards obvious need may be prompted by the emotion of pity. But a continued sense of obligation rests upon and expresses itself in rational calculations of the needs of others as compared with our own interests. A relation between the self and one other may be partly ecstatic; and in any case the calculation of relative interests may be reduced to a minimum. But as soon as a third person is introduced into the relation even the most perfect love requires a rational estimate of conflicting needs and interests. Even the love within a family avails itself of customs and usages which stereotype given adjustments between various members of the family in such a way that each action need not be oriented by a fresh calculation of competing interests.

The definitions of justice arrived at in a given community are the product of a social mind. Various perspectives upon common problems have been merged and have achieved a result, different from that at which any individual, class or group in the community would have arrived. The fact that various conceptions of a just solution of a common problem can be finally synthesized into a common solution disproves the idea that the approach of each individual or group is consistently egoistic. If it were, society would be an anarchy of rival interests until power from above subdued the anarchy.

Interests may indeed clash to such a degree that no arbitration of the conflict is possible, in which case the conflict is ended either by the victory of one side or the other, or by the submission of both to a superior coercive force. Martin Luther's and Thomas Hobbes' political views are informed by the belief that all conflicts of interest are of such a nature.

The achievements of democratic societies refute this pessimism; and with it the purely negative conception of the relation of government and systems of justice to the ideal of brotherhood. History reveals adjustments of interest to interest without the interposition of superior coercive force to be possible within wide limits. The capacity of communities to synthesize divergent approaches to a common problem and to arrive at a tolerably just solution proves man's capacity to consider interests other than his own. Nevertheless, the fact that a synthesis of conflicting interests and viewpoints is not easy, and may become impossible under certain conditions, is a refutation of a too simple trust in the impartial character of reason. It would be as false to regard rules and principles of justice, slowly elaborated in collective experience, as merely the instruments of the sense of social obligation, as to regard them merely as tools of egoistic interest.

An analysis of the development of social conscience on any current social issue, as for instance the community's sense of obligation to the unemployed, may clarify the complex factors involved in this development. The unemployment benefits which the community pays to those who are out of work is partly an expression of the sense of obligation of the more privileged members of the community towards those who are less fortunate. They find an advantage in meeting this obligation according to fixed principles instead of relying upon their own occasional feeling of pity for this or that needy person. They know furthermore that their own knowledge of comparative needs is very inadequate and that they require the more impartial and comprehensive perspective of the total community, functioning through its proper agencies. This function of principles of unemployment relief presents the most positive relation between specific rules and the sense of brotherhood.

On the other hand the benefits which are paid to the unemployed are almost always higher than the privileged would like to pay, even though they may be lower than the poor would like to receive. Some members of the privileged classes in modern communities have in fact obscured the issue of justice in regard to this problem by the most obvious and transparent of all ideologies. They have sought to maintain that the unemployed are the victims of sloth rather than of the caprices of an intricate industrial process; and that the fear of hunger might cure their sloth. The actual schedule of payments upon which the community finally decides represents the conclusions of the social, rather than any individual, mind, and is the consequence of a perennial debate upon the subject. It is probably a compromise between conflicting viewpoints and interests. It certainly is not an unconditionedly "just" solution of the social problem involved. The privileged may in fact accept it for no better reason than that they fear the revolt of the poor. This aspect of the situation proves the impossibility of completely separating the concept of "principles of justice" from the hopes and fears, the pressures and counter-pressures, of living communities, expressed below the level of a rational calculation of rights and interests.

The solution may nevertheless become a generally accepted social standard; and some privileged members of the community may welcome it, because it expresses their considered sense of social obligation upon which they would prefer to rely rather than upon the momentary power of pity. The poor as a whole may receive less from these benefits than an individual needy person might secure by appealing to a given sensitive and opulent individual. But they will certainly receive more than if all of them were dependent upon nothing but vagrant, momentary and capricious impulses of pity, dormant unless awakened by obvious need.

This positive relation between rules of justice and the law of love must be emphasized in opposition to sentimental versions of the love commandment, according to which only the most personal individual and direct expressions of social obligation are manifestations of Christian *agape*. Both sectarian and Lutheran analyses of the relation of love to justice easily fall into the error of excluding rules of justice from the domain of love.

Law and systems of justice do, however, have a negative as well as a positive relation to mutual love and brotherhood. They contain both approximations of and contradictions to the spirit of brotherhood. This aspect of their character is derived from the sinful element in all social reality. They are merely approximations in so far as justice presupposes a tendency of various members of a community to take advantage of each other, or to be more concerned with their own weal than with that of others. Because of this tendency all systems of justice make careful distinctions between the rights and interests of various members of a community. The fence and the boundary line are the symbols of the spirit of justice. They set the limits upon each man's interest to prevent one from taking advantage of the other. A harmony achieved through justice is therefore only an approximation of brotherhood. It is the best possible harmony within the conditions created by human egoism. This negative aspect of justice is not its only characteristic, as has been previously observed. Even if perfect love were presupposed, complex relations, involving more than two persons, require the calculation of rights. The negative aspect is nevertheless important.

The more positive contradiction to brotherhood in all schemes of justice is introduced by the contingent and finite character of rational estimates of rights and interests and by the taint of passion and self-interest upon calculations of the rights of others. There is no universal reason in history, and no impartial perspective upon the whole field of vital interests, which compete with and mutually support each other. Even the comparatively impartial view of the whole of a society, as expressed particularly in the carefully guarded objectivity of its juridical institutions, participates in the contingent character of all human viewpoints.

Such rules of justice as we have known in history have been arrived at by a social process in which various partial perspectives have been synthesized into a more inclusive one. But even the inclusive perspective is contingent to time and place. The Marxist cynicism in regard to the pretended moral purity of all laws and rules of justice is justified. Marxism is right, furthermore, in regarding them as primarily rationalizations of the interests of the dominant elements of a society. The requirements of "natural law" in the medieval period were obviously conceived in a feudal society; just as the supposed absolute and "self-evident" demands of eighteenth-century natural law were bourgeois in origin.

The relative and contingent character of these ideals and rules of justice refutes the claim of their unconditioned character, made alike by Catholic, liberal and even Marxist social theorists. Both Catholic and liberal social theories (and for that matter the Stoic theories in which both had their origin) make a distinction between "natural law" and the "positive" or "civil" law. The latter represents the actual and imperfect embodiment of the rules of justice in specific historical communities. The contingent and relative character of the latter type of law is recognized; but finality is ascribed to the former. This fundamental distinction must be challenged. It rests upon an untenable faith in the purity of reason; and it is merely another of the many efforts which men make to find a vantage point of the unconditioned in history. The effect of this pretended finality of "natural law" is obvious. It raises "ideology" to a higher degree of pretension, and is another of the many illustrations in history of the force of sin in the claim of sinlessness.

There is of course a tenable distinction between ideals of justice and their embodiment in historical or "civil" law. The latter is the consequence of pressures and counter-pressures in a living community. It is therefore subject to a greater degree of historical relativity than "natural law." In so far as thought is purer than action "natural law" is purer than "civil law." Furthermore it is important to recognize the validity of principles of justice, rationally conceived, as sources of criticism for the historical achievements of justice in living communities. If the medieval and modern secular theories of natural law claim too much for these rational principles of justice, both secular and Reformation relativists frequently dismiss them as irrelevant or dangerous. Karl Barth's belief that the moral life of man would possess no valid principles of guidance, if the Ten Commandments had not introduced such principles by revelation, is as absurd as it is unscriptural.

The practical universality of the prohibition of murder for instance in the moral codes of mankind is just as significant as the endless relativities which manifest themselves in the practical application of the general prohibition. There are essentially universal "principles" of justice moreover, by which the formulation of specific rules and systems of justice is oriented. Both "equality" and "liberty" are recognized in Stoic, medieval and modern theories of natural law as transcendent principles of justice; though the modern theories (both bourgeois and Marxist) falsely regard them as realizable rather than as transcendent principles. An analysis of one of them, the principle of equality, will serve to reveal the validity of both as transcendent principles of justice.

The perpetual recurrence of the principle of equality in social theory is a refutation of purely pessimistic conceptions of human nature, whether secular or religious. Its influence proves that men do not simply use social theory to rationalize their own interest. Equality as a pinnacle of the ideal of justice implicitly points towards love as the final norm of justice; for equal justice is the approximation of brotherhood under the conditions of sin. A higher justice always means a more equal justice. Special privilege may be frowned upon more severely by those who want it than those who have it; but those who have it are uneasy in their conscience about it. The ideological taint enters into the discussion of equality when those who suffer from inequality raise the principle of equality to the definitive principle of justice without recognizing that differences of need or of social function make the attainment of complete equality in society impossible. The beneficiaries of special privilege emphasize, on the other hand, that inequalities of social function justify corresponding inequalities of privilege. They may also assert, with some, but less, justification, that inequality of reward is a necessary inducement for the proper performance of social function. But they will seek to hide the historic fact that privileged members of the community invariably use their higher degree of social power to appropriate an excess of privileges not required by their function; and certainly not in accord with differences of need.

The validity of the principle of equality on the one hand and the impossibility of realizing it fully on the other, illustrates the relation of absolute norms of justice to the relativities of history. The fact that one class will tend to emphasize the absolute validity of the norm unduly, while another class will be inclined to emphasize the impossibility of achieving it fully, illustrates the inevitable "ideological taint" in the application of a generally valid principle, even if the principle itself achieves a high measure of transcendence over partial interest.

The complex character of all historic conceptions of justice thus refutes both the relativists who see no possibility of finding valid principles of justice, and the rationalists and optimists who imagine it possible to arrive at completely valid principles, free of every taint of special interest and historical passion.

The positive relation of principles of justice to the ideal of brotherhood makes an indeterminate approximation of love in the realm of justice possible. The negative relation means that all historic conceptions of justice will embody some elements which contradict the law of love. The interests of a class, the viewpoint of a nation, the prejudices of an age and the illusions of a culture are consciously and unconsciously insinuated into the norms by which men regulate their common life. They are intended to give one group an advantage over another. Or if that is not their intention, it is at least the unvarying consequence.

4. *Structures of Justice.* If rules and principles of justice ideally conceived and transcending the more dubious and ambiguous social realities of living societies have an equivocal relation to the ideal of brotherhood, this twofold character is even more obvious and apparent in the structures and systems, the organizations and mechanisms, of society in which these principles and rules are imperfectly embodied and made historically concrete. We have already noted the distinction between "natural law," as a rational statement of principle of justice, and "positive" law, which designates the historic enactments of living communities. But an analysis of the equivocal character of the "structures" of justice must include more than a mere consideration of "civil" or "positive" law. It must look beyond legal enactments to the whole structure and organization of historical communities. This structure is never merely the order of a legal system. The harmony of communities is not simply attained by the authority of law. *Nomos* does not coerce the vitalities of life into order. The social harmony of living communities is achieved by an interaction between the normative conceptions of morality and law and the existing and developing forces and vitalities of the community. Usually the norms of law are compromises between the rational-moral ideals of what ought to be, and the possibilities of the situation as determined by given equilibria of vital forces. The specific legal enactments are, on the one hand, the instruments of the conscience of the community, seeking to subdue the potential anarchy of forces and interests into a tolerable harmony. They are, on the other hand, merely explicit formulations of given tensions and equilibria of life and power, as worked out by the unconscious interactions of social life.

No human community is, in short, a simple construction of conscience or reason. All communities are more or less stable or precarious harmonies of human vital capacities. They are governed by power. The power which determines the quality of the order and harmony is not merely the coercive and organizing power of government. That is only one of the two aspects of social power. The other is the balance of vitalities and forces in any given social situation. These two elements of communal life—the central organizing principle and power, and the equilibrium of power—are essential and perennial aspects of community organization; and no moral or social advance can redeem society from its dependence upon these two principles.

Since there are various possibilities of so managing and equilibrating the balance of social forces in a given community that the highest possible justice may be achieved and since the organizing principle and power in the community is also subject to indeterminate refinement, communal order and justice can approximate a more perfect brotherhood in varying degree. But each principle of communal organization—the organization of power and the balance of power—contain possibilities of contradicting the law of brotherhood. The organizing principle and power may easily degenerate into tyranny. It may create a coerced unity of society in which the freedom and vitality of all individual members are impaired. Such a tyrannical unification of life is a travesty on brotherhood. Again, the principle of the balance of power is always pregnant with the possibility of anarchy. These twin evils, tyranny and anarchy, represent the Scylla and Charybdis between which the frail bark of social justice must sail. It is almost certain to founder upon one rock if it makes the mistake of regarding the other as the only peril.

No possible refinement of social forces and political harmonies can eliminate the potential contradiction to brotherhood which is implicit in the two political instruments of brotherhood—the organization of power and the balance of power. This paradoxical situation in the realm of social life is analogous to the Christian conception of the paradox of history as discerned in other realms of life. In order to explore the meaning of the paradox more fully it will be well to begin with an analysis of the nature and meaning of "power" in communal life. . . .

6. *Justice and World Community.* In the crisis of world history in which we stand, we have a particularly vivid example of the twofold character of all historic political tasks and achievements. The economic interdependence of the world places us under the obligation, and gives us the possibility, of enlarging the human community so that the principle of order and justice will govern the international as well as the national community. We are driven to this new task by the lash of fear as well as by the incitement of hope. For our civilization is undone if we cannot overcome the anarchy in which the nations live. This new and compelling task represents the positive side of historical development and reveals the indeterminate possibilities of good in history.

Unfortunately, however, many of the idealists who envisage this new responsibility think they can fulfill it best by denying the perennial problems of the political order. They think that world government is possible without an implied hegemony of the stronger powers. This hegemony is inevitable; and so is the peril of a new imperialism, which is inherent in it. The peril can best be overcome by arming all nations great and small with constitutional power to resist the exactions of dominant power. This is to say that the principle of the balance of power is implied in the idea of constitutional justice. But if the central and organizing principle of power is feared too much, and the central authority is weakened, then the political equilibrium degenerates once more to an unorganized balance of power. And an unorganized balance of power is potential anarchy.

Thus we face all the old problems of political organization on the new level of a potential international community. The new international community will be constructed neither by the pessimists, who believe it impossible to go beyond the balance of power principle in the relation of nations to each other; nor by the cynics, who would organize the world by the imposition of imperial authority without regard to the injustices which flow inevitably from arbitrary and irresponsible power; nor yet by the idealists, who are under the fond illusion that a new level of historic development will emancipate history of these vexing problems.

The new world must be built by resolute men who "when hope is dead will hope by faith"; who will neither seek premature escape from the guilt of history, nor yet call the evil, which taints all their achievements, good. There is no escape from the paradoxical relation of history to the Kingdom of God. History moves towards the realization of the Kingdom but yet the judgment of God is upon every new realization.

From Reinhold Niebuhr, *The Nature and Destiny of Man: A Christian Interpretation,* vols. 1 and 2 (New York: Charles Scribner's Sons, 1949). Vol. 1, pp. 178, 208–11, 250–54; copyright © 1941, (c) 1964 Charles Scribner's Sons, copyright renewed 1969 Reinhold Niebuhr. Vol. 2, pp. 246–58, 284–86; copyright © 1943 (c) 1964 Charles Scribner's Sons, copyright renewed 1971 Reinhold Niebuhr. Reprinted with permission of Simon & Schuster, Inc. from the Macmillan College text.

57.   Pope Leo XIII, *Rerum Novarum*

Although the encyclical Rerum Novarum *was issued in 1891, it is rightly considered the foundation of twentieth-century Catholic social doctrine. It represented the first serious effort by the church to come to terms with the Industrial Revolution, including labor organization, the "just wage," property rights, the new phenomenon of socialism, and the obligation of government to intervene for the "common good." The stance of the encylical at several of these points is not especially progressive by contemporary standards. But the importance of* Rerum Novarum *was demonstrated by the issuance of several later encyclicals marking decade anniversaries of this encyclical.*

30. . . . Acting as the mother of the rich owners of the means of production and of the poor alike and drawing upon the great fount of love which she everywhere creates, the Church has founded congregations of religious and many other useful institutions which have done their work so well that there is hardly any kind of need for which help is not provided. There are many today who follow the example of the heathens of old and find fault with the Church for showing such great charity. They argue that state welfare benefits should be provided instead. But there is no human device which can take the place of this Christian charity, which thinks of nothing other than to bring help where it is needed. . . .

31. However, it is not to be doubted that to do what needs to be done calls for everything that lies within men's powers. It is necessary for all who have a part to play to work and strain to do their share. As with the providence which governs the world so also here, we see that effects which depend upon a number of causes come about only when all are at work together.

32. The next step to take, therefore, is to ask what part of the remedy is to be looked for from the action of the state. . . .

33. The first task of rulers is to make use of the whole system of laws and institutions to give assistance both generally and to particular classes. Statesmanship consists in making the structure and administrative functioning of the state conduce of themselves to public and private prosperity. Bringing this about is the particular function of those who govern. The prosperity of a state is best served where there are sound morals, well-ordered family life, regard for religion and justice, moderate taxes equitably levied, growing industry and trade, a flourishing agriculture, and other provisions of a like kind which it is generally agreed will contribute to the greater well-being and happiness of the citizens. By these means rulers can benefit other classes and at the same time be of the greatest help to the unpropertied. It is fully within their right to act thus and since by virtue of its office the state ought to care for the common good they are not to be accused of excessive interference. The greater the abundance of opportunities which arise out of this general care, the less will be the need to try other measures to help the workers. . . .

34. But there is another aspect to be considered which is of very great importance in this connection. The one purpose for which the state exists is common to the highest and the lowest within it. By nature, the right of the unpropertied men to citizenship is equal to that of the wealthy owners of the means of production, for they through their families are among the true and living parts which go to form the body of the state. Indeed, it can be added, in every actual state they are greatly in the majority. Since it would be utterly absurd to care for one section of citizens and neglect another, it is evident that the public authority ought to take proper care to safeguard the lives and well-being of the unpropertied class. To fail in this would be to violate justice which bids us give to every man his due. As St. Thomas has wisely said: 'As a part and the whole are identical in a sense, so too in a sense that which is of the whole is also of a part' (*S. Theol.* II-II, Q.61, art.1, [and]2). Consequently, not the least nor the lightest of the duties which fall to rulers in their regard for the common good, but that which comes first of all, is to keep inviolate the justice which is called distributive by caring impartially for each and every class of citizen. . . .

44. . . . It is argued that, given that the scale of wages is decided by free agreement, it would appear that the employer fulfils the contract by paying the wage agreed upon, that nothing further is due from him and that injustice will be done only if the employer does not pay the full price or the worker does not perform the whole of his task. In these cases and not otherwise it would be right for the political authority to intervene and require each party to give to the other his due. This is an argument which a balanced judgment can neither entirely agree with nor easily accept. It does not take every consideration into account; and there is one consideration of the greatest importance which is omitted altogether. This is that to work is to exert oneself to obtain those things which are necessary for the various requirements of life and most of all for life itself. 'With sweat on your brow shall you eat your bread' (Gen. 3:19). Thus, human work has stamped upon it by nature, as it were, two marks peculiar to it. First, it is *personal*, because the force acting adheres to the person acting; and therefore it belongs entirely to the worker and is intended for his advantage. Second, it is *necessary*, because a man needs the results of his work to maintain himself in accordance with a command of nature itself which he must take particular care to obey. Were we to confine our attention to the personal aspect, we could take it for granted that the worker is free to agree to any rate of pay, however small. Since he works of his own free will, he is free to offer his work for a small payment, or for none at all.

45. But this position changes radically when to the personal we join the necessary aspect of labour, as we must. For although they can be separated in theory, in practice the two are inseparable. The reality is that it is every man's duty to stay alive. To fail in that is a crime. Hence arises necessarily the right to obtain those things which are needed to sustain life; and it is only the wage for his labour which permits the man at the bottom of the ladder to exercise this right. Let workers and employer, therefore, make any bargains they like, and in particular agree freely about wages; nevertheless, there underlies a requirement of natural justice higher and older than any bargain voluntarily struck: the wage ought not to be in any way insufficient for the bodily needs of a temperate and well-behaved worker. If, having no alternative and fearing a worse evil, a workman is forced to accept harder conditions imposed by an employer or contractor, he is the victim of violence against which justice cries out.

46. In these and similar cases—such, for instance, as the regulation of hours of labour in different industries or measures to safeguard health and safety at work—it is important to prevent the public authorities from thrusting themselves forward inconsiderately. Particularly because of the great variety of circumstances, times and places, it will be better to reserve such matters to the judgment of associations, of which more will be said later, or to find some other way by which the interests of wage-earners can be safeguarded. In the last resort appeal must be made to the help and protection of the state. . . .

47. If a worker earns a wage which enables him to make ample provision for the needs of himself, his wife and his children, he will find it easy to practise thrift. If he is sensible, does what nature itself advises him to do and cuts out excessive expenditure, he can contrive to acquire some little property. We have seen that effective efforts to put an end to the troubles facing us must start from the principle that the right to own privately must be maintained absolutely. For that reason the law should support this right and do what it can to enable as many as possible of the people to choose to exercise it. Most valuable consequences must follow from such action, the foremost among them being a more equitable distribution of wealth. The forces of social change have split states between two classes separated by an enormous gulf. On one side stands the extremely powerful party, because extremely rich; which, being in possession of the whole of industry and trade, turns all means of production to the service of its own ends and is able to take no small part in the government of the state. On the other side stands the multitude of the weak, destitute of resources, filled with bitterness and ever ready to revolt. However, if the efforts of the people were aroused by the hope of acquiring something of what the soil contains, it would gradually come about that class would move closer to class and the gulf which separates the greatest wealth from the deepest poverty be removed. . . .

48. Finally, employers and workers can do much themselves in this matter by means of institutions which can bring timely aid to the needy and draw class closer to class. Examples of these are mutual benefits societies; foundations of various kinds to provide security for workers and their widows and orphans in cases of sudden emergency, illness and death; and welfare organizations which provide for the protection of children, adolescents and older people.

48.1 But the most important are working-men's associations, the aims of which include almost all of those listed above. The good work done by the old guilds of artisans is well known. They brought benefit to the members themselves and also did much to develop the crafts, as many monuments show. Working-men's associations have to be adapted now to the greater demands which are made on people in an age of wider education and new ways of life. It is gratifying that everywhere societies of this kind are being formed, either by workers alone or by both classes together, and it is greatly to be desired that they should become both more numerous and more efficient. We have spoken of them more than once and this is the place to demonstrate that with their many advantages they exist of their own right and to discuss how they should be organized and what they ought to do. . . .

51. There will be occasions when the law may rightly intervene against private associations, as when some among them pursue policies which are plainly contrary to honesty, justice and the good of the state itself. In cases such as these the public authority may with justice prevent the formation of associations and dissolve them where they exist. However, great care must be taken lest the rights of the citizens be emptied of content and unreasonable regulations made under the pretence of public benefit. For laws have to be obeyed only when they accord with right reason and the eternal law of God. . . .

53. Associations in immense variety and especially unions of workers are now more common than they have ever been. This is not the place to enquire into the origins of most of them, their aims or the methods they employ. There is plenty of evidence to confirm the opinion that many are in the hands of secret leaders and are used for purposes which are inconsistent with both Christian principles and the social good. They do all that they can to ensure that those who will not join them shall not eat. In this state of affairs Christian workers have but two alternatives: they can join these associations and greatly endanger their religion; or they can form their own and, with united strength, free themselves courageously from such injustice and intolerable oppression. That the second alternative must be chosen cannot be doubted by those who have no desire to see men's highest good put into extreme danger.

54. High praise is due to the many Catholics who have informed themselves, seen what is needed and tried to learn from experience by what honourable means they might be able to lead unpropertied workers to a better standard of living. They have taken up the workers' cause, seeking to raise the incomes of families and individuals, introduce equity into the relations between workers and employers and strengthen among both groups regard for duty and the teaching of the Gospel—teaching which inculcates moderation, forbids excess and safeguards harmony in the state between very differently situated men and organizations. . . .

58.1. The condition of the workers is the question of the hour. It will be answered one way or another, rationally or irrationally, and which way it goes is of the greatest importance to the state. Christian workers can easily end matters by forming associations, choosing wise leaders and entering upon the same road as that which their fathers followed with singular advantage to themselves and to the whole community. Great though the power of prejudiced opinion and of greed may be, unless the sense of what is right be deliberately and wickedly stifled the good will of the citizens will come spontaneously to turn more and more towards those whom they see to be industrious and moderate, putting justice before gain and the sacredness of duty before all things else. A further advantage to be looked for from such a course of action is the hope and opportunity of a better life that will be offered to workers who now either altogether despise the Christian faith or live contrary to its requirements. These men know for the most part that they have been fooled by false hopes and lying appearances. They feel themselves to be treated with great inhumanity by their greedy employers who regard them as no more than so many instruments of gain; but if they are members of a union it will be of one which has no love and no affection at its heart and is torn apart by the internal strife which is the perpetual accompaniment of proud and unbelieving poverty. Broken in spirit, worn out in body, how many wish to free themselves from servitude and humiliation! But though their desire is strong, human respect or the fear of hunger holds them back. The self-governing unions of Catholics can be of immense benefit to all of these men if they will invite them, hesitant though they are, to join them in their search for a solution to their difficulties and will receive them with faith and aid and comfort as they do so.

From *Proclaiming Justice and Peace: Papal Documents from Rerum Novarum through Centesimus Annus,* edited by Michael Walsh and Brian Davies (Mystic, Conn.: Twenty-Third Publications, 1991), pp. 28–29, 33–39. Copyright © 1991 by compilation CAFOD. Copyright © 1991 introduction Michael J. Walsh.

58. Pope Pius XI,
Quadragesimo Anno

As the name indicates, this encylical was issued in 1931, the fortieth anniversary of Rerum Novarum. *It continues to discuss issues related to property and work and the role of the state. Its delineation of what came to be known as the doctrine of subsidiarity (at paragraphs 79 and 80) has taken on great importance in subsequent Catholic social teaching.*

49. It follows from what We have termed the individual and at the same time social character of ownership, that men must consider in this matter not only their own advantage but also the common good. To define these duties in detail when necessity requires and the natural law has not done so, is the function of those in charge of the State. Therefore, public authority, under the guiding light always of the natural and divine law, can determine more accurately upon consideration of the true requirements of the common good, what is permitted and what is not permitted to owners in the use of their property. . . . That the State is not permitted to discharge its duty arbitrarily is, however, clear. The natural right itself both of owning goods privately and of passing them on by inheritance ought always to remain intact and inviolate, since this indeed is a right that the State cannot take away. . . . Yet when the State brings private ownership into harmony with the needs of the common good, it does not commit a hostile act against private owners but rather does them a friendly service; for it thereby effectively prevents the private possession of goods, which the Author of nature in His most wise providence ordained for the support of human life from causing intolerable evils and thus rushing to its own destruction; it does not destroy private possessions, but safeguards them; and it does not weaken private property rights, but strengthens them.

50. Furthermore, a person's superfluous income, that is, income which he does not need to sustain life fittingly and with dignity, is not left wholly to his own free determination. Rather the Sacred Scriptures and the Fathers of the Church constantly declare in the most explicit language that the rich are bound by a very grave precept to practice almsgiving, beneficence, and munificence.

51. Expending larger incomes so that opportunity for gainful work may be abundant, provided, however, that this work is applied to producing really useful goods, ought to be considered, as We deduce from the principles of the Angelic Doctor, an outstanding exemplification of the virtue of munificence and one particularly suited to the needs of the times. . . .

52. That ownership is originally acquired both by occupancy of a thing not owned by any one and by labour, or, as is said, by specification, the tradition of all ages as well as the teaching of Our Predecessor Leo clearly testifies. For, whatever some idly say to the contrary, no injury is done to any person when a thing is occupied that is available to all but belongs to no one; however, only that labour which a man performs in his own name and by virtue of which a new form or increase has been given to a thing grants him title to these fruits.

53. Far different is the nature of work that is hired out to others and expended on the property of others. To this indeed especially applies what Leo XIII says is 'incontestible,' namely, that 'the wealth of nations originates from no other source than from the labour of workers.' For is it not plain that the enormous volume of goods that makes up human wealth is produced by and issues from the hands of the workers that either toil unaided or have their efficiency marvelously increased by being equipped with tools or machines? Every one knows, too, that no nation has ever risen out of want and poverty to a better and nobler condition save by the enormous and combined toil of all the people, both those who manage work and those who carry out directions. But it is no less evident that, had not God the Creator of all things, in keeping with His goodness, first generously bestowed natural riches and resources—the wealth and forces of nature—such supreme efforts would have been idle and vain, indeed could never even have begun. . . .

57. But not every distribution among human beings of property and wealth is of a character to attain either completely or to a satisfactory degree of perfection the end which God intends. Therefore, the riches that economic-social developments constantly increase ought to be so distributed among individual persons and classes that the common advantage of all, which Leo XIII had praised, will be safeguarded; in other words, that the common good of all society will be kept inviolate. By this law of social justice, one class is forbidden to exclude the other from sharing in the benefits. . . .

76. What We have thus far stated regarding an equitable distribution of property and regarding just wages concerns individual persons and only indirectly touches social order, to the restoration of which according to the principles of sound philosophy and to its perfection according to the sublime precepts of the law of the Gospel, Our Predecessor, Leo XIII, devoted all his thought and care.

77. Still, in order that what he so happily initiated may be solidly established, that what remains to be done may be accomplished, and that even more copious and richer benefits may accrue to the family of mankind, two things are especially necessary: reform of institutions and correction of morals.

78. When we speak of the reform of institutions, the State comes chiefly to mind, not as if universal well-being were to be expected from its activity, but because things have come to such a pass through the evil of what we have termed 'individualism' that, following upon the overthrow and near extinction of that rich social life which was once highly developed through associations of various kinds, there remain virtually only individuals and the State. This is to the great harm of the State itself; for, with a structure of social governance lost, and with the taking over of all the burdens which the wrecked associations once bore, the State has been overwhelmed and crushed by almost infinite tasks and duties.

79. As history abundantly proves, it is true that on account of changed conditions many things which were done by small associations in former times cannot be done now save by large associations. Still, that most weighty principle, which cannot be set aside or changed, remains fixed and unshaken in social philosophy: Just as it is gravely wrong to take from individuals what they can accomplish by their own initiative and industry and give it to the community, so also it is an injustice and at the same time a grave evil and disturbance of right order to assign to a greater and higher association what lesser and subordinate organizations can do. For every social activity ought of its very nature furnish help to the members of the body social, and never destroy and absorb them.

80. The supreme authority of the State ought, therefore, to let subordinate groups handle matters and concerns of lesser importance, which would otherwise dissipate its efforts greatly. Thereby the State will more freely, powerfully, and effectively do all those things that belong to it alone because it alone can do them: directing, watching, urging, restraining, as occasion requires and necessity demands. Therefore, those in power should be sure that the more perfectly a graduated order is kept among the various associations, in observance of the principle of 'subsidiary function,' the stronger social authority and effectiveness will be the happier and more prosperous the condition of the State.

From *Proclaiming Justice and Peace: Papal Documents from Rerum Novarum through Centesimus Annus*, edited by Michael Walsh and Brian Davies (Mystic, Conn.: Twenty-Third Publications, 1991), pp. 55–57, 62–63. Copyright © 1991 by compilation CAFOD. Copyright © 1991 introduction Michael J. Walsh.

59.   Pope John XXIII,
Pacem in Terris

Issued in 1963, during the "Cold War" (and during the Second Vatican Council), this encyclical is a plea for peace and world order. Developing the logic of the doctrine of subsidiarity, Pacem in Terris *argues that the world confronts new problems of global scale that cannot be solved by anything less than global institutions, such as the United Nations.*

130. Recent progress in science and technology has had a profound influence on man's way of life. This progress is a spur to men all over the world to extend their collaboration and association with one another in these days when material resources, travel from one country to another, and technical information have so vastly increased. This has led to a phenomenal growth in relationships between individuals, families and intermediate associations belonging to the various nations, and between the public authorities of the various political communities. There is also a growing economic interdependence between states. National economies are gradually becoming so interdependent that a kind of world economy is being born from the simultaneous integration of the economies of individual states. And finally, each country's social progress, order, security and peace are necessarily linked with the social progress, order, security and peace of every other country.

131. From this it is clear that no state can fittingly pursue its own interests in isolation from the rest, nor, under such circumstances, can it develop itself as it should. The prosperity and progress of any state is in part consequence, and in part cause, of the prosperity and progress of all other states.

132. No era will ever succeed in destroying the unity of the human family, for it consists of men who are all equal by virtue of their natural dignity. Hence there will always be an imperative need—born of man's very nature—to promote in sufficient measure the universal common good; the good, that is, of the whole human family.

133. In the past rulers of states seem to have been able to make sufficient provision for the universal common good through the normal diplomatic channels, or by top-level meetings and discussions, treaties and agreements; by using, that is, the ways and means suggested by the natural law, the law of nations, or international law.

134. In our own day, however, mutual relationships between states have undergone a far-reaching change. On the one hand, the universal common good gives rise to problems of the utmost gravity, complexity and urgency—especially as regards the preservation of the security and peace of the whole world. On the other hand, the rulers of individual nations, being all on an equal footing, largely fail in their efforts to achieve this, however much they multiply their meetings and their endeavours to discover more fitting instruments of justice. And this is no reflection on their sincerity and enterprise. It is merely that their authority is not sufficiently influential.

135. We are thus driven to the conclusion that the shape and structure of political life in the modern world, and the influence exercised by public authority in all the nations of the world are unequal to the task of promoting the common good of all peoples.

136. Now, if one considers carefully the inner significance of the common good on the one hand, and the nature and function of public authority on the other, one cannot fail to see that there is an intrinsic connection between them. Public authority, as the means of promoting the common good in civil society, is a postulate of the moral order. But the moral order likewise requires that this authority be effective in attaining its end. Hence the civil institutions in which such authority resides, becomes operative and promotes its ends, are endowed with a certain kind of structure and efficacy: a structure and efficacy which make such institutions capable of realizing the common good by ways and means adequate to the changing historical conditions.

137. Today the universal common good presents us with problems which are world-wide in their dimensions; problems, therefore, which cannot be solved except by a public authority with power, organization and means co-extensive with these problems, and with a world-wide sphere of activity. Consequently the moral order itself demands the establishment of some such general form of public authority.

138. But this general authority equipped with world-wide power and adequate means for achieving the universal common good cannot be imposed by force. It must be set up with the consent of all nations. If its work is to be effective, it must operate with fairness, absolute impartiality, and with dedication to the common good of all peoples. The forcible imposition by the more powerful nations of a universal authority of this kind would inevitably arouse fears of its being used as an instrument to serve the interests of the few or to take the side of a single nation, and thus the influence and effectiveness of its activity would be undermined. For even though nations may differ widely in material progress and military strength, they are very sensitive as regards their juridical equality and the excellence of their own way of life. They are right, therefore, in their reluctance to submit to an authority imposed by force, established without their cooperation, or not accepted of their own accord.

139. The common good of individual states is something that cannot be determined without reference to the human person, and the same is true of the common good of all states taken together. Hence the public authority of the world community must likewise have as its special aim the recognition, respect, safeguarding and promotion of the rights of the human person. This can be done by direct action, if need be, or by the creation throughout the world of the sort of conditions in which rulers of individual states can more easily carry out their specific functions.

140. The same principle of subsidiarity which governs the relations between public authorities and individuals, families and intermediate societies in a single state, must also apply to the relations between the public authority of the world community and the public authorities of each political community. The special function of this universal authority must be to evaluate and find a solution to economic, social, political and cultural problems which affect the universal common good. These are problems which, because of their extreme gravity, vastness and urgency, must be considered too difficult for the rulers of individual states to solve with any degree of success.

141. But it is no part of the duty of universal authority to limit the sphere of action of the public authority of individual states, or to arrogate any of their functions to itself. On the contrary, its essential purpose is to create world conditions in which the public authorities of each nation, its citizens and intermediate groups, can carry out their tasks, fulfil their duties and claim their rights with greater security. . . .

142. The United Nations Organization (UN) was established, as is well known, on 26 June 1945. To it were subsequently added lesser organizations consisting of members nominated by the public authority of the various nations and entrusted with highly important international functions in the economics, social, cultural, educational and health fields. The United Nations Organization has the special aim of maintaining and strengthening peace between nations, and of encouraging and assisting friendly relations between them, based on the principles of equality, mutual respect, and extensive co-operation in every field of human endeavour.

143. A clear proof of the far-sightedness of this organization is provided by the Universal Declaration of Human Rights passed by the United Nations General Assembly on 10 December 1948. The preamble of this declaration affirms that the genuine recognition and complete observance of all the rights and freedoms outlined in the declaration is a goal to be sought by all peoples and all nations.

144. We are, of course, aware that some of the points in the declaration did not meet with unqualified approval in some quarters; and there was justification for this. Nevertheless, we think the document should be considered a step in the right direction, an approach toward the establishment of a juridical and political ordering of the world community. It is a solemn recognition of the personal dignity of every human being; an assertion of everyone's right to be free to seek out the truth, to follow moral principles, discharge the duties imposed by justice, and lead a fully human life. It also recognized other rights connected with these.

145. It is therefore our earnest wish that the United Nations Organization may be able progressively to adapt its structure and methods of operation to the magnitude and nobility of its tasks. May the day be not long delayed when every human being can find in this organization an effective safeguard of his personal rights; those rights, that is, which derive directly from his dignity as a human person, and which are therefore universal, inviolable and inalienable. This is all the more desirable in that men today are taking an ever more active part in the public life of their own nations, and in doing so they are showing an increased interest in the affairs of all peoples. They are becoming more and more conscious of being living members of the universal family of mankind.

From *Proclaiming Justice and Peace: Papal Documents from Rerum Novarum through Centesimus Annus,* edited by Michael Walsh and Brian Davies (Mystic, Conn.: Twenty-Third Publications, 1991), pp. 148–51. Copyright © 1991 by compilation CAFOD. Copyright © 1991 introduction Michael J. Walsh.

60.   Vatican II, *Guadium et Spes*

The Second Vatican Council (1962–65) issued a series of declarations marking a watershed in twentieth-century Roman Catholic history. Not least of these was the declaration "The Church in the Modern World" (Guadium et Spes), which addresses a variety of social and cultural issues.

Chapter 2. ¶53. Man comes to a true and full humanity only through culture, that is through the cultivation of the goods and values of nature. Wherever human life is involved, therefore, nature and culture are quite intimately connected one with the other. . . .

54. The circumstances of the life of modern man have been so profoundly changed in their social and cultural aspect, that we can speak of a new age of human history. New ways are open, therefore, for the perfection and the further extension of culture. These ways have been prepared by the enormous growth of natural, human and social sciences, by technical progress, and advances in developing and organizing means whereby men can communicate with one another. Hence the culture of today possesses particular characteristics: sciences which are called exact greatly develop critical judgement; the more recent psychological studies more profoundly explain human activity; historical studies make it much easier to see things in their mutable and evolutionary aspects; customs and usages are becoming more and more uniform; industrialization, urbanization, and other causes which promote community living create a mass-culture from which are born new ways of thinking, acting and making use of leisure. The increase of commerce between the various nations and groups of men opens more widely to all the treasures of different civilizations and thus, little by little, there develops a more universal form of human culture, which better promotes and expresses the unity of the human race to the degree that it preserves the particular aspects of the different civilizations.

55. From day to day, in every group or nation, there is an increase in the number of men and women who are conscious that they themselves are the authors and the artisans of the culture of their community. Throughout the whole world there is a mounting increase in the sense of autonomy as well as of responsibility. This is of paramount importance for the spiritual and moral maturity of the human race. This becomes more clear if we consider the unification of the world and the duty which is imposed upon us, that we build a better world based upon truth and justice. Thus we are witnesses of the birth of a new humanism, one in which man is defined first of all by this responsibility to his brothers and to history. . . .

57.2. Furthermore, when man gives himself to the various disciplines of philosophy, history and of mathematical and natural sciences, and when he cultivates the arts, he can do very much to elevate the human family to a more sublime understanding of truth, goodness, and beauty, and to the formation of considered opinions which have universal value. Thus mankind may be more clearly enlightened by that marvellous wisdom which was with God from all eternity, composing all things with him, rejoicing in the earth, delighting in the sons of men.

57.3. In this way, the human spirit, being less subjected to material things, can be more easily drawn to the worship and contemplation of the creator. Moreover, by the impulse of grace, he is disposed to acknowledge the Word of God, who before he became flesh in order to save all and to sum up all in himself was already 'in the world' as 'the true light which enlightens every man' (John 1:9–10). . . .

58.3. The gospel of Christ constantly renews the life and culture of fallen man; it combats and removes the errors and evils resulting from the permanent allurement of sin. It never ceases to purify and elevate the morality of peoples. By riches coming from above, it makes fruitful, as it were from within, the spiritual qualities and traditions of every people and of every age. It strengthens, perfects and restores them in Christ. Thus the Church, in the very fulfilment of her own function stimulates and advances human and civic culture; by her action, also by her liturgy, she leads men toward interior liberty.

59. For the above reasons, the Church recalls to the mind of all that culture is to be subordinated to the integral perfection of the human person, to the good of the community and of the whole society. Therefore it is necessary to develop the human faculties in such a way that there results a growth of the faculty of wonder, of intuition, of contemplation, of making personal judgement, of developing a religious, moral and social sense.

59.1. Culture, because it flows immediately from the spiritual and social character of man, has constant need of a just freedom in order to develop; it needs also the legitimate possibility of exercising its autonomy according to its own principles. It therefore rightly demands respect and enjoys a certain inviolability within the limits of the common good, as long, of course, as it preserves the rights of the individual and the community, whether particular or universal. . . .

60. It is now possible to free most of humanity from the misery of ignorance. Therefore the duty most consonant with our times, especially for Christians, is that of working diligently for fundamental decisions to be taken in economic and political affairs, both on the national and international level, which will everywhere recognize and satisfy the right of all to a human and social culture in conformity with the dignity of the human person without any discrimination based on race, sex, nation, religion or social condition. Therefore it is necessary to provide all with a sufficient quantity of cultural benefits, especially of those which constitute the so-called basic culture lest very many be prevented from co-operating in the promotion of the common good in a truly human manner because of illiteracy and a lack of responsible activity.

60.1. We must strive to provide for those men who are gifted the possibility of pursuing higher studies; and in such a way that, as far as possible, they may occupy in society those duties, offices and services which are in harmony with their natural aptitude and the competence they have acquired. Thus each man and the social groups of every people will be able to attain the full development of their culture in conformity with their qualities and traditions.

60.2. Everything must be done to make everyone conscious of the right to culture and the duty he has of developing himself culturally and of helping others. Sometimes there exist conditions of life and of work which impede the cultural striving of men and destroy in them the eagerness for culture. This is especially true of farmers and workers. It is necessary to provide for them those working conditions which will not impede their human culture but rather favour it. Women now engage in almost all spheres of activity. It is fitting that they are able to assume their proper role in accordance with their own nature. It is incumbent upon all to acknowledge and favour the proper and necessary participation of women in cultural life.

61. Today it is more difficult to form a synthesis of the various disciplines of knowledge and the arts than it was formerly. For while the mass and the diversity of cultural factors are increasing, there is a decrease in each man's faculty of perceiving and unifying these things, so that the image of 'universal man' is being lost sight of more and more. Nevertheless it remains each man's duty to preserve an understanding of the whole human person in which the values of intellect, will, conscience and fraternity are pre-eminent. These values are all rooted in God the creator and have been wonderfully restored and elevated in Christ.

61.1. The family is, as it were, the primary mother and nurse of this education. There, the children, in an atmosphere of love, more easily learn the correct order of things, while proper forms of human culture impress themselves in an almost unconscious manner upon the mind of the developing adolescent.

61.2. Opportunities for the same education are to be found also in the societies of today, due especially to the increased circulation of books and to the new means of cultural and social communication which can foster a universal culture. With the more or less universal reduction of working hours, the leisure time of most men has increased. May this leisure be used properly to relax, to fortify the health of soul and body through spontaneous study and activity, through tourism which refines man's character and enriches him with understanding of others, through sports activity which helps to preserve an equilibrium of spirit even in the community, and to establish fraternal relations among men of all conditions, nations and races. Let Christians co-operate so that the cultural manifestations and collective activity characteristic of our time may be imbued with a human and a Christian spirit.

61.3. All these leisure activities however cannot bring man to a full cultural development unless there is at the same time a profound inquiry into the meaning of culture and science for the human person.

62. Although the Church has contributed much to the development of culture, experience shows that, because of circumstances, it is sometimes difficult to harmonize culture with Christian teaching.

62.1. These difficulties do not necessarily harm the life of faith, rather they can stimulate the mind to a deeper and more accurate understanding of the faith. The recent studies and findings of science, history and philosophy raise new questions which affect life and which demand new theological investigations. Furthermore, theologians, observing the requirements and methods proper to theology, are invited to seek continually for more suitable ways of communicating doctrine to the men of their times; for the deposit of faith or the truths are one thing and the manner in which they are enunciated, in the same meaning and understanding, is another. In pastoral care, sufficient use must be made not only of theological principles, but also of the findings of the secular sciences, especially of psychology and sociology, so that the faithful may be brought to a more adequate and mature life of faith.

62.2. Literature and the arts are also, in their own way, of great importance to the life of the Church. They strive to make known the proper nature of man, his problems and his experiences in trying to know and perfect both himself and the world. They have much to do with revealing man's place in history and in the world; with illustrating the miseries and joys, the needs and strengths of man and with foreshadowing a better life for him. Thus they are able to elevate human life, expressed in manifold forms in various times and places.

62.3. Efforts must be made so that those who foster these arts feel that the Church recognizes their activity and so that, enjoying orderly freedom, they may initiate more friendly relations with the Christian community. The Church acknowledges also new forms of art which are adapted to our age and are in keeping with the characteristics of various nations and regions. They may be brought into the sanctuary since they raise the mind to God, once the manner of expression is adapted and they are conformed to liturgical requirements.

62.4. Thus the knowledge of God is better manifested and the preaching of the gospel becomes clearer to human intelligence and shows itself to be relevant to man's actual conditions of life.

62.5. May the faithful, therefore, live in very close union with the other men of their time and judging, as expressed in their culture. Let them blend new sciences and theories and the understanding of the most recent discoveries with Christian morality and the teaching of Christian doctrine, so that their religious culture and morality may keep pace with their scientific knowledge and with the constantly progressing technology. Thus they will be able to interpret and evaluate all things in a truly Christian spirit.

62.6. Let those who teach theology in seminaries and universities strive to collaborate with men versed in the other sciences through a sharing of their resources and points of view. Theological inquiry should pursue a profound understanding of revealed truth; at the same time it should not neglect close contact with its own time that it may be able to help those men skilled in various disciplines to attain to a better understanding of the faith. This common effort will greatly aid the formation of priests, who will be able to present to our contemporaries the doctrine of the Church concerning God, man and the world, in a manner more adapted to them so that they may receive it more willingly. Furthermore, it is to be hoped that many of the laity will receive a sufficient formation in the sacred sciences and that some will dedicate themselves professionally to these studies, developing and deepening them by their own labours. In order that they may fulfil their function, let it be recognized that all the faithful, whether clerics or laity, possess a lawful freedom of inquiry, freedom of thought and of expressing their mind with humility and fortitude in those matters on which they enjoy competence.

Chapter 3. ¶63. In the economic and social realms, too, the dignity and complete vocation of the human person and the welfare of society as a whole are to be respected and promoted. For man is the source, the centre, and the purpose of all economic and social life.

63.1. Like other areas of social life, the economy of today is marked by man's increasing domination over nature, by closer and more intense relationships between citizens, groups, and countries and their mutual dependence, and by the increased intervention of the State. At the same time progress in the methods of production and in the exchange of goods and services has made the economy an instrument capable of better meeting the intensified needs of the human family.

63.2. Reasons for anxiety, however, are not lacking. Many people, especially in economically advanced areas, seem, as it were, to be ruled by economics, so that almost their entire personal and social life is permeated with a certain economic way of thinking. Such is true both of nations that favour a collective economy and of others. At the very time when the development of economic life could mitigate social inequalities (provided that it be guided and co-ordinated in a reasonable and human way), it is often made to embitter them; or, in some places, it even results in a decline of the social status of the underprivileged and in contempt for the poor. While an immense number of people still lack the absolute necessities of life, some, even in less advanced areas, live in luxury or squander wealth. Extravagance and wretchedness exist side by side. While a few enjoy very great power of choice, the majority are deprived of almost all possibility of acting on their own initiative and responsibility, and often subsist in living and working conditions unworthy of the human person.

63.3. A similar lack of economic and social balance is to be noticed between agriculture, industry, and the services, and also between different parts of one and the same country. The contrast between the economically more advanced countries and other countries is becoming more serious day by day, and the very peace of the world can be jeopardized thereby.

63.4. Our contemporaries are coming to feel these inequalities with an ever sharper awareness, since they are thoroughly convinced that the ampler technical and economic possibilities which the world of today enjoys can and should correct this unhappy state of affairs. Hence, many reforms in the socio-economic realm and a change of mentality and attitude are required for all. For this reason the Church down through the centuries and in the light of the gospel has worked out the principles of justice and equity demanded by right reason both for individual and social life and for international life, and has proclaimed them especially in recent times. This sacred council intends to strengthen these principles according to the circumstances of this age and to set forth certain guidelines, especially with regard to the requirements of economic development.

64. Today more than ever before attention is rightly given to the increase of the production of agricultural and industrial goods and of the rendering of services, for the purpose of making provision for the growth of population and of satisfying the increasing desires of the human race. Therefore, technical progress, an inventive spirit, an eagerness to create and to expand enterprises, the application of methods of production, and the strenuous efforts of all who engage in production—in a word, all the elements making for such development—must be promoted. The fundamental purpose of this production is not the mere increase of products nor profit or control but rather the service of man, and indeed of the whole man with regard for the full range of his material needs and the demands of his intellectual, moral, spiritual, and religious life; this applies to every man whatsoever and to every group of men, of every race and of every part of the world. Consequently, economic activity is to be carried on according to its own methods and laws within the limits of the moral order, so that God's plan for mankind may be realized.

65. Economic development must remain under man's determination and must not be left to the judgement of a few men or groups possessing too much economic power or of the political community alone or of certain more powerful nations. It is necessary, on the contrary, that at every level the largest possible number of people and, when it is a question of international relations, all nations have an active share in directing that development. There is need as well of the co-ordination and fitting and harmonious combination of the spontaneous efforts of individuals and of free groups with the undertakings of public authorities.

65.1. Growth is not to be left solely to a kind of mechanical course of economic activity of individuals, nor to the authority of government. For this reason, doctrines which obstruct the necessary reforms under the guise of a false liberty, and those which subordinate the basic rights of individual persons and groups to the collective organization of production must be shown to be erroneous. . . .

66. To satisfy the demands of justice and equity, strenuous efforts must be made, without disregarding the rights of persons or the natural qualities of each country, to remove as quickly as possible the immense economic inequalities, which now exist and in many cases are growing and which are connected with individual and social discrimination. Likewise, in many areas, in view of the special difficulties of agriculture relative to the raising and selling of produce, country people must be helped both to increase and to market what they produce, and to introduce the necessary development and renewal and also obtain a fair income. Otherwise, as too often happens, they will remain in the condition of lower-class citizens. Let farmers themselves, especially young ones, apply themselves to perfecting their professional skill, for without it, there can be no agricultural advance.

66.1. Justice and equity likewise require that the mobility which is necessary in a developing economy be regulated in such a way as to keep the life of individuals and their families from becoming insecure and precarious. When workers come from another country or district and contribute to the economic advancement of a nation or region by their labour, all discrimination as regards wages and working conditions must be carefully avoided. All the people, moreover, above all the public authorities, must treat them not as mere tools of production but as persons, and must help them to bring their families to live with them and to provide themselves with a decent dwelling; they must also see to it that these workers are incorporated into the social life of the country or region that receives them. Employment opportunities, however, should be created in their own areas as far as possible.

66.2. In economic affairs which today are subject to change, as in the new forms of industrial society in which automation, for example, is advancing, care must be taken that sufficient and suitable work and the possibility of the appropriate technical and professional formation are furnished. The livelihood and the human dignity especially of those who are in very difficult conditions because of illness or old age must be guaranteed.

67. Human labour which is expended in the production and exchange of goods or in the performance of economic services is superior to the other elements of economic life, for the latter have only the nature of tools.

67.1. This labour, whether it is engaged in independently or hired by someone else, comes immediately from the person, who as it were stamps the things of nature with his seal and subdues them to his will. By his labour a man ordinarily supports himself and his family, is joined to his fellow men and serves them, and can exercise genuine charity and be a partner in the work of bringing divine creation to perfection. Indeed, we hold that through labour offered to God man is associated with the redemptive work of Jesus Christ, who conferred an eminent dignity on labour when at Nazareth he worked with his own hands. From this there follows for every man the duty of working faithfully and also the right to work. It is the duty of society, moreover, according to the circumstances prevailing in it, and in keeping with its role, to help the citizens to find sufficient employment. Finally, remuneration for labour is to be such that man may be furnished the means to cultivate worthily his own material, social, cultural, and spiritual life and that of his dependants, in view of the function and productiveness of each one, the conditions of the factory or workshop, and the common good.

67.2. Since economic activity for the most part implies the associated work of human beings, any way of organizing and directing it which might be detrimental to any working men and women would be wrong and inhuman. It happens too often, however, even in our days, that workers are reduced to the level of being slaves to their own work. This is by no means justified by the so-called economic laws. The entire process of productive work, therefore, must be adapted to the needs of the person and to his way of life, above all to his domestic life, especially in respect to mothers of families, always with due regard for sex and age. The opportunity, moreover, should be granted to workers to unfold their own abilities and personality through the performance of their work. Applying their time and strength to their employment with a due sense of responsibility, they should also all enjoy sufficient rest and leisure to cultivate their familial, cultural, social and religious life. They should also have the opportunity freely to develop the energies and potentialities which perhaps they cannot bring to much fruition in their professional work. . . .

68.1. Among the basic rights of the human person is to be numbered the right of freely founding unions for working people. These should be able truly to represent them and to contribute to the organizing of economic life in the right way. Included is the right of freely taking part in the activity of these unions without risk of reprisal. Through this orderly participation joined to progressive economic and social formation, all will grow day by day in the awareness of their own function and responsibility, and thus they will be brought to feel that they are comrades in the whole task of economic development and in the attainment of the universal common good according to their capacities and aptitudes.

68.2. When, however, socio-economic disputes arise, efforts must be made to come to a peaceful settlement. Although recourse must always be had first to a sincere dialogue between the parties, the strike, nevertheless, can remain even in present-day circumstances a necessary, though ultimate, means for the defence of the workers' own rights and fulfillment of their just desires. As soon as possible, however, ways should be sought to resume negotiations and discussions leading towards reconciliation.

69. God intended the earth with everything contained in it for the use of all human beings and peoples. Thus, under the guidance of justice together with charity, created goods should be in abundance for all in an equitable manner. Whatever the forms of property may be, as adapted to the legitimate institutions of peoples, according to diverse and changeable circumstances, attention must always be paid to this universal goal of earthly goods. In using them, therefore, man should regard the external things that he legitimately possesses not only as his own but also as common in the sense that they should be able to benefit not only him but also others as well. On the other hand, the right of having a share of earthly goods sufficient for oneself and one's family belongs to everyone. The fathers and doctors of the Church held this opinion, teaching that men are obliged to come to the relief of the poor and to do so not merely out of their superfluous goods. If one is in extreme necessity, he has the right to procure for himself what he needs out of the riches of others. Since there are so many people prostrate with hunger in the world, this sacred council urges all, both individuals and governments to remember the aphorism of the fathers, 'Feed the man dying of hunger, because if you have not fed him, you have killed him,' and really to share and use their earthly goods, according to the ability of each, especially by supporting individuals or peoples with the aid by which they may be able to help and develop themselves.

69.1. In economically less advanced societies the common destination of earthly goods is partly satisfied by means of the customs and traditions proper to the community, by which the absolute essentials are furnished to each member. An effort must be made, however, to avoid regarding certain customs as altogether unchangeable, if they no longer answer the new needs of this age. On the other hand, imprudent action should not be taken against respectable customs which, provided they are suitably adapted to present-day circumstances, do not cease to be very useful. Similarly in highly developed nations a body of social institutions dealing with protection and security can, for its own part, bring to reality the common destination of earthly goods. Family and social services, especially those that provide for culture and education, should be further promoted. When all these things are being organized, vigilance is necessary to prevent the citizens from being led into a certain inertia vis-à-vis society or from rejecting the burden of taking up office or from refusing to serve. . . .

71. Since property and other forms of private ownership of external goods contribute to the expression of the personality, and since, moreover, they furnish one an occasion to exercise his function in society and in the economy, it is very important that the access of both individuals and communities to some ownership of external goods be fostered.

71.1. Private property or some ownership of external goods confers on everyone a sphere wholly necessary for the autonomy of the person and the family, and it should be regarded as an extension of human freedom. Lastly, since it adds incentives for carrying on one's function and duty, it constitutes one of the conditions for civil liberties.

71.2. The forms of such ownership of property are varied today and are becoming increasingly diversified. They all remain, however, a cause of security not to be underestimated, in spite of social funds, rights, and services provided by society. This is true not only of material goods but also of intangible goods such as professional skills.

71.3. The right of private ownership, however, is not opposed to the right inherent in various forms of public property. Goods can be transferred to the public domain only by the competent authority, according to the demands and within the limits of the common good, and with fair compensation. Furthermore, it is the right of public authority to prevent anyone from misusing his private property to the detriment of the common good.

71.4. By its very nature private property has a social quality which is based on the law of the common destination of earthly goods. If this social quality is overlooked, property often becomes an occasion of a passionate desire for wealth and serious disturbances, so that a pretext is given to those who attack private property for calling the right itself into question. . . .

Chapter 5. ¶78. Peace is not merely the absence of war; nor can it be reduced solely to the maintenance of a balance of power between enemies; nor is it brought about by dictatorship. Instead, it is rightly and appropriately called an enterprise of justice ([Isa.] 32:7). Peace results from that order structured into human society by its divine founder, and actualized by men as they thirst after ever greater justice. The common good of humanity finds its ultimate meaning in the eternal law. But since the concrete demands of this common good are constantly changing as time goes on, peace is never attained once and for all, but must be built up ceaselessly. Moreover, since the human will is unsteady and wounded by sin, the achievement of peace requires a constant mastering of passions and the vigilance of lawful authority.

78.1. But this is not enough. This peace on earth cannot be obtained unless personal well-being is safeguarded and men freely and trustingly share with one another the riches of their inner spirits and their talents. A firm determination to respect other men and peoples and their dignity, as well as the studied practice of brotherhood are absolutely necessary for the establishment of peace. Hence peace is likewise the fruit of love, which goes beyond what justice can provide.

78.2. That earthly peace which arises from love of neighbour symbolizes and results from the peace of Christ which radiates from God the father.

For by the cross the incarnate son, the prince of peace reconciled all men with God. By thus restoring all men to the unity of one people and one body, he slew hatred in his own flesh; and, after being lifted on high by his resurrection, he poured forth the spirit of love into the hearts of men.

78.3. For this reason, all Christians are urgently summoned to do in love what the truth requires (Eph. 4:15), and to join with all true peacemakers in pleading for peace and bringing it about.

78.4. Motivated by this same spirit, we cannot fail to praise those who renounce the use of violence in the vindication of their rights and who resort to methods of defence which are otherwise available to weaker parties too, provided this can be done without injury to the rights and duties of others or of the community itself.

78.5. In so far as men are sinful, the threat of war hangs over them, and hang over them it will until the return of Christ. But in so far as men vanquish sin by a union of love, they will vanquish violence as well and make these words come true: 'They shall turn their swords into plough-shares, and their spears into sickles. Nation shall not lift up sword against nation, neither shall they learn war any more' ([Isa.] 2:4).

79. In spite of the fact that recent wars have wrought physical and moral havoc on our world, war produces its devastation day by day in some part of the world. Indeed, now that every kind of weapon produced by modern science is used in war, the fierce character of warfare threatens to lead the combatants to a savagery far surpassing that of the past. Furthermore, the complexity of the modern world and the intricacy of international relations allow guerrilla warfare to be carried on by new methods of deceit and subversion. In many cases the use of terrorism is regarded as a new way to wage war.

79.1. Contemplating this melancholy state of humanity, the council wishes, above all things else, to recall the permanent binding force of universal natural law and its all-embracing principles. Man's conscience itself gives ever more emphatic voice to these principles. Therefore, actions which deliberately conflict with these same principles, as well as orders commanding such actions, are criminal, and blind obedience cannot excuse those who yield to them. The most infamous among these are actions designed for the methodical extermination of an entire people, nation or ethnic minority. Such actions must be vehemently condemned as horrendous crimes. The courage of those who fearlessly and openly resist those who issue such commands merits the highest commendation.

79.2. On the subject of war, quite a large number of nations have subscribed to international agreements aimed at making military activity and its consequences less inhuman. Their stipulations deal with such matters as the treatment of wounded soldiers and prisoners. Agreements of this sort must be honoured. Indeed they should be improved upon so that the frightfulness of war can be better and more workably held in check. All men, especially government officials and experts in these matters, are bound to do everything they can to effect these improvements. Moreover, it seems right that laws make humane provisions for the case of those who for reasons of conscience refuse to bear arms, provided however, that they agree to serve the human community in some other way.

79.3. Certainly, war has not been rooted out of human affairs. As long as the danger of war remains and there is no competent and sufficiently powerful authority at the international level, governments cannot be denied the right to legitimate defence once every means of peaceful settlement has been exhausted. Government authorities and others who share public responsibility have the duty to conduct such grave matters soberly and to protect the welfare of the people entrusted to their care. But it is one thing to undertake military action for the just defence of the people, and something else again to seek the subjugation of other nations. Nor, by the same token, does the mere fact that war has unhappily begun mean that all is fair between the warring parties.

79.4. Those too who devote themselves to the military service of their country should regard themselves as the agents of security and freedom of peoples. As long as they fulfil this role properly, they are making a genuine contribution to the establishment of peace.

80. The horror and perversity of war is immensely magnified by the increase in the number of scientific weapons. For acts of war involving these weapons can inflict massive and indiscriminate destruction, thus going far beyond the bounds of legitimate defence. Indeed, if the kind of instruments which can now be found in the armouries of the great nations were to be employed to their fullest, an almost total and altogether reciprocal slaughter of each side by the other would follow, not to mention the widespread devastation that would take place in the world and the deadly after-effects that would be spawned by the use of weapons of this kind.

80.1. All these considerations compel us to undertake an evaluation of war with an entirely new attitude. The men of our time must realize that they will have to give a sombre reckoning of their deeds of war for the course of the future will depend greatly on the decisions they make today.

80.2. With these truths in mind, this most holy synod makes its own the condemnations of total war already pronounced by recent popes, and issues the following declaration:

80.3. Any act of war aimed indiscriminately at the destruction of entire cities or extensive areas along with their population is a crime against God and man himself. It merits unequivocal and unhesitating condemnation.

80.4. The unique hazard of modern warfare consists in this: it provides those who possess modern scientific weapons with a kind of occasion for perpetrating just such abominations; moreover, through a certain inexorable chain of events, it can catapult men into the most atrocious decisions. That such may never happen in the future, the bishops of the whole world gathered together beg all men, especially government officials and military leaders, to give unremitting thought to their tremendous responsibility before God and the entire human race. . . .

82. It is our clear duty, therefore, to strain every muscle in working for the time when all war can be completely outlawed by international consent. This goal undoubtedly requires the establishment of some universal public authority acknowledged as such by all and endowed with the power to safeguard on the behalf of all, security, regard for justice, and respect for rights. But before this hoped-for authority can be set up, the highest existing international centres must devote themselves vigorously to the pursuit of better means for obtaining common security. Since peace must be born of mutual trust between nations and not be imposed on them through fear of the available weapons, everyone must labour to put an end at last to the arms race, and to make a true beginning of disarmament, not unilaterally indeed, but proceeding at an equal pace according to agreement, and backed up by adequate and workable safeguards. . . .

83. In order to build up peace the causes of discord among men, especially injustice, which foment wars must above all be rooted out. Not a few of these causes come from excessive economic inequalities and from putting off the steps needed to remedy them. Other causes of discord, however, have their source in the desire to dominate and in a contempt for persons. And, if we look for deeper causes, we find them in human envy, distrust, pride, and other egotistical passions. Man cannot bear so many ruptures in the harmony of things. Consequently, the world is constantly beset by strife and violence between men, even when no war is being waged. Besides, since these same evils are present in the relations between various nations as well, in order to overcome or forestall them and to keep violence once unleashed within limits, it is absolutely necessary for countries to co-operate to better advantage, to work together more closely, and jointly to organize international bodies and to work tirelessly for the creation of organizations which will foster peace.

84. In view of the increasingly close ties of mutual dependence today between all the inhabitants and peoples of the earth, the fitting pursuit and effective realization of the universal common good now require of the community of nations that it organize itself in a manner suited to its present responsibilities, especially towards the many parts of the world which are still suffering from unbearable want.

84.1. To reach this goal, organizations of the international community, for their part, must make provision for men's different needs, both in the fields of social life—such as food supplies, health, education, labour—and also in certain special circumstances which can crop up here and there, e.g., the need to promote the general improvement of developing countries, or to alleviate the distressing conditions in which refugees dispersed throughout the world find themselves, or also to assist migrants and their families. . . .

85. The present solidarity of mankind also calls for a revival of greater international co-operation in the economic field. Although nearly all peoples have become autonomous, they are far from being free of every form of undue dependence, and far from escaping all danger of serious internal difficulties. . . .

85.2. If an authentic economic order is to be established on a world-wide basis, an end will have to be put to profiteering, to national ambition, to the appetite for political supremacy, to militaristic calculations, and to machinations for the purpose of spreading and imposing ideologies.

86. The following norms seem useful for such co-operation:

86.1 (a) Developing nations should take great pains to seek as the object of progress to express and secure the total human fulfillment of their citizens. They should bear in mind that progress arises and grows above all out of the labour and genius of the nations themselves because it has to be based, not only on foreign aid, but especially on the full utilization of their own resources, and on the development of their own culture and traditions. Those who exert the greatest influence on others should be outstanding in this respect.

86.2 (b) On the other hand, it is a very important duty of the advanced nations to help the developing nations in discharging their above-mentioned responsibilities. They should therefore gladly carry out on their own home front those spiritual and material readjustments that are required for the realization of this universal co-operation. Consequently, in business dealings with weaker and poorer nations, they should be careful to respect their welfare, for these countries need the income they receive on the sale of their homemade products to support themselves.

86.3 (c) It is the role of the international community to co-ordinate and promote development, but in such a way that the resources earmarked for this purpose will be allocated as effectively as possible, and with complete equity. It is likewise this community's duty, with due regard for the principle of subsidiarity, so to regulate economic relations throughout the world that these will be carried out in accordance with the norms of justice. Suitable organizations should be set up to foster and regulate international business affairs, particularly with the underdeveloped countries, and to compensate for losses resulting from an excessive inequality of power among the various nations. This type of organization, in unison with technical, cultural, and financial aid, should provide the help which developing nations need so that they can advantageously pursue their own economic advancement. . . .

87.1. Governments undoubtedly have rights and duties, within the limits of their proper competency, regarding the population problem in their respective countries, for instance, with regard to social- and family-life legislation, or with regard to information concerning the condition and needs of the country. Since men today are giving thought to this problem and are so greatly disturbed over it, it is desirable in addition that Catholic specialists, especially in the universities, skilfully pursue and develop studies and projects on all these matters.

87.2. But there are many today who maintain that the increase in world population, or at least the population increase in some countries, must be radically curbed by every means possible and by any kind of intervention on the part of public authority. In view of this contention, the council urges everyone to guard against solutions, whether publicly or privately supported, or at times even imposed, which are contrary to the moral law. For in keeping with man's inalienable right to marry and generate children, the decision concerning the number of children they will have depends on the correct judgement of the parents and it cannot in any way be left to the judgement of public authority. But since the judgement of the parents presupposes a rightly formed conscience, it is of the utmost importance that the way be open for everyone to develop a correct and genuinely human responsibility which respects the divine law and takes into consideration the circumstances of the place and the time. But sometimes this requires an improvement in educational and social conditions, and, above all, formation in religion or at least a complete moral training. Men should judiciously be informed, furthermore, of scientific advances in exploring methods whereby spouses can be helped in regulating the number of their children and whose safeness has been well proven and whose harmony with the moral order has been ascertained.

88. Christians should co-operate willingly and wholeheartedly in establishing an international order that includes a genuine respect for all freedoms and amicable brotherhoods between all. This is all the more pressing since the greater part of the world is still suffering from so much poverty that it is as if Christ himself were crying out in these poor to beg the charity of the disciples. Do not let men then be scandalized because some countries with a majority of citizens who are counted as Christians have an abundance of wealth, whereas others are deprived of the necessities of life and are tormented with hunger, disease, and every kind of misery. The spirit of poverty and charity are the glory and witness of the Church of Christ.

88.1. Those Christians are to be praised and supported, therefore, who volunteer their services to help other men and nations. Indeed, it is the duty of the whole people of God, following the word and example of the bishops, to alleviate as far as they are able the sufferings of the modern age. They should do this too, as was the ancient custom in the Church, out of the substance of their goods, and not only out of what is superfluous.

88.2. The procedure of collecting and distributing aid, without being inflexible and completely uniform, should nevertheless be carried out in an orderly fashion in dioceses, nations, and throughout the entire world. Wherever it seems fitting, this activity of Catholics should be carried on in unison with other Christian brothers. For the spirit of charity does not forbid, but on the contrary commands that charitable activity be carried out in a careful and orderly manner. Therefore, it is essential for those who intend to dedicate themselves to the service of the developing nations to be properly trained in appropriate institutes. . . .

91. Drawn from the treasures of church teaching, the proposals of this sacred synod look to the assistance of every man of our time, whether he believes in God, or does not explicitly recognize him. If adopted, they will promote among men a sharper insight into their full destiny, and thereby lead them to fashion the world more to man's surpassing dignity, to search for a brotherhood which is universal and more deeply rooted, and to meet the urgencies of our age with a gallant and unified effort born of love.

91.2. Undeniably this conciliar programme is but a general one in several of its parts; and deliberately so, given the immense variety of situations and forms of human culture in the world. Indeed while it presents teaching already accepted in the Church, the programme will have to be followed up and amplified since it sometimes deals with matters in a constant state of development. Still, we have relied on the word of God and the spirit of the gospel. Hence we entertain the hope that many of our proposals will prove to be of substantial benefit to everyone, especially after they have been adapted to individual nations and mentalities by the faithful, under the guidance of their pastors.

92. By virtue of her mission to shed on the whole world the radiance of the gospel message, and to unify under one spirit all men of whatever nation, race or culture, the Church stands forth as a sign of that brotherhood which facilitates and invigorates sincere dialogue.

92.1. Such a mission requires in the first place that we foster within the Church itself mutual esteem, reverence and harmony, through the full recognition of lawful diversity. Thus all those who compose the one people of God, both pastors and the general faithful, can engage in dialogue with ever increasing effectiveness. For the bonds which unite the faithful are mightier than anything dividing them. Hence, let there be unity in essentials; freedom in doubtful matters; and in all things charity.

92.2. Our hearts embrace also those brothers and communities not yet living with us in full communion; to them we are linked nonetheless by our profession of the Father and Son and the Holy Spirit, and by the bond of charity. We are not unmindful of the fact that the unity of Christians is today awaited and desired by many, too, who do not believe in Christ; for the further it advances toward truth and love under the powerful impulse of the Holy Spirit, the more this unity will be a harbinger of unity and peace for the world at large. Therefore, by common effort and in ways which are today increasingly appropriate for seeking this splendid goal effectively, let us take pains to pattern ourselves after the gospel more exactly every day, and thus work as brothers in rendering service to the human family. For, in Christ Jesus this family is constituted to the family of the sons of God.

92.3. We think cordially too of all who acknowledge God, and who preserve in their traditions precious elements of religion and humanity. We want frank conversation to compel us all to receive the impulses of the Spirit faithfully and to act on them energetically.

92.4. For our part, the desire for such dialogue, which can lead to truth through love alone, excludes no one, though an appropriate measure of prudence must undoubtedly be exercised. We include those who cultivate outstanding qualities of the human spirit, but do not yet acknowledge the source of these qualities. We include those who oppress the Church and harass her in manifold ways. Since God the Father is the origin and purpose of all men, we are all called to be brothers. Therefore, if we have been summoned to the same destiny, human and divine, we can and we should work together without violence and deceit in order to build up the world in genuine peace.

From *Proclaiming Justice and Peace: Papal Documents from Rerum Novarum through Centesimus Annus,* edited by Michael Walsh and Brian Davies (Mystic, Conn.: Twenty-Third Publications, 1991), pp. 192–205, 210–19. Copyright © 1991 by compilation CAFOD. Copyright 1991 © introduction Michael J. Walsh.

61.   Pope John Paul II,
Veritatis Splendor

In this 1993 discussion of ethical method, John Paul II is especially critical of ethical consequentialism—judging acts principally on the basis of their consequences. He takes the occasion to reiterate long-standing papal condemnation of artificial contraception, abortion, and euthanasia as well as economic exploitation.

72. The morality of acts is defined by the relationship of man's freedom with the authentic good. This good is established as the eternal law by divine wisdom, which orders every being toward its end: This eternal law is known both by man's natural reason (hence it is "natural law"), and—in an integral and perfect way—by God's supernatural revelation (hence it is called "divine law"). Acting is morally good when the choices of freedom are in conformity with man's true good and thus express the voluntary ordering of the person toward his ultimate end: God himself, the supreme good in whom man finds his full and perfect happiness.

. . . Only the act in conformity with the good can be a path that leads to life.

The rational ordering of the human act to the good in its truth and the voluntary pursuit of that good, known by reason, constitute morality. Hence human activity cannot be judged as morally good merely because it is a means for attaining one or another of its goals or simply because the subject's intention is good. Activity is morally good when it attests to and expresses the voluntary ordering of the person to his ultimate end and the conformity of a concrete action with the human good as it is acknowledged in its truth by reason. If the object of the concrete action is not in harmony with the true good of the person, the choice of that action makes our will and ourselves morally evil, thus putting us in conflict with our ultimate end, the supreme good, God himself. . . .

73. . . . Consequently the moral life has an essential "teleological" character, since it consists in the deliberate ordering of human acts to God, the supreme good and ultimate end (*telos*) of man. . . .

74. But on what does the moral assessment of man's free acts depend? What is it that ensures this ordering of human acts to God? Is it the intention of the acting subject, the circumstances—and in particular the consequences—of his action or the object itself of his act?

This is what is traditionally called the problem of the *sources of morality*. Precisely with regard to this problem there have emerged in the last few decades new or newly revived theological and cultural trends which call for careful discernment on the part of the church's magisterium.

Certain ethical theories, called *teleological*, claim to be concerned for the conformity of human acts with the ends pursued by the agent and with the values intended by him. The criteria for evaluating the moral rightness of an action are drawn from the weighing of the nonmoral or premoral goods to be gained and the corresponding nonmoral or premoral values to be respected. For some, concrete behavior would be right or wrong according as whether or not it is capable of producing a better state of affairs for all concerned. Right conduct would be the one capable of "maximizing" goods and "minimizing" evils.

Many of the Catholic moralists who follow in this direction seek to distance themselves from utilitarianism and pragmatism, where the morality of human acts would be judged without any reference to the man's true ultimate end. They rightly recognize the need to find ever more consistent rational arguments in order to justify the requirements and to provide a foundation for the norms of the moral life. This kind of investigation is legitimate and necessary, since the moral order, as established by the natural law, is in principle accessible to human reason. Furthermore, such investigation is well-suited to meeting the demands of dialogue and cooperation with non-Catholics and nonbelievers, especially in pluralistic societies.

75. But as part of the effort to work out such a rational morality (for this reason it is sometimes called an *autonomous morality*) there exist false solutions, linked in particular to an inadequate understanding of the object of moral action. Some authors do not take into sufficient consideration the fact that the will is involved in the concrete choices which it makes: These choices are a condition of its moral goodness and its being ordered to the ultimate end of the person. Others are inspired by a notion of freedom which prescinds from the actual conditions of its exercise, from its objective reference to the truth about the good, and from its determination through choices of concrete kinds of behavior. According to these theories, free will would neither be morally subjected to specific obligations nor shaped by its choices while nonetheless still remaining responsible for its own acts and for their consequences. . . .

76. . . . Such theories however are not faithful to the church's teaching when they believe they can justify as morally good deliberate choices of kinds of behavior contrary to the commandments of the divine and natural law. These theories cannot claim to be grounded in the Catholic moral tradition. Although the latter did witness the development of a casuistry which tried to assess the best ways to achieve the good in certain concrete situations, it is nonetheless true that this casuistry concerned only cases in which the law was uncertain, and thus the absolute validity of negative moral precepts, which oblige without exception, was not called into question. The faithful are obliged to acknowledge and respect the specific moral precepts declared and taught by the church in the name of God, the Creator and Lord. . . .

77. In order to offer rational criteria for a right moral decision, the theories mentioned above take account of the intention and consequences of human action. Certainly there is need to take into account both the intention—as Jesus forcefully insisted in clear disagreement with the scribes and Pharisees, who prescribed in great detail certain outward practices without paying attention to the heart [cf. Mark 7:20–21; Matt. 15:19]—and the goods obtained and the evils avoided as a result of a particular act. Responsibility demands as much. But the consideration of these consequences, and also of intentions, is not sufficient for judging the moral quality of a concrete choice. The weighing of the goods and evils foreseeable as the consequence of an action is not an adequate method for determining whether the choice of that concrete kind of behavior is "according to its species" or "in itself" morally good or bad, licit or illicit. The foreseeable consequences are part of those circumstances of the act which, while capable of lessening the gravity of an evil act, nonetheless cannot alter its moral species.

Moreover, everyone recognizes the difficulty, or rather the impossibility, of evaluating all the good and evil consequences and effects—defined as premoral—of one's own acts: An exhaustive rational calculation is not possible. How then can one go about establishing proportions which depend on a measuring, the criteria of which remain obscure? How could an absolute obligation be justified on the basis of such debatable calculations?

78. The morality of the human act depends primarily and fundamentally on the "object" rationally chosen by the deliberate will, as is borne out by the insightful analysis, still valid today, made by St. Thomas. In order to be able to grasp the object of an act which specifies that act morally, it is therefore necessary to place oneself in the perspective of the acting person. The object of the act of willing is in fact a freely chosen kind of behavior. To the extent that it is in conformity with the order of reason, it is the cause of the goodness of the will; it perfects us morally and disposes us to recognize our ultimate end in the perfect good, primordial love. By the object of a given moral act, then, one cannot mean a process or an event of the merely physical order, to be assessed on the basis of its ability to bring about a given state of affairs in the outside world. Rather, that object is the proximate end of a deliberate decision which determines the act of willing on the part of the acting person. Consequently, as the Catechism of the Catholic Church teaches, "there are certain specific kinds of behavior that are always wrong to choose, because choosing them involves a disorder of the will, that is, a moral evil." And St. Thomas observes that "it often happens that man acts with a good intention, but without spiritual gain, because he lacks a good will. Let us say that someone robs in order to feed the poor: In this case, even though the intention is good, the uprightness of the will is lacking. Consequently, no evil done with a good intention can be excused. 'There are those who say: And why not do evil that good may come? Their condemnation is just' (Rom. 3:8)."

The reason why a good intention is not itself sufficient, but a correct choice of actions is also needed, is that the human act depends on its object, whether that object is capable or not of being ordered to God, to the one who "alone is good," and thus brings about the perfection of the person. An act is therefore good if its object is in conformity with the good of the person with respect for the goods morally relevant for him. Christian ethics, which pays particular attention to the moral object, does not refuse to consider the inner "teleology" of acting inasmuch as it is directed to promoting the true good of the person; but it recognizes that it is really pursued only when the essential elements of human nature are respected. The human act, good according to its object, is also capable of being ordered to its ultimate end. That same act then attains its ultimate and decisive perfection when the will actually does order it to God through charity. . . .

79. One must therefore reject the thesis, characteristic of teleological and proportionalist theories, which holds that it is impossible to qualify as morally evil according to its species—its "object"—the deliberate choice of certain kinds of behavior or specific acts apart from a consideration of the intention for which the choice is made or the totality of the foreseeable consequences of that act for all persons concerned.

The primary and decisive element for moral judgment is the object of the human act, which establishes whether it is capable of being ordered to the good and to the ultimate end, which is God. This capability is grasped by reason in the very being of man, considered in his integral truth, and therefore in his natural inclinations, his motivations and his finalities, which always have a spiritual dimension as well. It is precisely these which are the contents of the natural law. . . .

80. Reason attests that there are objects of the human act which are by their nature "incapable of being ordered" to God, because they radically contradict the good of the person made in his image. These are the acts which, in the church's moral tradition, have been termed "intrinsically evil" (*intrinsece malum*): They are such always and per se, in other words, on account of their very object and quite apart from the ulterior intentions of the one acting and the circumstances. Consequently, without in the least denying the influence on morality exercised by circumstances and especially by intentions, the church teaches that "there exist acts which per se and in themselves, independently of circumstances, are always seriously wrong by reason of their object." The Second Vatican Council itself, in discussing the respect due to the human person, gives a number of examples of such acts:

"Whatever is hostile to life itself, such as any kind of homicide, genocide, abortion, euthanasia and voluntary suicide; whatever violates the integrity of the human person, such as mutilation, physical and mental torture and attempts to coerce the spirit; whatever is offensive to human dignity such as subhuman living conditions, arbitrary imprisonment, deportation, slavery, prostitution and trafficking in women and children; degrading conditions of work which treat laborers as mere instruments of profit, and not as free responsible persons: All these and the like are a disgrace, and so long as they infect human civilization they contaminate those who inflict them more than those who suffer injustice, and they are a negation of the honor due to the Creator."

With regard to intrinsically evil acts and in reference to contraceptive practices whereby the conjugal act is intentionally rendered infertile, Pope Paul VI teaches:

"Though it is true that sometimes it is lawful to tolerate a lesser moral evil in order to avoid a greater evil or in order to promote a greater good, it is never lawful even for the gravest reasons to do evil that good may come of it (cf. Rom. 3:8)—in other words, to intend directly something which of its very nature contradicts the moral order and which must therefore be judged unworthy of man, even though the intention is to protect or promote the welfare of an individual, of a family or of society in general."

81. In teaching the existence of intrinsically evil acts, the church accepts the teaching of Sacred Scripture. The apostle Paul emphatically states: "Do not be deceived: Neither the immoral, nor idolators, nor adulterers, nor sexual perverts, nor thieves, nor the greedy, nor drunkards, nor revilers, nor robbers will inherit the kingdom of God" (1 Cor. 6:9–10).

If acts are intrinsically evil, a good intention or particular circumstances can diminish their evil, but they cannot remove it. They remain "irremediably" evil acts; per se and in themselves they are not capable of being ordered to God and to the good of the person. "As for acts which are themselves sins" (*cum iam opera ipsa peccata sunt*), St. Augustine writes, "like theft, fornication, blasphemy, who would dare affirm that by doing them for good motives (*causis bonis*), they would no longer be sins or, what is even more absurd, that they would be sins that are justified?"

Consequently, circumstances or intentions can never transform an act intrinsically evil by virtue of its object into an act "subjectively" good or defensible as a choice.

82. Furthermore, an intention is good when it has as its aim the true good of the person in view of his ultimate end. But acts whose object is "not capable of being ordered" to God and "unworthy of the human person" are always and in every case in conflict with that good. Consequently, respect for norms which prohibit such acts and oblige *semper et pro semper*, that is, without any exception, not only does not inhibit a good intention, but actually represents its basic expression.

From Pope John Paul II, "Encyclical 'Veritatis Splendor'," *Origins* vol. 23, no. 18 (1993): 319–22.

62. *The Oxford Conference*

Meeting in 1937, the Oxford Conference on Life and Work was an important ecumenical precursor to the World Council of Churches. Including delegates from dozens of Protestant and Eastern Orthodox communions, the conference had the benefit of insight from the leading theologians and some of the leading social theorists of the day. Its response to the rise of totalitarianism in the 1930s is especially striking.

Section 2.¶3. . . . The supreme duty of the Churches in all countries as they face the present situation in the world of states and nations is to repent before God, not only by corporate acts of repentance, but by awakening the spirit of repentance in all their members: repentance for things done and things left undone. Judgment must begin at the house of God. If as Christians we are deeply disquieted by the political development of our age and our time, we have to acknowledge a large share of responsibility. We have not lived up to the word of our Lord, "Ye are the salt of the earth and the light of the world." We have not expressed our faith in the redeeming Cross of Christ in terms of our social relations. We have accepted without clear protest existing social divisions. In like manner we recognize that Churches have at times substituted for the true totalitarianism of Christ which requires that every activity and every relation should be subject to the Will of God a forced totalitarianism, political in character. They have too often been far more concerned for their own security and prestige in this world than for fulfilling their Lord's commission and serving mankind in the spirit of self-sacrificing love. We to-day acknowledge with deep humility our share in this guilt.

With repentance must go reconsecration. Penitence, if sincere, must bear fruit in action. We therefore resolve by God's grace to do our utmost to prevent the repetition of such sins in the future; to discharge our duties as citizens in the spirit of Christian love; and, so far as in us lies, to create a spirit which will enable the State to fulfil its God-given task of maintaining justice and ministering to the welfare of the people.

Section 3.¶1. . . . The Church as the trustee of God's redeeming Gospel and the State as the guarantor of order, justice, and civil liberty have distinct functions in regard to society. The Church's concern is to witness to men of the realities which outlast change because they are founded on the eternal Will of God. The concern of the State is to provide men with justice, order, and security in a world of sin and change. As it is the aim of the Church to create a community founded on divine love, it cannot do its work by coercion, nor must it compromise the standards embodied in God's commandments by surrender to the necessities of the day. The State, on the other hand, has the duty of maintaining public order, and therefore must use coercion and accept the limits of the practicable.

The distinctive character of the Church's activity is the free operation of grace and love. The distinctive character of the State's activity, whatever its constructive function in the cultural and social life may be, is the power of constraint, legal and physical. In consequence there are certain social activities which clearly belong to the Church, others which clearly belong to the State; there are, however, still others which may be performed by either Church or State. In this area tension is unavoidable and solutions will vary in varying historical circumstances. It is true that our Lord told His disciples to render to Caesar the things that are Caesar's and to God the things that are God's. But it is God who declares what is Caesar's. Therefore, whatever the choice may be, the Christian must always, whether as a member of the Church or as a citizen, obey the Will of God.

2. . . . The primary duty of the Church to the State is to be the Church, namely, to witness to God, to preach His Word, to confess the faith before men, to teach both young and old to observe the divine commandments, and to serve the nation and the State by proclaiming the Will of God as the supreme standard to which all human wills must be subject and all human conduct must conform. These functions of worship, preaching, teaching, and ministry the Church cannot renounce whether the State consent or not.

From this responsibility certain duties follow for the Churches and for their members.

a. With reference to the individual State:

(i)   That of praying for the State, its people and its government;

(ii)   That of loyalty and obedience to the State, disobedience becoming a duty only if obedience would be clearly contrary to the command of God;

(iii)   That of co-operation with the State in promoting the welfare of the citizens, and of lending moral support to the State when it upholds the standards of justice set forth in the Word of God;

(iv)   That of criticism of the State when it departs from those standards;

(v)   That of holding before men in all their legislation and administration those principles which make for the upholding of the dignity of man who is made in the image of God;

(vi)   That of permeating the public life with the spirit of Christ and of training up men and women who as Christians can contribute to this end.

These duties rest upon Christians not only as individuals redeemed by Christ who must witness for Him in whatever position they may occupy in the State, but also upon the Church as a Christian community. The Church can serve the State in no better way than by illustrating in its own life the kind of life which is God's Will for society as a whole. Only in the measure that it seeks to realize this mission is it in a position to rebuke the State for its sins and failures for which both individual Christians and the Church in its organized capacity have been in no small measure responsible.

b. With reference to the State in its relations to other States:

In the interpretation of these duties it is important to keep constantly in mind that as the Church in its own sphere is a universal society, so to Christian faith the individual State is not itself the ultimate political unit, but a member of a family of nations with international relations and duties which it is the responsibility not only of the individual Christians but also of the Churches to affirm and to promote.

3. . . . In a State which is Christian by profession it is self-evident that the Church should be free to the fullest extent to fulfil its function.

It should also be evident that where in such a State there are majority and minority Churches the same essential liberty to carry out the Church's function should be enjoyed by minorities as well as by the majority. All Churches should renounce the use of the coercive power of the State in matters of religion. Membership in a minority Church should not be a reason for denying full civil and political equality.

In a State which acknowledges a liberal doctrine of rights it is equally evident that the Church, like other associations, should have the liberty which its function requires.

In countries where the Church finds in the theory and constitution of the State nothing on which to base a claim to right, this does not absolve the Church from its primary duty of witness. This duty must then include a witness against such a denial of fundamental justice. And if the State tries to hinder or suppress such witness, all other Churches have the duty of supporting this Church and giving it the utmost succour and relief in their power.

We recognize as essential conditions necessary to the Church's fulfilment of its primary duty that it should enjoy (a) freedom to determine its faith and creed; (b) freedom of public and private worship, preaching and teaching; (c) freedom from any imposition by the State of religious ceremonies and forms of worship; (d) freedom to determine the nature of its government and the qualifications of its ministers and members, and, conversely, the freedom of the individual to join the Church to which he feels called; (e) freedom to control the education of its ministers, to give religious instruction to its youth, and to provide for adequate development of their religious life; (f) freedom of Christian service and missionary activity, both home and foreign; (g) freedom to co-operate with other Churches; (h) freedom to use such facilities, open to all citizens or associations, as will make possible the accomplishment of these ends, as, e.g., the ownership of property and the collection of funds.

The freedom essential for the Church can in fact exist both in Churches organized as free associations under the general laws of a country or as established Churches in an organic or otherwise special connection with the State. If, however, this connection should result in impairing the Church's freedom to carry out its distinctive mission, it would then become the duty of its ministers and members to do all in their power to secure this freedom, even at the cost of disestablishment.

4. . . . What then follows from this survey as to the present tasks and opportunities of the Churches? This at least, that it is their duty—

(a)   to summon their own members to repentance, both as individuals and organized bodies, for their sins of omission and of commission and to pray for the spirit of consecration which shall make of them, both in their separate and in their united activities, agents which God may use for His purpose in the world;

(b)   to create within the local community, the nation, and the world such agencies of co-operative action as shall make it possible for them to discharge effectively such tasks as can be done in common;

(c)   to summon their individual members in their several callings, not only their clerical but also their lay members, men and women, to co-operate with the State in such constructive tasks as may be for the good of the whole;

(d) to guard for all Churches, both as groups of witnessing Christians and in their organized capacity, the opportunity of worship, of witness, of service, and of education which is essential to their mission, and this not for their own sake only, but for the sake of the State;

(e) to follow with sympathetic interest the fortunes of those, Christians and non-Christians, who are victims of cruelty and oppression, and to do what they can to secure for them a treatment compatible with the dignity of their human personality as children of God;

(f) to renounce publicly and for ever the use of all forms of persecution, whether by Christians against other Christians, or by Christians against adherents of other religions.

From the Oxford Conference, *The Churches Survey Their Task: The Report of the Conference at Oxford, July 1937, on Church, Community, and State* (London: George Allen & Unwin Ltd., 1937), pp. 80–86.

63. *World Council of Churches*

The World Council of Churches was inaugurated by 145 Protestant and Orthodox churches at the First Assembly at Amsterdam in 1948. Subsequent assemblies were held each six or seven years, with expanding numbers of denominational delegations. A developing body of social teaching has been produced by the assemblies. The World Council has attempted to define organizing concepts, such as the "responsible society" developed at Amsterdam and the later "just, participatory, and sustainable society." The Council has also analyzed major issues, such as racism and the conflict between economic systems, while also responding to particular problems.

Amsterdam (1948)

1. *The Disorder of Society.* The world to-day is experiencing a social crisis of unparalleled proportions. The deepest root of that disorder is the refusal of men to see and admit that their responsibility to God stands over and above their loyalty to any earthly community and their obedience to any worldly power. Our modern society, in which religious tradition and family life have been weakened, and which is for the most part secular in its outlook, underestimates both the depth of evil in human nature and the full height of freedom and dignity in the children of God.

The Christian Church approaches the disorder of our society with faith in the Lordship of Jesus Christ. In Him God has established His Kingdom and its gates stand open for all who will enter. Their lives belong to God with a certainty that no disorder of society can destroy, and on them is laid the duty to seek God's Kingdom and His righteousness.

In the light of that Kingdom, with its judgment and mercy, Christians are conscious of the sins which corrupt human communities and institutions in every age, but they are also assured of the final victory over all sin and death through Christ. It is He who has bidden us pray that God's Kingdom may come and that His will may be done on earth as it is in heaven; and our obedience to that command requires that we seek in every age to overcome the specific disorders which aggravate the perennial evil in human society, and that we search out the means of securing their elimination or control.

Men are often disillusioned by finding that changes of particular systems do not bring unqualified good, but fresh evils. New temptations to greed and power arise even in systems more just than those they have replaced because sin is ever present in the human heart. Many, therefore, lapse into apathy, irresponsibility and despair. The Christian faith leaves no room for such despair, being based on the fact that the Kingdom of God is firmly established in Christ and will come by God's act despite all human failure.

Two chief factors contribute to the crisis of our age. One of these is the vast concentrations of power—which are under capitalism mainly economic and under communism both economic and political. In such conditions, social evil is manifest on the largest scale not only in the greed, pride, and cruelty of persons and groups; but also in the momentum or inertia of huge organisations of men, which diminish their ability to act as moral and accountable beings. To find ways of realising personal responsibility for collective action in the large aggregations of power in modern society is a task which has not yet been undertaken seriously.

The second factor is that society, as a whole dominated as it is by technics, is likewise more controlled by a momentum of its own than in previous periods. While it enables men the better to use nature, it has the possibilities of destruction, both through war and through the undermining of the natural foundations of society in family, neighbourhood and craft. It has collected men into great industrial cities and has deprived many societies of those forms of association in which men can grow most fully as persons. It has accentuated the tendency in men to waste God's gift to them in the soil and in other natural resources.

On the other hand, technical developments have relieved men and women of much drudgery and poverty, and are still capable of doing more. There is a limit to what they can do in this direction. Large parts of the world, however, are far from that limit. Justice demands that the inhabitants of Asia and Africa, for instance, should have benefits of more machine production. They may learn to avoid the mechanisation of life and the other dangers of an unbalanced economy which impair the social health of the older industrial peoples. Technical progress also provides channels of communication and interdependence which can be aids to fellowship, though closer contact may also produce friction.

There is no inescapable necessity for society to succumb to undirected developments of technology, and the Christian Church has an urgent responsibility today to help men to achieve fuller personal life within the technical society.

In doing so, the churches should not forget to what extent they themselves have contributed to the very evils which they are tempted to blame wholly on the secularisation of society. While they have raised up many Christians who have taken the lead in movements of reform, and while many of them have come to see in a fresh way the relevance of their faith to the problems of society, and the imperative obligations thus laid upon them, they share responsibility for the contemporary disorder. Our churches have often given religious sanction to the special privileges of dominant classes, races and political groups, and so they have been obstacles to changes necessary in the interests of social justice and political freedom. They have often concentrated on a purely spiritual or other-worldly or individualistic interpretation of their message and their responsibility. They have often failed to understand the forces which have shaped society around them, and so they have been unprepared to deal creatively with new problems as they have arisen in technical civilisation; they have often neglected the effects of industrialisation on agricultural communities.

2. *Economic and Political Organisation.* In the industrial revolution economic activity was freed from previous social controls and outgrew its modest place in human life. It created the vast network of financial, commercial and industrial relations which we know as the capitalist order. In all parts of the world new controls have in various degrees been put upon the free play of economic forces, but there are economic necessities which no political system can afford to defy. In our days, for instance, the need for stability in the value of money, for creation of capital and for incentives in production, is inescapable and world-wide. Justice, however, demands that economic activities be subordinated to social ends. It is intolerable that vast millions of people be exposed to insecurity, hunger and frustration by periodic inflation or depression.

The Church cannot resolve the debate between those who feel that the primary solution is to socialise the means of production, and those who fear that such a course will merely lead to new and inordinate combinations of political and economic power, culminating finally in an omnicompetent State. In the light of the Christian understanding of man we must, however, say to the advocates of socialisation that the institution of property is not the root of the corruption of human nature. We must equally say to the defenders of existing property relations that ownership is not an unconditional right; it must, therefore, be preserved, curtailed or distributed in accordance with the requirements of justice.

On the one hand, we must vindicate the supremacy of persons over purely technical considerations by subordinating all economic processes and cherished rights to the needs of the community as a whole. On the other hand, we must preserve the possibility of a satisfying life for "little men in big societies." We must prevent abuse of authority and keep open as wide a sphere as possible in which men can have direct and responsible relations with one another as persons.

Coherent and purposeful ordering of society has now become a major necessity. Here governments have responsibilities which they must not shirk. But centres of initiative in economic life must be so encouraged as to avoid placing too great a burden upon centralised judgment and decision. To achieve religious, cultural, economic, social, and other ends it is of vital importance that society should have a rich variety of smaller forms of community, in local government, within industrial organisations, including trade unions, through the development of public corporations and through voluntary associations. By such means it is possible to prevent an undue centralisation of power in modern technically organised communities, and thus escape the perils of tyranny while avoiding the dangers of anarchy.

3. *The Responsible Society.* Man is created and called to be a free being, responsible to God and his neighbour. Any tendencies in State and society depriving man of the possibility of acting responsibly are a denial of God's intention for man and His work of salvation. A responsible society is one where freedom is the freedom of men who acknowledge responsibility to justice and public order, and where those who hold political authority or economic power are responsible for its exercise to God and the people whose welfare is affected by it.

Man must never be made a mere means for political or economic ends. Man is not made for the State but the State for man. Man is not made for production, but production for man. For a society to be responsible under modern conditions it is required that the people have freedom to control, to criticise and to change their governments, that power be made responsible by law and tradition, and be distributed as widely as possible through the whole community. It is required that economic justice and provision of equality of opportunity be established for all the members of society.

We therefore condemn:

1. Any attempt to limit the freedom of the Church to witness to its Lord and His design for mankind and any attempt to impair the freedom of men to obey God and to act according to conscience, for those freedoms are implied in man's responsibility before God;

2. Any denial to man of an opportunity to participate in the shaping of society, for this is a duty implied in man's responsibility towards his neighbour;

3. Any attempt to prevent men from learning and spreading the truth.

4. *Communism and Capitalism.* Christians should ask why communism in its modern totalitarian form makes so strong an appeal to great masses of people in many parts of the world. They should recognise the hand of God in the revolt of multitudes against injustice that gives communism much of its strength. They should seek to recapture for the Church the original Christian solidarity with the world's distressed people, not to curb their aspirations towards justice, but, on the contrary, to go beyond them and direct them towards the only road which does not lead to a blank wall, obedience to God's will and His justice. Christians should realise that for many, especially for many young men and women, communism seems to stand for a vision of human equality and universal brotherhood for which they were prepared by Christian influences. Christians who are beneficiaries of capitalism should try to see the world as it appears to many who know themselves excluded from its privileges and who see in communism a means of deliverance from poverty and insecurity. All should understand that the proclamation of racial equality by communists and their support of the cause of colonial peoples makes a strong appeal to the populations of Asia and Africa and to racial minorities elsewhere. It is a great human tragedy that so much that is good in the motives and aspirations of many communists and of those whose sympathies they win has been transformed into a force that engenders new forms of injustice and oppression, and that what is true in communist criticism should be used to give convincing power to untrustworthy propaganda.

Christians should recognise with contrition that many churches are involved in the forms of economic injustice and racial discrimination which have created the conditions favourable to the growth of communism, and that the atheism and the anti-religious teaching of communism are in part a reaction to the chequered record of a professedly Christian society. It is one of the most fateful facts in modern history that often the working classes, including tenant farmers, came to believe that the churches were against them or indifferent to their plight. Christians should realise that the Church has often failed to offer to its youth the appeal that can evoke a disciplined, purposeful and sacrificial response, and that in this respect communism has for many filled a moral and psychological vacuum.

The points of conflict between Christianity and the atheistic Marxian communism of our day are as follows: (1) the communist promise of what amounts to a complete redemption of man in history; (2) the belief that a particular class by virtue of its role as the bearer of a new order is free from the sins and ambiguities that Christians believe to be characteristic of all human existence; (3) the materialistic and deterministic teachings, however they may be qualified, that are incompatible with belief in God and with the Christian view of man as a person, made in God's image and responsible to Him; (4) the ruthless methods of communists in dealing with their opponents; (5) the demand of the party on its members for an exclusive and unqualified loyalty which belongs only to God, and the coercive policies of communist dictatorship in controlling every aspect of life.

The Church should seek to resist the extension of any system, that not only includes oppressive elements but fails to provide any means by which the victims of oppression may criticise or act to correct it. It is a part of the mission of the Church to raise its voice of protest wherever men are the victims of terror, wherever they are denied such fundamental human rights as the right to be secure against arbitrary arrest, and wherever governments use torture and cruel punishments to intimidate consciences of men.

The Church should make clear that there are conflicts between Christianity and capitalism. The developments of capitalism vary from country to country and often the exploitation of the workers that was characteristic of early capitalism has been corrected in considerable measure by the influence of trade unions, social legislation and responsible management. But

(1) capitalism tends to subordinate what should be the primary task of any economy—the meeting of human needs—to the economic advantages of those who have most power over its institutions. (2) It tends to produce serious inequalities. (3) It has developed a practical form of materialism in Western nations in spite of their Christian background, for it has placed the greatest emphasis upon success in making money. (4) It has also kept the people of capitalist countries subject to a kind of fate which has taken the form of such social catastrophes as mass unemployment.

The Christian churches should reject the ideologies of both communism and laissez-faire capitalism, and should seek to draw men away from the false assumption that these extremes are the only alternatives. Each has made promises which it could not redeem. Communist ideology puts the emphasis upon economic justice, and promises that freedom will come automatically after the completion of the revolution. Capitalism puts the emphasis upon freedom, and promises that justice will follow as a by-product of free enterprise; that, too, is an ideology which has been proved false. It is the responsibility of Christians to seek new, creative solutions which never allow either justice or freedom to destroy the other.

5. *The Social Function of the Church.* The greatest contribution that the Church can make to the renewal of society is for it to be renewed in its own life in faith and obedience to its Lord. Such inner renewal includes a clearer grasp of the meaning of the Gospel for the whole life of men. This renewal must take place both in the larger units of the Church and in the local congregations. The influence of worshiping congregations upon the problems of society is very great when those congregations include people from many social groups. If the Church can overcome the national and social barriers which now divide it, it can help society to overcome those barriers.

This is especially clear in the case of racial distinction. It is here that the Church has failed most lamentably, where it has reflected and then by its example sanctified the racial prejudice that is rampant in the world. And yet it is here that to-day its guidance concerning what God wills for it is especially clear. It knows that it must call society away from prejudice based upon race or colour and from the practices of discrimination and segregation as denials of justice and human dignity, but it cannot say a convincing word to society unless it takes steps to eliminate these practices from the Christian community because they contradict all that it believes about God's love for all His children.

There are occasions on which the churches, through their councils or through such persons as they may commission to speak on their behalf, should declare directly what they see to be the will of God for the public decisions of the hour. Such guidance will often take the form of warnings against concrete forms of injustice or oppression or social idolatry. They should also point to the main objectives towards which a particular society should move.

One problem is raised by the existence in several countries of Christian political parties. The Church as such should not be identified with any political party, and it must not act as though it were itself a political party. In general, the formation of such parties is hazardous because they easily confuse Christianity with the inherent compromises of politics. They may cut Christians off from the other parties which need the leaven of Christianity, and they may consolidate all who do not share the political principles of the Christian party not only against that party but against Christianity itself. Nevertheless, it may still be desirable in some situations for Christians to organize themselves into a political party for specific objectives, so long as they do not claim that it is the only possible expression of Christian loyalty in the situation.

But the social influence of the Church must come primarily from its influence upon its members through constant teaching and preaching of Christian truth in ways that illuminate the historical conditions in which men live and the problems which they face. The Church can be most effective in society as it inspires its members to ask in a new way what their Christian responsibility is whenever they vote or discharge the duties of public office, whenever they influence public opinion, whenever they make decisions as employers or as workers or in any other vocation to which they may be called. One of the most creative developments in the contemporary Church is the practice of groups of Christians facing much the same problems in their occupations to pray and to take counsel together in order to find out what they should do as Christians.

In discussing the social function of the Church, Christians should always remember the great variety of situations in which the Church lives. Nations in which professing Christians are in the majority, nations in which the Church represents only a few percent of the population, nations in which the Church lives under a hostile and oppressive government offer very different problems for the Church. It is one of the contributions of the ecumenical experience of recent years that churches under these contrasting conditions have come not only to appreciate one another's practices, but to learn from one another's failures and achievements and sufferings.

6. *Conclusion.* There is a great discrepancy between all that has been said here and the possibility of action in many parts of the world. Obedience to God will be possible under all external circumstances, and no one need despair when conditions restrict greatly the area of responsible action. The responsible society of which we have spoken represents, however, the goal for which the churches in all lands must work, to the glory of the one God and Father of all, and looking for the day of God and a new earth, wherein dwelleth righteousness.

From the World Council of Churches, *Man's Disorder and God's Design: The Amsterdam Assembly Series* (New York: Harper & Bros. Pub., 1948), pp. 189–97.

Evanston (1954)

(2) *The Incarnation.* Among many New Testament texts, three stand out as a basis for the agreement of the churches concerning the Incarnation and its bearing upon the race problem.

> And the Word was made flesh, and dwelt among us . . . [John 1:14]
>
> God was in Christ, reconciling the world into himself [2 Cor. 5:19]
>
> For God so loved the world, that he gave his only begotten Son. . . . [John 3:16]

The churches affirm that the Incarnation challenges us to effect a new relation between the peoples. Jesus Christ revealed God to be the Father of all. He was made "in human form," and he died for all men, rising from the dead that all might be born again. In him, men are therefore required to live in a new relation with one another. "By this all men will know that you are my disciples, if you have love for one another" [John 13:35]. His mission therefore confirms the equality and value of each person in the sight of God, in whose infinite love each sparrow [Luke 12:6] has its place, and who seeks and cares for each of those who are lost [Luke 15:1–10]. His mission restores the unity of mankind—lost through human sin in the Fall of man—with God and within itself.

Within those affirmations, it would also be agreed that Christ revealed God to be the Father, and that we are therefore brothers. But a few would maintain that this Fatherhood and this brotherhood are, as it were, recognizable and applicable only to those who have been particularly called or elected by God as His sons, or only to those who have found salvation in Christ Jesus. This view has tended to promote identification of a particular racial group as the chosen people. Most churches, however, would stress that being created by God we are His children, and would view the Father revealed by Jesus Christ as the Father of all men. As children of God, the "little ones" for whom Christ died, men of all sorts and conditions have equal value and status before God. Among them there is a new sense of brotherhood, in which there is no fundamental inequality and in which injustice, discrimination and segregation have no place. The brotherhood inaugurated by Christ is that which transforms our present sinful division and injustice into the original brotherhood of the race. The Fatherhood of God is thus a universal concept, and the brotherhood of man is, if not fully realized now, potentially a universal fellowship. Again, according to this view, the unity of the races, rather than a special designation of a single one, is fundamental.

(3) *The New Creation.*

> Therefore, if any one is in Christ, he is a new creation; the old is passed away, behold, the new has come. [2 Cor. 5:17, RSV]

The Kingdom of God is amongst us whenever His will is done; it will come in its fullness when His will is done on earth as it is in heaven. Thus it is, on the one hand, the hope by which we live in the present; and on the other, it is the goal toward which the Church is directed. The people of God, drawn from all the races, thus possess a common hope and a common goal, to which they must witness and which they must demonstrate.

Human beings suffer and are degraded because of the conflict among the races. The indignity and the frustration and the fear of those who are oppressed, and the warping of spirit and the fear of those who oppress, call alike for salvation and for hope. What hope does Christ hold out to them?

Christ gives us the hope for a new life now. He makes men into new men, establishing dignity in the human spirit, replacing fear with trust, and freeing the human spirit from its twisted confines. This is our first hope in Christ. "Therefore, if any one is in Christ, he is a new creation; the old is passed away, behold, the new has come."

Christ gives us hope for the future. His Kingdom, in which there is love and mercy, and in which evil and cruelty disappear, will come in its fullness. Part of His work of making men into new men is to give them the assurance that His Kingdom will come. The future is not, therefore, endless injustice and frustration for those who are oppressed. The future is determined by Christ, who will bring about "a new heaven and a new earth" toward which men are called to move. Men do not know His new creation, and neither is it made visible, unless it now becomes real in men's lives. When assumptions of superiority are turned into the recognition of equality in Christ; when frustration is turned into the purposeful work in and toward the Kingdom of God; when cruelty has been turned into love and mercy, the Kingdom of God is apparent on the earth. And as the Kingdom of God does appear among us, we know that it shall come in its fullness. Therein is our hope.

(4) *The Church.*

> For as the body is one, and hath many members, and all the members of that one body, being many, are one body: so also is Christ. For by one Spirit are we all baptized into one body, whether we be Jews or Gentiles, whether we be bond or free; and have been all made to drink into one Spirit [1 Cor. 12:12–13.]
>
> Be like men who are waiting for their master to come home from the marriage feast. [Luke 12:36, RSV]

Reported agreements from the churches reveal that they recognize a two-fold task.

First, they must proclaim and exemplify in the world at large the unity in Christ. In this task, they serve the Kingdom of God, which they know in part, but which shall be fully understood in the future. They must proclaim this unity to all men. Yet they do not. Even granting that the churches do not understand fully the goal toward which they move, they fail to live up to what they do see. Reconciliation in Christ is confessed by many Christians and churches who do not give evidence that they know or practice a reconciliation with men. Deep-going repentance is therefore needed, and connected inevitably with the task of the churches. As Christians strive, in constant repentance, to exemplify the unity of Christ, they are supported by the continuous witness of Word, sacrament and fellowship known by the Church through the ages. Here repentance is brought about and renewal of life is given.

Second, as part of their witness in the world, the churches affirm that they must seek to establish justice and reconciliation among the races. At least three measures are appropriate. In the first place, the churches can give encouragement and assistance to every good movement outside the churches which is working to better relationships among the races. Frequently the churches are silent when outside organizations strive to improve racial conditions, whereas a word of approval or actual participation in the effort would make the work of such organizations more effective. In the second place, the churches can assist the individual church member to see what his Christian duty is in his vocation and in his daily contact with members of other races. The individual Christian can never escape his responsibility to witness for his Lord in every area of his life. The churches can assist him to see more clearly what his Christian duty is in the area of race. Third, oppressed racial and ethnic groups can never receive justice until discriminating laws are abolished. The churches can study these laws and when they are found to be unjust, they can take appropriate initiative to get such laws changed or abolished.

Within these affirmations, there is a wide and serious variation of conviction. Agreeing that the people of God move toward an ultimate goal and end in which there is no distinction of race, there is disagreement as to the manner in which the churches at present should exemplify and set forth that ultimate unity. How shall they wait for the Master? For some, unity in Christ is a spiritual unity, not to be embodied in existing churches and social structures; such embodiment is to be avoided in the interests of upholding the order which God has established among the separate races. For most, the final unity of the Kingdom of God is to be approximated now, made visible by the workings of the Holy Spirit in the churches and in society. Here again, the unity of Creation, re-established by Christ, is the dominant concern. Moreover, the concept of justice and reconciliation among the races in society differs according to which of the views is held. One view, holding that a spiritual unity in Christ among those of different races is sufficient, calls for just treatment and right relationships among races which are separated from one another. The other view requires that the unity of the races will be exemplified in society as well as in the churches, and stresses that neither justice nor reconciliation can be effected until this unity is achieved. They recognize that to deny justice to any man or to impose segregation upon him because of race or color is to deny to him that dignity to which he is entitled as a child of God. It penalizes him for being what God has made him and for a condition which he cannot change. A person may change his church membership, this theology, his nationality; or he may improve his mind if ignorant, his economic status if poverty stricken; or his body if unclean; but he cannot change his color or physical characteristics. The growth of a unity, therefore, which recognizes and accepts the physical differences of various races and ethnic groups, is a prerequisite to the establishment of justice among them.

The churches affirm that a heavy responsibility in Christian discipleship rests with the individual. As the object of God's love, the lost sinner for whom Christ died, he cannot postpone or evade the requirements of obedience. These requirements call for rigid self-examination, which, in regard to race, necessitate honest scrutiny as to the extent and depth of prejudice within himself. No solution to race tension can be achieved unless this beam is first cast out. Every relationship which an individual has with other races will also come under review in the light of Christian principles. Some of these relationships will be direct and personal: social manners, language, friendships, indeed any expression of attitude will be screened for traces of prejudice in any of its subtle forms. Other relationships will be less direct and more impersonal. The support of organizations working for racial justice; the advocacy and support of governmental policy at all levels directed toward the same end; the seeking of full education and employment opportunities for all racial groups—these and a dozen other social duties rest upon the Christian individual. The Christian is, in fact, the "ambassador of Christ" to every realm of life. "No one who puts his hand to the plow and looks back is fit for the kingdom of God" (Luke 9:62).

From the Second Assembly of the World Council of Churches, *The Christian Hope and the Task of the Church* (New York: Harper & Bros. Pub., 1954), pp. 28–33. Copyright © 1954 by Harper & Brothers.

New Delhi (1961)

III. A. A Universal Organization of Nations

28. The structures and institutions of political government and international order offer no lasting security and stability and are subject to the constant flow of historical change. Our time is shaped by fundamental developments in the economic and social conditions of life all over the world, as well as in the forms of government and in the distribution of political power and influence in the international community. A growing number of formerly dependent peoples are entering the society of nations and are sharing the responsibilities of independence in a world that lacks harmony and order. This world is torn by deep antagonisms between political systems and by conflicts of power, and exists under a precarious equilibrium of terrible means of destruction.

29. Because of present divisions and tensions a perfected system of world-wide co-operation cannot be expected in the near future, but human society must move towards those ordered forms of universal political co-operation for the safeguarding of peace and the realization of social justice and the welfare of all nations, which modern technical development and the interdependence of peoples demand and make possible. Christians will recognize in this world of chaotic disorder and deep distrust the evidence of human fallibility. They will not cease to proclaim in a divided humanity the reign of love and justice and to strive for peace and for the fellowship of all men and nations.

30. In the present stage of transition and change the United Nations has

fulfilled an indispensable task. Even if its endeavours to secure disarmament have thus far failed and its efforts to prevent international conflicts have not always succeeded, the United Nations has facilitated the integration of newly rising states into the international society, has assisted world-wide co-operation in the economic development of all nations, has ensured talks and negotiations among opposing states in a time of crisis, and has defended the basic standards of justice, law and human dignity in international life.

31. To be equal to its role in international life, the United Nations must have the constant support of all its members. Work for the maintenance of peace and assistance given under the difficult conditions of peoples rising to full independence places heavy responsibilities and financial strains upon the United Nations. The churches should urge governments to discharge their full responsibilities towards the United Nations and to be prepared to increase their efforts for the common cause of peace and orderly progress. . . .

33. The United Nations is developing from a conference of national delegations into an organization with an authority of its own, empowered to undertake special responsibilities. This step forward requires an impartial and independent status for its administration.

34. Rapid de-colonization has overtaken the provisions of the Charter relating to the administration of dependent territories. Whilst these arrangements continue to function successfully in certain cases, an acute need is felt for institutions within the framework of the Charter which could more generally assist peoples in their transition to independence and prepare them for the responsibilities of full government either before or after the beginning of their independent status. Christian churches should urge upon governments concerned their obligation to provide for a timely and sufficient preparation of the people for their tasks in a free government.

35. Nations should not use the claim of sovereignty to exclude reasonable discussion of the international implications of their failures to protect human rights in their territories.

36. All nations should refrain from interfering for selfish interests in the full development of new states. . . .

C. Peaceful Change and Settlement

38. At the present time traditional methods of violence for effecting change have ceased to be accepted by international opinion as instruments of national policy. But in an age when all political and social forces of the world are in perpetual flux and the increase of populations and their migrations constantly create new dangers of unrest, the abrogation of war should not be identified with the mere maintenance of the status quo. Otherwise increasing tensions may finally result in violence and bloodshed.

39. The stability of international order and the respect for international law are basic elements of peace. The protection of the existing order, however, should be accompanied by the recognition of legitimate demands for its alteration, in so far as these further the maintenance of peace and serve the common good of the international community. That such changes can be brought about by mutual agreement is shown by the peaceful emergence in recent years of many newly independent states.

40. Christians should insist that governments and international organizations use to the full the available means for providing peaceful solutions by agreed change, and develop procedures for prompt international action for peace in emergencies.

41. So far as possible legal disputes between nations should be resolved by arbitration and judicial decisions. Governments should refrain from undermining the legal settlement of differences by making reservations which limit the general competence of international tribunals.

D. International Ethos

42. A deep foundation of moral values and ethical convictions underlies international order. From this it derives its authority and its basic principles.

43. Diversities of religion, culture and tradition, apparently so great between the main regions of the world, do not exclude the existence of a unified set of values, living and developing in the conscience of mankind. These do not in all cases derive from Christian sources but Christians have a special opportunity and duty to contribute to their articulation and development.

44. A more profound study of the nature and content of these moral foundations of international law and order will help nations of different traditions to understand and accept their common allegiance to basic ethical conceptions.

IV. A. Problems of Political Development

45. The mid-twentieth century has seen the emergence of many nations from a state of political subjection by alien powers to a status of political independence. We rejoice in this. We note, however, that there are nations and people still under foreign political domination. Such domination, recurring in human history, is not the result exclusively of any one particular political system. Wherever it occurs and under whatever system of political life, and wherever the consent of the governed is spurned and their welfare subordinated to the interests of the ruling power, this is unjust and the Christian conscience condemns it.

46. Both in the interests of human justice and international peace the transfer of political power to those to whom it should belong must be made without self-serving delay. We recognize that problems exist where a people has not been sufficiently prepared to assume the responsibilities of political independence. In such cases the process of necessary preparation must be greatly accelerated. To eliminate ambiguities in the role of ruling powers, and to expedite the achievement of independence, it is desirable that international assistance through agencies of the United Nations be associated with such a process.

47. Where other factors exist, such as the presence of ethnic or racial minorities, sufficient guarantees for the protection of the rights of these minorities should be assured by the people achieving independence. Where history has thrown two or more races or religious groups together in the same country, as the total welfare of all such people can be secured only through the mutual acceptance of each other as citizens of a common country and members of a common nation, it is necessary that no single group seek to perpetuate political advantage for itself at the cost of justice for all. While legitimate fears of minorities need to be allayed, no minority should be vested with such power of veto as to deny the rights of the majority and the welfare of the whole community.

48. Developing nations have to contend with many difficulties. Divisive tendencies arising from traditional patterns of life are a serious difficulty. In such a context, nationalism, cherished and fostered as bringing cohesion in the life of the peoples, has a creative role to play. On the other hand there is the danger that it may act as an impediment to creating a sense of community with neighbouring nations. Furthermore, when, in the general desire to create a sense of national identity, nationalism is confounded with a spurious revival of old customs, the latter becomes an enemy of progress.

49. It must be recognized that in the world of our day the interdependence of nations is a reality. The ideal that the Christian seeks along with all those interested in the promotion of human welfare, is a community of nations wherein each nation can develop its own life only in the context of an active and just international association.

B. Problems of Economic Development and Social Interdependence

50. It is a matter of gratification that many of the more advanced nations have sought to aid the progress of the economically less developed countries. Such aid is more than a matter of charity. Human justice demands a more equitable distribution of God-given resources to all the children of men. Human solidarity requires that nations collaborate for the creation of wealth for their common welfare. When economic co-operation is viewed thus, no political advantage can be sought by the donor of aid and the receiver of the aid has the obligation of using it responsibly.

51. To develop economic co-operation along these lines we urge a more adequate strategy for world development. The urgency of the situation in less developed countries and the rising expectations of their people call not only for a quantitative increase in assistance but for a qualitative planning, so that the best results may be secured within a reasonable span of time. Frustrated expectations may lead people to destructive revolt rather than along the path of peaceful revolution.

52. Donor countries should correlate their aid programmes. Unless bilateral aid is preferred by the parties concerned, both financial and technical aid should be channelled through international co-operative agencies like the United Nations. This should avoid waste and fruitless competition, and elicit a response free of suspicion from those receiving the aid. In developing countries, planning for a balanced development is absolutely necessary to avoid creating new problems and the compounding of old ones. All planning for development needs to be related to available and potential resources, including personnel, to execute such plans. The role of social change which is both created by development and aids such development must be taken into consideration.

53. In the long run trade, not aid, is the most effective instrument in furthering development. International co-operation to secure effective markets for the developing countries is necessary. Safeguards against the impact on the economics of these countries of changes in international monetary policies and of fluctuations in prices, both of primary commodities and of machinery for product purposes, have to be developed. Training for technological and administrative skills, supplemented by education to inculcate a sense of social responsibility, has to be stepped up. Accelerated programmes for education on a wide scale and the supply and pooling of resources for such plans must engage the continuing attention of both donor countries and receiving countries. Research in the special problems of developing countries is of paramount importance if sound plans are to be devised. A rational and co-operative regional distribution of productive enterprises needs to be encouraged more fully to meet consumer needs. In all these a more rational and correlated approach to development is imperative for all involved.

54. In this context special emphasis is laid on the need to control the growth of population, especially in developing countries. It is an error to think that such control is needed only in densely populated countries. The immediate necessity is to bring population pressures and economic growth into a more balanced relationship. It is known that even in countries where the national income has increased markedly within the last decade, the benefits of such increase have been largely off-set by mounting population pressures. As standards of health improve, mortality rates decrease dramatically, and unless birth rates are brought into balance many countries that have obtained political independence will find the prospects for genuine economic independence remote. While some developing countries have taken steps to promote responsible family planning, more energetic and comprehensive steps are needed even in such countries. The more developed countries should provide technical knowledge and assistance when so requested by developing countries.

55. Aid can never be and should not be a one-way affair. Out of their rich cultural heritage, the developing nations have much to contribute to the enrichment of the life of the people of the world as a whole. Nations should contribute to each other from the wealth of their wisdom, experience and other resources that the life of each may be the richer for it.

From the World of Council of Churches, *The New Delhi Report: The Third Assembly of the World Council of Churches, 1961* (New York: Association Press, 1961), pp. 270–76.

Vancouver (1983)

5.1 Statement on Peace and Justice

1. Humanity is now living in the dark shadow of an arms race more intense, and of systems of injustice more widespread, more dangerous and more costly than the world has ever known. Never before has the human race been as close as it is now to total self-destruction. Never before have so many lived in the grip of deprivation and oppression.

2. Under that shadow we have gathered here at the Sixth Assembly of the World Council of Churches (Vancouver, 1983) to proclaim our common faith in Jesus Christ, the Life of the World, and to say to the world:

—fear not, for Christ has overcome the forces of evil; in him are all things made new;
—fear not; for the love of God, rise up for justice and for peace;
—trust in the power of Christ who reigns over all; give witness to him in word and in deed, regardless of the cost.

3. Still we are moved to repentance as we consider with alarm the rapidity with which the threats to justice and survival have grown since we last met. The frantic race towards nuclear conflagration has accelerated sharply. In an incredibly short period of history, we have moved from the horrors of Hiroshima and Nagasaki, and the threat that they might be repeated elsewhere, to the likelihood, unless we act now, that life on the whole planet could be devastated. A moment of madness, a miscalculated strategic adventure, a chance combination of computer errors, a misperception of the other's intention, an honest mistake—any one could now set off a nuclear holocaust.

4. As we have been reminded dramatically during this Assembly, nuclear weapons claim victims even in the absence of war, through the lasting effects of nuclear bombings, weapons testing and the dumping of nuclear wastes.

5. For many millions, however, the most immediate threat to survival is not posed by nuclear weapons. Local, national and international conflicts rage around the world. The intersection of East-West and North-South conflicts results in massive injustice, systematic violation of human rights, oppression, homelessness, starvation and death for masses of people. Millions have been rendered stateless, expelled from their homes as refugees or exiles.

6. The World of Council of Churches has consistently drawn the attention of the churches to the economic threats to peace. Even without war, thousands perish daily in nations both rich and poor because of hunger and starvation. Human misery and suffering as a result of various forms of injustice have reached levels unprecedented in modern times. There is a resurgence of racism, often in itself a cause of war. Peoples continue to be driven, as a last resort, to take up arms to defend themselves against systematic violence, or to claim their rights to self-determination or independence.

7. While the equivalent of nearly two billion dollars (US) is being expended globally each day for armaments, the world economy is engulfed in a prolonged and deepening crisis which threatens every country and international security. The spectre of trade warfare, competitive devaluation and financial collapse is omnipresent. This crisis has contributed to even greater injustice for the developing countries, denying millions the basic necessities of life. The failure of UNCTAD VI has dashed hopes for meaningful North-South dialogue. While many factors are involved, the link between the arms race and economic development, the effects of rising defence budgets and accelerated reliance on arms production in the industrialized nations, and the ensuing strain on the international system as a whole pose special threats to peace and justice.

8. The peoples of the world stand in need of peace and justice. Peace is not just the absence of war. Peace cannot be built on foundations of injustice. Peace requires a new international order based on justice for and within all the nations, and respect for the God-given humanity and dignity of every person. Peace is, as the Prophet Isaiah has taught us, the effect of righteousness.

9. *The churches today are called to confess anew their faith, and to repent for the times when Christians have remained silent in the face of injustice or threats to peace. The biblical vision of peace with justice for all, of wholeness, of unity for all God's people is not one of several options for the followers of Christ. It is an imperative in our time.*

10. The ecumenical approach to peace and justice is based on the belief that without justice for all everywhere we shall never have peace anywhere. From its inception, peace with justice has been a central concern of the ecumenical movement. The World Council of Churches was conceived amid the rumblings of looming world wars. Ever since it was formed it has condemned war, and engaged almost constantly in efforts to prevent war, to aid the victims of war and to keep war from breaking out anew. It has exposed the injustices that lead to conflict, affirmed its solidarity with groups and movements struggling for justice and peace, and sought to establish channels of communication leading to the peaceful resolution of conflicts. It has repeatedly called the attention of the churches and through them the governments and the general public to the threats to peace, the threats to survival, and the deepening crisis. . . .

13. The blatant misuse of the concept of national security to justify repression, foreign intervention and spiralling arms budgets is of profound concern. No nation can pretend to be secure so long as others' legitimate rights to sovereignty and security are neglected or denied. Security can therefore be achieved only as a common enterprise of nations but security is also inseparable from justice. A concept of "common security" of nations must be reinforced by a concept of "people's security". True security for the people demands respect for human rights, including the right to self-determination, as well as social and economic justice for all within every nation, and a political framework that would ensure it.

14. In this connection the growing refusal of many governments to use the opportunities afforded by the United Nations to preserve international peace and security and for the peaceful resolution of conflicts, or to heed its resolutions, is deeply troubling. We call upon the governments to reaffirm their commitment to the United Nations Charter, to submit interstate conflicts to the Security Council at an early stage when resolution may still be possible short of the use of massive armed force, and to cooperate with it in the pursuit of peaceful solutions. *We draw special attention to the United Nations International Year of Peace (1986) and the World Disarmament Compaign, urging the churches to use them as important opportunities for the strengthening of international security and the promotion of disarmament, peace and justice.*

15. It is now a full decade since there has been any substantial, subsequently ratified measure of arms control. Since our last Assembly, global military expenditures have tripled. This past year has marked a new peak of confrontation between NATO and the Warsaw Treaty Organization. There is the real prospect, if the current negotiations in Geneva between the USA and the USSR fail to prevent it, that the world stockpile of nuclear weapons may increase dramatically in the next decade. The growing sophistication, accuracy and mobility of new generations of weapons now ready for deployment or currently being designed make them more dangerous and destabilizing than ever before. The failure of arms control among nuclear-weapon states has made the non-proliferation treaty, in practice, an instrument of invidious discrimination, incited the spread of nuclear weapons, and compounded the prospects for nuclear war in several areas of regional tension in the Southern hemisphere. Until the superpowers move decisively towards nuclear disarmament, efforts to contain nuclear proliferation are bound to fail.

16. *We call upon the churches, especially those in Europe, both East and West, and in North America, to redouble their efforts to convince their governments to reach a negotiated settlement and to turn away now, before it is too late, from plans to deploy additional or new nuclear weapons in Europe, and to begin immediately to reduce and then eliminate altogether present nuclear forces. . . .*

20. The Central Committee urged the churches to pay special attention to and take clear positions on a number of points developed in the report of the Amsterdam Hearing. We reiterate that appeal with respect to the following:

a) a nuclear war can under no circumstances, in no region and by no social system, be just or justifiable, given the fact that the magnitude of devastation caused by it will be far out of proportion to any conceivable benefit or advantage to be derived from it;

b) nuclear war is unlikely to remain limited, and therefore any contemplation of "limited" use of nuclear weapons should be discouraged as dangerous from the outset;

c) all nations now possessing nuclear weapons or capable of doing so in the foreseeable future should unequivocally renounce policies of "first use", as an immediate step towards building confidence;

d)   the concept of deterrence, the credibility of which depends on the possible use of nuclear weapons, is to be rejected as morally unacceptable and as incapable of safeguarding peace and security in the long-term;

e)   the production and deployment of nuclear weapons as well as their use constitute a crime against humanity, and therefore there should be a complete halt in the production of nuclear weapons and in weapons research and development in all nations, to be expeditiously enforced through a treaty; such a position supports the struggle to cause one's own nation to commit itself never to own or use nuclear weapons, despite the period of nuclear vulnerability, and to encourage and stand in solidarity with Christians and others who refuse to cooperate with or accept employment in any projects related to nuclear weapons and nuclear warfare;

f)   all nations should agree to and ratify a comprehensive test ban treaty as a necessary step to stopping the further development of nuclear weapons technology;

g)   all means leading to disarmament, both nuclear and conventional, should be welcomed as complementary and mutually reinforcing: multilateral conferences leading to effective decisions, bilateral negotiations pursued with daring and determination and unilateral initiatives leading to the relaxation of tensions and building of mutual confidence among nations and peoples.

21. In addition, we urge the churches to press their governments to abstain from any further research, production or deployment of weapons in space, and to prohibit the development and production of all weapons of mass destruction or indiscriminate effect, including chemical and biological means.

22. In our efforts since the last Assembly to accomplish the purpose of the World Council of Churches "to express the common concern of the churches in the service of human need, the breaking down of barriers between people, and the promotion of one human family in justice and peace", we have been encouraged and strengthened by the movement of the Holy Spirit among us, leading the churches to undertake new initiatives. In this process of conversion the insights and the leadership of women and youth have often been decisive. But our common faith and the times now demand much more of us as stewards of God's creation.

23. Christians cannot view the dangers of this moment as inherent in the nature of things. Nor can we give ourselves over to despair. As believers in the one Lord and Saviour, Jesus Christ, the Prince of Peace, we are stewards of God's hope for the future of creation. We know God's love and confess a Lord of history in whom we have the promise of the fullness of life.

God's mercy is everlasting, and the Holy Spirit is moving among us, kindling the love which drives out fear, renewing our vision of peace, stirring our imaginations, leading us through the wilderness, freeing us and uniting us. The peoples of the world are coming to their feet in growing numbers, demanding justice, crying out for peace. These are present signs of hope.

24. We have recognized that our approaches to justice and peace often differ, as do the starting points for discussion among the churches, due to the wide diversity of our histories, traditions and the contexts in which we live and witness. *We call upon the churches now to:*

a) *intensify their efforts to develop a common witness in a divided world, confronting with renewed vigour the threats to peace and survival and engaging in struggles for justice and human dignity;*

b) *become a living witness to peace and justice through prayer, worship and concrete involvement;*

c) *take steps towards unity through providing more frequent opportunities for sharing in and among the churches in order to learn more about and understand better each other's perspectives, defying every attempt to divide or separate us; and*

d) *develop more innovative approaches to programmes of education for peace and justice.*

25. According to the 1980 Geneva Convention, the use of certain weapons of indiscriminate effect is forbidden under international law. We believe nuclear weapons must be considered within that category. We join in the conviction expressed by the Panel of the WCC Public Hearing on Nuclear Weapons and Disarmament after it had examined the testimony of a broad range of expert witnesses: *"We believe that the time has come when the churches must unequivocally declare that the production and deployment as well as the use of nuclear weapons are a crime against humanity and that such activities must be condemned on ethical and theological grounds.* The nuclear weapons issue is, in its import and threat to humanity, a question of Christian discipline and faithfulness to the Gospel.

Canberra (1991)

Section I: Giver of Life—Sustain Your Creation!

"In the beginning God created the heavens and the earth . . . And God saw everything that God had made, and behold, it was very good" (Gen. 1:1, 31).

13. The universe in all its beauty and grandeur manifests the glory of the Triune God who is the source of all life. All things have been made in Christ, in whom God's creation comes to fulfilment. The divine presence of the Spirit in creation binds us as human beings together with all created life. We are accountable before God in and to the community of life, so that we understand ourselves as servants, stewards and trustees of the creation. We are called to approach creation in humility, with reverence, respect and compassion, and to work for the mending and healing of creation as a foretaste and pointer to the final gathering up of all things in Christ (cf. Eph. 1:10).

14. The earth was created by God out of nothing in a pure and simple act of love, and the Spirit has never ceased to sustain it. Yet our earth is in grave peril, the very creation groaning and travailing in all its parts (Rom. 8:22). This is a "sign of the times", calling us to return to God and to ask the Spirit to re-orient our lives. Through misunderstanding—and sometimes through deliberate choice—Christians have participated in the destruction of nature, and this requires our repentance. We are called to commit ourselves anew to living as a community which respects and cares for creation.

15. What is our place as human beings in the natural order? The earth itself, this little watery speck in space, is about 4.5 billion years old. Life began about 3.4 billion years ago. We ourselves came on the scene some 80,000 years ago, just yesterday in the twinkling of the Creator's eye. It is shocking and frightening for us that the human species has been able to threaten the very foundations of life on our planet in only about 200 years since modern industrialization began. So where do we belong in the Creator's purpose?

16. The Christian scriptures testify that God is the Creator of all, and that all that was created "was very good" (Gen. 1:31; cf. 1 Tim. 4:4). God's Spirit continually sustains and renews the earth (Ps. 104:30). Humanity is both part of the created world and charged to be God's steward of the created world (Gen. 1:26–27, 2:7). We are charged to "keep" the earth and to "serve" it (Gen. 2:15), in an attitude of that blessed meekness which will inherit the earth.

17. Human sin has broken the covenants which God has made and subjected the creation to distortion, disruption and disintegration—to "futility" (Rom. 8:20). In our own day we have brought the earth to the brink of destruction. But we confess that the redemptive work of Christ was the renewal not only of human life, but of the whole cosmos. Thus we confidently expect that the covenant promises for the earth's wholeness will be fulfilled, that in Christ "the creation itself will be set free from its bondage to decay and will obtain the glorious freedom of the children of God" (Rom 8:21).

18. The sacramental Christian perspective influences our approach to the creation; we confess that "the earth is the Lord's and all that is in it, the world, and those who live in it" (Ps. 24:1). In the whole of the Christian life we take up the created things of this world and offer them to God for sanctification and transfiguration so that they might manifest the kingdom, where God's will is done and the creation glorifies God forever.

19. We agree that some past understandings have led to domination, to forms of control which have been destructive of life, and to views of nature which regard it as subject to human "ownership" and unqualified manipulation. Many streams of the tradition have misunderstood human "dominion" (Gen. 1:28) as exploitation, and God's transcendence as absence. The more theology stressed God's absolute transcendence and distance from the material sphere, the more the earth was viewed as an "unspiritual" reality, as merely the object of human exploitation. While we repudiate these consequences of some theologies of creation, we also know that they are closely related to ways of life which have received theological sanction and support.

20. We are one in our confession of the Holy Spirit as the Source and Giver of Life, and have rejoiced in exploring together at this assembly the presence and the power of the Spirit. But much remains to be explored. How do we understand the relationship between the presence of the Spirit and "sustainability", and indeed the meaning of that word and relationship for our common life? These are life and death questions for humanity and for the planet as a whole.

21. Our exploration of a Spirit-centered theology of creation has led us to deeper understanding. The heritage of indigenous peoples and non-Western cultures, especially those who have retained their spirituality of the land, offers new insights for all. Worldwide, women and the land have often been seen and treated in parallel ways. The Spirit works to heal the wounds of both. Women's experience is invaluable in helping us to understand and to heal our relationships with the earth and with each other. The poor, who invariably suffer first and most from a degraded environment, also teach us things we must know for an adequate theology of creation. In a world so intimately interconnected, their struggles are the critical starting point for all. The community of scientists is also indispensable, for they carry the single most powerful set of tools for our understanding nature and nature's fragility in the face of human onslaught. And beyond this, our sense of the mystery of life and our awe and wonder at the Creator's handiwork is deepened by what we learn from science. We thank God for all these sources of insight, wisdom and understanding.

22. Opinion is divided, however, on how to relate inherited faith claims to the new cultural perspectives of emerging Christian voices, on how to relate Christian accounts of creation to creation stories from other traditions, and on how to relate faith to science in the continuing dialogue on creation.

23. Surely the Spirit blows where it wills. We hope that the WCC as a whole will join our plea to stand in its refreshing breezes, even as we carry on the necessary task of discerning together the spirits to see if they are of God. There are new perspectives and new partners in today's world. We cannot turn our back on them.

24. In the institutions of the sabbath, the sabbatical year and the jubilee year, the Bible has shown us how to reconcile economics and ecology, how to recreate people and society (Ex. 23, Lev. 25). Effective economics and stewardship of the earth's resources must be seen together. Law and mercy, discipline and social justice complement one another.

25. Reducing the destructive human domination over creation calls for a new, inclusive experience of community and sharing. The biblical vision is of an intimate and unbreakable relationship between development, economy and ecology. This vision is dimmed when progress is seen as the production and consumption of more and more material things, while development is equated with growth. The vision vanishes when wealth is cut off from the needs of the poor, and the world is divided between North and South, industrialized and non-industrialized nations. Exploitation of nation by nation, of people by companies, and of those who have only the work of their hands to offer by those who have access to powerful economic resources, leads inevitably to conflict. The unfair distribution of resources brings starvation to our neighbours, while destroying the integrity of our souls. In efforts to increase the gross *national* product, the gross *natural* product is diminished.

26. Any policy or action that threatens the sustainability of creation needs to be questioned. We cannot ignore the burden of debts that can never be repaid, bio-technologies through which human beings unsurp powers that belong to the Creator, or the fact that the root causes of population growth lie largely in the poverty and lack of social security still prevailing in two-thirds of our world. In facing these and other crucial issues we need the dynamic power of the Spirit which integrates faith and life, worship and action to overcome our fear of change.

27. The free-market economy facilitates rapid response to needs expressed in financial terms. But market and prices do not possess any inherent morality. The vast and shameful arms trade illustrates clearly the immorality of our world economic order; it is one of the root causes of the Gulf war. The international ecumenical movement has for years criticized the lack of economic democracy, social injustice, and the stimulation of human greed. But flagrant international inequality in the distribution of income, knowledge, power and wealth persists. Acquisitive materialism has become the dominant ideology of our day. The irresponsible exploitation of the created world continues. Changes will come only by active opposition and informed and responsible social pressure. We are now more than ever aware that the market economy is in need of reform, and to that end we suggest the following means: . . .

30. *Rethinking economics:* We should not lose sight of how the world community must be accountable to the whole creation, and how it is responsible for the economic and ecological choices to which the world system of trade leads. Market prices rarely reflect real long-term scarcities. Prices should reflect the need to conserve and to regenerate what nature offers; a market economy price is based on demand and supply, which are both being calculated on a very narrow, short-term basis. Non-material needs receive no price; hence they are often not satisfied through consumption, but only increased.

31. What we need, therefore, is a new concept of value, one based not on money and exchange but rather on *sustainability* and *use*. We need likewise a new concept of development as opposed to simple growth, a development which results in a self-sustaining whole. What is "just" and "right", then, must be found in social, biological, and physical relationships involving humanity and the earth. Such a true development focuses on the level of the eco-system as a whole.

32. *A universal declaration on human obligations towards nature:* The existing Universal Declaration of Human Rights serves as a moral standard for those charged with the responsibility of exercising power. In June 1992, the second United Nations Conference on Environment and Development that will take place in Brazil will present a plan for an "earth charter". It would comprise an international agreement on the obligations and responsibilities of governments to the global environment and to future generations. We think that the charter should include a section on the obligations of industrial and agricultural producers of goods and services, with special reference to global corporations, and a section on the responsibilities of consumers. There should be judicial mechanisms for the implementation of the charter from international to local levels. And an international organization, comparable to Amnesty International, should be formed to expose violations of the charter and to mobilize the public conscience. Collective action by consumers would be very helpful to this end. . . .

34. The church, a redeemed community which is a sign of the "new creation" in Christ, is called by God to a crucial role in the renewal of creation. Empowered by the Spirit, Christians are called to repent of their misuse and abuse of nature and to reflect critically upon the ways of understanding the Bible, and the theological systems which have been used to justify such abuse.

35. A new appreciation of the theology of creation and a fresh awareness of Christian responsibility towards all of creation may deepen the faith, and enrich the life and work, of the church.

Section II: Spirit of Truth—Set Us Free!

"For freedom Christ has set us free . . . For you were called to freedom, brothers and sisters . . ." (Gal. 5:1, 13). . . .

39. The Spirit of freedom and truth moves us to witness to the justice of the kingdom of God and to resist injustice in the world. We manifest the life of the Spirit by striving for the release of those who are captive to sin and by standing with the oppressed in their struggles for liberation, justice and peace. Liberated by the Spirit we are empowered to understand the world from the perspective of the poor and vulnerable and to give ourselves to mission, service and the sharing of our resources. . . .

41. Through the six preceding assemblies the World Council of Churches has called attention to the need to renew the international economic order. The ecumenical process on Justice, Peace and the Integrity of Creation (JPIC) confirmed the view that prevailing models of economic growth and world trade do not create conditions for a just and sustainable world society but rather destroy the ecological systems of the world, provoke massive migrations and lead to wars. The organization of the international market in ways which would promote life and justice for all remains a major challenge. We look for a review leading to more accountable and just economic and monetary structures, within the jurisdiction of the United Nations and the International Court of Justice. The creation of a just world economic order may require the creation of new international organizations.

42. Closely linked to the present economic order and the organization of the international market is the ongoing debt crisis which, since the end of the 1970s, has meant the impoverishment of the most deeply-indebted nations of Africa, Asia, the Caribbean, Latin America, and the Pacific. The debt crisis also threatens the economic prospects of the former "socialist" nations of Eastern Europe and is introducing tensions, financial instability and economic recession in North America, Western Europe and Japan. In this very serious situation the WCC and its member churches are called to share their energies and resources with those who suffer the effects of the world economic system. The critical reformulation of this system must be one of our priorities.

43. As Christians we seek a world of social and economic justice. This includes the empowerment of the victims of injustice and respect and care for those who are vulnerable, oppressed and dispossessed. The networks of concern that churches and Christian communities can build together and with other organizations can play a positive role in this process.

44. Racism, one of the terrible sins of humankind, is incompatible with the gospel of Christ. It is not simply exercised through personal prejudice but is also embodied in the structures and institutions of society. When members of one race or group seek to dominate those of another they are not truly free but are enslaved by their own fear and desire for control. Being oppressed and being an oppressor are both spiritually disabling. We see the need for both individual repentance of the sin of racism and for changes to abolish structural and institutional racism. The liberating voice of the Spirit calls us to embrace all our sisters and brothers in love and with justice. . . .

49. Communication in the light and power of the Spirit supports and sustains the building of a community of justice and equips us to challenge the powers which are opposed to the Spirit of truth. Our communication as Christians must be prophetic, serving the cause of justice, peace, and the integrity of creation. We are to communicate with one another in love, speaking the truth and listening to hear what is truly being said, rather than what we want to hear.

50. The mass media are powerful means of control, where the truth is often not told and we are unable to exercise an informed and free judgment. Control may be exercised by governments, the market, or the dominant culture. We are specially concerned about the influence on children of the media's promotion of violence, pornography and obscenity. Churches can seek ways to educate people to be discerning listeners, viewers and readers and to develop people's participation in communication. We encourage our churches to find ways to develop communications for liberation, to promote good interpersonal communication and the telling of the stories of the people. We encourage individual Christians who work in the field of communications to exercise their Christian witness in the work-place.

51. The search for lasting peace and meaningful security presents different challenges in the various regions of the world. The Seoul covenant (from the JPIC [Justice, Peace and the Integrity of Creation] process) with its four interlocking elements of protection of the environment, alleviation of debts, demilitarization of international relations and the rejection of racism, provides us with a helpful framework for our Christian commitment to peace with justice.

52. We affirm the roles of the United Nations and the International Court of Justice, and believe that these and other constructive international instruments for peace and security need to be developed and strengthened.

53. Churches are called to serve as examples of peace-making, not least by making peace among themselves. They must resist the use of religious factors to cause or exacerbate conflict, and we urge that they strengthen their regional solidarity in work for peace. The World Council of Churches could play a greater role in education for peace and in working for reconciliation in situations of conflict between churches and states.

54. The relationship between men and women is fundamental to the human condition although there are major cultural differences in the expression of such relationships. Sexual difference is a gift of God in creation but our human societies are often distorted by sexism (that is, discrimination based on gender). Specific aspects of sexism which concern us are the economic injustice experienced by many women and the growing phenomenon of the feminization of poverty (in other words the fact that increasingly the poor are women). In the work-place women are not only frequently underpaid and exploited but also are often forced to participate on male terms, which take little notice of their special needs and responsibilities. At work, at home and in society generally it is common for women and children to be the victims of male violence.

55. The Ecumenical Decade of the Churches in Solidarity with Women is an urgent call to the churches to give creative support to women's movements and groups which challenge oppressive structures in the global community and in the local community and church. The form which solidarity with women will take depends very much on local circumstances and on the needs and aspirations of women themselves, but we are sure that the full participation of women in our churches and societies will encourage the renewal of community.

56. As we affirm that "in Christ there is neither male nor female" (Gal. 3:28) we call on Christian communities and families to strive for equality in relationships, for mutual respect, a sharing of tasks and responsibilities and new models of caring and sharing. We acknowledge that churches differ in their approaches to the question of the ordination of women. Some see it as an issue of justice while others do not. In this situation we urge mutual respect for the other's position in the spirit of love and understanding.

From *Signs of the Spirit: Official Report,* edited by Michael Kinnamon (Geneva: World Council of Churches Publications, and Grand Rapids, Mich.: Wm. B. Eerdmans Publishing Corp., 1991), pp. 238–48. Copyright © 1991 by World Council of Churches.

64.   Gustavo Gutiérrez,
A Theology of Liberation

Peruvian Gustavo Gutiérrez (born 1928) is one of many Catholic priests who, encouraged by the Second Vatican Council and the 1968 Medellín conference of Latin American bishops, sought to develop a theology of praxis appropriate for a church that sees its purpose as service to the world. This "liberation theology," published in 1971 (English translation in 1973), uses aspects of Marxian social analysis in order to explicate God's "preferential option for the poor."

The function of theology as critical reflection on praxis has gradually become more clearly defined in recent years. . . .

For various reasons the existential and active aspects of the Christian life have recently been stressed in a different way than in the immediate past.

In the first place, *charity* has been fruitfully rediscovered as the center of the Christian life. This has led to a more biblical view of the faith as an act of trust, a going out of one's self, a commitment to God and neighbor, a relationship with others. It is in this sense that St. Paul tells us that faith works through charity: love is the nourishment and the fullness of faith, the gift of one's self to the Other, and invariably to others. This is the foundation of the *praxis* of the Christian, of his active presence in history. According to the Bible, faith is the total response of man to God, who saves through love. In this light, the understanding of the faith appears as the understanding not of the simple affirmation—almost memorization—of truths, but of a commitment, an overall attitude, a particular posture toward life. . . .

Moreover, today there is a greater sensitivity to the *anthropological aspects* of revelation. The Word about God is at the same time a promise to the world. In revealing God to us, the Gospel message reveals us to ourselves in our situation before the Lord and with other men. The God of Christian revelation is a God made man, hence the famous comment of Karl Barth regarding Christian anthropocentrism: "Man is the measure of all things, since God became man." All this has caused the revaluation of the presence and the activity of man in the world, especially in relation to other men. . . .

Vatican Council II has strongly reaffirmed the idea of a Church of service and not of power. This is a Church which is not centered upon itself and which does not "find itself" except when it "loses itself," when it lives "the joys and the hopes, the griefs and the anxieties of men of this age" (*Gaudium et spes*, no. 1). All of these trends provide a new focus for seeing the presence and activity of the Church in the world as a starting point for theological reflection.

What since John XXIII and Vatican Council II began to be called a theology of the *signs of the times* can be characterized along the same lines, although this takes a step beyond narrow ecclesial limits. It must not be forgotten that the signs of the times are not only a call to intellectual analysis. They are above all a call to pastoral activity, to commitment, and to service. . . .

To these factors can be added the influence of *Marxist thought,* focusing on praxis and geared to the transformation of the world. The Marxist influence began to be felt in the middle of the nineteenth century, but in recent times its cultural impact has become greater. Many agree with Sartre that "Marxism, as the formal framework of all contemporary philosophical thought, cannot be superseded." Be that as it may, contemporary theology does in fact find itself in direct and fruitful confrontation with Marxism, and it is to a large extent due to Marxism's influence that theological thought, searching for its own sources, has begun to reflect on the meaning of the transformation of this world and the action of man in history. Further, this confrontation helps theology to perceive what its efforts at understanding the faith receive from the historical praxis of man in history as well as what its own reflection might mean for the transformation of the world.

Finally, the rediscovery of the *eschatological dimension* in theology has also led us to consider the central role of historical praxis. Indeed, if human history is above all else an opening to the future, then it is a task, a political occupation, through which man orients and opens himself to the gift which gives history its transcendent meaning: the full and definitive encounter with the Lord and with other men. "To do the truth," as the Gospel says, thus acquires a precise and concrete meaning in terms of the importance of action in Christian life. Faith in a God who loves us and calls us to the gift of full communion with him and brotherhood among men not only is not foreign to the transformation of the world; it leads necessarily to the building up of that brotherhood and communion in history. Moreover, only by doing this truth will our faith be "veri-fied," in the etymological sense of the word. From this notion has recently been derived the term *orthopraxis,* which still disturbs the sensitivities of some. The intention, however, is not to deny the meaning of *orthodoxy,* understood as a proclamation of and reflection on statements considered to be true. Rather, the goal is to balance and even to reject the primacy and almost exclusiveness which doctrine has enjoyed in Christian life and above all to modify the emphasis, often obsessive, upon the attainment of an orthodoxy which is often nothing more than fidelity to an obsolete tradition or a debatable interpretation. In a more positive vein, the intention is to recognize the work and importance of concrete behavior, of deeds, of action, of praxis in the Christian life. . . .

To reflect upon the presence and action of the Christian in the world means, moreover, to go beyond the visible boundaries of the Church. This is of prime importance. It implies openness to the world, gathering the questions it poses, being attentive to its historical transformation. . . . It is precisely this opening to the totality of human history that allows theology to fulfill its critical function vis-à-vis ecclesial praxis without narrowness. . . .

This kind of theology, arising from concern with a particular set of issues, will perhaps give us the solid and permanent albeit modest foundation for the *theology in a Latin American perspective* which is both desired and needed. This Latin American focus would not be due to a frivolous desire for originality, but rather to a fundamental sense of historical efficacy and also—why hide it?—to the desire to contribute to the life and reflection of the universal Christian community. But in order to make our contribution, this desire for universality—as well as input from the Christian community as a whole—must be present from the beginning. To concretize this desire would be to overcome particularistic tendencies—provincial and chauvinistic—and produce something *unique,* both particular and universal, and therefore fruitful.

. . . The present in the praxis of liberation, in its deepest dimension, is pregnant with the future; hope must be an inherent part of our present commitment in history. Theology does not initiate this future which exists in the present. It does not create the vital attitude of hope out of nothing. Its role is more modest. It interprets and explains these as the true underpinnings of history. To reflect upon a forward-directed action is not to concentrate on the past. It does not mean being the caboose of the present. Rather it is to penetrate the present reality, the movement of history, that which is driving history toward the future. To reflect on the basis of the historical praxis of liberation is to reflect in the light of the future which is believed in and hoped for. It is to reflect with a view to action which transforms the present. But it does not mean doing this from an armchair; rather it means sinking roots where the pulse of history is beating at this moment and illuminating history with the Word of the Lord of history, who irreversibly committed himself to the present moment of mankind to carry it to its fulfillment.

It is for all these reasons that the theology of liberation offers us not so much a new theme for reflection as a *new way* to do theology. Theology as critical reflection on historical praxis is a liberating theology, a theology of the liberating transformation of the history of mankind and also therefore that part of mankind—gathered into *ecclesia*—which openly confesses Christ. This is a theology which does not stop with reflecting on the world, but rather tries to be part of the process through which the world is transformed. It is a theology which is open—in the protest against trampled human dignity, in the struggle against the plunder of the vast majority of people, in liberating love, and in the building of a new, just, and fraternal society—to the gift of the Kingdom of God.

. . . [W]e are faced with an increasing radicalization of social praxis. Contemporary man has begun to lose his naiveté as he confronts economic and socio-cultural determinants; the deep causes of the situation in which he finds himself are becoming clearer. He realizes that to attack these deep causes is the indispensable prerequisite for radical change. And so he has gradually abandoned a simple reformist attitude regarding the existing social order, for, by its very shallowness this reformism perpetuates the existing system. The revolutionary situation which prevails today, especially in the Third World, is an expression of this growing radicalization. To support the social revolution means to abolish the present status quo and to attempt to replace it with a qualitatively different one; it means to build a just society based on new relationships of production; it means to attempt to put an end to the domination of some countries by others, of some social classes by others, of some people by others. The liberation of these countries, social classes and people undermines the very foundation of the present order; it is the greatest challenge of our time.

This radicality has led us to see quite clearly that the political arena is necessarily conflictual. More precisely, the building of a just society means the confrontation—in which different kinds of violence are present—between groups with different interests and opinions. The building of a just society means overcoming every obstacle to the creation of an authentic peace among people. Concretely, in Latin America this conflict revolves around the *oppression-liberation axis*. Social praxis makes demands which may seem difficult or disturbing to those who wish to achieve—or maintain—a low-cost conciliation. Such a conciliation can be only a justifying ideology for a profound disorder, a device for the few to keep living off the poverty of the many. But to become aware of the conflictual nature of the political sphere should not mean to become complacent. On the contrary, it should mean struggling—with clarity and courage, deceiving neither oneself nor others—for the establishment of peace and justice among all people.

In the past, concern for social praxis in theological thought did not sufficiently take into account the political dimension. In Christian circles there was—and continues to be—difficulty in perceiving the originality and specificity of the political sphere. Stress was placed on private life and on the cultivation of private values; things political were relegated to a lower plane, to the elusive and undemanding area of a misunderstood "common good." At most, this viewpoint provided a basis for "social pastoral planning," grounded on the "social emotion" which every self-respecting Christian ought to experience. Hence there developed the complacency with a very general and "humanizing" vision of reality, to the detriment of a scientific and structural knowledge of socio-economic mechanisms and historical dynamics. Hence also there came the insistence on the personal and conciliatory aspects of the Gospel message rather than on its political and conflictual dimensions. We must take a new look at Christian life; we must see how these emphases in the past have conditioned and challenged the historical presence of the Church. This presence has an inescapable political dimension. . . . Participation in the process of liberation is an obligatory and privileged *locus* for Christian life and reflection. In this participation will be heard nuances of the Word of God which are imperceptible in other existential situations and without which there can be no authentic and fruitful faithfulness to the Lord.

If we look more deeply into the question of the value of salvation which emerges from our understanding of history—that is, a liberating praxis—we see that at issue is a question concerning *the very meaning of Christianity*. To be a Christian is to accept and to live—in solidarity, in faith, hope and charity—the meaning that the Word of the Lord and our encounter with him give to the historical becoming of mankind on the way toward total communion. To regard the unique and absolute relationship with God as the horizon of every human action is to place oneself, from the outset, in a wider and more profound context. It is likewise more demanding. We are faced in our day with the bare, central theologico-pastoral question: *What does it mean to be a Christian? What does it mean to be Church in the unknown circumstances of the future?* In the last instance, we must search the Gospel message for the answer to what according to Camus constitutes the most important question facing all people: "To decide whether life deserves to be lived or not."

These elements lend perhaps greater depth and a new dimension to the traditional problem. Not to acknowledge the newness of the issues raised under the pretext that in one way or another the problem has always been present is to detach oneself dangerously from reality; it is to risk falling into generalities, solutions without commitment, and, finally, evasive attitudes. But, on the other hand, to acknowledge nothing but the new aspects of the contemporary statement of the problem is to forego the contribution of the life and reflection of the Christian community in its historical pilgrimage. Its successes, its omissions, and its errors are our heritage. They should not, however, delimit our boundaries. The People of God march on "accounting for their hope" toward "a new heaven and a new earth." . . .

The theology of liberation attempts to reflect on the experience and meaning of the faith based on the commitment to abolish injustice and to build a new society; this theology must be verified by the practice of that commitment, by active, effective participation in the struggle which the exploited social classes have undertaken against their oppressors. Liberation from every form of exploitation, the possibility of a more human and more dignified life, the creation of a new man—all pass through this struggle.

But in the last instance we will have an authentic theology of liberation only when the oppressed themselves can freely raise their voice and express themselves directly and creatively in society and in the heart of the People of God, when they themselves "account for the hope," which they bear, when they are the protagonists of their own liberation. For now we must limit ourselves to efforts which ought to deepen and support that process, which has barely begun.

From Gustavo Gutiérrez, *A Theology of Liberation: History, Politics and Salvation,* 1st ed., translated and edited by Sister Caridad Inda and John Eagleson (Maryknoll, N.Y.: Orbis Books, 1973), pp. 6–15, 47–50, 307; 2nd ed. (Mary Knoll, N.Y.: Orbis Books and London: SCM Press, Ltd., 1988).

65.   Martin Luther King, Jr., *Letter from Birmingham City Jail*

This open letter by Martin Luther King, Jr. (1929–1968) was written while the great American civil rights leader was in prison. He had been arrested during the tense campaign in Birmingham, Alabama, in 1963. The letter is a classic statement of his theory of justice and nonviolent civil disobedience, and it contains a stern rebuke of the complacent church.

While confined here in the Birmingham City Jail, I came across your recent statement calling our present activities "unwise and untimely." Seldom, if ever, do I pause to answer criticism of my work and ideas. If I sought to answer all of the criticisms that cross my desk, my secretaries would be engaged in little else in the course of the day and I would have no time for constructive work. But since I feel that you are men of genuine goodwill and your criticisms are sincerely set forth, I would like to answer your statement in what I hope will be patient and reasonable terms.

I think I should give the reason for my being in Birmingham, since you have been influenced by the argument of "outsiders coming in." I have the honor of serving as president of the Southern Christian Leadership Conference, an organization operating in every Southern state with headquarters in Atlanta, Georgia. We have some eighty-five affiliate organizations all across the South—one being the Alabama Christian Movement for Human Rights. Whenever necessary and possible we share staff, educational, and financial resources with our affiliates. Several months ago our local affiliate here in Birmingham invited us to be on call to engage in a nonviolent direct action program if such were deemed necessary. We readily consented and when the hour came we lived up to our promises. So I am here, along with several members of my staff, because we were invited here. I am here because I have basic organizational ties here. Beyond this, I am in Birmingham because injustice is here. Just as the eighth century prophets left their little villages and carried their "thus saith the Lord" far beyond the boundaries of their home town, and just as the Apostle Paul left his little village of Tarsus and carried the gospel of Jesus Christ to practically very hamlet and city of the Graeco-Roman world, I too am compelled to carry the gospel of freedom beyond my particular home town. Like Paul, I must constantly respond to the Macedonian call for aid.

Moreover, I am cognizant of the interrelatedness of all communities and states. I cannot sit idly by in Atlanta and not be concerned about what happens in Birmingham. Injustice anywhere is a threat to justice everywhere. We are caught in an inescapable network of mutuality tied in a single garment of destiny. Whatever affects one directly affects all indirectly. Never again can we afford to live with the narrow, provincial "outside agitator" idea. Anyone who lives inside the United States can never be considered an outsider anywhere in this country.

You deplore the demonstrations that are presently taking place in Birmingham. But I am sorry that your statement did not express a similar concern for the conditions that brought the demonstrations into being. I am sure that each of you would want to go beyond the superficial social analyst who looks merely at effects, and does not grapple with underlying causes. I would not hesitate to say that it is unfortunate that so-called demonstrations are taking place in Birmingham at this time, but I would say in more emphatic terms that it is even more unfortunate that the white power structure of this city left the Negro community with no other alternative.

In any nonviolent campaign there are four basic steps: (1) collection of the facts to determine whether injustices are alive; (2) negotiation; (3) self-purification; and (4) direct action. We have gone through all of these steps in Birmingham. There can be no gainsaying of the fact that racial injustice engulfs this community. Birmingham is probably the most thoroughly segregated city in the United States. Its ugly record of police brutality is known in every section of this country. Its unjust treatment of Negroes in the courts is a notorious reality. There have been more unsolved bombings of Negro homes and churches in Birmingham than any city in this nation. These are the hard, brutal, and unbelievable facts. On the basis of these conditions Negro leaders sought to negotiate with the city fathers. But the political leaders consistently refused to engage in good faith negotiation.

Then came the opportunity last September to talk with some of the leaders of the economic community. In these negotiating sessions certain promises were made by the merchants—such as the promise to remove the humiliating racial signs from the stores. On the basis of these promises Rev. Shuttlesworth and the leaders of the Alabama Christian Movement for Human Rights agreed to call a moratorium on any type of demonstrations. As the weeks and months unfolded we realized that we were the victims of a broken promise. The signs remained. As in so many experiences of the past we were confronted with blasted hopes, and the dark shadow of a deep disappointment settled upon us. So we had no alternative except that of preparing for direct action, whereby we would present our very bodies as a means of laying our case before the conscience of the local and national community. We were not unmindful of the difficulties involved. So we decided to go through a process of self-purification. We started having workshops on nonviolence and repeatedly asked ourselves the questions, "Are you able to accept blows without retaliating?" "Are you able to endure the ordeals of jail?"

We decided to set our direct action program around the Easter season, realizing that with the exception of Christmas, this was the largest shopping period of the year. Knowing that a strong economic withdrawal program would be the by-product of direct action, we felt that this was the best time to bring pressure on the merchants for the needed changes. Then it occurred to us that the March election was ahead, and so we speedily decided to postpone action until after election day. When we discovered that Mr. Connor was in the run-off, we decided again to postpone action so that the demonstrations could not be used to cloud the issues. At this time we agreed to begin our nonviolent witness the day after the run-off.

This reveals that we did not move irresponsibly into direct action. We too wanted to see Mr. Connor defeated; so we went through postponement after postponement to aid in this community need. After this we felt that direct action could be delayed no longer.

You may well ask, "Why direct action? Why sit-ins, marches, etc.? Isn't negotiation a better path?" You are exactly right in your call for negotiation. Indeed, this is the purpose of direct action. Nonviolent direct action seeks to create such a crisis and establish such creative tension that a community that has constantly refused to negotiate is forced to confront the issue. It seeks so to dramatize the issue that it can no longer be ignored. I just

referred to the creation of tension as a part of the work of the nonviolent re-
sister. This may sound rather shocking. But I must confess that I am not
afraid of the word tension. I have earnestly worked and preached against
violent tension, but there is a type of constructive nonviolent tension that
is necessary for growth. Just as Socrates felt that it was necessary to create
a tension in the mind so that individuals could rise from the bondage of
myths and half-truths to the unfettered realm of creative analysis and objective appraisal, we must see the need of having nonviolent gadflies to create the kind of tension in society that will help men rise from the dark
depths of prejudice and racism to the majestic heights of understanding
and brotherhood. So the purpose of the direct action is to create a situation
so crisis-packed that it will inevitably open the door to negotiation. We,
therefore, concur with you in your call for negotiation. Too long has our
beloved Southland been bogged down in the tragic attempt to live in mono-
logue rather than dialogue.

One of the basic points in your statement is that our acts are untimely.
Some have asked, "Why didn't you give the new administration time to
act?" The only answer that I can give to this inquiry is that the new administration must be prodded about as much as the outgoing one before it
acts. We will be sadly mistaken if we feel that the election of Mr. Boutwell
will bring the millennium to Birmingham. While Mr. Boutwell is much
more articulate and gentle than Mr. Connor, they are both segregationists
dedicated to the task of maintaining the status quo. The hope I see in Mr.
Boutwell is that he will be reasonable enough to see the futility of massive
resistance to desegregation. But he will not see this without pressure from
the devotees of civil rights. My friends, I must say to you that we have not
made a single gain in civil rights without determined legal and nonviolent
pressure. History is the long and tragic story of the fact that privileged
groups seldom give up their privileges voluntarily. Individuals may see the
moral light and voluntarily give up their unjust posture; but as Reinhold
Niebuhr has reminded us, groups are more immoral than individuals.

We know through painful experience that freedom is never voluntarily
given by the oppressor; it must be demanded by the oppressed. Frankly I
have never yet engaged in a direct action movement that was "well timed,"
according to the timetable of those who have not suffered unduly from the
disease of segregation. For years now I have heard the word "Wait!" It
rings in the ear of every Negro with a piercing familiarity. This "wait" has
almost always meant "never." It has been a tranquilizing thalidomide, relieving the emotional stress for a moment, only to give birth to an ill-formed
infant of frustration. We must come to see with the distinguished jurist of
yesterday that "justice too long delayed is justice denied." We have waited
for more than three hundred and forty years for our constitutional and
God-given rights. The nations of Asia and Africa are moving with jet-like
speed toward the goal of political independence, and we still creep at horse
and buggy pace toward the gaining of a cup of coffee at a lunch counter.

I guess it is easy for those who have never felt the stinging darts of segregation to say wait. But when you have seen vicious mobs lynch your

mothers and fathers at will and drown your sisters and brothers at whim; when you have seen hate filled policemen curse, kick, brutalize, and even kill your black brothers and sisters with impunity; when you see the vast majority of your twenty million Negro brothers smothering in an air-tight cage of poverty in the midst of an affluent society; when you suddenly find your tongue twisted and your speech stammering as you seek to explain to your six-year-old daughter why she can't go to the public amusement park that has just been advertised on television, and see tears welling up in her little eyes when she is told that Funtown is closed to colored children, and see the depressing clouds of inferiority begin to form in her little mental sky, and see her begin to distort her little personality by unconsciously developing a bitterness toward white people; when you have to concoct an answer for a five-year-old son asking in agonizing pathos: "Daddy, why do white people treat colored people so mean?"; when you take a cross country drive and find it necessary to sleep night after night in the uncomfortable corners of your automobile because no motel will accept you; when you are humiliated day in and day out by nagging signs reading "white" men and "colored"; when your first name becomes "nigger" and your middle name becomes "boy" (however old you are) and your last name becomes "John," and when your wife and mother are never given the respected title "Mrs."; when you are harried by day and haunted by night by the fact that you are a Negro, living constantly at tip-toe stance never quite knowing what to expect next, and plagued with inner fears and outer resentments; when you are forever fighting a degenerating sense of "nobodiness";—then you will understand why we find it difficult to wait. There comes a time when the cup of endurance runs over, and men are no longer willing to be plunged into an abyss of injustice where they experience the bleakness of corroding despair. I hope, sirs, you can understand our legitimate and unavoidable impatience.

You express a great deal of anxiety over our willingness to break laws. This is certainly a legitimate concern. Since we so diligently urge people to obey the Supreme Court's decision of 1954 outlawing segregation in the public schools, it is rather strange and paradoxical to find us consciously breaking laws. One may well ask, "How can you advocate breaking some laws and obeying others?" The answer is found in the fact that there are two types of laws: There are *just* laws and there are *unjust* laws. I would be the first to advocate obeying just laws. One has not only a legal but moral responsibility to obey just laws. Conversely, one has a moral responsibility to disobey unjust laws. I would agree with Saint Augustine that "An unjust law is no law at all."

Now what is the difference between the two? How does one determine when a law is just or unjust? A just law is a man-made code that squares with the moral law or the law of God. An unjust law is a code that is out of harmony with the moral law. To put it in the terms of Saint Thomas Aquinas, an unjust law is a human law that is not rooted in eternal and natural law. Any law that uplifts human personality is just. Any law that degrades human personality is unjust. All segregation statues are unjust because segregation distorts the soul and damages the personality. It gives the segregator a false sense of superiority and the segregated a false sense of inferiority. To use the words of Martin Buber, the great Jewish philosopher, segregation substitutes an "I-it" relationship for the "I-thou" relationship, and ends up relegating persons to the status of things. So segregation is not only politically, economically, and sociologically unsound, but it is morally wrong and sinful. Paul Tillich has said that sin is separation. Isn't segregation an existential expression of man's tragic separation, an expression of his awful estrangement, his terrible sinfulness? So I can urge men to obey the 1954 decision of the Supreme Court because it is morally right, and I can urge them to disobey segregation ordinances because they are morally wrong.

Let us turn to a more concrete example of just and unjust laws. An unjust law is a code that a majority inflicts on a minority that is not binding on itself. This is *difference* made legal. On the other hand a just law is a code that a majority compels a minority to follow that it is willing to follow itself. This is *sameness* made legal.

Let me give another explanation. An unjust law is a code inflicted upon a minority which that minority had no part in enacting or creating because they did not have the unhampered right to vote. Who can say the legislature of Alabama which set up the segregation laws was democratically elected? Throughout the state of Alabama all types of conniving methods are used to prevent Negroes from becoming registered voters and there are some counties without a single Negro registered to vote despite the fact that the Negro constitutes a majority of the population. Can any law set up in such a state be considered democratically structured?

These are just a few examples of unjust and just laws. There are some instances when a law is just on its face but unjust in its application. For instance, I was arrested Friday on a charge of parading without a permit. Now there is nothing wrong with an ordinance which requires a permit for a parade, but when the ordinance is used to preserve segregation and to deny citizens the First Amendment privilege of peaceful assembly and peaceful protest, then it becomes unjust.

I hope you can see the distinction I am trying to point out. In no sense do I advocate evading or defying the law as the rabid segregationist would do. This would lead to anarchy. One who breaks an unjust law must do it *openly, lovingly* (not hatefully as the white mothers did in New Orleans when they were seen on television screaming "nigger, nigger, nigger") and with a willingness to accept the penalty. I submit that an individual who breaks a law that conscience tells him is unjust, and willingly accepts the penalty by staying in jail to arouse the conscience of the community over its injustice, is in reality expressing the very highest respect for law.

Of course there is nothing new about this kind of civil disobedience. It was seen sublimely in the refusal of Shadrach, Meshach, and Abednego to obey the laws of Nebuchadnezzar because a higher moral law was involved. It was practiced superbly by the early Christians who were willing to face hungry lions and the excruciating pain of chopping blocks, before submitting to certain unjust laws of the Roman Empire. To a degree academic freedom is a reality today because Socrates practiced civil disobedience.

We can never forget that everything Hitler did in Germany was "legal" and everything the Hungarian freedom fighters did in Hungary was "illegal." It was "illegal" to aid and comfort a Jew in Hitler's Germany. But I am sure that, if I had lived in Germany during that time, I would have aided and comforted my Jewish brothers even though it was illegal. If I lived in a communist country today where certain principles dear to the Christian faith are suppressed, I believe I would openly advocate disobeying these antireligious laws.

I must make two honest confessions to you, my Christian and Jewish brothers. First I must confess that over the last few years I have been gravely disappointed with the white moderate. I have almost reached the regrettable conclusion that the Negroes' great stumbling block in the stride toward freedom is not the White Citizens' "Counciler" or the Ku Klux Klanner, but the white moderate who is more devoted to "order" than to justice; who prefers a negative peace which is the absence of tension to a positive peace which is the presence of justice; who constantly says "I agree with you in the goal you seek, but I can't agree with your methods of direct action"; who paternalistically feels that he can set the time-table for another man's freedom; who lives by the myth of time and who constantly advises the Negro to wait until a "more convenient season." Shallow understanding from people of good will is more frustrating than absolute misunderstanding from people of ill will. Lukewarm acceptance is much more bewildering than outright rejection.

I had hoped that the white moderate would understand that law and order exist for the purpose of establishing justice, and that when they fail to do this they become the dangerously structured dams that block the flow of social progress. I had hoped that the white moderate would understand that the present tension in the South is merely a necessary phase of the transition from an obnoxious negative peace, where the Negro passively accepted his unjust plight, to a substance-filled positive peace, where all men will respect the dignity and worth of human personality. Actually, we who engage in nonviolent direct action are not the creators of tension. We merely bring to the surface the hidden tension that is already alive. We bring it out in the open where it can be seen and dealt with. Like a boil that can never be cured as long as it is covered up but must be opened with all its pus-flowing ugliness to the natural medicines of air and light, injustice must likewise be exposed, with all of the tension its exposing creates, to the light of human conscience and the air of national opinion before it can be cured.

In your statement you asserted that our actions, even though peaceful, must be condemned because they precipitate violence. But can this assertion be logically made? Isn't this like condemning the robbed man because his possession of money precipitated the evil act of robbery? Isn't this like condemning Socrates because his unswerving commitment to truth and his philosophical delvings precipitated the misguided popular mind to make him drink the hemlock? Isn't this like condemning Jesus because His unique God consciousness and never-ceasing devotion to His will precipitated the evil act of crucifixion? We must come to see, as federal courts have consistently affirmed, that it is immoral to urge an individual to withdraw his efforts to gain his basic constitutional rights because the quest precipitates violence. Society must protect the robbed and punish the robber.

I had also hoped that the white moderate would reject the myth of time. I received a letter this morning from a white brother in Texas which said: "All Christians know that the colored people will receive equal rights eventually, but is it possible that you are in too great of a religious hurry? It has taken Christianity almost 2000 years to accomplish what it has. The teachings of Christ take time to come to earth." All that is said here grows out of a tragic misconception of time. It is the strangely irrational notion that there is something in the very flow of time that will inevitably cure all ills. Actually time is neutral. It can be used either destructively or constructively. I am coming to feel that the people of ill will have used time much more effectively than the people of good will. We will have to repent in this generation not merely for the vitriolic words and actions of the bad people, but for the appalling silence of the good people. We must come to see that human progress never rolls in on wheels of inevitability. It comes through the tireless efforts and persistent work of men willing to be co-workers with God, and without this hard work time itself becomes an ally of the forces of social stagnation.

We must use time creatively, and forever realize that the time is always ripe to do right. Now is the time to make real the promise of democracy, and transform our pending national elegy into a creative psalm of brotherhood. Now is the time to lift our national policy from the quicksand of racial injustice to the solid rock of human dignity.

You spoke of our activity in Birmingham as extreme. At first I was rather disappointed that fellow clergymen would see my nonviolent efforts as those of the extremist. I started thinking about the fact that I stand in the middle of two opposing forces in the Negro community. One is a force of complacency made up of Negroes who, as a result of long years of oppression, have been so completely drained of self-respect and a sense of "somebodiness" that they have adjusted to segregation, and of a few Negroes in the middle class who, because of a degree of academic and economic security, and because at points they profit by segregation, have unconsciously become insensitive to the problems of the masses. The other force is one of bitterness and hatred and comes perilously close to advocating violence. It is expressed in the various black nationalist groups that are springing up over the nation, the largest and best known being Elijah Muhammad's Muslim movement. This movement is nourished by the contemporary frustration over the continued existence of racial discrimination. It is made up of people who have lost faith in America, who have absolutely repudiated Christianity, and who have concluded that the white man is an incurable "devil." I have tried to stand between these two forces saying that we need not follow the "do-nothing-ism" of the complacent or the hatred and despair of the black nationalist. There is the more excellent way of love and nonviolent protest. I'm grateful to God that, through the Negro church, the dimension of nonviolence entered our struggle. If this philosophy had not emerged I am convinced that by now many streets of the South would be flowing with floods of blood. And I am further convinced that if our white brothers dismiss us as "rabble rousers" and "outside agitators"—those of us who are working through the channels of nonviolent direct action—and refuse to support our nonviolent efforts, millions of Negroes, out of frustration and despair, will seek solace and security in black nationalist ideologies, a development that will lead inevitably to a frightening racial nightmare.

Oppressed people cannot remain oppressed forever. The urge for freedom will eventually come. This is what has happened to the American Negro. Something within has reminded him of his birthright of freedom; something without has reminded him that he can gain it. Consciously and unconsciously, he has been swept in by what the Germans call the *Zeitgeist*, and with his black brothers of Africa, and his brown and yellow brothers of Asia, South America, and the Caribbean, he is moving with a sense of cosmic urgency toward the promised land of racial justice. Recognizing this vital urge that has engulfed the Negro community, one should readily understand public demonstrations. The Negro has many pent-up resentments and latent frustrations. He has to get them out. So let him march sometime; let him have his prayer pilgrimages to the city hall; understand why he must have sit-ins and freedom rides. If his repressed emotions do not come out in these nonviolent ways, they will come out in ominous expressions of violence. This is not a threat; it is a fact of history. So I have not said to my people, "Get rid of your discontent." But I have tried to say that this normal and healthy discontent can be channeled through the creative outlet of nonviolent direct action. Now this approach is being dismissed as extremist. I must admit that I was initially disappointed in being so categorized.

But as I continued to think about the matter I gradually gained a bit of satisfaction from being considered an extremist. Was not Jesus an extremist in love? "Love your enemies, bless them that curse you, pray for them that despitefully use you." Was not Amos an extremist for justice—"Let justice roll down like waters and righteousness like a mighty stream." Was not Paul an extremist for the gospel of Jesus Christ—"I bear in my body the marks of the Lord Jesus." Was not Martin Luther an extremist—"Here I stand; I can do none other so help me God." Was not John Bunyan an extremist—"I will stay in jail to the end of my days before I make a butchery of my conscience." Was not Abraham Lincoln an extremist—"This nation cannot survive half slave and half free." Was not Thomas Jefferson an extremist—"We hold these truths to be self evident that all men are created equal." So the question is not whether we will be extremist but what kind of extremist will we be. Will we be extremists for hate or will we be extremists for love? Will we be extremists for the preservation of injustice— or will we be extremists for the cause of justice? In that dramatic scene on Calvary's hill three men were crucified. We must never forget that all three were crucified for the same crime—the crime of extremism. Two were extremists for immorality, and thus fell below their environment. The other, Jesus Christ, was an extremist for love, truth, and goodness, and thereby rose above His environment. So, after all, maybe the South, the nation, and the world are in dire need of creative extremists.

I had hoped that the white moderate would see this. Maybe I was too optimistic. Maybe I expected too much. I guess I should have realized that few members of a race that has oppressed another race can understand or appreciate the deep groans and passionate yearnings of those that have been oppressed, and still fewer have the vision to see that injustice must be rooted out by strong, persistent, and determined action. I am thankful, however, that some of our white brothers have grasped the meaning of this social revolution and committed themselves to it. They are still all too small in quantity, but they are big in quality. Some like Ralph McGill, Lillian Smith, Harry Golden, and James Dabbs have written about our struggle in eloquent, prophetic, and understanding terms. Others have marched with us down nameless streets of the South. They have languished in filthy, roach-infested jails, suffering the abuse and brutality of angry policemen who see them as "dirty nigger lovers." They, unlike so many of their moderate brothers and sisters, have recognized the urgency of the moment and sensed the need for powerful "action" antidotes to combat the disease of segregation.

Let me rush on to mention my other disappointment. I have been so greatly disappointed with the white Church and its leadership. Of course there are some notable exceptions. I am not unmindful of the fact that each of you has taken some significant stands on this issue. I commend you, Rev. Stallings, for your Christian stand on this past Sunday, in welcoming Negroes to your worship service on a non-segregated basis. I commend the Catholic leaders of this state for integrating Springhill College several years ago.

But despite these notable exceptions I must honestly reiterate that I have been disappointed with the Church. I do not say that as one of those negative critics who can always find something wrong with the Church. I say it as a minister of the gospel, who loves the Church; who was nurtured in its bosom; who has been sustained by its spiritual blessings and who will remain true to it as long as the cord of life shall lengthen.

I had the strange feeling when I was suddenly catapulted into the leadership of the bus protest in Montgomery several years ago that we would have the support of the white Church. I felt that the white ministers, priests, and rabbis of the South would be some of our strongest allies. Instead, some have been outright opponents, refusing to understand the freedom movement and misrepresenting its leaders; all too many others have been more cautious than courageous and have remained silent behind the anesthetizing security of stained glass windows.

In spite of my shattered dreams of the past, I came to Birmingham with the hope that the white religious leadership of this community would see the justice of our cause and, with deep moral concern, serve as the channel through which our just grievances could get to the power structure. I had hoped that each of you would understand. But again I have been disappointed.

I have heard numerous religious leaders of the South call upon their worshippers to comply with a desegregation decision because it is the law, but I have longed to hear white ministers say follow this decree because integration is morally right and the Negro is your brother. In the midst of blatant injustices inflicted upon the Negro, I have watched white churches stand on the sideline and merely mouth pious irrelevancies and sanctimonious trivialities. In the midst of a mighty struggle to rid our nation of racial and economic injustice, I have heard so many ministers say, "Those are social issues with which the Gospel has no real concern," and I have watched so many churches commit themselves to a completely other-worldly religion which made a strange distinction between body and soul, the sacred and the secular.

So here we are moving toward the exit of the twentieth century with a religious community largely adjusted to the status quo, standing as a tail light behind other community agencies rather than a headlight leading men to higher levels of justice.

I have travelled the length and breadth of Alabama, Mississippi, and all the other Southern states. On sweltering summer days and crisp autumn mornings I have looked at her beautiful churches with their spires pointing heavenward. I have beheld the impressive outlay of her massive religious education buildings. Over and over again I have found myself asking: "Who worships here? Who is their God? Where were their voices when the lips of Governor Barnett dripped with words of interposition and nullification? Where were they when Governor Wallace gave the clarion call for defiance and hatred? Where were their voices of support when tired, bruised, and weary Negro men and women decided to rise from the dark dungeons of complacency to the bright hills of creative protest?"

Yes, these questions are still in my mind. In deep disappointment, I have wept over the laxity of the Church. But be assured that my tears have been tears of love. There can be no deep disappointment where there is not deep love. Yes, I love the Church; I love her sacred walls. How could I do otherwise? I am in the rather unique position of being the son, the grandson, and the great grandson of preachers. Yes, I see the Church as the body of Christ. But, oh! How we have blemished and scarred that body through social neglect and fear of being nonconformist.

There was a time when the Church was very powerful. It was during that period when the early Christians rejoiced when they were deemed worthy to suffer for what they believed. In those days the Church was not merely a thermometer that recorded the ideas and principles of popular opinion; it was a thermostat that transformed the mores of society. Wherever the early Christians entered a town the power structure got disturbed and immediately sought to convict them for being "disturbers of the peace" and "outside agitators." But they went on with the conviction that they were a "colony of heaven" and had to obey God rather than man. They were small in number but big in commitment. They were too God-intoxicated to be "astronomically intimidated." They brought an end to such ancient evils as infanticide and gladiatorial contest.

Things are different now. The contemporary Church is so often a weak, ineffectual voice with an uncertain sound. It is so often the arch-supporter of the status quo. Far from being disturbed by the presence of the Church, the power structure of the average community is consoled by the Church's silent and often vocal sanction of things as they are.

But the judgment of God is upon the Church as never before. If the Church of today does not recapture the sacrificial spirit of the early Church, it will lose its authentic ring, forfeit the loyalty of millions, and be dismissed as an irrelevant social club with no meaning for the twentieth century. I am meeting young people every day whose disappointment with the Church has risen to outright disgust.

Maybe again I have been too optimistic. Is organized religion too inextricably bound to the status quo to save our nation and the world? Maybe I must turn my faith to the inner spiritual Church, the church within the Church, as the true *ecclesia* and the hope of the world. But again I am thankful to God that some noble souls from the ranks of organized religion have broken loose from the paralyzing chains of conformity and joined us as active partners in the struggle for freedom. They have left their secure congregations and walked the streets of Albany, Georgia, with us. They have gone through the highways of the South on torturous rides for freedom. Yes, they have gone to jail with us. Some have been kicked out of their churches and lost the support of their bishops and fellow ministers. But they have gone with the faith that right defeated is stronger than evil triumphant. These men have been the leaven in the lump of the race. Their witness has been the spiritual salt that has preserved the true meaning of the Gospel in these troubled times. They have carved a tunnel of hope through the dark mountain of disappointment.

I hope the Church as a whole will meet the challenge of this decisive hour. But even if the Church does not come to the aid of justice, I have no despair about the future. I have no fear about the outcome of our struggle in Birmingham, even if our motives are presently misunderstood. We will reach the goal of freedom in Birmingham and all over the nation, because the goal of America is freedom. Abused and scorned though we may be, our destiny is tied up with the destiny of America. Before the pilgrims landed at Plymouth, we were here. Before the pen of Jefferson etched across the pages of history the majestic words of the Declaration of Independence, we were here. For more than two centuries our foreparents labored in this country without wages; they made cotton "king"; and they built the homes of their masters in the midst of brutal injustice and shameful humiliation—and yet out of a bottomless vitality they continued to thrive and develop. If the inexpressible cruelties of slavery could not stop us, the opposition we now face will surely fail. We will win our freedom because the sacred heritage of our nation and the eternal will of God are embodied in our echoing demands.

I must close now. But before closing I am impelled to mention one other point in your statement that troubled me profoundly. You warmly commended the Birmingham police force for keeping "order" and "preventing violence." I don't believe you would have so warmly commended the police force if you had seen its angry violent dogs literally biting six unarmed, nonviolent Negroes. I don't believe you would so quickly commend the policemen if you would observe their ugly and inhuman treatment of Negroes here in the city jail; if you would watch them push and curse old Negro women and young Negro girls; if you would see them slap and kick old Negro men and young Negro boys; if you will observe them, as they did on two occasions, refuse to give us food because we wanted to sing our grace together. I'm sorry that I can't join in your praise for the police department.

It is true that they have been rather disciplined in their public handling of the demonstrators. In this sense they have been rather publicly "nonviolent." But for what purpose? To preserve the evil system of segregation. Over the last few years I have consistently preached that nonviolence demands that the means we use must be as pure as the ends we seek. So I have tried to make it clear that it is wrong to use immoral means to attain moral ends. But now I must affirm that it is just as wrong, or even moreso, to use moral means to preserve immoral ends. Maybe Mr. Connor and his policemen have been rather publicly nonviolent, as Chief Prichett was in Albany, Georgia, but they have used the moral means of nonviolence to maintain the immoral end of flagrant racial injustice. T. S. Eliot has said that there is no greater treason than to do the right deed for the wrong reason.

I wish you had commended the Negro sit-inners and demonstrators of Birmingham for their sublime courage, their willingness to suffer, and their amazing discipline in the midst of the most inhuman provocation. One day the South will recognize its real heroes. They will be the James Merediths, courageously and with a majestic sense of purpose, facing jeering and hostile mobs and the agonizing loneliness that characterizes the life of the pioneer. They will be old, oppressed, battered Negro women, symbolized in a seventy-two year old woman of Montgomery, Alabama, who rose up with a sense of dignity and with her people decided not to ride the segregated buses, and responded to one who inquired about her tiredness with ungrammatical profundity: "My feets is tired, but my soul is rested." They will be young high school and college students, young ministers of the gospel and a host of the elders, courageously and nonviolently sitting in at lunch counters and willingly going to jail for conscience sake. One day the South will know that when these disinherited children of God sat down at lunch counters they were in reality standing up for the best in the American dream and the most sacred values in our Judeo-Christian heritage, and thus carrying our whole nation back to great wells of democracy which were dug deep by the founding fathers in the formulation of the Constitution and the Declaration of Independence.

Never before have I written a letter this long (or should I say a book?). I'm afraid that it is much too long to take your precious time. I can assure you that it would have been much shorter if I had been writing from a comfortable desk, but what else is there to do when you are alone for days in the dull monotony of a narrow jail cell other than write long letters, think strange thoughts, and pray long prayers?

If I have said anything in this letter that is an overstatement of the truth and is indicative of an unreasonable impatience, I beg you to forgive me. If I have said anything in this letter that is an understatement of the truth and is indicative of my having a patience that makes me patient with anything less than brotherhood, I beg God to forgive me.

I hope this letter finds you strong in the faith. I also hope that circumstances will soon make it possible for me to meet each of you, not as an integrationist or a civil rights leader, but as a fellow clergyman and a Christian brother. Let us all hope that the dark clouds of racial prejudice will soon pass away and the deep fog of misunderstanding will be lifted from our fear-drenched communities and in some not too distant tomorrow the radiant stars of love and brotherhood will shine over our great nation with all of their scintillating beauty.

66.   James H. Cone,
A Black Theology of Liberation

A professor at Union Theological Seminary in New York, Cone (born 1938) is one of the major twentieth-century spokespersons for a distinctive African American theology. "Blackness," for Cone, symbolizes God's concern for the concreteness of human oppression as expressed in American racism. A Black Theology of Liberation was published in 1970.

. . . It is my contention that Christianity is essentially a religion of liberation. The function of theology is that of analyzing the meaning of that liberation for the oppressed community so they can know that their struggle for political, social, and economic justice is consistent with the gospel of Jesus Christ. Any message that is not related to the liberation of the poor in the society is not Christ's message. Any theology that is indifferent to the theme of liberation is not Christian theology.

In a society where men are oppressed because they are *black*, Christian theology must become *Black Theology*, a theology that is unreservedly identified with the goals of the oppressed community and seeking to interpret the divine character of their struggle for liberation. "Black Theology" is a phrase that is particularly appropriate for contemporary America because of its symbolic power to convey both what whites mean by oppression and what blacks mean by liberation. However, I am convinced that the patterns of meaning centered in the idea of Black Theology are by no means restricted to the American scene, since blackness symbolizes oppression and liberation in any society.

. . . . There will be no peace in America until white people begin to hate their whiteness, asking from the depths of their being: "How can we become black?" It is hoped that enough people will begin to ask that question that this country will no longer be divided on the basis of color. But until then, it is the task of the Christian theologian to do theology in the light of the concreteness of human oppression as expressed in color, and to interpret for the oppressed the meaning of God's liberation in their community. . . .

Unfortunately, American white theology has not been involved in the struggle for black liberation. It has been basically a theology of the white oppressor, giving religious sanction to the genocide of Indians and the enslavement of black people. From the very beginning to the present day, American white theological thought has been "patriotic," either by defining the theological task independently of black suffering (the liberal northern approach) or by defining Christianity as compatible with white racism (the conservative southern approach). In both cases theology becomes a servant of the state, and that can only mean death to black people. It is little wonder that an increasing number of black religionists are finding it difficult to be black and also to be identified with traditional theological thought forms.

The appearance of Black Theology on the American scene then is due exclusively to the failure of white religionists to relate the gospel of Jesus to the pain of being black in a white racist society. It arises from the need of black people to liberate themselves from white oppressors. Black Theology is a theology of liberation because it is a theology which arises from an identification with the oppressed blacks of America, seeking to interpret the gospel of Christ in the light of the black condition. It believes that the liberation of black people *is* God's liberation.

The task of Black Theology then is to analyze the nature of the gospel of Jesus Christ in the light of oppressed black people so they will see the gospel as inseparable from their humiliated condition, bestowing on them the necessary power to break the chains of oppression. This means that it is a theology of and for the black community, seeking to interpret the religious dimensions of the forces of liberation in that community.

There are two reasons why Black Theology is Christian theology and possibly the only expression of Christian theology in America. First, there can be no theology of the gospel which does not arise from an oppressed community. This is so because God in Christ has revealed himself as a God whose righteousness is inseparable from the weak and helpless in human society. The goal of Black Theology is to interpret God's activity as he is related to the oppressed black community.

Second, Black Theology is Christian theology because it centers on Jesus Christ. There can be no Christian theology which does not have Jesus Christ as its point of departure. Though Black Theology affirms the black condition as the primary datum of reality which must be reckoned with, this does not mean that it denies the absolute revelation of God in Jesus Christ. Rather it affirms it. Unlike white theology which tends to make the Christ-event an abstract, intellectual idea, Black Theology believes that the black community itself is precisely where Christ is at work. The Christ-event in twentieth-century America is a black-event, that is, an event of liberation taking place in the black community in which black people recognize that it is incumbent upon them to throw off the chains of white oppression by whatever means they regard as suitable. This is what God's revelation means to black and white America, and why Black Theology may be the only possible theology in our time.

It is to be expected that some persons will ask, "Why Black Theology? Is it not true that God is color blind? Is it not true that there are others who suffer as much as, if not more in some cases than, black people?" These questions reveal a basic lack of understanding regarding Black Theology, and also a superficial view of the world at large. There are at least three points to be made here.

First, in a revolutionary situation there can never be just theology. It is always theology identified with a particular community. It is either identified with those who inflict oppression or with those who are its victims. A theology of the latter is authentic Christian theology, and a theology of the former is a theology of the Antichrist. Insofar as Black Theology is a theology arising from an identification with the oppressed black community and seeks to interpret the gospel of Jesus Christ in the light of the liberation of that community, it is Christian theology. American white theology is a theology of the Antichrist, insofar as it arises from an identification with the white community, thereby placing God's approval on white oppression of black existence.

Second, in a racist society, God is never color blind. To say God is color blind is analogous to saying that God is blind to justice and injustice, to right and wrong, to good and evil. Certainly this is not the picture of God revealed in the Old and New Testaments. Yahweh takes sides. On the one hand, he sides with Israel against the Canaanites as she makes her settlement in Palestine. On the other hand, he sides with the poor within the community of Israel against the rich and other political oppressors. In the New Testament, Jesus is not *for all*, but for the oppressed, the poor and unwanted of society, and against oppressors. The God of the biblical tradition is not uninvolved or neutral regarding human affairs; rather he is quite involved. He is active in human history, taking sides with the oppressed of the land. If God is not involved in human history, then all theology is useless, and Christianity itself is a mockery, a hollow, meaningless diversion.

The meaning of this message for our contemporary situation is clear: God, because he is a God of the oppressed, takes sides with black people. He is not color blind in the black-white struggle, but has made an unqualified identification with black people. This means that the movement for black liberation is the work of God himself, effecting his will among men.

Thirdly, there are, to be sure, many people who suffer, and they are not all black. . . . It is not the purpose of Black Theology to minimize the suffering of others, including white people. Black Theology merely tries to discern the activity of the Holy One as he effects his purpose in the liberation of man from the forces of oppression. We *must* make decisions about where God is at work so we can join him in his fight against evil. But there is no perfect guide for discerning God's movement in the world. Contrary to what many conservatives would say, the Bible is not a blueprint on this matter. It is a valuable symbol for pointing to God's revelation in Christ, but it is not self-interpreting. We are thus placed in an existential situation of freedom in which the burden is on us to make the decision without a guaranteed ethical guide. This is the risk of faith. For the black theologian God is at work in the black community, vindicating black people against white oppression. It is impossible for him to be indifferent on this issue. Either God is for black people in their fight for liberation and against the white oppressors, or he is not. He cannot be both for us and for white oppressors at the same time.

In this connection we may observe that Black Theology takes seriously Paul Tillich's description of the symbolic nature of all theological speech. Man cannot describe God directly; he must use symbols that point to dimensions of reality that cannot be spoken of literally. Therefore to speak of Black Theology is to speak with the Tillichian understanding of symbol in mind. The focus on blackness does not mean that *only* blacks suffer as victims in a racist society, but that blackness is an ontological symbol and a visible reality which best describes what oppression means in America. The extermination of Indians, the persecution of the Jews, the oppression of Mexican Americans, and every other conceivable inhumanity done in the name of God and country—these brutalities can be analyzed in terms of America's inability to recognize humanity in persons of color. If the oppressed of this land want to challenge the oppressive character of white society, they must begin by affirming their identity in terms of that reality which is antiwhite. Blackness, then, stands for all victims of oppression who realize that their humanity is inseparable from man's liberation from whiteness. . . .

The definition of Christ as black is crucial for Christology if we truly believe in his continued presence today. Taking our clue from the historical Jesus who is pictured in the New Testament as the Oppressed One, what else, except blackness, could adequately tell us the meaning of his presence today? Any statement about Christ today that fails to consider blackness as the *decisive* factor about his Person is a denial of the New Testament message.The life, death and resurrection of Jesus reveal that he is the man for others, disclosing to them what is necessary for their liberation from oppression. If this is true, then Christ must be black with black people so they can know that their liberation is his liberation.

The Black Christ is also an important theological symbol for an analysis of Christ's presence today because we must make decisions about where he is at work in the world. Is his presence synonymous with the work of the oppressed or the oppressors, blacks or whites? Is he to be found among the wretched or among the rich? Of course our clever white theologians would say that it is not either/or. Rather he is to be found somewhere in between, a little black and a little white. Such an analysis is not only irrelevant for our times but also irrelevant for the time of the historical Jesus. Jesus was not for and against the poor, for and against the rich. He was for the poor and against the rich, for the weak and against the strong. Who can read the New Testament and fail to see that Jesus took sides and accepted freely the problem of being misunderstood? If the historical Jesus is any clue for an analysis of the contemporary Christ, then he must be where men are enslaved. To speak of him is to speak of the liberation of the oppressed. In a society that defines blackness as evil and whiteness as good, the theological significance of Jesus is found in the possibility of human liberation through blackness. Jesus is the Black Christ!

From James H. Cone, *A Black Theology of Liberation*, (Philadelphia: J. B. Lippincott Co., 1970), pp. 11–12, 22–28, 214–15. Copyright © 1990 by Orbis Books, Maryknoll, New York.

67. Rosemary Radford Ruether, *Sexism and God-Talk*

One of the leading feminist theologians of the late twentieth century, Rosemary Radford Ruether, in this 1983 book explored the importance of theological language in the perpetuation of the oppression of women.

An explanatory word is appropriate about the words for the divine used in this work. When speaking of the understanding of the divine of the ancient Near East, I speak of Gods and Goddesses, making clear that paired male and female concepts were used. These terms are capitalized, rejecting the traditional Western usage that left them lowercase to signal that these were false deities and not the true (Judeo-Christian) God. When speaking of the divine within the Judeo-Christian tradition, I use the term God. This is understood to be a male generic form and thus inadequate to express the vision of the divine sought in this theology. It does not imply, however, that there are not usable and authentic intimations of divinity found within traditional Jewish and Christian understandings of God.

Finally, when discussing fuller divinity to which this theology points, I use the term God/ess, a written symbol intended to combine both the masculine and feminine forms of the word for the divine while preserving the Judeo-Christian affirmation that divinity is one. This term is unpronounceable and inadequate. It is not intended as language for worship, where one might prefer a more evocative term, such as Holy One or Holy Wisdom. Rather it serves here as an analytic sign to point toward that yet unnameable understanding of the divine that would transcend patriarchal limitations and signal redemptive experience for women as well as men. . . .

Although the predominantly male images and roles of God make Yahwism an agent in the sacralization of patriarchy, there are critical elements in Biblical theology that contradict this view of God. By patriarchy we mean not only the subordination of females to males, but the whole structure of Father-ruled society: aristocracy over serfs, masters over slaves, king over subjects, racial overlords over colonized people. Religions that reinforce hierarchical stratification use the Divine as the apex of this system of privilege and control. The religions of the ancient Near East link the Gods and Goddesses with the kings and queens, the priests and priestesses, the warrior and temple aristocracy of a stratified society. The Gods and Goddesses mirror this ruling class and form its heavenly counterpart. The divinities also show mercy and favor to the distressed, but in the manner of noblesse oblige.

Yahweh, as tribal God of Israel, shows many characteristics similar to those of the Near Eastern deities, as mighty king, warrior, and one who shows mercy and vindicates justice. But these characteristics are put in a new and distinct context: Yahweh is unique as the God of a tribal confederation that identifies itself as liberated slaves. The basic identity of Yahweh as God of this confederation lies in "his" historical action as the divine power that liberated these slaves from bondage and led them to a new land. This confederation is not an ethnic people, but a bonding of groups of distinct backgrounds. A core group experienced the escape from bondage in Egypt that formed the primary identity of Israel. They were joined by nomadic groups from the desert and hill peoples in Canaan in revolt against the feudal power of the city-states of the plains. Norman Gottwald reconstructs the premonarchical formation of this tribal confederation (1250–1050 B.C.). The identification of Yahweh with liberation from bondage allowed this diverse group to unite in a new egalitarian society and to revolt against the stratified feudal society of the city-states that oppressed the peasant peoples of the hills with taxes and forced labor.

The Davidic monarchy represents a capitulation of Judaic leadership to the city-state model of power, but the prophets of Israel continue the tradition of protest against the hierarchical, urban, landowning society that deprives and oppresses the rural peasantry. This established at the heart of Biblical religion a motif of protest against the status quo of ruling-class privilege and the deprivation of the poor. God is seen as a critic of this society, a champion of the social victims. Salvation is envisioned as deliverance from systems of social oppression and as restoration of an egalitarian peasant society of equals, "where each have their own vine and fig tree and none need be afraid" (Micah 4:4).

Although Yahwism dissents against class hierarchy, it issues no similar protest against gender discrimination. There are several reasons (not to be seen as "excuses") for this. First, there is always a sociology of knowledge in social ideology, even in liberation ideology. Those male prophets who were aware of oppression by rich urbanites or dominating empires were not similarly conscious of their own oppression of dependents—women and slaves—in the patriarchal family. Only the emergence of women conscious of their oppression could have applied the categories of protest to women. This did not happen in Yahwism. Second, although Hebrew religion was to shape systems of patriarchal law that emphasize gender dualism and hierarchy, in its protest against Canaanite urban society it would have known powerful females, queens, priestesses, and wealthy landowners who functioned as oppressors. It would have been difficult to recognize women as an oppressed gender group when the primary social stratification integrated some women into roles of power. Indeed, perhaps it was not until the early modern period that the perception of women as marginalized by gender became stronger than the perception of women as divided by class. Only then could a feminist movement arise that protested the subjugation of women as a group.

The New Testament contains a renewal and radicalization of prophetic consciousness, now applied to marginalized groups in a universal, nontribal context. Consequently, it is possible to recognize as liberated by God social groups overlooked in Old Testament prophecy. Class, ethnicity, and gender are now specifically singled out as the divisions overcome by redemption in Christ. In the New Testament stories, gender is recognized as an additional oppression within oppressed classes and ethnic groups. Women, the doubly oppressed within marginalized groups, manifest God's iconoclastic, liberating action in making "the last first and the first last." All women are not doubly oppressed; there are also queens and wealthy women. But women's experience of oppression has begun to become visible and to be addressed by prophetic consciousness (very likely because of the participation of women in the early Christian movement).

A second antipatriarchal use of God-language occurs in the Old and New Testaments when divine sovereignty and fatherhood are used to break the ties of bondage under human kings and fathers. Abraham is called into an adoptive or covenanted relation with God only by breaking his ties with his family, leaving behind the graves of his ancestors. The God of Exodus establishes a relationship with the people that breaks their ties with the ruling overlords. As the people flee from the land of bondage, Pharaoh and his horsemen are drowned. God's kingship liberates Israel from human kings. The antimonarchical tradition inveighs against Israel's capitulation to the customs of the surrounding people by adopting kingship.

These Old Testament traditions are developed in Jesus' teaching. It has been often pointed out that Jesus uses a unique word for God. By adopting the word *Abba* for God, he affirms a primary relationship to God based on love and trust; *Abba* was the intimate word used by children in the family for their fathers. It is not fully conveyed by English terms such as *Daddy*, for it was also a term an adult could use of an older man to signify a combination of respect and affection. But is it enough to conclude from this use of *Abba* that Jesus transforms the patriarchal concept of divine fatherhood into what might be called a maternal or nurturing concept of God as loving, trustworthy parent?

The early Jesus movement characteristically uses this concept of God as *Abba* to liberate the community from human dominance-dependence relationships based on kinship ties or master-servant relationships. In the Gospel tradition, joining the new community of Jesus creates a rupture with traditional family ties and loyalties. In order to follow Jesus one must "hate" (that is, put aside one's loyalty to) father and mother, sisters and brothers (Luke 14:26; Matt. 10:37–38). The patriarchal family is replaced by a new community of brothers and sisters (Matt. 12:46–50; Mark 3:31–35; Luke 8:19–21). This new community is a community of equals, not of master and servants, father and children. Matthew 23:1–10 states that the relationship to God as *Abba* abolishes all father-child, master-servant relations between people within the Jesus community: "You are to call no man father, master or Lord," The relationship between Christians is to be one of mutual service and not of mastery and servitude. At the end of the Gospel of John, Jesus tells the disciples that their relationship has now become one of equals. They now have the same *Abba* relation to God as he does and can act out of the same principles: "No longer do I call you servants, . . . but I have called you friends" (John 15:15). These traditions reverse the symbolic relation between divine fatherhood and sovereignty and the sacralization of patriarchy. Because God is our king, we need obey no human kings. Because God is our parent, we are liberated from dependence on patriarchal authority.

But the language used in this tradition creates an obvious ambivalence. It works to establish a new liberated relationship to a new community of equals for those in revolt against established authorities. This is true not only in the formation of Israel and in the rise of the Jesus movement; again and again throughout Christian history this antipatriarchal use of God-language has been rediscovered by dissenting groups. The call to "obey God rather than men" has perhaps been the most continuous theological basis for dissent in the Christian tradition. Throughout Christian history women discovered this concept of direct relation to God as a way to affirm their own authority and autonomy against patriarchal authority. God's call to them to preach, to teach, to form a new community where women's gifts were fully actualized overruled the patriarchal authority that told them to remain at home as dutiful daughters or wives.

But once the new community becomes a part of the dominant society, God as father and king can be assimilated back into the traditional patriarchal relationships and used to sacralize the authority of human lordship and patriarchy. The radical meaning of *Abba* for God is lost in translation and interpretation. Instead, a host of new ecclesiastical and imperial "holy fathers" arises, claiming the fatherhood and kingship of God as the basis of their power over others. In order to preserve the prophetic social relationships, we need to find a new language that cannot be as easily co-opted by the systems of domination.

A third Biblical tradition that is important to a feminist theology is the proscription of idolatry. Israel is to make no picture or graven image of God; no pictorial or verbal representation of God can be taken literally. By contrast, Christian sculpture and painting represents God as a powerful old man with a white beard, even crowned and robed in the insignia of human kings or the triple tiara of the Pope. The message created by such images is that God is both similar to and represented by the patriarchal leadership, the monarchs and the Pope. Such imaging of God should be judged for what it is—as idolatry, as the setting up of certain human figures as the privileged images and representations of God. To the extent that such political and ecclesiastical patriarchy incarnates unjust and oppressive relationships, such images of God become sanctions of evil.

The proscription of idolatry must also be extended to verbal pictures. When the word *Father* is taken literally to mean that God is male and not female, represented by males and not females, then this word becomes idolatrous. The Israelite tradition is circumspect about the verbal image, printing it without vowel signs. The revelation to Moses in the burning bush gives as the name of God only the enigmatic "I am what I shall be." God is person without being imaged by existing social roles. God's being is open-ended, pointing both to what is and to what can be.

Classical Christian theology teaches that all names for God are analogies. The tradition of negative or *apophatic* theology emphasizes the unlikeness between God and human words for God. That tradition corrects the tendency to take verbal images literally; God is like but also unlike any verbal analogy. Does this not mean that male words for God are not in any way superior to or more appropriate than female analogies? God is both male and female and neither male nor female. One needs inclusive language for God that draws on the images and experiences of both genders. This inclusiveness should not become more abstract. Abstractions often conceal androcentric assumptions and prevent the shattering of the male monopoly on God-language, as in "God is not male. He is Spirit." Inclusiveness can happen only by naming God/ess in female as well as male metaphors.

As there are Biblical examples of such naming of God/ess in female as well as male metaphors that are truly equivalent images, that is, not "feminine" aspects of a male God? The synoptic Gospels offer some examples of this in the parallel parables, which seem to have been shaped in the early Christian catechetical community. They reflect the innovation of the early Christian movement of including women equally in those called to study the Torah of Jesus. Jesus justifies this practice in the Mary-Martha story, where he defends Mary's right to study in the circle of disciples around Rabbi Jesus in the words "Mary has chosen the better part which shall not be taken from her" (Luke 10:38–42).

In the parables of the mustard seed and the leaven the explosive power of the Kingdom, which God, through Jesus, is sowing in history through small signs and deeds, is compared to a farmer sowing the tiny mustard seed that produces a great tree or a woman folding the tiny bit of leaven in three measures of flour which then causes the whole to rise (Luke 13:18–21; Matt. 13:31–33). The parables of the lost sheep and the lost coin portray God seeking the sinners despised by the "righteous" of Israel. God is compared to a shepherd who leaves his ninety-nine sheep to seek the one that is lost or to a woman with ten coins who loses one and sweeps her house diligently until she finds it. Having found it, she rejoices and throws a party for her friends. This rejoicing is compared to God's rejoicing with the angels in heaven over the repentance of one sinner (Luke 15:1–10).

These metaphors for divine activity are so humble that their significance has been easily overlooked in exegesis, but we should note several important points. First, the images of male and female in these parables are equivalent. They both stand for the same things, as paired images. One is in no way inferior to the other. Second, the images are not drawn from the social roles of the mighty, but from the activities of Galilean peasants. It might be objected that the roles of the women are stereotypical and enforce the concept of woman as housekeeper. But it is interesting that the women are never described as related to or dependent on men. The small treasure of the old woman is her own. Presumably she is an independent householder. Finally, and most significantly, the parallel male and female images do not picture divine action in parental terms. The old woman seeking the lost coin and the woman leavening the flour image God not as mother or father (Creator), but as seeker of the lost and transformer of history (Redeemer).

The four preceding Biblical traditions may not be adequate for a feminist reconstruction of God/ess, but they are suggestive. If all language for God/ess is analogy, if taking a particular human image literally is idolatry, then male language for the divine must lose its privileged place. If God/ess is not the creator and validator of the existing hierarchical social order, but rather the one who liberates us from it, who opens up a new community of equals, then language about God/ess drawn from kingship and hierarchical power must lose its privileged place. Images of God/ess must include female roles and experience. Images of God/ess must be drawn from the activities of peasants and working people, people at the bottom of society. Most of all, images of God/ess must be transformative, pointing us back to our authentic potential and forward to new redeemed possibilities. God/ess-language cannot validate roles of men or women in stereotypic ways that justify male dominance and female subordination. Adding an image of God/ess as loving, nurturing mother, mediating the power of the strong, sovereign father, is insufficient.

Feminists must question the overreliance of Christianity, especially modern bourgeois Christianity, on the model of God/ess as parent. Obviously any symbol of God/ess as parent should include mother as well as father. Mary Baker Eddy's inclusive term, *Mother-Father God,* already did this one hundred years ago. Mother-Father God has the virtue of concreteness, evoking both parental images rather than moving to an abstraction (Parent), which loses effective resonance. Mother and father image God/ess as creator, as the source of our being. They point back from our own historical existence to those upon whom our existence depends. Parents are a symbol of roots, the sense of being grounded in the universe in those who have gone before, who underlie our own existence.

But the parent model for the divine has negative resonance as well. It suggests a kind of permanent parent-child relationship to God. God becomes a neurotic parent who does not want us to grow up. To become autonomous and responsible for our own lives is the gravest sin against God. Patriarchal theology uses the parent image for God to prolong spiritual infantilism as virtue and to make autonomy and assertion of free will a sin. Parenting in patriarchal society also becomes the way of enculturating us to the stereotypic male and female roles. The family becomes the nucleus and model of patrarichal relations in society. To that extent parenting language for God reinforces patriarchal power rather than liberating us from it. We need to start with language for the Divine as redeemer, as liberator, as one who fosters full personhood and, in that context, speak of God/ess as creator, as source of being.

Patriarchal theologies of "hope" or liberation affirm the God of Exodus, the God who uproots us from present historical systems and puts us on the road to new possibilities. But they typically do this in negation of God/ess as Matrix, as source and ground of our being. They make the fundamental mistake of identifying the ground of creation with the foundations of existing social systems. Being, matter, and nature become the ontocratic base for the evil system of what is. Liberation is liberation out of or against nature into spirit. The identification of matter, nature, and being with mother makes such patriarchal theology hostile to women as symbols of all that "drags us down" from freedom. The hostility of males to any symbol of God/ess as female is rooted in this identification of mother with the negation of liberated spirit. God/ess as Matrix is thought of as "static" immanence. A static, devouring, death-dealing matter is imaged, with horror, as extinguishing the free flight of transcendent consciousness. The dualism of nature and transcendence, matter and spirit as female against male is basic to male theology.

Feminist theology must fundamentally reject this dualism of nature and spirit. It must reject both sides of the dualism: both the image of mother-matter-matrix as "static immanence" and as the ontological foundation of existing, oppressive social systems and also the concept of spirit and transcendence as rootless, antinatural, originating in an "other world" beyond the cosmos, ever repudiating and fleeing from nature, body, and the visible world. Feminist theology needs to affirm the God of Exodus, of liberation and new being, but as rooted in the foundations of being rather than as its antithesis. The God/ess who is the foundation (at one and the same time) of our being and our new being embraces both the roots of the material substratum of our existence (matter) and also the endlessly new creative potential (spirit). The God/ess who is the foundation of our being-new being does not lead us back to a stifled, dependent self or uproot us in a spirit-trip outside the earth. Rather it leads us to the converted center, the harmonization of self and body, self and other, self and world. It is the *Shalom* of our being.

God/ess as once and future *Shalom* of being, however, is *not* the creator, founder, or sanctioner of patriarchal-hierarchical society. This world arises in revolt against God/ess and in alienation from nature. It erects a false system of alienated dualisms modeled on its distorted and oppressive social relationships. God/ess liberates us from this false and alienated world, not by an endless continuation of the same trajectory of alienation but as a constant breakthrough that points us to new possibilities that are, at the same time, the regrounding of ourselves in the primordial matrix, the original harmony. The liberating encounter with God/ess is always an encounter with our authentic selves resurrected from underneath the alienated self. It is not experienced against, but in and through relationships, healing our broken relations with our bodies, with other people, with nature. We have no adequate name for the true God/ess, the "I am who I shall become." Intimations of Her/His name will appear as we emerge from false naming of God/ess modeled on patriarchal alienation.

68. Carl F. H. Henry,
Aspects of Christian Social Ethics

As editor of Christianity Today *magazine, Carl Henry (born 1913) represented the voice of post–World War II "neo-evangelicalism." In this 1963 lecture given at Fuller Theological Seminary, Henry argues that the strategy of personal regeneration is God's revealed method for social change.*

The Christian task force is divided today about the best method for improving social conditions. The problem may be stated this way: In seeking a better social order, to what extent shall we rely on *law* and to what extent on *grace*? How much shall we trust *legislation* and how much shall we trust *regeneration* to change the social setting? What should we expect the *State* to contribute, what should we expect the *Church* to contribute, if we are seeking a society ruled by justice and love?

Many issues on which twentieth-century churchmen disagree, and laymen as well, turn on this question. It underlies the behind-the-scenes controversy between Billy Graham and Reinhold Niebuhr: whether the evangelist by his emphasis on spiritual decision and dedication offers a solution too simple for presumably insoluble social problems, and whether the professor by his reliance on legislation and compulsion as the means of social betterment minimizes and neglects the transforming power of the Holy Spirit. It is involved in one's attitude (if he takes a reasoned attitude) toward the crusade for civil rights and for racial integration. It is involved in the debate over government and public welfare: is the welfare state a normal exercise of governmental function (as the socialists would have it), or should the State (except in times of emergency) refrain altogether from welfare programs?

In our century, as I see it, Protestant forces seeking a better social order in

America have mostly neglected the method of *evangelism* and the dynamic of supernatural *regeneration* and *sanctification*. Instead, they have resorted to a series of alternative forces—at first, moral propaganda and education, then legislation, and more recently, nonviolent public demonstrations and even mob pressures against existing laws. Now it is true that the Church has a legitimate and necessary stake in education and legislation as means of *preserving* what is worth preserving in the present social order, but it must rely on spiritual regeneration for the *transformation* of society. The neglect of this latter resource accounts mainly for the social impotence of contemporary Christianity.

Social action begins, of course, only where there is some sense of the immorality of the *status quo*, a witness against social evils, and a creative challenge to the established attitudes and patterns of society. Social passivity is no strategy at all. Hence we ignore that mood of indifference settling on some churches in their recoil from Protestant Liberalism's substitution of social betterment for spiritual redemption. In these churches the sole preoccupation is private saintliness, preaching "Christ crucified" in absolute isolation from socio-political affairs, and promoting the piety of the local church in total unconcern over social disorders and evils.

The reconstruction or renewal of society may be attempted through a number of different strategies. . . .

The strategy of *revolution* not only proposes to rectify social evils, but it denies the existence of divinely given structures in history and society. It would destroy and displace *ultimate norms*, whether in respect to marriage, property, or the State. The obvious example in modern times is Communism. In place of the time-honored social forms validated by revealed religion, and still widely accepted as normative by society in general, Communism substitutes novel patterns of social life based on the totalitarian state, which takes control of family, of economic and political life, and of culture itself. Communist theory assails the *status quo* along lines that are anti-Christ (that is, it opposes Christian patterns of marriage, economics, and limited government) and anti-God (since it opposes the whole idea of supernaturally willed orders of responsibility).

The strategy of *regeneration*, by contrast, expresses the classic Christian view. It deplores any socio-historical revolt against the divine order of creation, while through spiritual renewal it seeks to secure man's respect for, and return to, the divine intention in society. The purpose of redemption, therefore, is to bind man's will afresh to the purpose of the Creator and the Lord of life.

Both the strategies of *revolution* and *regeneration* express indignation over the *status quo*; the one is fundamentally destructive of the past and the other reconstructive of it: the one radically anti-supernaturalistic and the other radically anti-naturalistic. The former brings the whole socio-historic movement under the criticism of Marx in order to destroy it, and the latter under the criticism of Christ in order to renew it.

Between these opposite poles we may locate the strategies of social *reform* and of social *revaluation*. While both aim to revise the existing social situation, neither involves a critique as radical as that of *revolution* or of *regeneration*. Why do *reform* and *revaluation* lack thoroughgoing indignation over the cultural order? The *reform* strategy builds upon the developmental (that is, evolutionary) philosophy of a gradually emerging ideal society. The *revaluation* strategy, on the other hand, emphasizes transcendent values discoverable in human experience. Both approaches, therefore, must find in the presently existing social order a significant area of contact. . . .

The historic Christian view sets the social problem in the larger theological framework of divine revelation and redemption, and cultural objectives in the context of the Christian mission. This fact distinguishes the strategy of *regeneration* from the other patterns of social action, in which the social issue tends to become ultimate. Christian leaders do not regard themselves primarily as social reformers. They give no quarter to the illusion that Christianity is primarily an ethical idealism engaged in denouncing political and social injustice, or aiming at social reform as an end in itself. Even in the social thrust they preserve Christianity's basic nature as a religion of supernatural redemption for sinners. . . .

The *regeneration* strategy insists that revelational theology is prior, and depicts the Living God as dealing simultaneously with man's spiritual and material condition. The Church derives her social message from divinely revealed principles. By contrast, the other strategies exalt the social issue above the theological, and prize the Christian religion mainly as a tool for justifying an independently determined course of social action. They show little concern for the Creator-Redeemer God and his holy commandments; for Palestine as the geographic theater of the drama of human destiny; for the specially-inspired Scriptures; for the Law and the Gospel; for the social crisis viewed within man's larger problem of created dignity and sinful corruption; and for human rights and responsibilities "under God."

In defining and delineating the fundamental perspectives of an ideal social order, the other strategies invoke moral criteria independent of the Bible. They do not all, like Communism, rail at the commandments and scorn the Bible. . . . While they may prize the Bible for high moral insights, they nonetheless single out only those premises in the scriptural revelation congenial to their own presuppositions. Humanists treasure such generalities as democracy, brotherhood and justice, or other social conclusions presumably "inhering in the Christian Gospel" (in which they have no genuine interest whatever). Idealists hail Christianity as the supreme religion of ethical idealism whose primary end is social reconstruction. But capitalizing on the social and minimizing the personal message of Christianity, and thereby obscuring the special framework of revelation and redemption on which both depend, has serious consequences. By divorcing the social from the personal, it deals with human rights in abstraction from human responsibilities, or rather, from the divine obligation of man. It obscures the supernatural source and sanction of human rights and duties, and fractures them (Roosevelt's famous "four freedoms," for example) through loss of a comprehensive overview. Vagueness results just where precision is most needed today, that is, in stipulating the content of the life of social righteousness and personal virtue. It should surprise nobody, then, that in respect to personal no less than to social morality the twentieth century has moved into an age of rebellion and revolution against biblical patterns of conduct. The reason for this tendency is found mainly in neglect of the Hebrew-Christian view of God and the world.

The strength of the strategy of *regeneration* lies in this: in contrast to the other modern social philosophies, it flows from the revelation of the Creator-Redeemer God. The biblical message is basically one of supernatural redemption from sin, and the problem of social justice is placed in necessary relationship to man's need and God's provision of salvation. Hence such concepts as the will of God; man's fall; the revealed commandments; the law of love; the prophetic promise of a Redeemer and its fulfillment in Jesus Christ; the need for personal holiness and the gift of the Holy Spirit; the Church as a society of twice-born men and women in union with Christ; the ultimate triumph of the right and the final judgment of the wicked, become central considerations in the Christian approach to the social crisis. Amid the modern crusade for social betterment, therefore, the strategy of *regeneration* proclaims the hard news that social evils contradict man's dignity and destiny by creation, but also the good news of a "new heaven and new earth" assured in Jesus Christ. . . .

The strategy of *regeneration* . . . relies primarily on spiritual dynamic for social change. It aims not merely to re-educate man (although it knows that the Holy Spirit uses truth—particularly the truth of the Gospel—as a means of conviction), but to renew the whole man morally and spiritually through a saving experience of Jesus Christ. The power on which it relies for social change is not totalitarian compulsion, nor is it the power, *per se*, of legislated morality, education, and unregenerate conscience. *Regeneration* rests upon spiritual power. The Gospel of Christ is the Church's peculiar *dynamis* for facing the entire world. Christian social action condones no social solutions in which personal acceptance of Jesus Christ as Saviour and Lord is an optional consideration. Personal regeneration and redemption are inherent in its hope for the social order. It proclaims the Kingdom of God as the new order, not some secular counterpart. And "except a man be born again he cannot see the kingdom of God" (John 3:3). The new birth restores man to fellowship with God, and lifts him not only to the vision of truth and goodness but also qualifies him with a new nature and moral power to place his energies in the service of righteousness. The Holy Spirit sunders the shackles of human sin, requiring men first to recognize social evils in the light of personal wickedness. While personal sin often finds its occasion in the prevailing community situation, the Christian pulpit and personal witness encourage effective solution of social evils by calling out a race of renewed men united in devotion to God's purpose in creation and redemption.

From Carl F. H. Henry, *Aspects of Christian Social Ethics* (Grand Rapids, Mich.: Wm. B. Eerdmans Publishing Co., 1964), pp. 15–25.

69. John Howard Yoder,
Nonresistance and the Aeons

Drawing on New Testament scholarship that emphasized the depiction of Jesus in the Gospels as an eschatological prophet and also drawing on the pacifism of his own Mennonite tradition, John Howard Yoder (born 1927) reacted against the Christian Realism of mid–twentieth-century ethicists such as Reinhold Niebuhr. In Yoder's view, the path of Christian discipleship was not realistic at all. Rather, the gospel made claims for commitment so intense and demanding they could only be understood in terms of the ultimate goal of eschatological meaning.

The New Testament sees our present age—the age of the church, extending from Pentecost to the Parousia—as a period of the overlapping of two aeons. These aeons are not distinct periods of time, for they exist simultaneously. They differ rather in nature or in direction; one points backward to human history outside of (before) Christ; the other points forward to the fullness of the kingdom of God, of which it is a foretaste. Each aeon has a social manifestation: the former in the "world," the latter in the church or the body of Christ. The new aeon came into history in a decisive way with the incarnation and the entire work of Christ. Christ had been awaited eagerly by Judaism for centuries; but when he came he was rejected, for the new aeon he revealed was not what people wanted. Jesus' contemporaries were awaiting a new age, a bringing to fulfillment of God's plan; but they expected it to confirm and to vindicate their national hopes, prides, and solidarities. Thus Christ's claims and kingdom were to them scandalous.

The new aeon involves a radical break with the old; Christ also was forced to break with the Jewish national community to be faithful to his mission. The gospel he brought, even though expressed in terms borrowed from the realm of government (kingdom) and involving definite consequences for the social order, proclaimed the institution of a new kind of life, not of a new government. All through his ministry, from the temptation in the desert to the last minute in Gethsemane, violent means were offered him from all sides as short cuts to the accomplishment of his purposes, and he refused to use them. . . .

Jesus' interest was in people; the reason for his low esteem for the political order was his high, loving esteem for concrete people as the object of his concern. Christ is *agape*; self-giving, nonresistant love. At the cross this nonresistance, including the refusal to use political means of self-defense, found its ultimate revelation in the uncomplaining and forgiving death of the innocent at the hands of the guilty. This death reveals how God deals with evil; here is the only valid starting point for Christian pacifism or nonresistance. The cross is the extreme demonstration that *agape* seeks neither effectiveness nor justice and is willing to suffer any loss or seeming defeat for the sake of obedience.

But the cross is not defeat. Christ's obedience unto death was crowned by the miracle of the resurrection and the exaltation at the right hand of God. . . .

Effectiveness and success had been sacrificed for the sake of love, but this sacrifice was turned by God into a victory that vindicated to the utmost the apparent impotence of love. The same life of the new aeon that was revealed in Christ is also the possession of the church, since Pentecost answered the Old Testament's longings for a "pouring out of the Spirit on all flesh" and a "law written in the heart." The Holy Spirit is the "down payment" on the coming glory, and the new life of the resurrection is the path of the Christian now. But before the resurrection there was the cross, and Christians must follow their Master in suffering for the sake of love.

Nonresistance is thus not a matter of legalism but of discipleship, not "thou shalt not" but "as he is, so are we in this world" (1 John 4:17), and it is especially in relation to evil that discipleship is meaningful. Every strand of New Testament literature testifies to a direct relationship between the way Christ suffered on the cross and the way the Christian, as disciple, is called to suffer in the face of evil (Matt. 10:38; Mark 10:38f; 8:34f; Luke 14:27). Solidarity with Christ ("discipleship") must often be in tension with the wider human solidarity (John 15:20; 2 Cor. 1:5; 4:10; Phil. 1:29; 2:5–8; 3:10; Col. 1:24f; Heb. 12:1–4; 1 Pet. 2:21f; Rev. 12:11).

It is not going too far to affirm that the new thing revealed in Christ was this attitude to the old aeon, including force and self-defense. The cross was not in itself a new revelation; Isaiah 53 foresaw already the path that the Servant of YHWH would have to tread. Nor was the resurrection essentially new; God's victory over evil had been affirmed, by definition one might say, from the beginning. Nor was the selection of a faithful remnant a new idea. What was centrally new about Christ was that these ideas became incarnate. But superficially the greatest novelty and the occasion of stumbling was his willingness to sacrifice in the interest of nonresistant love, all other forms of human solidarity, including the legitimate national interests of the chosen people. Abraham had been told that in his seed all the nations would be blessed, and most of his descendants had understood this promise as the vindication of their nationalism. Jesus revealed that the contrary was the case: the universality of God's kingdom contradicts rather than confirms all particular solidarities and can be reached only by first forsaking the old aeon (Luke 18:28–30).

. . . . Nationalism and pragmatism are both rejected in the life of the people of the new aeon, whose only purpose is love in the way of the cross and in the power of the resurrection.

Christ is not only the Head of the church; he is at the same time Lord of history, reigning at the right hand of God over the principalities and powers. The old aeon, representative of human history under the mark of sin, has also been brought under the reign of Christ (which is not identical with the consummate kingdom of God, 1 Cor. 15:24). The characteristic of the reign of Christ is that evil, without being blotted out, is channelized by God, in spite of itself, to serve God's purposes. Vengeance itself, the most characteristic manifestation of evil, instead of creating chaos as is its nature, is harnessed through the state in such a way as to preserve order and give room for the growth and work of the church. Vengeance is not thereby redeemed or made good; it is nonetheless rendered subservient to God's purposes, as an anticipation of the promised ultimate defeat of sin.

. . . When the New Testament attributes this lordship over history and the powers to Christ, it means that the essential change that has taken place is not without the realm of the old aeon, vengeance and the state, where there is really no change; it is rather that the new aeon revealed in Christ takes primacy over the old, explains the meaning of the old, and will finally vanquish the old. The state did not change with the coming of Christ; what changed was the coming of the new aeon that proclaimed doom for the old one.

Romans 13 and the parallel passages in 1 Timothy 2 and 1 Peter 2 give us the criteria for judging to what extent a state's activities (since the state incarnates this semi-subdued evil) are subject to Christ's reign. If the use of force is such as to protect the innocent and punish the evildoers, to preserve peace so that "all might come to the knowledge of the truth," then that state may be considered as fitting within God's plan, as to that extent subject to the reign of Christ. This positive evaluation cannot apply to a given state in all that it does, but at best in one case at a time, each time it chooses the best alternative rather than adding evil to evil. It is, however, possible, and even frequent, for a state to abandon this function, to deny any sort of submission to a moral order higher than itself, and in so doing to punish the innocent and reward the guilty. That state is what we find in Revelation 13, best described as demonic. . . .

The consummation will mean the fulfillment of the new aeon and the collapse of the old. The "world" in the sense of creation becomes after purgation identical with the new aeon, after having been the hostage of the old. It is in the light of this promised fulfillment that life in the new aeon, which seems so ineffective now, is nevertheless meaningful and right.

. . . The church's suffering, like the Master's suffering, is the measure of the church's obedience to the self-giving love of God. Nonresistance is right, in the deepest sense, not because it works, but because it anticipates the triumph of the Lamb that was slain.

The apparent complicity with evil that the nonresistant position involves has always been a stumbling block to nonpacifists. Here we must point out that this attitude, leaving evil free to be evil, leaving sinners free to separate themselves from God and sin against humanity, is part of the nature of *agape* itself, as revealed already in creation. . . . God's love for us begins right at the point where God permits sin against himself and against others, without crushing the rebel under his/her own rebellion. The word for this is divine *patience*, not complicity.

But this gracious divine patience is not the complete answer to evil. We have seen that evil is already brought into check by the reign of Christ; the consummation of this reign is the defeat of every enemy by the exclusion of evil. Just as the doctrine of creation affirms that God made us free and the doctrine of redemption says this freedom of sin was what led agape to the cross, so also the doctrine of hell lets sin free, finally and irrevocably, to choose separation from God. Only by respecting this freedom to the bitter end can love give meaning to history. Any universalism that would seek, in the intention of magnifying redemption, to deny to the unrepentant sinner the liberty to refuse God's grace would in reality deny that human choice has any real meaning at all. With judgment and hell the old aeon comes to its end (by being left to itself) and the fate of the disobedient is exclusion from the new heaven and new earth, the consummation of the new society begun in Christ.

It is abundantly clear in the New Testament, as all exegetes agree, that this final triumph over evil is not brought about by any human or political means.The agent in judgment is not the church, for the church suffers nonresistantly. . . . Nor is the agent the state, as it is for the judgments of God within history; for in fact the king or the state, refusing ever more demonically Christ's dominion, becomes God's major enemy (Antichrist). God's agent is his own miraculous Word, the sword coming from the mouth of the King of kings and Lord of lords who is astride the white horse (Rev. 19). Just as has been the case ever since the patriarchs and most notably at Christ's cross, the task of obedience is to obey, and the responsibility for bringing about victory is God's alone, God's means beyond human calculation. God's intervention, not human progress, is the vindication of human obedience. The Christian's responsibility for defeating evil is to resist the temptation to meet it on its own terms. To crush the evil adversary is to be vanquished by him because it means accepting his standards.

The term "interim ethics" has often been used to describe the ethics of the New Testament. Customarily (according to the line of thought derived from Albert Schweitzer) this term means that Christ and the New Testament writers were led by their expectancy of an early end of time to an irresponsible attitude to ethics in society. This analysis springs from the attempt to judge on the basis of the old aeon. The New Testament view is rather: "Were you not raised to life with Christ? Then aspire to the realm above" (Col. 3:1). It means being longsighted, not shortsighted; it means trusting God to triumph through the cross. Faith is just this attitude (as the examples of Heb. 11:1–12:4 show), the willingness to accept the apparently ineffective path of obedience, trusting in God for the results. Faith, even in Hebrews 11:1f., does not mean doctrinal acquiescence to unproved affirmations, but the same trust in God that Christ initiated and perfected in itself (12:3). Again, the example is the cross, which was right in itself even though its rightness (in terms of ultimate effect) was not yet apparent.

From John H. Yoder, "The Original Revolution," in *The Royal Priesthood: Essays Ecclesiological and Ecumenical*, edited and with an introduction by Michael G. Cartwright (Grand Rapids, Mich.: Wm. B. Eerdmans Publishing Co., 1994), pp. 146–52. Reprinted by permission of Herald Press.

70. Bernard Häring, *The Law of Christ*

In this 1963 work, Bernard Häring illustrates an important movement by twentieth-century Roman Catholic moral theologians to combine long-standing moral traditions based upon Thomistic natural law with fresh emphasis upon God's grace revealed in Christ.

In our friendship with Christ our love is always the love of the disciple of Christ. The disciple is always anxious to learn; he seeks to be a truly submissive disciple and never to fail to manifest his appreciation of the Master's authority through his obedience. Obviously the perfection of the disciple's obedience is found only in his love. The world must be made to recognize in our manifestation of obedience to Christ the evidence of our love as Christ attested His love for the Father through His obedience. "But he comes that the world may know that I love the Father, and that I do as the Father has commanded me" [John 14:31].

As love implies obedience, so it implies law, and love and law are essentially and mutually interchangeable. Obedience of love is surely more comprehensive than mere legal obedience for mere observance of law is the lowest degree of obedience. Mere legal obedience is not yet in the shadow of love. External laws are no more than universal regulations and therefore basically only minimum requirements. Universal rules cannot in fact even prescribe what is highest and best, since the best is not universal and cannot be demanded from men universally. On the contrary, love by its very nature strives for the highest and best and seeks the most perfect manifestation of its ideals in actions.

How can any one who does not fulfill the minimum requirements of the law progress toward that which is higher and better? Since the minimum requirements are basic for the fulfillment of the law of love, love may never violate or ignore the law. At the same time one who truly loves may not remain at the lowest level of obedience and be satisfied with the bare legal minimum.

In order to avoid confusion in this important matter we must clarify the term *law* as used here. If we understand by law the lowest limits of the least requirement (prescriptive laws), then indeed one must demand of love that in fulfilling the law (which it may never violate) it refuse to rest content with mere observance, but seek constantly to surpass the law. However, if by law (in its total meaning) we understand the directive toward ever loftier heights (laws directed to ends and ideals rather than merely to the prescription or prohibition of acts), then love and only love fulfills the law entirely. "Love . . . is the fulfillment of the law" [Rom. 13:10]. "For the whole law is fulfilled in one word: Thou shalt love thy neighbor as thyself" [Gal. 5:14]. "Now the purpose of this charge is charity" [1 Tim. 1:5].

The new law which embraces everything is the love of Christ [John 13:34f.; Matt. 22:36ff.]. Each individual law or command, each individual precept is intended as an expression and a directive or application of the great commandment of love. Hence one can fulfill the individual laws according to their profoundest significance, only if one obeys them in the spirit of love, for only love divines and carries out the deepest purposes of every law.

As much as the virtue of love and the law are intimately correlated, so much do the spirit of love and the spirit of sheer legalism stand in irreconcilable opposition to each other. Love is entirely personal. It regards the person of the lawgiver, it has insight into his mind and purpose and the intention of the law. One possessed of this personal love feels called in person by the law giver, summoned to respond with all his powers and according to all the circumstances of the situation. One who is motivated by sheer legalism faces the impersonal law (even though it may not be the mere letter of the law) and asks only: what is the minimum requirement of the law, in order that I may avoid violation of law?

If love demands only this: what must be exactly done or avoided to shun loss of grace and the fall from love, it is very imperfect. But if the fulfillment of the law is still realized through such effort to avoid the total loss of love, the concern is not to be characterized as sheer legalism. Though such love is far from perfect, it is not without real value and genuinely fulfills the law.

Genuine charity, the great-hearted and magnanimous love of the disciple for the Master, is not satisfied with the minimum requirement of the law as ultimate norm, but looks to the loftiest ideals as its ultimate goal. But of course the disciple must be prudent! True charity will prompt him to ask humbly and modestly: In my own present situation, with the capacities now at my disposal (perhaps these are not very prepossessing), what is the better course for me, what is most pleasing to God for me? . . .

The attempt on the part of infidel states to suppress Christian charitable endeavor or, more specifically, to control it and take it over, is due to a basic misconception of the distinction between law and love. It is a mad attempt to legalize the activity of love. Human welfare has a legal side but also a charitable one, which is no less significant. Only the legal phase and only that which is strictly the obligation of justice can and should be legislated by the state according to norms of law. Even though the state should temporarily be able through legal pressures to take over by some external control and operation a portion of the Church's charitable activities, this very intervention would repel that which is best, the free movement of love. But should the spirit of voluntary charitable endeavor wane, then the minimum measure of love would also disappear from society. The love which is prerequisite for the clear knowledge and realization of legal social duties would cease to be effective. This is obvious from the many misconceptions prevalent among the leaders in pagan states. (There is little realization of the duty of the state to protect the rights of the unborn child, no understanding of the evils involved in certain types of birth restriction, little grasp of the duty of the state to avoid educational monopoly and to treat all children equally in the distribution of state funds for educational purposes, etc.)

The state by seeking to take over the charitable institutions of the Christian communities, even only externally, while permitting the communities to operate them, would involve itself in an absurd contradiction; for the inner vitality of the very communities placed under duress would be sorely constricted. Moreover, for the state to force such massive control in every area is most destructive of all human right and freedom. The more the Church is excluded from the works of charity, the more she is forced to withdraw from the work which is proper to her as the institution of love, the more exclusively will mere impersonal and purely legalistic concepts and, eventually, merely pragmatic motives enter into what was once the abode of love. Thus the state, far from promoting justice, will eventually destroy charity, and ultimately be the source of the gravest social injustice.

Not only should the state shun all unjust interference in the work of the Church; it should welcome the service of love performed by her through the communities of love, welcome and in some manner include it in the grand project of human welfare promoted by public authority. This inclusion, however, must always allow for that indispensably free action of the Church's charity and, paradoxically, also for unimpeded acceptance of material means to further her work. For this reason public funds should not furnish all the means for the Church's institutions, since the gifts which she herself procures through free love for charitable activity are in every way more precious and fruitful than the money obtained by pressure of taxation—which scarcely anyone looks upon as a gift of love.

Except for the actual dechristianization of the schools nothing is so destructive of the care of souls as the undermining and cramping of the charitable work of the Church, particularly through the expulsion of Catholic sisterhoods from hospitals and institutions of care for the needy. Countless men have opened their hearts to divine love in the sacred moment when human misery met with the tenderness of Christlike love, when divine grace turned sinners to a Christian life or at least prepared them for a Christian death.

The obligatory nature of almsgiving can be studied correctly only in the total context of the universal obligation of the social use of material goods, from which use it must be clearly distinguished.

Charitable endeavor bereft of a sense of justice cannot be genuine love. Nor is it effective and fruitful. It may even prove very baneful. This is not to deny that love is queen in the hierarchy of virtues, but to make plain the inescapable fact that charity rests on justice. Justice is an essential support for the right order of love.

First Principle: Commutative justice demands compensation for work according to the principle of exchange, like value to be given for like value. An employer who does not pay wages according to this principle does not redress his wrong conduct by giving the equivalent of the defrauded wages in the form of alms. He must restore the amount to the worker who earned it, as a recompense for the work itself, and not as alms or other form of gratuity.

Second Principle: Legal justice obliges us to pay the tax which the state justly levies for the general welfare. Only in instances of great need in which the state cannot or will not render necessary assistance is one permitted, under certain circumstances, to substitute for the tax imposed or other payment required a form of direct contribution under the guise of alms to the individual concerned.

Third Principle: Social justice (this means the social direction inherent in the earthly goods themselves as God created them, and even more emphatically in the sum total of created reality as saved and redirected by Christ who offered Himself in Sacrifice for all men) requires that all property be used with a sense of social responsibility. Superfluous goods must be so used as to contribute to the good and welfare of society. This is the same as to say they must be used for the good of our neighbor.

Only a thorough understanding of the social and economic situation can determine in individual instances the most appropriate use of superfluous goods in the social order. Suggested as more effective in promoting the general welfare than indiscriminate or massive distribution of gratuities are the following: construction of adequate housing, promotion of widespread employment, furnishing of loans interest free or at a low rate of interest for construction of homes. In general it is socially and morally more advisable to create a sound economic and social order in which the individual is encouraged to work, to save, to exercise thrift, and to care for himself and his family.

Fourth Principle: In determining concretely and in individual instances what goods are to be classed as superfluous, strict social justice will prove less flexible than expansive and generous love of neighbor. After a manner of speaking, we may set up a doubly relative standard. On the one hand, we must look to the vast acquisition of wealth far beyond the individual and family needs of the possessors, and on the other, to the appalling misery of countless human beings the world over. In the light of these two extremes one must form the sincere judgment: how much of my wealth is superfluous, unnecessary for me, capable of relieving human misery and distress?

A standard based on the concept *station in life* must meet with many difficulties. It is entirely too relative and too readily misapplied. In a world saturated with passion for self-indulgence, egoism, cupidity, the Christian can scarcely find a valid standard, particularly if he is dealing with the wealthier classes on the basis of the customary standard of living among our rich. In fact, experience proves that the very rich rarely, if ever, are disturbed in conscience by the realization that the *station in life* is also to be gauged by the general condition of human needs, not merely by the life to which one is accustomed. It is contrary to social justice that one social class should lay claim to an affluence and luxury suited to its so-called rank and station in life while vast masses do not have the minimum essential to sustain health. Nothing could be more perverted than to have moral theology confirm an erroneous conscience through false teaching regarding the standard of living in accordance with one's station in life. True Christian life is not to be judged by its conformity to the special privileges or prerogatives of a station in life, but rather by conformity to the teaching and example of Christ. Nevertheless, there is a correct sense in which we may use the term, *station in life.* For example, one's office or one's position in life or society has a bearing on the education of one's children. One's position may determine the type of education and training which is to be provided for them. The cultivation of one's home life, the cultural activity of individual and family, all the efforts for cultural progress depend very largely on one's social attainments and status.

Fifth Principle: Not even charity (not to speak of social justice) requires that one devote all one's superfluities to almsgiving. A socially sound and fruitful use of material goods in other ways may frequently prove more advantageous to the furtherance of the true welfare of our neighbor than the distribution of alms. The sharp utterances of many Fathers of the Church declaring that there is an obligation in charity, or even in justice, to give all one's superfluous goods in alms may reasonably be interpreted to mean that there is a real obligation to devote the total superfluity to the welfare of one's neighbors, primarily in the form of alms. Ambrose's statement directed to the rich almsgiver, "You return to the poor something of his own," is according to all theologians literally true if the poor who receive the gift are in desperate need. As to other instances Ambrose means merely that the goods of this earth have an absolute and immutable destination to the welfare of all, and therefore also of those who are in need through no fault of their own. Augustine repeatedly stresses that all superfluities of the rich exist in order to serve the poor in their misery. Particularly sharp in this context are the following words: *Res alienae possidentur, cum superflua possidentur* (One who possesses superfluous goods is in possession of another's property.) "The superfluity of the rich is necessary for the poor. Hence to cling to superfluous wealth is to possess the property of others." These bold assertions of Augustine are not at all pious rhetorical exaggeration. St. Thomas also says that the refusal to give alms from one's superfluity in instances where our neighbor is in great need is a violation of legal justice.

In weighing the gravity of these words of the Fathers or similar expressions we must always bear in mind that in the economic system of the period, the superfluous goods to which Augustine directly and immediately referred were not productive, but unproductive, amassed, inherited wealth. Augustine and the Fathers did not have in mind the alternative between a use of wealth in the social order through almsgiving and the consequent relief of distress and the use in some other responsible form. The only alternative in mind was either the use of superfluous wealth for the alleviation of distress by almsgiving or clinging to amassed wealth which had no social value or very little social value at all. In any instance the position of Augustine is quite clear. He holds that the withholding of superfluity by refusal to contribute to the alleviation of the misery of others is a violation of the right order in the use of material goods. It is not easy to determine whether the great Doctor has in mind the violation of legal (or, more specifically, social) justice, or perhaps a violation of charity. But the saint surely refers to the objective order inherent in the material values as such and in their relation to us, not merely the order of our love to our fellows. With this thought of Augustine in mind, we may assert that no earthly possession is free from the claim of social justice. Every earthly possession is stamped with this claim. And the possession of the disciples of Christ bear the mark of yet another claim in the social order. Christ Himself by His example has placed upon them the special mark of His redemptive possession: He Who has the right of ownership to all earthly things and Who redeemed all things with the price of His Blood kept nothing, not even His garments, when He died naked on the Cross.

Very sharp are the words of St. Gregory the Great in reference to the rich man in the Gospel: "No one should feel secure even though he can say, 'I have not stolen anything belonging to others, and what belongs to me I use lawfully.' For that rich man (Dives of the Gospel) was delivered into hell because he used the wealth given him for luxury and closed his heart to the misery of the poor."

No one who studies the passages just cited—and there are many others in the Fathers—can escape the conclusion that, at the very least, there is an obligation to use all one's superfluous goods in a socially responsible way for the needy. The sharp stress of almsgiving by the Fathers, however, is also conditioned by the sociological factors of their time, and must be so understood.

Sixth Principle: From what we have just said it is clear not only that there is an obligation to make a social use of the entire superfluity we may possess, but that a certain portion must be distributed as alms. The amount depends on the greatness of the necessity and the extent of one's wealth.

In the Old Testament a tithe for worship and a tithe for the poor was prescribed. Every seventh year the poor were allowed to reap the harvest. They also had a claim to the annual gleanings (Ex. 23:11; [Lev.] 19:9f.; 23:22). But beyond all this, the generous loan without interest or profit and the giving of alms are particularly stressed ([Deut.] 15:7ff.).

Even though the state should demand and expend huge sums for welfare in many forms, even though wealth is used intelligently and with great vision for the common welfare, there is still a constant need related to the care of souls and divine worship for various types of charity, all of which call for almsgiving. Little appeals are always directed to us wherever we may be. So many are the demands on the charity of every openhearted man, due to extraordinary distress ("The poor you have always with you." [John 12:8]), that total refusal to give alms must be considered sinful.

From Bernard Häring, *The Law of Christ*, vol. 2 (Westminster, Md.: The Newman Press/Paulist Press, 1963), pp. 94–95, 398–403.

Acknowledgments

In addition to the source material following each selection, grateful acknowledgment is made to the following.

Augsburg Fortress, for material from *Luther's Works*: Vol. 31, edited by Harold Grimm, copyright © 1959 Fortress Press; Vol. 45, edited by Walther I. Brandt, copyright © 1962 Muhlenberg Press; Vol. 46, edited by Robert C. Schultz, copyright © 1967 Fortress Press.

Beacon Press, for material from Rosemary Radford Ruether, *Sexism and God-Talk*, copyright © 1983, 1993 by Rosemary Radford Ruether.

Columbia University Press, for material from:

Marsilius of Padua, Defensor Pacis, translated by Alan Gerwith, copyright © 1938 by Columbia University Press.

Medieval Handbooks of Penance, edited by John T. McNeill and Helena M. Gamer, copyright © 1990 by Columbia University Press.

Joan Daves Agency, for material from Martin Luther King, Jr., "Letter from Birmingham Jail," in *A Testament of Hope*, edited by James M. Washington. Copyright © 1963 by Martin Luther King, Jr., copyright renewed 1991 by Coretta Scott King.

Herald Press, for material from *The Original Revolution*, by John H. Yoder, 1972.

ICS Publications, for material from *The Collected Works of St. Teresa of Ávila*, Vols. 1 and 2, translated by Kiernan Kavanaugh and Otilio Rodriguez, copyright © 1976, 1980 by Washington Province of Discalced Carmelites, ICS Publications.

Orbis Books, for material from *The Selected Writings of Dorothy Day*, edited by Robert Ellsberg, copyright © 1983, 1992 by Robert Ellsberg and Tamar Hennessey.

Oxford University Press, for material from Paul Tillich, *Love, Power, and Justice*. Copyright © 1954 Oxford University Press.

Paulist Press, for material from:

Bernard of Clairvaux: Selected Works, translated by G. R. Evans. Copyright © 1987 Gillian R. Evans.

Catherine of Siena: The Dialogue, translated by Suzanne Noffke, O.P. Copyright © 1980 by The Missionary Society of St. Paul the

Acknowledgments

Apostle in the State of New York.

Hildegard of Bingen: Scivias, translated by Mother Columba Hart and Jane Bishop. Copyright © 1990 by the Abbey of Regina Laudis.

Julian of Norwich: Showings, translated by Edmund Colledge, O.S.A. and James Walsh, S.J. Copyright © 1978 by The Missionary Society of St. Paul the Apostle in the State of New York.

Simon & Schuster, for material from:

Dietrich Bonhoeffer, *The Cost of Discipleship,* translated from German by R. H. Fuller, with some revision by Irmgard Booth. Copyright © 1959 in the English translation by SCM Press, Ltd. Dietrich Bonhoeffer, *Ethics,* translated from German by Neville Horton Smith and edited by Eberhard Bethge. Copyright © 1955 in the English translation by SCM Press, Ltd. Copyright © 1955 by Macmillan Publishing Company.

Reinhold Niebuhr, *The Nature and Destiny of Man,* Vol. 1, copyright © 1941, (c) 1964 Charles Scribner's Sons. Copyright renewed 1969 Reinhold Niebuhr; Vol. 2, copyright 1943, (c) 1964 Charles Scribner's Sons. Copyright renewed 1971 Reinhold Niebuhr.

Walter Rauschenbusch, *A Theology for the Social Gospel,* copyright © 1917 by Macmillan Publishing Company. Copyright renewed 1945 Pauline E. Rauschenbusch.

Index of Subjects

Index of Subjects

enemies, love of, 26, 28, 48, 67, 198. *See also* prayer
epicurism, 38
equality, 160, 164–65, 171, 278, 296–97, 303, 319, 322–23, 365. *See also* gender equality
eschatology, 342, 373. *See also* parousia
ethics, x, 190, 191–92, 242–43, 250–53, 268, 307–10, 376. *See also* social gospel; social ethics
euthanasia, 307, 310
evil, 2, 51, 67, 90–91, 263, 309–11, 315, 372, 375–76. *See also* good: and evil

faith, xi, 93, 105–6, 113–14, 124, 127, 147, 162, 170, 172, 173, 175, 261, 341, 345, 376. *See also* justification: by faith/grace
family, 294, 298, 299, 304. *See also* birth control; children
fasting, 11, 13, 67, 196, 247
feminism, 232, 364–69
force, use of. *See* nonresistance; sword
forgiveness, 10, 163, 198, 199, 259, 260
fornication, 10, 14, 15, 20, 84–85, 311
fortitude, 62, 92
freedom, 8, 121–22, 127, 147, 165, 167, 243, 252, 264, 269, 272, 293, 295, 305, 307, 314, 315, 320, 338–40, 348, 353, 361. *See also* liberty
free will, 22, 51, 53–54, 83, 114, 134–39, 308, 368, 376

gender equality, 15–16, 99–100, 218, 220, 221, 222, 224–27, 228–30, 232, 246–47, 340, 362, 364–69
genocide, 359, 361
gifts, use of. *See* stewardship
giving. *See* offerings
gluttony, 38–39, 50, 67, 83–84, 147
Gnosticism, 2
God, ix, 19, 54, 134, 170, 230; accountability to, 26, 40; as creator, 18, 21, 23; fear of, 9, 69, 162; feminine aspects of, 117–19, 362–69; grace of, 117, 121–22, 125, 135–36, 251, 376, 377; image of, 100, 176, 366–67; judgment of, 26, 31, 60, 265–66, 356; kingdom of, 234, 281, 316, 322, 324, 338, 373, 374, 375; knowledge of, 102, 105–6, 216; love of. *See* love: of God; mercy of, 135, 137, 172, 265–66, 363; rebellion against. *See* sin; transcendence of, 32–33; union with, 65; will of, 5, 135, 177, 190, 193, 239, 272, 313; word of, 18, 124, 228, 250, 260, 264, 292, 376; wrath of, 140
God-consciousness, 170, 188–91
good, 44, 45–46, 65, 81, 90, 101, 103–4, 239, 250, 251, 280, 292, 307; deeds, 5, 6, 181, 250; and evil, 37, 46, 51–52, 130, 134, 199, 309; works, 121, 125, 134, 146, 162
goodness, 90, 239, 251, 292
government, 7, 106–8, 130, 162, 164–66, 281. *See also* state

grace, 121, 135–36, 232, 259–61, 265, 292, 312, 369. *See also* God: grace of

happiness, 61, 92–93, 95, 102–3, 104–6, 162, 220
holiness, 5, 146, 163
Holy Spirit, 372, 374
homelessness, 330
homosexuality, 10
hope, 93, 323, 368
hospitality, 50, 111, 156
human rights. *See* rights: human
humanism, 292, 371
humility, 5, 6, 7, 14, 56, 68–71, 80, 81, 82, 198, 199
hunger, 247, 266, 299, 330
husbands and wives, 8, 9, 17, 31, 50–51, 72, 154. *See also* gender equality
hypocrisy, 14, 15, 207–8, 271

"ideology," 277, 278
idolatry, 12, 15, 57, 270–71, 365–67
imprisonment, 24, 30, 310
incarnation, 321, 322
incest, 21, 22, 28
income. *See* wages
individualism, 170, 231, 287
indulgences, 121
Industrial Revolution, 231, 236, 241, 281, 317
industry/-ization, 161, 276, 292, 298, 317
inequality. *See* equality
injustice, 269, 330, 337, 338, 355, 371. *See also* justice
intemperance, 39, 170, 179

justice, 25, 42, 44–45, 47, 62, 80, 81, 92, 135, 230, 292, 300, 346, 351, 363; commutative, 379; economic, 318, 330–34, 339; and love, 266–68, 273–74, 320, 325, 378; and power, 266–67; "proximate," 268; rules and laws of, 274–79, 381; social, 170, 232, 296, 312, 317, 324, 325, 339, 343–44, 348, 354, 380; structures of, 274, 279–81
justification, 121–22, 173, 177, 260; by deeds/works, 5, 128; by faith/grace, 125, 137, 260, 261, 263–64
just war, 51, 59, 107, 151–52, 157–60, 255–56, 302

kindness, 4, 80
kingdoms, two, 122, 123, 128–31, 236–37, 244. *See also* rulers

labor. *See* work
law, 95–98, 127, 377–78; civil, 109–10, 277–78; divine, 39–40, 97, 111, 112–13, 170, 191–92, 213–14, 244, 307; international, 289–91, 326–27, 334; moral, 121, 144–46, 169, 192, 239, 251, 304, 349; natural, 39, 89, 96, 98, 128–29, 143, 169, 213–14, 277–78, 279, 301, 307–8, 377; obedience to, 17, 20, 172

386